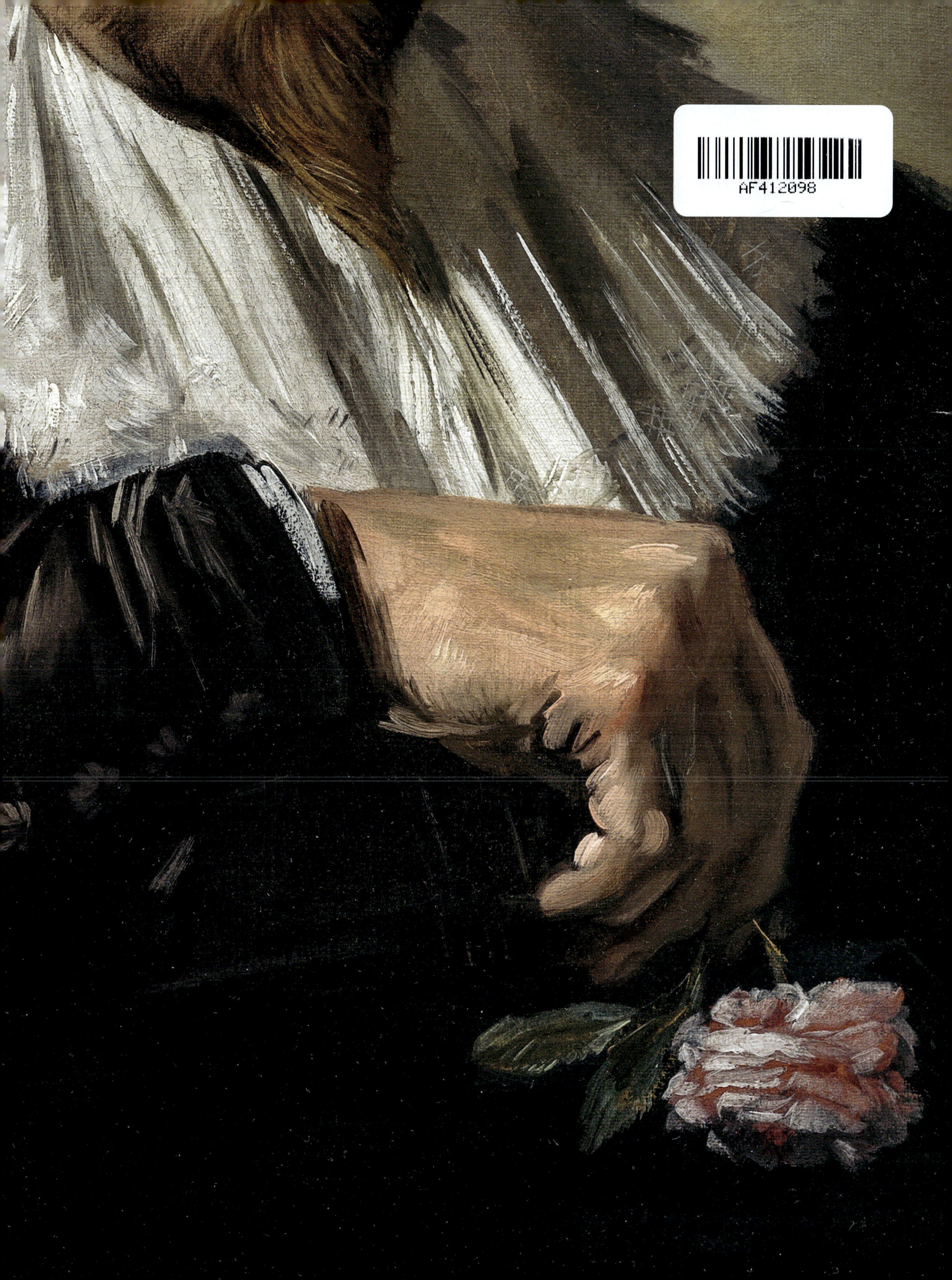
AF412098

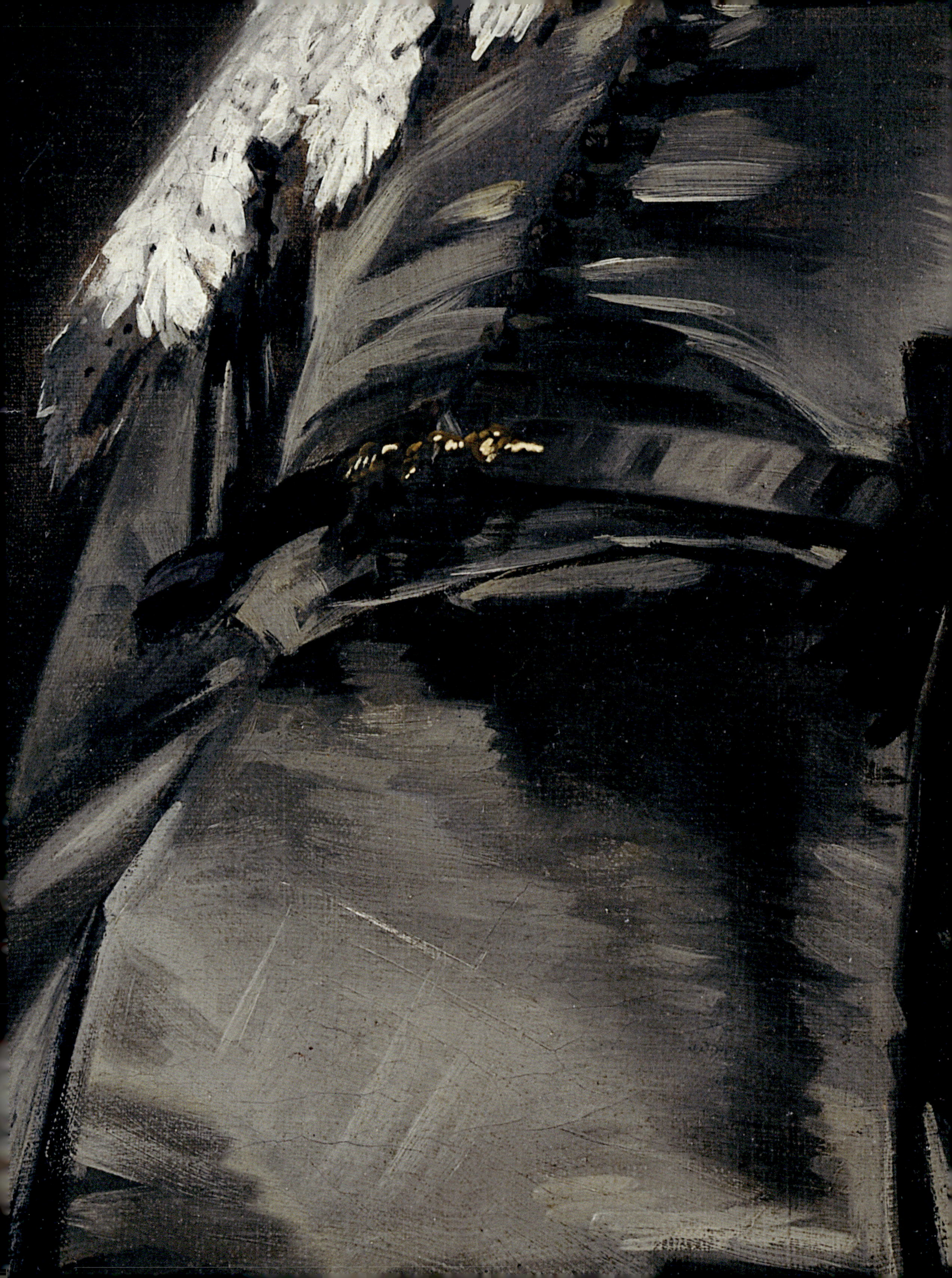

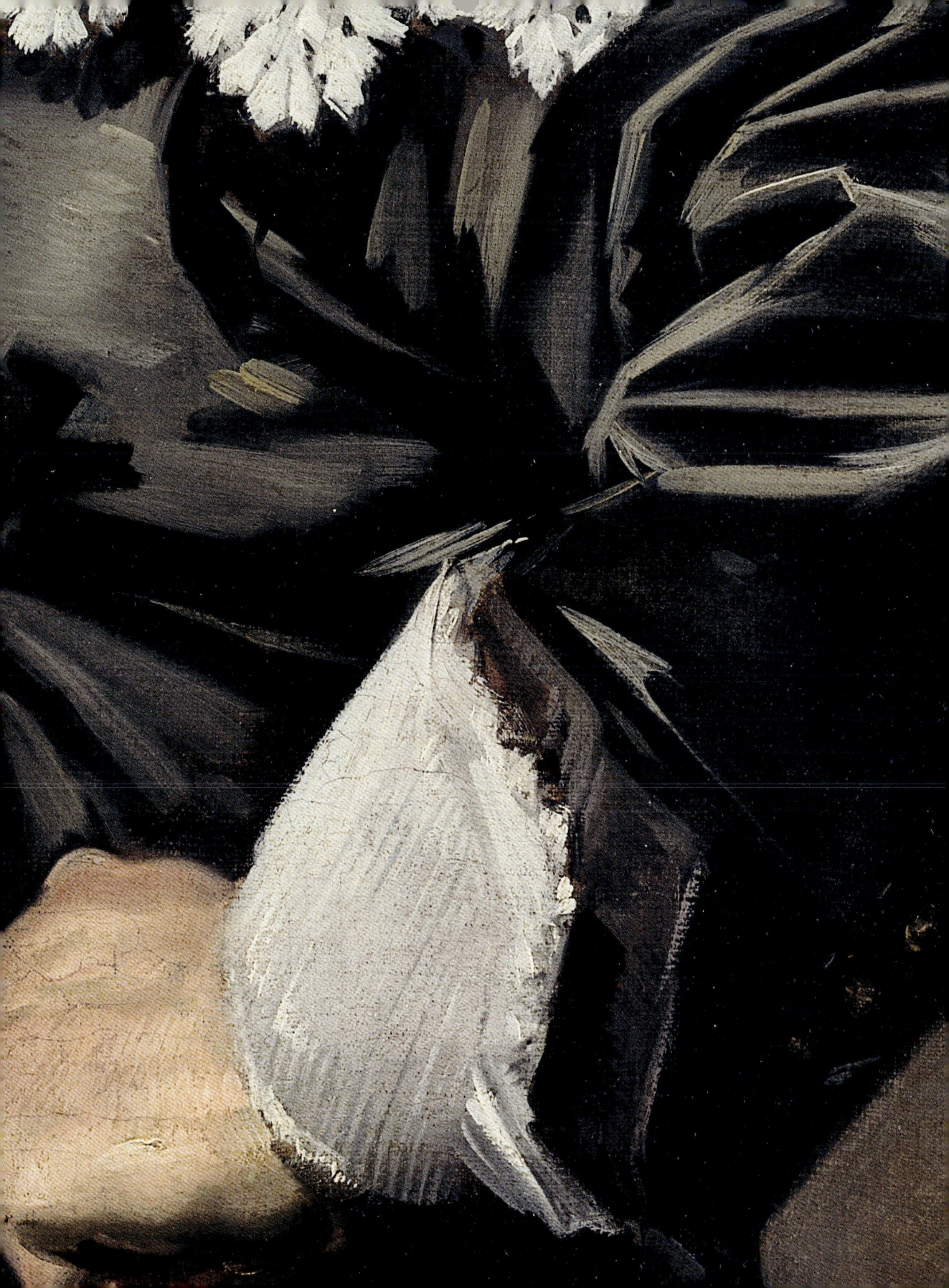

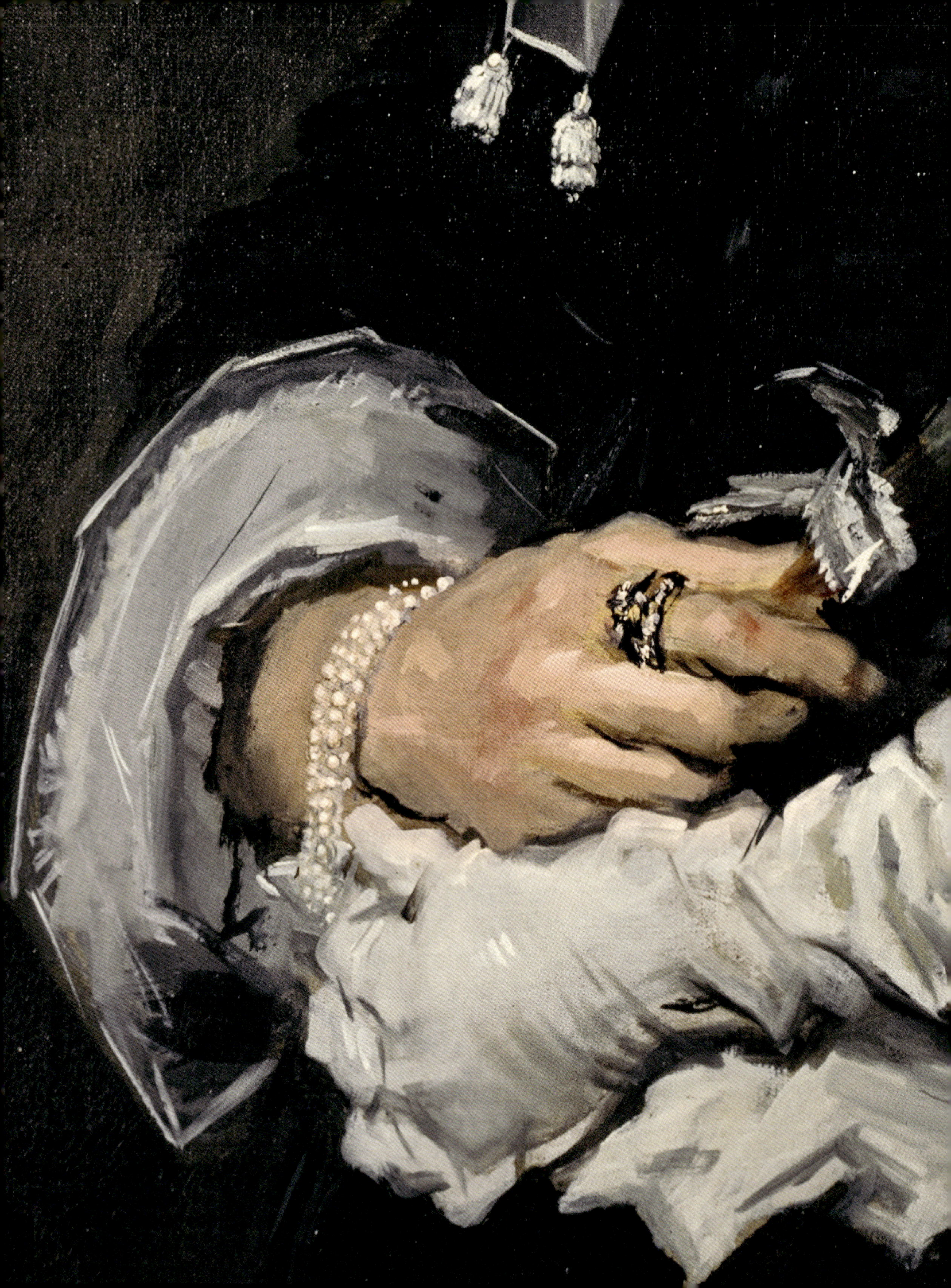

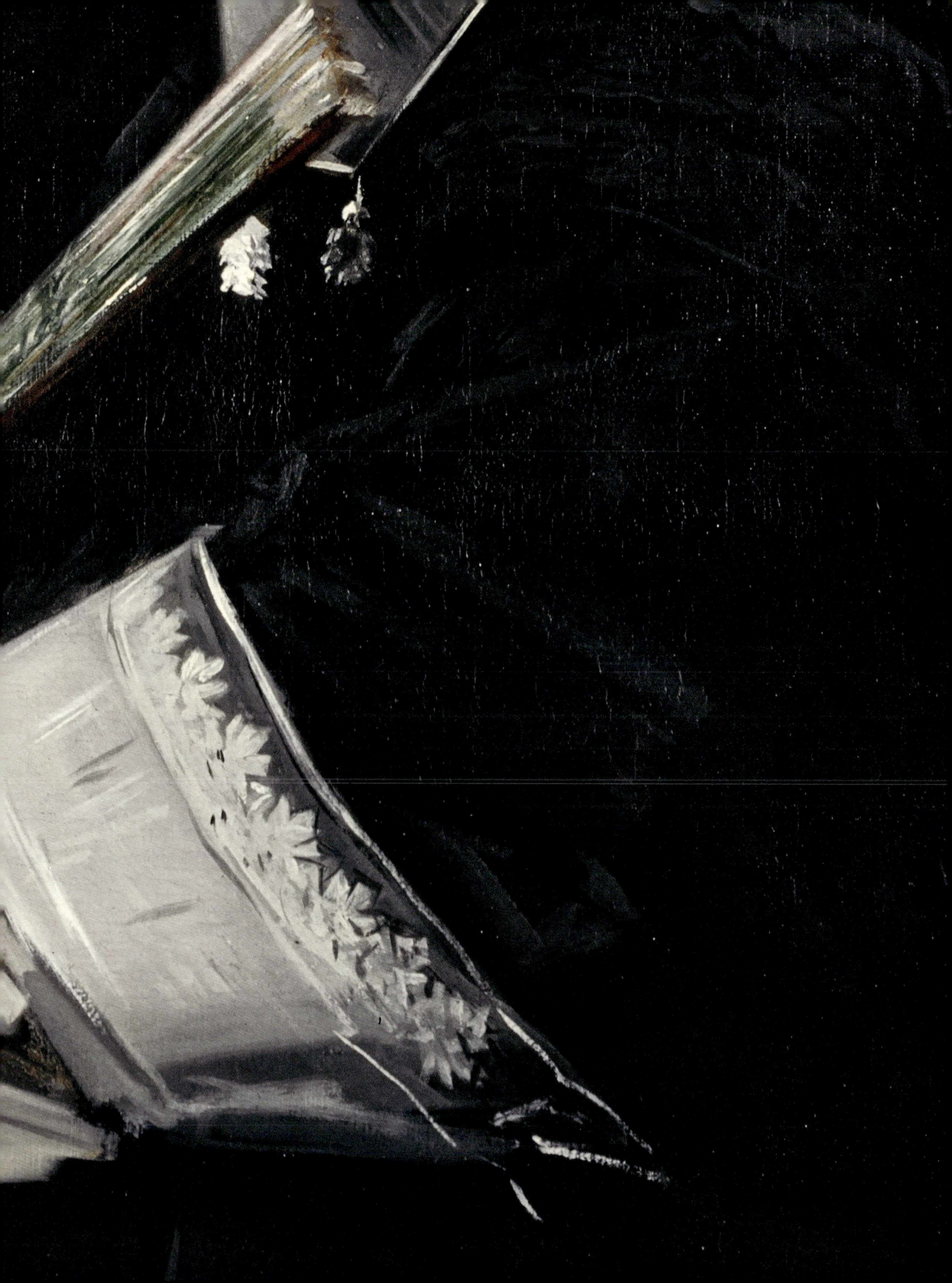

BART CORNELIS

FRISO LAMMERTSE

JUSTINE RINNOOY KAN

JAAP VAN DER VEEN

Frans Hals

PUBLISHED BY NATIONAL GALLERY GLOBAL, LONDON
IN ASSOCIATION WITH THE RIJKSMUSEUM, AMSTERDAM
DISTRIBUTED BY YALE UNIVERSITY PRESS

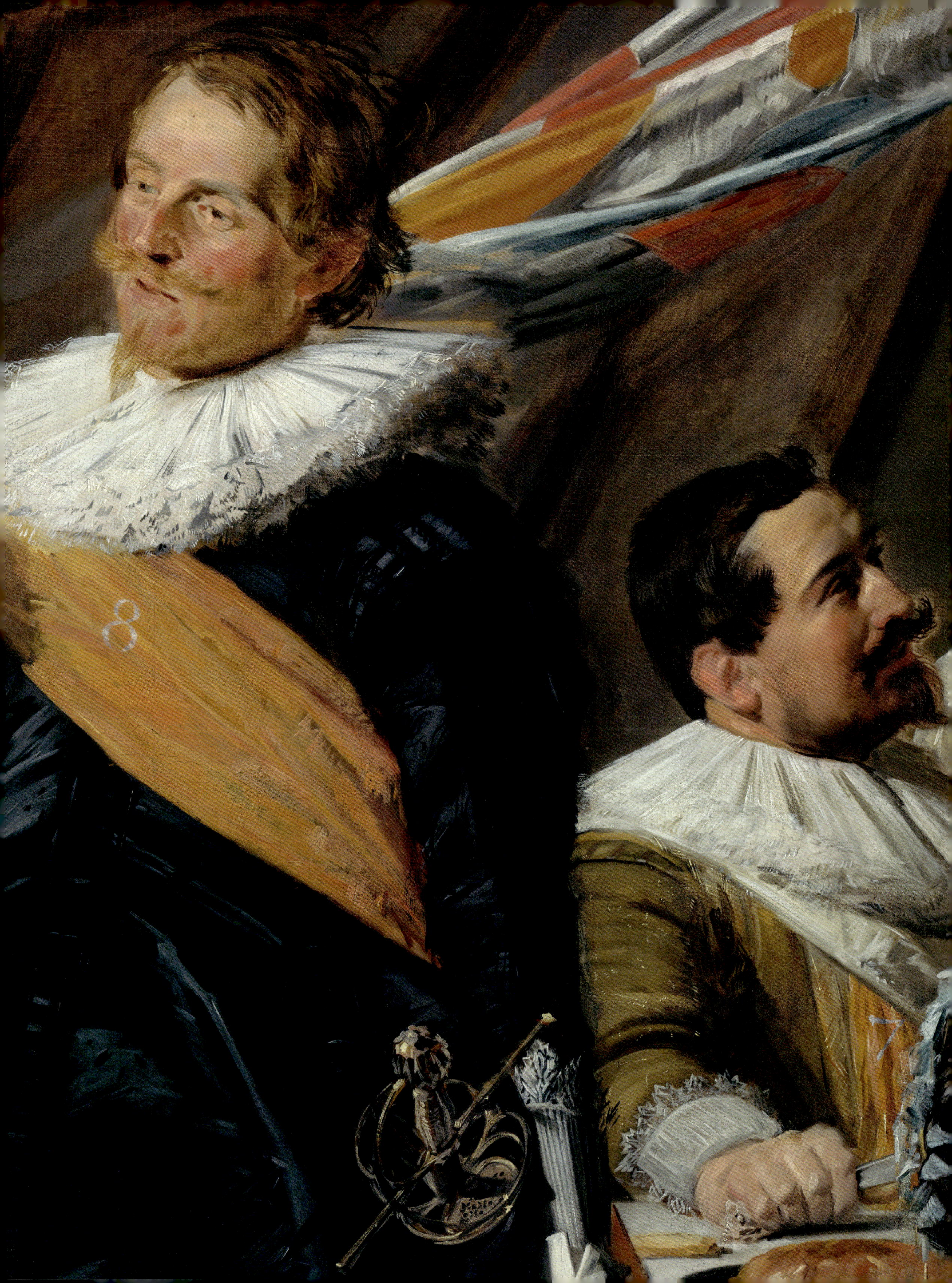

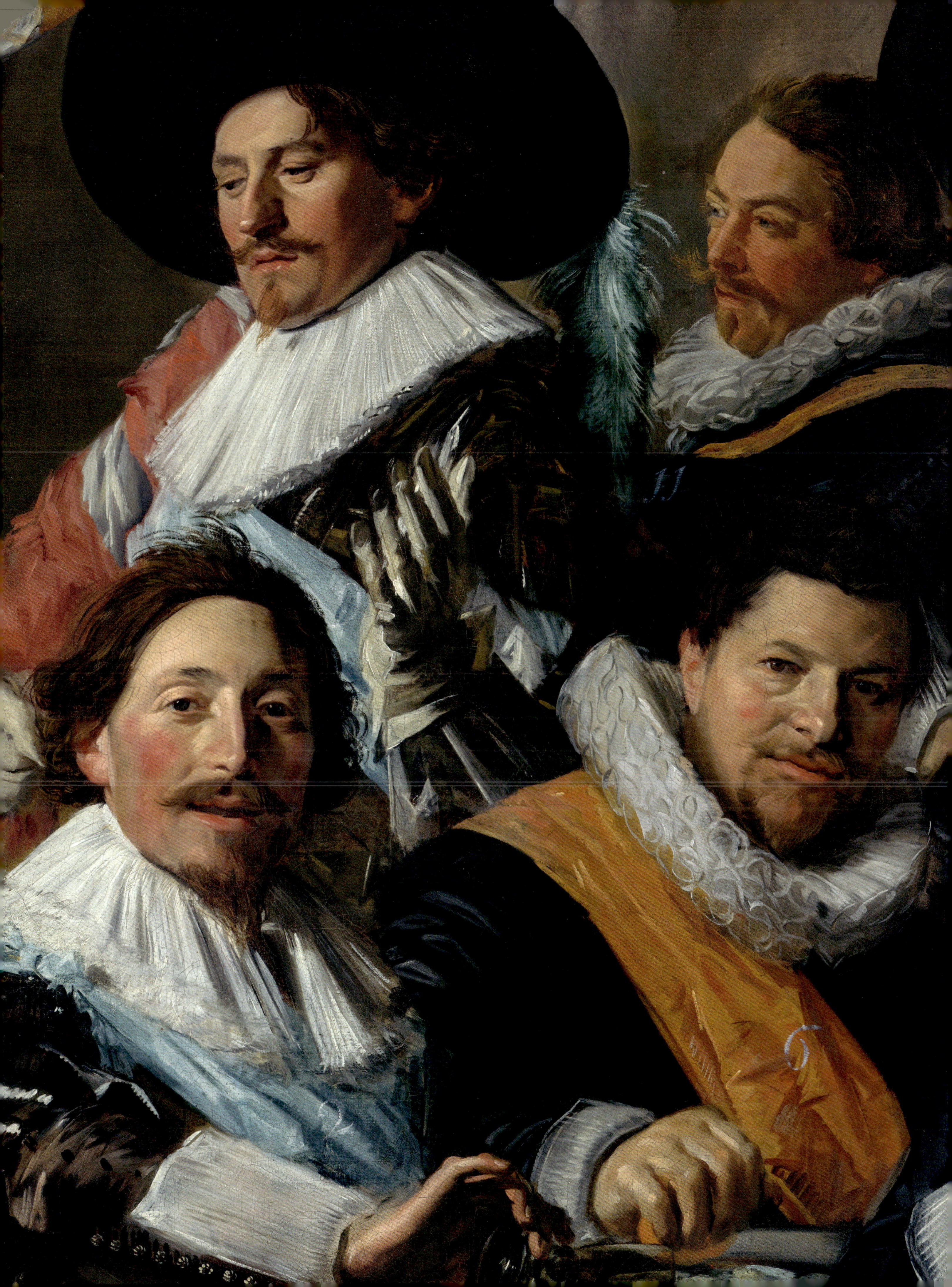

Published to accompany

The Credit Suisse Exhibition
Frans Hals
The National Gallery, London
30 September 2023–21 January 2024

Frans Hals
Rijksmuseum, Amsterdam
16 February–9 June 2024

Frans Hals
Gemäldegalerie, Berlin
12 July–3 November 2024

Exhibition organised by the National Gallery, London, the Rijksmuseum, Amsterdam, and the Gemäldegalerie, Staatliche Museen zu Berlin, with the special collaboration of the Frans Hals Museum, Haarlem.

Exhibition sponsored by

CREDIT SUISSE

Partner of the National Gallery

With additional support from
The Thompson Family Charitable Trust

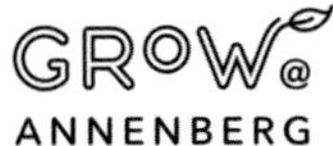

ANNENBERG

Gregory Annenberg Weingarten

Katrin Henkel
Marco Voena

And other donors

This exhibition has been made possible by the provision of insurance through the Government Indemnity Scheme. The National Gallery would like to thank HM Government for providing Government Indemnity and the Department for Culture, Media and Sport and Arts Council England for arranging the indemnity.

Published by National Gallery Global, London, in association with Rijksmuseum, Amsterdam.

© National Gallery Global Limited 2023

Texts by Bart Cornelis and Justine Rinnooy Kan
© National Gallery Global Limited 2023
Texts by Friso Lammertse and Jaap van der Veen
© Rijksmuseum, Amsterdam 2023

The authors have asserted their rights under the Copyright, Designs and Patents Act, 1988, to be identified as the Authors of this work.

All rights reserved. No part of this publication may be transmitted in any form or by any means, electronic or mechanical, including photocopy, recording, or any storage and retrieval system, without the prior permission in writing from the publisher.

First published in 2023 by
National Gallery Global Limited
Trafalgar Square
London WC2N 5DN
www.shop.nationalgallery.org.uk

ISBN 978 1 85709 712 2
1052665

British Library Cataloguing-in-Publication Data
A catalogue record is available from the British Library
Library of Congress Control Number: 2023938163

For the National Gallery
Publisher Laura Lappin
Managing Editor Diana Adell
Copy-editors Marieke de Jong (Rijksmuseum) and Johanna Stephenson
Proofreader Felicity Maunder
Indexer Hilary Bird
List of works Tamar van Riessen (Rijksmuseum), with the contribution of Justine Rinnooy Kan
Picture Researcher Rebecca Thornton
Production Jane Hyne and Justine Montizon

For the Rijksmuseum
Project management Barbera van Kooij
Copy-editor Marieke de Jong

Translation from Dutch by Pierre Bouvier ('The Life of Frans Hals', 'Portrait Prints') and Michael Hoyle ('Honoured and Famed', 'Antwerp and Haarlem', 'The Studio', 'Laughter').

Design IBO
Origination ALTA
Printer Gomer Press, Wales

All works are by Frans Hals unless otherwise stated.
All measurements give height before width.

Cover Detail from *The Lute Player* (fig. 177)

CONTENTS

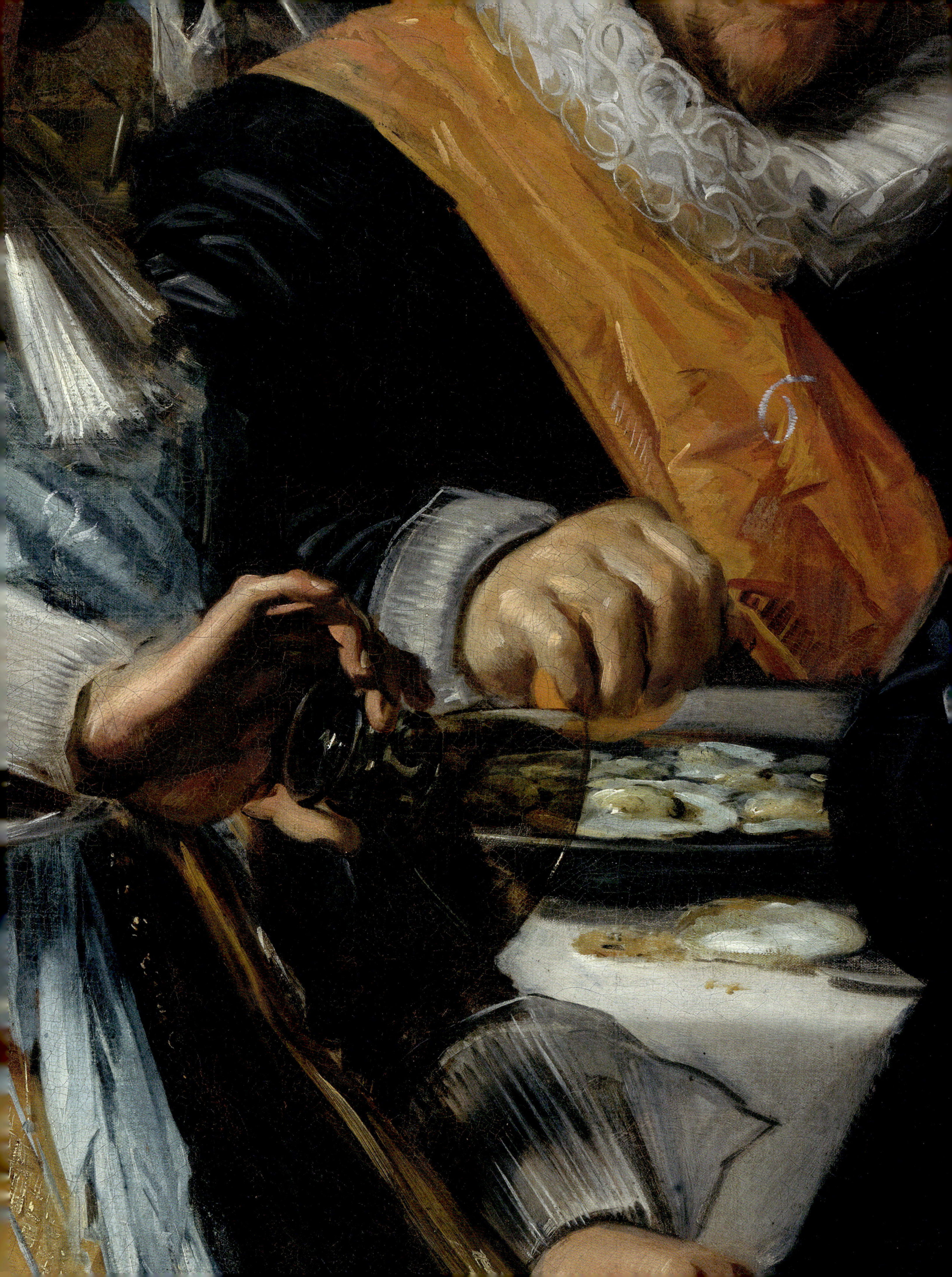

DIRECTORS' FOREWORD

This catalogue accompanies the first major loan exhibition in more than three decades to present the remarkable talents of Frans Hals (1582/4–1666), a true master of portraiture and genre painting. The exhibition, organised with the special collaboration of the Frans Hals Museum in Haarlem, takes place first in London's National Gallery and then at the Rijksmuseum in Amsterdam. It will also travel, in a different configuration, to the Gemäldegalerie – Staatliche Museen zu Berlin and we would like to thank their Director, Dagmar Hirschfelder, for her invaluable support of the project and her resolve to bring Hals's work to a German audience.

The show aims to demonstrate Frans Hals's unparalleled ability to capture the essence of his subjects and to breathe life into their likenesses. His extraordinary facility with the brush allowed him to create vibrant portraits that transcend the inherently commemorative and dynastic functions of portraiture. Whether it is the confident gaze of a military officer, the playful smile of a young child or the pensive expression of an elderly woman, Hals had a unique gift for revealing the individuality of his subjects. Such is the power of his portraiture that the identities and biographies of his sitters are by no means necessary for viewers to realise that we are looking at great works of art. Hals's expressive but meticulously controlled brushwork reveals his mastery of technique in the service of making his sitters come to life. He applied his virtuoso technique with equal enthusiasm to his genre paintings, which similarly brim with life and joy.

It is a joy that pervades his entire oeuvre, and one that we hope visitors to this exhibition will experience for themselves, whether it be the joy of witnessing his technical bravura, the visceral experience of encountering people who lived centuries ago but whose humanity speaks to us as if they are our contemporaries, or indeed the literal joy of laughter, for Hals is one of the few artists who knew how to paint people smiling and laughing. This is epitomised in what is arguably his most famous painting, *The Laughing Cavalier* from the Wallace Collection. This illustrious picture, which has never left London's Manchester Square since the Wallace Collection opened in 1900, has been allowed very exceptionally to join our celebration of Hals's work at both the National Gallery and the Rijksmuseum. We are enormously grateful to the Trustees and Director of the Wallace Collection.

Another first is that two of Hals's early group portraits – the *Banquet of the Officers of the St George Civic Guard* of 1616 and of around 1627 – have been allowed to leave the city of Haarlem for the first time since they were painted. We are greatly indebted to the Frans Hals Museum and the municipality of Haarlem for agreeing to lend these superb demonstrations of Hals's ability to invest his sitters with life and character; they also show that Hals thrived when confronted with the considerable challenge of incorporating a large number of likenesses into a single work.

This exhibition would not have been possible without the generosity of all our lenders, including museums in the United Kingdom, the Netherlands and elsewhere, as well as private collectors, all of whom graciously agreed to part with their precious paintings for the duration of the show. We are deeply grateful to all of them.

Curated by Bart Cornelis at the National Gallery and Friso Lammertse at the Rijksmuseum, this exhibition is the result of a fruitful collaboration between our two museums. We want to thank the catalogue authors for their contribution to this publication. We also want to express our appreciation to the Gemäldegalerie curators, Katja Kleinert and Erik Eising, for the helpful mutual exchange and inspiring discussions about the project.

In London we want to thank Credit Suisse, Partner of the National Gallery, for supporting this exhibition and for their long-term commitment towards the National Gallery's exhibition programme. In addition, we would like to express our gratitude to the trustees of the Thompson Family Charitable Trust for their generous grant towards this exhibition and their ongoing support of the Gallery. Thanks are also due to Katrin Henkel, Marco Voena, Gregory Annenberg Weingarten and GRoW@Annenberg, and the other donors who have helped to make this exhibition possible.

In Amsterdam we want to thank our sponsor Philips, as well as our main partners Friends Lottery, ING and KPN, for their loyal support of the Rijksmuseum. In addition, we are grateful to Ammodo for generously supporting our exhibition programme, including *Frans Hals*. We would also like to extend our gratitude to the Rijksmuseum International Circle and the Rijksmuseum Patrons for their contributions to the realisation of this exhibition.

Gabriele Finaldi
Director, The National Gallery, London

Taco Dibbits
General Director, Rijksmuseum, Amsterdam

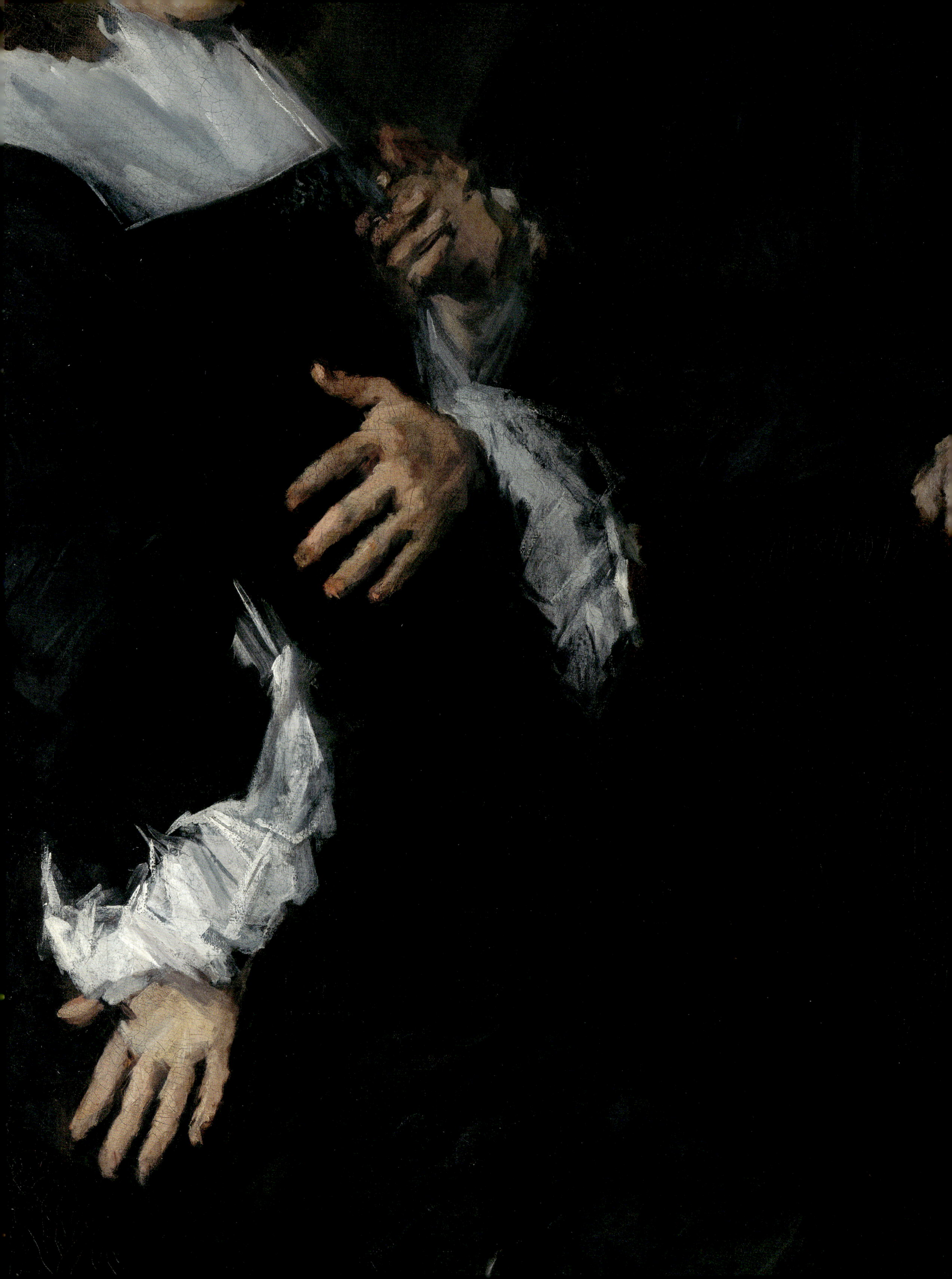

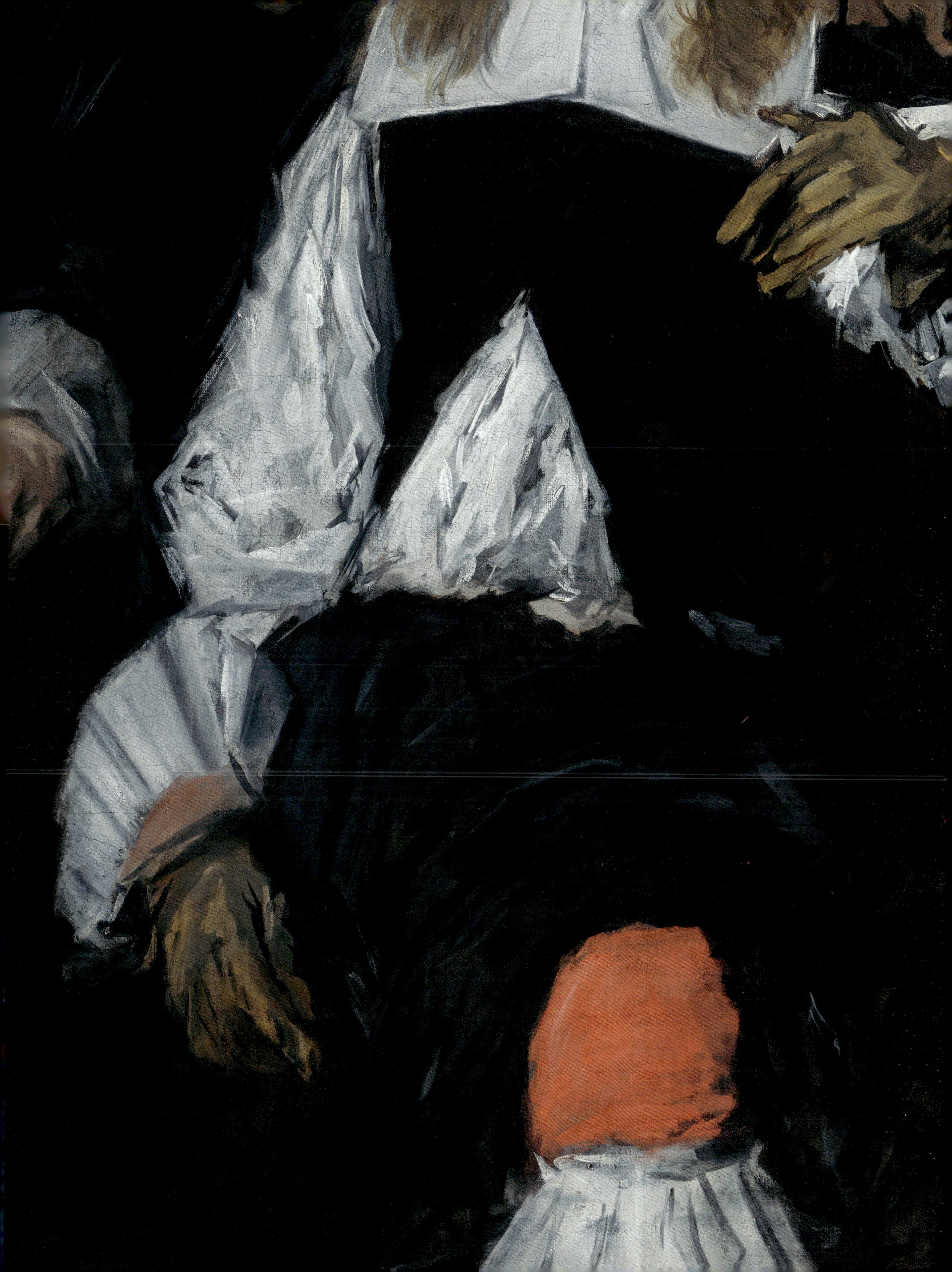

HONOURED AND FAMED

FRISO LAMMERTSE AND
BART CORNELIS

At the end of August 1902 the American artist James Abbott McNeill Whistler travelled from The Hague to Haarlem to view the civic guard pieces and regent portraits by Frans Hals in the town hall there (fig. 1). When he caught sight of one of them he was unable to control himself and wriggled his way under the railing to take a closer look. The attendant arrived and told him sternly that he was misbehaving, and Whistler was forced to wriggle his way back out again. But he did not give up. After the chief attendant had recognised that he was Whistler, 'the great painter', they let him go behind the barrier once the other visitors had left. He was even allowed to stand on a chair in order to study the *Regentesses of the Old Men's Alms House* more closely. Enraptured, 'he moved tenderly with his fingers over the face of one of the old women'.[1]

Whistler was not alone in his awe of the master. Frans Hals began attracting more and more attention in the second half of the nineteenth century. This was due mainly to the influential French art critic Théophile Thoré, who was also blowing the dust of ages off Johannes Vermeer, and from 1857 started to proclaim Hals's greatness in several of his publications.[2] Like Whistler, he was particularly struck by the two late group portraits of the regents and regentesses (figs 3, 4). According to him, the ardour ('fougue') with which they had been painted put all other painters with an extremely vigorous handling of the brush ('quel brosseur des plus enragés') in the shade, among them Rubens, Rembrandt and El Greco.[3]

Many painters, such as Gustave Courbet, John Singer Sargent, Vincent van Gogh and Max Liebermann, saw that Hals was not only a great artist but a soulmate too.[4] For his extraordinary brushwork, which Thoré likened to a fencer wielding his sabre, he was regarded as one of the most important forerunners of the loose manner of painting that was becoming popular at the time.[5] But it was also the way in which Hals characterised his contemporaries that really pleased them. In their eyes he had portrayed his sitters as they truly were, devoid of any kind of frippery. Thoré, and many others with him, regarded seventeenth-century Dutch society as a lodestar for the ideal society that they wanted to create, a society that was not run by the aristocracy and the Church but by ordinary citizens. They saw republican ideals reflected in Dutch painting, with its preference for daily life rather than stories from the Bible, complex allegories or classical myths. Hals was soon being hailed as the undisputed master of the first generation of Dutch seventeenth-century masters.[6] Van Gogh felt that Hals's work was worth as much as that of Michelangelo, Raphael and the artists of Greek antiquity, precisely because Hals painted portraits of people of every kind with an unfeigned naturalism, no matter whether they were respectable citizens, drunkards, fishwives or the painter himself with his wife, 'as young lovers on a turf bench in a garden, after their first wedding night'.[7] The latter description was an allusion to a double portrait in a landscape, which people at the time generally but wrongly thought depicted Frans Hals and his second wife, Lysbeth Reyniers (fig. 61).

As Hals's fame grew, so did the prices for his work. At a sensational auction in 1865 in Paris, James Mayer de Rothschild and London's National Gallery were pipped at the post when the fabulously rich Marquess of Hertford bid 51,000 francs for *The Laughing Cavalier* (fig. 78). That was 11 times the price paid for it by the former owner, a French count, in the Netherlands in 1822. Two months later Baron de Rothschild bought his Hals, a small panel in which Willem van Heythuysen is precariously seated on a tilted chair, for 35,000 francs (fig. 50).[8] At that moment the prices for Hals's paintings matched those for Rubens, Rembrandt, Van Dyck and Velázquez.[9] In the second half of the nineteenth century Hals's star rose to giddying heights, but he had never been entirely forgotten, certainly not in the Netherlands, and had been a highly valued artist in his own day. Urban historians such as Samuel Ampzing and Theodorus Schrevelius in Haarlem ranked him among the city's most important artists.[10] The Southern Netherlandish notary and writer Cornelis de Bie stated in 1662 that Hals was 'miraculously excellent' as a portrait

painter, and the French diplomat Balthasar de Monconys noted in his travel journal a year later that Hals was rightly admired by the greatest painters.[11] In 1686, twenty years after his death, he was lauded as a true phoenix in a New Year's poem for the Guild of St Luke in Haarlem.[12] However, it was above all Arnold Houbraken's 1718 biography that was to secure his reputation in the centuries that followed.[13]

The majority of those who later wrote about Hals eagerly recited the juicy details that Houbraken had dished up, whether Jacob Campo Weyerman in 1729, Jean-Baptiste Descamps in 1753 or Everhardus Johannes Potgieter in 1837.[14] But not everyone did. The Haarlem writer and publisher Adriaan Loosjes, for instance, focused almost exclusively on Hals's work in a lyric poem that he recited at a prize-giving event at the Haarlem Drawing Academy in 1789. According to Loosjes, Hals only wanted to paint the truth. He had no interest in history paintings or allegories, but had an eye, Loosjes said, for the heroes of the fatherland, namely the 'faithful and useful citizens, with honest faces'.[15]

The emphasis that Houbraken placed on Hals's fondness for alcohol was viewed with growing scepticism in the second half of the nineteenth century. People refused to believe that such a great artist was a tippler. Thoré announced with satisfaction that Hals had lived an honourable life, according to archival research in Haarlem.[16] For Whistler, Hals's paintings were proof that the maker of such works could never have been a drunkard or coarse.[17]

The growing interest in Frans Hals's work turned Haarlem into a place of pilgrimage for his admirers. In 1862 two rooms were opened in the town hall that had been built specifically to house the municipal art collection.[18] Needless to say, Hals's five civic guard pieces and three regent portraits were the top attractions. From his first group portrait, *Banquet of the Officers of the St George Civic Guard* of 1616 (fig. 68), up to and including the two group portraits of the regents and regentesses of the Old Men's Alms House of about 1664 (figs 3, 4), the works gave visitors an unparalleled visual history of Hals's long career.

In the decades that followed Haarlem responded to local chauvinism by organising a range of events to honour the artist and keep the memory of his work alive. The celebrations reached their peak with the unveiling of a statue of Hals by Henri Scholtz in Florapark on 14 June 1900. This was accompanied by a three-day festival that included a parade of local residents wearing seventeenth-century dress, and festive songs during which girls scattered flowers around Scholtz's monument (fig. 2).[19] This made Hals the second seventeenth-century artist (after Rembrandt) to be honoured with a statue in the Netherlands. When the Haarlem art collection was moved 13 years later from the town hall to the renovated Old Men's Alms House, the building was renamed the Frans Hals Museum. This was an exceptional honour: no other Dutch municipality had renamed its local museum after

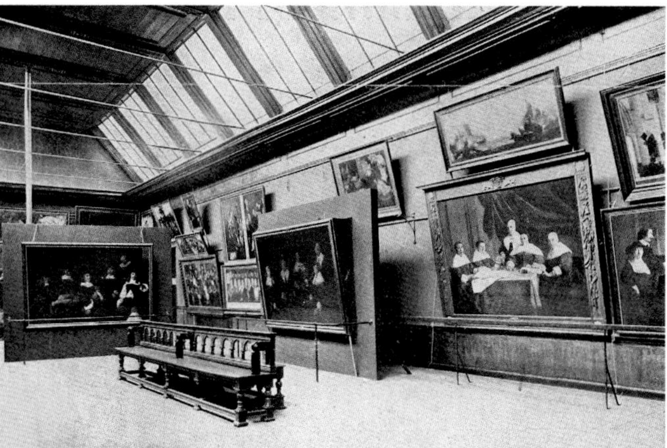

Fig. 1 The large gallery in the Haarlem town hall, with Frans Hals's two late regent paintings on the left, 1912 Noord-Hollands Archief, Haarlem

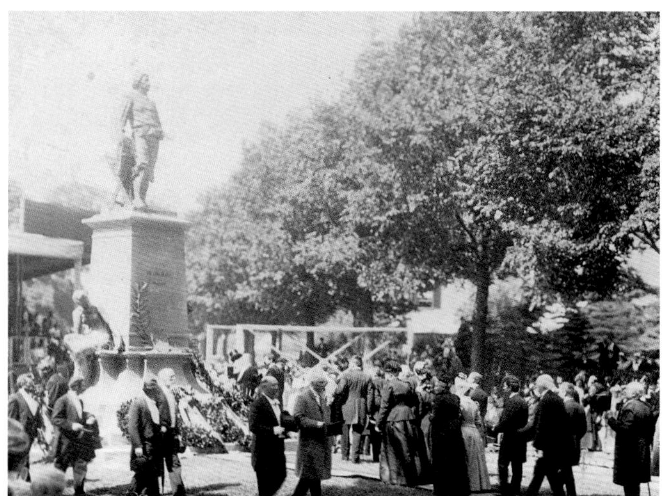

Fig. 2 Willem Hendrik Dikkenberg, wreath-laying ceremony at the statue of Frans Hals in Florapark, Haarlem, 14 June 1900 Rijksmuseum, Amsterdam

HONOURED AND FAMED

an artist, merely giving them neutral names like 'city' or 'municipal'. The Hals Museum, though, turned into a true champion of the master, not only with its permanent collection but increasingly through special exhibitions, the standard way of generating interest in an artist in the twentieth and twenty-first centuries. The major retrospectives in 1937, 1962 and 1990, in particular, attracted international interest.[20]

HALS'S STYLE OF PAINTING

> Praise be to art, loftily elevated,
> To colour plain canvas
> And, driven by a wondrous power,
> To create *life* with the stroke of a brush.

These are the opening words of an ode sung in the Church of St Bavo in Haarlem to mark the unveiling of Scholtz's statue of Frans Hals. The paean of praise repeatedly referred to the enchantment with which the artist gave life to his works.[21] The idea that artists can breathe life into their creations is a topos, but it was rarely said as often as it was about Hals. Schrevelius wrote as early as 1647 that there was 'life' in his paintings, while a friend described Schrevelius's portrait by Hals as 'lively'. Loosjes wrote in his poem that Hals's brush bestowed 'spirit and life' on his paint.[22] He gave his sitters a sense of energy and motion, outdoing his peers in creating the impression that he had captured a moment in time. This is brilliantly illustrated by Van Heythuysen leaning back in his chair (fig. 50) or the flute player looking down sideways (fig. 162). The viewer automatically expects Van Heythuysen to lean forward at any second and set all four legs of his chair on the floor, or the musician to raise his eyes at the last moment to meet our gaze. But it is not just the poses adopted by the figures that create their sense of movement, it is also Hals's loose touch.

Frans Hals stands apart for his daring brushwork. His contemporaries were all too aware of that: Schrevelius speaks of his 'uncommon manner' and in 1662 De Bie praises Hals's touch as 'very rough and bold'.[23] The fact that his brushstrokes were so clearly visible was deliberate, for they demonstrated his adherence to the most recent ideas about painting.[24] Houbraken writes that Hals carefully allowed the different tones of paint to merge 'meltingly' into each other, and only then added his characteristic brushstrokes, with the words 'Now to give it the master's touch'.[25]

De Bie stresses that Hals's portraits were 'pleasing and ingenious' when seen from a distance, although Whistler could not get close enough to them. This was perhaps because, unlike De Bie, he was a painter himself. But it is also a case of an altered view of art: De Bie, typically for his day, regarded the loose touch as a way of heightening the illusion, which required the viewer to step back a little. The point for Whistler was simply to take a close look at Hals's wild brushstrokes – he was less

interested in seeing reality imitated as accurately as possible. The viewer had to be aware that the painter worked with paint. This was also why Whistler and so many other nineteenth- and twentieth-century artists felt that Frans Hals was way ahead of his time.

Art historical research on Hals got under way after Thoré wrote his articles on the artist. The first monograph appeared in 1871 and was written by the influential Wilhelm Bode, later the director of the Kaiser-Friedrich-Museum in Berlin and a friend of Liebermann.[26] Bode's was the first in a stream of publications on Hals that has continued to the present day. In particular, many art historians have been kept busy deciding what is by the master and what is not.

In 1648 Schrevelius wrote that there were 'incredibly many' works by Hals, at a time when the master still had almost twenty years ahead of him.[27] Thus it is not surprising that so many paintings have been attributed to Hals in the past. The last two oeuvre catalogues, however, by Seymour Slive in 1970–4 and Claus Grimm in 1989, only give him 222 and 145 paintings respectively.[28] This would mean that Hals painted between three and five works a year in his career of more than fifty years – not very many, even if one assumes that they included a good number of group portraits and that works have undoubtedly been lost down the years. It now looks as if scholars may have been too critical.

In the present publication, which accompanies the exhibition of the same title, the emphasis is on the paintings that are almost unanimously regarded as autograph works by Frans Hals. Little work has been done to identify the contribution of assistants, mainly because technical research into Hals's work is still at a very early stage, certainly compared to that on Rembrandt and Vermeer. Such an investigation is an important aid for getting a better idea of the genesis of a painting. The discussions of attributions to date have been based largely on rather personal views of Hals and how his studio operated. This research mainly takes the form of various attempts to distinguish the hand of one of his assistants in addition to his own in certain works. So the reader will not find a chapter on attributions in this book. However, there is a chapter on Hals's studio, which is there because we felt that it was important to put together all the available information so as to get a better idea of his working practice. The other chapters are devoted to his life; the contacts between Antwerp (where Hals was born) and Haarlem (where he lived and worked); Hals's portraits; the prints after his portraits; and the genre paintings and the almost universal broad smiles of his genre figures.

THE 'BIG THREE'

In the second half of the nineteenth century and the beginning of the twentieth, Frans Hals was raised to the rank of hero, alongside Rembrandt and Vermeer. These were the 'big three' masters of the Dutch Golden Age.

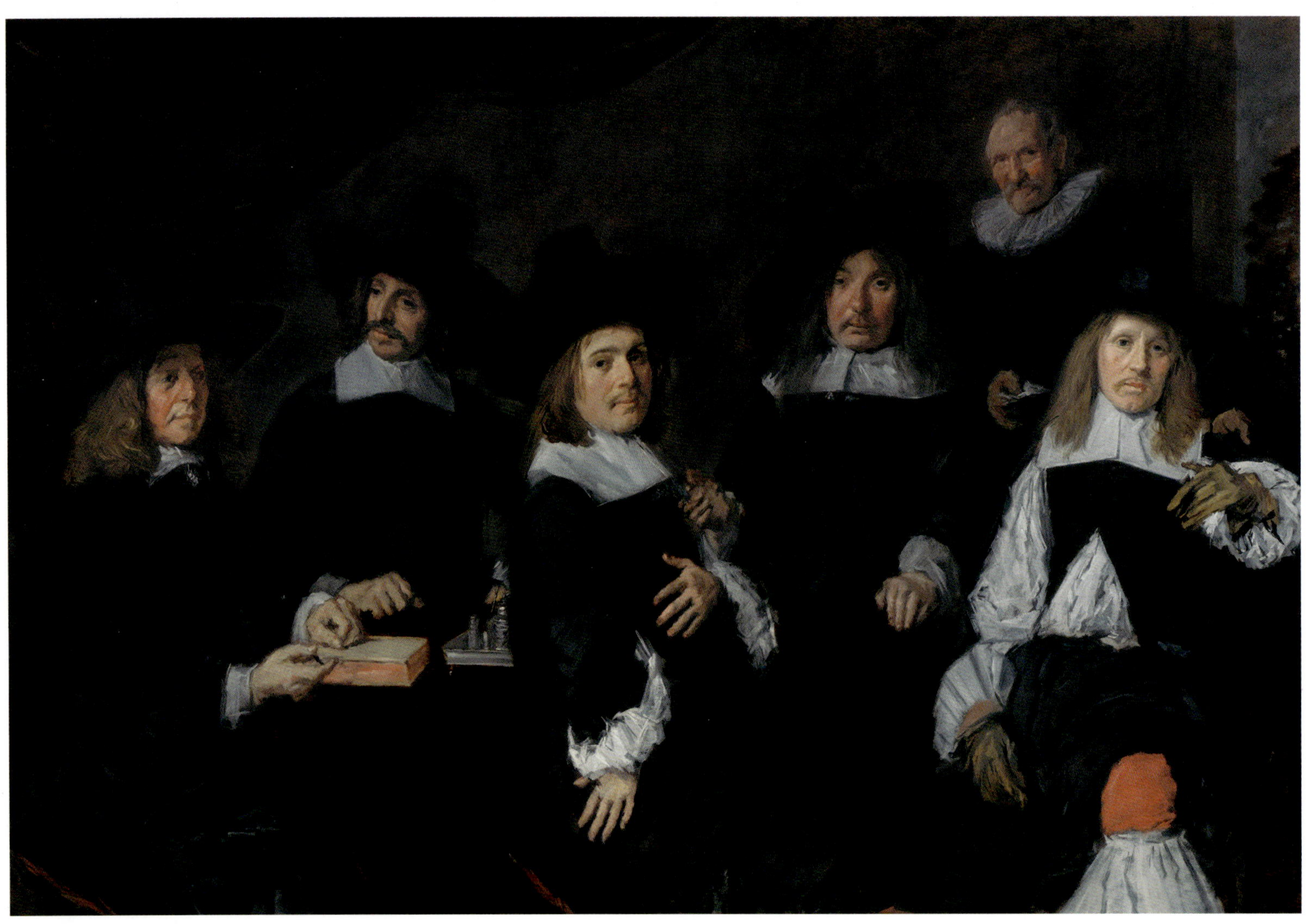

Fig. 3 *Regents of the Old Men's Alms House*, about 1664
Oil on canvas, 172.3 × 256 cm
Frans Hals Museum, Haarlem

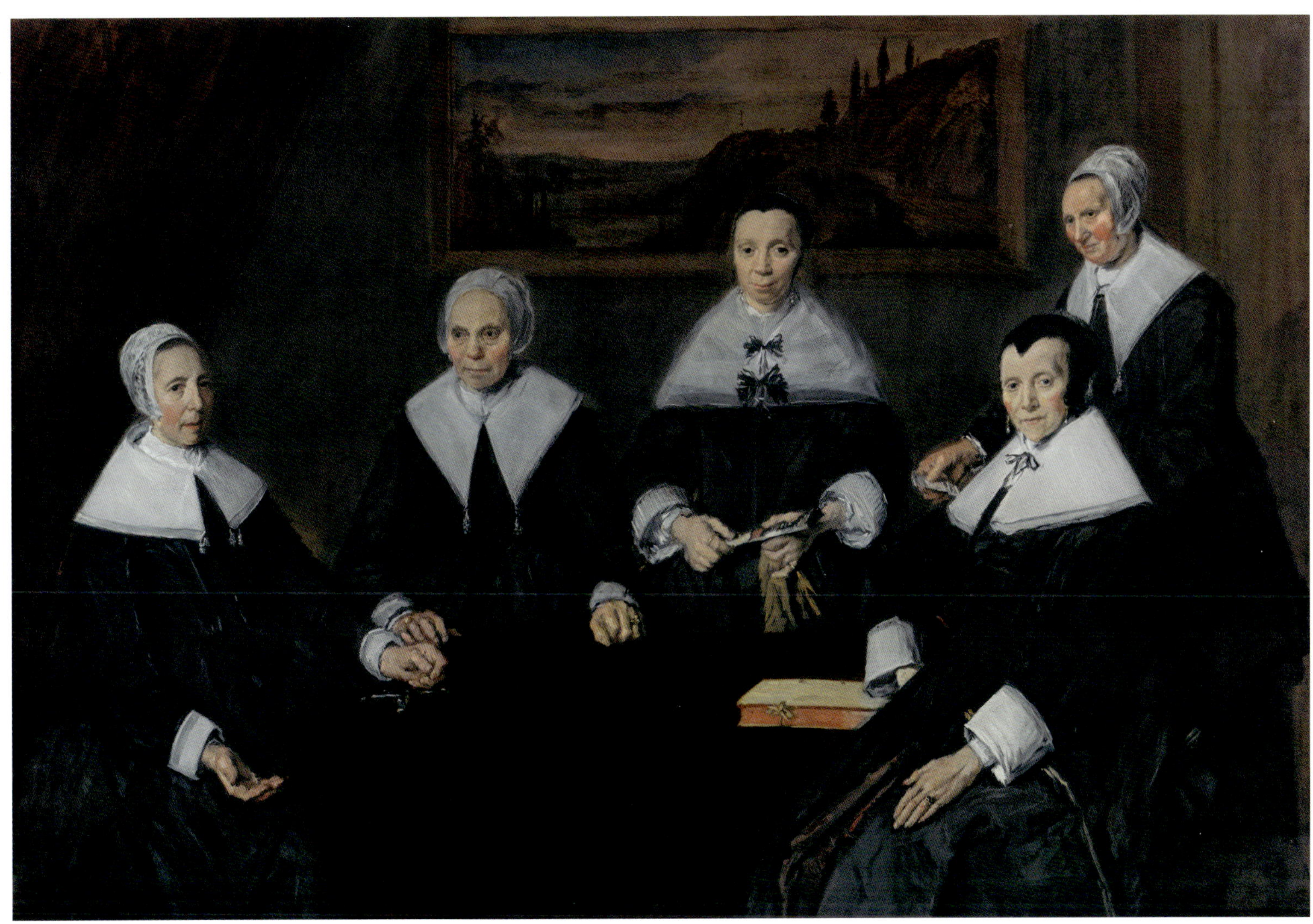

Fig. 4 *Regentesses of the Old Men's Alms House*, about 1664
Oil on canvas, 170.5 × 249.5 cm
Frans Hals Museum, Haarlem

But whereas Rembrandt retained his position after the Second World War and Vermeer's star rose spectacularly, Hals faded more or less into the background. Was this because people no longer found his style so exceptional, despite the fact that it had made such a deep impression on painters in the nineteenth century? A loose touch had become common practice as a by-product of Impressionism and Expressionism, and as a result, somewhat ironically, Hals lost his reputation as a revolutionary. In addition, the waning interest in his work was due in part to the fact that portraits, which made up five-sixths of his total oeuvre, had become less popular compared to scenes from daily life or landscapes. But perhaps the most important factor is the loss of admiration for virtuoso brushwork. This is typified by the pronouncement of Kenneth Clark, former Director of the National Gallery, who observed in his popular television programme *Civilisation* and book of the same name that he found Hals's paintings 'revoltingly cheerful and odiously skilful'.[29] Technical mastery was no longer a precondition and absolutely not evidence of good art any more. This applied to contemporary art, but it is significant that seventeenth-century painters like Adriaen Coorte and Jacobus Vrel, who were regarded until recently as well-intentioned but slightly naive amateurs, have become popular with a large public for their tranquil compositions.

The current exhibition and accompanying book owe their existence to the conviction that Hals is an exceptional artist who has not, in our opinion, been receiving the attention he deserves for some decades. The present publication provides background information to assist a viewing of his paintings. Given the risk to people and art, it is not recommended that anyone tries to repeat Whistler's behaviour in Haarlem. But his words tug at our heartstrings: with his frail body (he was 68 and had barely recovered from a serious illness), he clambered on to a chair to inspect the *Regentesses of the Old Men's Alms House* and whispered: 'Look at it – just look – look at the beautiful colour – the flesh – look at the white – that black – look how those ribbons are put in. O, what a swell he was.'[30]

HONOURED AND FAMED

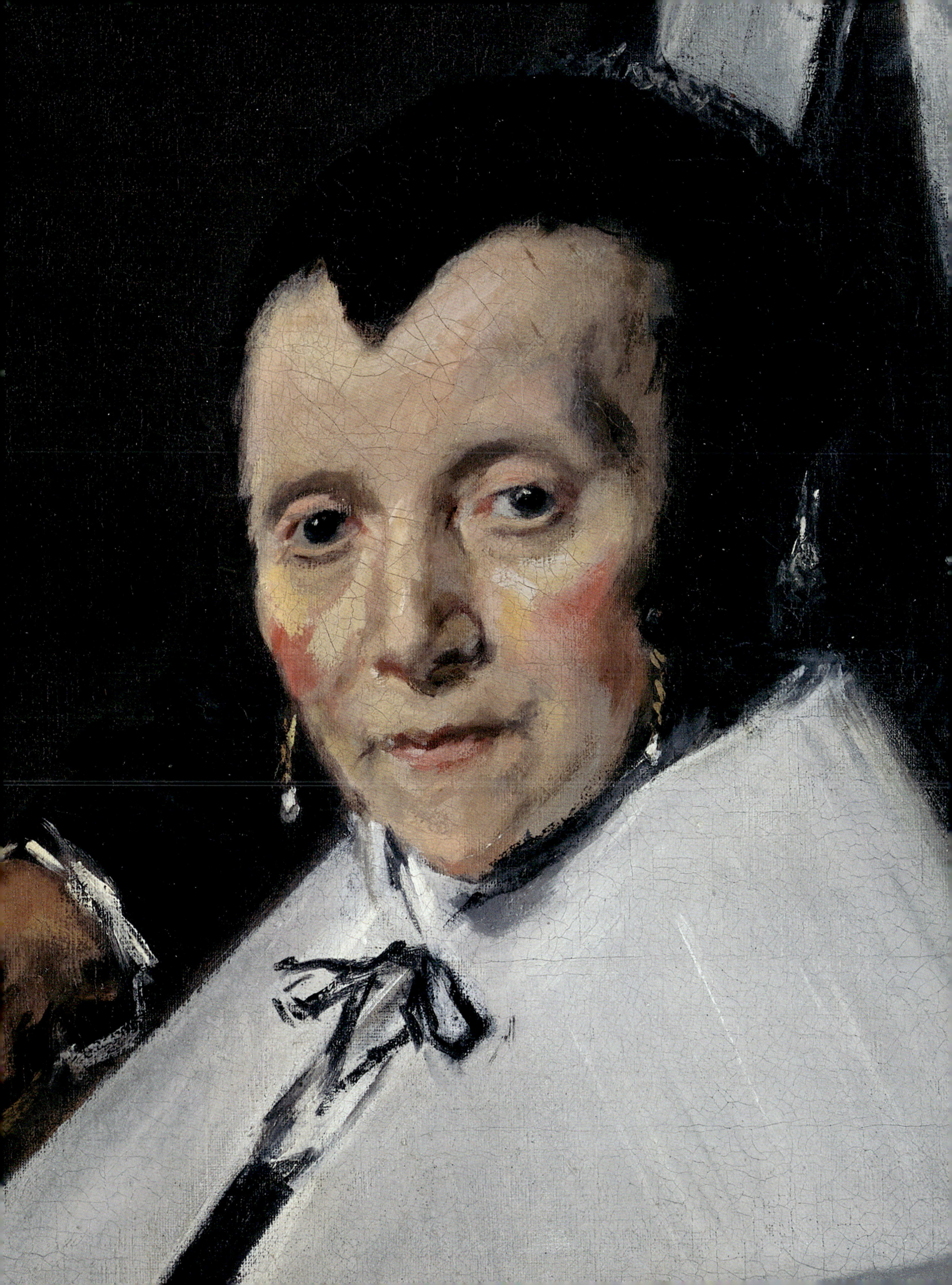

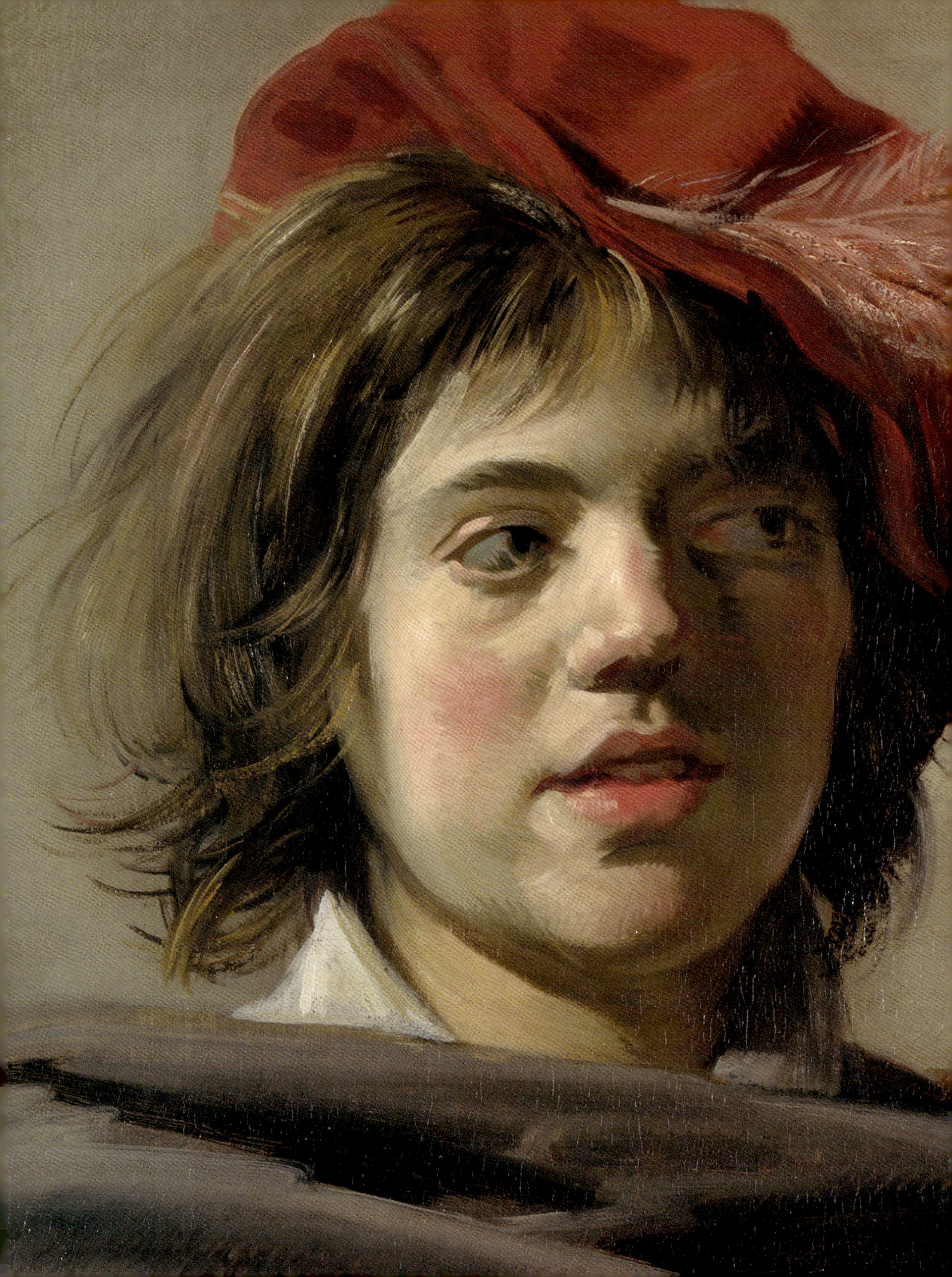

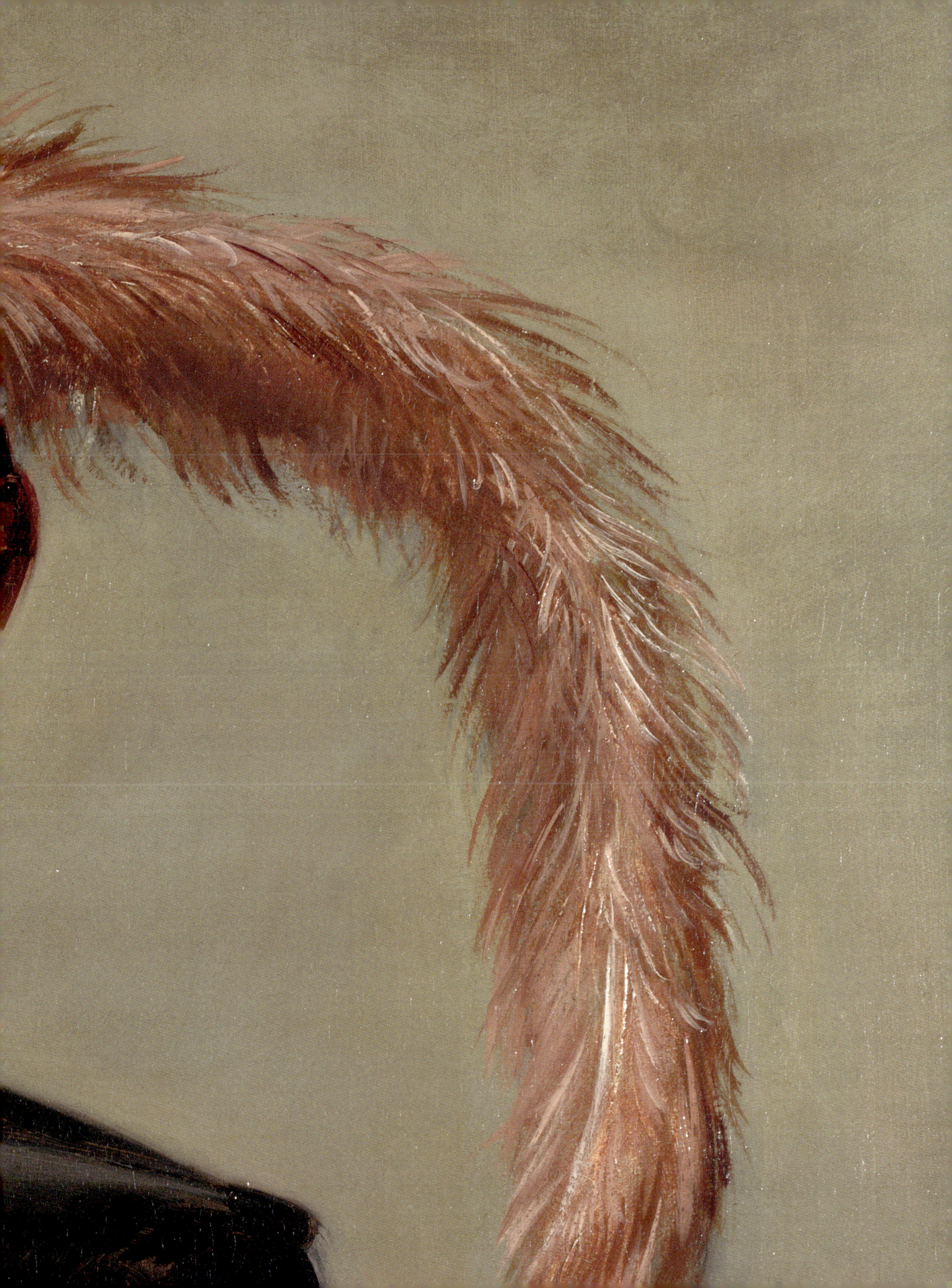

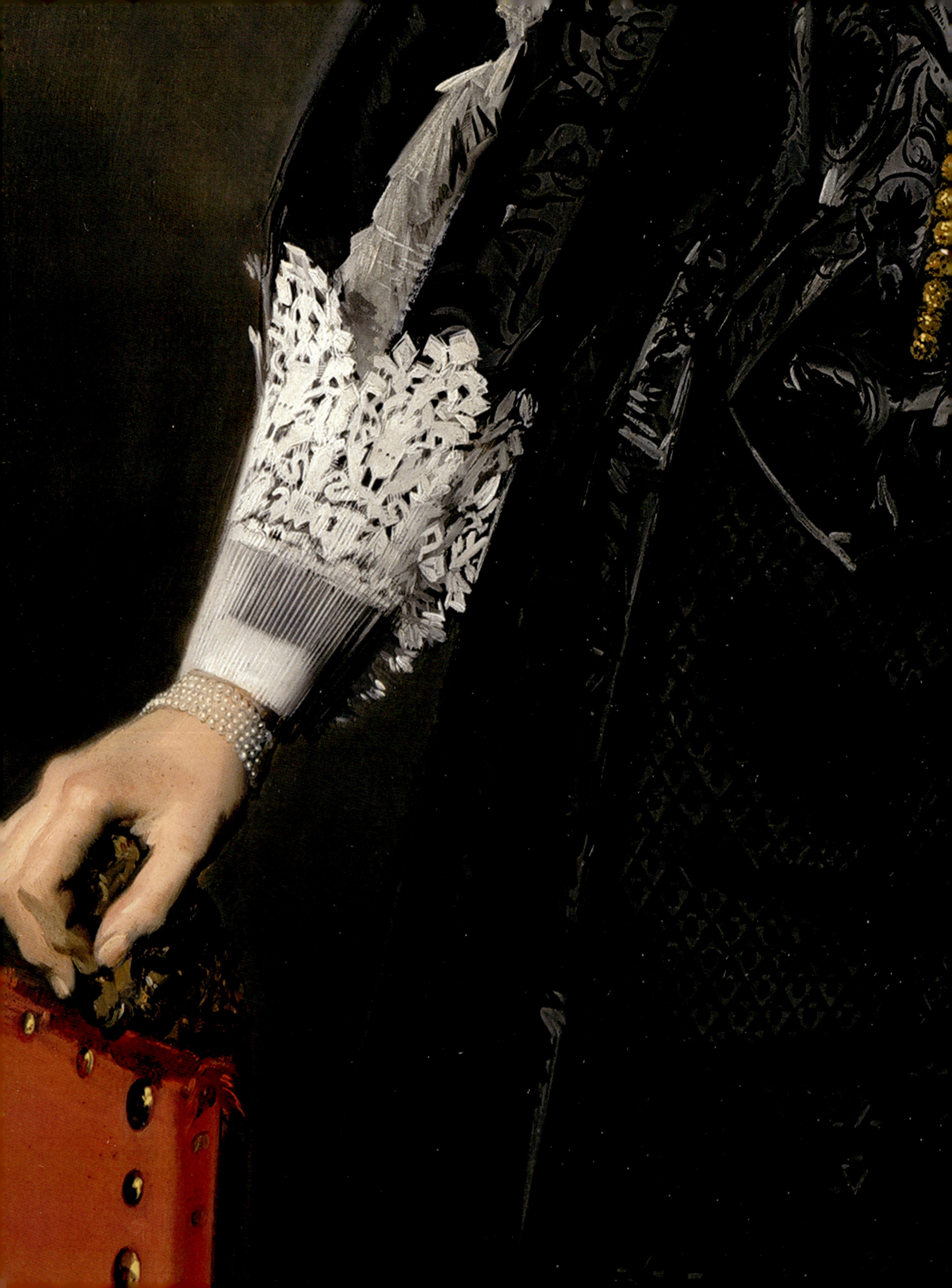

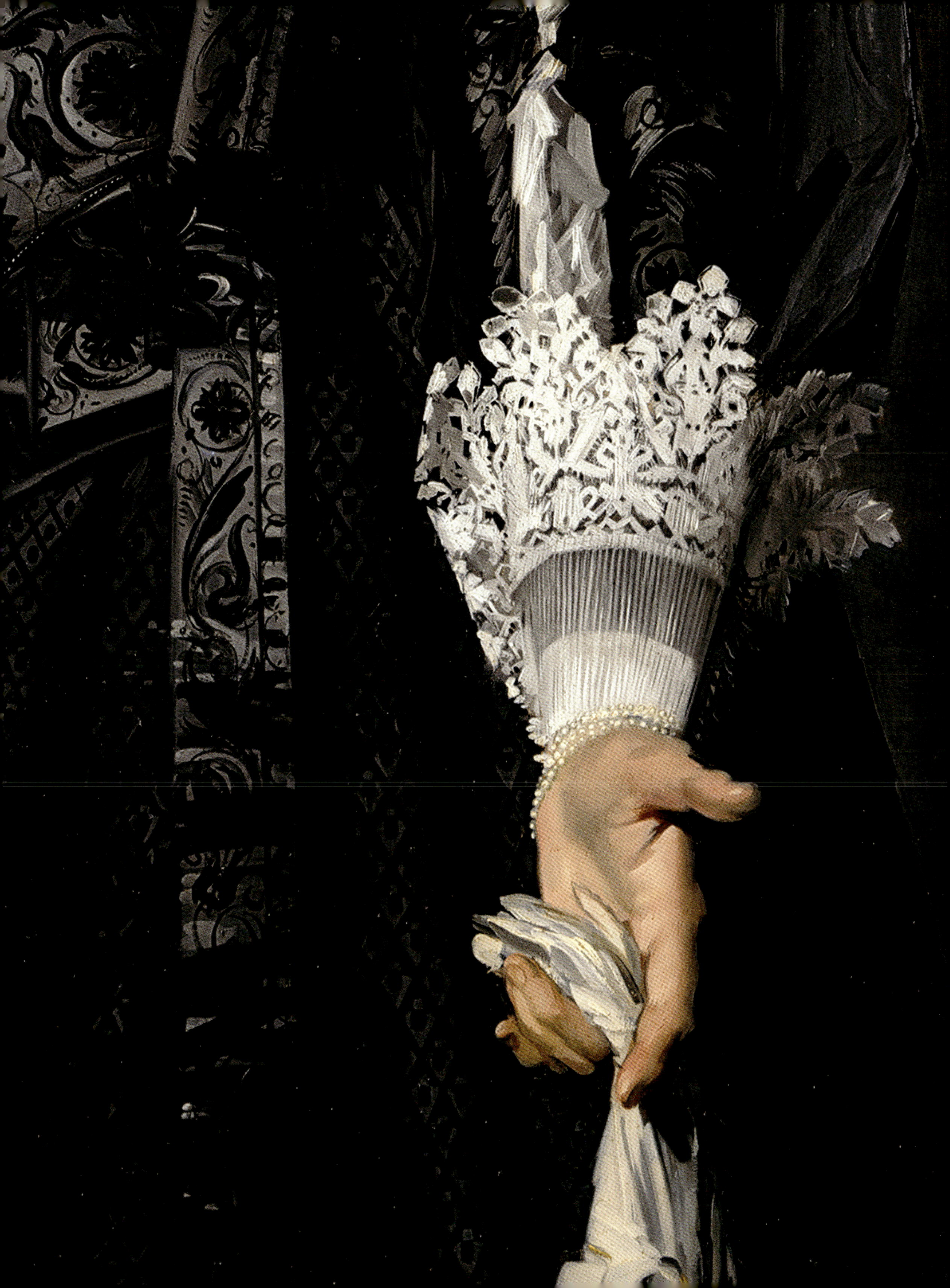

THE LIFE OF FRANS HALS

JAAP VAN DER VEEN

In 1679 the painter Matthias Scheits, born and later active in Hamburg, scribbled a few notes about painters he considered significant in his copy of Karel van Mander's *Schilder-Boeck* (Book of Painting, 1604): Rubens, Jacques Jordaens, Rembrandt, Frans Hals and Philips Wouwerman. He qualified these artists as 'outstanding masters whose art I, M.S., have known and who are deceased'.[1] Wouwerman's name jars somewhat among such renowned artists but was probably included because he had been Scheits's teacher. This period of instruction took place sometime between 1640 and 1651 in Haarlem, where Scheits would have interacted directly with Hals.[2] He would have heard a thing or two about this painter, not least from his own master, for Wouwerman had been taught in turn by Frans Hals.[3] After his apprenticeship, Scheits returned to Hamburg but he stayed in touch with his colleagues in the Dutch Republic, some of whom visited him in his home-town.[4] He travelled at least once more to the Netherlands: in 1669 he visited Jordaens at his home in Antwerp and may well have gone north on the way there or on his journey home. Scheits was aware, for example, that Rembrandt had died in Amsterdam in September of that year.[5]

The fact that Scheits knew personally the leading artists of his time, with the exception of Rubens, is what makes his annotations so valuable, however summary. 'The exceptional portrait painter Frans Hals of Haarlem', he writes, 'studied under Carel Vermander of Molebeke'. He may have heard about this during his period of training in Haarlem and was later able to read about it in Van Mander's book. The second edition of the *Schilder-Boeck* (1618) includes an anonymous biography of the author, by then deceased, listing Frans Hals among his prominent students.[6]

The course of Frans Hals's life can be traced in broad outline thanks to documents found about him and his relatives.[7] He was born in the Southern Netherlands and moved with his parents at a young age to Haarlem, where he worked as a portrait painter between 1610 and 1666. Little is known about the lives of virtually any seventeenth-century Dutch painters, in particular concerning the day-to-day operations of their studios. This is no different for Hals. In his case we do not even have the kind of source material that has survived for many of his colleagues, such as a will or an estate inventory. The sparse information that we do have seldom concerns his activities as a painter, including how he acquired clients as a portraitist. We do know what he looked like: he pictured himself in *Officers and Sergeants of the St George Civic Guard* around 1639 (fig. 67, see detail opposite). The image of Hals that has emerged over time was defined to a significant degree by details mentioned by the artist biographer Arnold Houbraken. In the first volume of his *De groote schouburgh der Nederlantsche konstschilders en schilderessen* (The Great Theatre of the Netherlandish Painters and Paintresses), published in 1718, he portrayed Hals as someone who frequented drinking establishments daily. Houbraken also recorded several remarkable anecdotes about the painter but their veracity is considered dubious. What follows is a sketch of the life of Frans Hals and then an examination of Houbraken's text, which has so influenced, rightly or wrongly, our view of the artist.

EARLY YEARS

The gaps in our knowledge of the life of Frans Hals start with the year of his birth, which cannot be determined with certainty. His father, Franchoys Fransz Hals, and mother, Ariaentje van Geertenrijck, must have been married in Antwerp in early 1582 or shortly before. Their son Frans was probably born the same year, or at the latest in early 1584.[8] Both parents had been married before. Hals senior's profession was that of 'lakenbereider' (cloth-shearer).[9] The couple had two more sons: Joost, born around 1585, and Dirck, who was baptised at the Dutch Reformed Church in Haarlem in 1591. When Antwerp fell into Spanish hands during the Eighty Years' War in 1585, the family, like many others, fled north, sometime between the summer of 1585 and July 1586.[10] The fact that they settled immediately in the Northern Netherlands is not insignificant: the conditions of surrender of

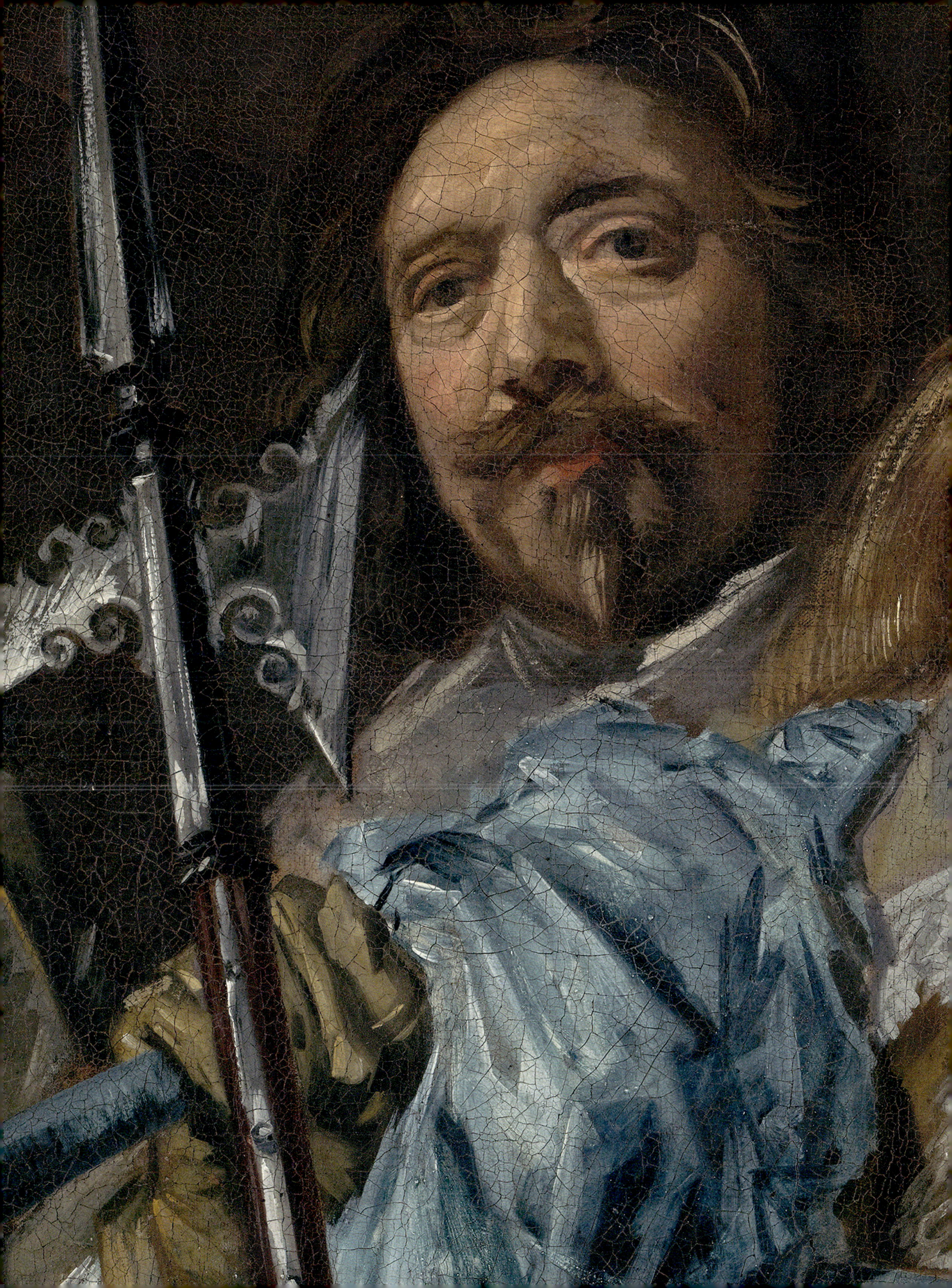

Antwerp stipulated that fleeing to the rebellious provinces could result in the confiscation of any property left behind. If refugees first went to neutral territory, however, they would retain their rights to their belongings. For example, the parents of Pieter de Molijn, later a leading landscape painter in Haarlem, initially spent time in London before going to the Dutch Republic.[11] The fact that Hals senior and his wife did not do this, settling immediately in Haarlem instead, suggests that they had left no assets of any significance in Antwerp.

Hals's parents were among the stream of refugees who fled north from the Southern Netherlands from the late 1570s onwards for economic, political or religious reasons. Many of the Flemings and Brabanders who settled in Haarlem worked in the textile industry. Among the migrants were also various artists, including Meulebeke-born Karel van Mander. Given that Hals's presumed master left Haarlem in 1603, the apprenticeship must have taken place before this. By this time Hals was about 21 years old, an age at which formal training for an artist would normally have been completed. In many cases this would be followed by a period as a 'knecht' or 'gezel' (journeyman) for a painter. This was probably the path that Hals followed, for he would not register with Haarlem's Guild of St Luke until 1610, when he was definitely no longer a youth. In the absence of any documentation we can do no more than speculate about what he was doing in the intervening years. One possibility is that he was residing in Antwerp, to which he would later return for a time in 1616.[12]

Hals's late start as an independent master in Haarlem may have been caused by something other than a period of work elsewhere. The aforementioned Scheits notes the following about him: 'in his youth he led a rather *lüstich* [lusty] life'.[13] The basis for this remark, written in a mixture of Dutch and German, cannot be found in any contemporary publication: Scheits probably gleaned the information during his apprenticeship in Haarlem and felt it worth recording many years later. The word 'youth' would have referred not to Hals's teenage years but to the period before he attained his legal majority, which began at the age of 25 or upon marriage. The passage suggests that Hals was living it up: the word 'lüstich' implies a dissolute lifestyle, at a time when young men, and artists in particular, had a reputation for it. The author of a pamphlet published in 1662 condemned what he considered the ostentatious attire of his contemporaries, prescribing who should and should not be permitted to wear costly fabrics. But what was to be done about painters? These varied markedly in terms of their work and income, and many, concluded the pamphleteer, were also 'mad of spirit'.[14] It seems that these artists were often arrogant and probably displayed bohemian-like behaviour.

This is reminiscent of the adage Van Mander cites in his text *Den grondt der edel vry schilder-const* (The Foundation of the Noble, Free Art of Painting): 'hoe Schilder hoe wilder' (the more painter the wilder).[15] He describes this as a 'volcx' (popular) proverb; it must therefore have

been widely used. The adage presumably reflected the fact that some painters, especially the more successful among them, did not take much notice of prevailing norms and deemed themselves 'free'. In this context we might consider the gatherings of artists in inns, for example, where things could get boisterous. Upon completing his training, Frans Hals was 'free' in two ways: he was a bachelor and did not yet have his own studio, with all the attendant responsibilities. Both situations would change almost simultaneously.

PAINTER IN HAARLEM

In 1610 Hals both joined the Guild of St Luke of Haarlem and established his social status. From 1612 he served as a musketeer in the third company of the St George Civic Guard. The fact that he had settled down is also evidenced by his marriage: around 1610 he married Anneke Harmens, the daughter of a Haarlem bleacher.[16] The couple had three children, of whom two were still living when Anneke died at the age of 25 in 1615, including a son, Harmen (born in 1611). Two years later Hals married Lysbeth Reyniers, whose father, a glazier, must have been one of his acquaintances, since his profession was also part of the Guild of St Luke. Between 1617 and 1634 it seems that the couple had 11 children, of whom Frans, Jan, Reynier and Claes, along with their half-brother Harmen, became painters. The baptismal registration of eight of the children has been found, all in the Dutch Reformed Church. Serving as witnesses were relatives of both parents and several individuals who can be considered close friends of the family, among them Flemish merchant Isaac Massa and innkeeper Barend van Someren. Other witnesses included colleagues such as the painters Franchoys Elaut and Nicolaes de Kemp the Elder, the print publisher and art seller Jan Pietersz Berendrecht and the draughtsman and graphic artist Jan van de Velde the Younger. They remained in close contact with the family: Berendrecht published prints of paintings by Frans and his brother Dirck Hals between 1626 and 1632, while in the same period Van de Velde produced prints of seven paintings by Frans Hals.

We know of virtually no signed and dated paintings from the first years after Hals registered with the Haarlem Guild of St Luke. His breakthrough came around 1615, the year in which he was probably commissioned to paint a banquet of officers of the St George Civic Guard, which he completed in 1616 (fig. 68). In the preceding years he was presumably building his reputation as an artist. His signing up in 1616 as a member of the Haarlem chamber of rhetoric De Wijngaertrancken (Vine Tendrils) also indicates a breakthrough: people would join a chamber of rhetoric when they became socially successful.[17]

Hals specialised in portrait painting from the outset. This deliberate choice is notable in that Van Mander, in his treatise, advised young painters to focus on history painting, which he considered most important, while realising that not every artist had either the opportunity

THE LIFE OF FRANS HALS

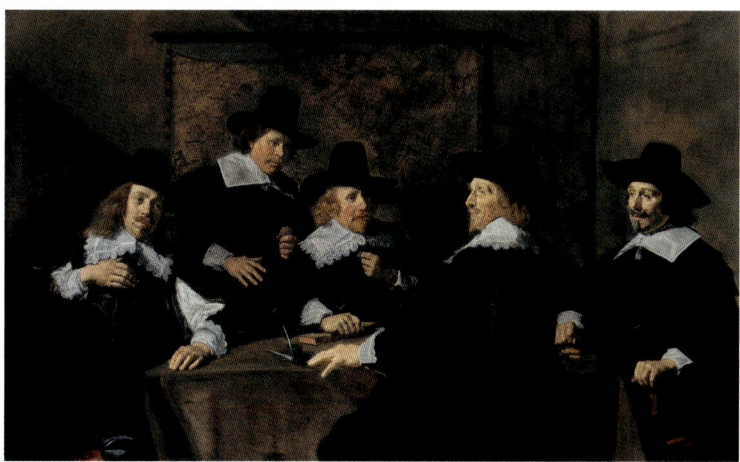

Fig. 5 *Regents of St Elizabeth's Hospital in Haarlem*,
about 1641. Oil on canvas, 153 × 252 cm
Frans Hals Museum, Haarlem

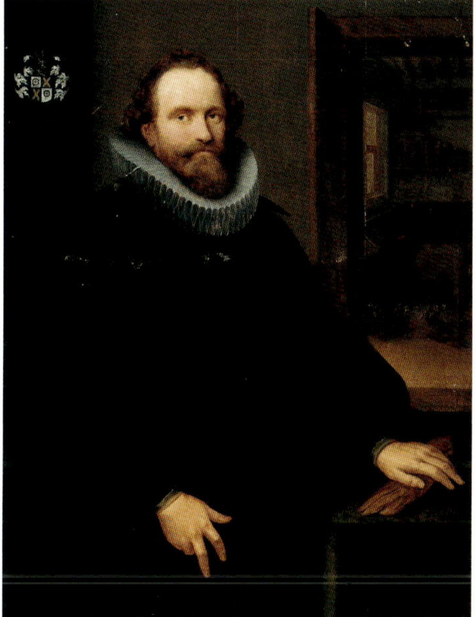

Fig. 6 Frans Pietersz de Grebber,
Portrait of Job Claesz Gijblant, 1611
Oil on wood, 129 × 101 cm
Frans Hals Museum, Haarlem

or the talent for it. He writes that around 1600, due to a dearth of commissions, many turned to painting portraits and were thus able to successfully support themselves.[18] A portrait painter had a regular income but less freedom to develop, since the expectation was to conform to the wishes of the clients in respect of format, general composition and pose. Clients' demands could be very specific, as evidenced by the five Haarlem civic guard paintings that Hals produced between 1616 and 1639 (figs 65–9). In none of these are the figures portrayed full-length, whereas this is not the case in his only Amsterdam civic guard painting from the same period (fig. 70). This seems to have been at the request of the clients rather than the painter's choice. Clients' wishes regarding execution would have been less explicit, given the fact that most were familiar with Hals's painting style. He was certainly able to produce fine likenesses of his models. Not only is there no surviving evidence of a complaint about a likeness – as is the case with other portraitists – but the many portraits that Hals continued to make throughout his career are proof of his reputation.

In addition to his six civic guard paintings, Hals painted a regents portrait around 1641 (fig. 5) and two group portraits of the regents and regentesses of the Haarlem Old Men's Alms House around 1664 (figs 3–4). These nine paintings depicted a total of around a hundred people. We can only guess the number of individual portraits that Hals produced. Author and poet Theodorus Schrevelius, who lived in Haarlem for many years, writes about Hals's production in *Harlemias…*, the Dutch edition of his ode to the city, published in 1648. Schrevelius praises the unusual painting style of Hals's portraits, 'which is unique to him', of which he says there are 'unbelievably many'.[19] These do not include the portraits contained in the civic guard paintings, as he mentions these later. What did Schrevelius mean by 'unbelievably many'? His assertion cannot simply be ignored, for as a fellow townsman and contemporary of Hals he must have been well informed and had himself, in 1617, posed for Hals (fig. 106). The catalogue of Hals's works compiled by art historian Seymour Slive lists fewer than two hundred individual likenesses, a number that would not necessarily qualify as 'unbelievably many'. Schrevelius probably exaggerated somewhat; this also occurred with the commentaries that other authors made on the production of other artists.[20] The assumption that portraits by Hals have been lost over time offers only a partially satisfactory explanation. In any event, he was popular as a portraitist and in his most successful period, until the mid-1640s, he was definitely not short of work.

Hals had to carve out a place for himself in the art market as a portrait painter. In Haarlem he had to compete with, among others, renowned artists from an earlier generation, including Cornelis Cornelisz, who was active as a painter from 1580, and Cornelis Engelsz, the father of Johannes Verspronck, who was commissioned to paint civic guard portraits in 1612 and 1618. His greatest competitor must have been Frans Pietersz

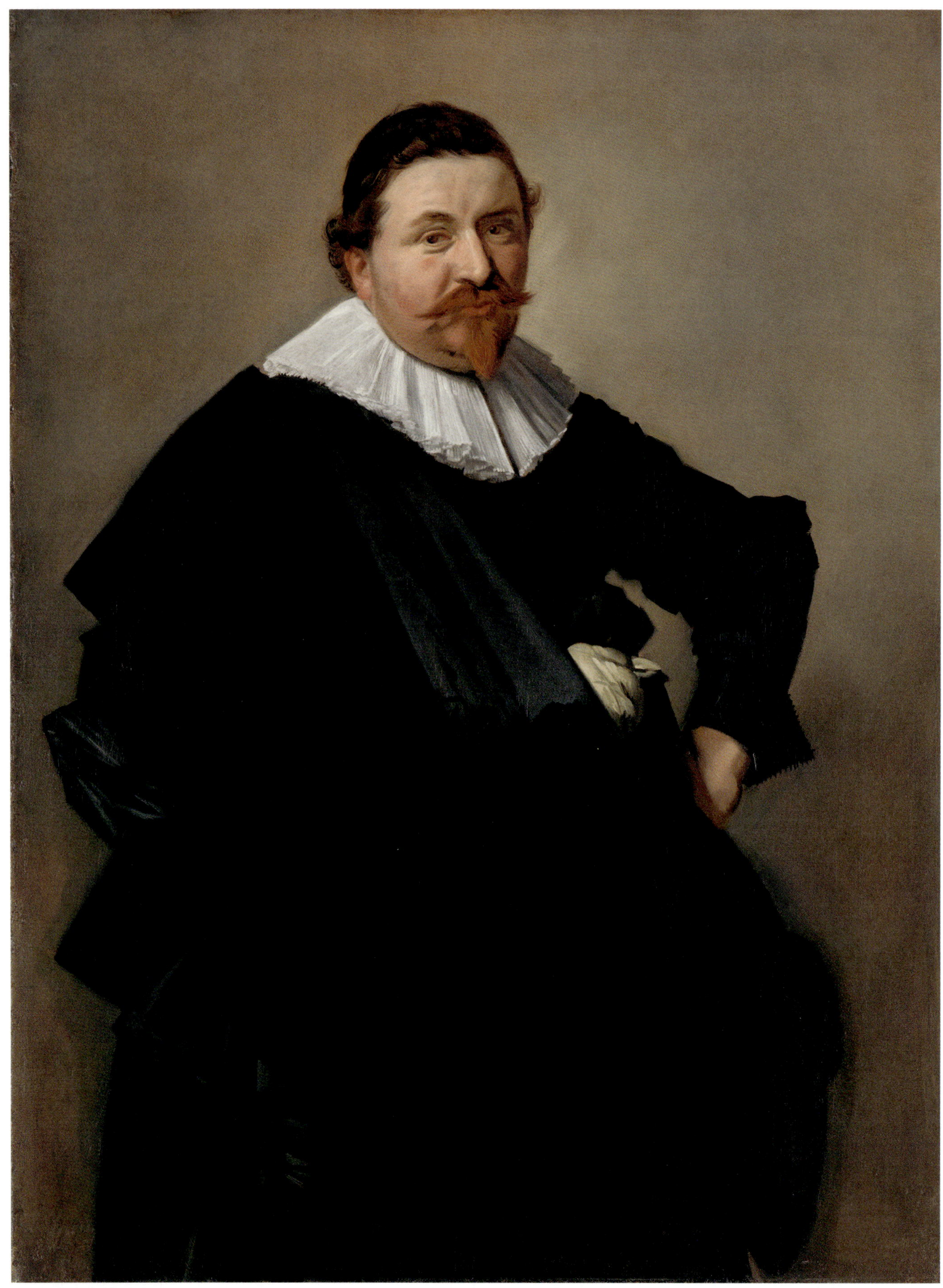

Fig. 7 *Portrait of Lucas de Clercq*, about 1635
Oil on canvas, 121.6 × 91.5 cm
Rijksmuseum, Amsterdam

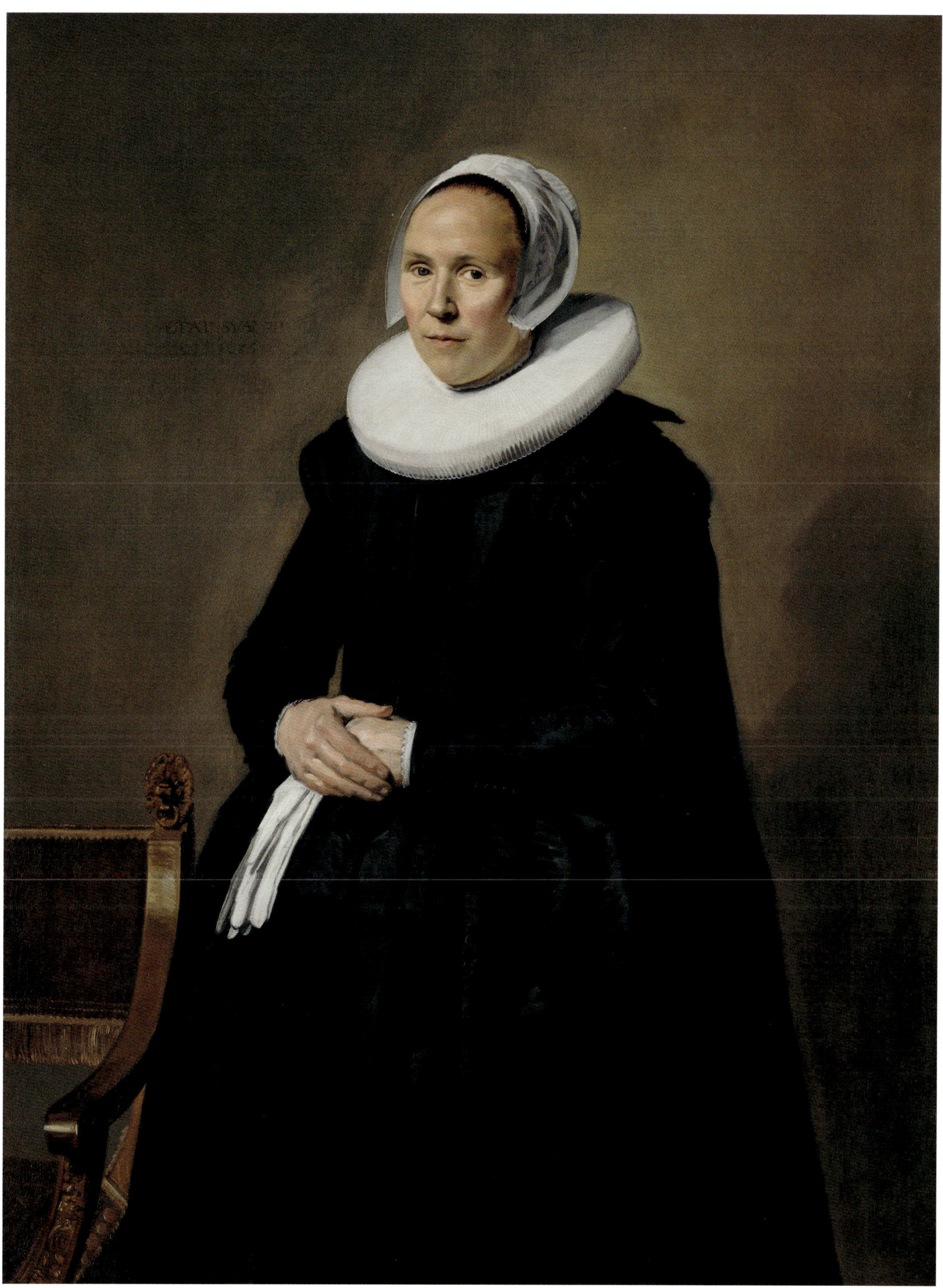

Fig. 8 *Portrait of Feyntje van Steenkiste*, 1635
Oil on canvas, 121.9 × 91.5 cm
Rijksmuseum, Amsterdam

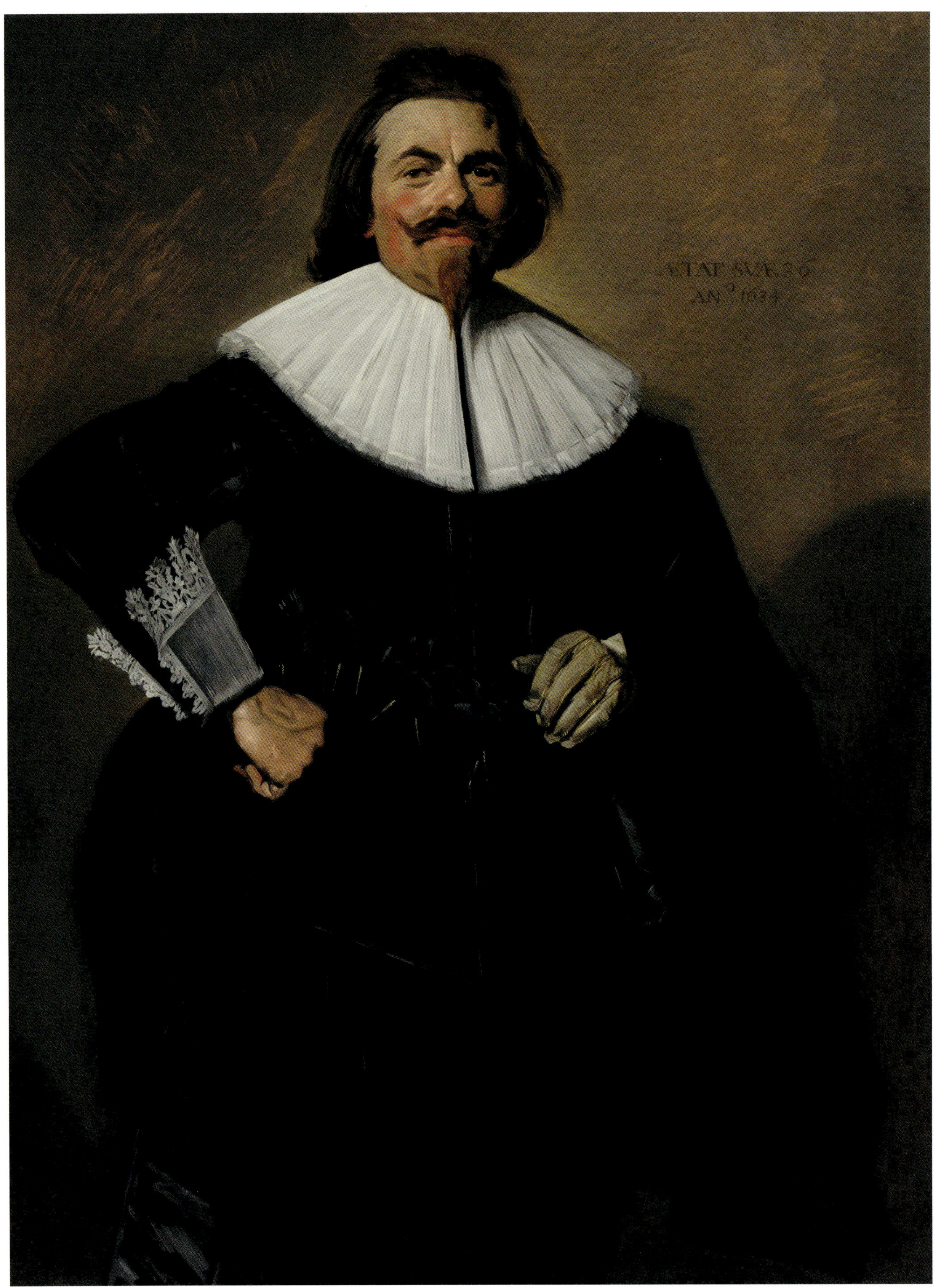

Fig. 9 *Portrait of Tieleman Roosterman*, 1634
Oil on canvas, 117 × 87 cm
The Cleveland Museum of Art

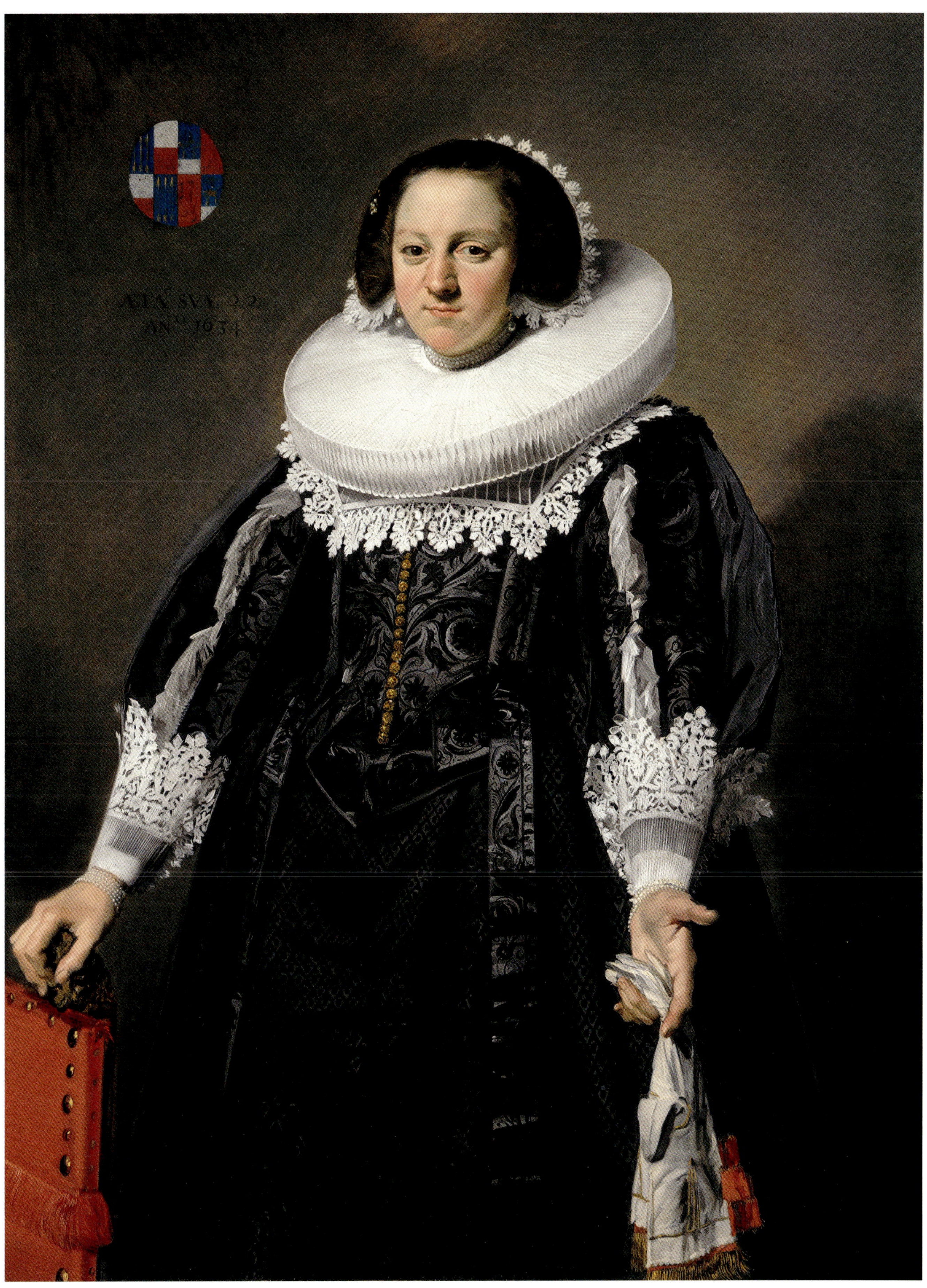

Fig. 10 *Portrait of Catharina Brugman*, 1634
Oil on canvas, 115 × 85 cm
Private collection

de Grebber, who from 1594 painted portraits – including life-size work – as well as history paintings in Haarlem and ran a studio with a series of pupils and assistants. Between 1600 and 1624, De Grebber made five Haarlem civic guard group portraits. It is worth noting that it was him and not Hals who in 1611 painted the portrait of the Haarlem brewer and alderman Job Claesz Gijblant (fig. 6), who was closely connected to Hals: he had served as guardian to his niece Anneke Harmens prior to her marriage to Hals. Apparently it was not self-evident that such a portrait commission should go to a relative by marriage. Not that Hals had much to complain about in terms of commissions in the meantime: a few years later it was him and not De Grebber who was awarded the commission for the aforementioned civic guard banquet painting finished in 1616.

His commissions reveal that Hals quickly made his name as a portraitist. His clients included members of the political and economic elite of Haarlem, including wealthy cloth merchants and beer brewers (figs 7–10, 41–2). Over a period of several years he painted at least 18 portraits of members of the well-to-do Olycan brewing family and their relatives.[21] Scholarly writers also employed him to paint their portraits, usually small likenesses intended to be made into prints. His portrait of Schrevelius is one such example.[22] Hals's clientele was made up of the city's elite: only affluent citizens could afford to commission a portrait from an artist of his standing.

Yet Hals also made portraits of acquaintances and colleagues, not always on commission or for a fee. The two portraits of the parents (or parents-in-law) of painter Nicolaes de Kemp the Elder, which may not have been preserved, belong in this category. Born around 1574, De Kemp also practised his profession in Haarlem and maintained close relations with Hals.[23] Karel van Mander's anonymous biographer writes that De Kemp, like Hals, had studied under Van Mander; between 1614 and 1621 he was a 'beminnaer' (member) of De Wijngaertrancken (Vine Tendrils), the chamber of rhetoric to which Hals also belonged at that time,[24] and he served as a witness at the baptism of Claes, the son born to Hals and his second wife in 1628. Hals's two portraits are listed in a document of 1656, which states that Willem Buytewech produced the painted frame.[25] Since this artist worked in Haarlem between 1612 and 1617, it is probable that Hals painted the portraits in this period, although it is not possible, based on the document, to determine whether the portraits are of De Kemp's parents or his wife's. If the former, Hals must have worked from existing portraits, since the couple were already deceased; if the latter, they could have been painted from life since De Kemp's in-laws were still living in Haarlem at the beginning of the seventeenth century.

While most of Hals's clients lived in Haarlem or had connections with the city, people found their way to his studio from further afield as well, such as members of the Soop family of Amsterdam, owners of a glass factory who commissioned several portraits from Hals. In 1632 civic guardsmen in Amsterdam sought a painter for the group portrait of their company, and it is significant that they selected Hals. In the seventeenth century it was extremely uncommon – and in fact went against the rules of the guild – to engage an artist working elsewhere for such a commission.

Frans Hals thus dedicated himself to painting commissioned portraits, but over time he also began making genre paintings of cheerful revellers and types such as a *rommelpot* player and the comic theatrical character Pekelharing (figs 153–4, 172). In addition, he painted *tronies* (expressive facial or head studies) as well as fisherboys and girls (figs 164, 167–8), works in which his fluid brushwork came into its own even more than in his portraits. Such pieces were sold at public auctions, contributing to Hals's name recognition. An early document that has so far gone unnoticed in the literature on Hals must be related to this kind of work. In 1621 the Amsterdam merchant Dirck Rodenburg sent a memorandum to Christian IV, in which he provided the Danish king with the names of entrepreneurs and artisans willing to work for him in his country. The Haarlem painter Salomon de Bray, for example, was open to working in Copenhagen. Rodenburg sent a list of about 350 paintings that he had taken with him to Denmark and from which the king could select. The merchant had purchased the works of art in Antwerp, Amsterdam, Delft and Haarlem; in the latter he had spoken with De Bray. The list features the names of such Haarlem masters as Karel van Mander, Hendrick Goltzius, Cornelis Cornelisz van Haarlem and Hendrick Vroom, as well as Frans Hals.[26] Rodenburg did not specify subjects, writing only that the inventory would be worth no less than 20,000 rijksdaalders, thus indicating that he was offering the king the best of the best. For this reason the paintings by Hals are unlikely to have been his insignificant *tronies*, genre pieces or portraits. It is most likely that Hals's work on Rodenburg's list included paintings such as the *Merrymakers at Shrovetide* (fig. 149) or *The Rommel-Pot Player* (fig. 172), which may have been painted by 1621.

TWO IMPORTANT CLIENTS

Hals painted portraits of at least two of the witnesses present at his children's baptisms. The first is Pieter van den Broecke, a cloth merchant's son born in Antwerp in 1585. In his youth he travelled to Africa and Asia and later held an important position in the Dutch East India Company: he was a factory director in Surate, a trading post on the north-west coast of present-day India. On returning to the Dutch Republic in 1630 he published his travel experiences. His portrait, painted by Hals in 1633 (fig. 11), was made into a print by Adriaen Jacobsz Matham and included in this book, which was published in 1634. Matham, as was his wont, may have made a drawing from the painted portrait to use as the basis for the print.[27] We cannot exclude the possibility that Hals painted a small-format portrait especially for the printmaker

THE LIFE OF FRANS HALS

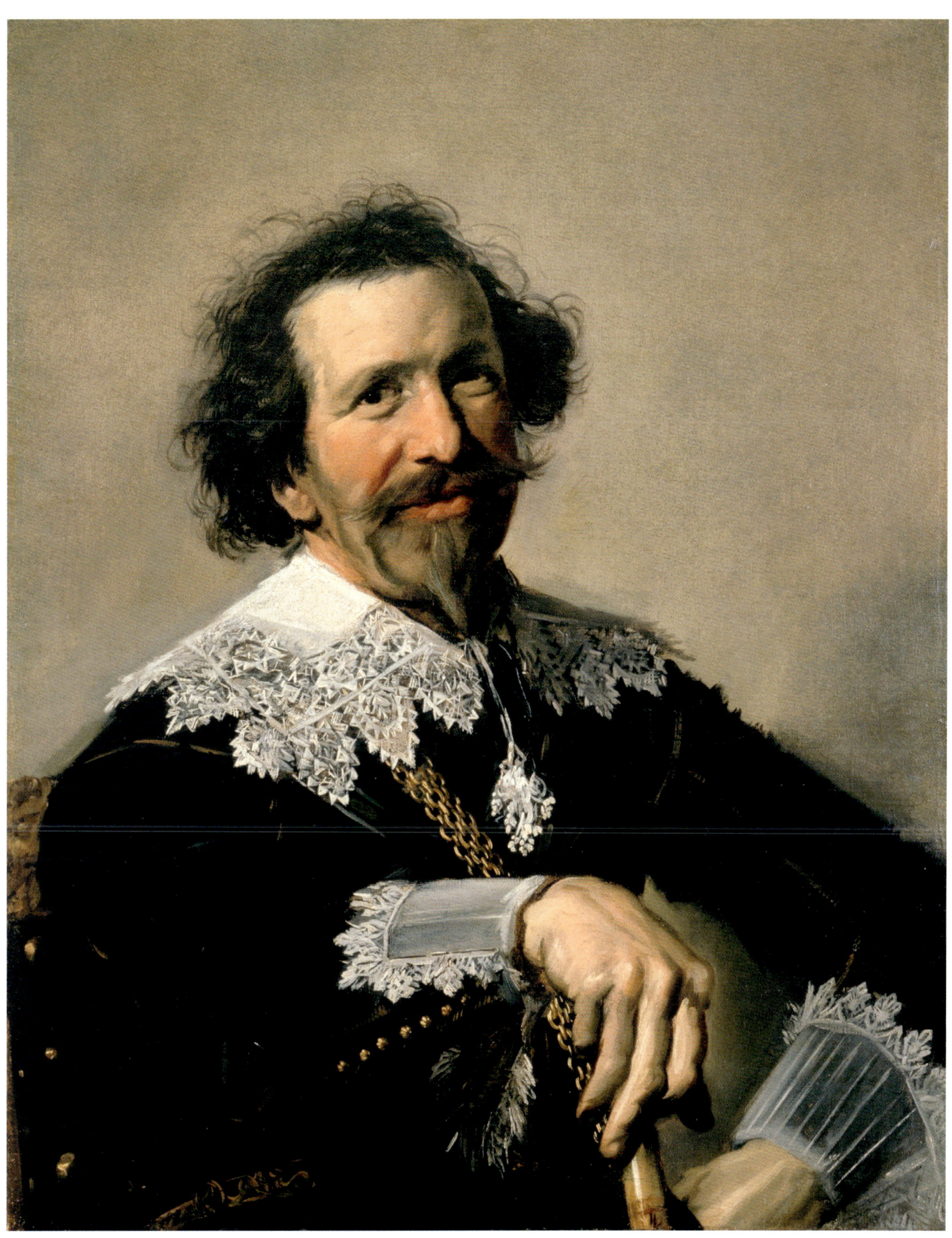

Fig. 11 *Portrait of Pieter van den Broecke*, 1633
Oil on canvas, 68.3 × 54.9 cm
English Heritage, The Iveagh Bequest (Kenwood, London)

and that he subsequently (at the request of the sitter) made a portrait of him in a larger format. The idea of approaching Hals is more likely to have come from the publisher, Passchier van Wesbusch, than from Van den Broecke himself. Since his arrival in Haarlem in 1601, Van Wesbusch had sold, among other things, chamber of rhetoric texts by his fellow Mennonite Karel van Mander as well as his *Schilder-Boeck*. His son, Hans Passchiers van Wesbusch, expanded his father's business and also sold prints, including work by Jan van de Velde the Younger. The successful collaboration between those involved in Van den Broecke's publication is evidenced by Van de Velde's presence at the baptism of Hals's daughter Susanna on 26 January 1634. The second witness, listed only by his first name and patronym as Adriaen Jacobs, can be none other than Adriaen Jacobsz Matham.[28]

The Haarlem merchant Isaac Massa, who traded in Russia and lived there for a time as well, is the other witness to the baptism of a child of Hals and his second wife to have his portrait painted by Hals. Unlike Pieter van den Broecke, who seems to have been in professional contact with Hals only once, Massa kept in touch with the painter for an extended period of time. If the portrait of the man with his arms crossed painted by Hals in 1622 (fig. 94) does indeed represent Massa, as argued elsewhere in this book, they already knew each other by this date.[29] A certain familiarity between the two, as with Van den Broecke, seems to have resulted from the commission, and Massa was a witness at the baptism of Hals's daughter Ariaentje on 21 July 1623.[30] Other members of the Massa and Hals families also knew each other. For example, Susanna Massa, one of Isaac's sisters, served as a witness alongside the aforementioned draughtsman and printmaker Jan van de Velde the Younger at the baptism of a daughter of Dirck Hals in 1624. Hals painted portraits of Isaac Massa in 1626 (fig. 93) and again in 1635, the latter a small-format sketch intended to be made into a print by Adriaen Matham (figs 112, 133).

Isaac Massa married Beatrix van der Laen in 1622, and after her death in 1639 he married Maria van Wassenbergh the following year. He died in 1643, his second wife in 1652, whereupon, with an eye to the interests of the minor children, an inventory of their joint possessions was drawn up. In this estate inventory, which is unpublished, are no fewer than five portraits of Isaac Massa.[31] None is attributed to an artist but three of them must have been painted by Hals.[32] In addition to two portraits of Massa's second wife, the inventory lists around twenty other paintings but only three with makers' names. These include various landscapes, a single work with a secular theme and a few biblical scenes, including *Job on the Dung Heap* and *Joseph and Mary*. The three attributed paintings bear Hals's name: 'a small painting of music by Master Hals, with a black ebony frame' and 'two round *tronies* by Frans Hals'.[33] One of Massa's portrait commissions may have led to the purchase of these small works. Or did Hals perhaps gift these to his client? The 'small painting of music' may

have been a representation of children playing music, comparable to Hals's *Two singing Boys* – although this cannot be described as small.[34] The two other works may possibly be identified as Hals's *Laughing Boy with a Wine Glass* (fig. 165) and *Laughing Boy with a Flute* (fig. 166), given their round, small format and the fact that they are pendant paintings.[35]

Hals's children may have served as models for his paintings of boys and girls.[36] The 'two square portraits of the children of Hals done in Haarlem by the same' listed in a Leiden inventory in 1644 may be Hals's *Girl singing* (fig. 12) and *Boy playing the Violin* (fig. 13), both now in a private collection.[37] Besides the fact that these works are square (diamond-shaped), which is practically never found in Hals's oeuvre, they are also pendant paintings. One Haarlem resident, who by his own account had known most of Hals's children, told Houbraken that they were keen musicians. This supports the idea that the boys and girls playing music depicted by Hals may have been his own children.

The number of paintings in Isaac Massa's estate inventory does not directly suggest that he was an important art collector. However, it was not drawn up until nine years after his death, so some of his property may have been sold or moved elsewhere in the intervening years. What is certain is that Massa spent time with artists: besides Hals he was also particularly well acquainted with De Grebber and Pieter de Molijn. In 1653 De Molijn declared, at the request of fellow Haarlem resident and art dealer Olivier Jacobsz, that he had maintained 'great familiarity' with Jacobsz and Isaac Massa (who had died in the meantime) for many years.[38] According to this same declaration, De Molijn, on the instructions of Jacobsz, had gone to Massa's home in about 1634 and spoken with him about a painting by Moyses van Wtenbrouck, which Jacobsz had sold to Massa. This transaction had not been successfully completed.[39] As an art dealer, Jacobsz represented the interests of several Haarlem painters, and apparently Massa also did business with him.[40]

HALS'S FINANCIAL POSITION

One would assume that the steady stream of portrait commissions provided Frans Hals with a sizeable income. In addition there was also the income from his teaching and paintings sold from his studio. Hals received a considerable sum in 1615 from the estate of his first wife's grandfather. The inheritance had to be split among a large number of people, but Hals nevertheless received about 565 guilders.[41] Such a sum far exceeded the annual income of most artisans.

It is worth noting the attitude Hals adopted in his conflict with the Amsterdam civic guard officers. When the group portrait they had commissioned was still not finished in 1636, the clients summoned Hals to fulfil his obligations.[42] In his reply he made no attempt whatsoever to meet the gentlemen halfway. Indeed, he exacer-

THE LIFE OF FRANS HALS

bated the situation by suggesting that they should travel to Haarlem, knowing all too well that this would not happen: it had previously proved difficult to persuade the men to attend sittings even in their own city. One of the documents on this issue shows that Hals had already received part of the agreed payment.[43] For such commissions it was not unusual for part of the fee – sometimes even half – to be paid in advance. Hals had to paint the portraits of a total of 16 individuals, each of whom was expected to pay 60 guilders out of his own pocket, totalling 960 guilders. In reality the total was more: in the meantime the clients had agreed with Hals that he would be paid an additional six guilders per person if he was willing to carry out the work in Amsterdam, which came to 1,056 guilders. In not being inclined to be accommodating to his clients – who judged Hals's reply to their request 'frivolous', if not downright insolent – the painter was forfeiting a very large sum. If he had received half in advance, this was almost 500 guilders, and otherwise even more. This is not exactly something that an artist in dire financial straits would do. Clearly Hals could afford to do this, or he felt that he could.

Until the 1640s he must have been doing well financially. Yet it is often thought that he was then already living in precarious circumstances. His many changes of address, for example, do not indicate a carefree existence. Hals never bought a house; he always rented and he regularly moved with his family.[44] The precise locations on each street are unknown, so we do not know how large these houses were, let alone what their floorplans were like. However, his residence on the Groot Heiligland could not have been small: in his reply of 20 March 1636 to the Amsterdam civic guard officers regarding the completion of their group portrait, Hals proposed that the gentlemen should come to Haarlem, where he would finish the painting – of hardly modest dimensions – 'in his own house'.[45]

It has been said that Hals was regularly harassed by creditors, yet this was not particularly exceptional: in the seventeenth century the extension of considerable and long-term credit was commonplace.[46] Shopkeepers and suppliers, often bakers, had to exercise enormous patience with slow payers. When they insisted on payment, this did not always take place in currency: an outstanding debt might be fulfilled in kind. In Hals's case these were relatively small sums – and it is by no means certain that the debts were always his. 'Hals' was a common name in Haarlem, while later mentions may also refer to his son of the same name. In 1654, however, he did incur a considerable debt. In that year a Haarlem baker claimed that he owed 200 guilders for bread delivered and money loaned. Hals paid off the debt in kind with some household items and five paintings: a *Sermon of John the Baptist* by Karel van Mander; a *Gathering of the Manna by the Israelites* by Maarten van Heemskerck; another *Sermon of John the Baptist* painted by his eldest son, Harmen; as well as a work by Hals himself and another by one of his sons, neither otherwise specified. The creditor, however,

allowed Hals to continue to keep these items.[47] Hals presumably dealt in works of art, like many of his colleagues, and it is also possible that he used such paintings in his studio as teaching aids. It is no coincidence that the painting by his eldest son was a *Sermon of John the Baptist* – possibly a copy of Van Mander's.

There are other indications that Hals's finances were not in good shape in the 1650s. A passage in the will of his son Claes Hals, drawn up on 31 March 1656, names Claes's wife as his heir and stipulates what his parents should receive. It was usual for parents to be allocated a legal inheritance, but here they were given a choice of three options, all of which amounted to less than the inheritance to which they were entitled. Claes Hals asked his parents to be content with this, since by his own account he had brought hardly any assets into his marriage exactly one year previously.[48] In 1655, therefore, he had received practically nothing from his parents. Another indication of Frans Hals's poor financial position is his signing up on 8 October 1655 as a member of the Dutch Reformed congregation of Haarlem, which was presumably connected with the possibility of receiving support from the parish. To be eligible, one had to be registered as a member.

In the mid-1650s Hals was about 70 years old. By this time his production was no longer as sizeable as in earlier years, as Matthias Scheits implies. Once Hals had reached an advanced age 'and could no longer make a living with his art (which was not as before)', he turned to the municipality of Haarlem for financial support. His request was granted, Scheits says, because of the quality of his art.[49] Hals did indeed receive support at the end of his life, and not just from the Haarlem city authorities: in 1661 the governors of the Guild of St Luke gave him a dispensation from the annual contribution, and in the last four years of his life, 'in his very urgent need', Hals received financial and material assistance from the city.[50] He reached the respectable age of about 84. Scheits gives the year of his death as either 1665 or 1666, stating that the painter had died very old: 'As far as I can guess', he writes, Hals 'was 90 years old or not much less'.[51] Houbraken is more precise, taking the date of Hals's burial from a funeral notice on which was a handwritten note that the painter had died on 29 August 1666 'at the age of 85 or 86'.

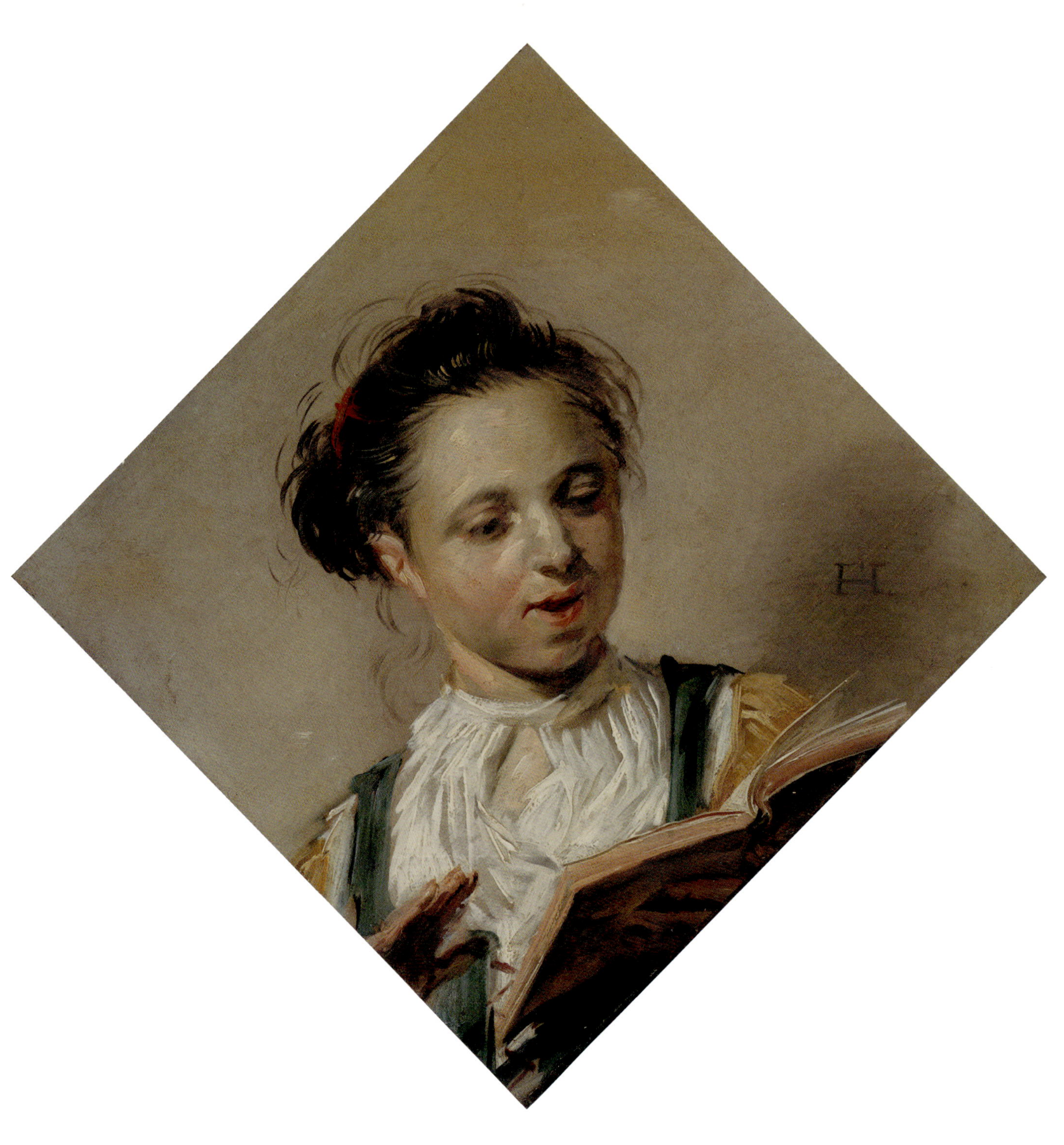

Fig. 12 *Girl singing*, about 1628
Oil on wood, 20.3 × 20.3 cm
The Jordan and Thomas A. Saunders III Collection,
on loan to the Virginia Museum of Fine Arts

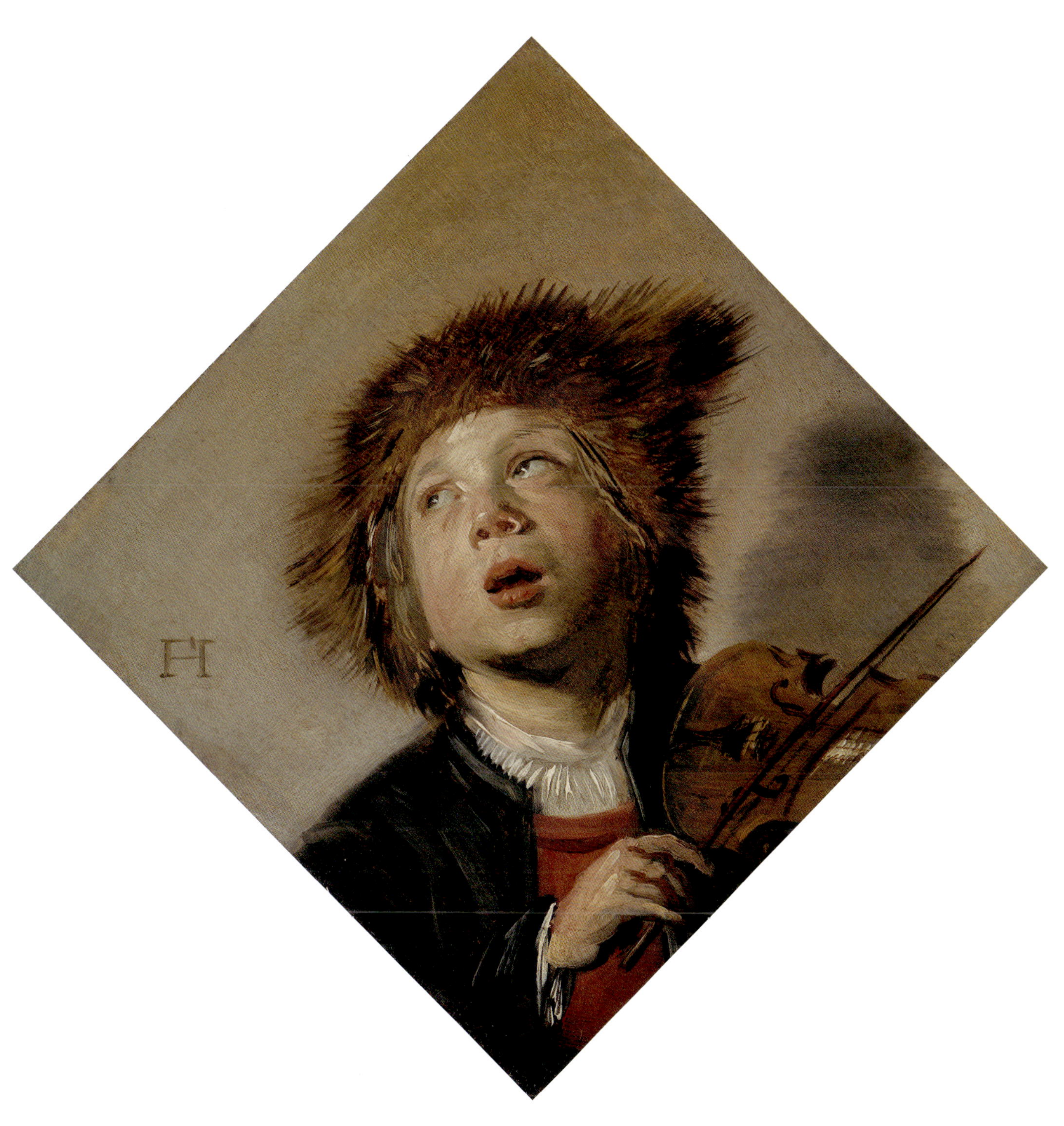

Fig. 13 *Boy playing the Violin*, about 1628
Oil on wood, 20.3 × 20.3 cm
The Jordan and Thomas A. Saunders III Collection,
on loan to the Virginia Museum of Fine Arts

HOUBRAKEN ON HALS

Our knowledge of the life of Frans Hals is based on no more than a handful of primary sources that inevitably provide a fragmentary picture. Arnold Houbraken offers a few further details in his *Groote schouburgh*, published between 1718 and 1721. In the first volume he includes an extensive text on Hals, in which he inserts, as he often did, several anecdotes that add considerably to its readability.[52] However, it is not known how reliable these stories are: their historical value is considered dubious, since most are unverifiable.[53] This applies, for instance, to the meeting that Houbraken describes between Frans Hals and the Antwerp painter Anthony van Dyck. On his way to England to enter the service of the English king, Van Dyck apparently felt the need to see Hals. Once in Haarlem he found that the painter was not at home and had to be dragged out of a pub. Hals, who supposedly did not know who his visitor was, was asked to paint his portrait. Once he had done so, Van Dyck suggested that he should depict Hals. From the way his visitor held his palette and brushes, Hals realised he was in the company of a painter; his identity became clear when he looked at the portrait. According to Houbraken, Hals embraced and kissed his visitor with the words: 'Thou art Van Dyck, for no other man can do such a thing'.

Houbraken's anecdote, reinforced by the fact that he supposedly reports the exact words of the artists, seems too good to be true. The artists' meeting is therefore considered apocryphal – all the more because it is preceded by a passage in which the story taken from Pliny the Elder about the meeting between Apelles and Protogenes is related in detail. Apelles, the celebrated painter of Ancient Greece, travelled to Rhodes in order to meet his colleague and rival Protogenes but did not find him at home. On a canvas he found in the studio he drew 'a fine line' – an outline, most likely of a body part – and asked the servant to give this to her master. As soon as Protogenes saw it he recognised the hand of Apelles, 'for no one else can do such a thing'. He then drew his own line on the canvas and gave it back to the servant to show to Apelles, should he return. Apelles indeed saw it and drew another line through it, in a different colour, so masterfully that Protogenes admitted his defeat and 'lovingly dealt with' Apelles. Houbraken concludes his tale with Anthony van Dyck taking the portrait with him, still wet, and giving the children of the family money on his departure – which their father promptly spent on drink. Houbraken asserts that Van Dyck tried hard to lure Hals to England but that Hals refused, because he did not wish to abandon his 'bad way of life'.[54]

Houbraken does not reveal how he discovered the story about the encounter between Hals and Van Dyck, beyond a mere 'they say'. He based his book on the testimony of various informants whom he often identifies in full, but in this case he remains silent. Neither does he reveal his source for the anecdote describing how Hals's students once played a clever trick on their master. According to Houbraken, Hals was wont to spend every evening drinking hard in the pub. His students were so fond of him that the eldest of them would take turns collecting him, bringing him home safely and putting him to bed. Hals supposedly had the habit, however drunk he was, of muttering a nightly prayer, always concluding it with the wish 'Dear Lord, take me up quickly to your high Heaven'.[55] Curious, the students decided to find out whether he really meant this. Above each corner of Hals's bed they drilled a hole in the ceiling, through which they lowered ropes from the attic and attached them to the bed. The following night they once again helped their master to bed and crept upstairs. When Hals mumbled his usual words, the four of them pulled up the bed in unison. At this Hals cried out: 'Not so soon, dear Lord, not so soon!' The students then lowered the bed and Hals supposedly never expressed his 'wish' again. Afterwards his students would regularly recall the incident among themselves, which 'frequently made them laugh'.[56]

Houbraken's account describes how Adriaen Brouwer and Dirck van Delen were involved in the four-poster bed prank.[57] Brouwer (fig. 14), who enjoyed a reputation among his contemporaries as a consummate prankster, played the leading role in what was seen at the time as another comic episode in Hals's studio. The artist's wife, who had something to do away from home, asked Brouwer, who was working in the house, to watch over her young child, Ariaentje. Brouwer dutifully took the child in his arms and laid her over his shoulder. He bounced her up and down so enthusiastically that she soiled him from head to toe. The young painter could not let this pass: he dropped his breeches and repaid the child in kind. Houbraken had heard this story from the painter Michiel Carré, who, he writes, was a close confidant of Pieter van Roestraten and his wife in London in 1695. The wife was no other than Ariaentje Hals, whom the young Brouwer had once babysat. She and her husband had often retold this story to Carré – 'usually for the joke', Houbraken adds.[58] As well as living in London, Michiel Carré also lived in Amsterdam, where he worked for several years from 1686 onwards and again from around 1715. Thus he was a fellow townsman of Houbraken, who frequently cites him as a source.[59] The first- and second-hand testimony inspires a certain confidence in the veracity of the story, all the more since it supposedly came from the protagonist herself, Ariaentje Hals, and her husband, who had worked as a student and assistant for Frans Hals.

In his biography of Adriaen Brouwer, Houbraken discusses the period during which Brouwer worked for Hals at length, basing his account on a text provided by a student of the painter Karel de Moor. This source is not known to us but it is unlikely to have been an invention: Houbraken and De Moor knew each other very well and the latter was still alive when the last volume of *De groote schouburgh*, in which he is cited as an informant, was published.[60] The young Brouwer had been given a space

THE LIFE OF FRANS HALS

Fig. 14 Workshop of Arnold Houbraken after an unknown example,
Portrait of Adriaen Brouwer, in Houbraken's *De groote schouburgh*
(1718–21), vol. 1, opposite p. 326 (detail)
Rijksmuseum Research Library, Amsterdam

Fig. 15 Workshop of Arnold Houbraken after an unknown example,
Portrait of Frans Hals, in Houbraken's *De groote schouburgh*
(1718–21), vol. 1, opposite p. 90 (detail)
Rijksmuseum Research Library, Amsterdam

of his own in the attic of Hals's house. Although he worked diligently for his master, he felt short-changed. Dissatisfied with the situation and goaded by Adriaen van Ostade and others, Brouwer decided to leave. Having no idea where to find somewhere else to live, he came back with his tail between his legs – and Hals subsequently treated him better, keen not to lose the income from Brouwer's work. Brouwer nevertheless left a second time, this time for Amsterdam, where he wished to work for someone dealing in art. There, according to Houbraken, he found 'a certain van Zomeren, at the time innkeeper of 't schilt van Vrankryk'. This innkeeper 'took him in, and set him to work painting'.[61]

If the details about Brouwer and Hals were indeed taken from this unknown source, it did contain reliable elements. Brouwer's new patron in Amsterdam was in fact Barend van Someren, a painter who combined the professions of innkeeper and art dealer. The contact between the two can even be specified with greater precision: a notarial deed drawn up between Van Someren and the painter Adriaen van Nieulandt on 23 July 1626 was signed by Adriaen Brouwer as witness.[62] Notarial deeds had to be drawn up and signed in the presence of two witnesses and Brouwer was evidently close at hand. Perhaps he paid for his room and board with his own art. At the auction held in 1635, three years after Van Someren's death, in his inn, Het Schild van Frankrijk on the Dam, a large number of Brouwer's drawings were sold; a small round painting by Brouwer was later listed among the possessions of Van Someren's widow.[63]

Houbraken's account implies that Brouwer met Van Someren more or less by chance. However, there may have been prior business dealings between the innkeeper-art dealer and Frans Hals, or perhaps these took place at the time of Brouwer's move from Haarlem to Amsterdam in 1626. On 12 November 1631 Van Someren served as a witness at the baptism of Hals's daughter Maria.[64] It would be no casual thing to invite someone from outside the family to be a baptism witness. Since several details incorporated by Houbraken seem to be historically accurate, this source material cannot simply be dismissed as fictitious. Could the anecdote about the four-poster bed, in which Brouwer specifically played such a prominent role, originate from the same document?

Houbraken was at pains to be well informed about Frans Hals and his relatives. In Haarlem he spoke with several of the sons of Vincent van der Vinne, who had studied under Hals. From the eldest son he obtained the funeral notices of Frans and Dirck Hals, on which their father had scribbled information.[65] In addition to their years of death (1666 and 1656), Houbraken noted that they both came from Mechelen. Strictly speaking this is wrong – Frans Hals was born in Antwerp, Dirck Hals in Haarlem – but Mechelen would have been listed in the funeral notices as the family's place of origin. In Haarlem Houbraken also gained access to the archives of the Guild of St Luke. From a register he noted the names of Frans Hals's sons Harmen, Jan, Frans and Claes, as well as that of a grandson. One of them was still living in the East Indies, where he married – undoubtedly for her money, Houbraken opines scornfully – a '*Mestys*' woman, who was born to a white man and a local Black woman. This descendant of Frans Hals built a house in the tropics that he decorated 'in the Holland manner' with paintings.[66] He was reputedly appreciated more as a musician than for his painting. Did Houbraken obtain these specific details from a reliable informant? Or was he making it up? The latter does not seem to be the case.

One of Frans Hals's painter sons, Reynier Hals, had six children with his second wife, Elisabeth Pieters Groen, in Amsterdam; their sons Jan and Jacob were still alive in 1689, by which time both parents had died. The Hals-Groen estate was administered by the commissioners of the Orphan Chamber of Amsterdam, who noted in their records that both brothers were living in the East Indies in the aforementioned year.[67] In 1694 Jan Hals was back in Amsterdam, where he received his share of the inheritance. Five years later the remaining share, intended for Jacob Hals, was deducted and transferred to the Orphan Chamber Commissioners of Colombo in Ceylon (present-day Sri Lanka).[68] The latter had informed their colleagues in Amsterdam that 'the soldier Jacob Hals, son of Reynier Hals and Elisabet Groen' had asked them to make over to him the money from his parents' estate. Having attained his majority, it was reported from Colombo that Jacob Hals had decided 'to settle in these lands' and could make good use of the money. In that same year he was made a 'free citizen' of Colombo and served as a deacon of the Dutch Reformed Church there, while from about 1700 he took on the post of Orphan Chamber Commissioner for several years without interruption. He was still listed as such in 1731.[69]

Not all the information supplied by Houbraken can be verified, but the core of his story is true: a grandson of Frans Hals settled in the East Indies. Houbraken's informant is likely to have been a member of the Hals family who lived in Amsterdam, perhaps Jacob's brother Jan Hals, who had received his share of the inheritance from the Orphan Chamber Commissioners in 1694.[70] It is possible that it was also thanks to him that Houbraken obtained access to a portrait of Frans Hals which he had made into a print for his *Groote schouburgh* (fig. 15). This portrait shows Hals at a younger age than another likeness that has survived in several copies.[71] Houbraken must have seen it at the home of one of the painter's descendants, very likely his grandson Jan Hals. Whether Jan's brother Jacob was a painter, as Houbraken suggests, is difficult to ascertain; he may have assumed this because a number of Hals's sons and grandsons did take up painting. Noting that this descendant of Frans Hals was a celebrated musician in the East Indies, Houbraken then observed that musicality seemed to be inborn in the Hals children: 'J. Wieland, an old *Liefhebber* [art lover or amateur dealer], and who knew most of them, testifies: that all of F. Hals's children were light of spirit, and lovers of singing and playing music.'[72] Joan Wielant, who

related this to Houbraken, registered as a painter with the Haarlem Guild of St Luke on 2 October 1696 and died in the city in 1717.[73] He may be the same person as Johannes Wielant, who had his marriage banns read in Amsterdam in 1670, stating that he was 34 years old, a schoolmaster by profession and originally from Haarlem.[74] The fact that he left Haarlem for Amsterdam (and possibly then returned to Haarlem) makes it conceivable that he was familiar with the Hals family, of whom Reynier, Claes and their sister Ariaentje all lived in Amsterdam. It is also possible that it was Wielant who gave Houbraken access to the archives of the Haarlem Guild of St Luke, of which he was made a 'vinder' (governor) in 1702.

BRIMFUL OF DRINK

Young artists, Houbraken says, should take the art of Frans Hals as an example. However, he condemned Hals's lifestyle severely. According to Houbraken, the painter indulged in excessive drinking on a daily basis and must 'generally have been filled to the throat with drink every night'.[75] It has been argued that Houbraken spoke to several people in Haarlem and Amsterdam who were able to inform him about Hals and his family; there is no reason to suppose that his statement about Hals's consumption of alcohol in inns and pubs is an invention. Why should Houbraken, who so admired Hals's painting, wish to speak ill of him? He mentions the waste of money and time through excesses away from home in his accounts of various painters, while emphasising that others spent little if any time with cronies or frequenting drinking establishments.[76] He was, incidentally, conscious of the fact that social mores of the early seventeenth century were still rather loose and that a high consumption of alcohol was more common than in his own time: 'engaging in indecent activities, and in particular excessive wallowing in wine, was especially in vogue among painters, and was adopted as a fashion'. He then observes, with some relief, 'that this has long since subsided' and, to the credit of painters, that there is almost no drunkard to be found among them.[77]

One factor of which Houbraken took no account was the importance of the inn as a meeting place for artists and their potential clients, and as a venue for publicising their art. The latter is demonstrated in a written declaration made by two Haarlem residents in 1637 at the request of Dirck Hals.[78] Although it is not stated in so many words in this document, in all probability one of his paintings had been sold by Jan Bossu (since deceased) and his wife, innkeepers of the Haarlemmerhout, without Hals getting his money from them; the testimony would have served to support his claim. One of the witnesses reported having been in the inn on several occasions and having seen on display, in a small room next to the chimney, a painting by Dirck Hals of 'modern images' (young people in fashionable attire). The innkeepers tried to sell this painting to various individuals, explicitly mentioning

THE LIFE OF FRANS HALS

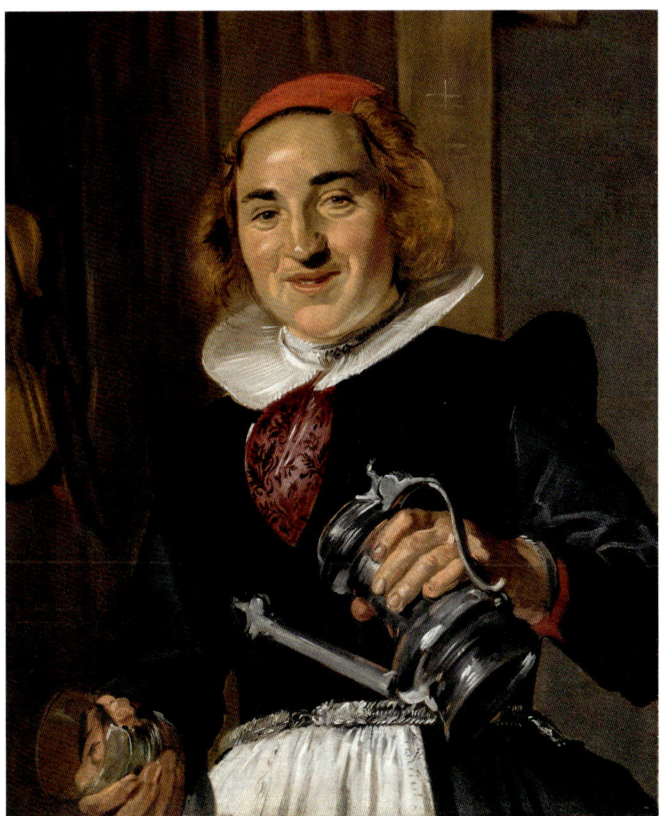

Fig. 16 *Woman holding a Glass and a Flagon*,
about 1630. Oil on canvas, 77.3 × 63.5 cm
David Koetser, Zurich

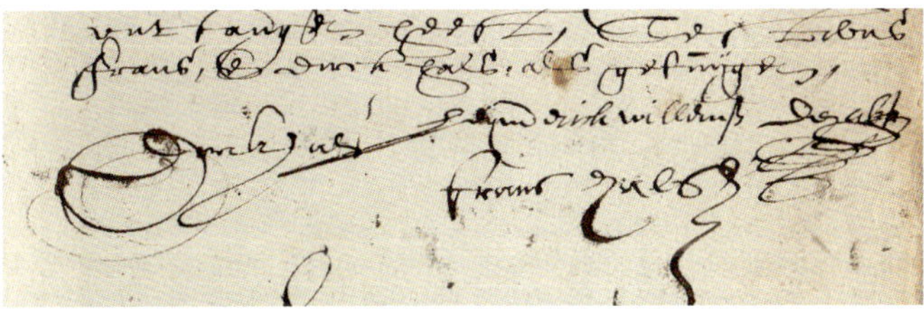

Fig. 17 Frans Hals's signature, with those of Dirck Hals and
Hendrick Willemsz den Abt, on a document dated 29 March 1630
Noord-Hollands Archief, Haarlem (notary W. Crousen de Jonge,
inv. 155, fol. 208, 29 March 1630)

that it belonged to its maker. The witness had heard them say that they could have earned 60 guilders from the sale. This suggests that either the couple or the painter had a higher price in mind. The intermediaries no doubt received a commission for their involvement.

The relations between Frans Hals and the Amsterdam innkeeper and art dealer Barend van Someren are discussed above. Van Someren had a colleague in Haarlem, Hendrick Willemsz den Abt, who was well known as a painter and owner of an inn where painters gathered.[79] He was also an art dealer and used his inn as an exhibition gallery and auction room. In 1631 he organised an auction of paintings, including several originating from Hals's studio: originals and copies of paintings by Frans and Dirck Hals, five pieces by Harmen Hals and four small *tronies* by the then still young painter Jan Miense Molenaer.[80] A year and a half earlier Frans and Dirck Hals had witnessed and signed a statement given by Den Abt (fig. 17).[81] Frans Hals frequented Den Abt's inn for many years. After the innkeeper's death in 1650, his son Willem and his widow, Josina van Nesten, claimed over 31 guilders from Hals, for 'previously consumed fare'.[82] It is tempting to identify Hals's *Woman holding a Glass and a Flagon* as Den Abt's wife (fig. 16).[83] Her clothing suggests that the woman, who holds a pitcher in one hand and a glass in the other, represents an innkeeper. Behind her (on a slate?) we see lines recording a customer's outstanding tab. Her stance, with a slightly turned torso, suggests that there may once have been a pendant portrait. Among the possessions that she brought to her second marriage were around seventy paintings (among which there was a series on the five senses and another small work by Dirck Hals) that included two pairs of portraits of Josina and her first husband. The pair of pendant portraits described first were painted by Hendrick Pot. The maker of the second pair is unidentified but since Frans Hals maintained close relations with Den Abt and his wife for many years, it cannot be ruled out that they were his work.[84]

While in all probability alcohol flowed freely in the Hals household, this in no way diminishes the importance of culture within the family. The children became familiar with music at a young age at home. As a member of a chamber of rhetoric, Hals participated in gatherings of kindred spirits at which poems were exchanged and discussions took place. There is no doubt that he received a good education, his stylish signature showing a practised writer's hand. Trained by Karel van Mander, Hals would have had a thorough theoretical grounding in painting and literature, which would have served him well as a portrait painter attracting distinguished and learned clients throughout his working life.

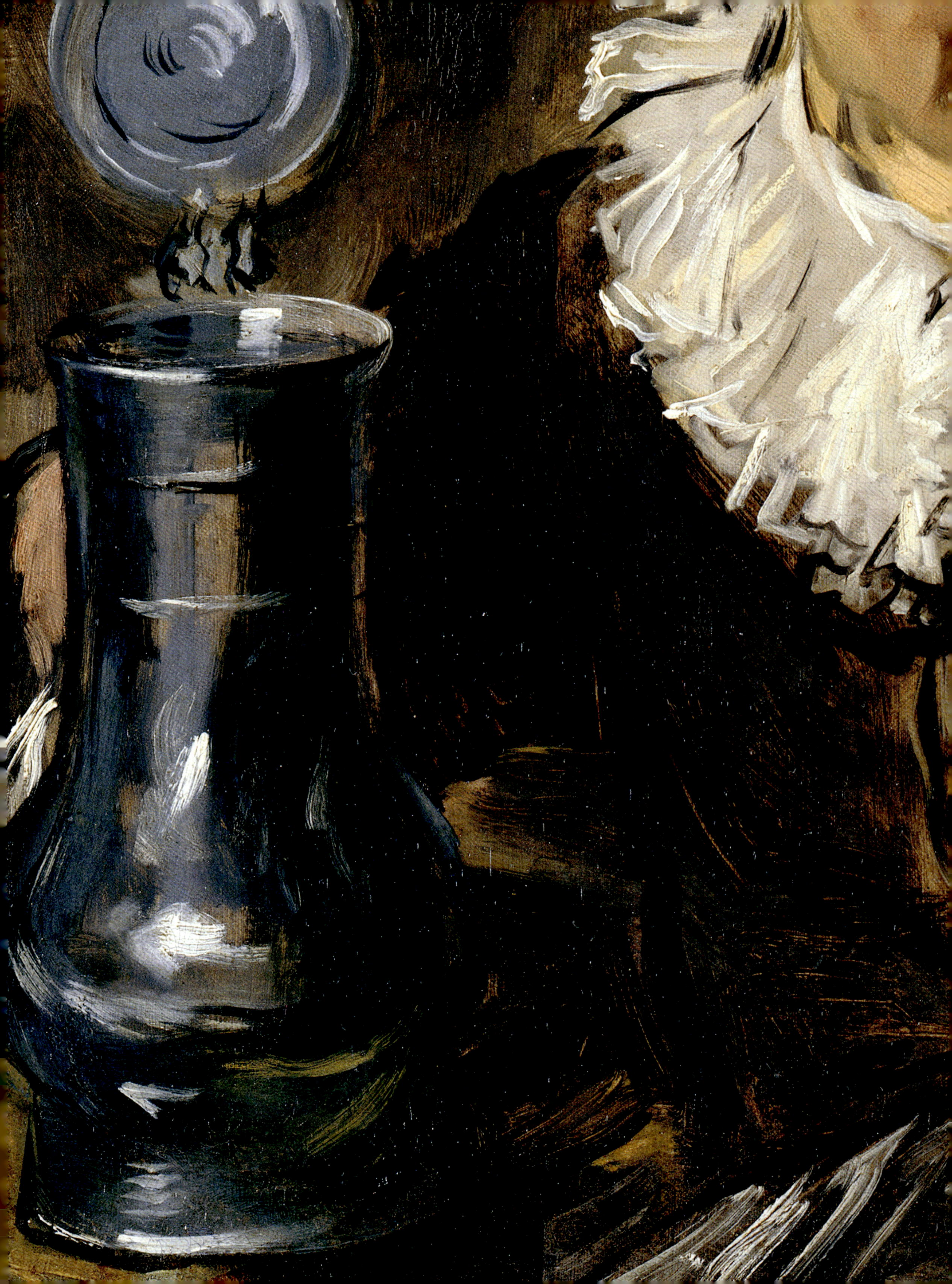

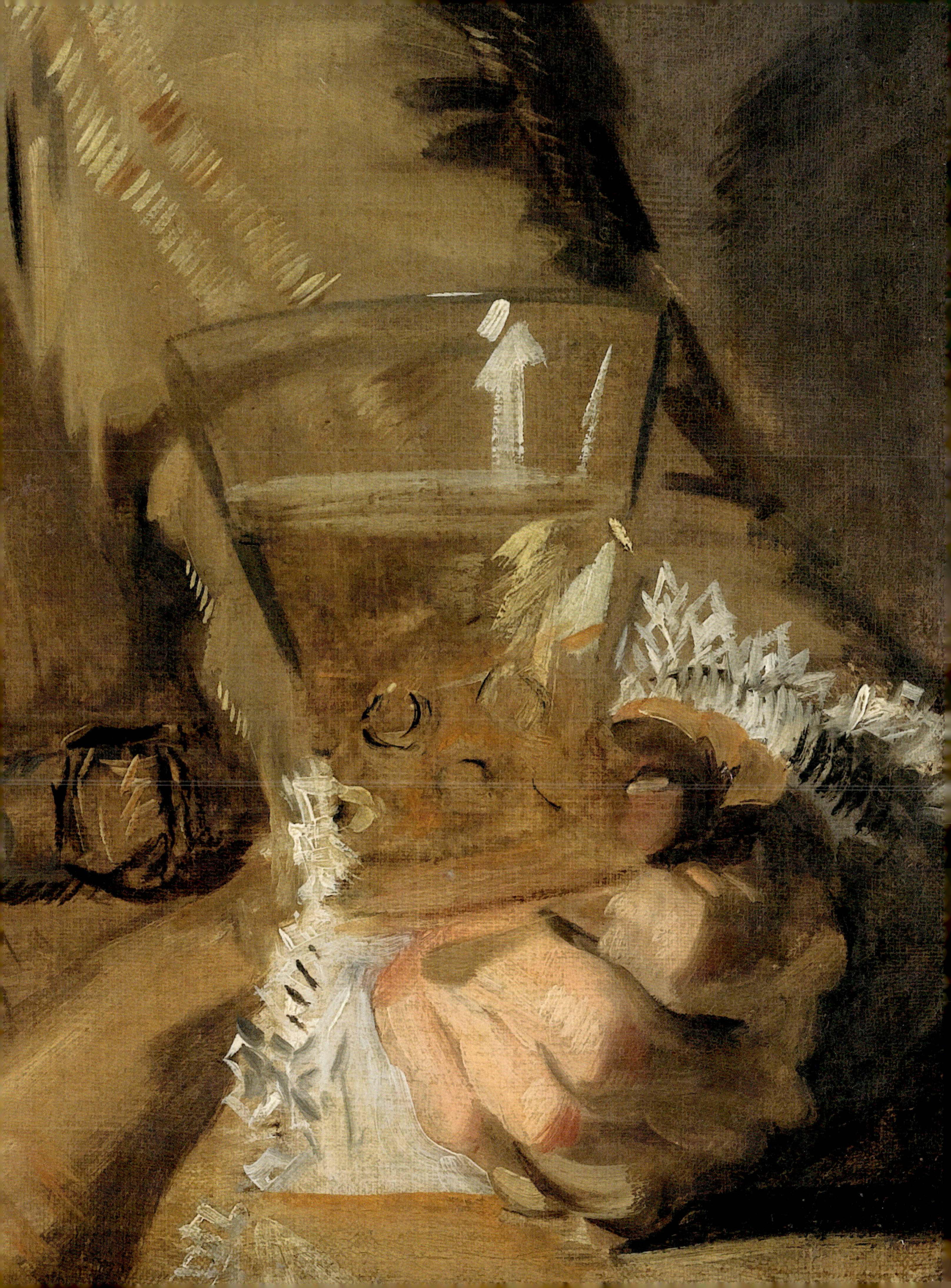

ANTWERP AND HAARLEM

FRISO LAMMERTSE AND
JAAP VAN DER VEEN

On 6 August 1616 a receiver presented himself at the Court of Petty Sessions in Haarlem in connection with a debt owed by Frans Hals. The painter owed 4 guilders and 15 stuivers for the purchase of a painting from an estate administered by the receiver. The court usher informed the receiver that the case would have to be held over because Hals, the 'gedaechde' (respondent), was 'wonachtig' (living) in Antwerp.[1] The timing of Hals's absence is significant. His wife, Anneke Harmens, had died a little over a year earlier, whereupon he had entrusted their two young children to the care of a woman of whom nothing is known apart from her name, Neeltje Leendersdr.[2] It was in 1616, too, that he completed his first large militia painting of the officers of the St George Civic Guard at their farewell banquet (fig. 68). What Hals was doing back in his native Antwerp is not documented. The word 'wonachtig' implies more than a short stay. Had the young widower with a well-filled purse (for the guardsmen would have paid him handsomely on completion of their group portrait) travelled south on a family visit, or, who knows, for pleasure? Or was he on a business trip? It is not inconceivable that he was working on a commission in Antwerp, or perhaps he was toying with the idea of working there for a longer period. This, though, is not what happened. He stayed for just a few months, for in November he was back in Haarlem.[3]

The fact that Hals spent some time in Antwerp comes as no surprise, for this was a time of heightened exchanges between the Northern and Southern Netherlands, certainly on an artistic level. In fact, the remarkable advances in painting made in the Dutch Republic at the beginning of the seventeenth century would not have been possible without developments taking place in the South. This also applied to Hals's work, for his style at the time displays parallels with that of some of his Antwerp contemporaries. However, the lack of reliable sources makes it difficult to see precisely how that influence took place. The mention of his stay in Antwerp in 1616 is the only proof of his presence there at the time when he was an active painter. Perhaps he visited the city more often, or was in regular contact with people there, but

we know nothing of this for certain. In order to get an idea of the relationship between Antwerp and Haarlem that was so important for Hals we will examine the cultural exchanges between the two cities, and above all shine a light on a few artists for whom there are surviving documents that testify to lively contacts between them.

ANTWERP

The Hals family fled from Antwerp in 1585 or 1586, when Frans was still just a few years old. It is not known precisely why they left but, as with so many others in the same period, it undoubtedly had something to do with the war with Spain, the economic downturn or religious persecution, or a mixture of all three. Antwerp had been the leading trade metropolis by far in north-western Europe in the sixteenth century (fig. 18) and for a long time it had had little to fear from competition from the northern provinces; but that all changed in the last quarter of the century. There was growing dissatisfaction with the way Spain was ruling the provinces, above all as regards their economy and religion. The unrest ultimately exploded in a rebellion that King Philip II of Spain tried to put down by force. Spanish troops under the command of the Duke of Parma regained control of the provinces of Flanders and Brabant, but did not advance any further. The result was the establishment of a dividing line between the northern and southern provinces of the Netherlands. Antwerp was badly damaged by the politico-military events. It was besieged from July 1584 to August 1585 before being captured by Spanish troops. Supporters of the Reformation were given four years to either recant or leave the city with their belongings. Countless numbers, including the Hals family, took the latter option, and the city rapidly emptied. There are no exact figures for the size of the exodus but there are rough approximations. Around 1579 Antwerp had a population of more than 100,000; 20 years later there were a mere 42,000 left, at most. When Hals stayed there in 1616 the city was still a desolate shell. In that year Dudley Carleton, the English ambassador in The Hague, made

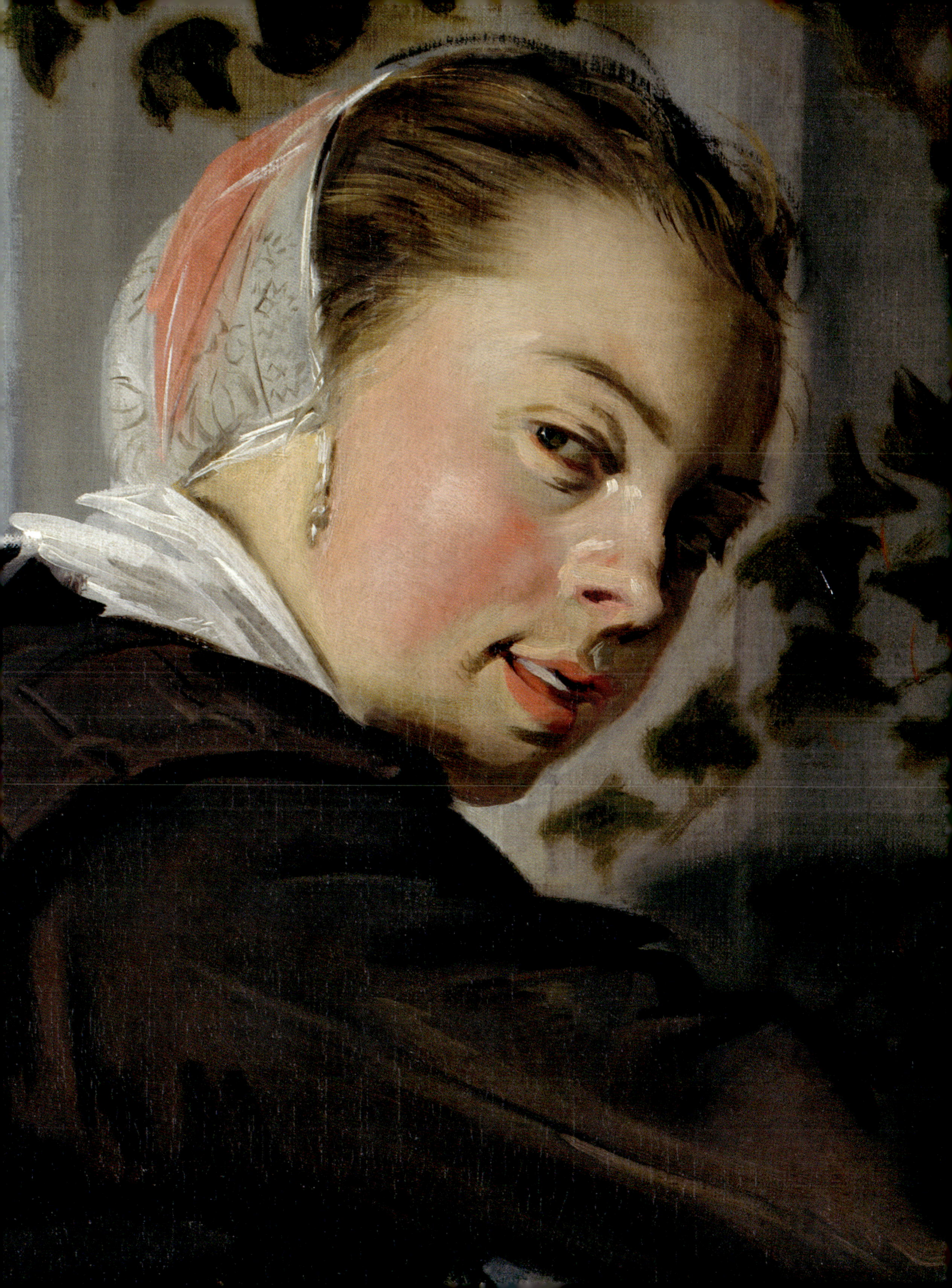

a striking comparison between Antwerp and Amsterdam. 'I saw the whole town', he said of Amsterdam, 'and observed this difference from Antwerp, that there was a town without people and here a people as it were without a town'.[4]

Antwerp would never recover the position it had enjoyed in the sixteenth century but, remarkably enough, the fine arts flourished. The artistic revival was due in part to the countless orders for religious paintings and statues to replace those that had been smashed to pieces in churches and monasteries during the iconoclasm of 1566. Once Spanish rule had been reinstated, pious Catholics eagerly set about restoring the buildings to their former glory. While it was mainly private citizens who paid for the repairs and redecoration, the patronage of the court in Brussels was extremely important, especially during the period of Albert of Austria and his wife, Isabella, who governed the Spanish Netherlands from 1598. They built up a large art collection and took artists into their service, headed by Rubens, who was appointed court painter in 1609. Contrary to the custom with court artists, Rubens did not have to move to Brussels but was allowed to continue living in Antwerp. His large studio there was a hive of industry, producing paintings, often very large ones, for numerous private individuals and institutions at home and abroad. But Rubens was not entirely responsible for this extraordinary outpouring of art. In Antwerp alone other artists included Jacques Jordaens, Jan Brueghel the Elder, Frans Snijders, Anthony van Dyck, Hendrick van Balen the Elder, David Teniers, Cornelis Schut, Andries van Eertvelt, Jan Wildens and dozens of other masters.

Albert and Isabella governed the Netherlands until the latter's death in 1633, in a period that partly coincided with the temporary cessation of hostilities between the rebellious provinces and Spain. In 1609 a truce lasting for 12 years was signed between the Dutch Republic and the Spanish Netherlands, which had the effect of greatly easing and intensifying relations between the two sides.[5] The borders were immediately reopened and traffic flowed in both directions once again. It was in this period that contacts of every kind are documented, among them Hals's stay in Antwerp. That was also the case with Clara Geerts, the mother of the Antwerp artist Van Eertvelt, who travelled to see relatives in Amsterdam in 1612 and while she was there bought a consignment of wood and had it sent back to Antwerp.[6] This combination of private and commercial activities was very common during these years. In addition to the increased trade between the regions, the truce stimulated artistic relations between North and South. Painters and art dealers in Antwerp found a new market in the North, and it was not long before they were flooding the Republic with artworks that were often at the cheap end of the market.[7]

A number of Southern Netherlandish painters and dealers regularly travelled to do business in the North and some of them settled there for good, while staying in touch with their native cities. One of them was Andries Snellingh, who was active in Haarlem. In 1628 the local preacher and writer Samuel Ampzing ranked this still-life painter among the city's famous artists; in 1634 Snellingh was a member of the Haarlem Guild of St Luke.[8] The fact that documents record him as a merchant indicates that he was also an art dealer. It is not known when he settled in the Republic but in 1613 he stated that he was 'born in Antwerp' and was 'presently living in Haarlem'.[9] From his arrival there until his death in 1638 he kept in close touch with relatives and business associates in Antwerp, where he owned a house that he rented out. For a while he did business as an art dealer with the Haarlem painter Frans Pietersz de Grebber[10] and in 1629 the pair of them held a public sale of pictures that attracted the interest of Frans Hals. Hals bought works at the auction but did not pay for them right away, so a guarantor had to be found; it was his brother Dirck who agreed to act as such.[11] Given Snellingh's connections with Antwerp, it is very possible that the sale included works from masters there.[12] De Grebber acted for Snellingh in Antwerp at least on one occasion. In 1640 Snellingh's widow claimed 47 guilders from De Grebber that he had supposedly received in Antwerp years earlier. However, De Grebber denied that he owed her any money, pointing out that no one had raised the matter in 17 years,[13] his form of words indicating that he must have been in Antwerp around 1623.

De Grebber's name also appears in Rubens's correspondence. In a letter of 1618 he describes a certain 'François Pieterssen' as his 'agent'.[14] Precisely when Rubens appointed De Grebber as such is not documented, nor when they got to know each other. The fact that they were co-religionists may have played a part. In 1618 De Grebber travelled to Antwerp with his son Pieter, who was about 18 years old. He had gone there in connection with a transaction that Rubens was making with Dudley Carleton, mentioned above.[15] In exchange for a valuable group of classical sculptures belonging to Carleton, Rubens was supplying a series of tapestries and several paintings by himself and studio assistants, including works that are still famous, such as *Prometheus bound* (fig. 20), *Achilles among the Daughters of Lycomedes* and *Daniel in the Lions' Den*.[16] De Grebber acted as Rubens's agent for the transaction, checking the quality of the sculptures and accompanying the shipment from The Hague to Antwerp. Rubens spoke highly of him, describing him as his friend, and a trustworthy and 'honourable person, of good repute'.[17]

People in the North must have had the opportunity to see work by Rubens at an early date, not only with Carleton in The Hague but also with collectors in other cities. For instance, his *Supper at Emmaus* and a *Venus and Adonis* were in Delft and his *Head of Medusa* was hanging in Amsterdam.[18] The Amsterdam merchant Marten van den Heuvel, whose brother Nicolaes commissioned Hals to paint the portraits of himself and his family (fig. 22), owned Rubens's monumental *Ixion*

ANTWERP AND HAARLEM

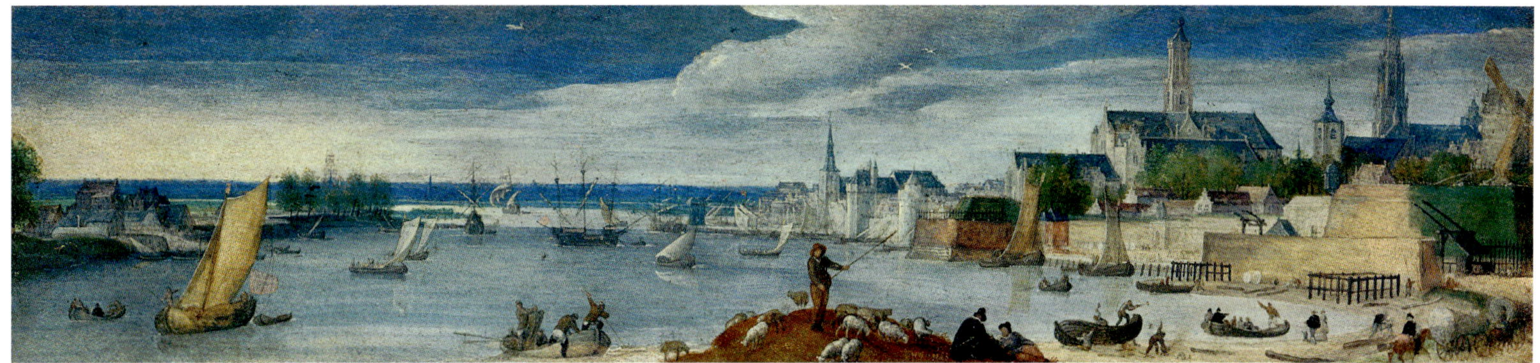

Fig. 18 Hans Bol, *A View of Antwerp Harbour*, 1583
Tempera and gouache on parchment (transferred to panel), 5.9 × 23 cm
Museum Rockoxhuis, Antwerp

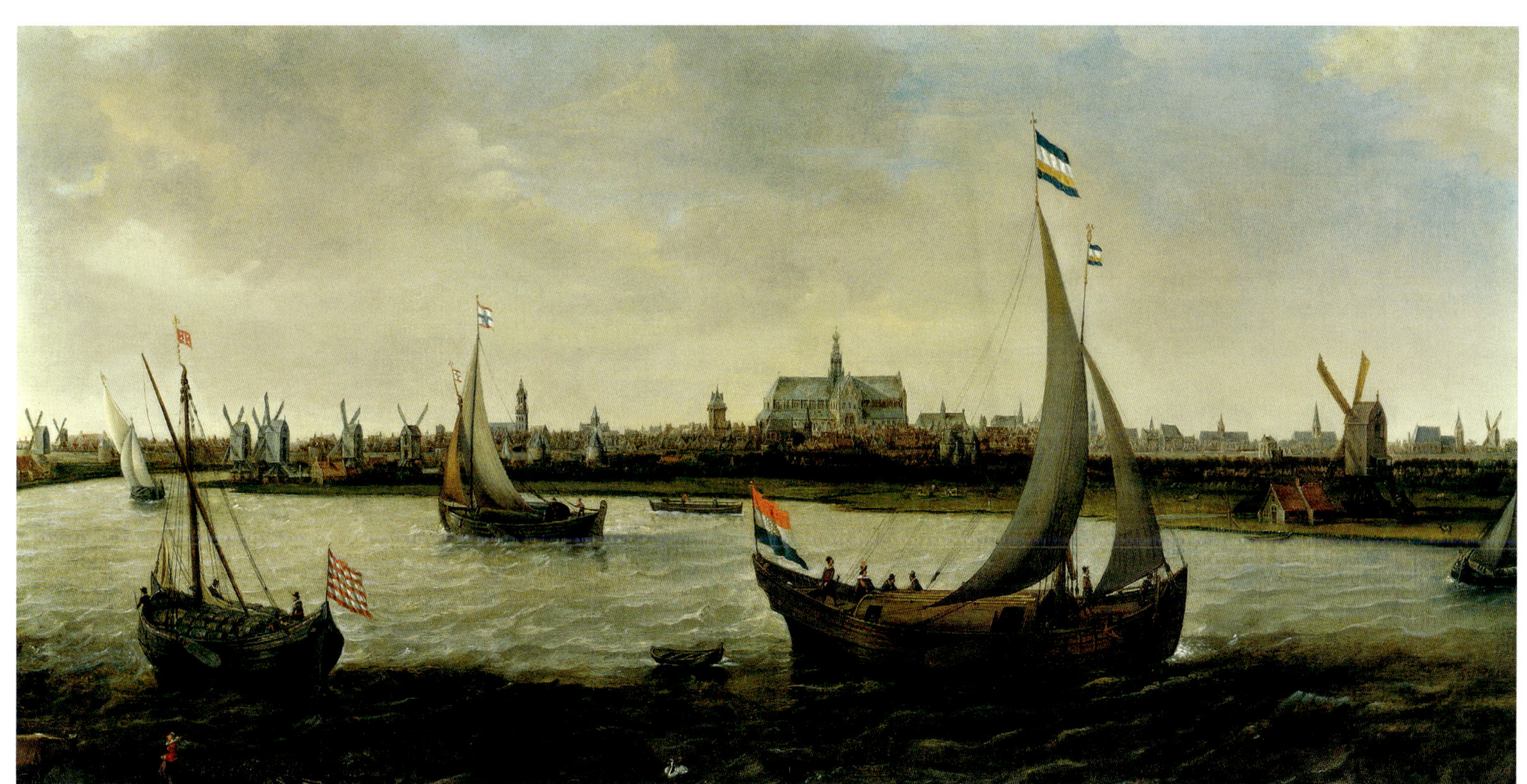

Fig. 19 Hendrick Vroom, *View of Haarlem from the Noorder-Spaarne River*, 1625
Oil on canvas, 61 × 122.5 cm
Frans Hals Museum, Haarlem

deceived by Juno (fig. 21).[19] It is striking that several Haarlem artists seem to have been influenced by Rubens's art, more so than was the case in other Dutch cities. Willem Buytewech made various etchings after his designs, and the work of painters like Salomon de Bray, Pieter Soutman and above all Pieter de Grebber (son of Frans de Grebber) would be inconceivable without his example.[20] This is easily explained in the case of Soutman, for he had studied with Rubens and remained in Antwerp for some time after 1619 as an independent master. Here he was in contact with Anthony van Dyck, who had worked with Rubens at the same time as himself. Van Dyck made a superb, very loosely painted portrait of Soutman (fig. 23), who took it with him when he returned to his native Haarlem in 1628 and displayed it in his house, together with other pictures by Van Dyck.[21] In a letter of 8 February 1645 he wrote to the Antwerp art dealer Matthijs Musson about this portrait, saying that it was regarded in Haarlem as the artist's very best work and that he would not sell it for any less than 300 guilders.[22]

HAARLEM

The Fall of Antwerp had major consequences for Haarlem. Around 1570 it had a population of roughly 18,000, but 50 years later that had grown to almost 40,000 (fig. 19), largely due to immigration from the Southern Netherlands.[23] The migrants came to Haarlem for its textiles industry, which was stimulated by the city government's policy of attracting skilled artisans, whom it regarded as vital for helping the city to recover from its disastrous siege and occupation by Spanish troops in 1572–3 and the enormous damage caused by a devastating fire in 1576. The authorities judged that the severely impoverished population would be unable to rebuild the city and restore its economy. They expressed the hope that 'some good folk from elsewhere' would come to take up 'their residence in Haarlem'.[24] The policy paid off but that was not thanks to just 'some good folk'. At the beginning of the seventeenth century roughly half the population consisted of 'incomers' from the Southern Netherlands and their descendants.

Many former Brabanders and Flemings worked in the Haarlem textile industry, like Frans Hals's father, who was a cloth-shearer. Others followed careers as merchant, faiencier, gold- and silversmith, schoolmaster, or cobbler or printer. There were also a few painters. Although the migrants made a major contribution to the development of painting in Haarlem and laid the foundations for a period of great growth, the city already had a reputation as an artistic centre before they arrived. The painter Karel van Mander, who came from Meulebeke in the South, near Courtrai (Kortrijk), and settled in Haarlem in 1583 as one of the first newcomers, reported in his *Schilder-Boeck* of 1604 that the city had a long history of producing excellent artists of the stature of Albert van Ouwater, Geertgen tot Sint Jans and Maarten van

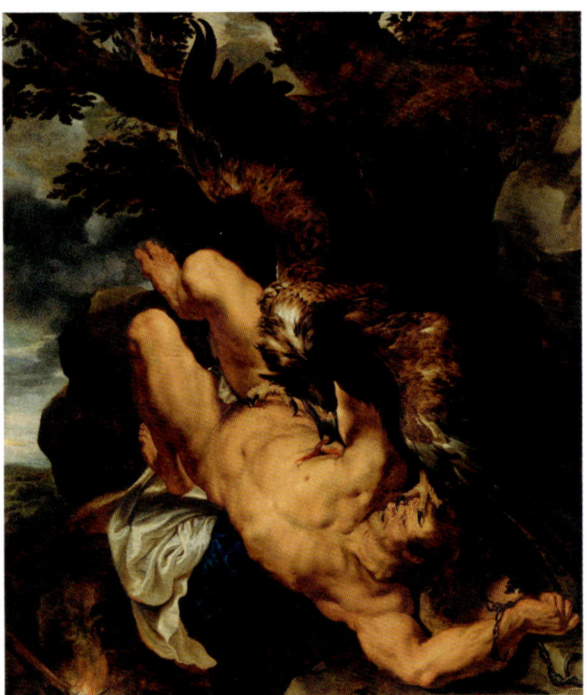

Fig. 20 Peter Paul Rubens and Frans Snijders, *Prometheus bound*, about 1611–18
Oil on canvas, 242.6 × 209.6 cm
Philadelphia Museum of Art;
purchased with the W. P. Wilstach Fund, 1950

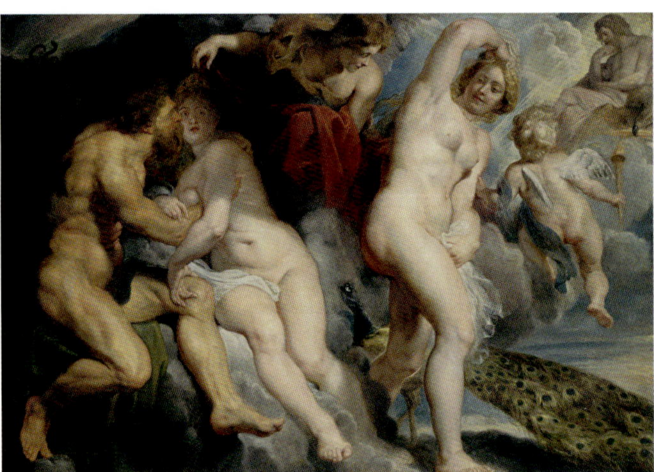

Fig. 21 Peter Paul Rubens, *Ixion deceived by Juno*, about 1620. Oil on canvas, 171 × 245 cm
Musée du Louvre, Paris, Paintings Department

ANTWERP AND HAARLEM

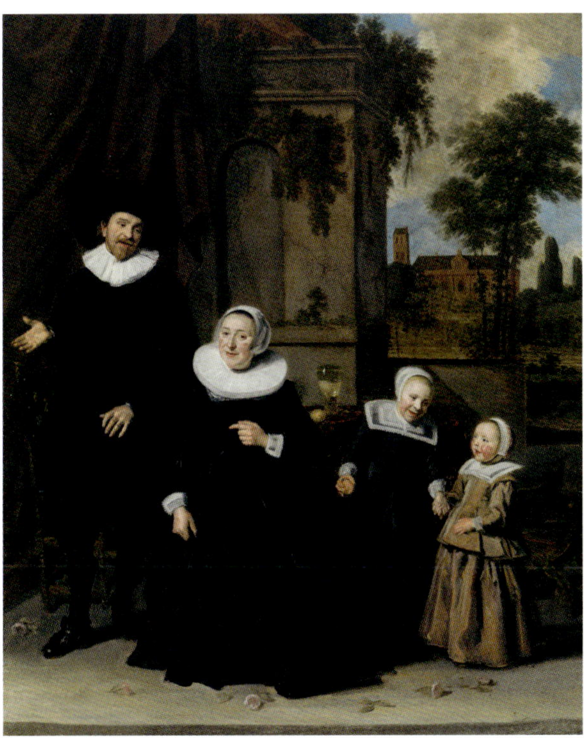

Fig. 22 *Portrait of Nicolaes van den Heuvel, his Wife Susanna van Halmael, their Daughter Maria and an Unknown Daughter,* about 1635. Oil on canvas, 111.7 × 91.6 cm
Cincinnati Art Museum, Cincinnati, Ohio; Bequest of Mary M. Emery

Fig. 23 Anthony van Dyck, *Portrait of Pieter Soutman,* about 1620–8. Oil on canvas, 75.5 × 58.3 cm
Kunsthistorisches Museum, Vienna

Heemskerck. When Van Mander himself arrived, he was astonished that such fine painters as Hendrick Goltzius, Cornelis Cornelisz van Haarlem and Hendrick Vroom were living there. One could perhaps suspect Van Mander of a dose of civic pride, but the Southern Netherlandish notary and writer Cornelis de Bie also speaks of the 'art-bearing city of Haarlem'.[25] On the occasion of his recent visit there, Dudley Carleton claimed in his letter cited above that its painters were 'the chiefest curiosity' of the city. He felt that three of them deserved special mention: Cornelis Cornelisz, whose colouring pleased him but who, in his opinion, 'errs in proportions'; Vroom, whose seascapes he praised but considered expensive; and Goltzius, whose 'art decays with his body'.[26]

Carleton's visit to Haarlem took place in a period of far-reaching innovations in the visual arts. Between 1610 and 1614 Frans Hals, Willem Buytewech, Hercules Segers, Esaias van de Velde and his cousin Jan van de Velde were among those who had registered as masters with the local Guild of St Luke.[27] The last four, as draughtsmen, painters and printmakers, pioneered a more naturalistic depiction of the Dutch landscape. Esaias van de Velde and Buytewech also specialised in scenes of daily life, above all showing elegant young people enjoying music, dancing and drinking; these soon after became the speciality of Frans Hals's younger brother, Dirck. Not only were these subjects new; so, too, was the way in which the young artists working in Haarlem depicted them. As one of the first in the North, Frans Hals abandoned the almost invisible brushstroke that had been common up until then, in favour of the 'bold', rough approach.[28] It was now that draughtsmen also began taking an interest in a similarly loose style. Chief among them was Buytewech, who collaborated with Frans Hals and displayed a remarkable sketchiness in his pen drawings.

In his letter Carleton only mentioned the work of established masters in Haarlem. Did he not have an eye for this trail-blazing art? In any event the new generation was not blind to the city's importance as a centre of adventurous artistic excellence. Many were drawn to it as if to a magnet. These included various young painters who went on to make names for themselves, such as Jan van Goyen from Leiden, who was apprenticed to Esaias van de Velde in 1617; Gerard ter Borch of Zwolle, who trained with Pieter de Molijn from 1633 to 1635; and Paulus Potter, who moved from Amsterdam to Haarlem in 1642 to study under Jacob de Wet the Elder.[29] De Grebber, too, trained many pupils over the years, among them Pieter van der Faes of The Hague (although born in Soest near Arnsberg), who became a portraitist in high demand in England under the name Peter Lely. Fully fledged painters also found their way to Haarlem. Jan Porcellis, for example, who played a key part in the development of marine painting, went to live there around 1622 after working in Rotterdam and Antwerp.[30]

FRANS HALS'S CONTACTS IN ANTWERP

Several of those whose portraits Frans Hals painted in Haarlem had a background in Antwerp. Their common origin may have been why they chose him, but there could have been other reasons as well. Many of the new-comers from Antwerp, especially the wealthier among them, looked and behaved differently from the people who had already been living in the North for some time. They had a more uninhibited lifestyle and wore more colourful and fashionable clothes. Some whom Hals portrayed are not wearing the kind of sober black suits that were common at the time, but are depicted in luxurious clothing and eye-catching poses. Isaac Massa, for instance, is seated in a chair with his upper body turned towards the viewer, and in another picture he crosses his arms (figs 93–4). Most other portrait painters showed their sitters looking grave, but Hals sometimes gave them a merry look, possibly after consultation with the client. He portrayed Pieter van den Broecke sitting in a chair like Massa, but looking out at the viewer with a friendly, almost mischievous gaze (fig. 11). Both men had their roots in Antwerp.

Hals would have been personally familiar with several artists from Antwerp. It is known that Rubens visited the city at least once, probably in or around 1612,[31] but the precise reason for this is not known. For a long time it was assumed that he was looking for printmakers there who could have made prints after his paintings, but that idea has now been ruled out.[32] It may have been a pleasure trip, possibly combined with business; the fact that Hendrick Goltzius lived there would undoubtedly have been an added incentive.[33] Goltzius was known throughout Europe for his prints and Rubens himself had made drawn copies after Goltzius's *Passion of Christ* at the beginning of his career.[34] Rubens's stay in the city must have been a memorable occasion, not only because he had been regarded as the leading painter of the Low Countries since his return from Italy in 1608, and had even been nicknamed 'god among the painters',[35] but also because of a practical joke that was played during the visit. After Rubens, Jan Brueghel the Elder, Hendrick van Balen and several of their unnamed travelling companions had left the city, they were arrested in a neighbouring village by a group of strangers.[36] This turned out to be a prank dreamed up by Hendrick Goltzius and other Haarlemers who had made themselves unrecognisable as a manner of joke. In fact they simply wanted to bid the famous painters a second farewell, pay their respects and raise a glass to wish them a safe journey.

It is no longer possible to say who else was involved in the reception for this illustrious company or its later 'arrest' – including Frans Hals. He had registered as a master with the Guild of St Luke two years previously, and it seems unlikely that he would have passed up the chance to have a little fun. The memory of the visit was possibly one of the reasons for his own trip to Antwerp a few years later. It seems inconceivable, anyway, that he

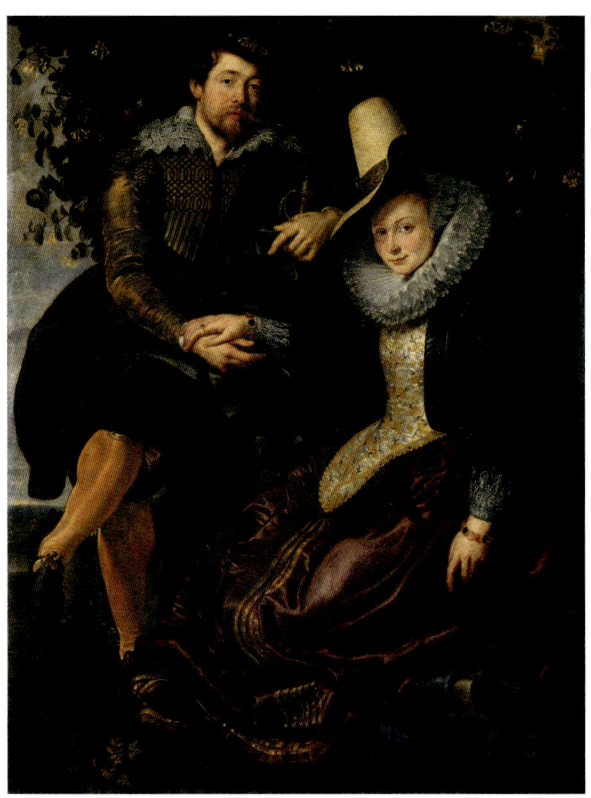

Fig. 24 Peter Paul Rubens, *Self portrait with Isabella Brant in the Honeysuckle Arbor*, about 1609–10
Oil on canvas mounted on wood, 178 × 136.5 cm
Alte Pinakothek, Munich

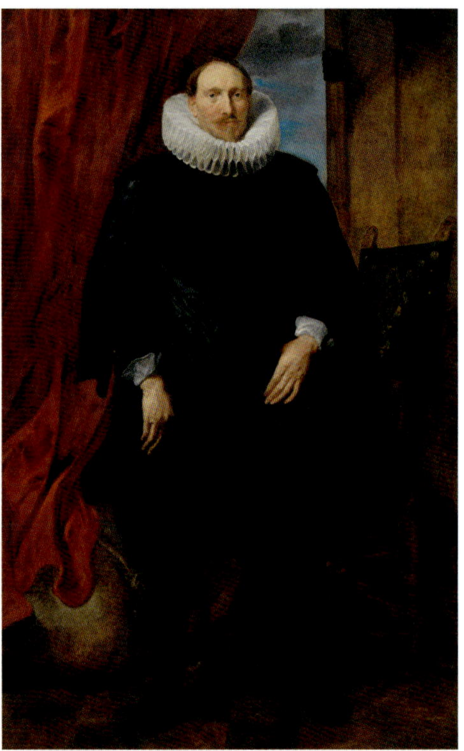

Fig. 25 Anthony van Dyck, *Portrait of a Man, possibly Alexander or Jan Vinck*, 1616 or before
Oil on canvas, 199 × 126 cm
Royal Museum of Fine Arts, Antwerp

ANTWERP AND HAARLEM

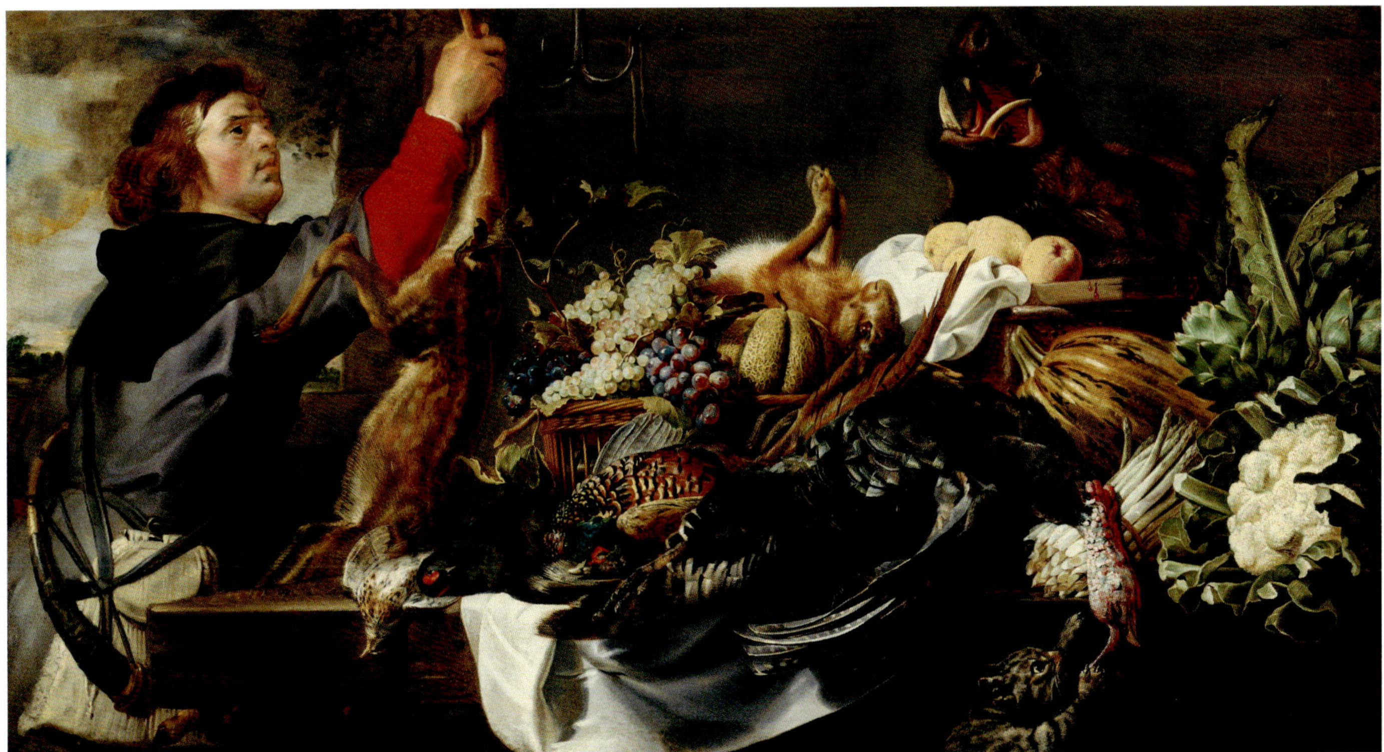

Fig. 26 Frans Snijders and an unknown Antwerp artist,
Still Life with Huntsman, about 1615
Oil on canvas, 113.7 × 205.5 cm
Mauritshuis, The Hague

would not have taken the opportunity while he was there to call at Rubens's studio, where both Anthony van Dyck and Jacques Jordaens were working at the time. However, it is not so easy to determine how his meetings with these and other artists actually influenced him. It has been pointed out that his double portrait of the two sitters who may be Isaac Massa and Beatrix van der Laen displays similarities to Rubens's famous self portrait with his wife Isabella Brant of a decade earlier (figs 61, 24).[37] The portraits that Van Dyck (fig. 25) and Jordaens were making around 1616 may also have had an influence on Hals.[38] The crowded composition of his *Merrymakers at Shrovetide* (fig. 149) has been likened to works by Jordaens from the same period.[39] One of Hals's most 'Flemish' paintings is the large market scene that he and Claes van Heussen made jointly in 1630 (fig. 27), which clearly recalls pictures by Frans Snijders and other Antwerp still-life painters (fig. 26).

Yet there is no question that Hals borrowed literally from such works. Rather than being interested in certain details or compositions, Hals seems to have been inspired by his southern colleagues' brushwork. His teacher Karel van Mander must have drawn his attention to the fact that there were both 'neat' and 'rough' ways of painting.[40] Although he wrote at the beginning of the seventeenth century that the latter manner was becoming increasingly popular, there were barely any examples to be found in the Northern Netherlands. Rubens,

Jordaens and Van Dyck, however, were all virtuosi with the brush, and the latter excelled with his very rough touch indeed.[41] It was this interest in style that must have had a particular appeal to Hals.

It was around twenty years after Rubens's visit to Haarlem that his former pupil Van Dyck came to the Republic before leaving for England. If one is to believe Houbraken, Van Dyck made a point of going to Haarlem to call on Hals.[42] It is known that he was staying in The Hague in January 1631, where he painted the portrait of Constantijn Huygens the Elder.[43] He left for London three months later. It is not certain whether Van Dyck did indeed travel up to Haarlem in the meantime; Houbraken is the only one to mention this. According to him, Van Dyck went to Hals's studio, where the two artists painted each other's portrait without Hals realising who the other man was. However, when he saw the portrait of himself he immediately recognised Van Dyck's touch and kissed him.[44] Houbraken undoubtedly embellished the story but that is not to say that it lacks a kernel of truth. Be that as it may, it is a nice idea that the two virtuosi born in Antwerp, who were among the finest portraitists of their age, embraced in Haarlem.

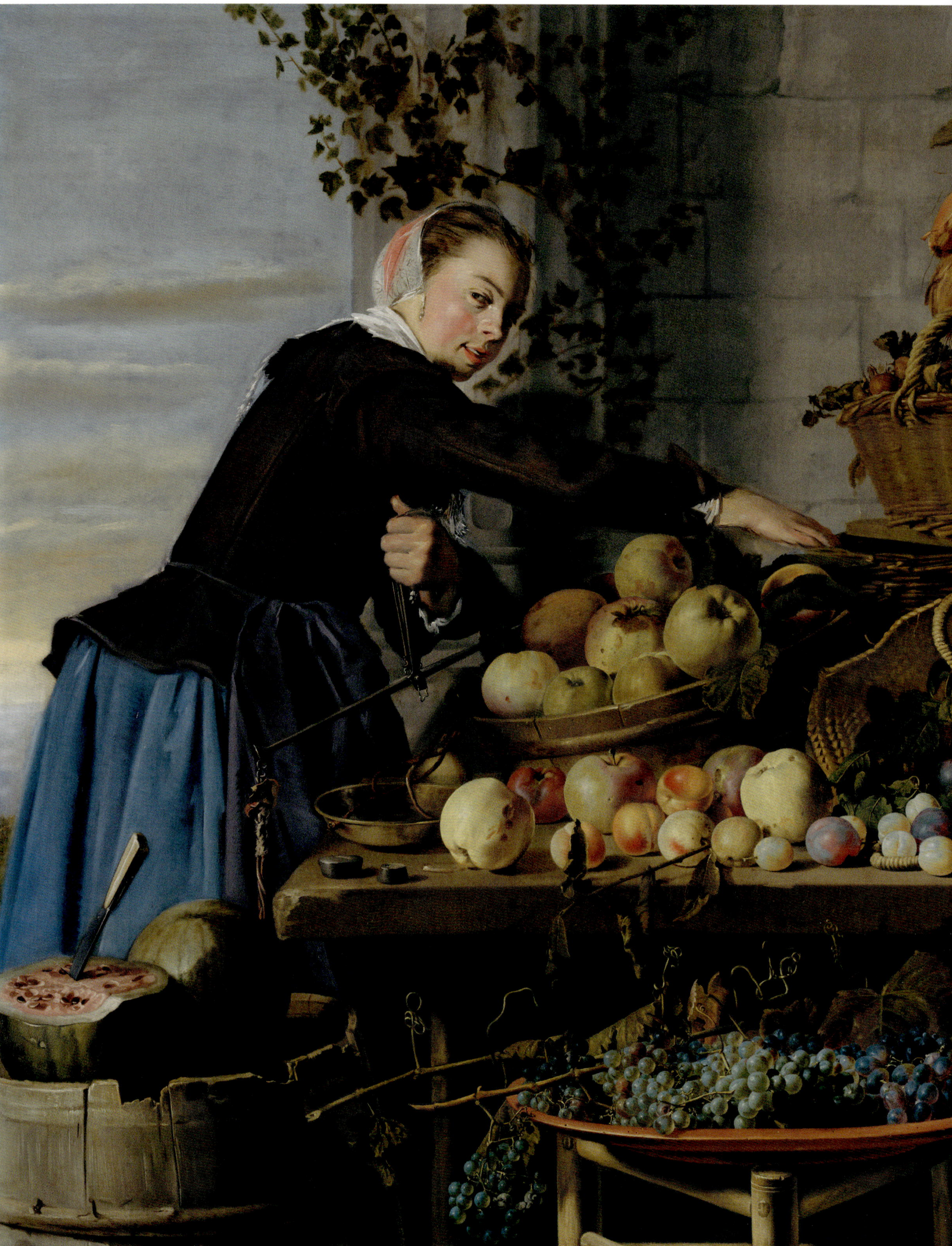

Fig. 27 Frans Hals and Claes van Heussen,
Young Woman with a Display of Fruit and Vegetables, 1630
Oil on canvas, 157 × 200 cm
Private collection

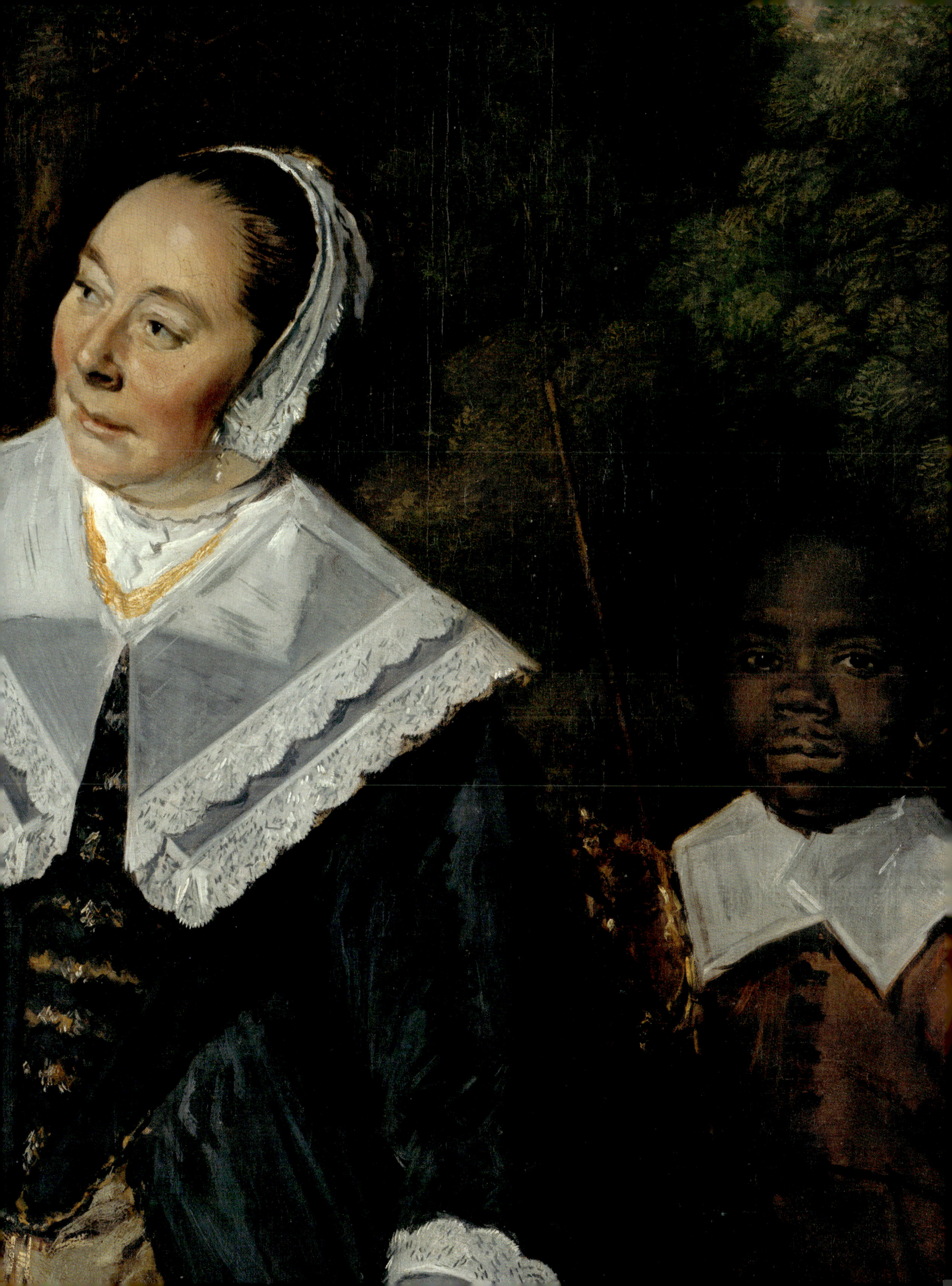

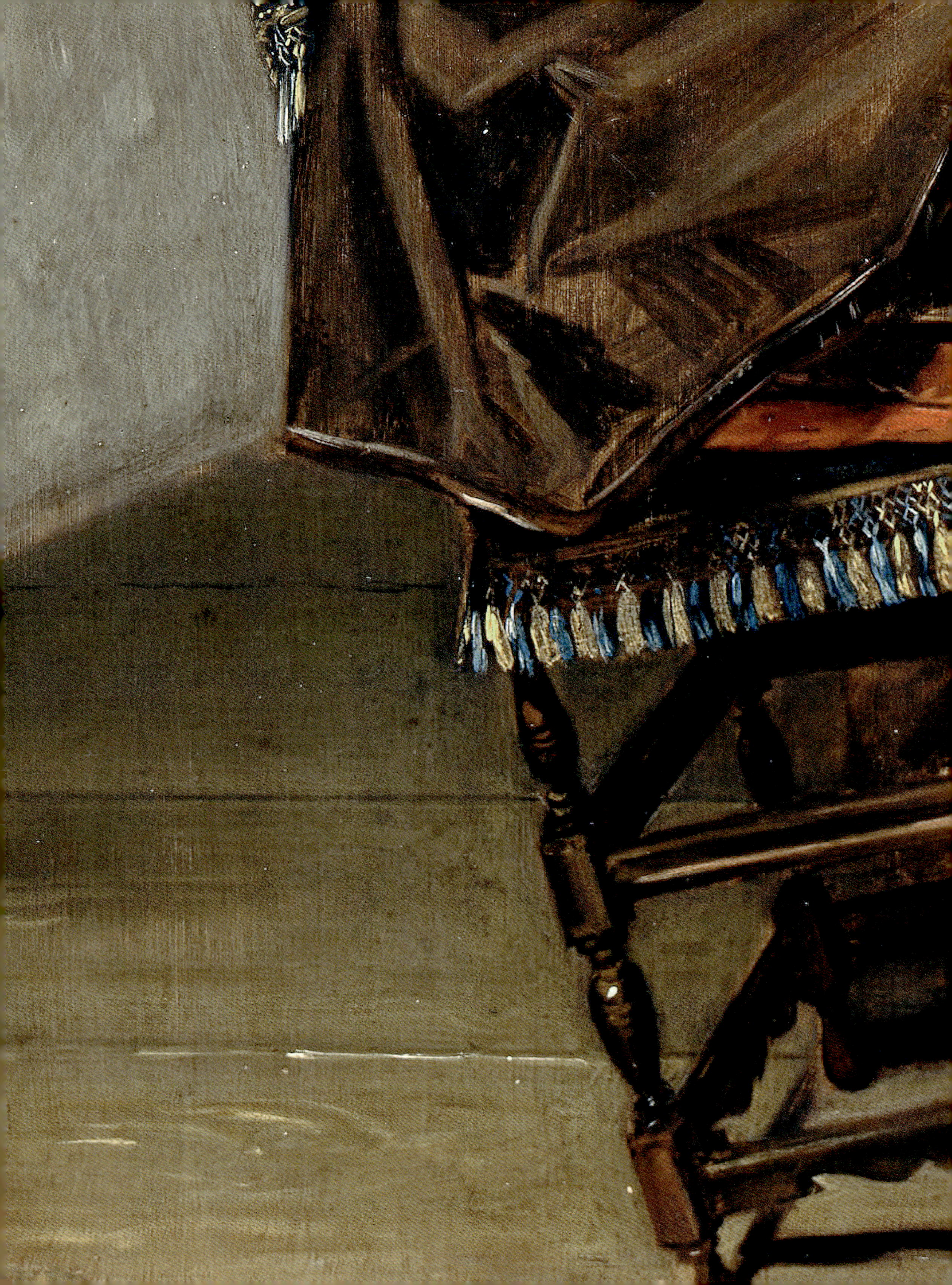

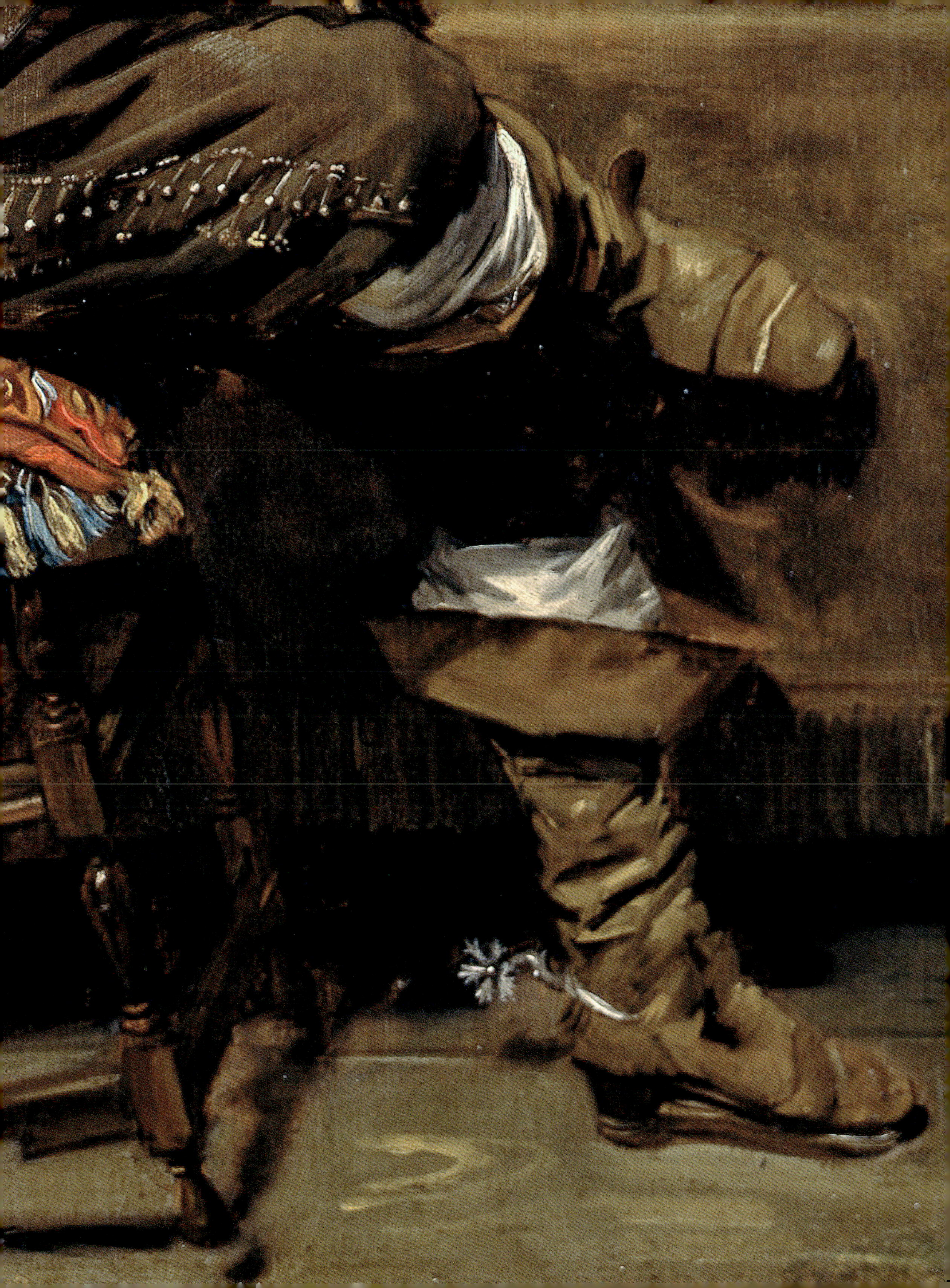

THE STUDIO

FRISO LAMMERTSE AND
JAAP VAN DER VEEN

In 1636 the civic guardsmen of District 11 in Amsterdam, who had ordered a group portrait from Frans Hals three years previously, decided that they had been kept waiting for long enough. They asked him to come and complete the painting in Amsterdam as soon as possible. Hals was not in the least bit obliging. He replied that he had tried to work on the portrait in Amsterdam, but several of the guardsmen had not turned up for their sittings at the agreed time, so he was unable to work on the painting any further and had incurred a great deal of extra expense into the bargain. He asked the guardsmen in question to come to Haarlem, which was the original agreement. In his own house, he announced, he would be able to finish the work 'with greater enthusiasm' than in Amsterdam, because being with 'zijn volck' (his people) he could 'keep an eye on them'.[1] His clients refused, and carried out their earlier threat to have the painting completed by another painter, Pieter Codde, who lived close by in Amsterdam (fig. 70).

By 'his people' Hals meant the employees in his studio. Karel van Mander used the term in the same sense in his *Schilder-Boeck* when he described Lambert Lombard asking Frans Floris 'what kind of people he had there in his shop'.[2] This puts the figure at two or more people; how many more one can only guess, but it does give an idea of how busy the studio was. This was not only where Hals painted on his own but where he also had pupils to teach and assistants who worked for him. Back in those days the employees were often called 'discipelen' (disciples) or 'knechten' (assistants).[3] The first word is equivalent to 'pupil', meaning both the beginner receiving his first drawing or painting lessons as well as the more advanced student. The assistant was someone who had completed his formal apprenticeship but was not yet running his own workshop. He would continue working with his teacher or would move to another studio to make paintings for sale as a fully qualified artist. He could also supervise the apprentices in the house. A third kind of employee was the '(werck)gesel' (working journeyman) or 'vrij gast' (free craftsman), who often came from another town and sought employment for a shorter

or longer period. The term 'leerknecht' (teaching assistant), which is found sporadically in the archives, could refer either to a fully trained assistant who was not yet working as an independent artist but was learning how to develop into one, or to a painter who trained his master's apprentices. It was certainly not unusual, as also with Frans Hals, for a pupil to spend years with the same master, graduating from disciple to assistant. Some even stayed on a good deal longer.[4]

Sources with concrete information about Hals's 'people' are scarce. This chapter is devoted to what is known about his workshop. Who worked in his studio? What did they do? How did Hals teach his pupils? Since painters were bound by the rules of the guild statutes governing the training of apprentices and the practice of their craft, we will first examine the statutes, specifically those governing the lives of apprentices and journeymen.

THE STATUTES OF THE HAARLEM GUILD OF ST LUKE

In 1610 Frans Hals enrolled as a member of the Haarlem Guild of St Luke. In those days anyone who wanted to practise a craft had to be registered with the guild that represented their profession. This was laid down in the statutes, bylaws decreed by the city authorities that had to be obeyed by members of a specific professional category. The Guild of St Luke board, members of which served for a year, consisted of a dean (chairman) and several wardens (other board members). When Hals joined the guild it was governed by the statutes of 1590.[5] The first of these 14 articles dealt with the membership. Anyone who wanted to join had to be a burgess of the city and pay an admission fee, half of which was paid to the city and the other half to the guild. The other 13 articles specified all kinds of financial obligations, among them the payments to the guild and fines for transgressions, as well as regulations for the sale of paintings. The ordinance says remarkably little about practical arrangements in the studios and almost nothing about the quality of the work to be produced there. For example, a

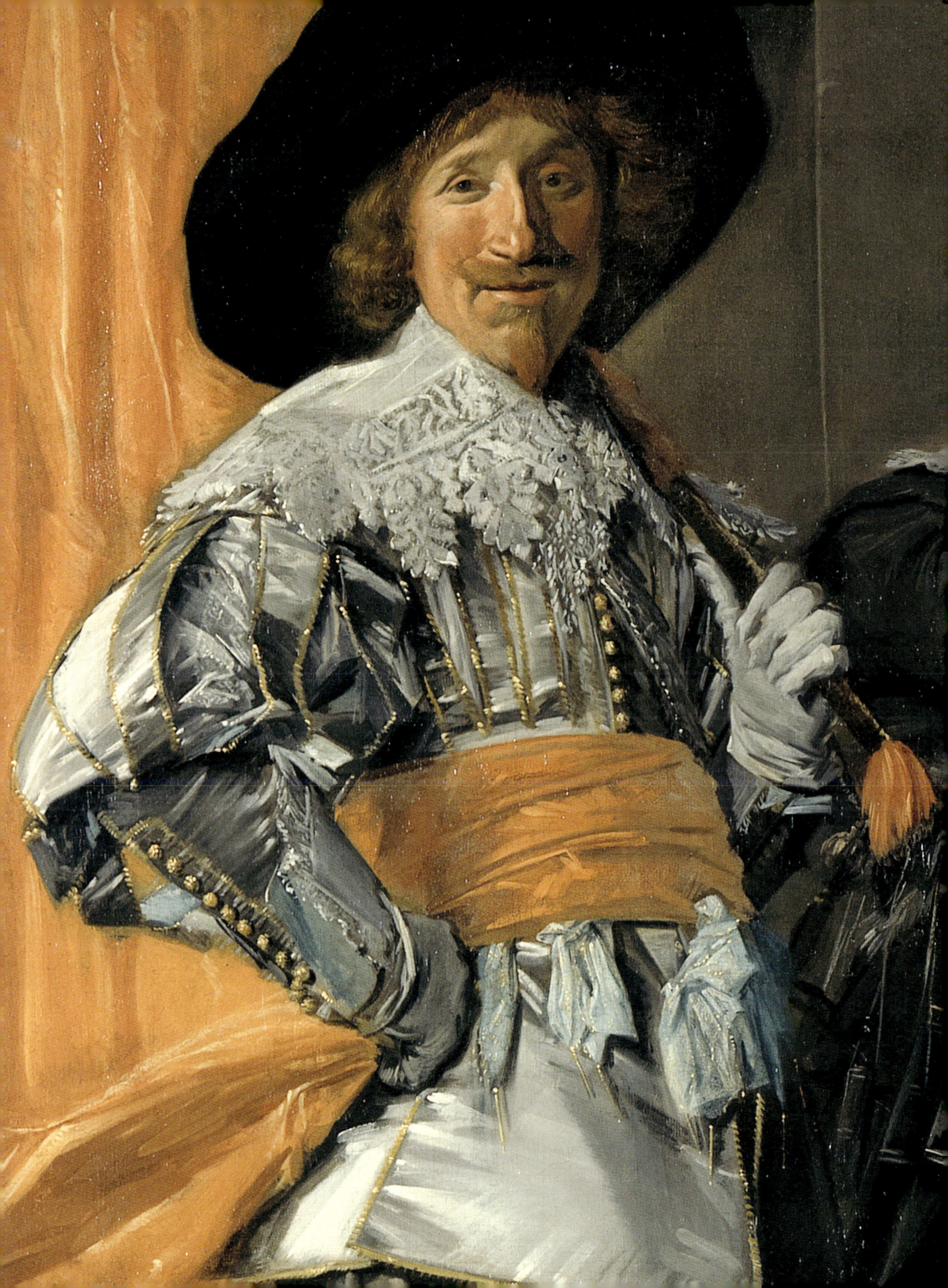

budding artist did not have to produce a masterpiece, which was required by most other professions. The statutes do, however, stipulate details of the training to be given, specifically about taking on pupils and the work of journeymen.

The guild charged 12 stuivers for each apprentice. A master had to register a new apprentice with the guild within six weeks of application; failure to do so was penalised with a fine of 12 stuivers. A master painter could have no more than two apprentices at a time, but if he entered into a contract for one of them for just one year he could take on a third. This was stipulated in the fifth article of the statutes, which made further exceptions. If a master wanted to take on more apprentices he could submit a request to the burgomasters of the city and the guild wardens. If a pupil had completed his apprenticeship and was promoted to journeyman, he was still not allowed to work immediately as an independent artist. He could only do this when he had painted with a master for a year. The statutes allowed journeymen in Haarlem to work for a master for a fortnight without having to pay anything to the guild; if they worked for longer, they had to pay 2 stuivers.

Although the Haarlem statutes put a limit on the number of employees in a workshop, a master could still have two or three apprentices at any one time, plus at least one assistant and an undefined number of journeymen. The statutes did not specify how many assistants were permitted, possibly because they were paid for their work.

The 1590 statutes remained in force throughout the seventeenth century and were only superseded by a new decree in 1751. Although a number of artists drew up new regulations in 1631 that were submitted to the authorities, they were rejected by the burgomasters. These were discussed by the college of wardens in 1634 but never ratified.[6] The 1631 draft, which may have reflected the situation at the time, or perhaps because of its hierarchical classification of professions, specified the regulations that the drafters wanted to be implemented and envisaged an increase in the number of employees. Article 26 states that a master could have three apprentices at any one time but foresaw that a situation could arise, 'by request or increase of applicants', that would almost force the master to take on even more. If he did so, the master had to pay 3 guilders to the guild for every extra apprentice. However, that did not apply to the 'free craftsmen' who worked 'for payment' and were apparently not subject to any limitation. It is true that this draft was never implemented but it would have reflected the desire to set many hands to work. Haarlem was a thriving artistic centre at the time and many up-and-coming artists moved there to train as painters.[7]

It is not easy to determine how strictly the rules were followed in practice. Reference has been made in this respect to Frans Pietersz de Grebber, who trained many pupils. In 1640 this fellow townsman and contemporary of Hals was admonished by the guild for not paying the contribution for no fewer than 16 of 'his disciples'. He would not have been training them all at the same time, as has been assumed, but the large number is certainly striking. The matter came up again two years later and the guild took him to task once more, this time not just for the number of pupils for whom he had failed to pay, but also for his 'unregistered pupils' and the payment for 'his craftsmen'. Because De Grebber was not in the city at the time, there was no immediate reply, whereupon the exasperated board resolved that on his return they would again ask him 'how many assistants he had who have failed to pay'.[8]

FRANS HALS'S 'PEOPLE'

In 1635 the guild wardens discussed a complaint that Judith Jansdr Leyster had lodged with the dean.[9] A young apprentice called Willem Woutersz had withdrawn from her studio and joined Frans Hals's. The guild servant was ordered to tell Hals that he could not keep the boy, whom he had not registered: the statutes did not permit it, on pain of a fine of 3 guilders. Six weeks later Judith appeared in the boardroom to settle the affair with the pupil's mother. The boy had been ordered to spend three months with Leyster for 8 guilders, after which time they could separate or carry on together.[10] The mother considered it unfair that she had to pay the full sum as her son had only spent three or four days with Leyster. Besides, the mother argued, she had earlier treated Leyster well and therefore did not owe her anything. After an argument, the women agreed that they would accept the wardens' decision; both then agreed that the mother had to pay 4 guilders. Judith Leyster, who was fined for not registering her pupil, released him 'to go wherever he wishes' and promised to have 'her assistant' give him his belongings that were still in her house. She took the opportunity to register her pupils Hendrick Jacobs and David de Bary with the guild. When the guild servant called on her she said that she would pay the outstanding sum. It says a great deal about the size of a studio at the time that a 26-year-old painter had three apprentices and an assistant working for her simultaneously. The boy in question remained with Frans Hals. The wardens summoned him to appear before them about 'retaining his disciple' but it is not known whether Hals obeyed.

Willem Woutersz joined Frans Hals's studio at the time when the latter spoke of his 'people' in his reply to his Amsterdam clients. There is no precise information about the number of apprentices and journeymen he had in his studio. The ledgers with their names have not been preserved and the surviving minutes of the guild board are only fragmentary. The names of studio employees are only known by chance. Some artists, including a handful of Haarlem painters, kept their own records. Jacob de Wet the Elder, for instance, recorded the names of apprentices who came to draw or paint with him in a notebook that has come down to us.[11] Cornelis Dusart did the same: his 'memorandum book with the names of disciples' is recorded in his probate inventory as being in his house, but it has not survived. In the case of Frans de

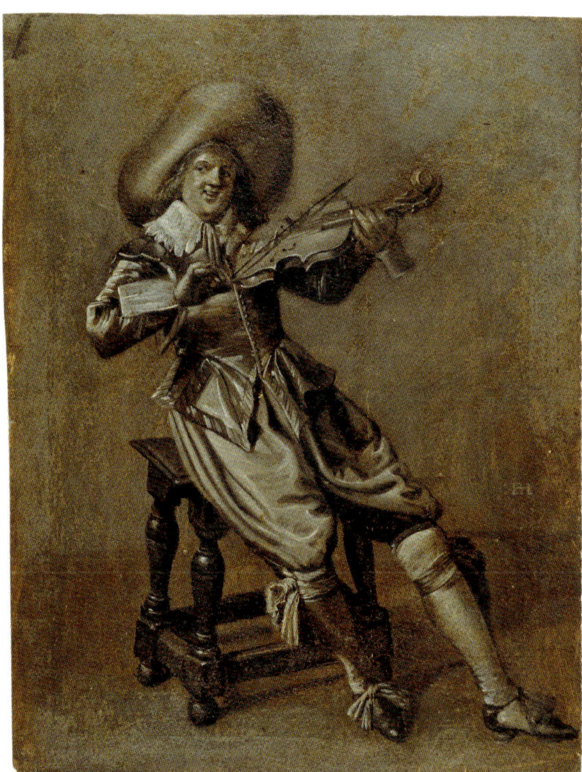

Fig. 28 Dirck Hals, *A Seated Man playing the Violin*, 1629
Oil on paper, 21.3 × 16.5 cm
Fitzwilliam Museum, Cambridge

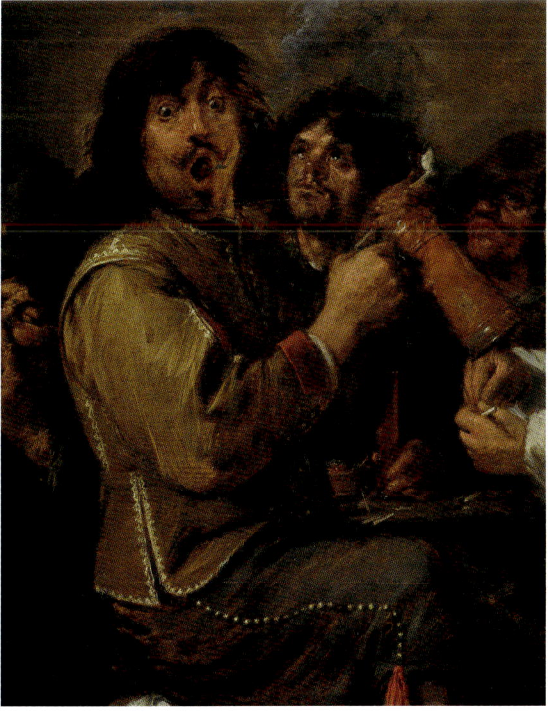

Fig. 29 Adriaen Brouwer's self portrait from *The Smokers* (detail),
about 1636. Oil on wood, 46.4 × 36.8 cm
The Metropolitan Museum of Art, New York; The Friedsam
Collection, Bequest of Michael Friedsam, 1931

Grebber, there are records in 1620 and 1642 of a book in which he recorded the names of his pupils, together with the dates when he took them on, so that he could calculate their tuition fees.[12] Written contracts between a painter and pupil, statements testifying to the fact that the tuition period was completed satisfactorily or receipts for tuition fees received are generally scarce, and in Hals's case completely unknown.[13]

Although there are no precise records about the number of apprentices and assistants that Hals had, one can hazard some cautious speculations. As a master joining the guild in 1610 and still working as an artist at an advanced age, he must have been active as a painter for around 50 years. If one assumes that he taught for 30 of those years and had two pupils a year, he would have taught a grand total of 60 pupils. Since some of these would have stayed with him for longer, the total number could have been lower. In addition, Hals must have had assistants on the payroll. If he had just one (although there would probably have been more), then a significant number of artists would have contributed to the output of the studio. It is conceivable that Hals preferred to take on advanced pupils who had already had drawing lessons from other masters and had even learned the basic principles of painting, because he could set them to work straight away, unlike beginners. It is a mistake, in our view, to assume that in the first half of the 1620s, when Hals seems to have been less productive, he had no need for assistance in the studio or was unable to afford to take someone on.[14] Teaching was a not inconsiderable source of income for most artists. Judith Leyster lost 8 guilders for three months of tuition for the pupil who had 'passed her by', as she put it, which would have represented 32 guilders per annum. In any event, she still had two other pupils. More experienced painters charged more. De Wet, mentioned above, initially charged 48 guilders a year for painting lessons, later increasing to 60 guilders, and a minimum of 40 guilders for drawing instruction. Philips Wouwerman charged his pupils 60 guilders a year and Nicolaes Berchem as much as 72 guilders. Hals probably charged at least as much as De Wet.

PUPILS AND ASSISTANTS

It is known with some degree of certainty that 14 named artists (including the Willem Woutersz who had decamped to Frans Hals from Judith Leyster) definitely studied with Frans Hals for some length of time or worked in his studio, while in the case of others there are good reasons for assuming that they also did so.

DIRCK HALS

It seems likely that Dirck Hals learned painting from his elder brother, who was eight years his senior. From around 1616 he started making oil sketches on paper that are close to Frans's style (fig. 28).[15] He may then have spent some time working for Esaias van de Velde and Willem Pietersz Buytewech, whose influence is clearly visible in his popular depictions of merry companies of elegantly dressed young pleasure-seekers.[16] In any event, it was probably not long before Dirck returned to his brother's studio. His earliest dated painting of young merrymakers is from 1619; there are dozens more, signed and dated from then until 1627, when he joined the Guild of St Luke as a master at the age of 35 or 36. He must therefore have made these paintings in the studio of someone other than Van de Velde or Buytewech, both of whom had left Haarlem in 1617. It is only logical to assume that his brother Frans gave Dirck a space to work. This would have been financially attractive, as they then paid less to the guild and there were many other advantages in sharing a studio. As we shall see, Dirck's subsequent role would have been similar to the way in which Frans first taught his own sons and then had them work with him.

ADRIAEN BROUWER

The artists' biographer Arnold Houbraken explicitly states that Adriaen Brouwer was one of Hals's pupils (fig. 29). Frans Hals may have got to know Adriaen through his brother Joost, who was a cartoon painter. According to Houbraken, Adriaen Brouwer worked for his mother painting textiles with ornamental foliage and birds. Recent research into his background has shown that his family were tapestry weavers active in Gouda, where cartoon painters also worked.[17] It is thought that Brouwer's time with Hals overlapped with the apprenticeship of Adriaen van Ostade, whom Hals probably taught around 1626–7.

Houbraken also states that Pieter Gerritsz van Roestraten, another very well-documented pupil of Hals, married his master's daughter Ariaentje after his period of study. When Ariaentje was very young it was said that her mother, Lysbeth Reyniers, once asked Brouwer whether he would look after her child 'when he was still young and was learning art from F. Hals'. He carried the little girl around and danced with her to stop her crying. The child, who had not yet been house-trained, then 'beshat' him.[18] If one believes this anecdote, which Houbraken had heard from an artist friend of his, who had been told in turn by Hals's daughter and her husband, it is possible to pin down Brouwer's apprenticeship with Hals more precisely. Ariaentje was born in July 1623, which means that Brouwer would have been working in Hals's Haarlem studio between that year or earlier and 1627.

Brouwer is presented by Arnold Houbraken as a fledgling pupil of Hals and, when he started making great progress as an artist, as an advanced assistant or journeyman whose painting Hals sold. It was said that Hals set Brouwer to work in an attic in his house, 'apart from his other pupils',[19] evidence that he was not the only person training with Hals at the time. A tale related by Houbraken about a trick with a four-poster bed mentions four pupils.[20]

Brouwer joined the Haarlem guild at an unknown date after working with Hals, probably around 1628. He left for Antwerp three years later, where he died at an early age.

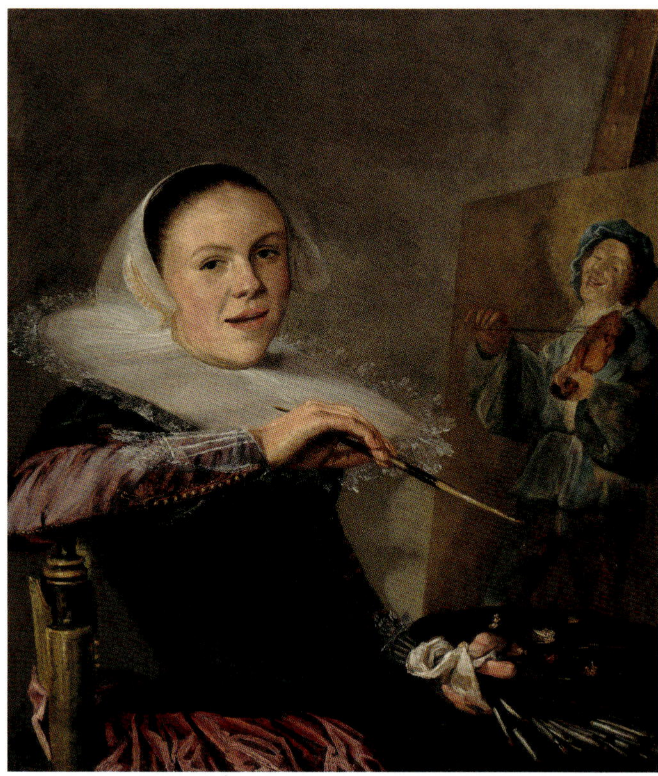

Fig. 30 Judith Leyster, *Self Portrait*, about 1630. Oil on canvas, 74.6 × 65.1 cm National Gallery of Art, Washington; Gift of Mr and Mrs Robert Woods Bliss

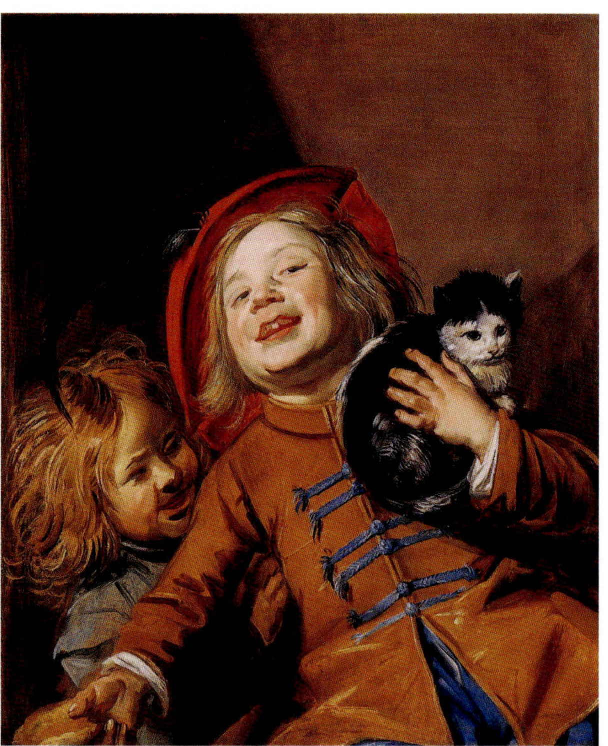

Fig. 31 Judith Leyster, *Two Children with a Cat*, about 1630. Oil on canvas, 61 × 52 cm Private collection

     THE STUDIO

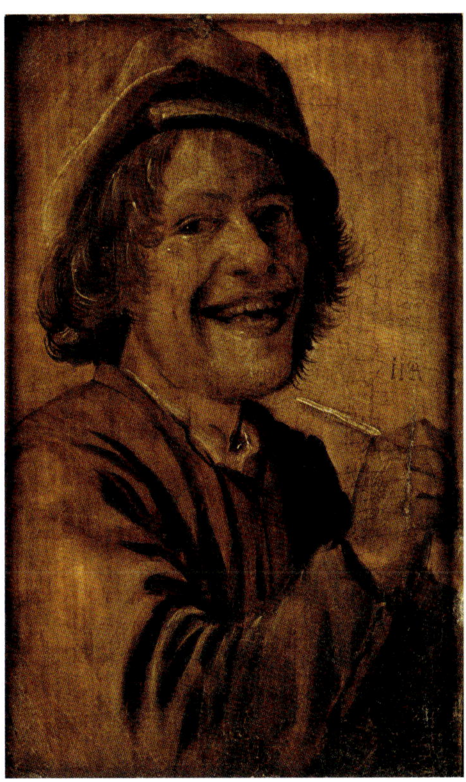

Fig. 32 Jan Miense Molenaer, *Laughing Youth with a Stylus*, about 1629. Oil on paper, transferred on to panel, 16 × 11 cm Museum Mayer van den Bergh, Antwerp

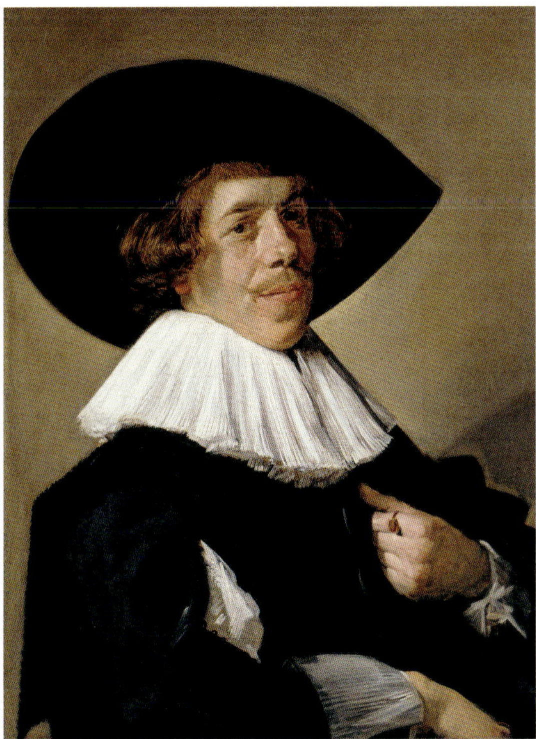

Fig. 33 *Portrait of a Man, possibly Jan Miense Molenaer*, about 1634. Oil on canvas, 75.7 × 61.4 cm Staatliche Museen zu Berlin, Gemäldegalerie

JUDITH LEYSTER

Judith Leyster, who was born in Haarlem in 1609, was placed with a painter by her parents. This turned out to be a wise decision, as she worked professionally after her apprenticeship (fig. 30). Painting was a very unusual choice of profession for a woman at this time. There is no firm information about her training but her early work provides some clues. The paintings that she made between 1629 and 1631 are of a markedly Caravaggist character, so the likeliest explanation is that she was influenced by a follower of Caravaggio active in Utrecht. This is supported by the fact that around 1625/6 her parents moved from Haarlem to Vreeland, just outside Utrecht.[21] From 1628 she would have worked for some years in Haarlem as an assistant or journeyman, very probably for Frans Hals. During this time she produced paintings close to Hals's in subject matter, and especially in style, such as *The Serenade* (fig. 176), *Two Children with a Cat* (fig. 31) and *A Fool holding a Jug, known as 'The Jolly Drinker'*.[22] Her documented but lost portrait painted by Frans Hals, who more than once portrayed a pupil or former pupil, is also evidence of their close contact.[23] Leyster started working independently in 1633 and was soon taking on pupils of her own. She painted genre scenes and a few portraits, and the occasional still life following her marriage in 1636 to Jan Miense Molenaer.[24]

JAN MIENSE MOLENAER

Although Jan Miense Molenaer's apprenticeship is not documented, it is assumed that he trained in the studio of Frans and Dirck Hals.[25] An important pointer is his oil sketch *Laughing Youth with a Stylus* (fig. 32), which bears his distinctive 'IMR' monogram.[26] Oil sketches by Dutch artists from the first decades of the seventeenth century are uncommon, particularly if they are on paper, but Dirck Hals was one of the few painters who made them. Molenaer's sketch is similar to his work but the composition and wide grin point more in the direction of Frans Hals. It is possible that this is a self portrait that Molenaer made while in Hals's studio, or perhaps depicts a fellow pupil.[27]

The influence of both Frans and Dirck Hals can be seen in the subject matter and execution of Molenaer's paintings from 1629. The earliest mention of his work is at an auction held by Hendrick Willemsz den Abt in 1631. No fewer than four 'heads' by the barely 21-year-old artist were on offer, along with paintings by Frans (including another head study) and Dirck Hals, several anonymous copies after works by both brothers, and five pieces by the 'young Hals', namely Harmen Hals.[28] Seventeenth-century probate inventories frequently mention paintings by Frans Hals and his family, in combination with works by artists who worked in his studio or had done so, which probably also came from the Hals studio.[29]

As far as Molenaer's assumed apprenticeship with Frans Hals is concerned, there is also a mention of his portrait by Frans Hals (fig. 33), together with that of his wife, Judith Leyster, in their probate inventory of 1668.[30] Hals painted several portraits of former pupils, so those of Molenaer and Leyster may fall into the same category. In addition to two works by Harmen Hals and two more 'by Hals', the inventory lists four by Adriaen Brouwer (as well as one made to his design), plus a scene of tric-trac players in dead-colouring by Brouwer that was completed by Molenaer.[31]

In 1634 Molenaer settled in Haarlem as a master and two years later moved to Amsterdam. Here he continued to depict subjects that he had painted as a pupil. As it will be discussed below, he also remained to some extent indebted to Adriaen Brouwer's style.

ADRIAEN VAN OSTADE

Houbraken writes in his biography of Adriaen van Ostade that he and Adriaen Brouwer were pupils of Frans Hals 'at the same time'.[32] Van Ostade was born in 1610 and would have arrived in Hals's studio around 1626–7, or a little earlier if he was younger when apprenticed. It is not known how long he stayed there. He is very probably the man with a hat painted by Frans Hals (fig. 34), which is therefore another of Hals's pupil portraits.

In his early years as an independent painter Van Ostade specialised in genre pieces and peasant scenes. An affidavit from the summer of 163w2 relates to his agreement to paint a woman eating pottage and a man smoking.[33] A couple of years later he delivered two drawings that he had made for a collector's album, one of a peasant on a bench drinking and the other of a man in a chair with a small pipe in his hand.[34] It is known that Adriaen Brouwer and other pupils of Hals did a great deal of drawing, but there is not a single known sheet by Frans Hals, nor has a mention of one yet been found in contemporary inventories and other source material, suggesting that they were trained in this by some other artist.[35]

PHILIPS WOUWERMAN

The Brabant rhetorician and jurist Cornelis de Bie explicitly states in his book of painters' biographies of 1662 that Philips Wouwerman (fig. 35) was a pupil of Frans Hals.[36] Wouwerman's name also appears in the notebook of mid-seventeenth-century art lover Joannes Sysmus, who recorded the names of artists, sometimes adding details such as the name of a teacher or characteristics of their work. According to Sysmus, Wouwerman excelled in the depiction of horses and battles, calling him a 'disciple of Frans Hals, painter'.[37] Although Sysmus sometimes took information from De Bie, that does not appear to be the case here since their texts do not match.

Born in Haarlem in 1619, Wouwerman probably received his first lessons from his father, Pouwels Joostensz Wouwerman. He served his apprenticeship to Hals before 1638, when he is recorded earning a living in the Hamburg studio of Evert Decker, probably as a journeyman. Wouwerman registered with the Guild of St Luke in 1640, when he was back in Haarlem. He was in close touch with Pieter van Roestraten, who claimed that he knew not only the Hals family 'very well', but also several other Haarlem artists, Wouwerman among them.[38]

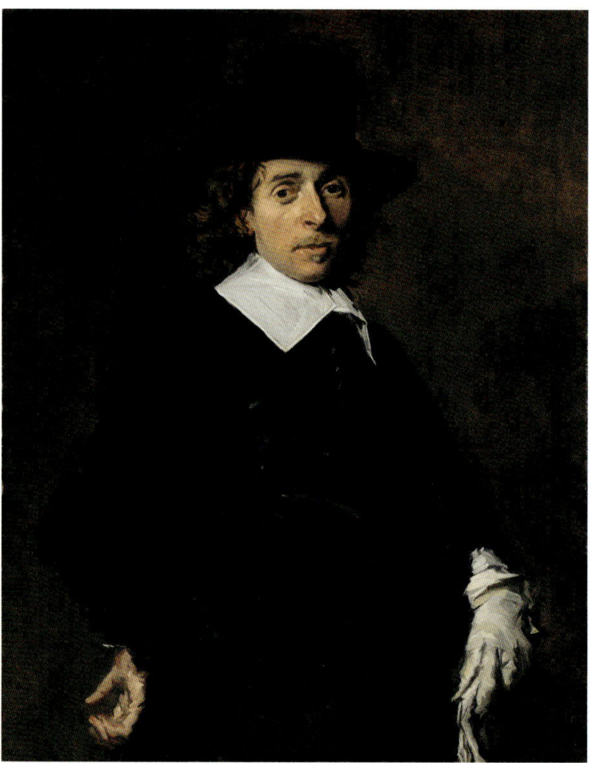

Fig. 34 *Portrait of a Man, possibly Adriaen van Ostade*, about 1647. Oil on canvas, 94 × 75 cm
National Gallery of Art, Washington; Andrew W. Mellon Collection

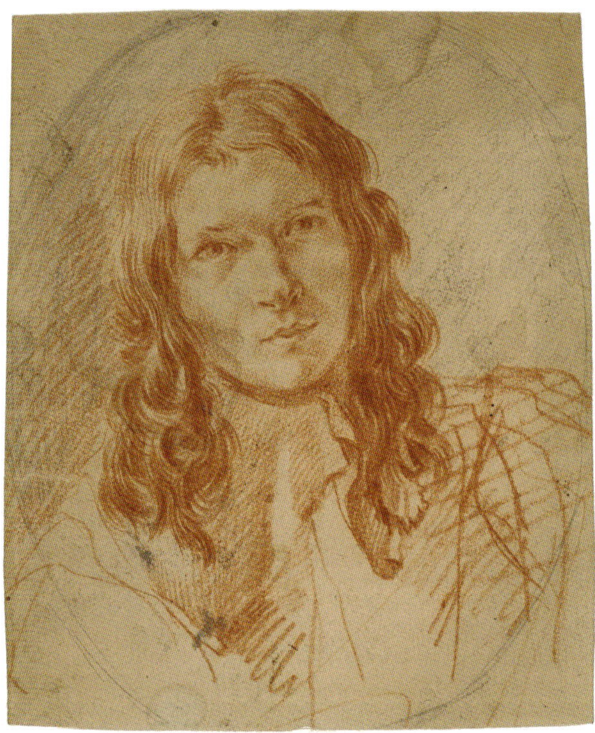

Fig. 35 Philips Wouwerman, *Self Portrait*, about 1649. Red and black chalk, 17.5 × 14.6 cm
British Museum, London

THE STUDIO

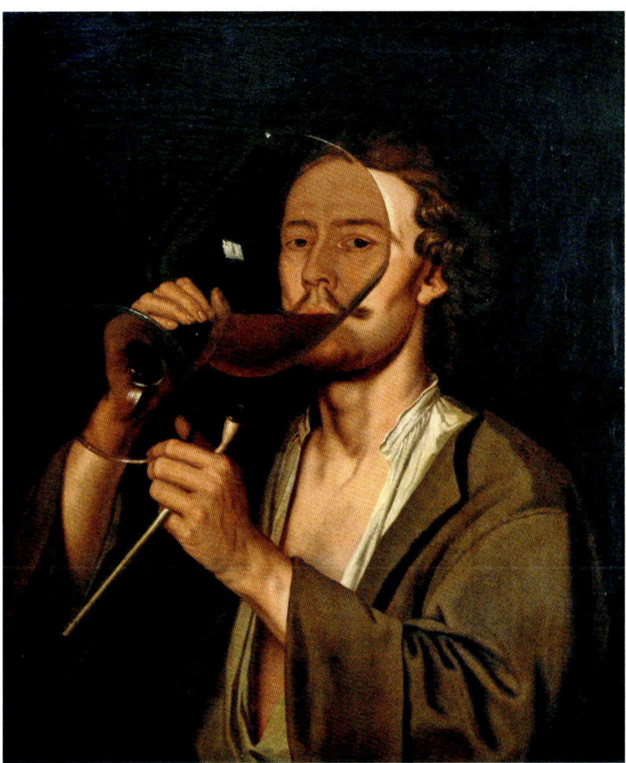

Fig. 36 Pieter Gerritsz van Roestraten, *Self Portrait, drinking from a Large Glass*, about 1670(?). Oil on canvas, 72 × 62.5 cm
Present whereabouts unknown

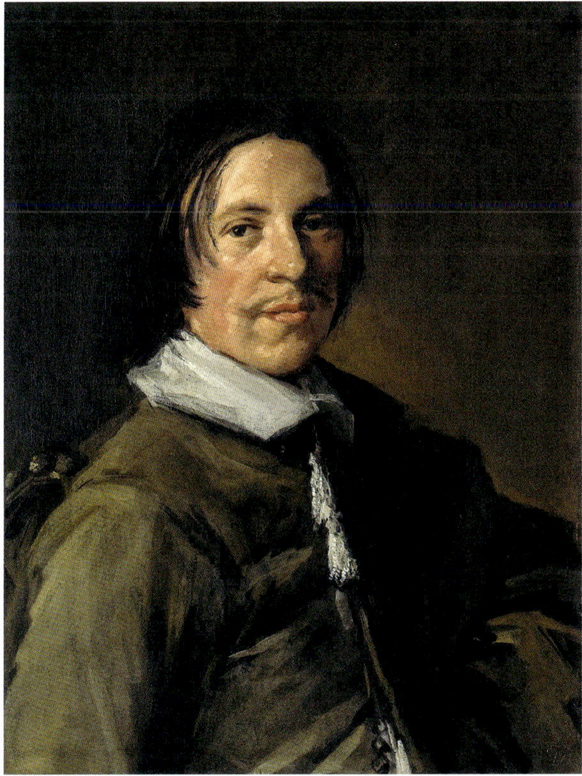

Fig. 37 *Portrait of Vincent Laurensz van der Vinne*, about 1658. Oil on canvas, 64.7 × 48.9 cm
Art Gallery of Ontario, Toronto; Bequest of Frank P. Wood, 1955

PIETER GERRITSZ VAN ROESTRATEN

Houbraken's account of Pieter van Roestraten's period of apprenticeship with Frans Hals was confirmed in an affidavit dated 6 October 1651. At the request of Frans Hals's wife, Lysbeth, Van Roestraten and one other appeared in the office of an Amsterdam notary to sign an affidavit concerning Hals's son Anthonie, who had sailed to the East Indies in 1646 and died in Tonkin in 1650. It was customary for signatories to explain how they knew the person for whom they were testifying. Van Roestraten stated that he had 'worked for the petitioner and her husband for five years',[39] which suggests that this was now in the past. He was still living in Haarlem at the time of the affidavit, so if this refers to a period in the recent past, he would have arrived in Hals's studio in 1646 or a little earlier. Since he was born in 1630, he would have started as an apprentice and subsequently remained as an assistant. In 1654 he married one of his teacher's daughters, Ariaentje. When the banns were read in Amsterdam, Van Roestraten was supported by Claes Hals, one of the painter sons of Frans Hals.

Van Roestraten is known as a painter of still lifes. Most of these date from his time in London, to which he and his wife moved in 1663. Frans Hals would have taught him to paint portraits and genre scenes, so it is with good reason that the membership roll of the Haarlem Guild of St Luke, which was compiled in the eighteenth century from old lists, has the word 'pourtraitschilder' (portrait painter) after his name.[40] Houbraken writes that Peter Lely was also working in London, having trained with Frans de Grebber in Haarlem. Lely was unhappy about having Van Roestraten as a competing portraitist, so asked him not to accept any portrait commissions; he repaid his promise by regularly buying paintings from him.[41] Two self portraits demonstrate Van Roestraten's skill: one of them has survived as a reproductive print (fig. 174); the other one, a painting, is a combination of portrait and genre scene (fig. 36). In addition to portraits, he no doubt painted the occasional tavern interior in his early Haarlem period, as well as drawing figure studies in red and black chalk. One intriguing detail is the mention in 1936 of the head of an old Haarlem fisherman painted by Van Roestraten, which would have been related to the fisherboys from Hals's studio.[42]

VINCENT LAURENSZ VAN DER VINNE

In his brief biography of Vincent Laurensz van der Vinne, Houbraken records Frans Hals's advice to his apprentices to work boldly. According to Houbraken, the young Van der Vinne was a local friend of Hals's sons. This fact, and his enthusiasm for drawing and painting, persuaded his parents to apprentice him to Hals. In the studio he soon mastered his teacher's daring manner and felt that he could stand on his own two feet. The versatile Van der Vinne turned his hand to every medium: he made easel paintings, painted signboards and decorated rooms. Houbraken believed that in his portraits he was extremely 'good at capturing' ('gelukkig in 't treffen') his subjects, painting with a 'bold brush' ('stout penceel') following the example of his master, Frans Hals.[43]

A surviving genealogy reveals that Van der Vinne was born in Haarlem in 1628 or 1629 (the first year being altered into the second) and that he was apprenticed to Hals at the age of 18 in 1646–7. According to the same source, he remained with Hals for nine months and never had another teacher. In 1649 he became a member of the guild and made at least two self portraits around the same time.[44] Some years after Hals painted his portrait, as he so often did with former pupils (fig. 37).[45]

FRANS HALS'S FIVE SONS

Frans Hals and his first wife, Anneke Harmens, had three children, of whom only one son, Harmen (born 1611), survived into adulthood. His second wife, Lysbeth Reyniers, bore him some 11 children, among them at least four sons: Frans (born 1618), Jan (born about 1620), Reynier (born 1627) and Claes (born 1628). With their elder half-brother they followed their father's profession, trained by him, as was customary at the time, in his studio. This is explicitly stated in the inscription below the portrait of Harmen Hals, who is identified as the 'son and disciple of Frans Hals' (fig. 38).[46] Hals's workshop can therefore rightly be described as a family business, his children becoming involved in its daily routine while they were still young and some serving as models.

While they followed in their father's footsteps, Hals's sons did not slavishly imitate his style and subject matter. The inscription below Harmen's portrait describes him as 'geselschapschilder' ('painter of companies') and his extant works comprise tavern scenes and small pictures of peasants drinking and smoking. Not a single work can be attributed to Frans Hals the Younger with any certainty. Inventories do occasionally speak of 'the young Hals' but that could equally well be one of the other sons. Jan painted portraits, but not exclusively, in his father's studio. In 1668 a Haarlem couple are recorded as settling a debt by selling property, including their own portraits by Frans Hals. The same document also mentions a portrait of the sitter's brother with his wife and son, depicted 'as large as life by Jan Hals' ('soo groot als 't leven gedaen van Jan Hals'), a figure painting by Jan and two pieces by Dirck Hals.[47] Jan Hals also painted head studies: an inventory of 1676 mentions two studies of boys' heads by him and three by Frans Hals, probably his father. Reynier Hals, who lived in Haarlem after serving in the Dutch East India Company in 1643–5, specialised in genre and interior scenes. He did not register with the guild there, so probably worked in his father's studio. He moved to Amsterdam after marrying in 1653.[48] The youngest of the artist's sons, Claes, painted landscapes, a few cityscapes and possibly also genre pieces. Among these is a small 'tobacco smoker' described in an inventory of 1700, bearing the 'C.H.' monogram with which Claes signed his paintings.[49]

If a painting is unsigned, it can be difficult to make out which family member made it. Contemporaries had similar

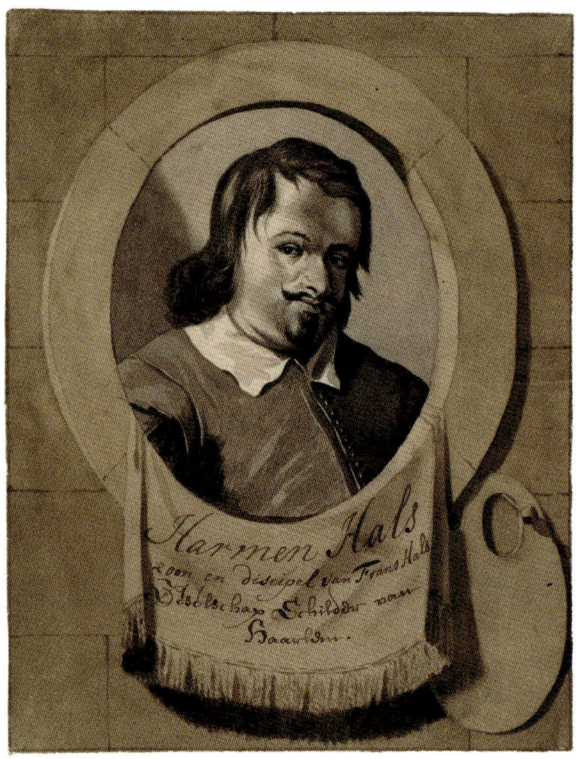

Fig. 38 Anonymous, *Portrait of Harmen Hals*, in or after 1735. Pen and brush, 21.3 × 16.4 cm Noord-Hollands Archief, Haarlem

THE STUDIO

difficulty, as seen in the mention of 'a painting by Claes or Dirck Hals' in a Haarlem inventory of 1669.[50] That kind of uncertainty over the maker is found frequently in connection with works by the Hals family.

OTHER POSSIBLE APPRENTICES OR JOURNEYMEN

This overview of apprentices and assistants known with some certainty to have worked with Frans Hals can be expanded with the names of others associated with his studio in one way or another. Two of these can be dealt with briefly.[51] It has been suggested that Pieter Codde was asked to finish the civic guard piece started by Hals because he was a member of this civic guard company – he may even have included a depiction of himself, possibly as one of the guardsmen.[52] However, in 1636, the year in which he must have been working on the painting, a detailed inventory was made of Codde's possessions but does not mention paraphernalia associated with the civic guard.[53] It has been observed more than once that Codde's contribution to *The Meagre Company'* was skilled, and that it is not immediately evident which parts of the picture he painted (fig. 70). Could he so easily have imitated Frans Hals's manner? Is it not possible that he was once apprenticed to Hals, or worked under him as a fully fledged assistant? This would offer an alternative explanation for the choice of the guardsmen. In addition, it seems that Codde had connections with Haarlem. His estate contained paintings by masters active there, such as Pieter Claesz, Salomon van Ruysdael, Pieter de Molijn and Adriaen Brouwer, as well as Frans Hals.[54] Jan Miense Molenaer's probate inventory lists a work of his own done 'after Codde', which would have been a copy from Molenaer's Haarlem period. And in a Haarlem house in 1673 there was a 'female card player by Pieter Codde' ('een caertspeelstertje van Pieter Codde'), which could well have been painted in the city, as was a small work by Codde described in Delft in 1659, in which the landscape 'was done by Pieter Molijn'.[55]

Dirck van Delen was described by Houbraken as a disciple of Frans Hals, although this has been in doubt for some time.[56] Nevertheless, a connection with Hals's studio cannot be ruled out. It has long been assumed that the figures in some of Van Delen's interiors were painted by Dirck Hals, although it is more likely that Van Delen provided his own staffage but occasionally borrowed figures from Dirck Hals's pictures. A case in point involves a small group of three palatial architecture paintings of 1628, two of which are signed by Dirck Hals and one by Van Delen.[57] The signature relates to the figures, because the other parts of two of these pictures have been convincingly attributed to the Hague painter and architect Bartholomeus van Bassen.[58] Hals's figures are considerably freer than Van Delen's. There is a suspicion that Van Delen was in touch with Dirck Hals in Haarlem in 1628, and it is possible that he had been apprenticed previously to Frans Hals. This suggestion depends on the reliability of Houbraken's anecdote about a trick that Adriaen Brouwer played on Frans Hals, his teacher, which also involved his contemporary, Dirck van Delen.[59]

AT HOME

In Frans Hals's day, private and work lives were closely entwined. Painters and other craftsmen usually worked at home, their houses serving both as family homes and as workshops. Here the master worked with his pupils and other employees, some of whom paid for board and lodging. Paintings, finished or in various stages of preparation, were kept here, where the artists were at work. Clients came into the 'shop' ('winckel') to examine paintings, and if the artist also made portraits, for sittings and discussions as well. A sitter might show an interest in another of the artist's works, or commission a portrait after buying a genre scene, for instance. It is not unusual for contemporary probate inventories to list portraits alongside other paintings by a particular artist and his studio.[60] For example, the estate of the widow of trader Isaac Massa included not only five portraits of her husband, at least three of them by Frans Hals, but also three other works by the same artist.[61] Aletta Hanemans, whose portrait and that of her first husband, the Haarlem brewer Jacob Pietersz Olycan, were painted by Frans Hals, left an estate in 1653 that included these two marriage paintings, another from his studio with children by Hals, and three pictures by Dirck Hals.[62]

The combination of home and business made for a busy house, especially when the head of the workshop had a large family and many employees, which was certainly the case with Frans Hals. As a popular portrait painter he would also have had regular visits from prospective customers: in his reply of 20 March 1636 to the Amsterdam guardsmen urging completion of their group portrait he wrote that they should come to Haarlem, where he could finish it 'at home'. This document also gives the location of his house in Groot Heiligland. Hals moved house quite often in Haarlem.[63] It is not known how large his homes were, nor how they were laid out. He would certainly have felt the need for space with so many people to accommodate.

An apprentice or assistant could sit with an easel in the same room as the master, or in a separate one if the house was big enough. And that, it seems, is what Hals did, for Houbraken states that Brouwer was given his own workspace in the attic. Houbraken himself had experienced something similar when he was apprenticed to the Dordrecht painter Samuel van Hoogstraten. As the eldest pupil he was given a room above his master's, while the other apprentices were crowded together in a room on the other side of the inner courtyard. When his master was away on a visit somewhere, Houbraken would keep in touch with his fellow pupils through his upstairs window.[64] It emerges from his description of his apprenticeship with Van Hoogstraten that there were at least three pupils working there at any one time. Similar numbers are also mentioned in connection with other masters, so the situation with Frans Hals would have been much the same.[65]

Family members often played a role in the business, as was certainly the case in the Hals household. His sons, and some of his daughters too, would have been involved in the joint enterprise, thus contributing to the output and income. Quite often the woman of the house also had a specific part to play, while young pupils and the master's children would act as models. A probate inventory drawn up in Leiden in 1644 mentions two paintings by Hals portraying two of his children, while the inventory made in 1653 after the death of Aletta Hanemans, the widow of a Haarlem brewer, mentions another.[66] None of these would have been formal portraits, but rather genre scenes or study heads for which the children posed. The 1644 example makes it clear that even people outside Haarlem knew that the children in such scenes were Hals's. It is tempting to include in this group Hals's *Laughing Boy* in the Mauritshuis (fig. 164), the two paintings of boys in Schwerin (figs 165–6), and above all the *Girl singing* and *Boy playing the Violin* (figs 12–3) now in a private collection.[67]

TRAINING

Almost nothing is known of Frans Hals's ideas about training his pupils. He himself had been taught by Karel van Mander, whose treatise *Den grondt der edel vry schilder-const* (The Foundation of the Noble, Free Art of Painting) shows him to have been keenly interested in the teaching of art. In his *Schilder-Boeck*, too, Van Mander identifies the teacher or teachers of almost every artist in their biographies, regularly detailing their educational accomplishments. Oddly enough, the only known advice that Frans Hals gave his pupils was diametrically opposed to the ideas of his master. According to Houbraken, Hals used to tell his apprentices: 'You must slap it on boldly, if you become secure in art the neatness will come of its own accord'.[68] Van Mander, on the other hand, advised his pupils to become accustomed to 'neatness' and only then try working in a looser manner.[69] Perhaps Houbraken found Hals's advice worth mentioning because it ran counter to contemporary ideas.

The training of painters traditionally took place in several stages. A young apprentice was first instructed in drawing, and once he had mastered this he could start on painting. The basic activities, in Van Mander's words, consisted of helping 'to keep the workshop in good repair', that is to say cleaning brushes and palettes and other painters' tools.[70] The pupils then learned how to grind the pigments for paint and prepare panels and canvases.[71] Hals could prepare his canvases in advance and keep them in stock without much difficulty, as a considerable amount of both his genre paintings and his portraits have similar dimensions.[72] The question is the extent to which Hals left this to his assistants, for specialist shops also supplied ready-made prepared panels and canvases.

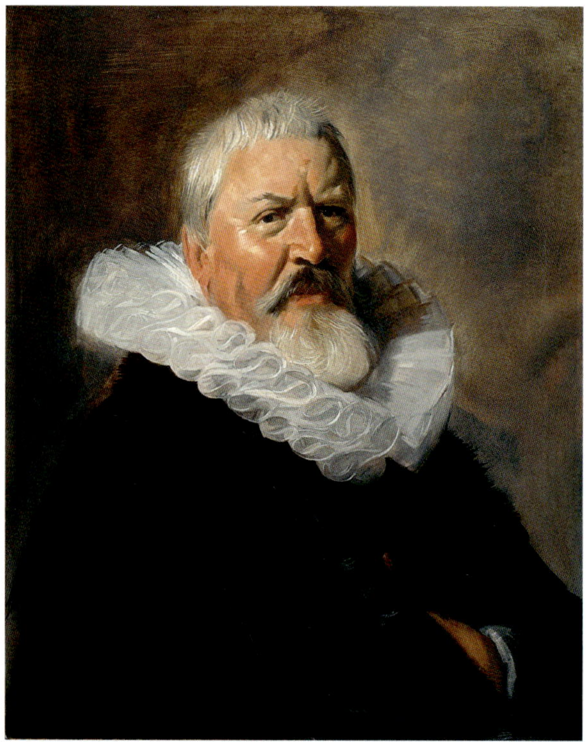

Fig. 39 Workshop of Frans Hals, *Portrait of Pieter Jacobsz Olycan*, about 1640
Oil on wood, 66.2 × 56.2 cm
Private collection

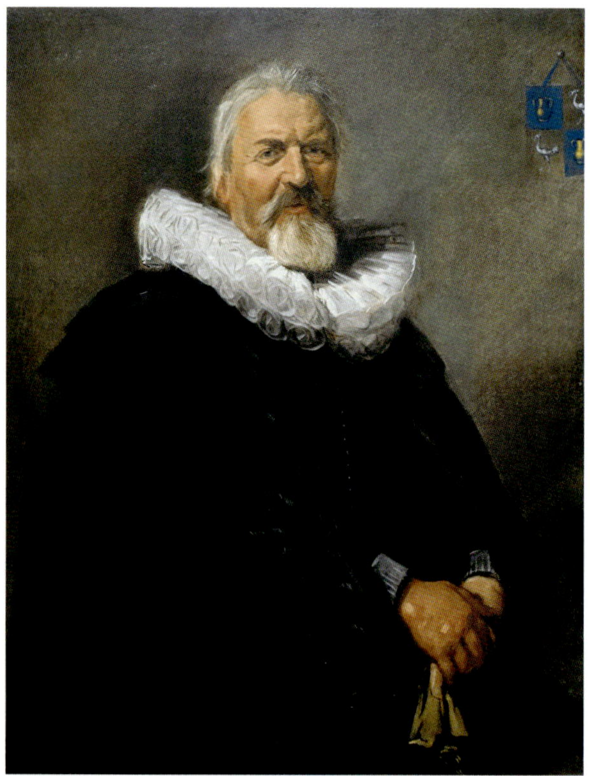

Fig. 41 *Portrait of Pieter Jacobsz Olycan*, about 1639. Oil on canvas, 111.1 × 86.7 cm
The John and Mable Ringling Museum, Sarasota;
Bequest of John Ringling, 1936

THE STUDIO

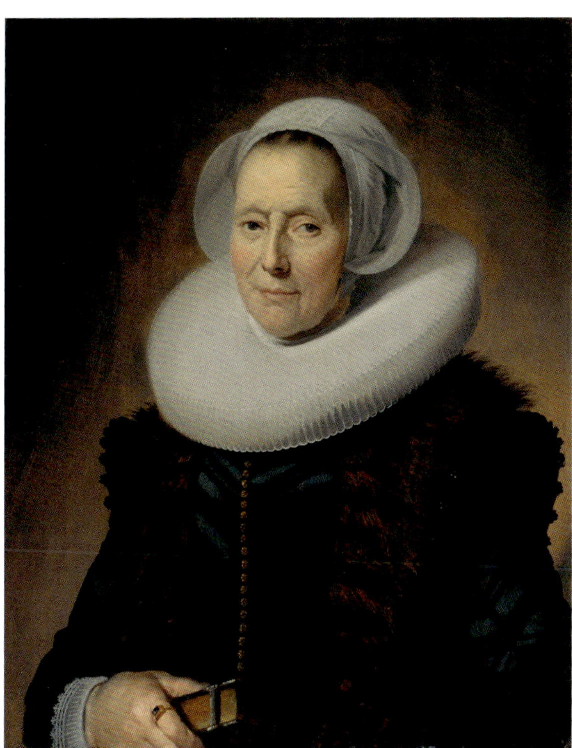

Fig. 40 Workshop of Frans Hals, *Portrait of Maritge Claesdr Vooght*, about 1640
Oil on wood, 66.2 × 56.7 cm
Present whereabouts unknown

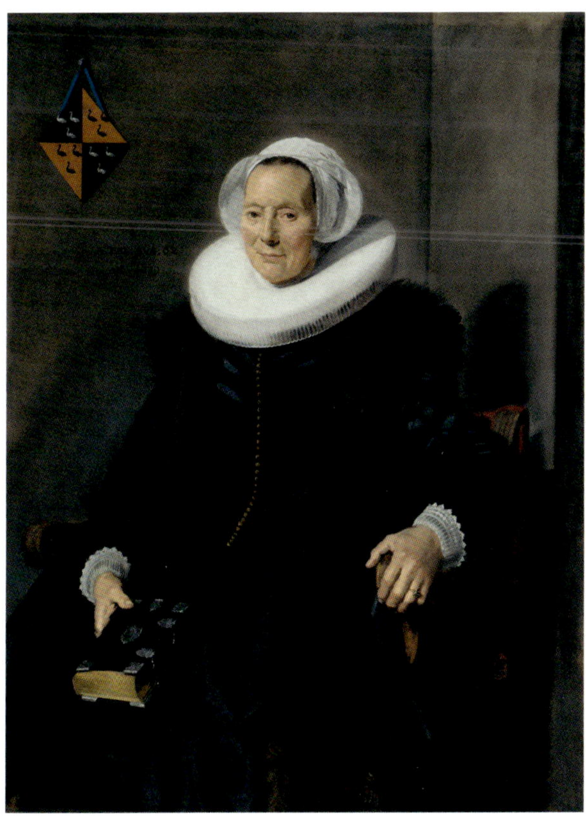

Fig. 42 *Portrait of Maritge Claesdr Vooght*, 1639
Oil on canvas, 126.4 × 93.2 cm
Rijksmuseum, Amsterdam. On loan from the
City of Amsterdam (A. van der Hoop Bequest)

COPIES AND IMITATION

An important part of an apprentice's training consisted of copying paintings. This was regarded as a way of developing skills, and had the not inconsiderable advantage of producing saleable results. The benefit was so great that copies were also produced without any educational purpose. Apprentices copied works by their master but also by other artists, preferably famous ones.[73] This gave them experience with a variety of styles and compositional methods. Hals owned paintings by several famous Haarlem masters, such as Maarten van Heemskerck, Karel van Mander and Hendrick Goltzius, which he may well have recommended to his pupils as examples.[74] He was first and foremost a portrait painter but the market for copies of portraits was limited, unless they were of famous rulers, naval heroes or generals. The production of new versions of portraits of Prince Maurits, his half-brother Frederik Hendrik and other family members was a significant source of income for the studio of Michiel van Mierevelt, for example.[75] Hals did not fill that need. It is true that there are several versions of portraits of René Descartes, his most famous model, but only a few of them seem to have been made in his studio.[76] It was a regular practice for a client to order one or more copies of a portrait of himself, a family member or an acquaintance. The copies of Hals's likenesses of the Haarlem burgomaster Pieter Jacobsz Olycan (figs 39, 41) and his wife, Maritge Claesdr Vooght (figs 40, 42), which hung in the house of one of their daughters, were probably the result of one such order.[77] A work that is well documented is the copy after the small portrait of the wealthy bachelor Willem van Heythuysen (figs 49–50). In August 1653, three years after Van Heythuysen's death, Hals was paid 36 guilders for a copy of the picture that he had made around 1638, this second version being for the governors' chamber of the alms house founded with money from the deceased.[78]

Hals's study heads and genre scenes must have been copied far more often than his portraits. Their popularity is clear from the number that still survive today. For instance, there are no fewer than at least 13 versions of *The Rommel-Pot Player* (fig. 172).[79] Many of the copies are only known from mentions in old records and photographs, so it is often impossible to say whether they were painted in the seventeenth century, let alone in Hals's studio. But there can be no doubt that works of this kind originated there. Copies after his work are often mentioned in documents, from which it can be deduced that the earliest mentions are connected with his shop. For instance, in 1631 the above-mentioned Hendrick den Abt already had 'various copies after Frans Hals'; in 1649 there were 'three heads, being copies of Frans Hals' in a Leiden estate; and a record from the same year in Haarlem lists not only two small paintings by Hals but also 'a copy of or by Hals'.[80]

In addition to making copies that followed the original composition reasonably faithfully, the more advanced pupils were given a freer hand to make a variant.[81] Rembrandt followed this method in his studio and Hals encouraged his apprentices to do the same. A striking example is the *Malle Babbe* in the Metropolitan Museum of Art in New York, a painting that is in essence a mirror-image version of the famous work in the Gemäldegalerie in Berlin, but the sitter's hands are folded rather than holding a pewter tankard (figs 43, 171). The composition of the small variant of *The Rommel-Pot Player* is almost identical to Hals's original (figs 44, 172)[82] except that the copyist has altered details of the children's headgear, coiffures and clothing. If *The Serenade* by Judith Leyster was indeed made in Hals's studio, then it is a superb example of how pupils could create very free variations, in this case of Hals's *The Lute Player* (figs 176–7). The musician's pose, glance and hands are clearly based on the model, but the clothing and, above all, the stronger chiaroscuro give the painting a character that is totally original.

As soon as a pupil had sufficient skill he could start assisting his master on autograph works. It is difficult to say whether that happened in Hals's studio and, if so, when it started and how often. Nor is it clear how much he worked up the paintings by his pupils. In 1640 the Leiden burgomaster and art lover Jan Jansz Orlers described a painting belonging to his daughter as 'A small painting of a brothel painted over by Hals',[83] which could refer either to Frans or Dirck. Houbraken says that Frans Hals was in the habit of 'laying his portraits on thickly and meltingly', only applying his clearly visible brushstrokes later, with the words: 'Now to give it the master's touch'.[84] One wonders whether he only did this with the paintings that he had laid in himself, or gave those by his pupils that typical Hals touch to make them more marketable.

Due to the almost total lack of written or printed records, the only way of deciding on the possible contribution of a pupil or assistant is by distinguishing stylistic differences. But since the aim in the studios of leading artists was to imitate the master's touch as closely as possible, this is a tricky undertaking, certainly in the case of Frans Hals. Art historians are still locked in discussions about which works attributed to him really are autograph. It is generally assumed that he was not responsible for faithful copies, although according to some the second, 1653 version of the portrait of Willem van Heythuysen mentioned above actually is the master's work.[85] Conversely, it is agreed that *The Lute Player* in the Rijksmuseum (fig. 45) is not. While the brushwork is close, it does not match the virtuoso heights of the original in the Louvre (fig. 177), which is dated around 1623. However, its high quality and date (it was painted soon after the original) suggest that it was probably painted under Hals's supervision. In 1624 the Leiden painter David Bailly made a drawn copy after the Amsterdam painting;[86] certain details found only in the Amsterdam piece show that he did not work from the original. The differences are only minor, but they are unmistakable.[87]

Different working methods may be at play in the variants of a prototype. The execution of *Malle Babbe* in New York is a pale echo of the sparkling touch of the

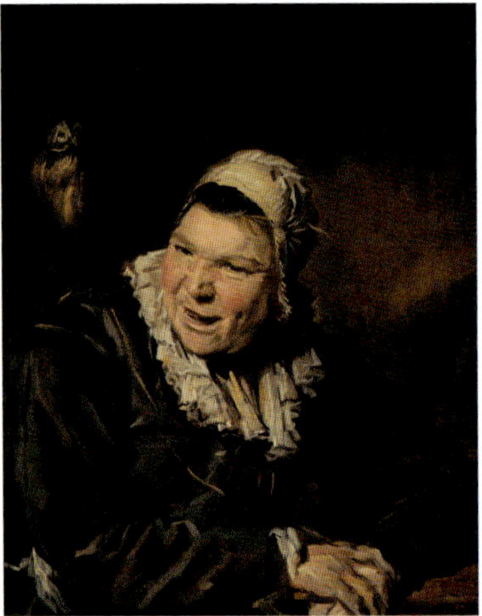

Fig. 43 Workshop of Frans Hals, *Malle Babbe*, about 1625–40. Oil on canvas, 74.9 × 61 cm The Metropolitan Museum of Art, New York; purchase, 1871

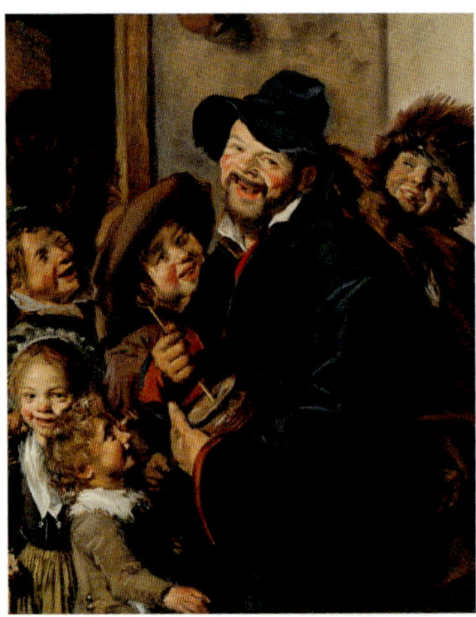

Fig. 44 Workshop of Frans Hals, *The Rommel-Pot Player*, 1625–35. Oil on wood, 39.1 × 30.5 cm The Art Institute of Chicago; Charles H. and Mary F.S. Worcester Collection

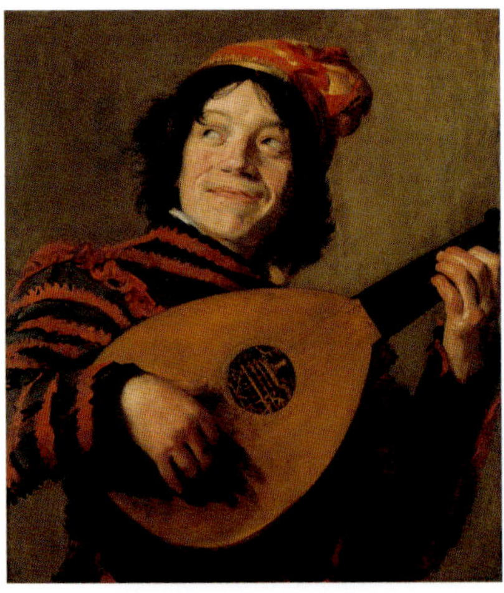

Fig. 45 Workshop of Frans Hals, *The Lute Player*, about 1624. Oil on canvas, 67 × 60 cm Rijksmuseum, Amsterdam; Dupper Wzn. Bequest, Dordrecht

THE STUDIO

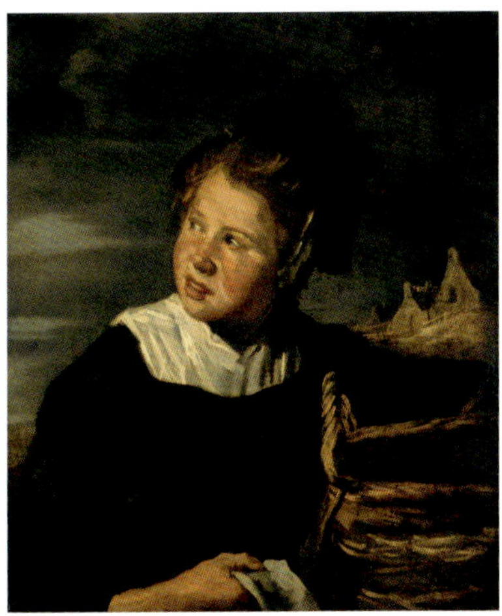

Fig. 46 Workshop of Frans Hals, *Fisher Girl*,
about 1630(?). Oil on canvas, 65.5 × 56 cm
Wallraf-Richartz-Museum &
Fondation Corboud, Cologne

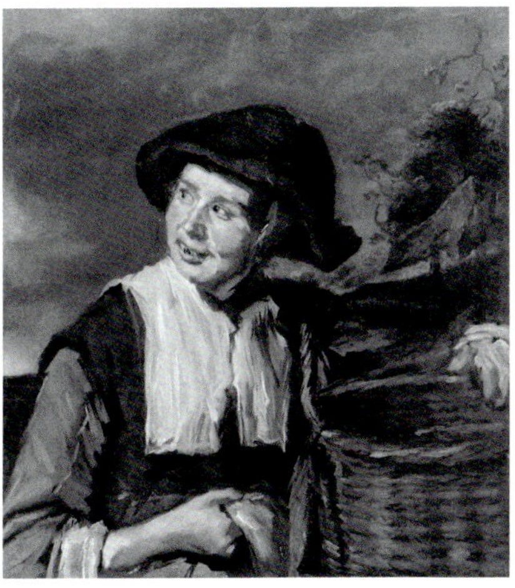

Fig. 47 Workshop of Frans Hals,
Fisher Girl, about 1630(?)
Oil on canvas, 69 × 64 cm
Present whereabouts unknown

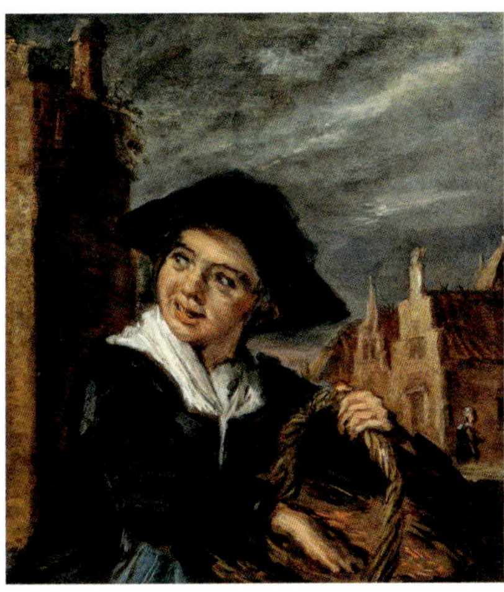

Fig. 48 Workshop of Frans Hals,
Fisher Girl, about 1630(?)
Oil on wood, 32 × 27.5 cm
Private collection

Berlin picture, so is probably the work of an assistant (figs 43, 171).[88] The two versions of *Pekelharing* in Kassel and Leipzig (figs 153–4), which like the two *Malle Babbe* paintings are essentially reversed variants of each other, seem to have been made by Hals himself.[89] There are three versions of a fisher girl looking up to the left (figs 46–8). The composition is similar, but with differences in clothing, pose and background. There is no autograph original, so one wonders whether it is lost or if this is a work that Hals left to his assistants for its execution, composition and variants.[90]

The painting *Two Children with a Cat* (fig. 31), which bears Judith Leyster's monogram, is even more in Hals's style than her *Serenade*. The Amsterdam printmaker Cornelis Danckerts made an engraving of the composition on which he stated that it was made after a painting by Frans Hals ('f. Hals. pinxit'). Since a painting of the subject by Leyster is mentioned as being in Amsterdam in 1642, it seems very likely that this was the engraver's model.[91] Did he engrave Hals's name on the print because he was more famous, or because he knew or believed that although it was executed by Leyster it was actually composed by Hals?[92] Art historians are tempted to assume that a painting bearing the slightest resemblance in style and technique to a known work by Hals must have been made in his studio. If based solely on stylistic similarities, this must remain an assumption and one cannot rule out the possibility that such works were also made outside his studio. Thus Judith Leyster would have painted in his style not only when she worked with him but also when she had her own studio.

The same applies to Jan Hals, by whom there are signed portraits that are entirely in his father's manner.[93] In addition, there were other artists who never worked for Frans Hals but were very good at imitating his brushwork: see, for example, the 1652 copy by the Rotterdam artist Ludolf de Jongh after Hals's portrait of the theologian Nicolaes Stenius painted two years earlier.[94] Conversely, not all the copies and variants made in Hals's studio are in his style. Often this would have reflected the copyist's skill – one pupil being more successful in imitating the master's manner than another – but perhaps it was not always considered necessary to copy his distinctive manner. In the case of the copies after the portraits of Olycan and Vooght, the execution of the former is so close to Hals that it has also been attributed to him, while the portrait of the wife, which must also have been painted in the studio, bears little relationship to the master's original.[95] The brushwork of a second version of *The Laughing Cavalier*, in which the sitter is bareheaded, has little or nothing that recalls Hals, but it must have been made around the same time as the first version (figs 51, 78).[96] Was the copy painted by a studio assistant who was allowed his own interpretation – or was it not made in the studio at all?

The fact that not all the paintings from Hals's studio are in his style would have had something to do with his ideas about training. Imitation was important, but a good teacher taught his pupils to develop their own inventiveness and style. After Karel van Mander's biographer lists a selection of his pupils, Frans Hals among them, he states that all of them were to be praised for their 'wealth of inventions and boldness of painting and drawing'.[97] Van Mander had trained them in such a way that they could develop independently of him.

THE DEVELOPMENT OF INDIVIDUAL STYLES

Adriaen Brouwer is probably the best illustration of a pupil whom Frans Hals encouraged to develop his own style and subject matter. When he discovered how talented his pupil was, Hals set him rigorously to work in the attic, isolated from the others, where, according to Houbraken, he was not expected to imitate his master. On the contrary, Hals seems to have been deeply impressed by the personal characteristics Brouwer displayed in his work. Houbraken stresses not so much the emphasis on training but the independence of the young artist, despite the fact that he was working in Hals's studio, and the financial benefit. Hals supposedly praised Brouwer's work as that of the 'foreign master' ('vremden meester') from whom he derived great profit, because he had the exclusive right to Brouwer's work, and art lovers were eager to own something by this new, still unknown artist. It is difficult to make out just how accurate Houbraken was in stressing that Hals was rather secretive about his treatment of Brouwer. He writes of 'Frans's secret dealings': he did not want the other pupils taking a peep in Brouwer's room. They did so anyway, and according to reports bought small works from him for a few stuivers.[98]

The paintings that Brouwer made in Hals's house must have been his characteristic small-figured peasant scenes, a subject that Hals rarely, if ever, depicted.[99] It seems that after Brouwer's departure, scenes of this kind continued to be produced in the studio by Molenaer, Van Roestraten and a few of Hals's sons. A small group of coastal scenes is attributed to Molenaer, featuring fishermen's children based on pictures in Hals's studio (fig. 52).[100] In contrast to his life-size half-length figures, the people in these scenes are small full-lengths in a broad landscape. The attribution to Molenaer is not certain, but the conclusion that they were made in Hals's studio seems likely, despite the difference in style.[101] It is otherwise difficult to explain how the artist had access to so many models by Hals.

That Hals encouraged the adoption of individual styles is also clear from the work made by his pupils Adriaen van Ostade, Philips Wouwerman and Pieter van Roestraten when they became independent artists. With his brother Dirck, Frans no doubt agreed specific arrangements about who could paint what, and how. Such arrangements would have been influenced not only by the brothers' personal preferences but also by their wish to avoid competing with each other. For example, there are only a few small autonomous portraits by Dirck: although he had a talent for portraiture, he probably left

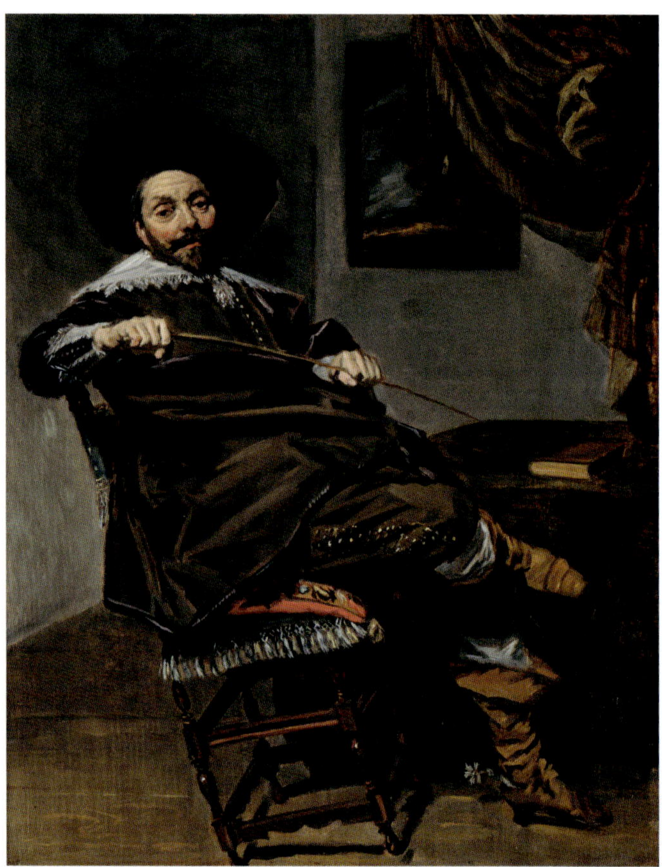

Fig. 49 *Portrait of Willem van Heythuysen*, about 1653. Oil on wood, 46.9 × 37.5 cm
Royal Museums of Fine Arts of Belgium, Brussels

THE STUDIO

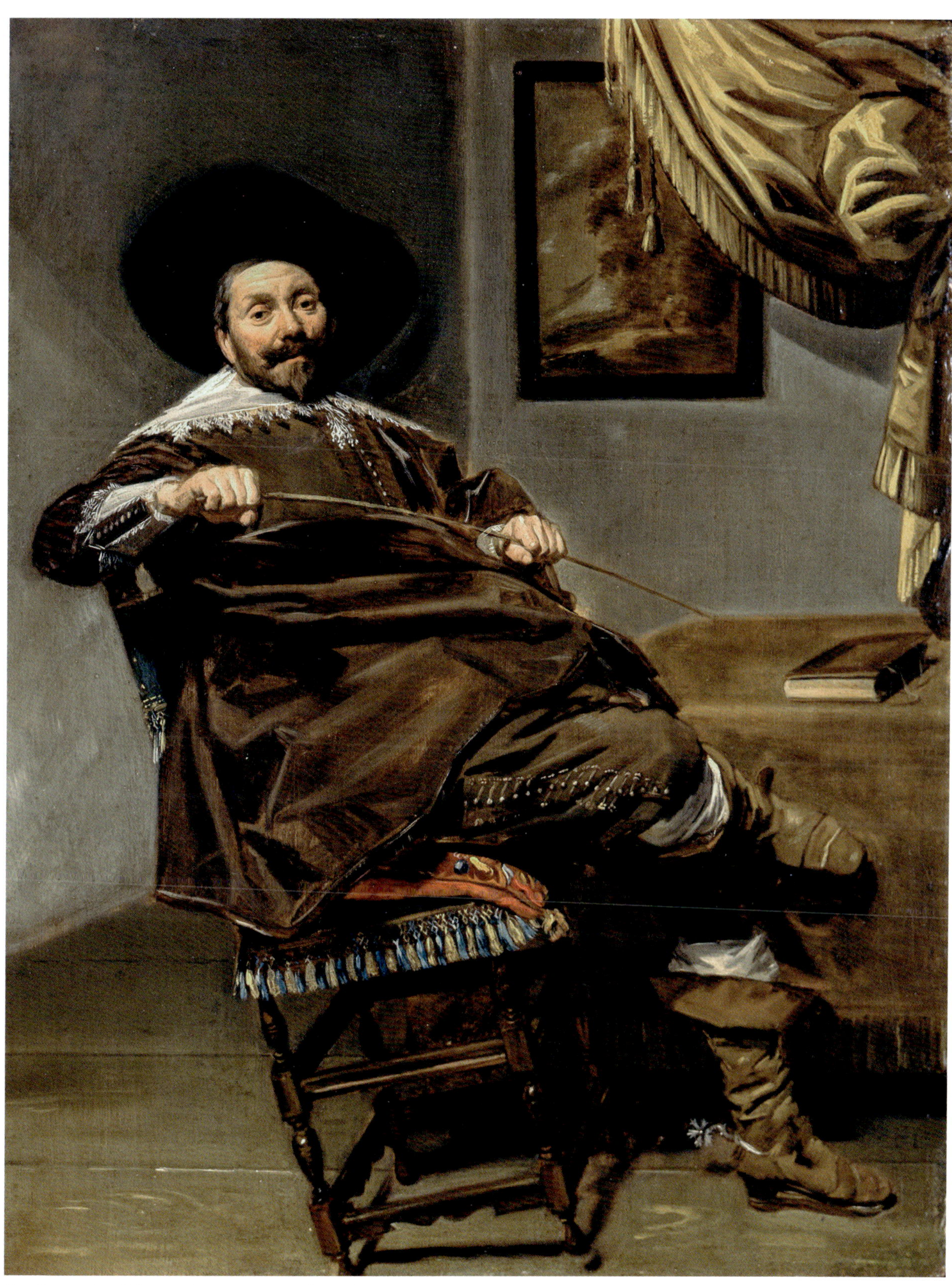

Fig. 50 *Portrait of Willem van Heythuysen seated in a Chair*, about 1638
Oil on wood, 47 × 36.7 cm
Private collection, Courtesy Richard Nagy Ltd., London

these to his brother Frans and concentrated instead on genre scenes with small figures. His pictures of merry companies occasionally include a portrait, such as one of the painter Johannes Torrentius.[102] Yet this was a different kind of work from the much larger, commissioned portraits in which Frans specialised. While Frans, in his turn, likely made a few small-figured genre scenes, his output was dominated by portraits as well as genre scenes with large half-lengths.[103] Dirck occasionally copied or quoted from his brother's work, but even then he retained his own style and signed with his own name.[104]

The apprentices in Hals's studio also influenced each other, particularly the experienced artists impacting younger pupils. For instance, the influence of Dirck Hals and Adriaen Brouwer on the work of the young Jan Miense Molenaer and Adriaen van Ostade is unmistakable. Just how well Molenaer knew and imitated the subject matter and style of Adriaen Brouwer is implied in the mention of a peasant company by his hand that was 'as if painted by Brouwer'.[105] His familiarity with Brouwer's work is also evidenced in a previously unpublished document of 1642 with an account of someone from Haarlem showing Molenaer two small paintings by Brouwer. Molenaer asked how much they cost and the man replied that he wanted 12 Flemish pounds (72 guilders) for them. Molenaer was amazed and reacted with aplomb, saying: 'I will supply you with 12 pieces, each one as good as those for 12 pounds' and promised to deliver them a month later. The man from Haarlem proposed showing Molenaer's paintings to experts to test whether they were indeed as good as the two little works by Brouwer, to which the young artist replied, 'yes, and even better than that'. They sealed the deal with a handshake in the presence of Molenaer's wife, Judith Leyster. Molenaer then promised to supply the man with an original work by Adriaen Brouwer for 18 guilders. This transaction was sealed in the same way, again in the presence of Judith Leyster.[106]

From time to time Frans Hals worked with fully qualified painters outside his studio. For example, he and Claes van Heussen worked together on a magnificent market scene, for which Van Heussen provided the highly detailed still life and Hals the broadly brushed young woman (fig. 27). The composition and subject appear to have been influenced by paintings made in Antwerp, as was the idea of having two artists who differed so much in their brushwork collaborate on the same painting. For instance, Peter Paul Rubens and Jacques Jordaens supplied the figures for several monumental still lifes by Frans Snijders,[107] and it has been suggested on stylistic grounds that the landscapes in a number of portraits by Frans Hals are the work of Pieter de Molijn – although they may rather be the work of a studio assistant who was skilled in landscape. A contemporary source mentions two portraits by Hals in a setting painted by Willem Buytewech,[108] which could have been executed outside Hals's studio.

Fig. 51 Workshop(?) of Frans Hals, *The Laughing Cavalier*, about 1624. Oil on wood, 69.7 × 59.8 cm
Private collection

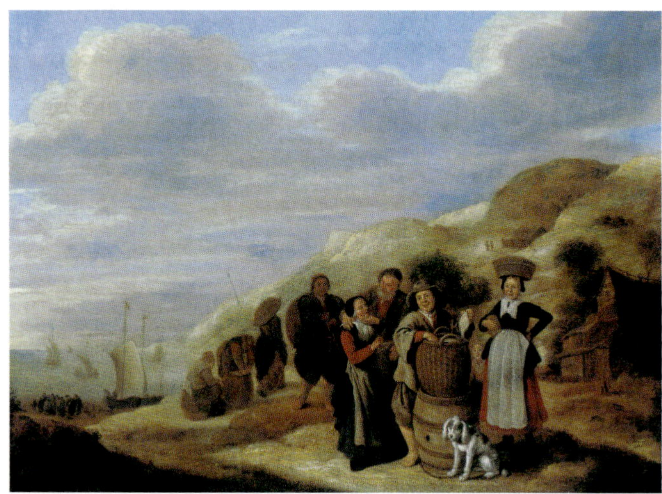

Fig. 52 Jan Miense Molenaer, *Beach Scene with Fishermen*, about 1630–40. Oil on canvas, 66 × 91 cm
Present whereabouts unknown

THE STUDIO

The Amsterdam guardsmen were not impressed by Frans Hals's argument that he could keep an eye on his people if he worked in his own house. They simply ignored him and sent the remaining work out to be finished by a different artist, Pieter Codde, who lived locally. However, Hals's suggestion is perfectly understandable: it is still the case today that adolescents and young adults working close together need some supervision, and it was no different in the seventeenth century. The studio must have been busy during Hals's more productive period. The family formed its foundation: at least five of his sons and probably his brother Dirck, possibly also their brother Joost, who died in 1626. Ariaentje married one of her father's former pupils, while Dirck's only son, Anthonie, born in 1621, also became a painter. But it was far more than just a family business. In addition, some other 8 painters are known or thought to have trained or worked with Hals, but he would have taught many more in his long career. Of those whose names are known, it can be said that they went on to make a name for themselves through their later output. Many of their works have survived, so they are still known today. This is not true of young Willem Woutersz, however, who absconded from Judith Leyster's tutelage and whose apprenticeship to Hals is recorded in an account that survived through sheer chance.

It is striking that Hals's pupils, with the exception of Adriaen Brouwer, all came from Haarlem, and remarkable how many talented artists must have been working together in his studio at times. Gathered together under one roof, often painting in the same room, they would have influenced each others' work, and it seems that their teacher gave them plenty of scope to do so. In the 1620s Dirck Hals and Adriaen Brouwer were active in his studio, and in the second half of the decade they may have been joined by Judith Leyster, Adriaen van Ostade and Jan Miense Molenaer. They were taught the art of portraiture, Frans Hals's speciality, and that of depicting the human figure with a view to the production of genre scenes. Most struck out on different paths once they became independent artists. Although there are known portraits by Adriaen Brouwer, Judith Leyster, Jan Miense Molenaer, Adriaen van Ostade, Pieter van Roestraten and Vincent van der Vinne, ultimately they all specialised in other genres and styles that had little in common with that of their former teacher. It is clear that Hals did not constrain them but gave them the artistic freedom they needed. Perhaps this is the chief reason why his 'people', according to Houbraken, held him in such 'high regard'.[109]

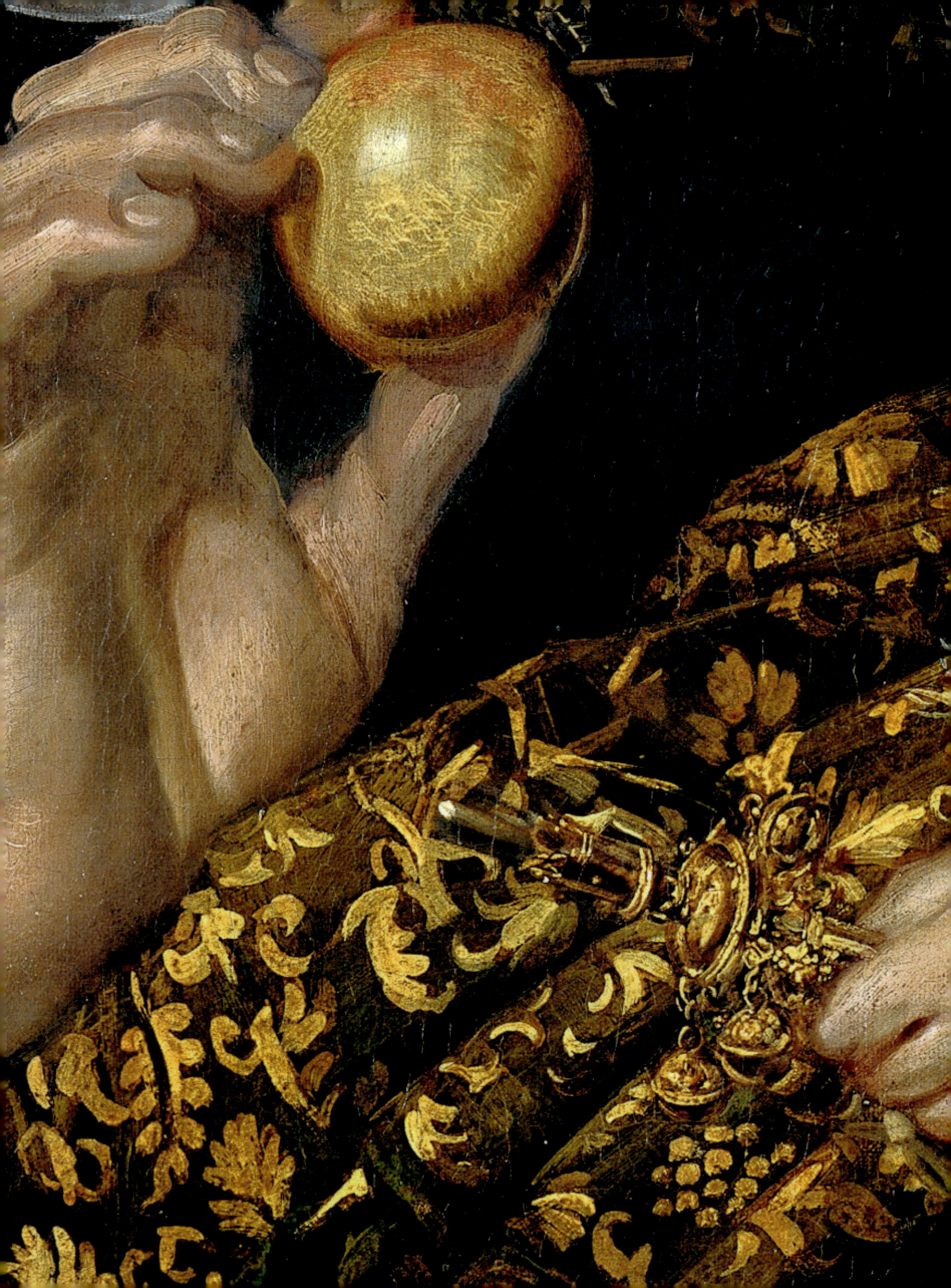

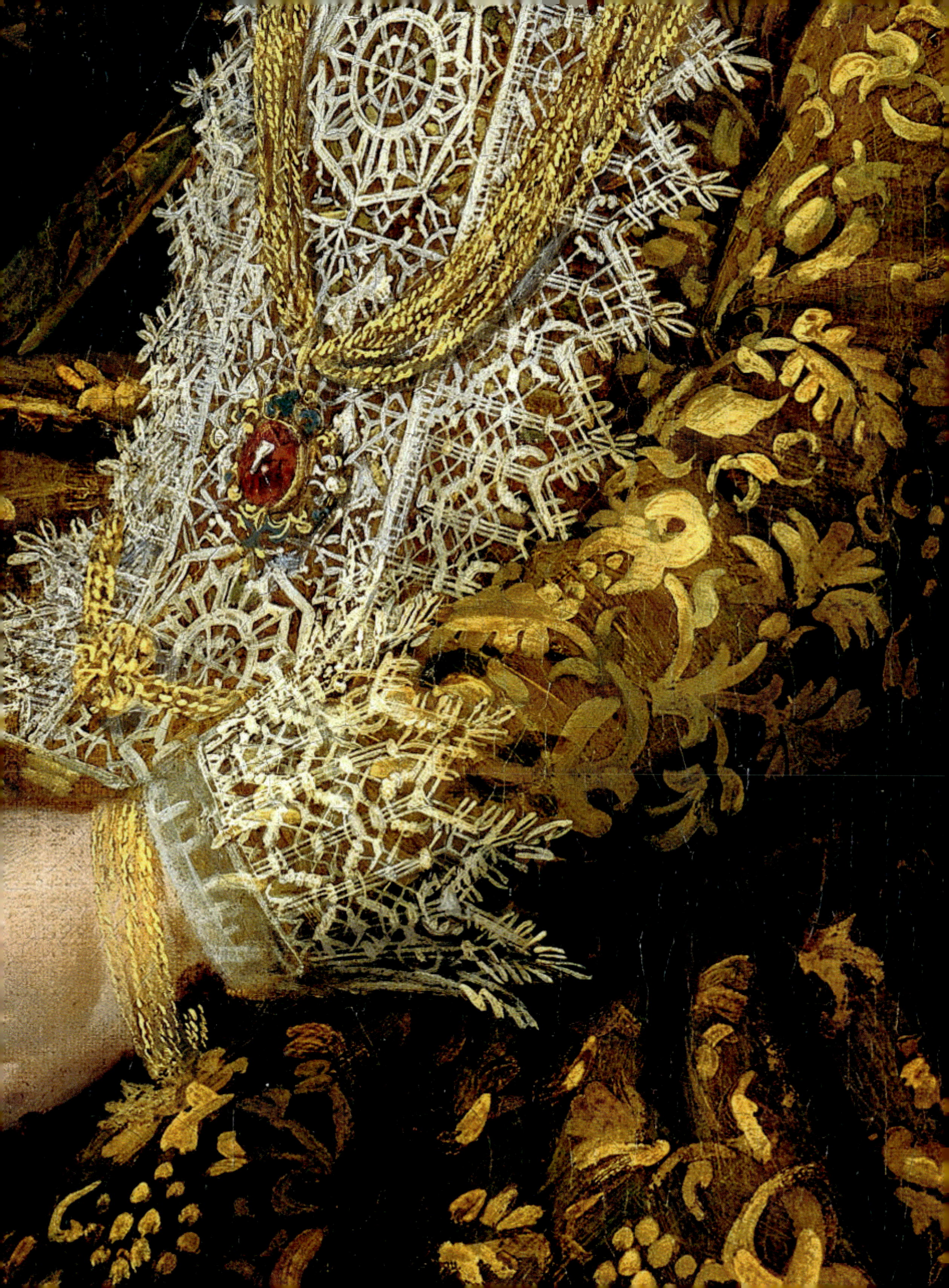

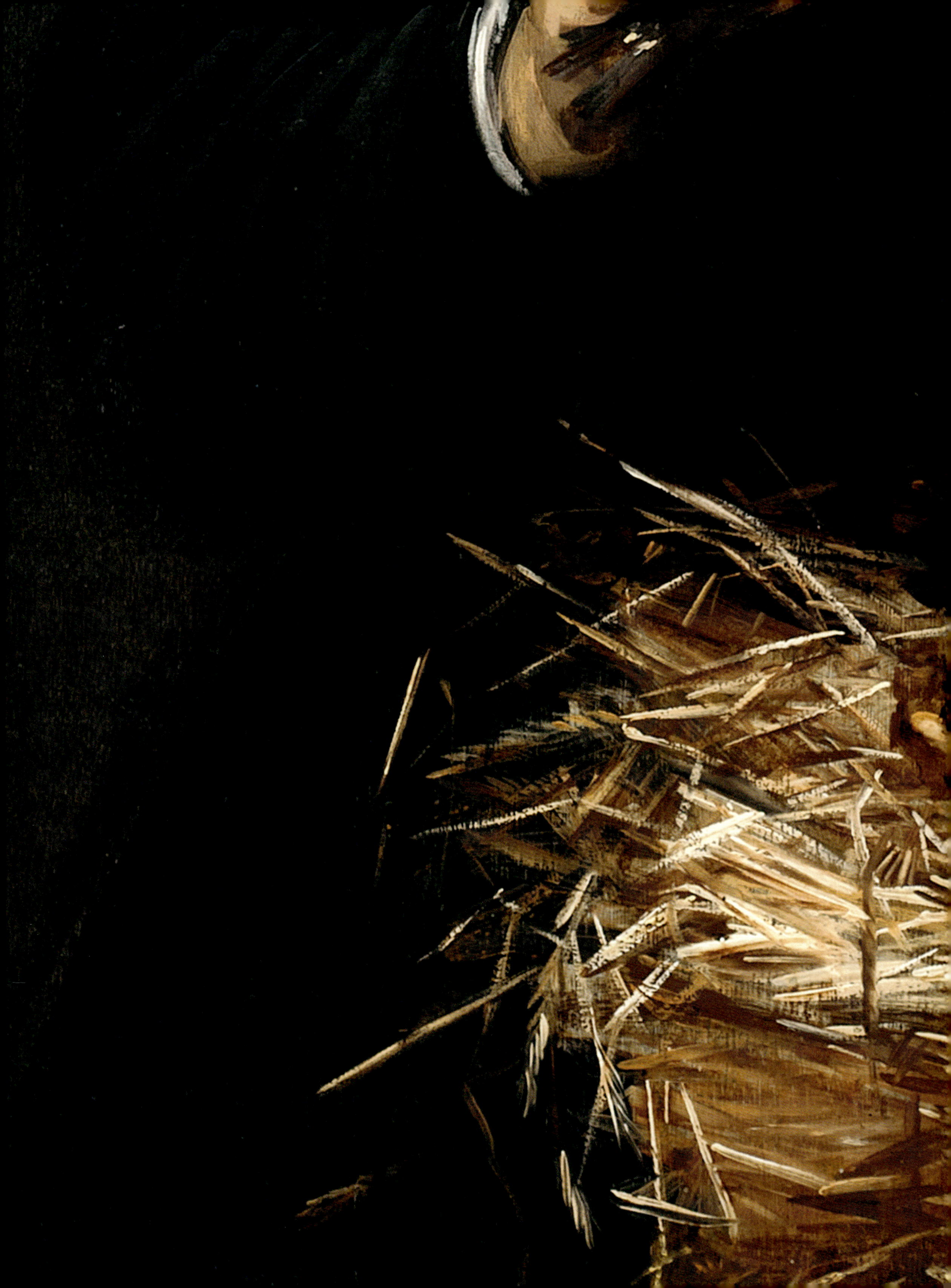

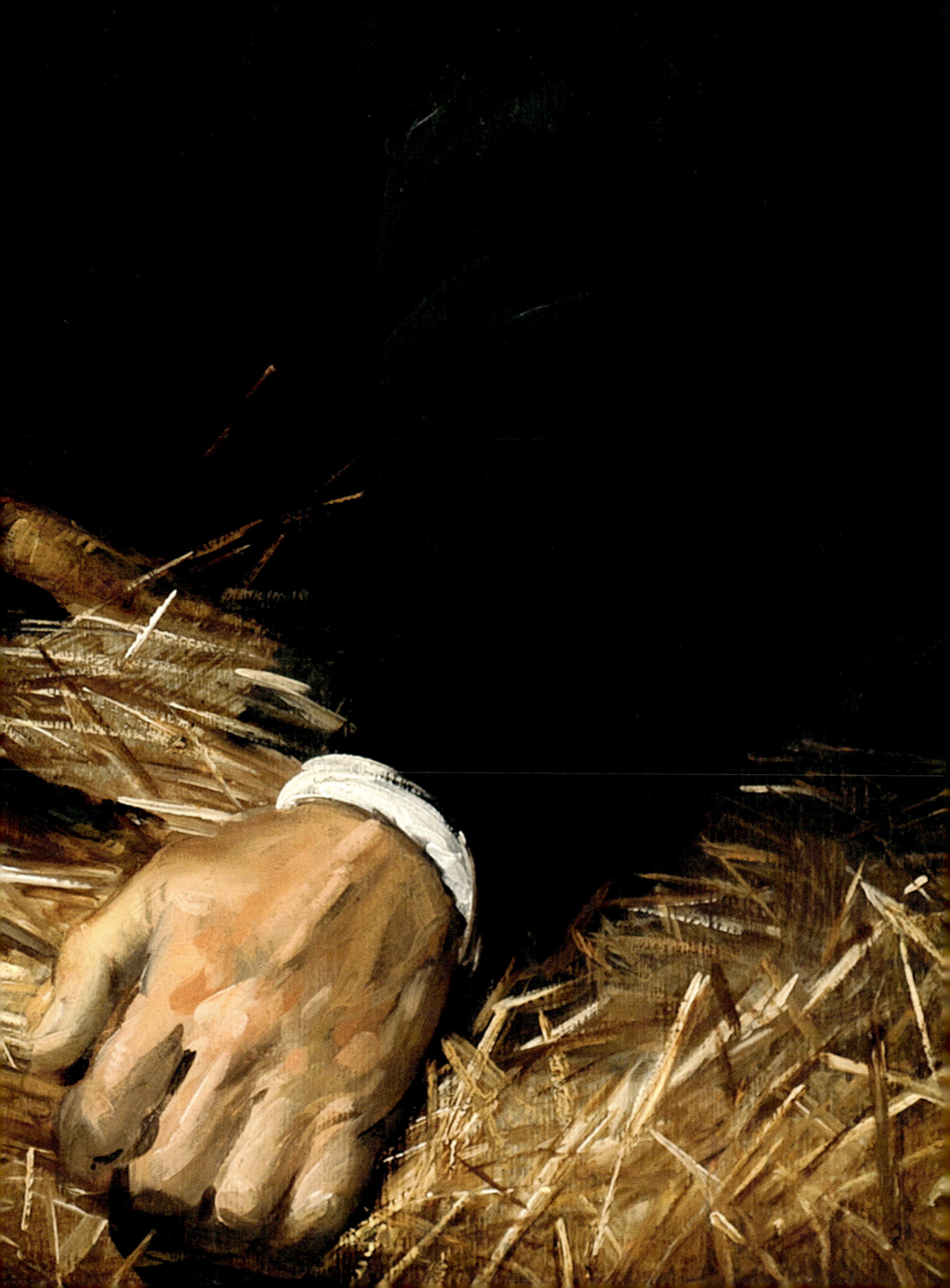

PORTRAITURE INTO ART

BART CORNELIS

Portraiture is but a 'side-road of art', wrote the artist and author Karel van Mander in his *Schilder-Boeck* of 1604.[1] Creating a likeness after life, Van Mander reasoned, was a task that required only slavish imitation. There being a healthy demand for portraits, it was an undertaking that could bring financial reward, but in Van Mander's eyes it could only be compared unfavourably to the higher calling of depicting the human figure in paintings representing biblical or mythological stories. The latter required artists to use their knowledge and imagination to present their audiences with narratives that would elevate the mind. In modern parlance it might be described as the difference between the competence of a good portrait photographer and the compelling imagination of a great cinematographer. Van Mander's casual dismissal of this 'side-road of art' can be found in his biography of the portrait painter Michiel van Mierevelt. To be fair to Van Mander, it is preceded by a caveat in his opening lines of the biography: 'He who is outstanding and surpasses others in at least one single category, deserves praiseworthy fame in our art and to remain free from all scorn', while a little further on he also concedes that 'one can also make something worthwhile from a portrait: that a face, after all the most important part of the human body, contains quite enough so as to be able to disclose and reveal the quality and efficacy of art'.[2]

Van Mierevelt's work embodies, perhaps like no other, the dynastic function of portraiture. He (and his busy studio) excelled at producing tremendously skilful if rather matter-of-fact portraits of leading citizens of Delft (figs 53–4). Recognition of his skill found expression in the fact that in 1607 he became the official painter to the court of the stadtholder, producing numerous portraits of members of the House of Orange and foreign diplomats residing in The Hague. His clients would commission him to portray themselves and their families to give expression to their power and status and to have their family line represented and preserved for posterity. Such portraits would adorn the rooms and corridors of their houses in much the same way as today's board-room might be lined with portraits of chief executives past and present. That this was their overriding function is borne out by the fact that there was a steady demand for replicas, so that such dynastic lineage and power could be on display in more than one place. Van Mierevelt ran such a large workshop to cater for this demand that a recent exhibition devoted to his work went under the title *The Portrait Factory of Michiel van Mierevelt*.[3] There is some truth in Van Mander's observation that his was perhaps not the highest calling in art.

Seen in that light, there is some irony in the fact that the man who dismissed portraiture as 'a side-road of art' counted among his pupils a young Frans Hals, who would go on to become one of the greatest portrait painters of all time. But why do we now think so highly of Hals's portraits? What makes him so different from his predecessors? What methods did he employ to make his sitters come to life in his portraits in such an unprecedented way? How did Hals rise above the constraints put on portraiture by its predominantly dynastic function? In short, how did he turn portraiture into art?

THE LATE START OF A PRODIGY

Although originally from Antwerp, the Hals family moved to Haarlem when Hals was still a toddler, so one cannot ascribe any influence on the works he would later produce to have originated in the first few years of his life. And yet there is a certain Flemish trait in his paintings in general, and especially in his earliest works. For example, there is a Rubensian quality to the luminous flesh tones in his *Portrait of a Woman standing* in the Devonshire Collections at Chatsworth (fig. 59); her pose is also reminiscent of Flemish examples (fig. 57).

The Chatsworth painting looks resplendent after its recent conservation treatment, as does the portrait of her husband at the Barber Institute of Fine Arts in Birmingham (fig. 58), which was treated at the same time.[4] The male portrait looks traditional enough, in some ways harking back to sixteenth-century examples.

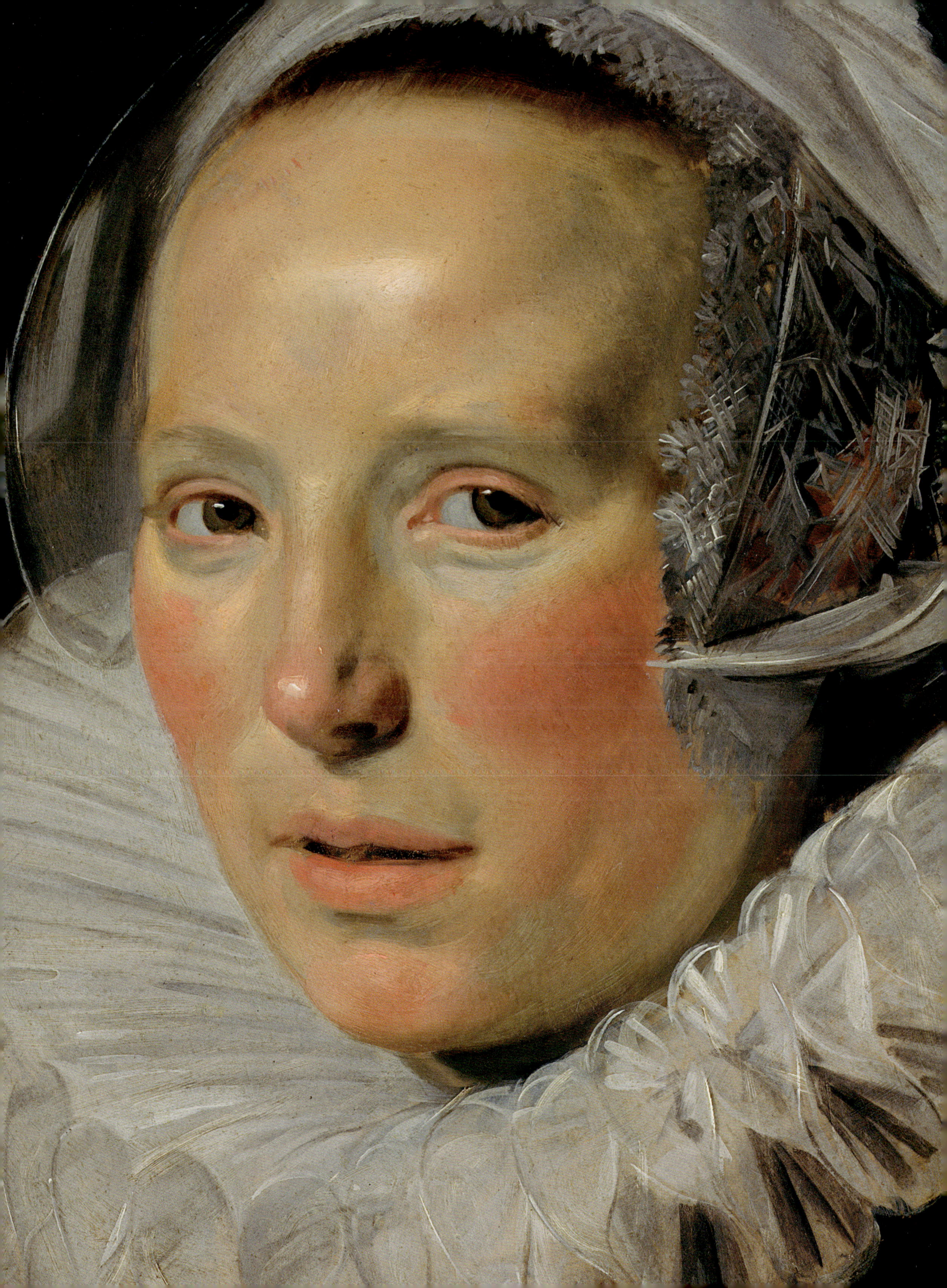

Although the landscape background has disappeared, in other respects it still has echoes of works such as the *Portrait of Pompejus Occo* of 1531 by Dirck Jacobsz (fig. 55), with the skull – alluding to the transience of life – giving both portraits an allegorical twist. Somewhat closer to it in date, the *Portrait of the Shell Collector Jan Govertsen van der Aer* of 1603 by Hals's fellow townsman Hendrick Goltzius springs to mind (fig. 56). The pendants by Hals are still relatively static: there is little sense of movement in them. The woman subtly lifts the gold chain suspended from her ornate clothes. This suggests her wealth and status but may also have been intended to extend the theme of transience in her husband's portrait by drawing attention to the futility of earthly possessions.

But for all their conformity, both works already display elements that anticipate one aspect of Hals's greatness: his incredible facility with the brush. This can be seen in the starched cambric ruff around the man's neck and the pleated cuff at the wrist of his right hand, which are exceptionally freely brushed. Such forms are suggested but not meticulously described, in stark contrast to what we see in Van Mierevelt's works (figs 53–4). In the pendant we can admire the immense confidence with which Hals used rapid flicks of the brush to indicate the various details of the woman's lace inner cap and cambric outer cap, which form a masterclass in dazzlingly effective brushwork.

It is not entirely clear when exactly these portraits should be dated. Some have suggested around 1612 while others prefer to date them a few years later, but they must anyhow be among Hals's earliest-known works. It is worth pointing out that he was therefore in his late twenties when he painted them and certainly no longer a budding artist. But the two pendants are far too skilful to be considered his earliest attempts at portraiture, so something must have gone before them, except that we do not know what. Nor do these works betray his apprenticeship with Karel van Mander, who tried to practise what he preached and mostly painted biblical subjects.[5] Even though Van Mander had occasionally painted scenes from daily life, these can hardly be said to have had a profound influence on the younger artist's genre paintings. Hals's early career therefore remains shrouded in mystery. All we know for certain is that in 1610 he enrolled in the Guild of St Luke, as was required for an artist who wanted to set up shop as a painter.

The inevitable dynastic function of portraits means that knowledge of the identity of the sitters was more likely to be preserved if a portrait remained with their descendants, who could refer to family traditions handed down through the generations. But portraits did sometimes change hands, perhaps more readily if their artistic quality was much higher than was strictly speaking necessary for a dynastic 'photograph'. It is a fate that must have befallen the Barber and Chatsworth pendants. We have the satisfaction of experiencing an encounter with people who, despite having lived some four centuries ago, seem alive and relatable, but we do not have the

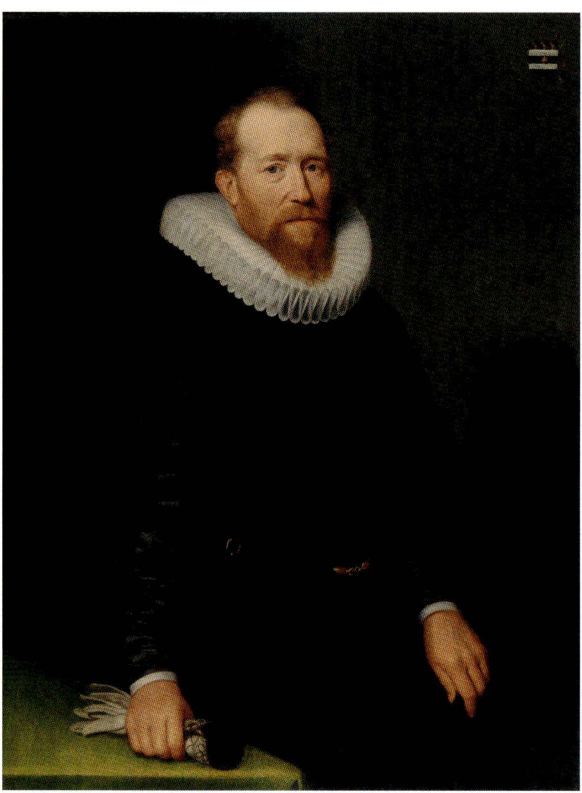

Fig. 53 Michiel van Mierevelt, *Portrait of Arent van der Graeff*, 1618
Oil on wood, 113.5 × 85.5 cm. Museum Het Prinsenhof, Delft;
loan Cultural Heritage Agency of the Netherlands

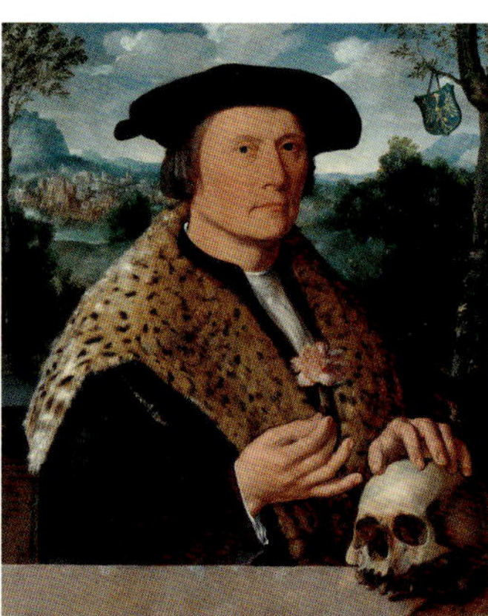

Fig. 55 Dirck Jacobsz,
Portrait of Pompejus Occo, 1531
Oil on wood, 66.5 × 55.1 cm
Rijksmuseum, Amsterdam;
purchased with a contribution
from the J. Loudon Bequest

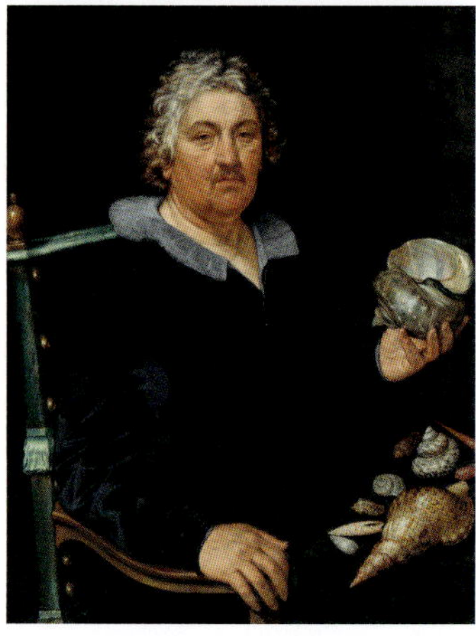

Fig. 56 Hendrick Goltzius,
*Portrait of the Shell Collector
Jan Govertsen van der Aer*, 1603
Oil on canvas, 107.5 × 82.7 cm
Museum Boijmans Van Beuningen,
Rotterdam, on loan from P. & N.
de Boer Foundation, 1960

PORTRAITURE INTO ART

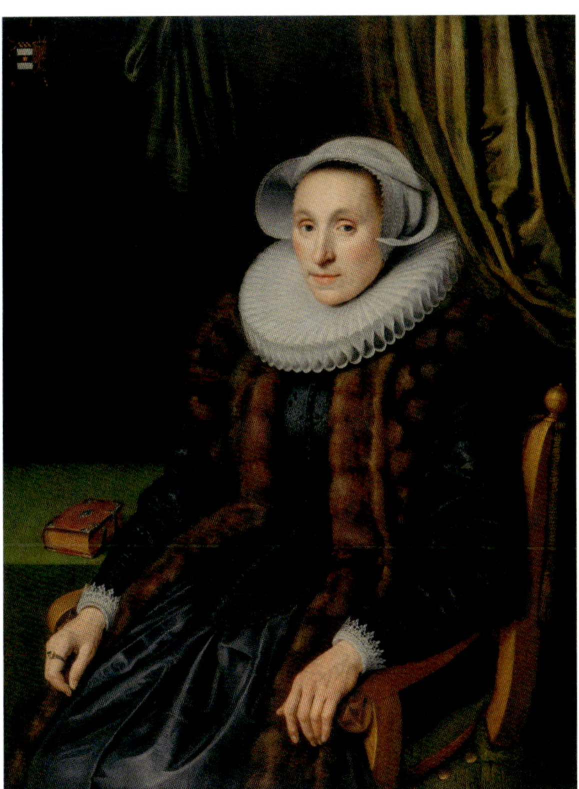

Fig. 54 Michiel van Mierevelt, *Portrait of Sara Bosschaert*, 1619
Oil on wood, 113.5 × 85.5 cm. Museum Het Prinsenhof, Delft;
loan Cultural Heritage Agency of the Netherlands

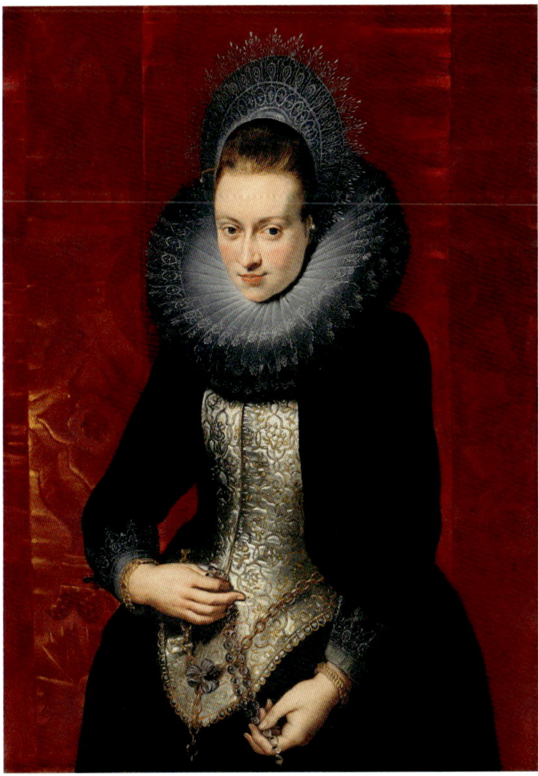

Fig. 57 Peter Paul Rubens, *Portrait of
a Young Woman with a Rosary*, about 1609
Oil on wood, 107 × 76.7 cm
Museo Nacional Thyssen-Bornemisza, Madrid

pleasure of knowing their names. Our knowledge is restricted to their considerable age difference: inscriptions on the panels tell us that the man was 60 years old, while his wife was 32 years of age. Attempts to identify the family coats of arms seen in the background of both pictures have so far proved fruitless. This couple may represent one of the earliest manifestations of Hals's art, but they must, for now, remain nameless.[6]

We do know the name of the man depicted in another early work, preserved in Pittsburgh. Hals's *Portrait of Pieter Cornelisz van der Mersch* of 1616 (fig. 151)[7] displays even more daring brushwork, especially in the straw in the basket that the sitter clutches in his left hand. This type of brushwork would remain a hallmark of Hals's style throughout his career. In his *Schilder-Boeck* Van Mander had advised young artists that employing such a broad technique was perhaps tempting but far from straightforward. He recommended 'to make a lot of effort at first and to accustom yourself, diligently, to a clean technique and a neat beginning'.[8] His remark comes in a passage devoted to Titian, who, Van Mander concedes, had mastered such a loose and rough manner; but he also warned that this could only be achieved through extensive practice, and that 'several masters who wanted to imitate this in their work have made nothing decent out of it but instead created a lot of ugly things'.[9] We do not know whether Van Mander's most famous pupil ignored those warnings right from the start, although his earliest-known works suggest that he was not an artist who was instinctively inclined to work in 'a clean technique'. And such was Hals's talent that he applied a loose manner with great success. But his transformation of the art of portraiture extends to other aspects as well.

CHARACTERISATION

Although the works discussed so far are still relatively static, they already show signs of Hals's extraordinary ability to make his sitters come to life. It is this quality that represents arguably Hals's greatest achievement, remarked upon as early as 1628 when the Haarlem minister and poet Samuel Ampzing exclaimed in his book devoted to the city of Haarlem: 'How dashingly Frans paints people from life!'[10] A more elaborate observation in a similar vein is found in a later book on Haarlem by the writer and poet Theodorus Schrevelius, who in 1648 wrote that Hals

excels almost everyone with the superb and uncommon manner of painting which is uniquely his. His paintings are imbued with such force and vitality that he seems to defy nature herself with his brush. This is seen in all his portraits, so numerous as to pass belief, which are coloured in such a way that they seem to live and breathe.[11]

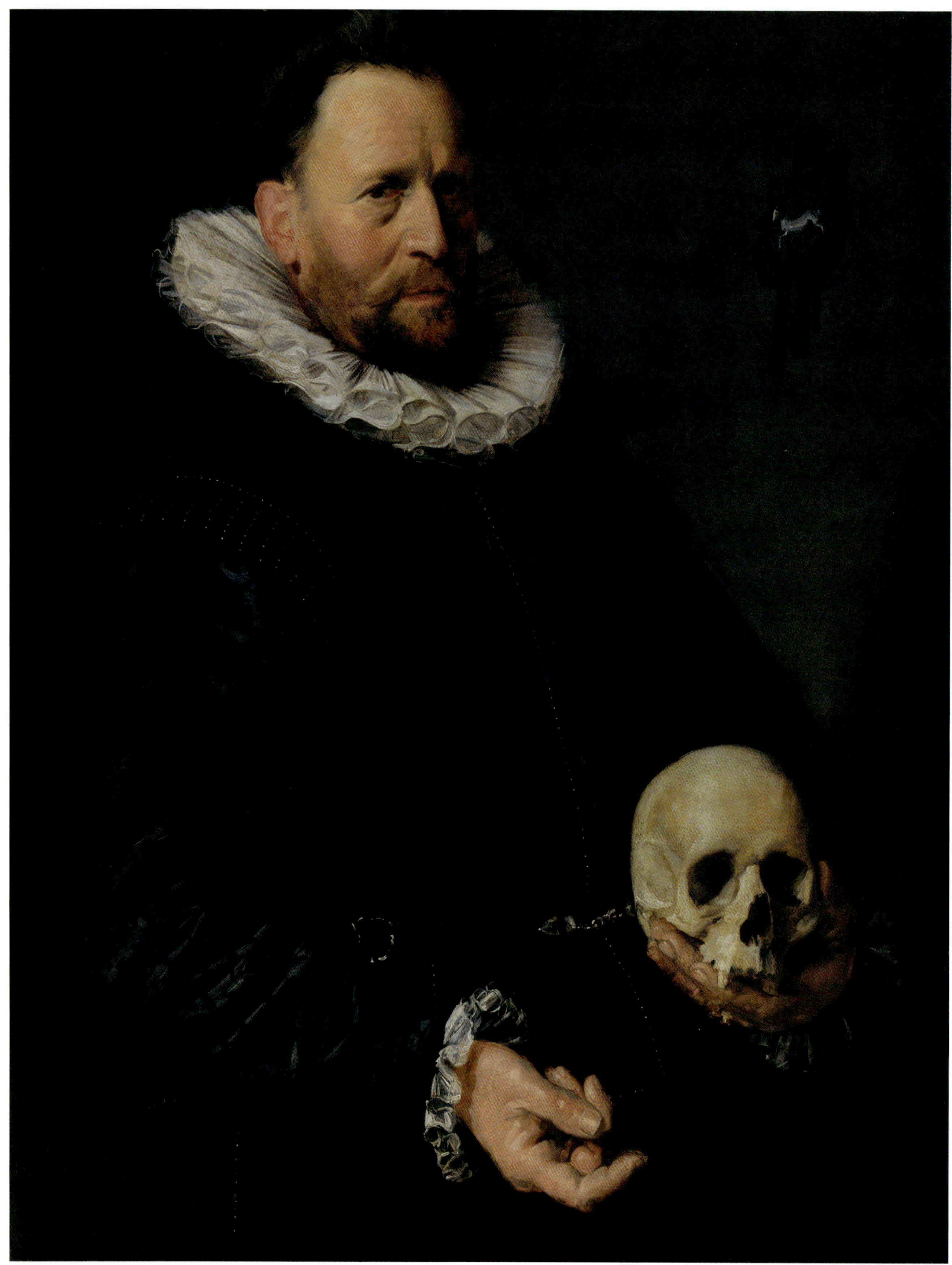

Fig. 58 *Portrait of a Man holding a Skull*, about 1612
Oil on wood, 92.8 × 71.2 cm
The Henry Barber Trust, the Barber Institute of Fine Arts, University of Birmingham

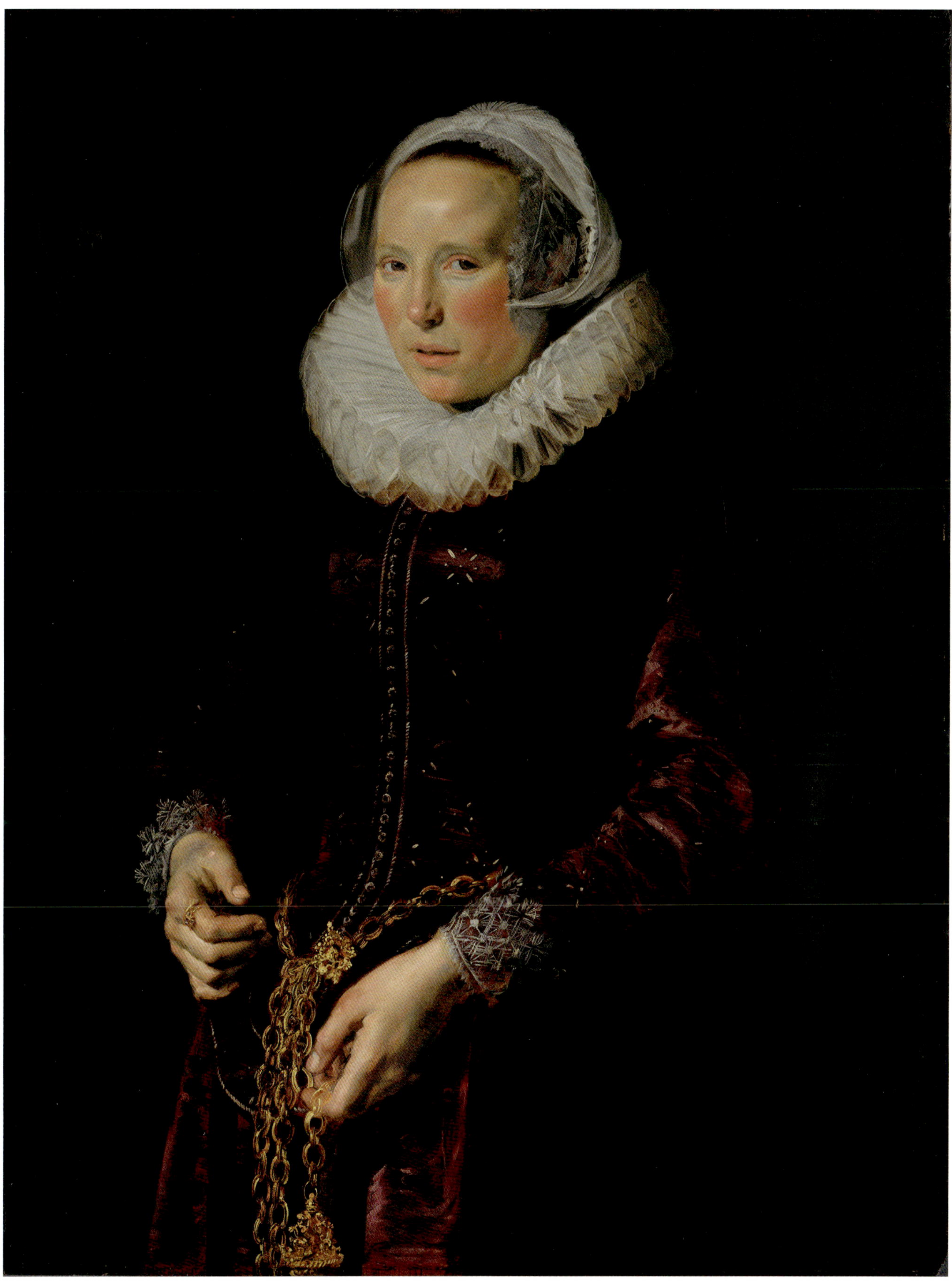

Fig. 59 *Portrait of a Woman standing*, about 1612
Oil on wood, 94.2 × 71.1 cm
The Devonshire Collections, Chatsworth

With the words 'living' and 'breathing' Schrevelius did not employ a worn cliché but provided a perfectly apt observation. Although his loose brushwork certainly helped Hals to bring out the characters of his sitters, he succeeded above all because he was clearly an exceedingly astute observer of facial expressions. He must also have had a tremendous sense of how people interact with each other – witness the people we see within a single composition, as in his family or group portraits (figs 62, 65–9), but also in his pendant paintings of couples, in which the sitters sometimes reach out to each other across the divide. In this he even includes the viewer, who is made to feel as if they can interact with his sitters. Looking at Hals's portraits is an almost visceral experience: we feel that we are in the presence of men and women of flesh and blood whom we can easily imagine meeting in real life. They exert a magnetic pull on us.

A striking example among Hals's early works is his portrait of Catharina Hooft with her nurse (fig. 60). In a superficial sense the portrait seems unassuming, which is why it is easy to overlook how unconventional it is. It was anyhow unusual to portray a child with her nurse rather than her mother, but it must have seemed just as novel to contemporary audiences that they should have been depicted in such a seemingly spontaneous moment. The toddler's arm stretches out to her nurse in the way small children do, the gesture sending mixed messages: it expresses affection as much as conveying that a certain distance should be observed, something that also helps Hals to tell the viewer that the main sitter is not the nurse but the splendidly dressed Catharina Hooft. And yet Hals could not have depicted the former in a more sympathetic light, her endearing smile and captivating eyes inviting us to engage with her devotion to the child, as indicated more explicitly by her presenting her charge with a small apple. And although it is hard for a painter to breathe much life into the smooth skin of a young child, Hals nevertheless managed to capture her in such an engaging way that we feel we should respond to her slightly mischievous gaze.

It is often said that seventeenth-century Dutch portraits of men tend to be more engaging than those of women. There is generally some truth in this, but *Portrait of Catharina Hooft with her Nurse* illustrates that Hals could be equally alert to female faces. In fact, examples abound of his extraordinary capacity to capture the character of his female sitters, and they encompass Hals's entire career. Arguably the most astonishing example is the female sitter in the double portrait of about 1622 now in the Rijksmuseum (fig. 61), probably depicting Beatrix van der Laen and her husband, Isaac Massa. It is hard to think of another artist of the period who could make a woman's smile and gaze equally disarming and evocative. On a superficial level, the double portrait recalls Rubens's famous self portrait with his wife, Isabella Brant (fig. 24),[12] but with Hals a jolt of pure joy has been injected into the scene by the woman's priceless expression alone. A more solemn example is the

facial expression of the wife looking at her husband in the family portrait of some 25 years later in the Museo Thyssen-Bornemisza in Madrid (fig. 62), which, paradoxically, is both tender and slightly forbidding. There is a peerless animation to the cheerful look of adoration that Isabella Coymans bestows on her husband, Stephanus Geraerdts, in their pendant portraits of about 1650 (figs 82–3). A far more subtle but no less evocative characterisation of a woman is seen in the poignant *Portrait of a Young Woman* of around 1658 (fig. 63), now in the Ferens Art Gallery in Hull, whose direct yet slightly hesitant expression stops us in our tracks. The picture is impossible to forget.

Hals's portraits have such life in them that one could reasonably wonder whether his sitters were required to sit still during a lengthy session posing for him.[13] The couples we see in his more conventional pendant portraits (figs 7–10, 86–7) seem to have posed in this manner, but many of the postures and facial expressions we encounter in his more adventurous portraits are almost incompatible with the notion of sitting or standing still. We can only speculate about Hals's studio practice in this regard because there are no records that tell us one way or the other. He obviously needed time to observe his sitters, but posing for Hals may in some cases have been a relatively relaxed affair, with changes in the sitters' facial expressions (and perhaps even their poses) a help rather than a hindrance in capturing what could be described, for want of a better word, as the 'aura' of a person.

Hals's genre paintings, most of which date from the 1620s, are illuminating in this context. In these he records types rather than portraits. And yet they are clearly after live models, with some reappearing in other works. Unrestrained by the requirements of portraiture, Hals allowed the main characters in his genre paintings to come to life through facial expressions that brim with life and movement. There are, of course, exceptions. In *Young Man holding a Skull (Vanitas)* (fig. 64) – its subject a straightforward allegory reminding us of our mortality – we see a relatively static face, the picture deriving its dynamism not so much from the young man's expression as from the way he extends his gesturing hand towards us, jutting into the space of the viewer, the foreshortening handled with an apparently impossible economy of means. But it seems highly unlikely that the subjects in his pictures of various musicians (figs 157, 162, 177) would have sat still, maintaining their poses and facial expressions. Nor can this have been the case when he painted what is in effect a portrait of *Malle Babbe* (fig. 171), in which only the tankard and the owl are static counterweights to the frenetic energy that pervades the rest of the picture. Although it looks like a genre painting, Malle Babbe was in fact an actual person.[14] As her frenzied appearance and fiendish grimace suggest, she would hardly have been one to sit still.

All the visual evidence suggests that Hals must have been a very keen observer of people's behaviour and facial expressions, but it is not easy to determine how he

PORTRAITURE INTO ART

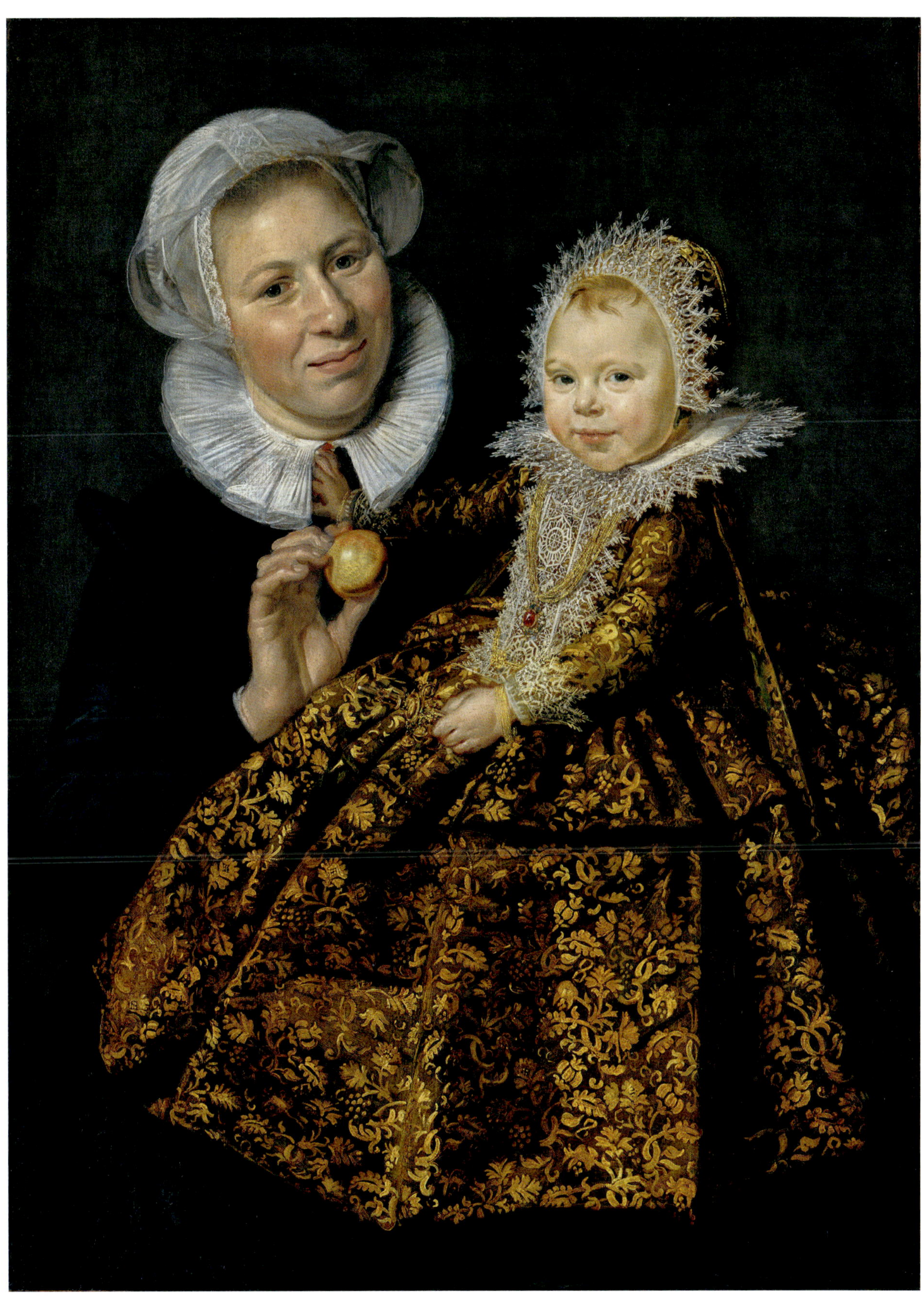

Fig. 60 *Portrait of Catharina Hooft with her Nurse*, 1619–20
Oil on canvas, 91.8 × 68.3 cm
Staatliche Museen zu Berlin, Gemäldegalerie

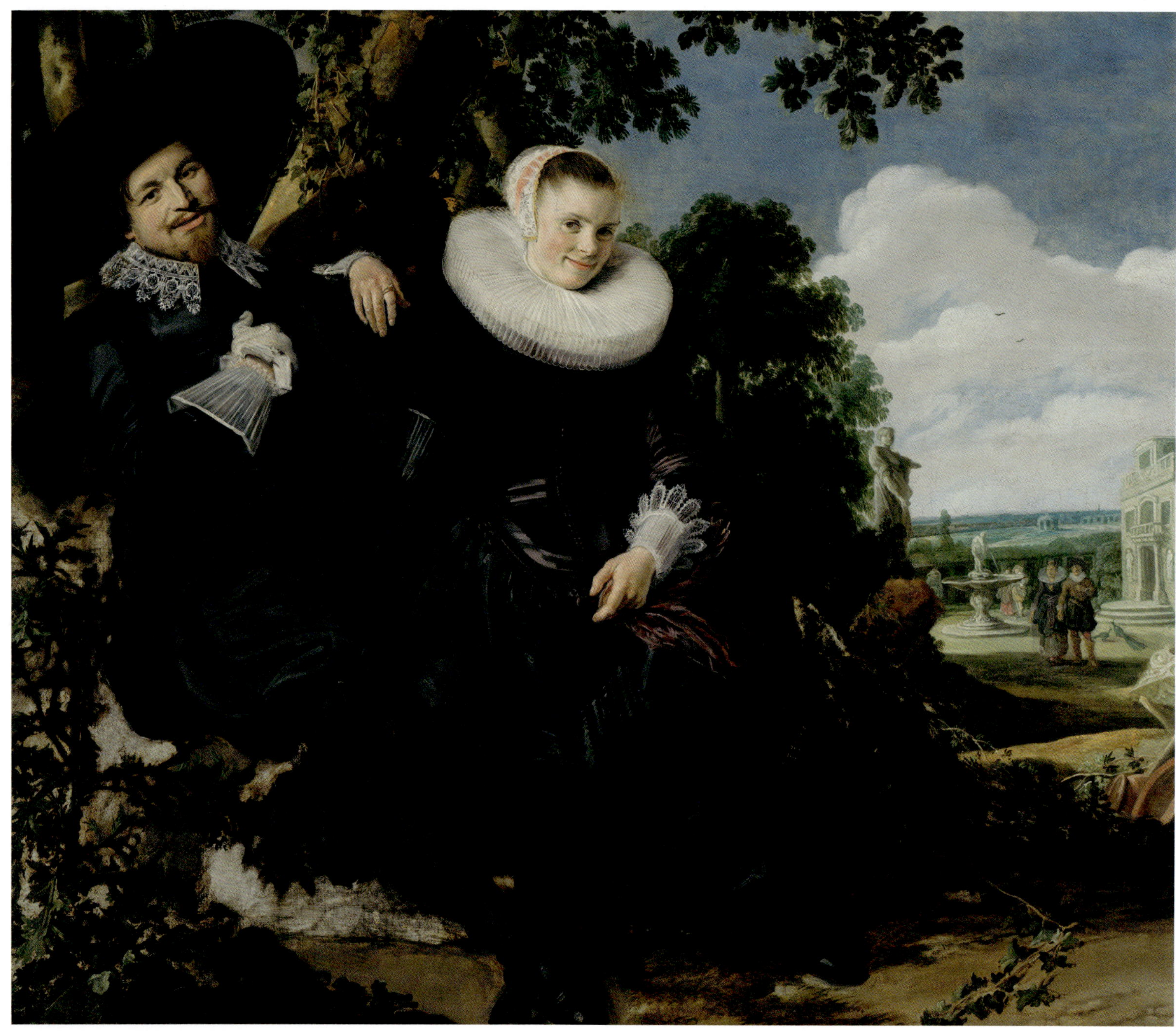

Fig. 61 *Portrait of a Couple, probably Isaac Abrahamsz Massa and Beatrix van der Laen*, about 1622
Oil on canvas, 140 × 166.5 cm
Rijksmuseum, Amsterdam

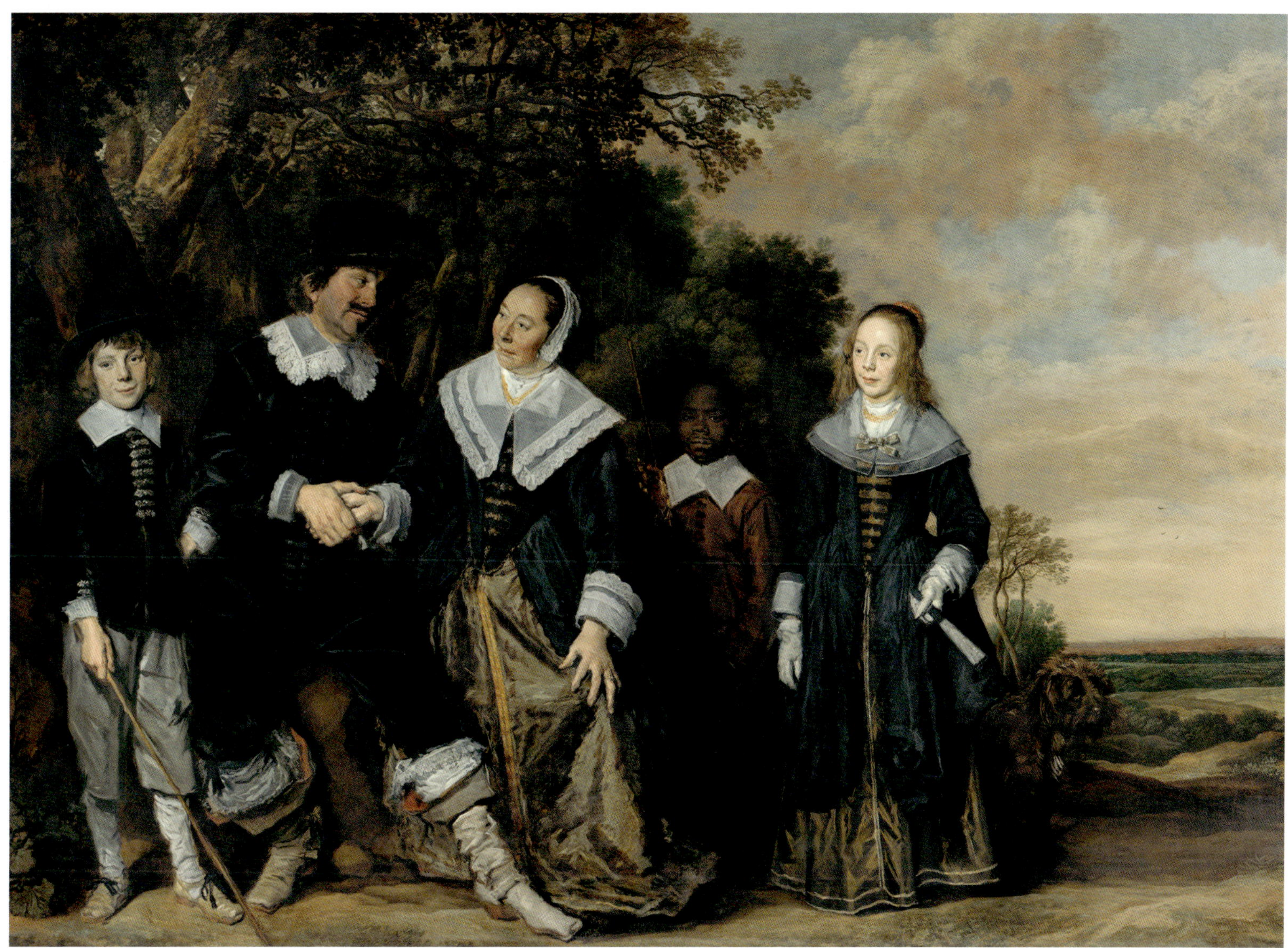

Fig. 62 *Family Group in a Landscape*, about 1646
Oil on canvas, 202 × 285 cm
Museo Nacional Thyssen-Bornemisza, Madrid

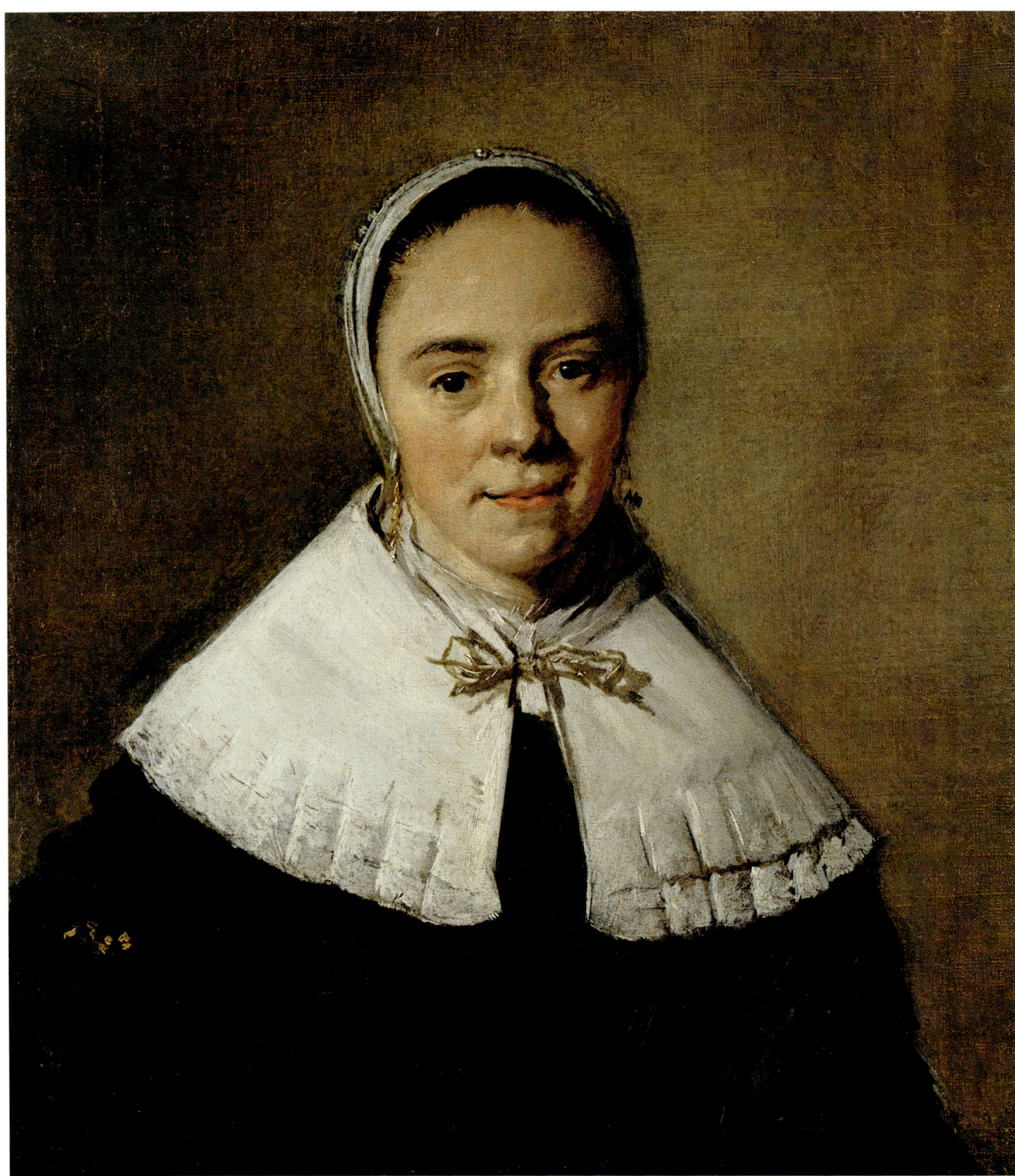

Fig. 63 *Portrait of a Young Woman*, about 1658
Oil on canvas, 60 × 55.5 cm
Ferens Art Gallery: Hull Museums

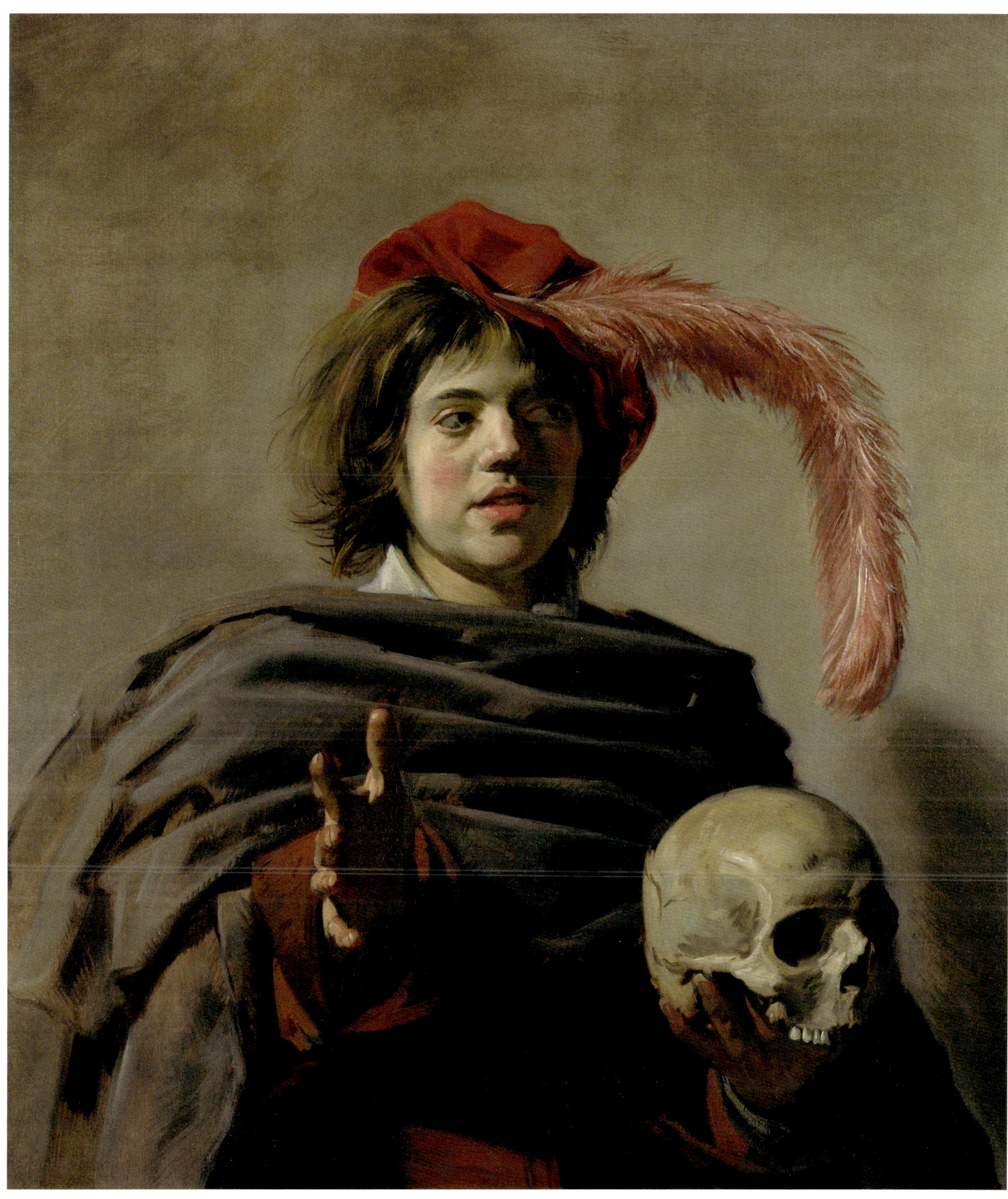

Fig. 64 *Young Man holding a Skull (Vanitas)*, about 1627
Oil on canvas, 92.2 × 80.8 cm
The National Gallery, London

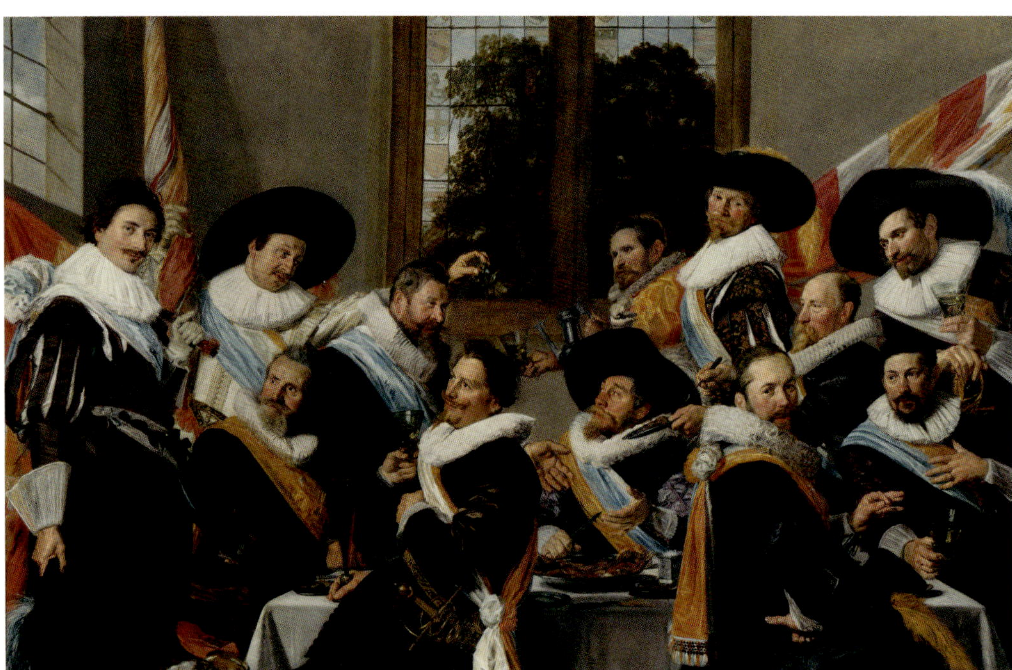

Fig. 65 *Banquet of the Officers of the Calivermen Civic Guard*, about 1627
Oil on canvas, 183 × 266.5 cm
Frans Hals Museum, Haarlem

converted such impressions into paintings that are not just convincing but also affecting.[15] In addition to the mystery of his early years, there is the conundrum that the artist seems never to have made drawings or sketches to record his impressions. The question arises as to whether Hals necessarily studied his models or sitters through a time-consuming examination of their outward appearance. For the most part his portrayal of types and sitters steers clear of caricature. Yet the liveliness in many of his portraits and genre pictures is such that one is inclined to draw a parallel with how some caricaturists prefer to work from moving images of their subjects rather than photographic representations, for it is a person's gait and their ever-changing facial expressions that bring them to life and establish their character. If the term 'impressionistic' is sometimes used to describe the way Hals suggested surfaces and materials, one could extend the term to include the way he depicted faces and poses, the liveliness depending on an impression of a sitter's face and bearing. Sensitivity to the essence of a person's expression, posture and demeanour in itself is nothing unusual: it is an essential part of how we all instantly recognise the people we know. The miracle lies in the fact that Hals knew how to convert this sensitivity into the paint flowing from his brush, creating likenesses that instantly engender in the viewer the sense that we are becoming familiar with the person in question. This is all the more remarkable when we consider that we cannot check the likenesses of people who lived before the age of photography.[16] And yet Hals's best portraits provoke a visceral response that creates a moment of 'recognition', even without further knowledge of the sitters.[17] Perhaps this is what Van Mander meant when he wrote that 'a face, after all the most important part of

the human body, contains quite enough so as to be able to disclose and reveal the quality and efficacy of art'. What is certain, however, is that in the hands of great artists – whether Rembrandt, Rubens, Velázquez or Hals – Van Mander's 'side-road of art' takes a definite turn towards the main road.

A salient example is Hals's *Portrait of Pieter van den Broecke* of about 1633 (fig. 11), which looks like a snapshot far more than it resembles an official portrait. The sitter was one of the main traders of the Dutch East India Company, rewarded for his 17 years of service with the golden chain he wears in his portrait. One would perhaps expect a more solemn portrait reflecting the status of the sitter, but instead his appearance can only be described as jovial. Hals may have felt he could take some liberties because Van den Broecke was a friend.[18] The result is that we believe we are getting to know the sitter's character, in much the same way as we instantly relate to Hals's famous *'Merry Drinker'* of only a few years earlier (fig. 175), in which the artist blurred the boundaries between genre and portraiture to such an extent that it is difficult to tell whether we are looking at a character study of a man in a particularly jolly mood, or a portrait of an actual civic guardsman in his military outfit inviting us to join him in enjoying a glass of wine.[19] The fact that the work is so very loosely brushed might suggest that it is the former, because there would have been no reason for Hals to hold back if the conventions of portraiture could be ignored, but the comparable treatment seen in the portrait of Pieter van den Broecke counts against that idea. It is clear that Hals increasingly felt that the full extent of his loose technique and casual approach could be called upon in his portraits as much as in his genre pictures, and many of his clients evidently agreed.

   PORTRAITURE INTO ART

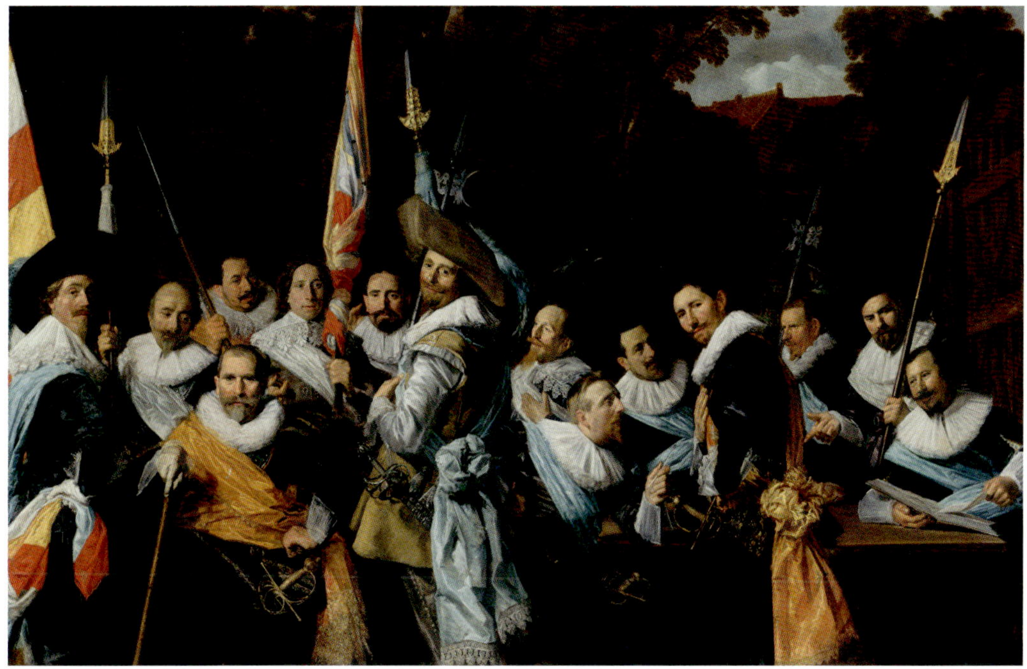

Fig. 66 *Meeting of the Officers and Sergeants of the Calivermen Civic Guard*, about 1633
Oil on canvas, 207 × 337 cm
Frans Hals Museum, Haarlem

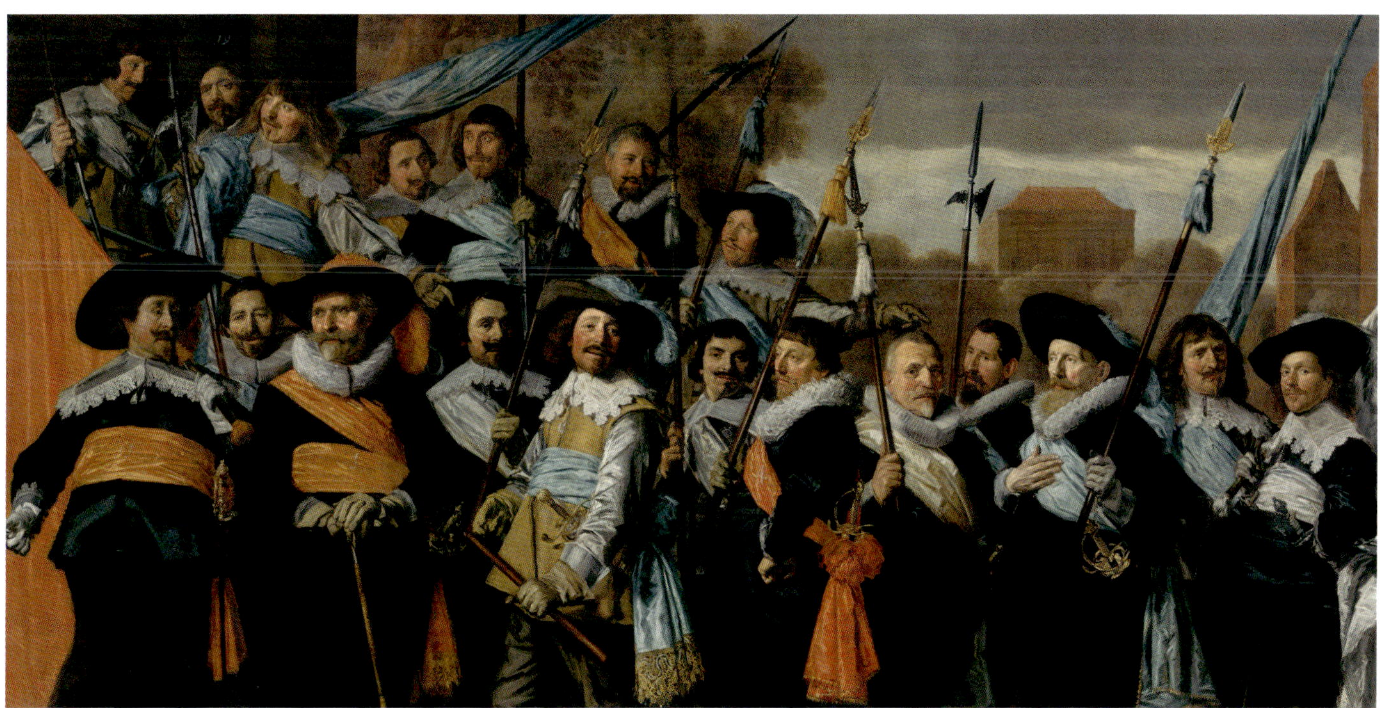

Fig. 67 *Officers and Sergeants of the St George Civic Guard*, about 1639
Oil on canvas, 218 × 421 cm
Frans Hals Museum, Haarlem

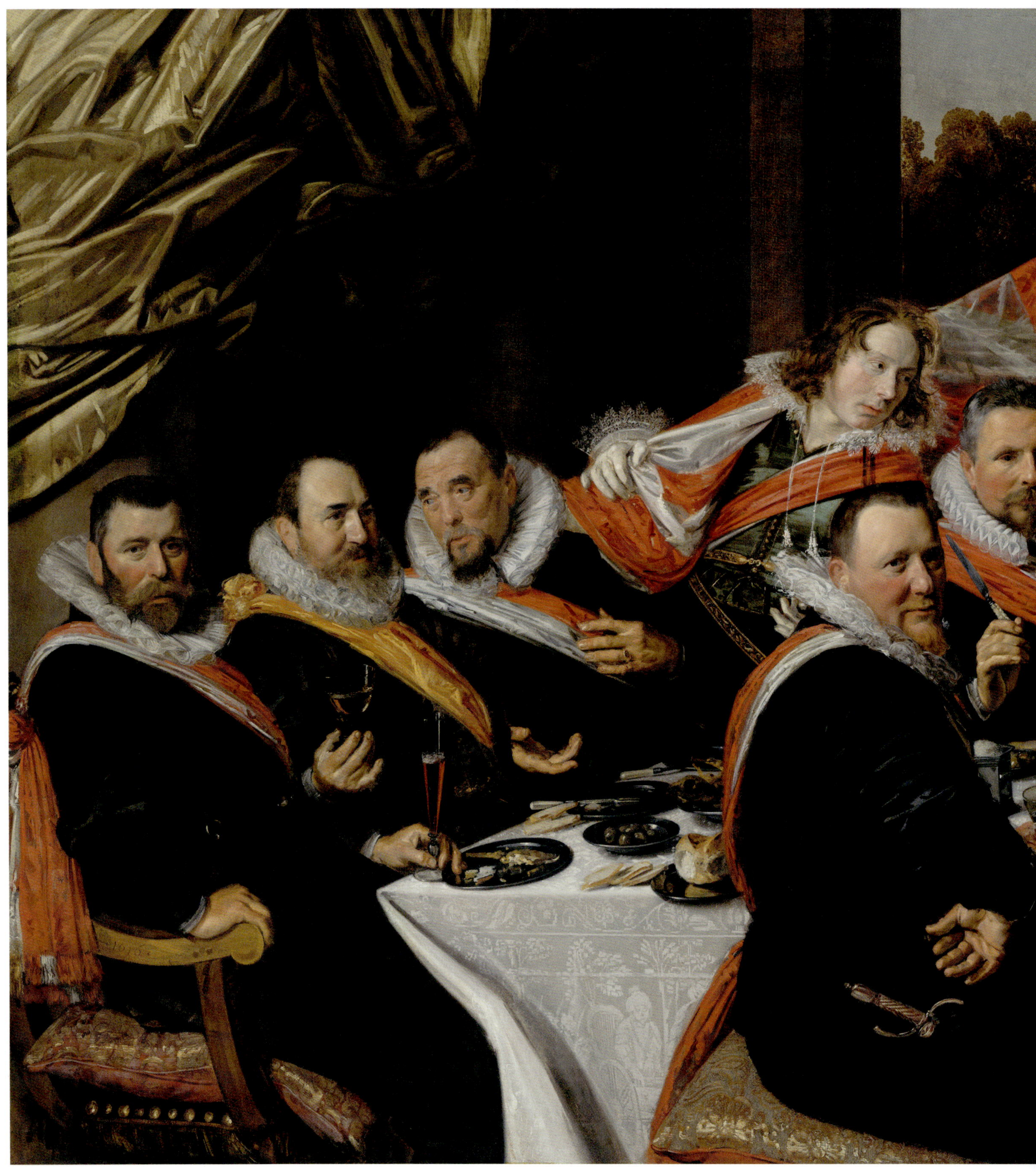

Fig. 68 *Banquet of the Officers of the St George Civic Guard*, 1616
Oil on canvas, 175 × 324 cm
Frans Hals Museum, Haarlem

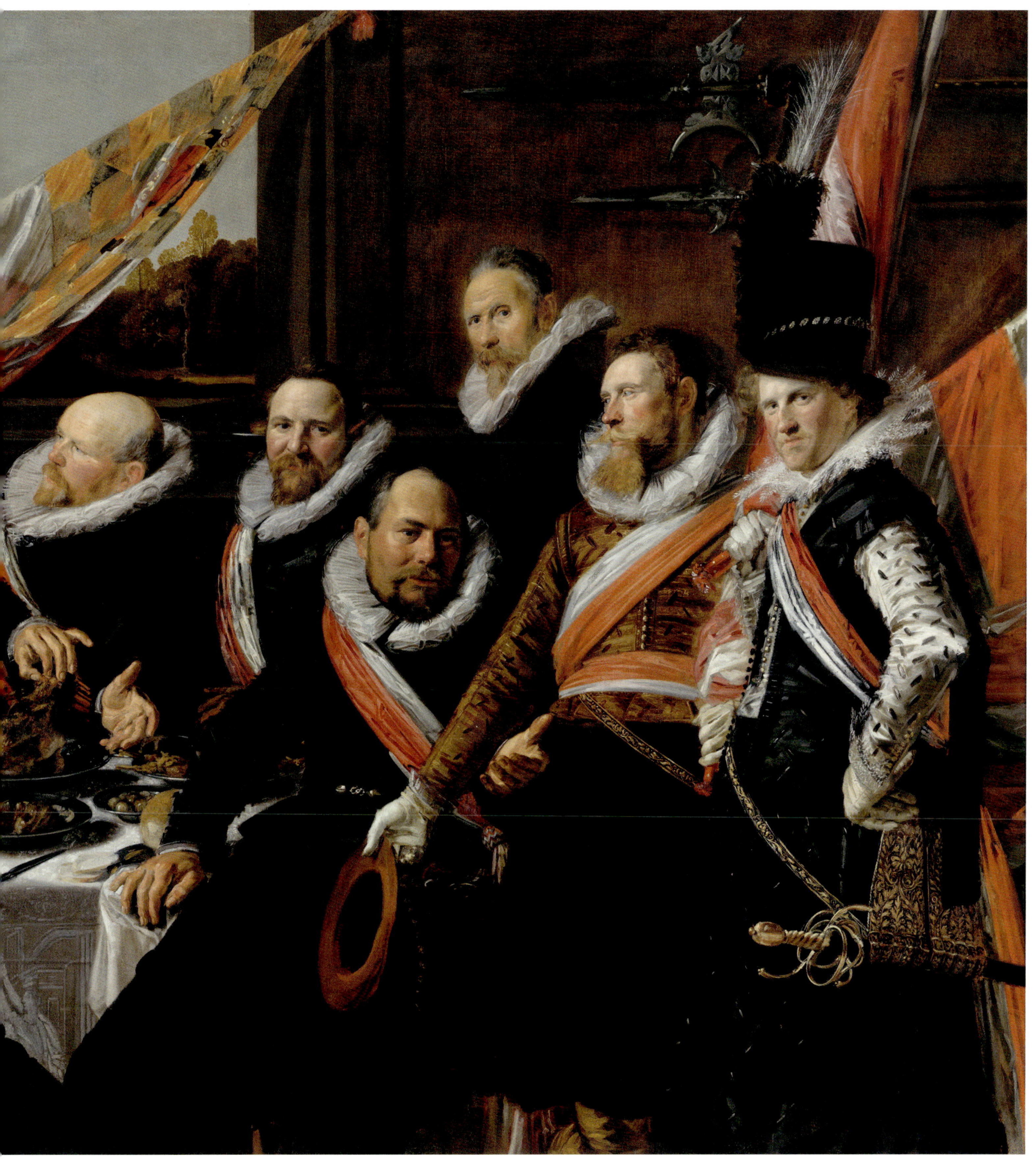

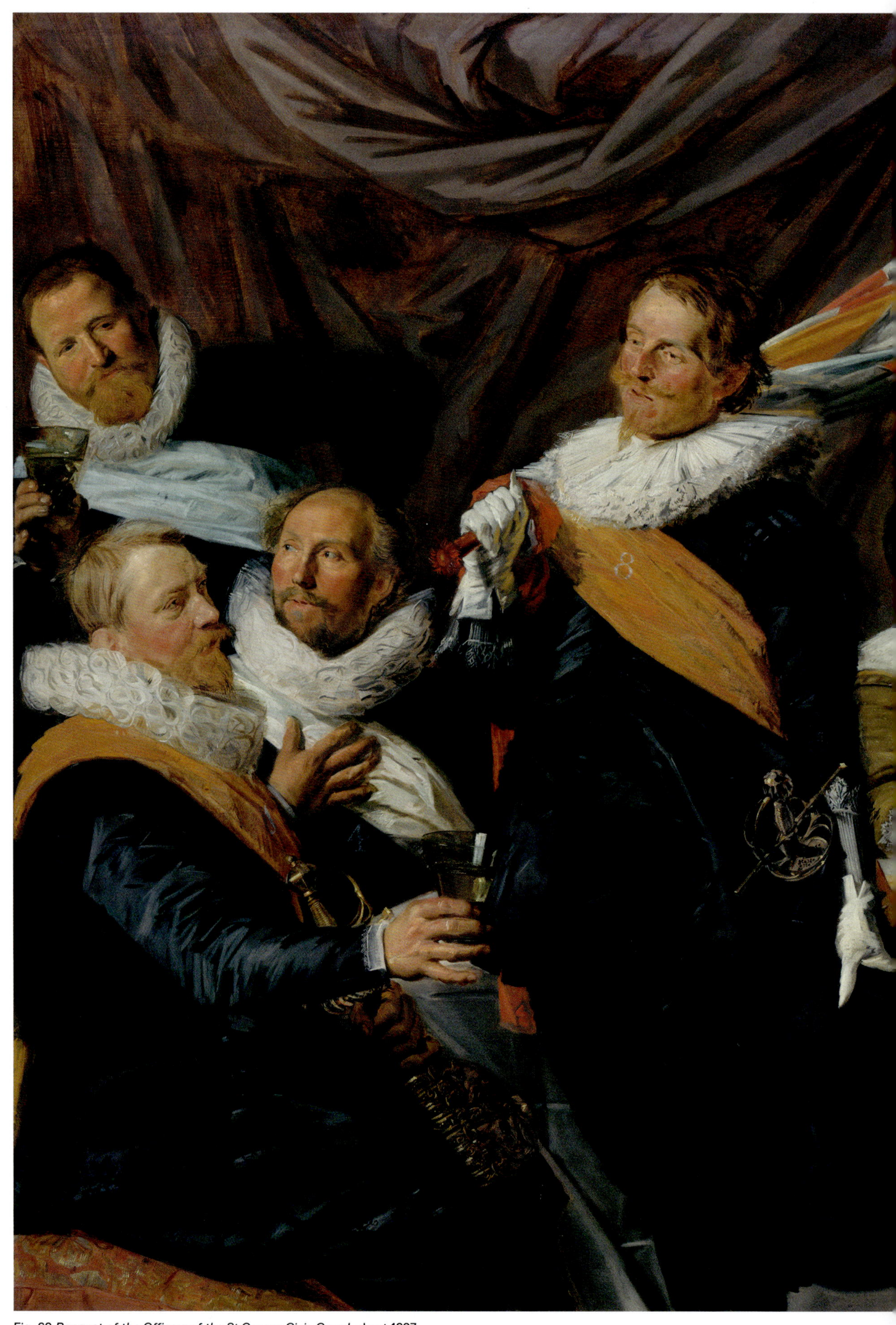

Fig. 69 *Banquet of the Officers of the St George Civic Guard*, about 1627
Oil on canvas, 179 × 257.5 cm
Frans Hals Museum, Haarlem

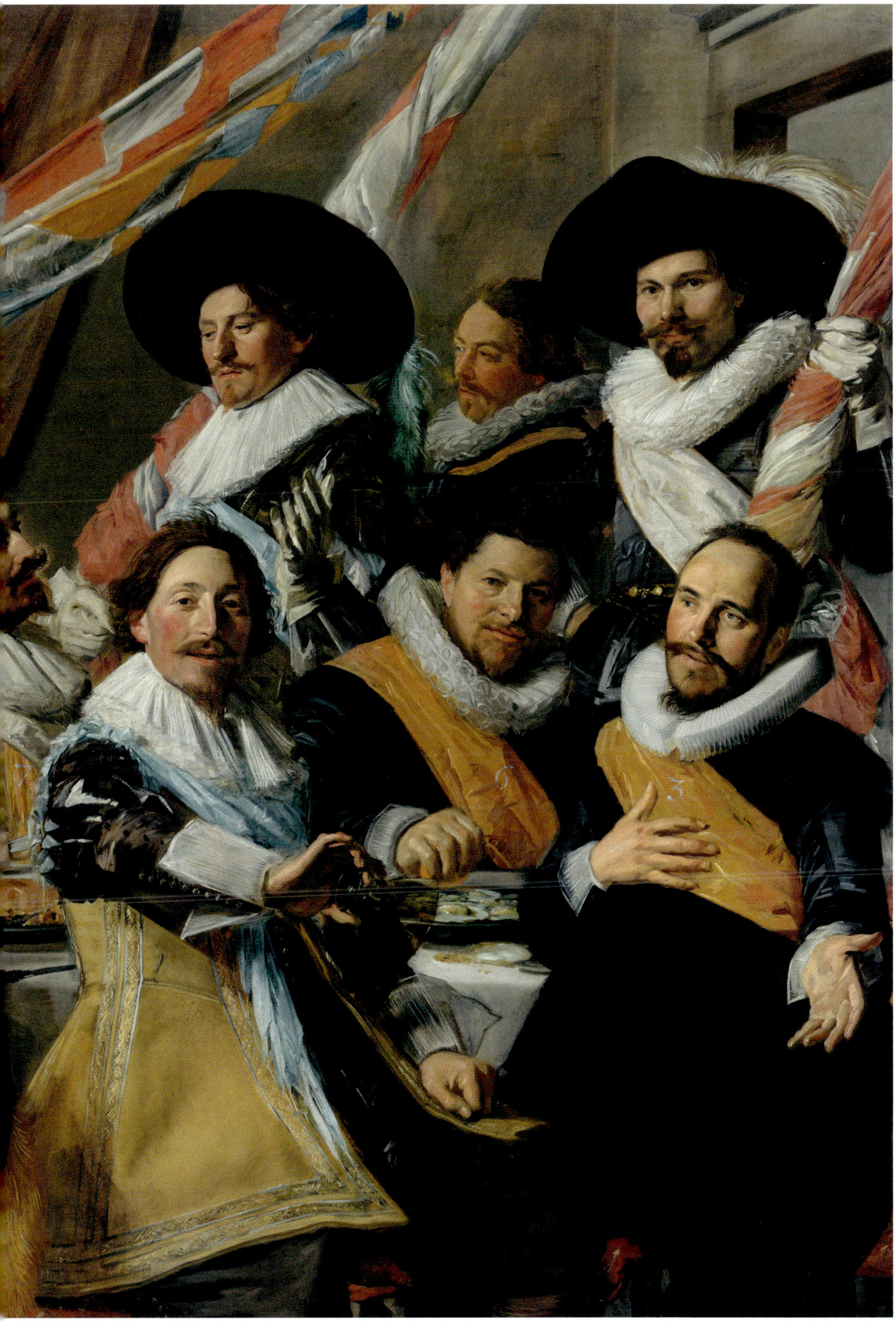

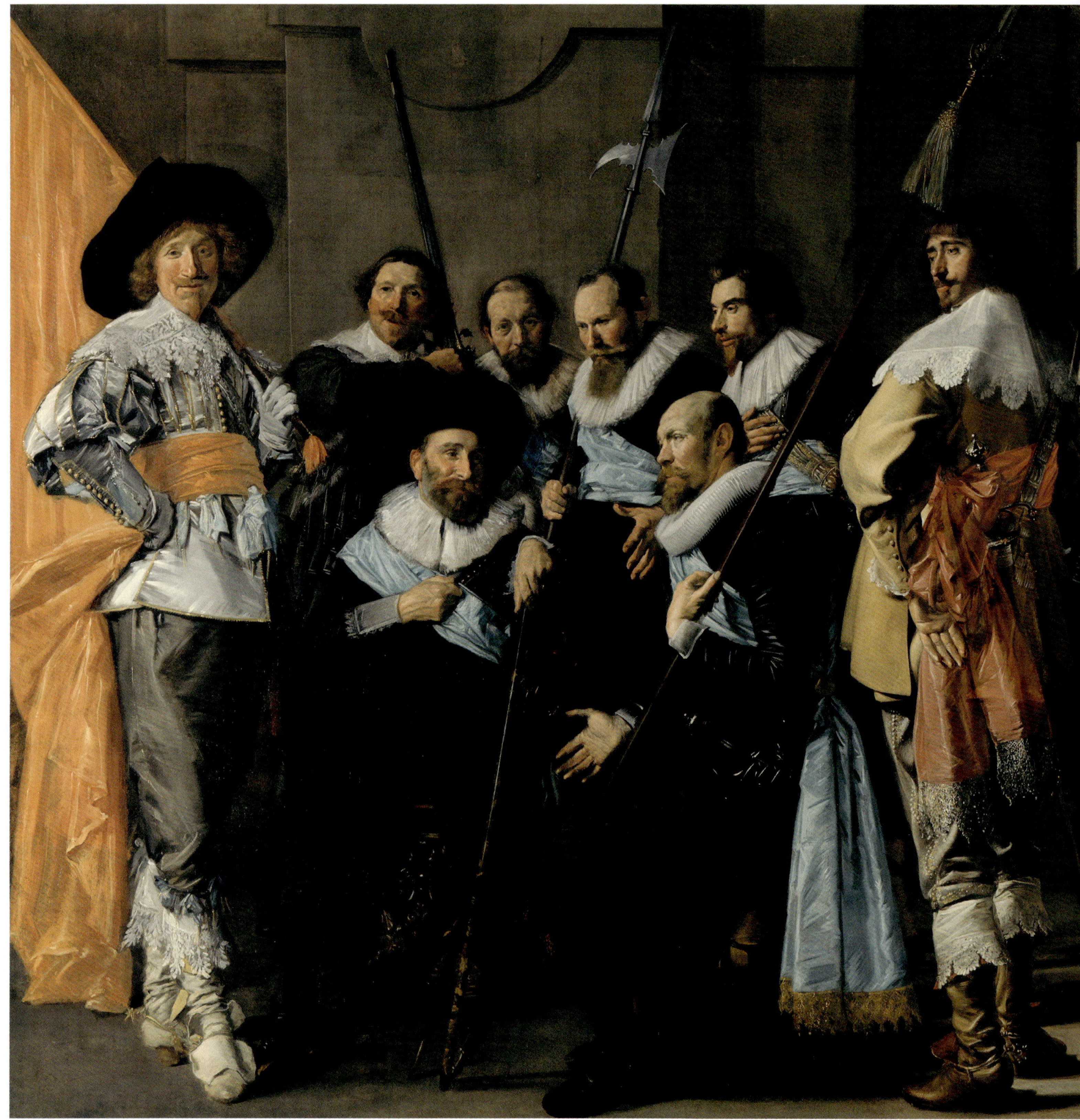

Fig. 70 *Militia Company of District XI under the Command of Captain Reynier Reael,
known as 'The Meagre Company'*, 1633 (completed by Pieter Codde, 1637)
Oil on canvas, 209 × 429 cm
Rijksmuseum, Amsterdam. On loan from the City of Amsterdam

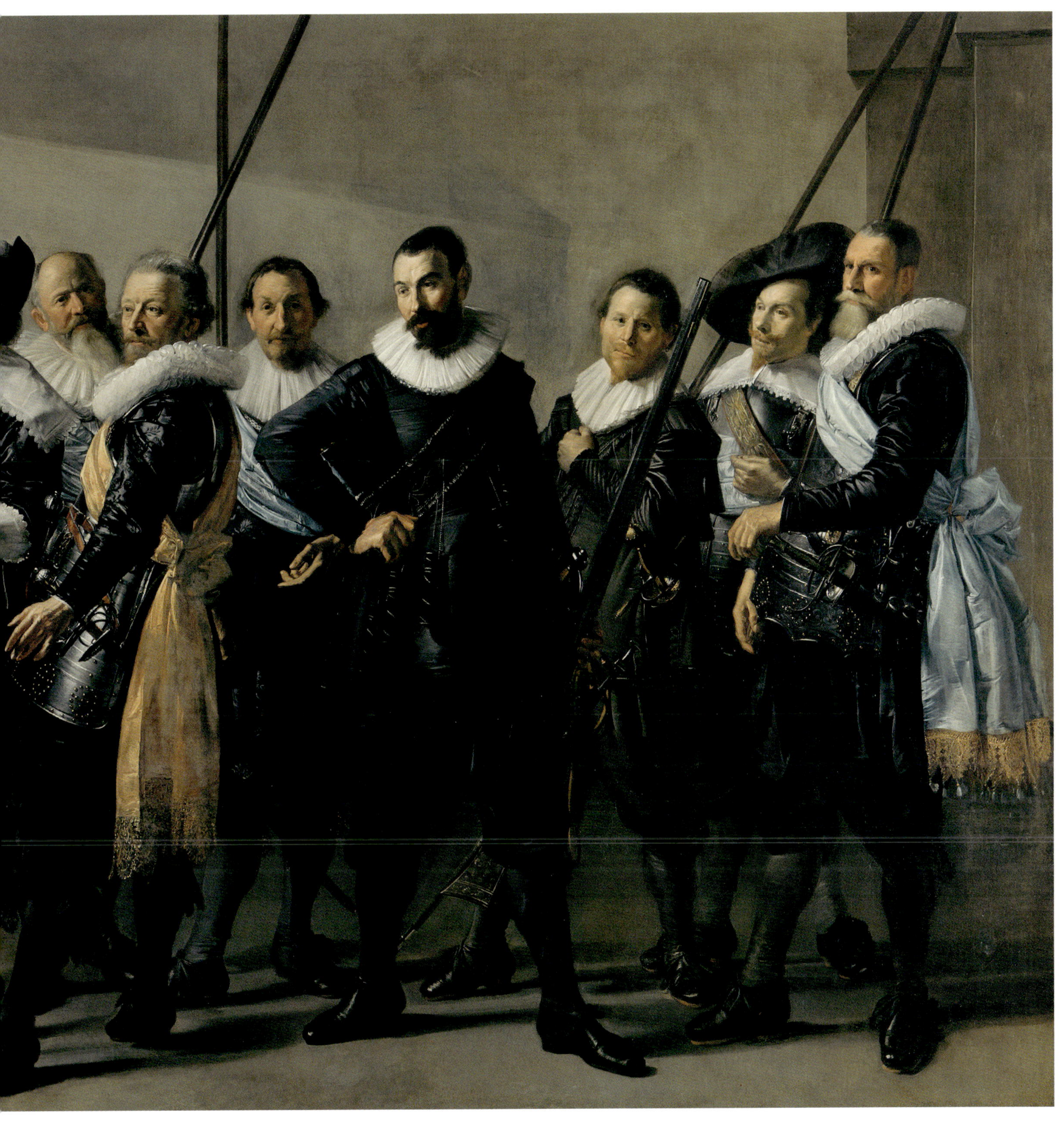

POSES

Frans Hals amplified his skill in conveying a sitter's character by employing a great variety of poses and gestures. These run the gamut from delightfully subtle to extravagantly exuberant, helping him to suggest traits ranging from modesty and worthiness (figs 7–8, 63) to ostentatiousness (figs 9–10, 86–7), nonchalance (figs 50, 61, 93), unequivocal arrogance (figs 73, 88) and defiance (fig. 94). Some sitters seem to have been relatively unconcerned with questions of decorum, while others appear keen to avoid expressive gestures or dynamic poses, which may occasionally reflect their more puritanical outlook on life.[20]

A veritable catalogue of poses can be found in Hals's large group portraits of Haarlem militia companies, which rightly count as among the artist's greatest achievements (figs 65–70). Militia companies helped the local authorities to defend a town or city from attacks, whether from outside or, in the case of a revolt, from within. They were originally organised as guilds under the patronage of a saint, which is how the two Haarlem militias seen in Hals's paintings came to be named after St George and St Adrian. By the early seventeenth century, each Haarlem militia consisted of three companies; the city magistrates, themselves part of an urban elite, chose the officers of each company from among the more affluent citizens, who were required to pay for their own weapons and uniforms. The highest-ranking officer was the colonel, followed by the provost, after which came the three captains and three lieutenants of each company. The ensigns were always young bachelors, and in group portraits of the period are often the ones wearing the most extravagant outfits. Each company consisted of a hundred or so guardsmen recruited from the middle classes, who were assigned to a company depending on the ward in which they lived. By the early seventeenth century there was a long tradition to adorn the rooms where a company congregated with group portraits of its principal members.

From 1612 to 1624 Hals was himself a member of the third company of the St George Civic Guard. It was not unusual for a painter-member to be commissioned to paint the militia company's group portrait; moreover, Hals's reputation must already have been such that he was an obvious choice. Especially in his paintings of the St George Civic Guard, first in 1616 and again around 1627 (figs 68, 69), he went to town in every respect, producing showpieces in which he demonstrated his unparalleled ability to imbue his works with life and energy. These have a panache that lifts the genre to a whole new level.

The arrangement of the officers in group portraits of militia companies followed a strict military protocol to reflect their hierarchical structure. Incorporating a substantial number of portraits into one composition forms a tremendous challenge, and most sixteenth-century depictions of guardsmen attending a banquet show

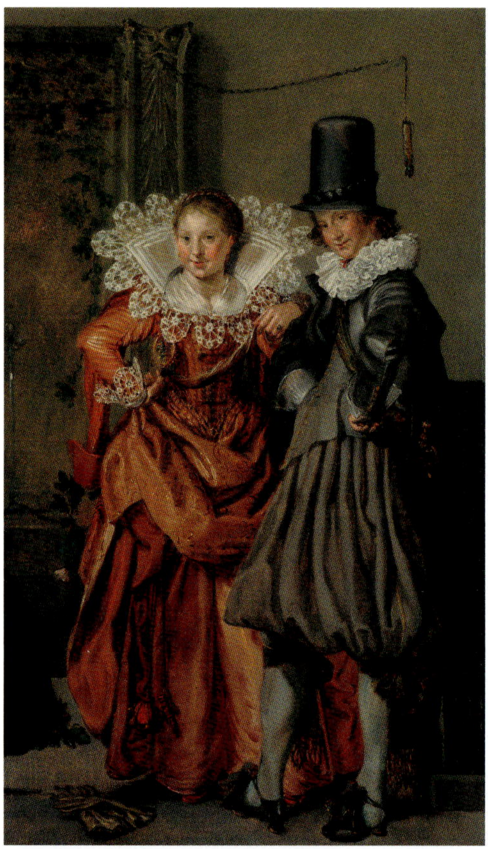

Fig. 71 Willem Buytewech, *Elegant Couples courting* (detail), about 1616–20. Oil on canvas, 56.3 × 70.5 cm
Rijksmuseum, Amsterdam; purchased with the support of the Commissie voor Fotoverkoop

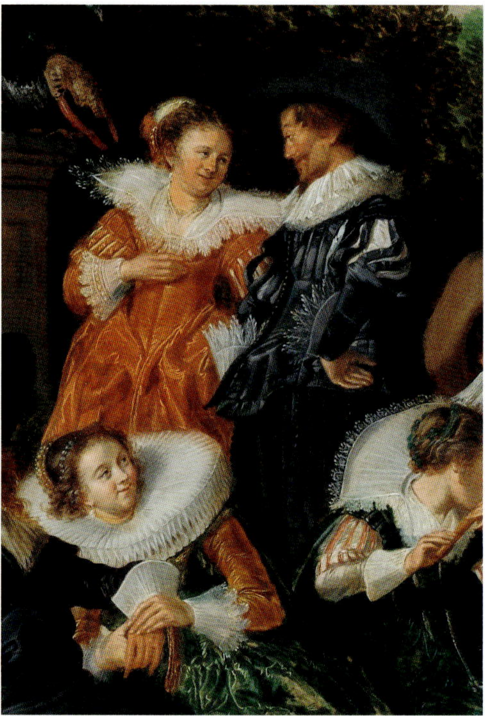

Fig. 72 Dirck Hals, *Fête champêtre* (detail), 1627
Oil on wood, 77.6 × 135.7 cm
Rijksmuseum, Amsterdam

PORTRAITURE INTO ART

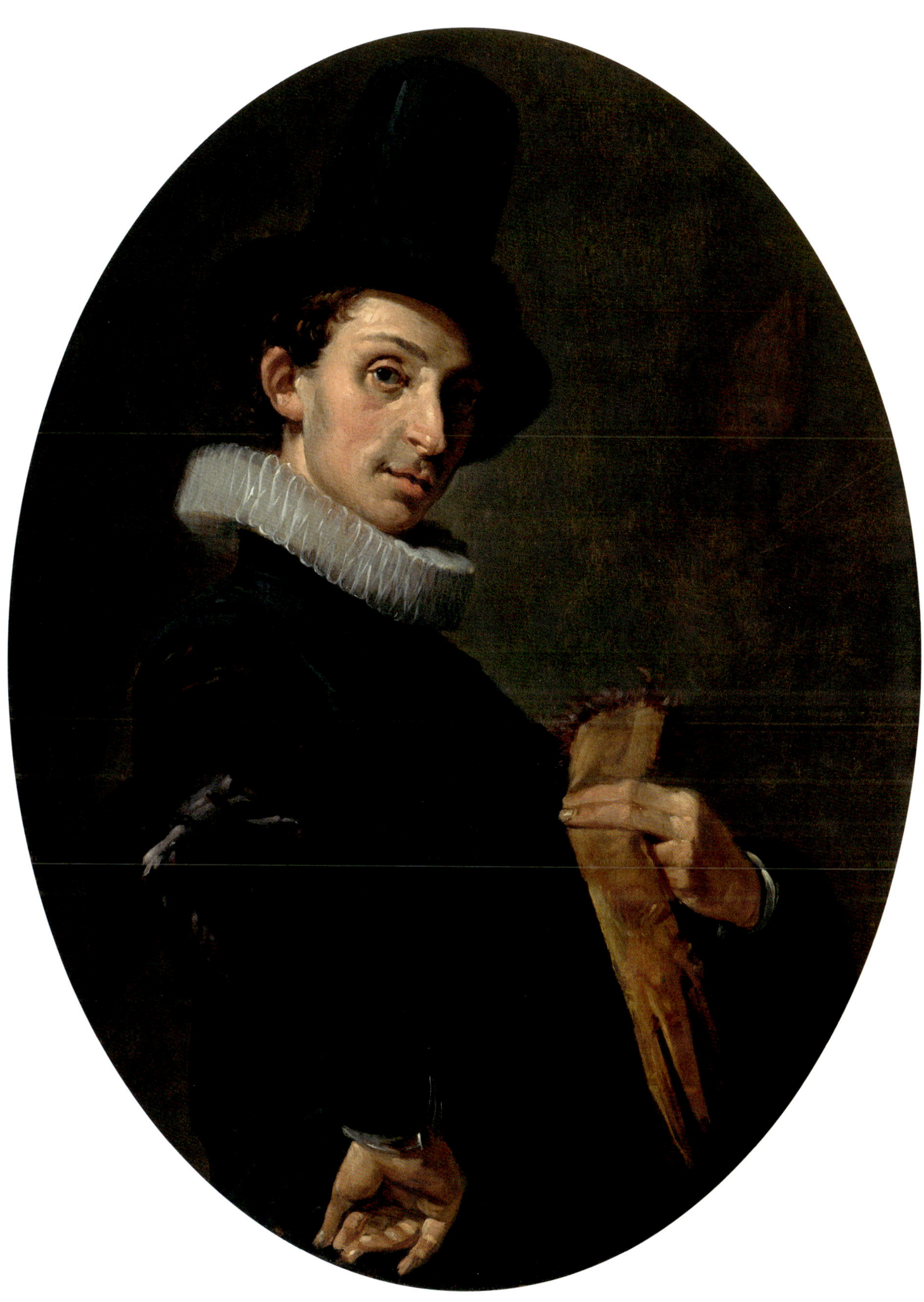

Fig. 73 *Portrait of a Young Man holding a Pair of Gloves*, about 1619
Oil on wood, 24.5 × 19 cm
Rose-Marie and Eijk de Mol van Otterloo Collection

decidedly rigid compositions that are essentially an accumulation of individual portraits, the sitters barely interacting. By 1583 Cornelis van Haarlem managed to introduce plenty of lively interaction and characterisation of individuals in his *Banquet of Members of the Haarlem Calivermen Civic Guard* (fig. 75), but the arrangement in tiers still feels unnatural, while the way the members are huddled together makes for a crowded scene. That something more engaging and natural was afoot can already be seen in a spirited drawing of about 1600 by Hals's fellow townsman Hendrick Goltzius for a militia piece that was probably never executed (fig. 74).

It is this approach that is perfected in Hals's first attempt at such a group portrait of 1616 (fig. 68). The colonel, Hendrick van Berckenrode, is seated at the head of the table at left. He is the only one wearing an orange sash. He is accompanied on his right by the provost, Johan van Napels, and on his left by captain Jacob Laurensz, whose high cheekbones, slightly weathered face and commanding presence Hals has captured so brilliantly that we immediately feel we know 'the type'. What unfolds further to the right is a cast of ruddy-faced captains and lieutenants seated around a richly laden table, with three rather more youthful-looking ensigns standing around them. An older servant stands in the background. For the first time in the history of the genre, a group portrait of this type in no way feels contrived: we are made to feel as if we have stumbled upon this merry company, with some members looking at us as if they have only just become aware that they are being watched.

Punctuating the scene at regular intervals are three people with their elbows jutting out towards us. Johan van Napels flanks the scene on the left, followed in the middle by Nicolaes Woutersz van der Meer and, on the far right, by the dashing ensign Boudewijn van Offenberg, portrayed again 11 years later as the central ensign in Hals's portrait of the same company in 1627 (fig. 65). This is a time-honoured device to give depth to the foreground of a scene. Hals repeated the ploy by having the gesturing hand of lieutenant Pieter Adriaensz Verbeek peep through towards us from under the outstretched arm holding the hat of ensign Gerrit Cornelisz Vlasman. He here proves himself to be the undisputed master of choreography, but that choreography only reveals itself on close analysis of the composition; the care he has taken to arrange the sitters does not at any point impede the overall impression of artlessness. It is for the same reason that the obviously deliberate triangular composition of the group is not even the first thing we notice.

Having one arm akimbo at an angle towards the viewer was certainly not a Hals invention, although he seems to have employed the stance more enthusiastically than any of his peers. It is seen in many Renaissance portraits – Pontormo's *Portrait of a Halberdier* is a famous example[21] – and is therefore often referred to as the 'Renaissance elbow'.[22] In fact, the arm akimbo goes back further still and has its roots in the portrayal of defiance and power in depictions of mythological or biblical

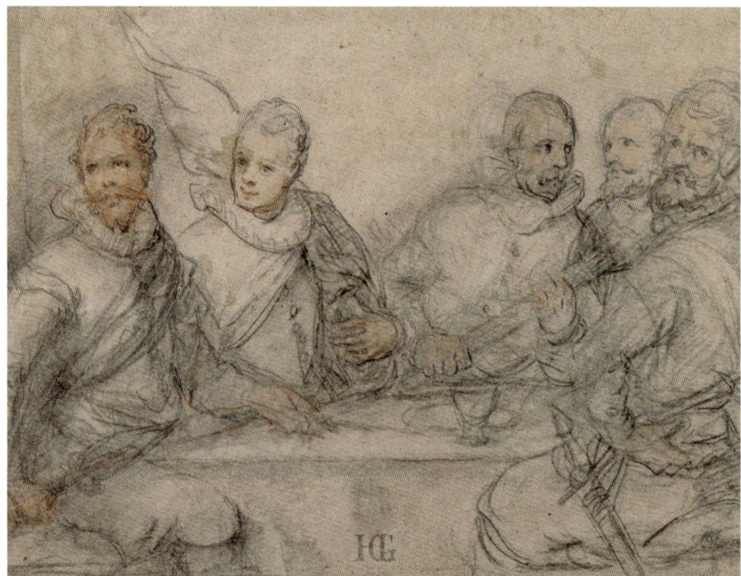

Fig. 74 Hendrick Goltzius, *Study for a Group of Militia Officers*, about 1600. Black and red chalk on paper, 24 × 31.8 cm
Rijksmuseum, Amsterdam; purchased with the support of the Vereniging Rembrandt

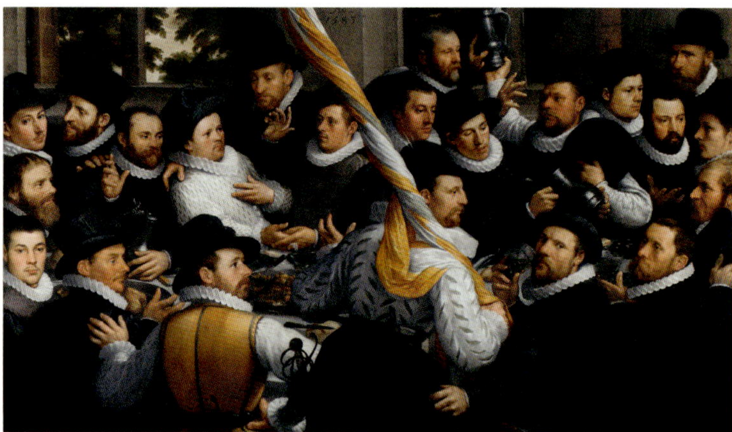

Fig. 75 Cornelis van Haarlem, *Banquet of Members of the Haarlem Calivermen Civic Guard*, 1583
Oil on wood, 135 × 233 cm
Frans Hals Museum, Haarlem

PORTRAITURE INTO ART

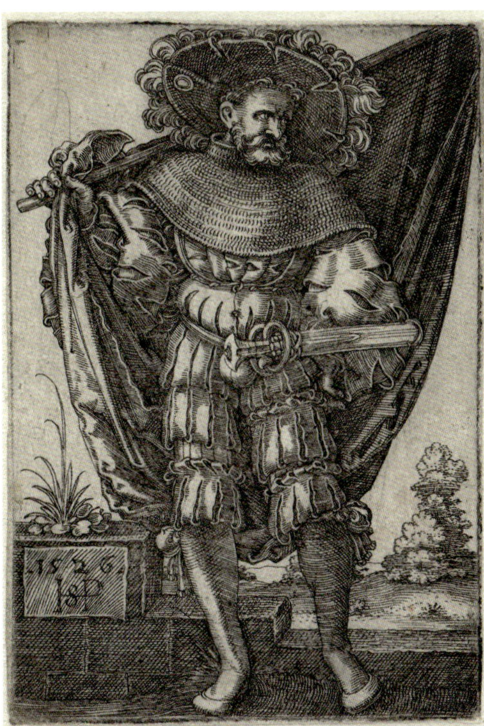

Fig. 76 Hans Sebald Beham,
Standard Bearer, 1526
Engraving, 7.2 × 5.1 cm
Rijksmuseum, Amsterdam

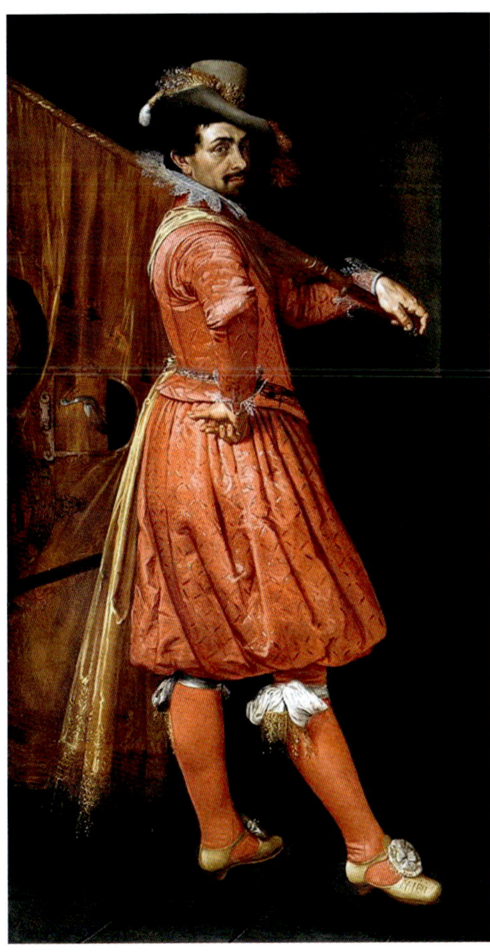

Fig. 77 Evert van der Maes,
Willem Jansz Cock as a Standard Bearer, 1617
Oil on canvas, 198 × 102 cm
Haags Historisch Museum, The Hague

figures, the most famous examples being Donatello's sculptures of David.[23] The pose suggests that the person is a force to be reckoned with, in the same category as what we today call the 'power stance' (the legs placed far apart) sometimes adopted by those who wish to be perceived as dominant. But while the 'power stance' in the politician or chief executive often leads to an awkward or even comical look, in its swagger the arm akimbo or 'Renaissance elbow' combines power with elegance. It is above all this latter quality that Hals exploited (and of necessity in his portrayal of children, who are too young to claim a powerful position in society; see the young boy at the far left in fig. 62).

The proud figure of the ensign in the St George Civic Guard painting (fig. 68) lends itself to the pose, which in real life is a practical (and in art a visual) counterweight to the bearing of the standard with the other arm. Only unmarried men were allowed to fulfil the role of ensign in a guard company (in an actual conflict an ensign could be required to defend the standard with his life) and bachelors were free to indulge in the kind of extravagant clothing that married men were expected to trade in for a more sober outfit. Their exuberant appearance and one arm akimbo were already being singled out in sixteenth-century prints (fig. 76). In the seventeenth century ensigns were very occasionally painted in isolation to commemorate this colourful aspect of their young lives, as in a splendid painting of 1617 (fig. 77) by Evert van der Maes.[24] Although the sitter is not a standard bearer, exactly the same comportment is seen in a small oval portrait of a young man that has only recently been convincingly attributed to Hals (fig. 73),[25] the youthful arrogance in the subject's face captured with the kind of brushwork that is entirely characteristic of the artist. Like the ensign on the right in Hals's 1616 militia painting (fig. 68), the oval portrait is reminiscent of similar figures in contemporary genre pictures such as *Elegant Couples courting* by Willem Buytewech (fig. 71), or indeed in works by Hals's younger brother, Dirck (fig. 72).[26]

Hals employed the 'Renaissance elbow' in roughly one third of his male portraits, of which about two thirds are from the 1620s and 1630s. It occurs in all kinds of portraits, whether the subjects are bachelors in all their finery or married men in more sober attire (with or without pendant portraits of their wives), while outside this category the pose is frequently found in his group portraits. The most famous example is *The Laughing Cavalier* of 1624 (fig. 78).[27] We do not know the identity of the smiling (rather than laughing) man portrayed in this picture, but judging from his opulent clothing it seems reasonably certain that in 1624 he was still a bachelor. This is one of the most successful examples of how the arm-akimbo pose not only lends dynamism to a portrait but also generates a tremendous sense of depth, the elbow hiding beneath a luxuriously decorated sleeve entering the viewer's space. The effect is heightened by bringing the sitter very close to the picture plane. Much the same is seen in the 'excellent picture of a man in a

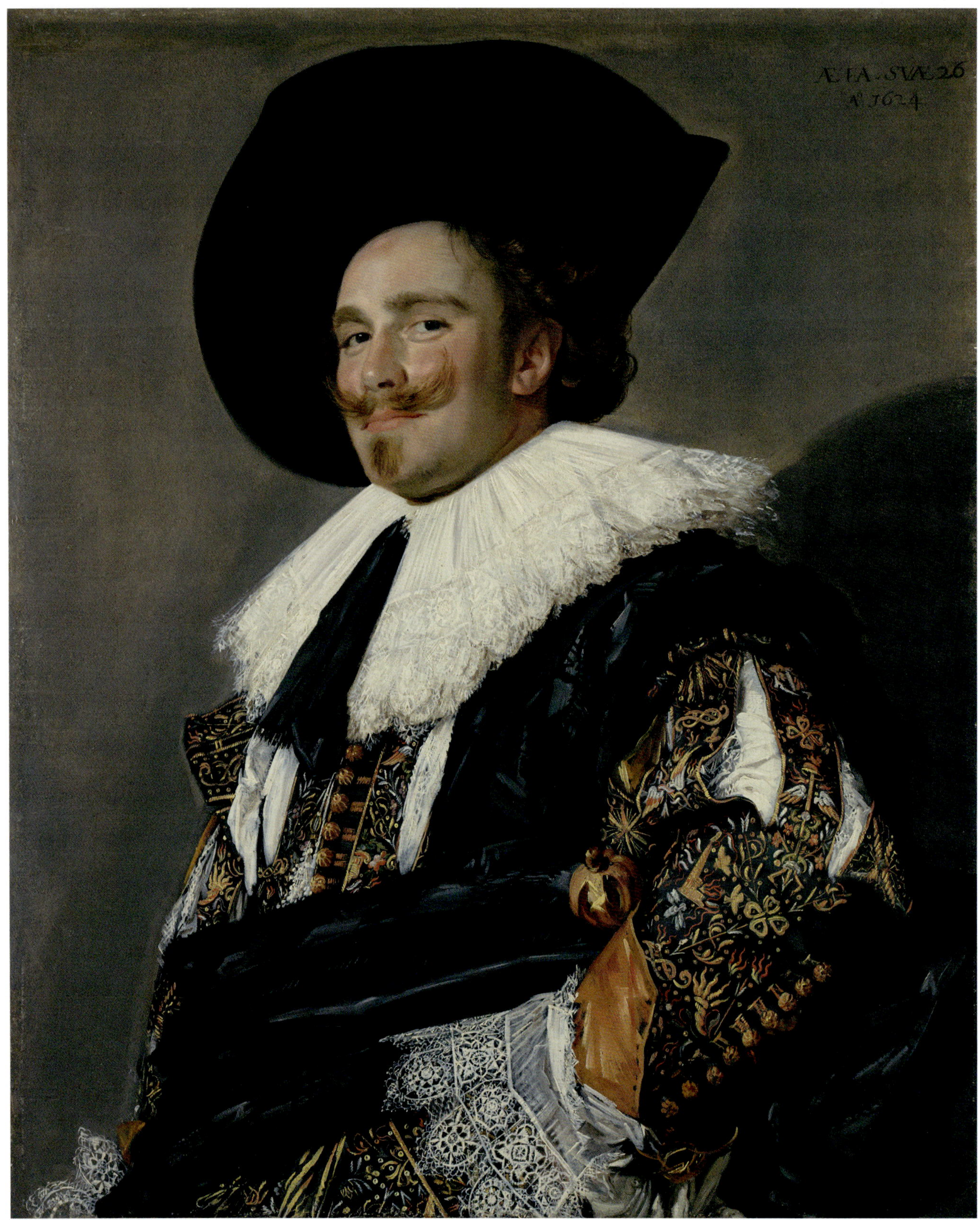

Fig. 78 *The Laughing Cavalier*, 1624
Oil on canvas, 83 × 67.3 cm
The Wallace Collection, London

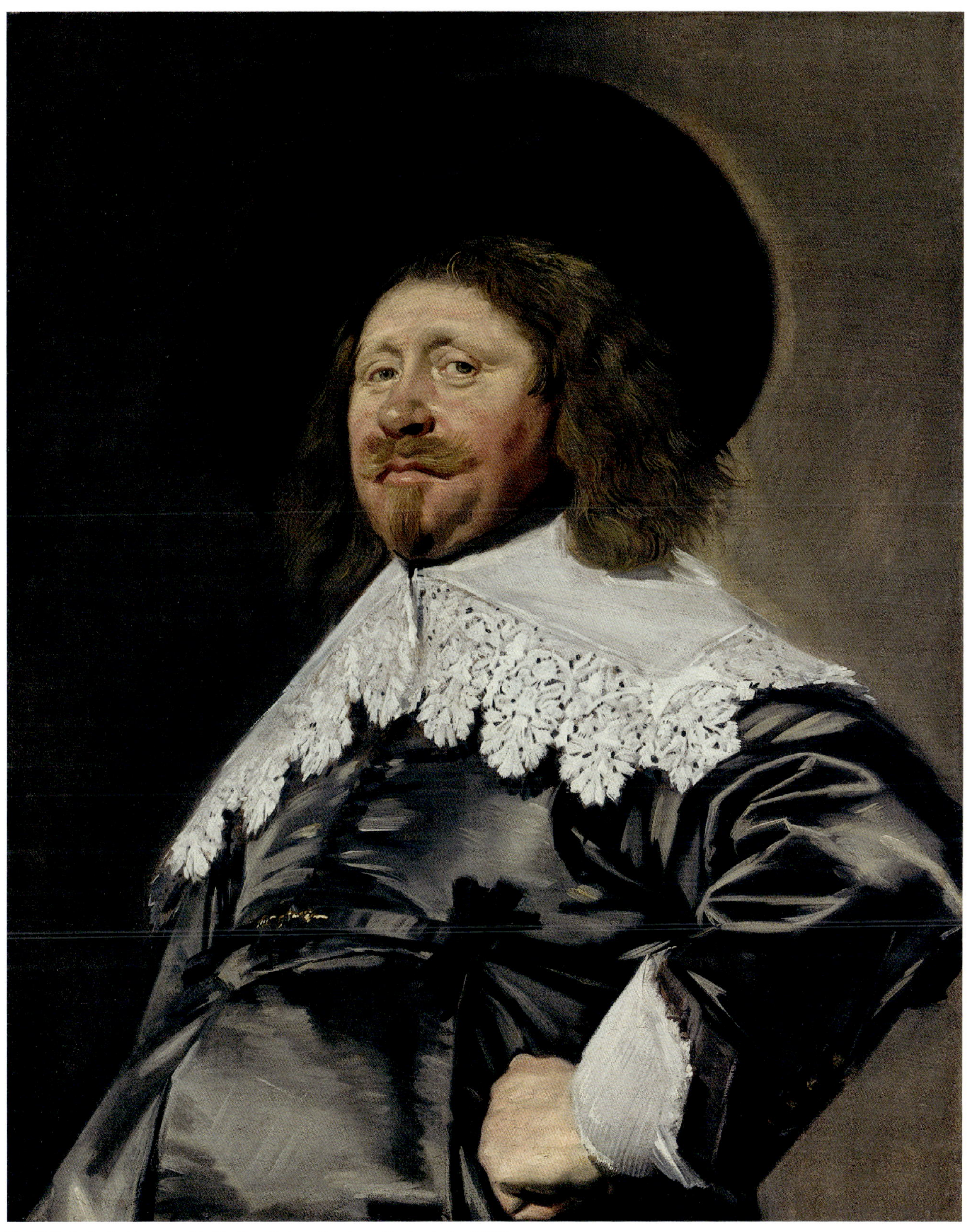

Fig. 79 *Portrait of a Man, possibly Nicolaes Pietersz Duyst van Voorhout*, about 1637
Oil on canvas, 80.6 × 66 cm
The Metropolitan Museum of Art, New York

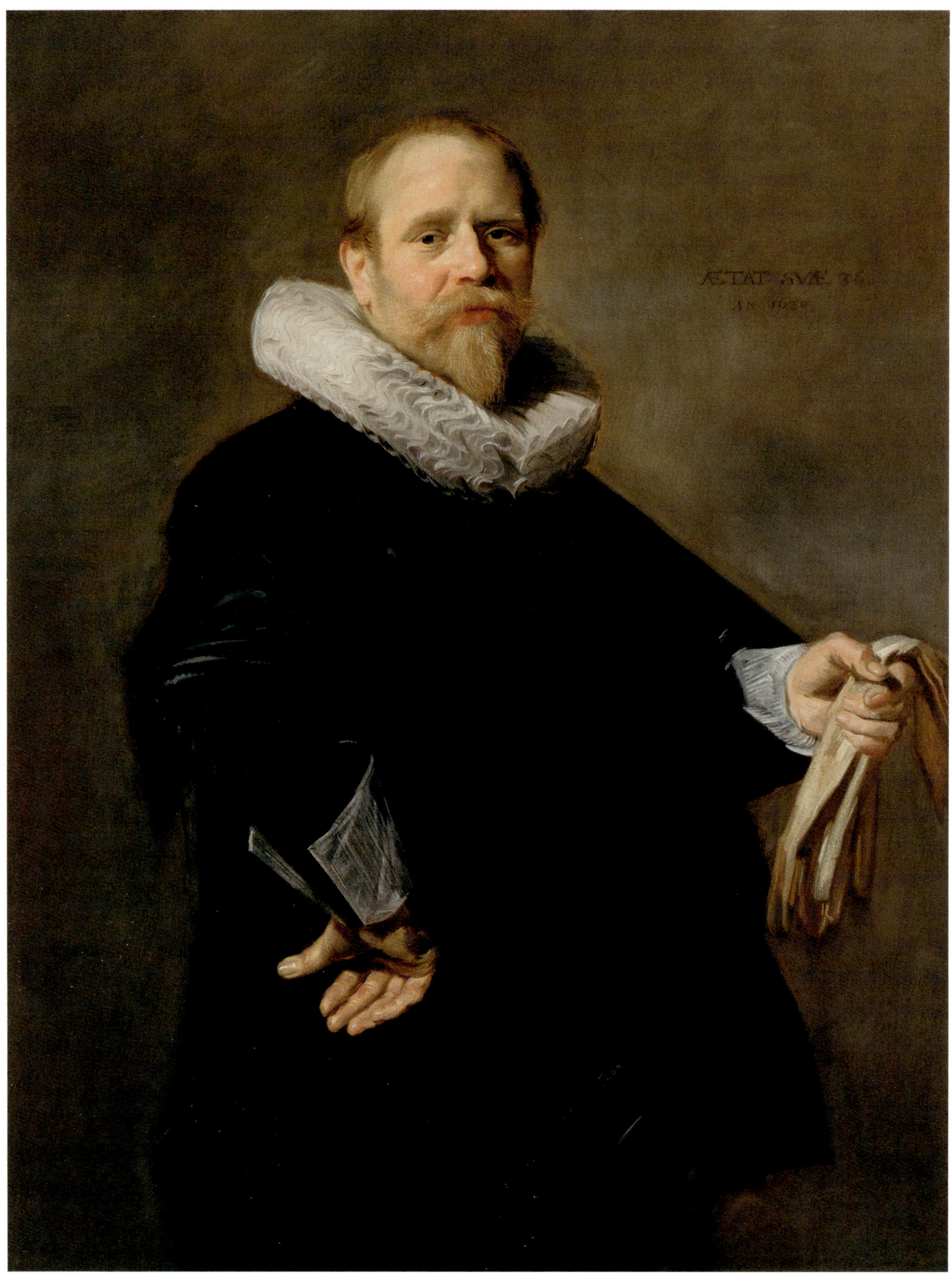

Fig. 80 *Portrait of a Man*, 1630
Oil on canvas, 116.7 × 90.2 cm
The Royal Collection / HM King Charles III

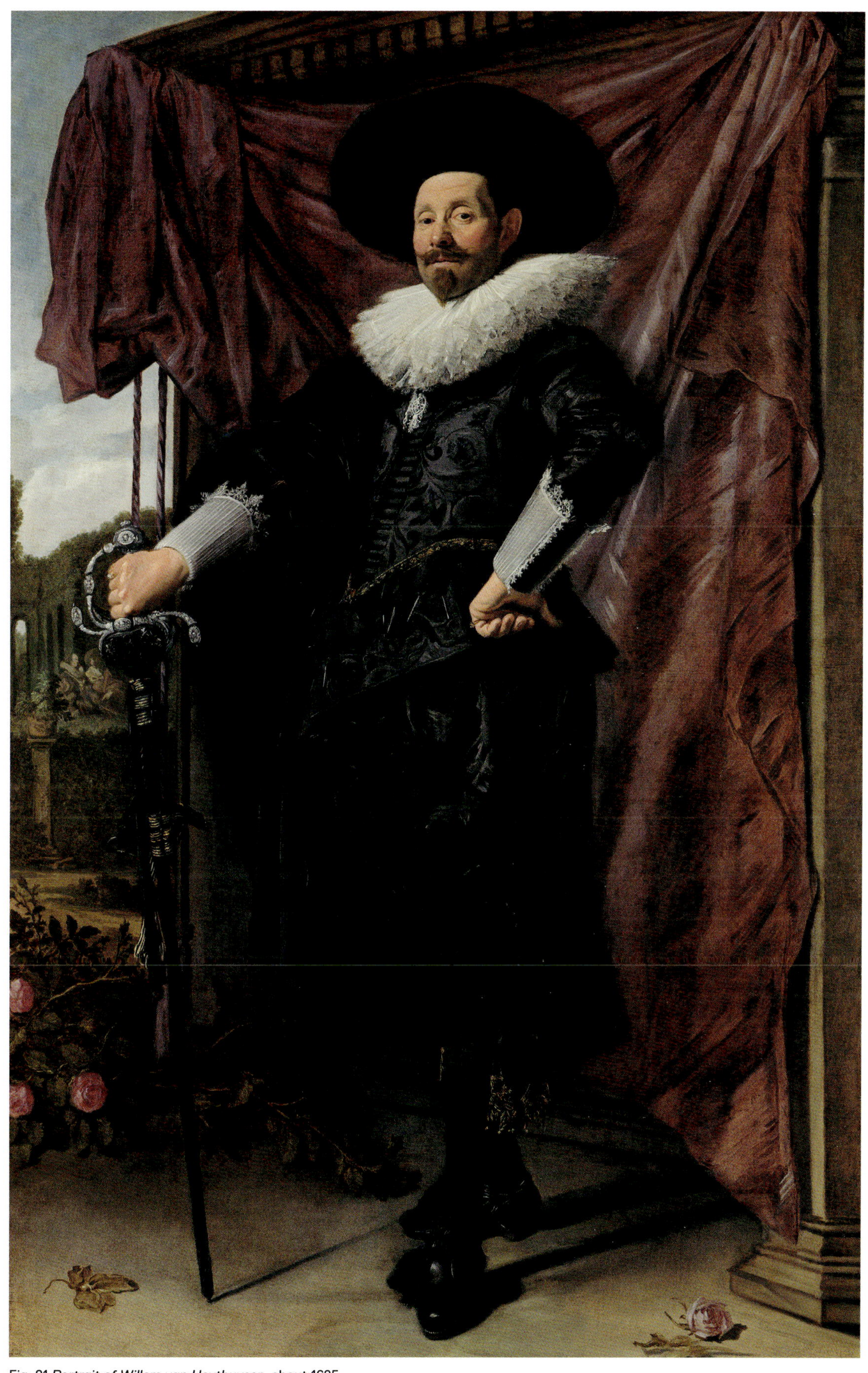

Fig. 81 *Portrait of Willem van Heythuysen*, about 1625
Oil on canvas, 204.5 × 134.5 cm
Bayerische Staatsgemäldesammlungen München – Alte Pinakothek

broad-brimmed hat, with his left hand on his hip, and his eyes and cheeks telling of many a sacrifice to Bacchus', as the nineteenth-century connoisseur Gustav Waagen in 1854 described a portrait now in New York (fig. 79) but at that time at Petworth House in Sussex.[28] Waagen was equally enamoured of the portrait of a man, 'left hand holding a glove, the right resting on his hip', that he saw at Buckingham Palace (fig. 80), describing it as 'unusually spirited and animated, even for Frank [*sic*] Hals'. He continued that in his opinion,

> the real value of this painter in the history of Dutch art has never been sufficiently appreciated. He was the first who introduced the broad manner of Rubens into Holland, where it was adopted and followed up with the greatest success by Rembrandt, who was born twenty years later.[29]

Waagen was certainly right to evoke Rubens in his assessment of Hals's achievements, but the picture above all demonstrates yet again how Hals's brush can turn a portrait into a palpable presence, and that the identity of the sitter is in no way crucial to our appreciation of a portrait of exceptional quality, in much the same way as we do not need to know the identity of *The Laughing Cavalier* to recognise its pre-eminence as a work of art.

We do know the identity of the supremely confident person in Hals's only known full-length portrait (fig. 81). The wealthy cloth merchant Willem van Heythuysen has his eyes firmly trained on the viewer, his arm-akimbo pose reinforced by his resolutely placing his sword on the ground in front of him with his outstretched right arm. His pose is a little unnerving, the imposing effect heightened by the fact that he is seen from a low viewpoint. It is curious that the sitter who had himself depicted life-size and in such a stately manner (the picture is some 2 metres high) had himself portrayed over a decade later in one of Hals's smallest and most casual portraits (fig. 50), less than 50 cm in height. The latter shows Van Heythuysen in a decidedly more playful mood, resting his right leg on his left knee while bending his hunting crop and perilously tilting his chair back. The riding gear leaves little doubt that Van Heythuysen was keen to express his social status here as well, but this is evidently a far more personal image. Indeed, we know that it was hanging in one of the intimate rooms of his Haarlem residence.[30] Its informality is akin to genre pictures of the period, the sitter's pose reminiscent of figure studies in oil on paper by Hals's brother Dirck.[31]

Although in Dutch portrait painting the arm-akimbo pose was almost exclusively a male preserve, in Hals's oeuvre there is one glorious exception of a woman adopting the stance (fig. 85). It has only recently been established that this portrait represents Cunera van Baersdorp and that it is a pendant of a similarly unusual portrait of a man (fig. 84) that depicts her husband, Michiel de Wael, a successful Haarlem merchant and owner of the city's De Son and Het Rode Hert brew-

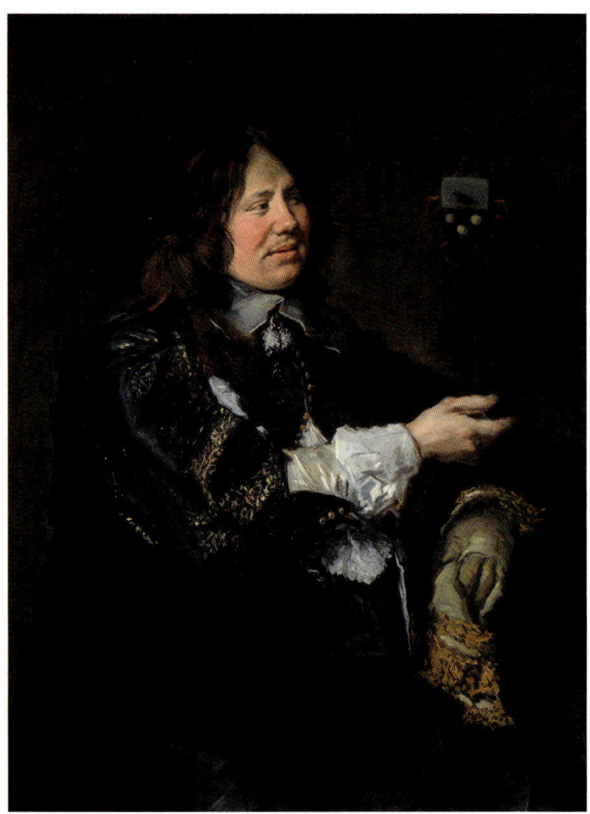

Fig. 82 *Portrait of Stephanus Geraerdts*, about 1650. Oil on canvas, 114.5 × 86.5 cm
Royal Museum of Fine Arts, Antwerp

eries.[32] It will not have been lost on contemporary audiences that such a powerful posture was unusual in a female portrait, and some may well have thought of it as unbecoming.[33] Hals's teacher Van Mander advised painters that decorum should be observed in the depiction of gesture and comportment, so that, for example, men act like men and women like women.[34] As we have seen, it is not the only piece of advice by his master that Hals did not necessarily follow.

The boldness of Cunera van Baersdorp's portrait is mirrored in that of her husband. It was customary in pendant portraits of married couples not only to have the man on the left and the woman on the right, but also to have them turning to one another (figs 7–10, 86–7). But Michiel de Wael, like his wife, has his left arm placed on his hip, and consequently his body turns away from her to take on a more frontal stance. For this reason one is inclined to 'read' the pendants from right to left, starting with Cunera van Baersdorp's commanding pose before turning our attention to her husband. This does not in any way feel inappropriate; on the contrary, despite their unconformity, there is a wonderful unity and continuity between the two pictures. Michiel de Wael's pose not only echoes that of his wife, he is also holding his glove in his right hand where she is holding a handkerchief in hers. Hals also achieved unity by contrasting their comportment: while her stance is firm, he is caught mid-flow

PORTRAITURE INTO ART

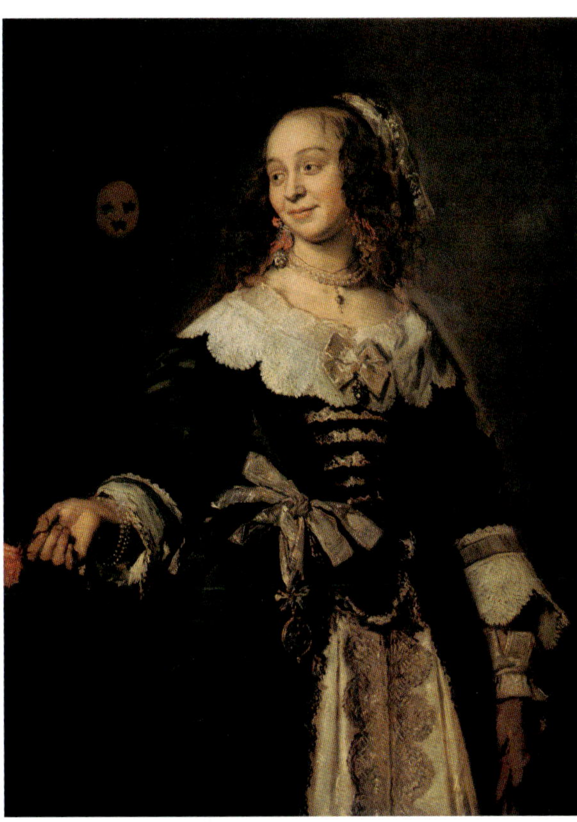

Fig. 83 *Portrait of Isabella Coymans*,
about 1650. Oil on canvas, 116 × 86 cm
Private collection

in a majestic movement across the canvas towards our left. And when we look at them together, it is Cunera van Baersdorp who takes the lead in the choreography played out across these two canvases. In these pendants we see Hals at his most inventive, surpassed only by his pendant portraits of Stephanus Geraerdts and Isabella Coymans of a quarter of a century later (figs 82–3), in which the roles played by husband and wife are similar. Isabella Coymans turns her body away from her husband but stretches out her right arm to offer him a rose, a gift that he is clearly anticipating. Here, too, we 'read' the pendants from right to left, the gestures towards each other across the divide creating a heart-warming connection of playful affection. Both sets of pendants are a class apart, even by Hals's standards.

We see the same Michiel de Wael at the centre of the *Banquet of the Officers of the St George Civic Guard* of around 1627 (fig. 69), arguably Hals's greatest militia piece (he appears once more, now aged, in a similarly central position in Hals's portrait of the same company painted in 1639, fig. 67). Compared to the 1616 militia painting (fig. 68), the dynamics in the 1627 picture have changed. As in the earlier painting, the colonel, Aernout Druyvesteyn, is seated at the head of the table at the far left, but instead of the officers following according to their rank from left to right, they are now largely arranged from near to far, with the captains in the foreground and

the lieutenants behind the table. We have also come a lot closer to the action, which is even more casual than in the earlier work. There are spirited encounters between the colonel and the ensign (Boudewijn van Offenberg) standing in front of him, and between a seated lieutenant (Jacob Pietersz Olycan) who looks up to the ensign (Dirck Dicx) standing next to him. Brilliantly observed details include a lieutenant in the background (Frederick Coning) squeezing a lemon over a plate of oysters, and Michiel de Wael in the foreground turning his glass upside down. There is animation and movement throughout the composition, with even the servant who has just come in through the door on the right looking as if he is in motion. The scene is bookended by two men with one arm akimbo: on the far left Cornelis Boudewijnsz raises his glass with his other hand, while on the far right ensign Jacob Cornelisz Schout firmly holds on to his standard with his. The banquet is a celebration of colour, too, with accents in orange, white, light blue and red in the sashes and standards (the first three colours representing the three companies), set against the dark and ochre tones of the men's costumes. All this is unusually freely brushed, even for Hals.

That Hals's extraordinary gift as a painter of group portraits was noted elsewhere is clear from the fact that in 1633 the officers of a company of the Amsterdam Crossbow Civic Guard took the unusual step of commissioning a painter from Haarlem for their group portrait, now best known as *'The Meagre Company'* (fig. 70). They may well have regretted their decision not to commission a local artist – as was the tradition – once it became clear what kind of logistical problems it entailed. Hals started the painting but eventually could not come to an agreement with his patrons as to how he would complete it.[35] Four years later, Pieter Codde was given the unenviable task of finishing the painting. The result is a curious hybrid, with Hals responsible for most of the left half of the figures, although technical evidence shows that his underdrawing in oil means that he was responsible for the overall composition. He had only begun but not finished six or seven heads and some of the clothing when he abandoned the work. They are all on the left and include the seated captain Reynier Reael and lieutenant Cornelis Michielsz Blaeuw – the only ones whose identity we know for certain – as well as the standing figures around them. Comparing them to the other figures to the right of this group is an object lesson in how to distinguish between the hand of the master and an imitator. One cannot fault Codde's attempt to adapt his painting technique to that of Hals to unify the handling in the work, but he also inadvertently illustrates how Van Mander had good reason to warn artists against merely imitating a loose manner (see above); there is a great deal of difference, especially in the treatment of the faces and hands, which in Hals's section looks assured but in Codde's feels derivative and contrived. The ensign at the far left, his 'Renaissance elbow' as prominent as can be, must be one of the most glorious

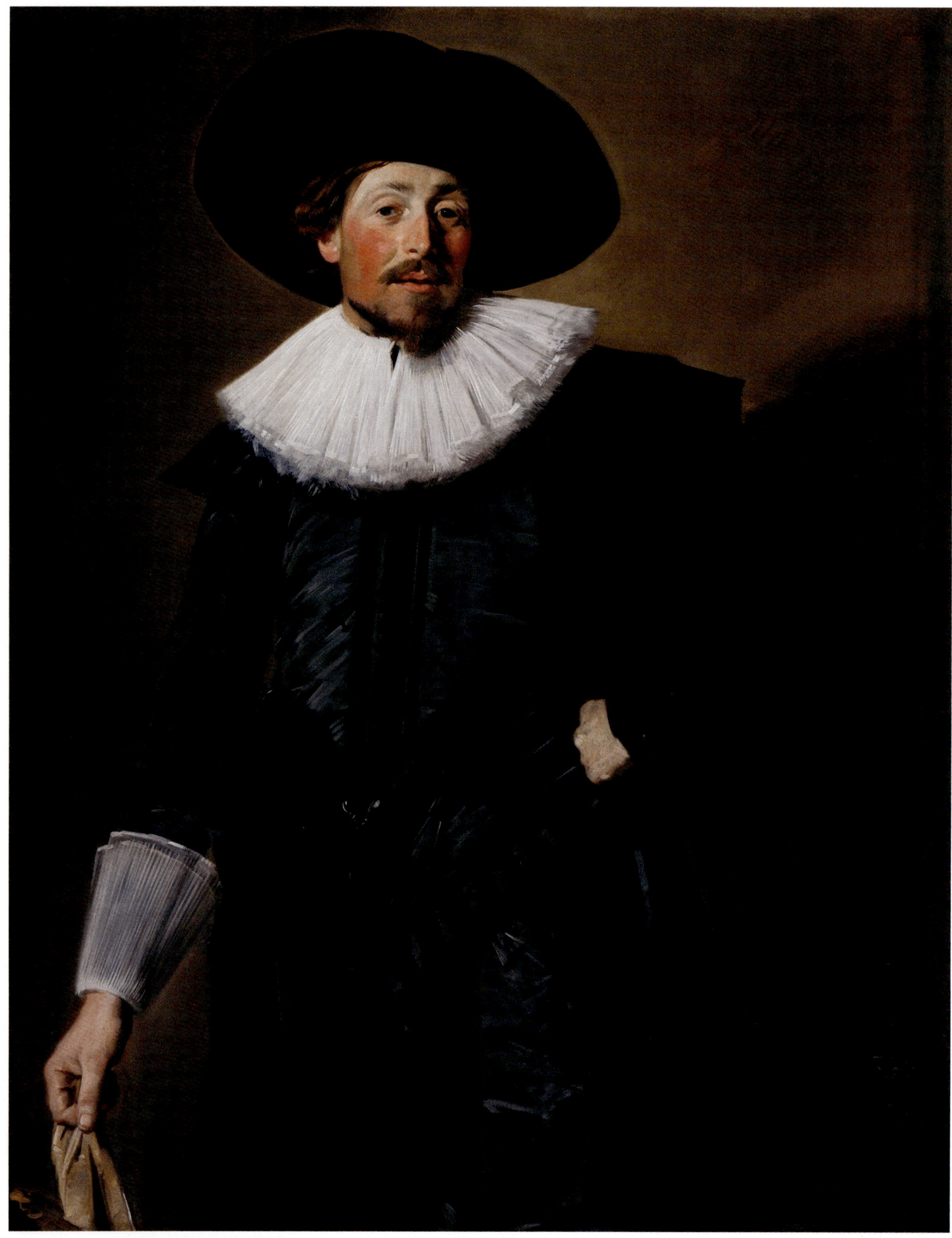

Fig. 84 *Portrait of Michiel de Wael*, about 1625
Oil on canvas, 118.8 × 95.3 cm
Taft Museum of Art, Cincinnati, Ohio

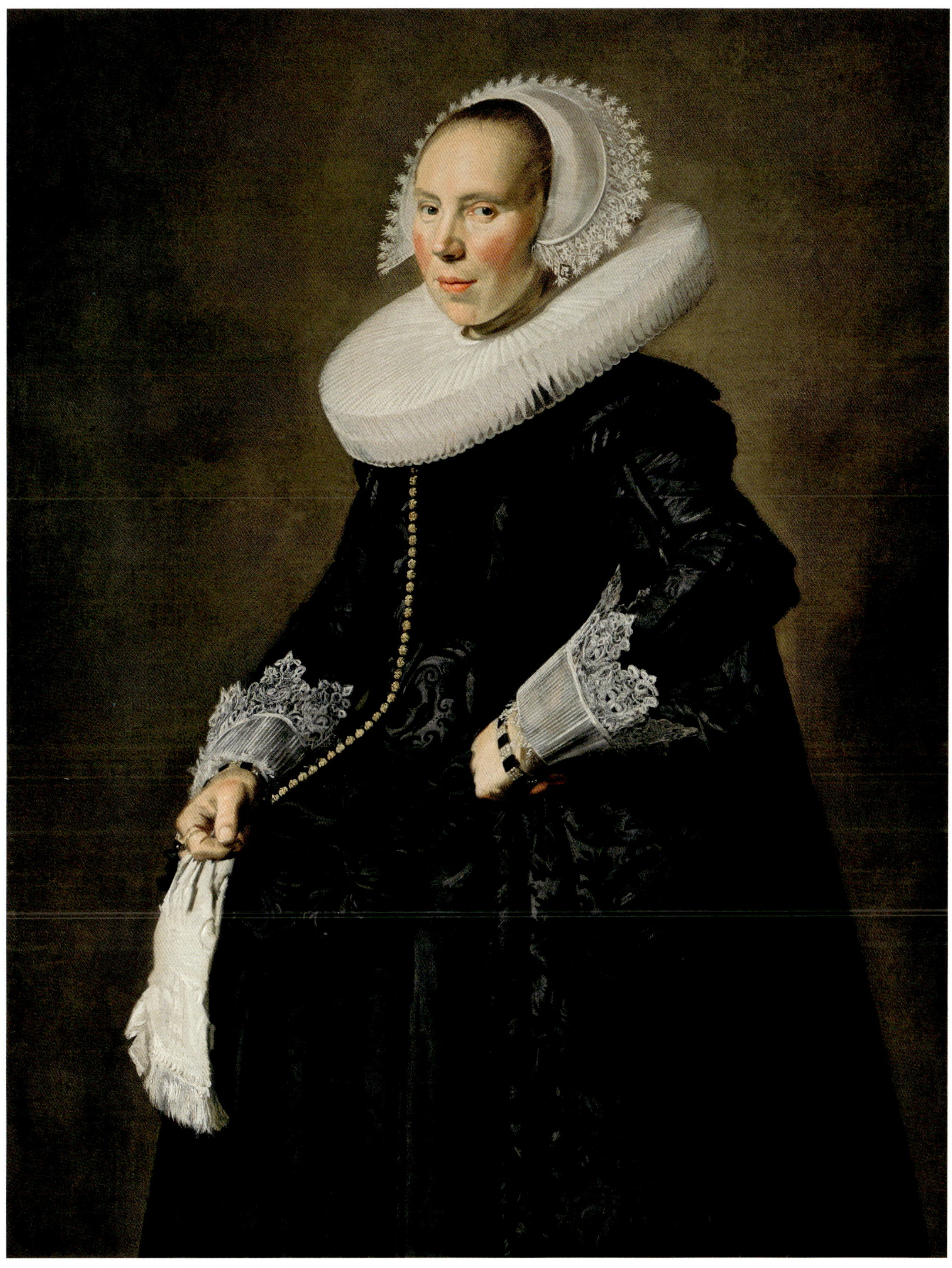

Fig. 85 *Portrait of Cunera van Baersdorp*, about 1625
Oil on canvas, 123.8 × 95.3 cm
Susan and Matthew Weatherbie Collection

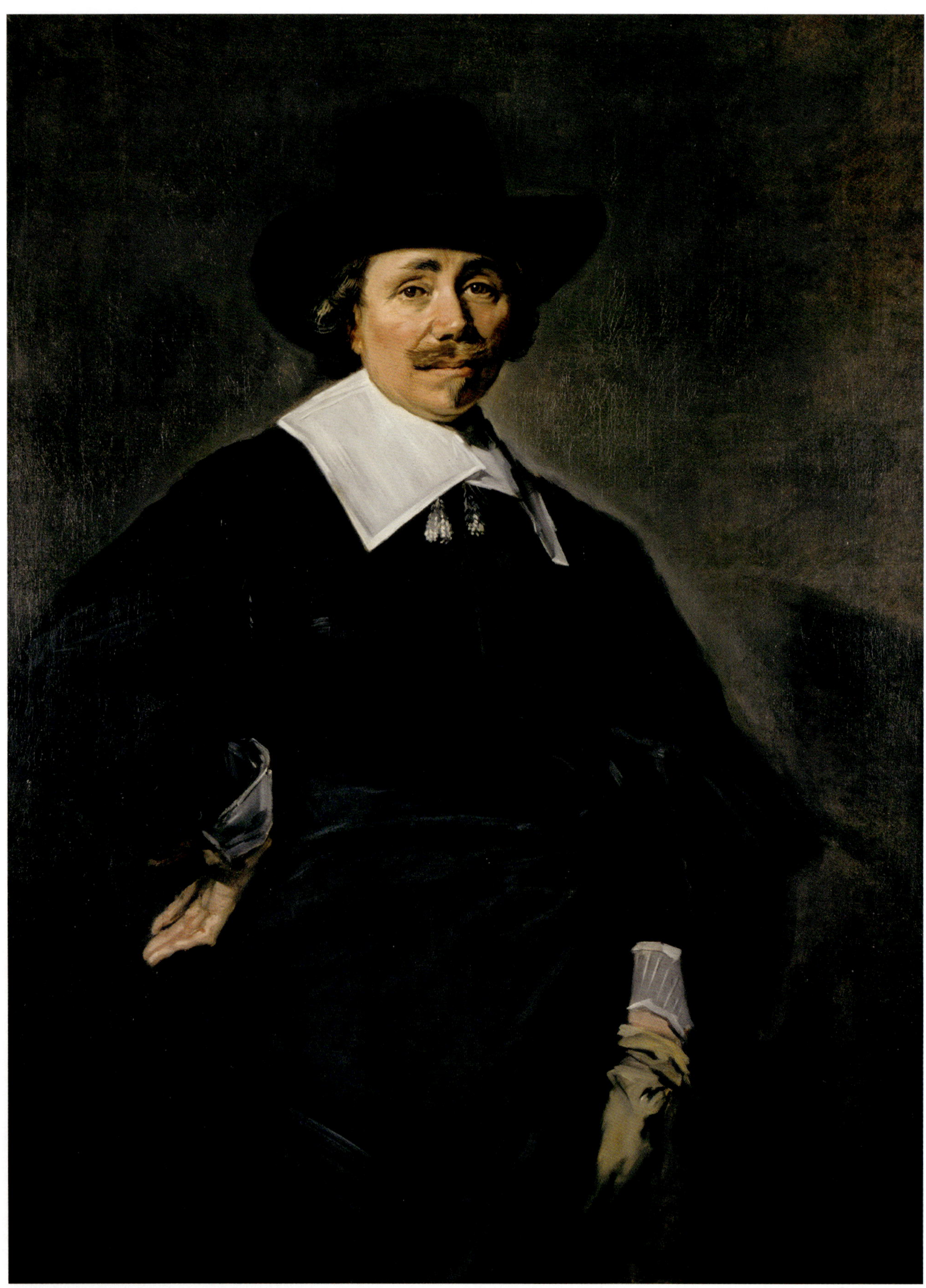

Fig. 86 *Portrait of François Wouters*, about 1645
Oil on canvas, 115 × 86.1 cm
National Galleries of Scotland

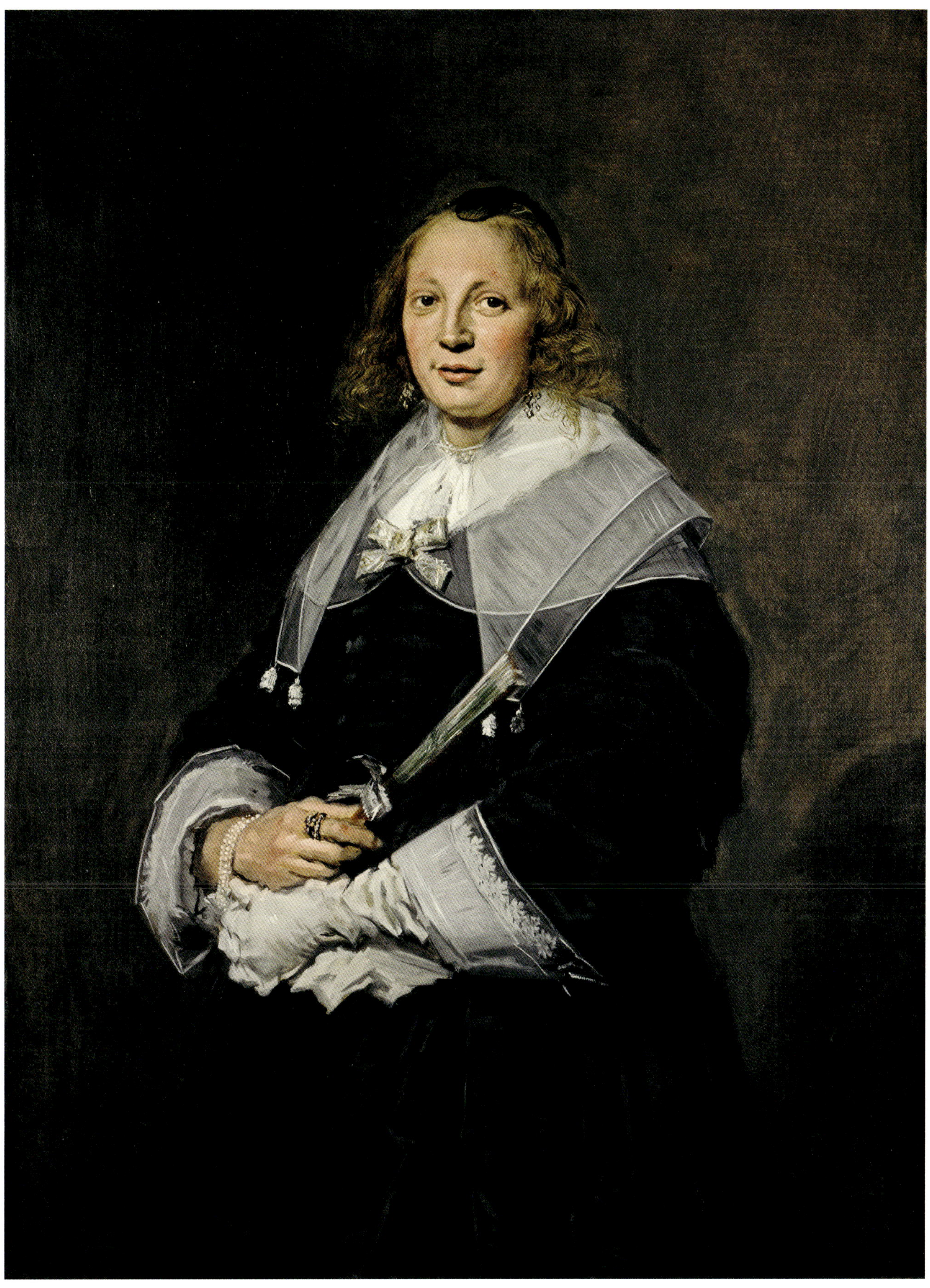

Fig. 87 *Portrait of Susanna Baillij*, about 1645
Oil on canvas, 115 × 85.8 cm
National Galleries of Scotland

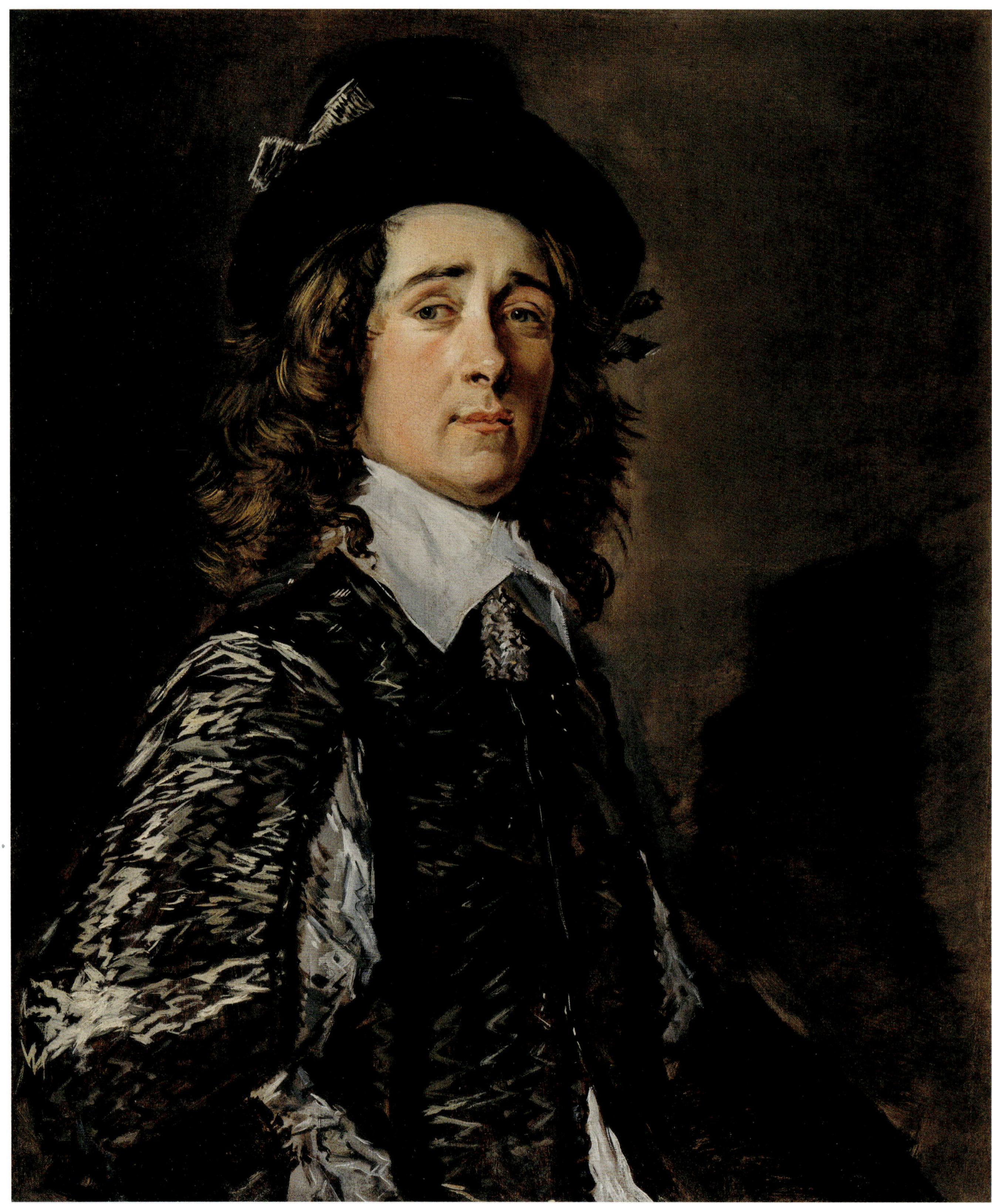

Fig. 88 *Portrait of Jasper Schade*, 1645
Oil on canvas, 80 × 67.5 cm
National Gallery Prague

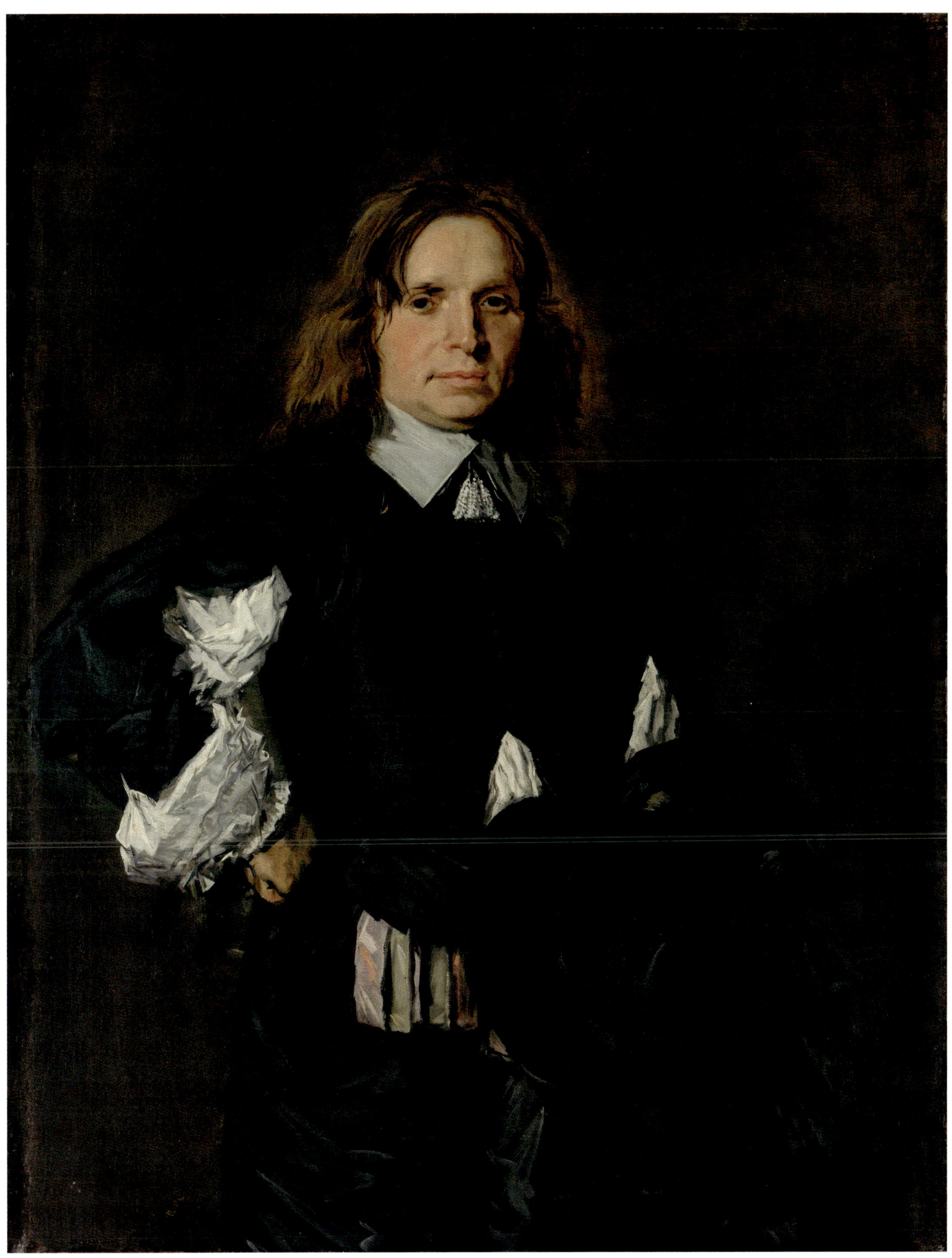

Fig. 89 *Portrait of a Man*, about 1650
Oil on canvas, 110.5 × 86.4 cm
The Metropolitan Museum of Art, New York

figures Hals ever painted. The entire painting, but especially this figure, famously stopped Vincent van Gogh in his tracks when he first saw it in 1885, writing to his brother Theo that on encountering the work he was 'literally rooted to the spot', adding on the subject of the ensign that he had 'seldom seen a more divinely beautiful figure'.[36] The painting inspired some of the most lyrical passages in Van Gogh's letters.[37]

The finest rendition of the arm-akimbo pose must be Hals's portrait of Jasper Schade of the mid-1640s (fig. 88), in which we are confronted with the rather condescending gaze and extravagant outfit of a young man who was overly concerned with looking stylish and fashionable. It is not surprising to learn from contemporary correspondence between his uncle Louis van Kinschot and his cousin Kaspar van Kinschot that Jasper had a reputation for spending excessive amounts on his clothes.[38] The sleeve of Schade's spectacular taffeta jacket thrusts into our space and provided Hals with a chance to dazzle the viewer with his virtuoso brushwork. Throughout the jacket, but especially in the sleeve, we can delight in the artist's brush dancing over the surface of the picture. Tracing every rapid stroke with our eyes takes almost as long as it took Hals to paint them. How his brushwork evolved over time is immediately apparent when we compare Schade's sleeve with the equally assured but still rather more precise handling of the sleeve of *The Laughing Cavalier*, painted some two decades earlier.

Far more stately examples of the pose include the portraits of Lucas de Clercq (fig. 7), Tieleman Roosterman (fig. 9) and François Wouters (fig. 86) of the 1630s and 1640s. The pose becomes almost completely frontal in Hals's magisterial *Portrait of a Man* of about 1650 (fig. 89). Here, once again, he exploited the sitter's 'Renaissance elbow' to impress the viewer with his ever more daring flickering brushwork in the whites of the man's frilly cuff, or indeed in the small accents of lilac, grey-green and rose in the ribbons at his waist, audacious details in an image largely consisting of whites and blacks.

Few artists can do nonchalance as well as Hals. The relaxed poses of the couple in the Rijksmuseum double portrait (fig. 61) suggest that they are completely at ease with each other. We hardly notice that he has his arm akimbo because our attention is drawn to the unselfconscious manner in which his wife, seated at the centre of the composition, rests her hand on it. There is probably no more captivating image of love and affection in seventeenth-century Dutch painting. Although this central message is alluded to in various details in the composition that symbolise love and fidelity in marriage,[39] it finds its most eloquent expression in the couple's relaxed attitude. There is no conclusive proof, but it seems likely that the double portrait represents the wealthy grain merchant Isaac Abrahamsz Massa and his wife, Beatrix van der Laen, and that it was painted on the occasion of their marriage in 1622. In 1623 Isaac Massa was a witness at the baptism of Hals's daughter Ariaentje, which

suggests that he and Hals knew one another well.[40] It would certainly make sense for a friend of the artist to have encouraged him to create such an exceptionally informal portrait.

Their friendship would also explain the informal pose in a securely identified portrait of Isaac Massa (fig. 93), which shows him turning in a chair, his arm resting on its back. We all know the pose – most of us will have adopted it at some point in our lives – but Hals appears to be the first artist ever to employ it in a portrait.[41] This is yet another example of how, much more than any of his peers, Hals used a person's comportment as much as their facial resemblance to create a successful portrait.

MEANINGFUL ATTRIBUTES

While in the Toronto portrait (fig. 93) Massa holds a sprig of holly, which may be understood as an emblem of friendship,[42] Pieter Tjarck has a pink rose as an unambiguous symbol of love in the pendants depicting him and Marie Larp (figs 91–2), whom he married in 1634. Also seated on a chair, Tjarck adopts the same pose as Massa, but in a more composed manner, as befits a portrait that must have been painted to mark his marriage. He nevertheless looks positively relaxed compared with his wife, who sits as upright as can be, rigidly holding her hand to her chest. We cannot be sure that her gesture reciprocates his offering by indicating that love resides in the heart, but it certainly draws attention to her faultless posture. [43]

Such meaningful details or attributes in Hals's portraits are relatively rare. We have already seen how the skull in his early portrait of a man (fig. 58) functions as a symbol of vanitas. Elsewhere in this book the question is discussed of how a specific meaning may be attached to the red herring held by Pieter Cornelisz van der Mersch (fig. 151).[44] There is the rather bizarre attribute of a jawbone in Hals's portrayal of Verdonck (fig. 90), as he is identified in a contemporary print after it by Jan van de Velde. It has been convincingly argued that this jawbone alludes to how, in an ongoing dispute between factions of the Mennonite community, Verdonck (probably a Pieter Verdonck from Haarlem) crushed his enemies – like the biblical figure of Samson with his jawbone of a donkey – albeit figuratively rather than literally, with the power of his words.[45]

In the Toronto portrait of Isaac Massa (fig. 93) we see in the background a window offering a view of a landscape with conifers. This almost certainly alludes to Massa's activities in Russia and the Baltic.[46] He was a successful grain merchant who repeatedly travelled on business to Moscow, where from 1614 he also performed diplomatic services for the Dutch States General; he had similarly good contacts in Sweden, where in 1625 King Gustavus Adolphus granted him a patent of nobility.[47] We also know, however, that other Dutch merchants with business dealings in Russia were quick to object to Massa's diplomatic and business activities in Moscow,

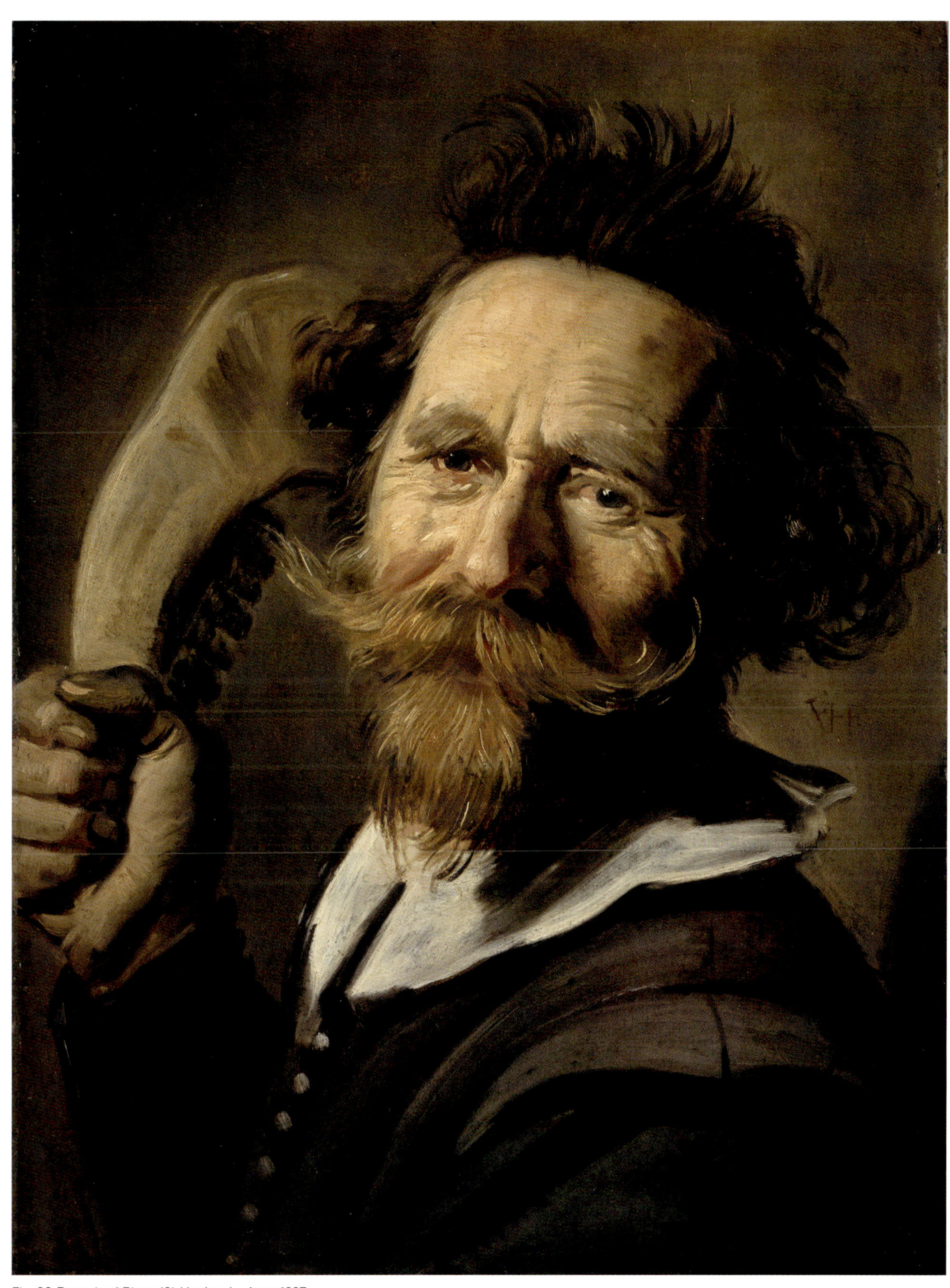

Fig. 90 *Portrait of Pieter(?) Verdonck*, about 1627
Oil on wood, 46.7 × 35.5 cm
National Galleries of Scotland

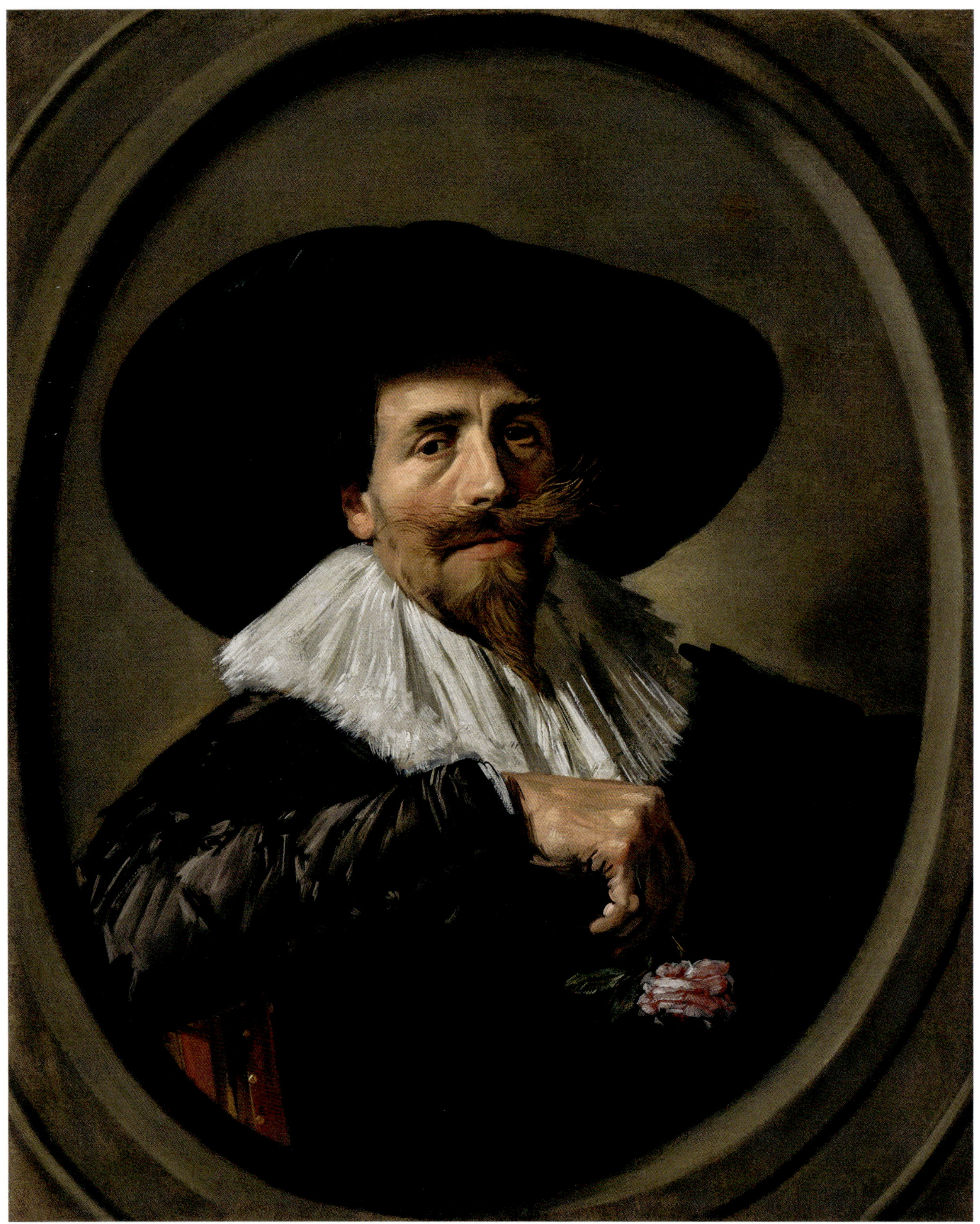

Fig. 91 *Portrait of Pieter Dircksz Tjarck*, about 1635
Oil on canvas, 85.3 × 69.9 cm
Los Angeles County Museum of Art

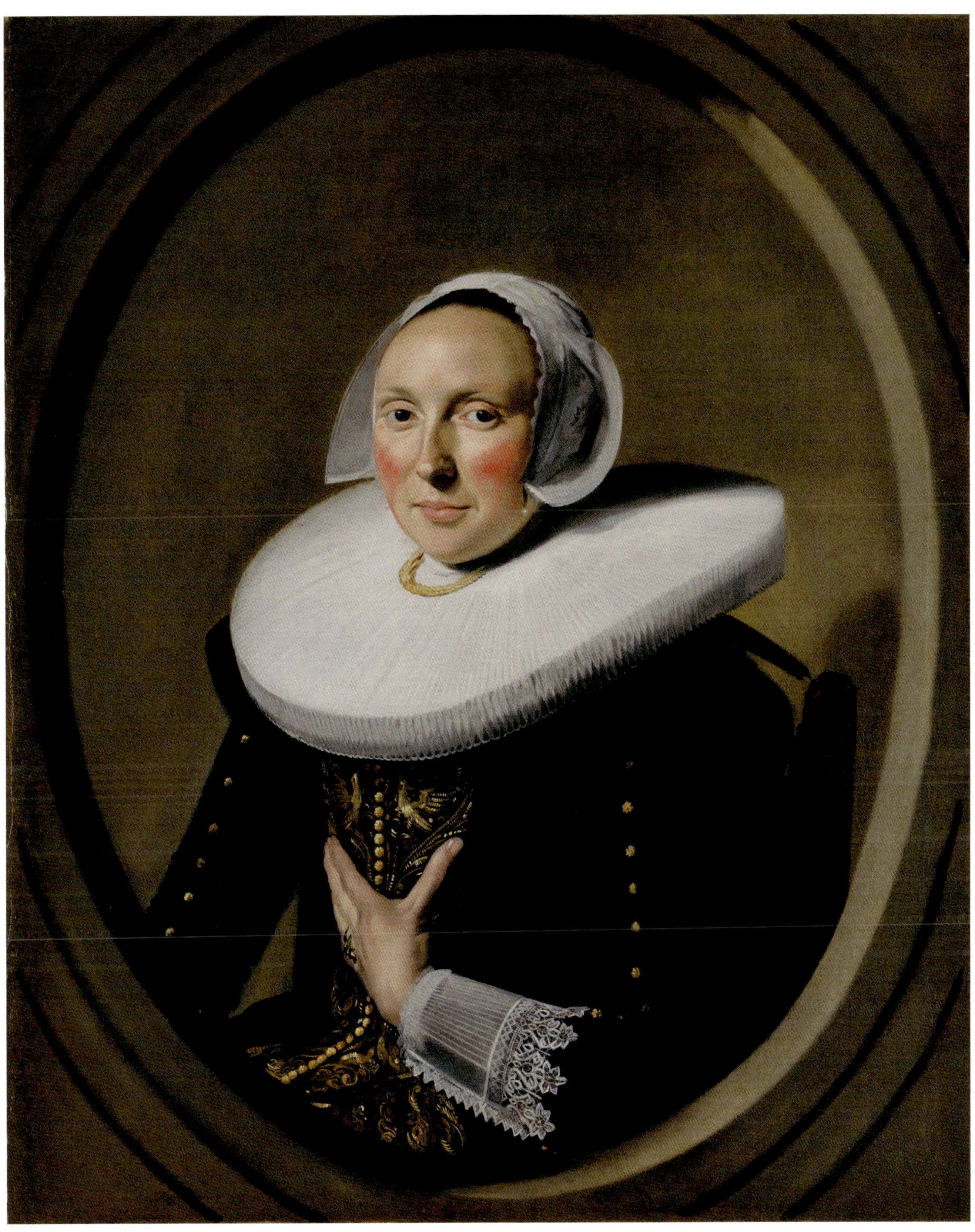

Fig. 92 *Portrait of Marie Larp*, about 1635
Oil on canvas, 83.4 × 68.1 cm
The National Gallery, London

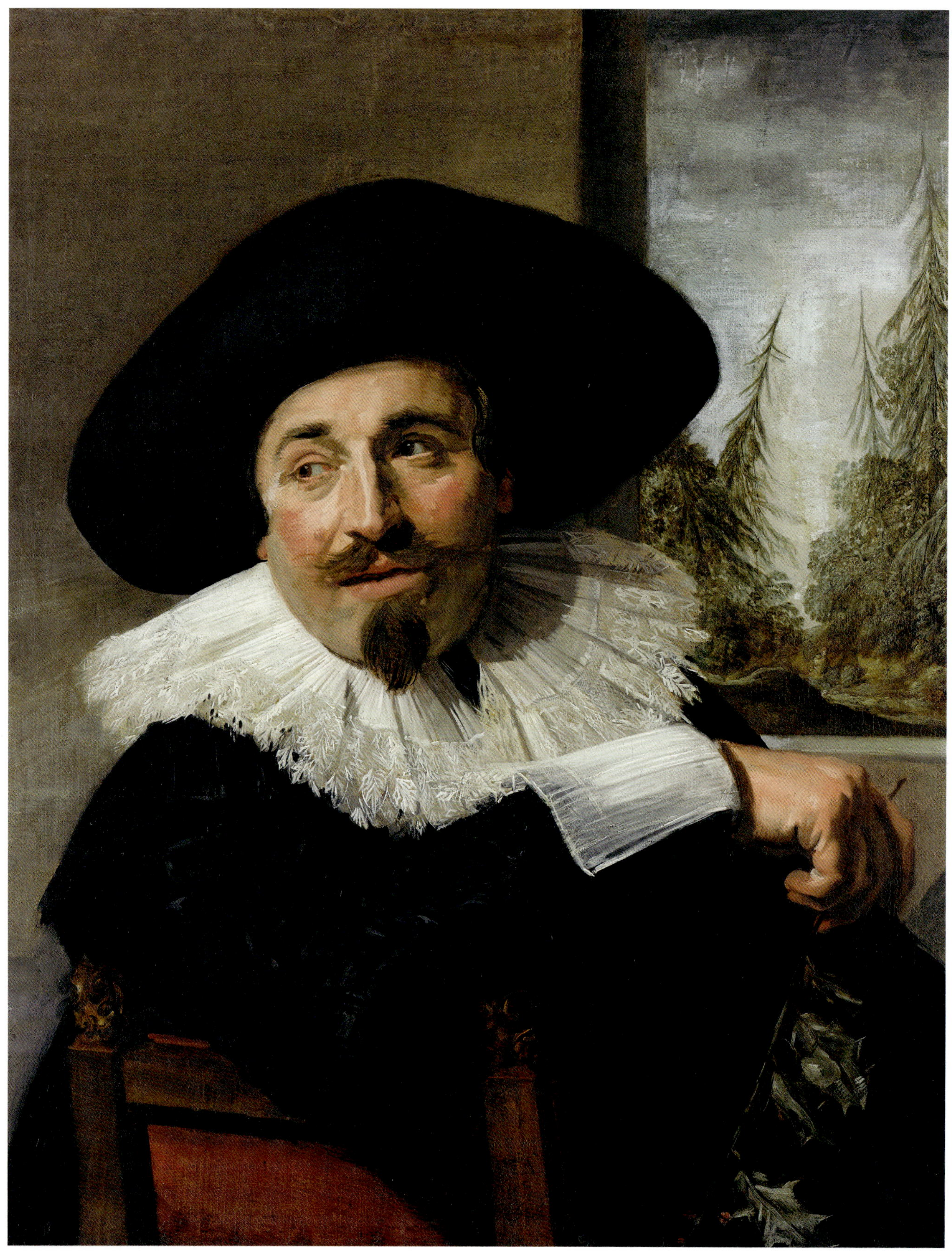

Fig. 93 *Portrait of Isaac Abrahamsz Massa*, 1626
Oil on canvas, 79.7 × 65.1 cm
Collection Art Gallery of Ontario, Toronto

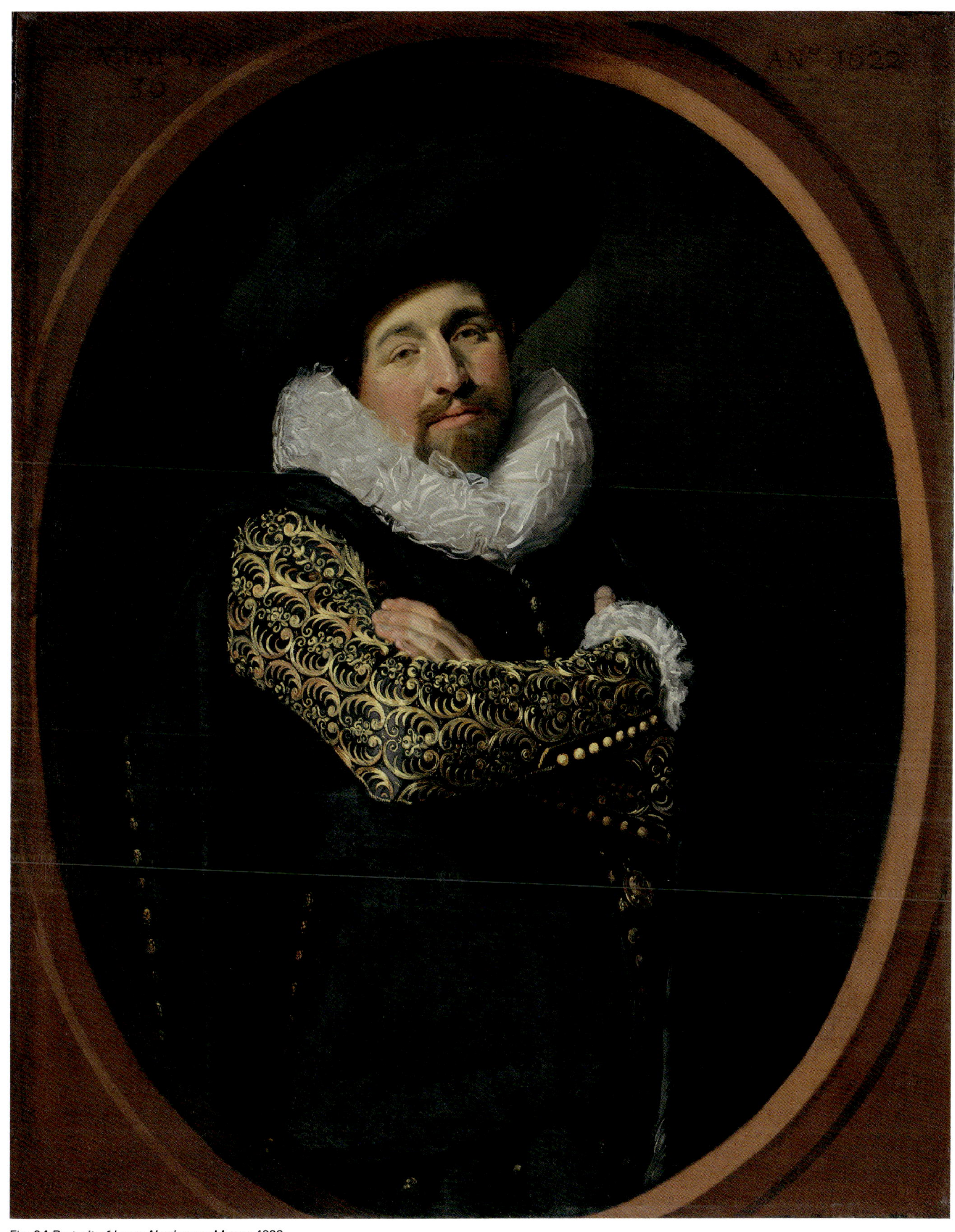

Fig. 94 *Portrait of Isaac Abrahamsz Massa*, 1622
Oil on canvas mounted on wood, 107 × 85 cm
The Devonshire Collections, Chatsworth

which, they claimed, were detrimental to their own interests – and even disingenuous.[48] There is an oblique reference to Massa's awareness of his detractors in the caption accompanying the print that was made after Hals's small portrait of Massa painted about 1635 (figs 112, 133). In addition to championing Massa's diplomatic and trading accomplishments, the caption mentions the word *Nijt* (Envy) no fewer than three times. Massa clearly felt 'Pursued by hatred and envy', as the opening line of the caption puts it, but he had

> obtained honour from Emperor, King and Lord and sought their favour, while fulfilling the commissions entrusted to him by the States. When envy brought accusations upon him, he continued on his way, trusting in God, and obtained greater honours from the commander of the Goths, while laughing at envy. Promoted to the nobility, and having become rich, he now calmly awaits his eternal bliss.[49]

It has been suggested, based on facial resemblance, that the sitter in Hals's extraordinary portrait of a man with his arms folded across his chest (fig. 94) also shows Isaac Massa.[50] The pose is unique in Hals's oeuvre. It has been observed that it is difficult to say whether it signifies 'defiance, insolent arrogance, impatience, sloth or incredulity'.[51] Interestingly, it has recently proved possible through technical examination – carried out during recent conservation treatment of the picture at the National Gallery[52] – to establish that the first option of defiance must be the correct one. Details found hiding beneath later overpaint covering the background of the portrait prove beyond doubt that we are indeed looking at a portrait of Isaac Massa, and that this portrait can be seen as the visual equivalent of the caption to the print quoted above.

The infrared reflectogram of the work (fig. 95) reveals that there were originally two figures looming from behind the sitter's left shoulder: one clearly a skull together with part of the associated skeleton and the other some kind of monstrous creature. Over Massa's other shoulder we see the more conventional detail of a coat of arms, but also a scroll sloping down from his right shoulder with what seems to be lettering on it, although the details of both these features are difficult to see. Further technical examination suggested that all this belongs to the original composition.[53] The monstrous creature consists of a head that appears to have snakes for hair. As can be seen in fig. 97, this figure must have had reddish eyes and was holding something red in front of its mouth. There can be little doubt that it is in fact a personification of Envy, who invariably has snakes for hair and, crucially, tends to hold a heart in front of her mouth, as we can see in an engraving of 1593 by Jacob Matham after a design by Hendrick Goltzius (fig. 98). This print would have been readily available in Hals's time, especially in Haarlem, the city where both Matham and Goltzius were active, and it may well have been this very image that

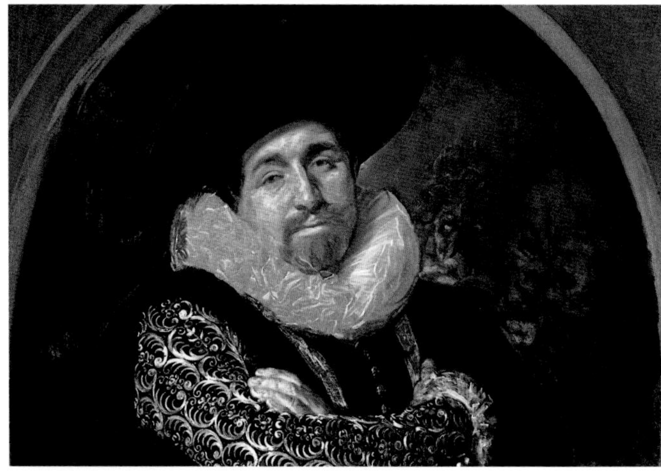

Fig. 95 Detail of infrared reflectogram of fig. 94

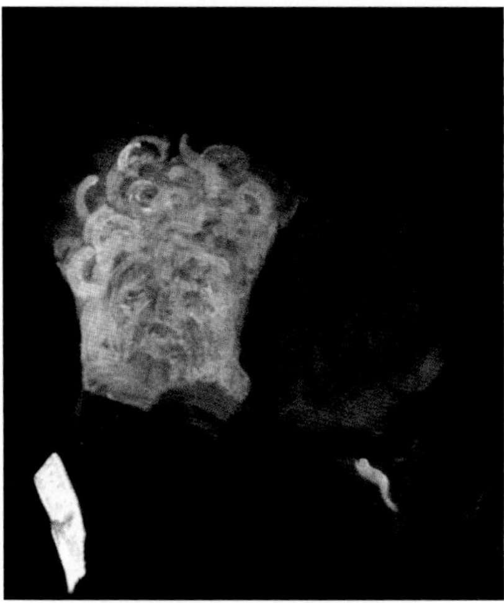

Fig. 96 Detail of copper X-ray fluorescence (XRF) map (Cu-KA) of fig. 94

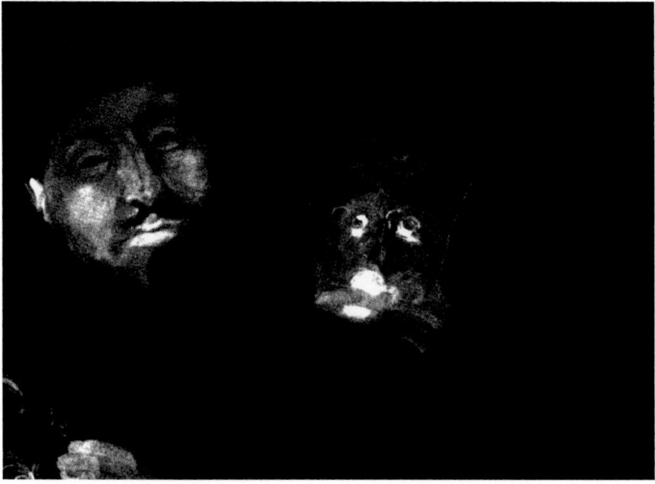

Fig. 97 Detail of mercury X-ray fluorescence (XRF) map (Hg-LA) of fig. 94

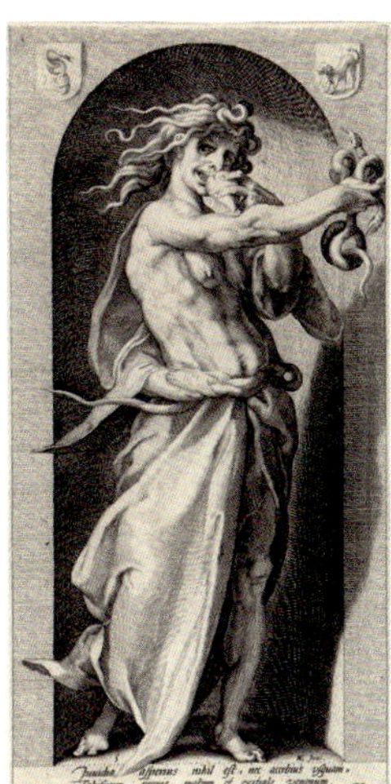

Fig. 98 Jacob Matham after Hendrick Goltzius, *Envy*, 1593
Engraving, 32.2 × 16.7 cm
Rijksmuseum, Amsterdam

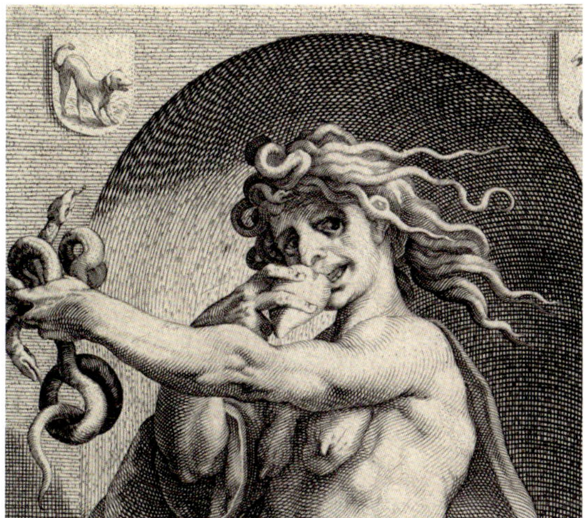

Fig. 99 *Envy* (reversed, detail of fig. 98), 1593

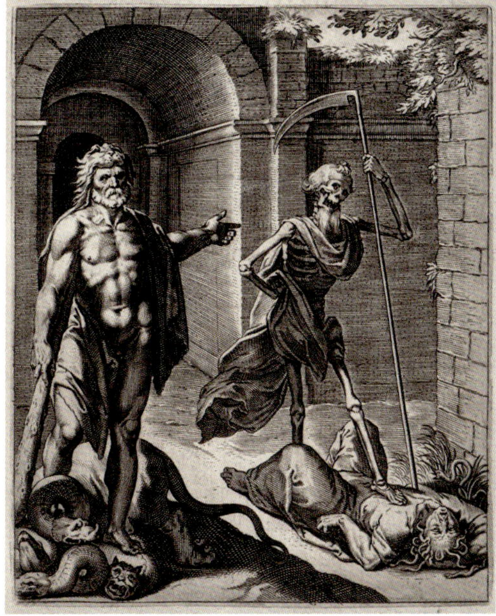

Fig. 100 Otto van Veen (Vaenius), *Q. Horatii Flacci Emblemata*, Antwerp 1612 (first edition 1607), p. 172

Hals used as inspiration for his depiction of the personification: when reversed, the resemblance is uncanny, including the way Envy holds the heart to her mouth and the wavy snake hair extends to the right, appearing from behind the skull (figs 96, 99).

But why is Envy accompanied by a personification of Death? The answer may be found in a well-known early seventeenth-century emblem book by Otto van Veen (Vaenius), which contains an image of Envy being trampled by Death (fig. 100). This is accompanied by the Latin motto 'Post Mortem Cessat Invidia' (after death, envy ceases). The image is accompanied by an explanation that reads:

> Hercules has conquered many large monsters in his day / But only Death has ever managed to tame the dark force of Envy. For as long as one lives / she will devour a good reputation with her sharp teeth: Only reputations of the dead are set free / They will no longer be disturbed by her.

When seen in relation to Massa's biography, all these details fit the bill. Clearly, he was aware of his detractors and seems to have decided that his feeling of being 'Pursued by hatred and envy' should find expression in his portrait by Hals. We can therefore also make sense of his unusual pose, which is evidently one of defiance in the face of those he perceived as his enemies. The additional message that Massa appears to have been keen to include is that in the long run death will bring every form of envy to an end. It is a peculiar message to convey in a painted portrait, which as a consequence will have looked not only cluttered but also fairly lugubrious. One cannot entirely blame those who, probably not long after Massa's death in 1643, decided to have such distracting details painted out, leaving us with just his bold cross-armed pose.[54]

Massa will have specifically requested his portrait to be accompanied by such meaningful details. Such a rather learned slant chimes with what we know about him, an educated man involved in geography and cartography and who had immersed himself in Russian history, writing several treatises on Russia that appeared in both Dutch and Latin. His two life-size portraits demonstrate that he was keen to include in them allusions to his personal circumstances. That Massa clearly had a penchant for symbolism adds yet more weight to the idea that the marriage portrait in the Rijksmuseum (fig. 61), with its flora alluding to love and fidelity, does indeed show Isaac Massa and his wife.

Hals used the pose he introduced in his Toronto portrait of Massa (fig. 93) throughout his career, most famously in a portrait best known by its German nickname, 'Schlapphut' (slouch, floppy hat), a late work in which the artist's broad painting technique has entered its most audacious phase (fig. 101). As in Massa's portrait, the anonymous man in the much later work sits by an open window, hinting at the world outside. It is as if Hals has reprised the earlier work to demonstrate that he could do the same just as effectively using even bolder brushstrokes. Just how bold his late style was is also seen in a similar unidentified portrait, once again showing the arm-akimbo pose (fig. 102). Here again, his broad application of paint is superbly effective despite having been executed in what can only be described as a rush, as evidenced by the wet paint dripping down the canvas at lower right.

It is worth mentioning that by the time Hals painted these two portraits he was around 80 years old. While at such an advanced age the human eye rarely sees as clearly as it once may have done, it is unnecessary to attribute Hals's late style to diminishing eyesight. His tendency towards an ever broader and more detached application of paint in his later years was undoubtedly a deliberate artistic choice. Similarly, Titian before him and Rembrandt around the same time decided that their true metier was in a bold – even rough – painting style, a logical conclusion to their lifelong practices. This certainly did not chime with a general classicising trend towards a smooth style in Dutch painting of the later seventeenth century. Yet both Rembrandt and Hals resolved to lean into their methods: it would have been more surprising had they not done so. In both cases there were patrons who preferred their style, and possibly their fame, over what was fashionable at the time.

Hals's late style found its purest expression when he was one last time confronted with the difficult task of painting group portraits, this time of the regents and regentesses of the Old Men's Alms House, resulting in what became two veritable icons of seventeenth-century Dutch painting (figs 3–4). Both works are possibly somewhat darker than they would originally have appeared, but it is not difficult to enjoy Hals's adventurous brushwork in its most extreme form in the dark clothes in both works – although it is most obvious in the flesh tones and the white details of the sitters' attire. The handling of paint in the two men closest to us in the foreground of the regents portrait in particular – in one of them the arm akimbo making one of its last appearances – is nothing short of miraculous. The whites, greys and blacks of their dress, or indeed the ochre of a glove, have been applied with an enviable certainty of touch. The audacious inclusion of what is essentially a block of red paint for the stocking of the man on the right constitutes an unforgettable piece of painting. Every stroke of the brush in the picture is essential to our understanding of the forms they describe, and yet standing at an arm's length distance from the painting, it can be difficult to understand how Hals managed to keep track of the organisation of his brushstrokes. A lifetime of experience informs not only the breathtaking handling of paint, but also the deeply felt portrayal of the human condition. One need only look at the long hand of the elder woman seated in the right foreground of the regentesses painting to realise that Hals knew how to convey the frailty of old age. We know far less about these men and women than we do about the sitters in Hals's earlier group portraits. Although we have names for those who were portrayed, there is no record of which name belongs to whom. But such knowledge is ultimately immaterial to us recognising that we are looking at great works of art.

Van Gogh waxed lyrical about Hals on several occasions. In a letter to his brother Theo of 13 October 1885 he mused about various seventeenth-century Dutch painters, including Hals, astutely observing that 'A great lesson that the old Dutch masters teach, it seems to me, is this: to regard drawing and colour as one'. His observation describes Hals's technique in a nutshell, and in the process may well provide the reason why Hals never seems to have made any drawings. A week later Van Gogh put Hals in the correct company in another letter to Theo, writing that 'Frans Hals is a colourist among colourists, a colourist like Veronese, like Rubens, like Delacroix, like Velázquez'. But in the context of the present essay, Van Gogh's most relevant observations concern Hals's repertory being largely limited to portraiture. On 30 July 1888 he writes about Hals in a letter to Emile Bernard: 'Never did he paint Christs, annunciations to shepherds, angels or crucifixions and resurrections; never did he paint voluptuous and bestial naked women. He painted portraits; nothing nothing nothing but that', adding a little further on that Hals 'doesn't know much more than that, but it is worth as much as Dante's Paradise and the Michelangelos and Raphaels and even the Greeks'.[55] A faint echo of Van Mander's 'side-road of art' cited at the start of this essay can still be heard in his remark, yet Van Gogh also proves himself to be our star witness in making the case that Hals succeeded in turning portraiture into art.

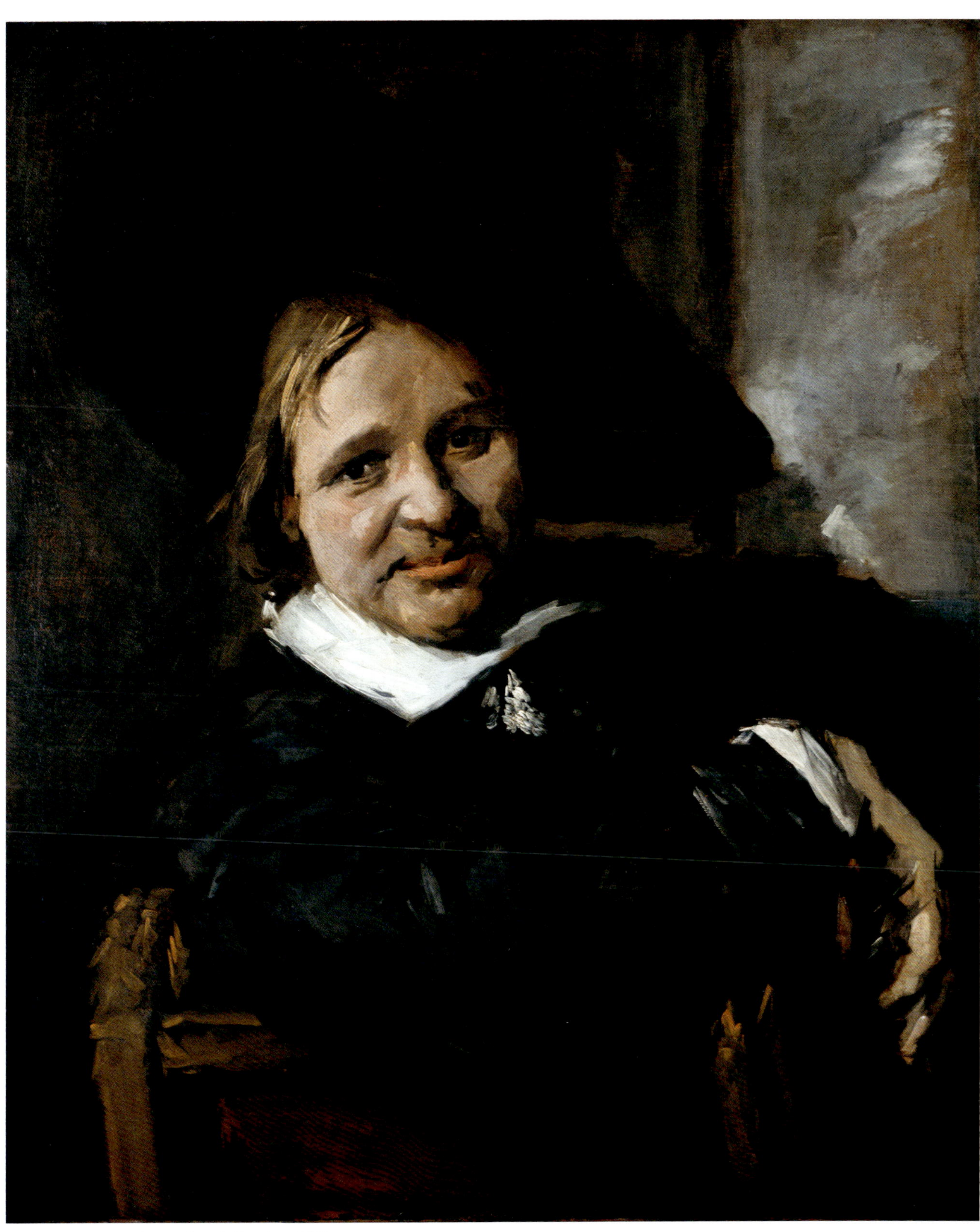

Fig. 101 *Portrait of a Man in a Slouch Hat*, about 1660
Oil on canvas, 79.5 × 66.5 cm
Hessen Kassel Heritage

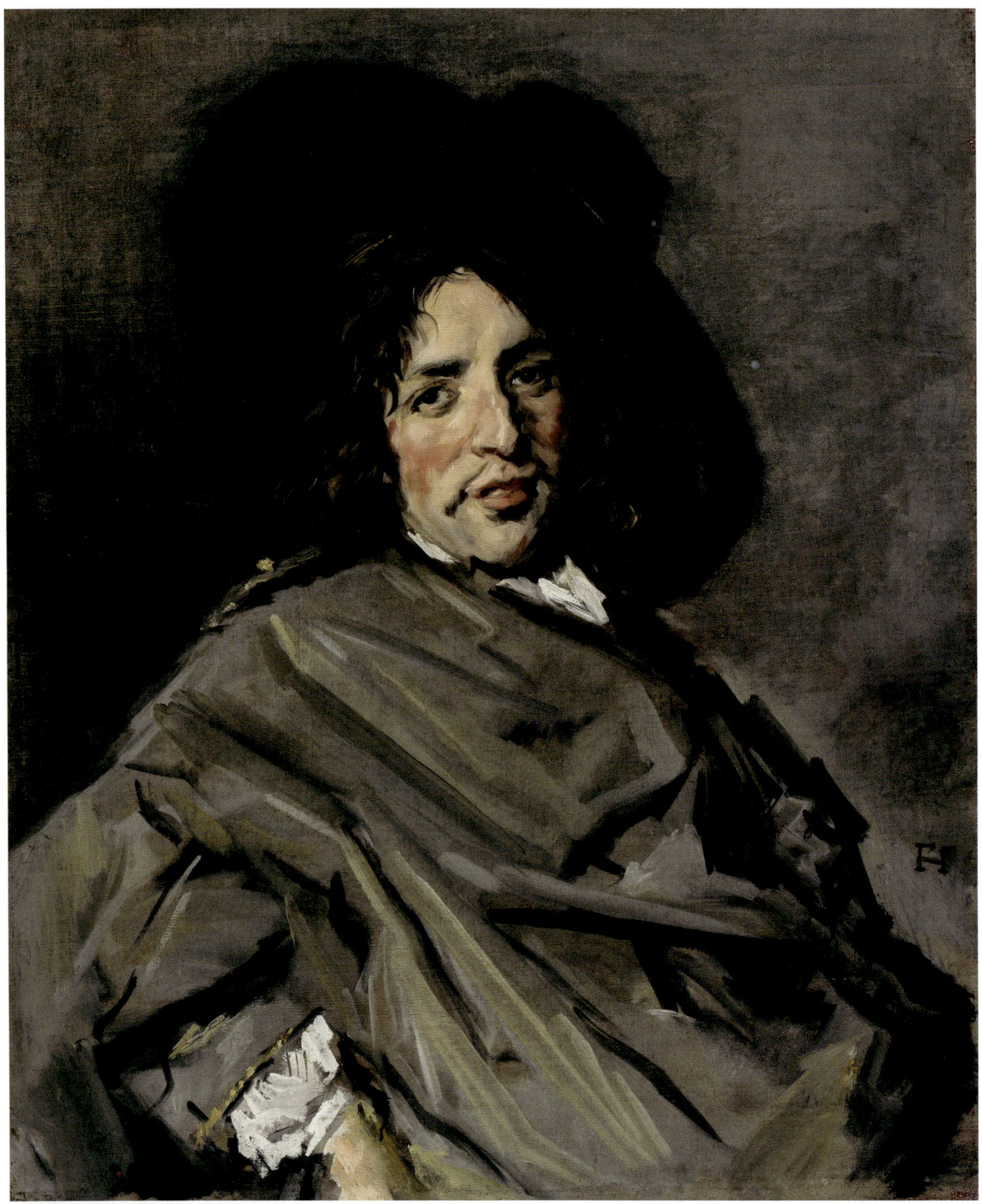

Fig. 102 *Portrait of an Unknown Man*, about 1660
Oil on canvas, 80 × 67 cm
The Syndics of the Fitzwilliam Museum,
University of Cambridge

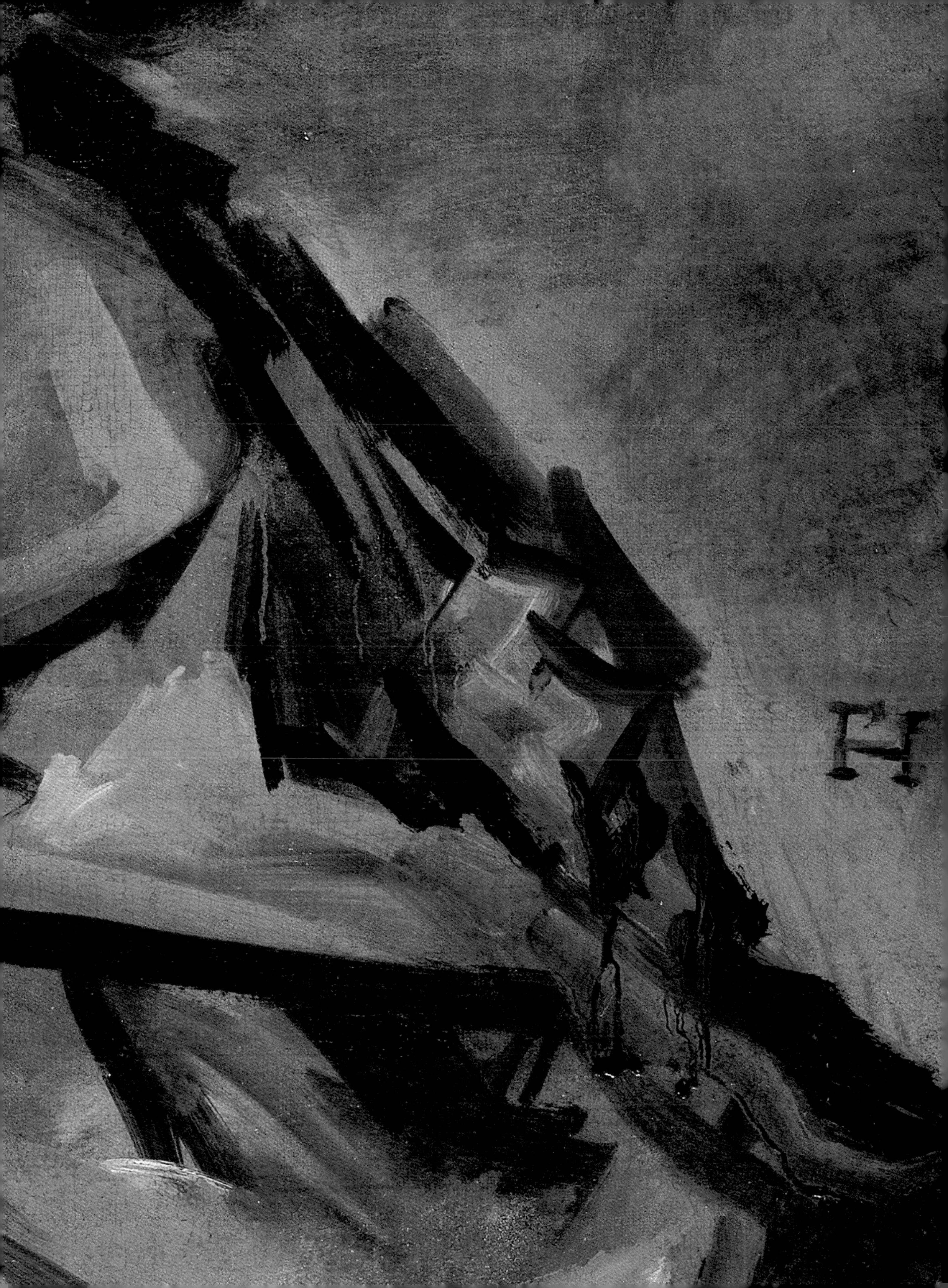

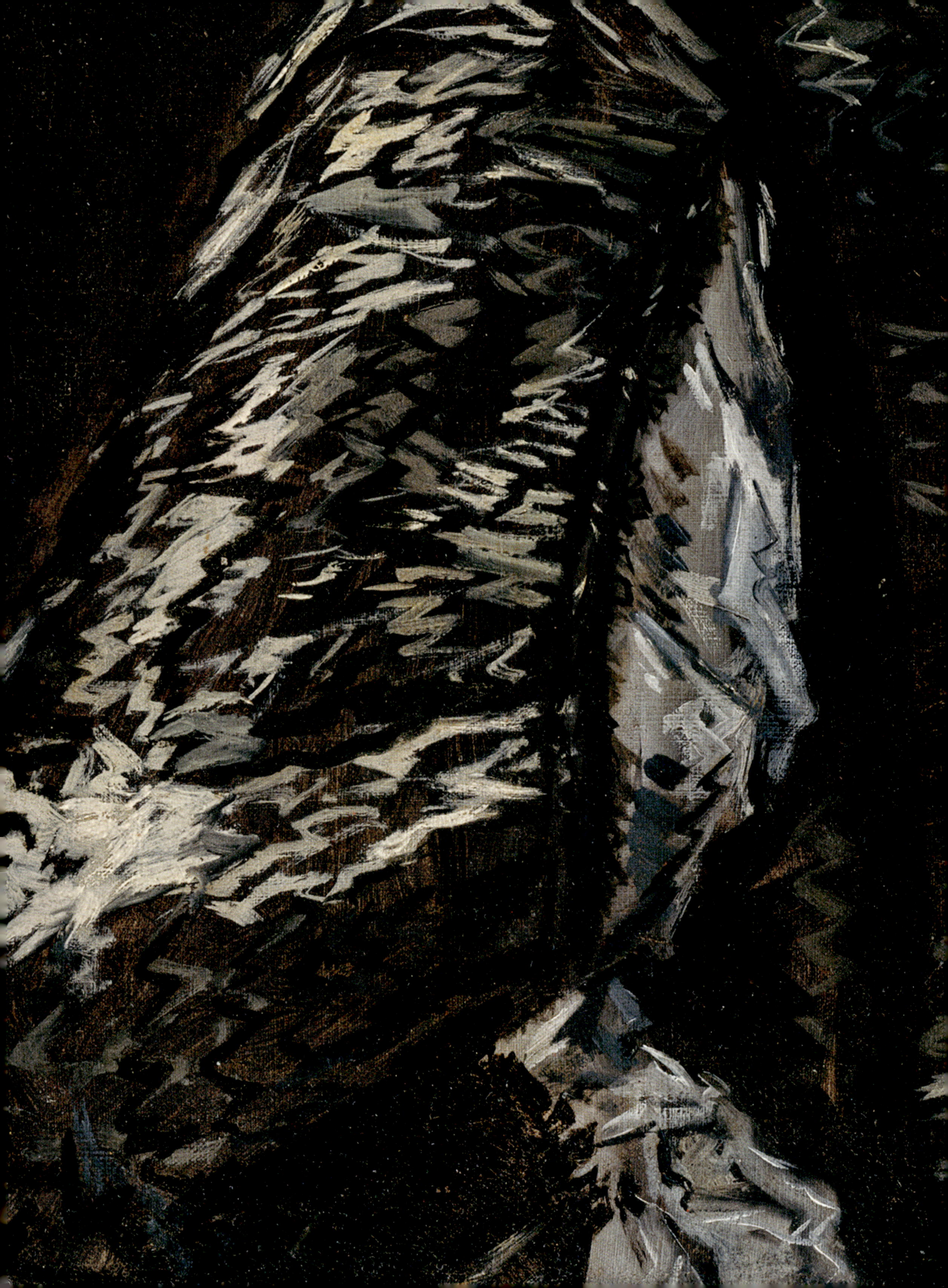

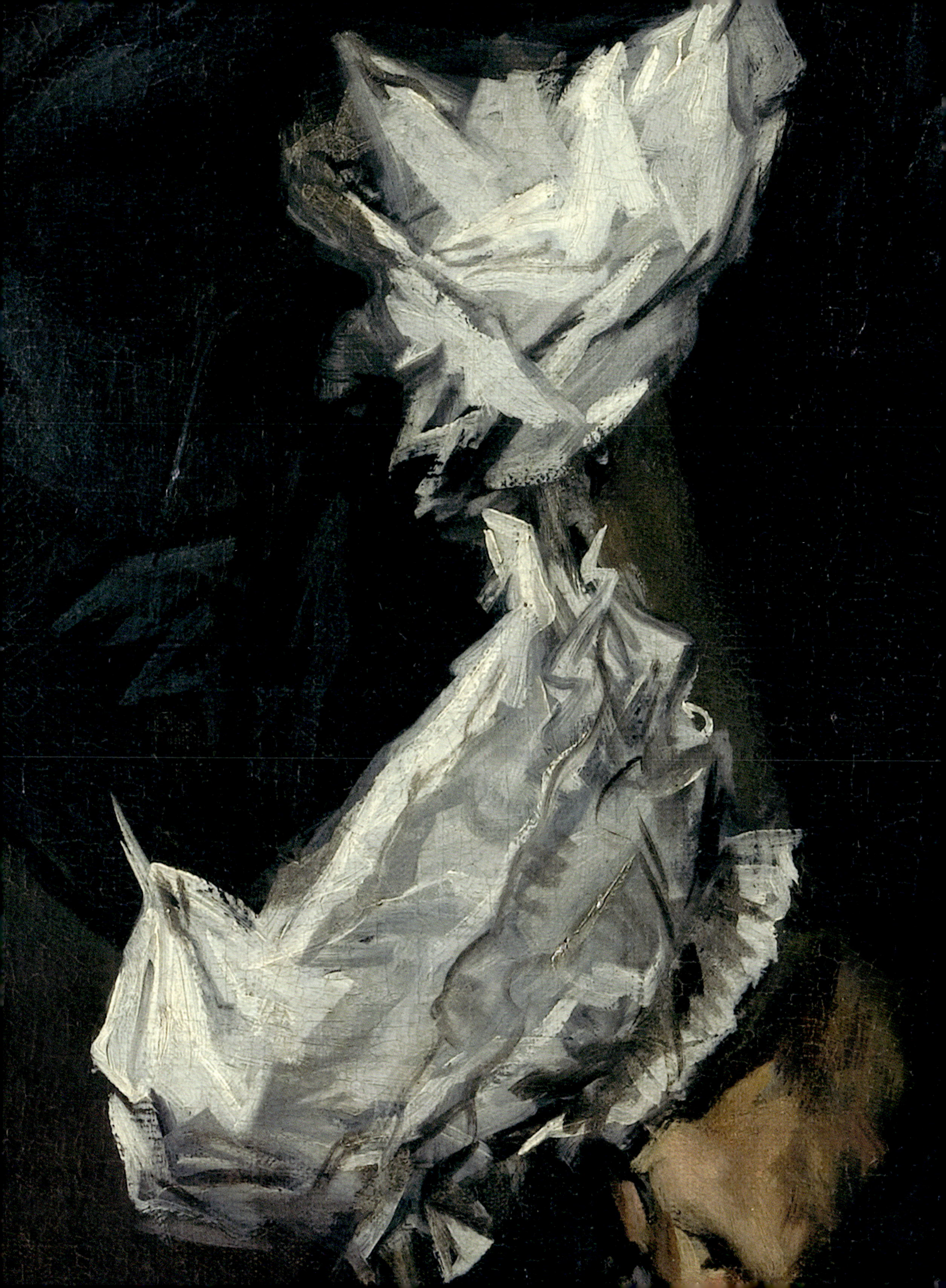

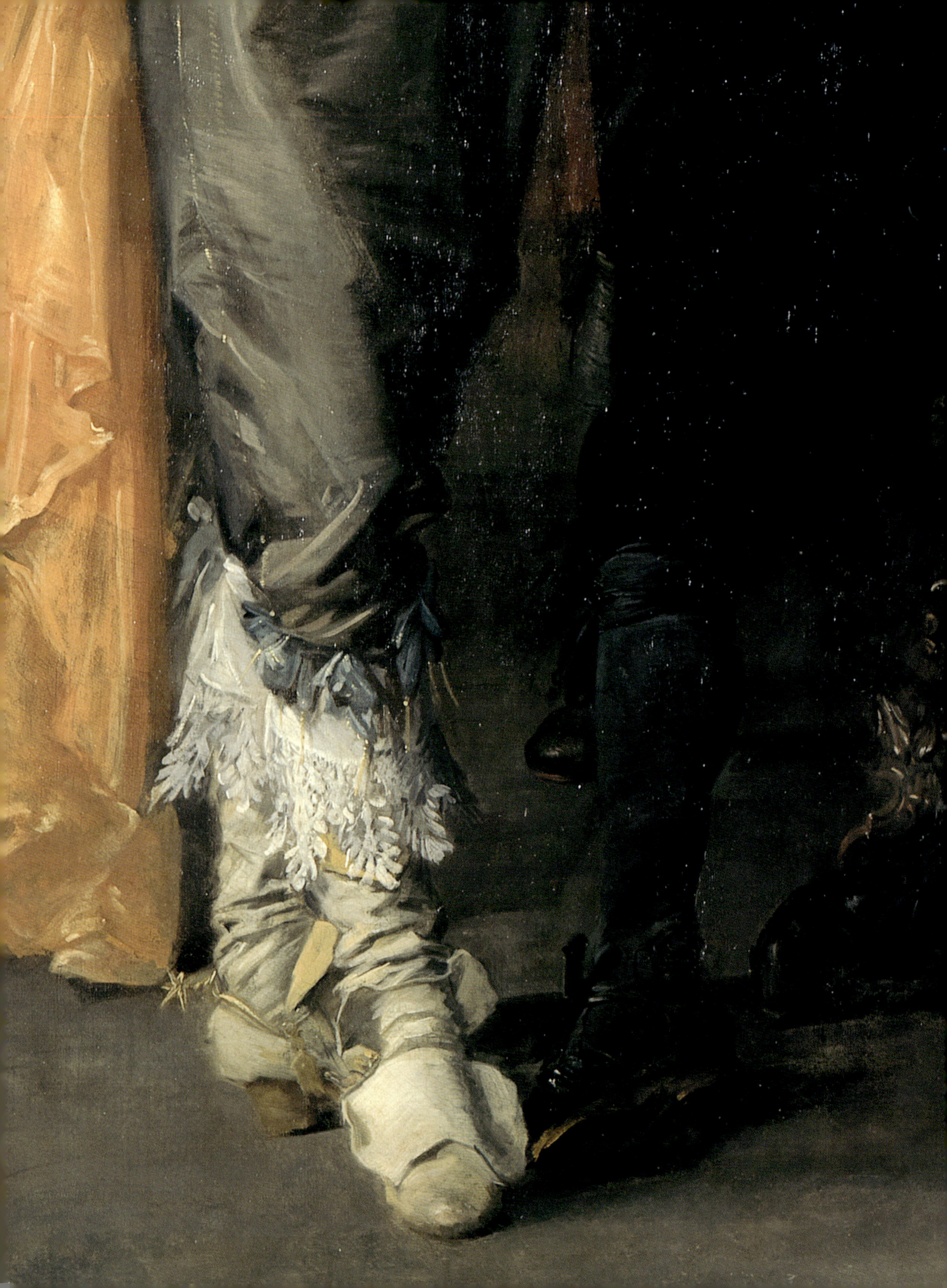

PORTRAIT PRINTS

JUSTINE RINNOOY KAN

'What a jewel that little Frans Hals is!' In 1860 the art critic and collector Théophile Thoré expressed his great admiration for a small portrait that would be lost four years later in a fire at the Museum Boymans in Rotterdam. Thoré, who played a significant role in Hals's nineteenth-century revival, was ecstatic to find that this 'fiery artist' of large paintings, which he considered on a par with the masterpieces of Rembrandt, Velázquez and Titian, 'was also a portraitist in miniature!' He continued:

> Here in Rotterdam, Frans Hals enclosed his man in an oval medallion 22 centimetres high; only the bust, but with one hand. It is the historian Pieter Bor Christiaanszoon … at the age of 75 … His moustache and beard are entirely white; on his bald pate a small black cap; elegant black silk suit and large ruff. The hand, in full light, holds a quill. Lively and expressive physiognomy. All of this is of such skill, such knowledge, such freedom, such spirit![1]

A print of this lost 1634 work (fig. 103), made by engraver Adriaen Matham, gives an idea of what the painted portrait must have looked like.[2] Other small portraits painted by Hals were also engraved on copper plate, making a print edition possible. The names of both artists are included in the prints: 'Hals pinxit' (painted) and '[printmaker's name] sculpsit' (engraved).[3] There are many seventeenth-century prints made after paintings, but few paintings were made with the intention of being produced in print form. There are hints that Hals did create his smallest works in the knowledge that they would serve as originals for prints. For example, the almost identical dimensions of portraits by Hals and of the corresponding engravings is remarkable. As a result, the engravers did not need to reduce their scale on the printing plates.

This chapter focuses on the smallest portraits by Hals, with particular attention to their function as models for prints. What were the links between Hals, his clients and the engravers? How did the process from painting to print unfold? But first: how many of these works are there?

PORTRAIT PRINTS AFTER HALS

Of the over 220 known paintings by Frans Hals, about 70 per cent are painted on canvas. There are three known works on copper; the rest were produced on panel.[4] When Hals's oeuvre is ranked from large to small, at a height of 55 cm there is an abrupt change from canvas to panel and copper.[5] For his smaller work Hals consistently opted for a hard surface and about forty small portraits on panel and copper have survived. Among the very smallest, with a height of about 27 cm or less, an intriguing group stands out: 11 of these little paintings were produced as prints at virtually the same scale during Hals's lifetime (see pp. 152–3).[6] The painted works were created over a span of several decades and do not form a planned series. The sparse information available on the creation of Hals's smallest portraits means that it is not always certain whether he made these paintings simply as ordinary, relatively affordable works of art or whether it was clear from the outset that they were intended as models for prints. For instance, a portrait of an anonymous man painted on copper (fig. 104), now in the Gemäldegalerie in Berlin, fits in well with the other works in terms of dimensions and composition but there is no known corresponding print.[7]

The reverse is also true, in the sense that, as we have seen, sometimes the portrait print is all that remains of a lost painting. In part thanks to Thoré, we know the dimensions of the painted portrait of Pieter Christiaansz Bor, so that we can be certain that these matched those of the print.[8] When the print reads 'Hals pinxit' but the dimensions of the original painting were not recorded, the correspondence between the two objects remains unknown. The 1628 posthumous print of clergyman Johannes Bogaert, engraved by Jan van de Velde the Younger (fig. 105), illustrates the complexity of this particularly well.[9] It has been suggested that this is the earliest example of a small painted portrait made expressly for use as a print, having been created before the preacher's death in 1614.[10] As the painting's current location is unknown, however, little can be said on this with any

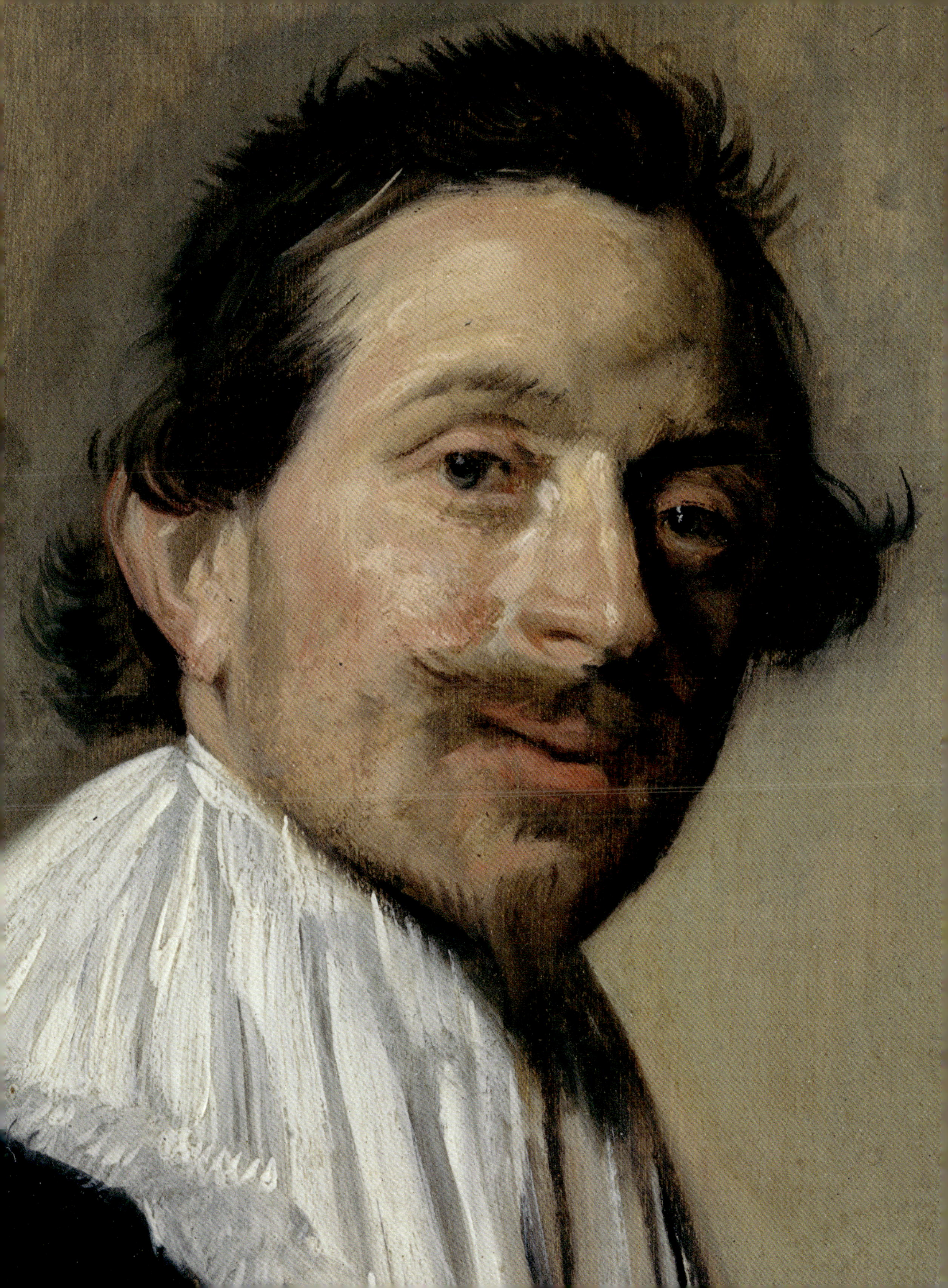

certainty: it might just as easily have been a larger (or perhaps life-size) portrait that was reproduced as a reduced-scale print in 1628.

Even when both a print and a painting of the same sitter have survived, ambiguities may still exist, such as with the portrait print of René Descartes made from a painting by Hals (fig. 142). This print, made by Jonas Suyderhoef and published by Pieter Goos in Amsterdam, was advertised in a newspaper on 11 June 1650. The text notes that Hals painted 'the pre-eminent mathematician and philosophising nobleman Renatus Descartes from life'.[11] There are several life-size copies of this portrait painted by anonymous artists, as well as a small, damaged and possibly trimmed version probably painted by Hals himself (fig. 141).[12] Was this latter work the original for the print, in which the face is depicted just a little larger than in the painting? Or was the engraving made at a reduced scale from a lost life-size work? In the absence of further information, these questions remain unanswered.

Larger portraits, which comprise the lion's share of Hals's oeuvre, were also produced in print intermittently during the artist's lifetime, with the print in each case being a significantly reduced version of the painted portrait. In these instances it is commonly assumed that the commissions for the painting and for the print were not directly linked.[13]

THE TRADITION OF PORTRAIT PRINTS

The portrait prints produced after paintings by Hals are part of a long tradition in Europe. Collecting likenesses of heroes, artists and scholars dates back to antiquity.[14] The advent of the Renaissance saw a surge of interest in this practice.[15] Painted portraits of eminent men, *viri illustres*, were collected for physical galleries.[16] In the sixteenth century, portrait prints experienced a boom: the handy, relatively affordable prints made rapid and widespread distribution possible, and a thriving international trade developed in prints of role models, distinguished people past and present.[17] Humanists would send letters to their colleagues accompanied by their likenesses, in lieu of a face-to-face encounter.[18]

Thousands of Dutch portrait prints from Hals's century have survived.[19] A large proportion of these consists of loose sheets intended for sale.[20] Portraits of famous contemporaries were assured widespread interest in the Dutch Republic. Even with a limited budget, one could hang the portrait of a hero on the wall or collect sheets and keep them in portfolios. Furthermore, many portrait prints were produced as illustrations in books, whether as images to accompany the text or as a portrait of the author. There were even publications consisting exclusively of portrait prints.[21] In addition, some prints were made primarily for private circulation, for example among friends, relatives or colleagues, often on the initiative of the portrait sitters or their immediate circle. While this group represents only a relatively small proportion of portrait print production as a whole, it includes some of the most beautiful examples.[22]

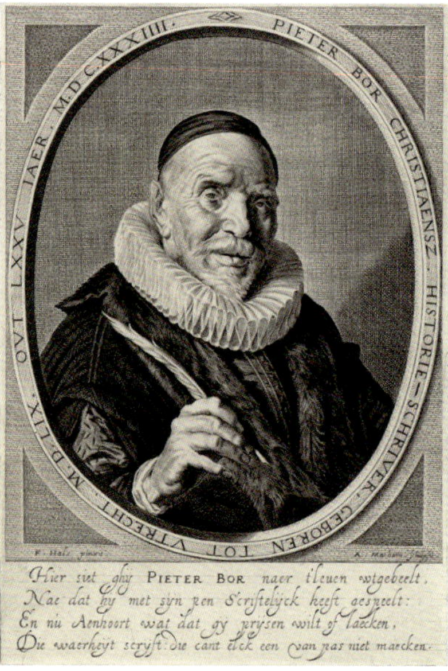

Fig. 103 Adriaen Matham after Frans Hals, *Portrait of Pieter Christiaansz Bor*, 1634
Engraving, 25 × 17.2 cm
Rijksmuseum, Amsterdam

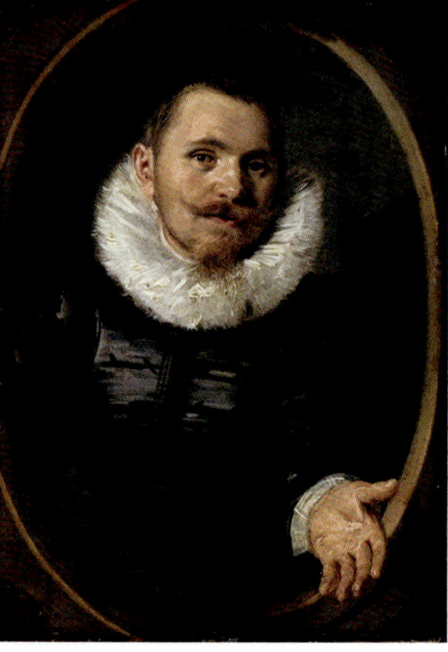

Fig. 104 *Portrait of an Unknown Man*, 162[...], possibly 1627
Oil on copper, 20 × 14.2 cm
Staatliche Museen zu Berlin, Gemäldegalerie

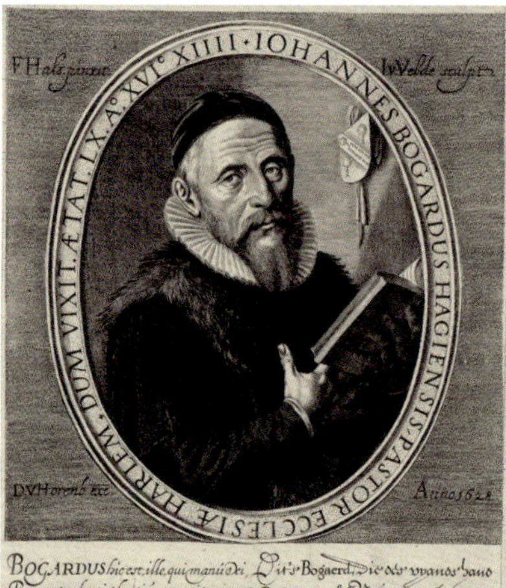

Fig. 105 Jan van de Velde the Younger after Frans Hals, *Portrait of Johannes Bogaert*, 1628
Engraving, 23.4 × 16.7 cm
Rijksmuseum, Amsterdam

PORTRAIT PRINTS

The prints made to scale after small portraits by Hals are predominantly likenesses of intellectuals, such as scholars and clergymen. Private circulation of these would have played a far greater role than it would for portrait prints of famous heroes and rulers. Hals frequently immortalised these distinguished sitters holding a book or a pen: these were the people who published city histories of Haarlem, educated the populace through their sermons or at the Latin or French school, and moved in the same intellectual circles. Their often Latinised names illustrate that Hals successfully secured commissions in their scholarly milieu in which, for example, Dirk Schrevel styled himself Theodorus Schrevelius.

SCHREVELIUS AS TRENDSETTER

The earliest-known portrait by Hals likely to have originated as a model for a print is that of Schrevelius (fig. 106, reproduced to scale). Since the sitter's age is noted on the painting – according to the inscription, he was 44 years old – it can be ascertained that it dates from before 25 July 1617.[23] This work on copper is the smallest in Hals's entire oeuvre: at 14.5 by 12 cm it fits easily into an adult hand. In 1618 Jacob Matham, one of Haarlem's finest engravers, produced a print after the little painting, adding a decorative frame featuring the Ancient Roman gods Minerva and Mercury (fig. 107, reproduced to scale).[24] Since both print and painting are well documented, and the painting is arguably the earliest example of Hals's small portraits for prints, these works are worth a closer look.

After he finished school Schrevelius left Haarlem for Leiden, where he initially studied theology, intending to become a clergyman; he eventually focused on *litterae humaniores* (humanities).[25] After his studies he began as a schoolmaster at the Latin school in Leiden. His accomplishments did not go unnoticed in his hometown: in 1597, at the age of 24, he was made deputy headmaster at the Latin school in Haarlem.[26] In 1609 he became headmaster and had himself immortalised in this role by Hals in painting and print years later.

The absence of any mention of a publisher on the print, normally listed as '[name] excudit', may be an indication that the portrait print was a self-publication. Additional evidence is provided by a letter that Schrevelius wrote in 1618 to his close friend Petrus Scriverius, an antiquarian with extensive expertise in subjects including Dutch history and classical literature, who lived as an independent, private scholar in Leiden. In their youth the near-namesakes had together attended the Latin school where Schrevelius now worked. In his letter Schrevelius reminds Scriverius of his request to provide a caption for his portrait print. It is rare to find sources that offer such keen insight into the creation process of a specific print. On 17 June 1618 Schrevelius writes:

The engraver Matham has at last put the final touches to a work that he began long ago [and placed] under the protection of Minerva and Mercury, for he has

engraved my portrait, painted in lively colours, in copper and so preserved it for posterity. The maker of this prototype wished me to send it to you...[27]

This implies that Matham took quite some time turning the painted portrait by Hals into an engraving, and alludes to an important function of the print in Schrevelius's view, namely his own legacy. It is also remarkable to know that a print *avant la lettre* (that is, to which the caption has not yet been added) was sent along at the request of the engraver. No copy of this stage of the print has survived.

The mention of 'lively colours' ('vivis coloribus') merits extra attention. This is the earliest-known description of a painting by Hals, albeit a succinct one. Such contemporaneous assessments are very scarce. The painter is not named, so the compliment only reveals itself once the letter is matched to the correct print.[28] In his copious notes on art the Utrecht antiquarian Arnoldus Buchelius also writes in positive terms about the portrait in question.[29] In 1620 Schrevelius was dismissed as headmaster due to the political and religious intrigues in Haarlem and ordered to leave the city.[30] He moved back to Leiden, where he was appointed headmaster of the Latin school in 1625.[31] Buchelius visited Schrevelius twice in Leiden. Following his first visit, in 1621, Buchelius made a note of 'a portrait of Schrevelius, small, very well done at Haarlem'.[32] Of his second visit, in May 1628, he writes that his host showed him a small, very lively portrait by Hals.[33]

Clergyman, poet and antiquarian Samuel Ampzing wrote about the painter at about the same time. This former pupil of Schrevelius published several city histories of Haarlem with assistance from Scriverius.[34] Frans Hals features in the one from 1621, although merely listed in an overview of artists working in the city.[35] In the 1628 edition Ampzing writes enthusiastically: 'How dashingly Frans paints the people from life!'[36] Twenty years later Schrevelius himself wrote a city history of Haarlem, in which he remarks that portraits by Hals 'are coloured in such a way that they seem to live and breathe'.[37] 'Lively' as a characterisation has become an intrinsic element of the literature about Hals; the language used by Buchelius, Ampzing and Schrevelius are at the root of this.

Scriverius supplied the caption requested by Schrevelius to complete the portrait print. Here he states that the sitter, thanks to his many accomplishments as a strict teacher, is worthy of an engraving by Matham, which will save him from potential oblivion.[38] The function of the print in keeping the memory of Schrevelius alive, to which he himself had alluded in his letter, is echoed in many inscriptions on portrait prints. The same applies to the glorification of the person portrayed. The implicit compliment to the engraver illustrates how highly prints by Matham were valued.

The print combines the work of two outstanding artists, Hals and Matham; in this it forms a prestigious vehicle for the self-promotion of the sitter during his lifetime

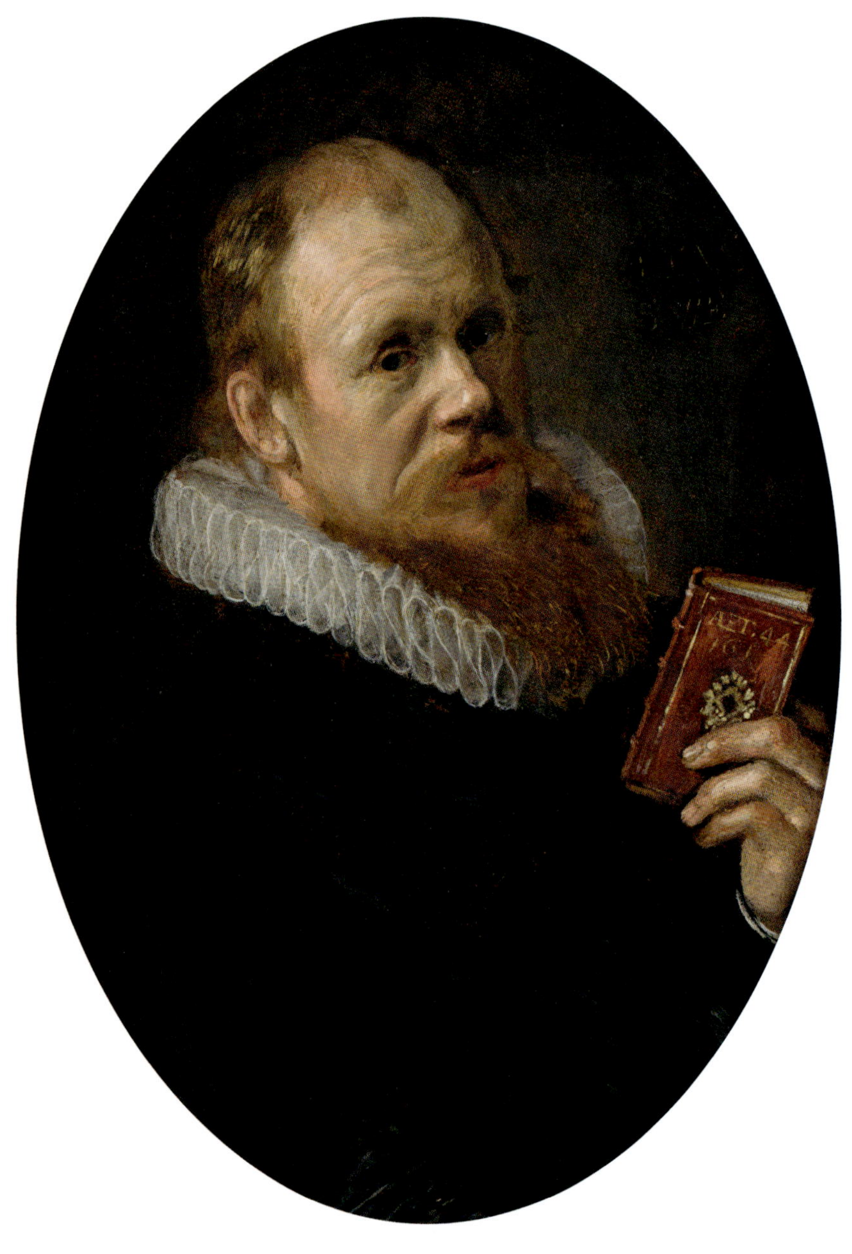

Fig. 106 *Portrait of Theodorus Schrevelius*, 1617
Oil on copper, 14.5 × 12 cm
Frans Hals Museum, Haarlem

Fig. 107 Jacob Matham after Frans Hals,
Portrait of Theodorus Schrevelius, 1618
Engraving, 26.2 × 16 cm
Rijksmuseum, Amsterdam

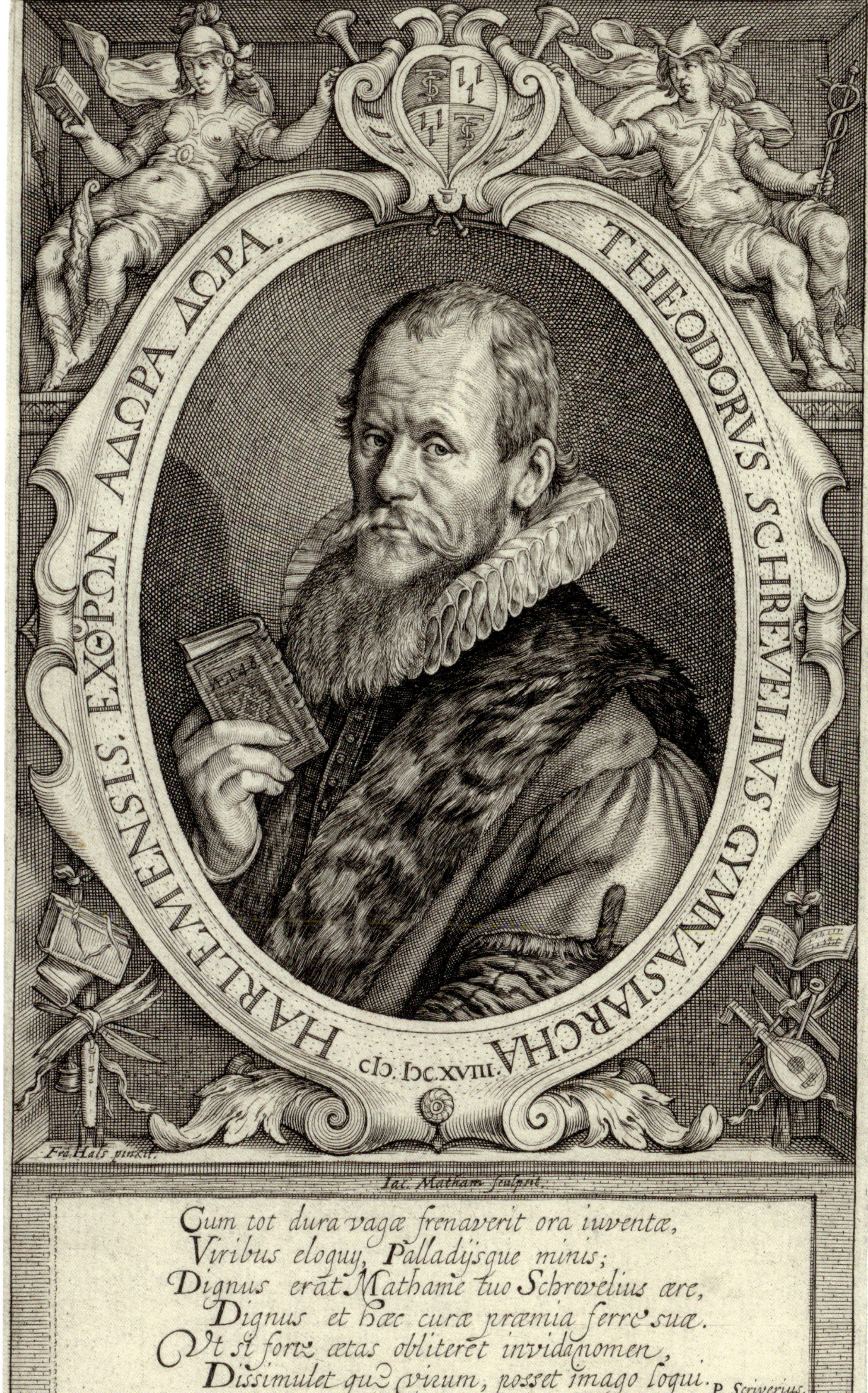

Cum tot dura vagæ frenaverit ora iuventæ,
Viribus eloquy, Palladijsque minis;
Dignus erat Mathame tuo Schrevelius ære,
Dignus et hæc curæ præmia ferre suæ.
Vt si fortɀ ætas obliteret invida nomen,
Dissimulet quɔ virum, posset imago loqui. P. Scriverius.

and beyond. Might Schrevelius have wanted not only a small painting but also a portrait print from the start? The short interval between the creation of the painting and the engraving, as well as the matching dimensions of the artworks, indicate that this may have been the case, certainly since the print seems to be self-published. Designs for prints were usually drawings, as painted portraits were relatively expensive. Perhaps Schrevelius wanted the print design to be as lifelike as possible and therefore chose Hals, who could achieve that effect like no other. There are no known drawings by Hals, so the choice of a print design by him may have meant commissioning a small painting as well. Its very limited size was no doubt reflected in a relatively low price. Thus Schrevelius got not only a small painting by Hals, a painter he admired, but also a print design. So the modest dimensions of the portrait probably had little to do with personal modesty: he was recorded not just once but multiple times, thanks to the print run of the engraving.

The combination of a painted portrait by Hals and a beautiful print after it must have also appealed to Scriverius. In 1626 he commissioned Hals to paint small portraits on panel of himself and his wife, Anna van der Aar (figs 124–5). The print of Scriverius's portrait was published soon after, engraved by Jan van de Velde the Younger, a successful former pupil of Jacob Matham (fig. 108). After Schrevelius's 1617 portrait, this is the earliest dated example of a small painting with a corresponding print made to scale. With pendant portraits of male public figures and their spouses, as a rule only the former would be published as prints.[39] The correspondence and *album amicorum* of Scriverius that have been preserved provide an idea of the many learned men with whom he was in contact and among whom he possibly distributed his print.[40] Buchelius noted that he received two copies of Scriverius's portrait print from Schrevelius, during his visit in 1628.[41] This illustrates how prints could also be circulated via mutual friends of portrait sitters.

Around 1630 Hals painted a small-size portrait of Samuel Ampzing on copper, which was also published in print by Jan van de Velde the Younger (figs 129–30), shortly before or after Ampzing's untimely death on 29 July 1632.[42] From Ampzing's city history of 1628, in which he discusses those he considered important citizens of Haarlem, we find that he was aware of the inscriptions on the portrait prints made from small paintings by Hals. All four dating from before 1628 are included: Scriverius, Schrevelius, Bogaert and Acronius (about whom more later).[43] Ampzing incorporated the inscriptions in their entirety. First he transcribed the original Latin inscription 'Versus in Effigiem [name]' and provided his readers with a Dutch translation in verse, 'Verzen op de Afbeeldinge van (Verses on the Image of) [name]', followed in some cases by his own ode to the person in question. The inscription on Ampzing's own portrait print of 1632 was written by Scriverius.[44]

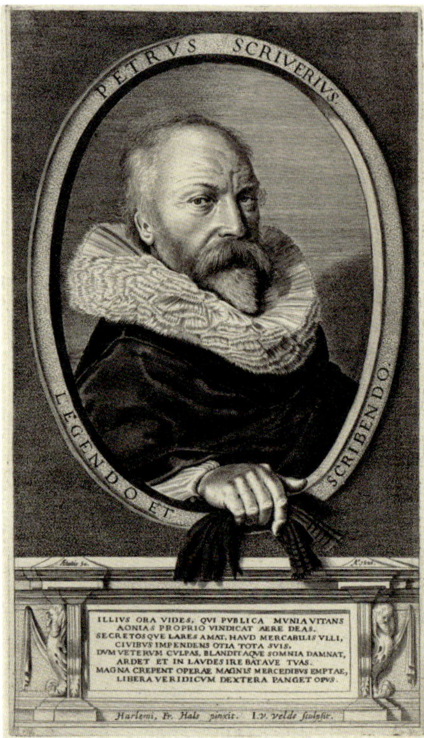

Fig. 108 Jan van de Velde the Younger after Frans Hals, *Portrait of Petrus Scriverius*, 1626. Engraving, 26.9 × 15.6 cm Rijksmuseum, Amsterdam; D. Franken Bequest, Le Vésinet

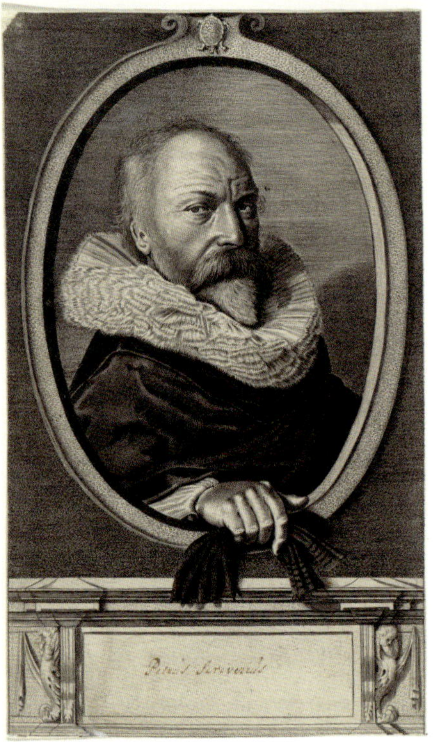

Fig. 109 Jan van de Velde the Younger after Frans Hals, *Portrait of Petrus Scriverius*, 1626. Engraving, 26 × 15.4 cm Rijksmuseum, Amsterdam

PORTRAIT PRINTS

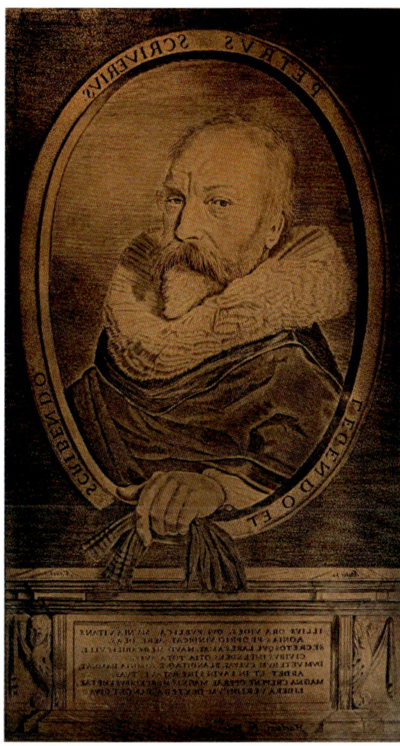

Fig. 110 Jan van de Velde the Younger
after Frans Hals, *Portrait of Petrus Scriverius*, 1626
Copper plate, 26 × 15.4 cm
Stichting Familie van Hoogstraten

RELATIONS WITH ENGRAVERS

When it comes to the prints made after paintings by Hals, it is difficult to determine precisely who took the initiative to produce them. The sitter, the portraitist, the engraver and, as we will see, sometimes the publisher all had a stake in the work: who had the idea first was not recorded. Admirers may also have suggested it. Because of Hals's close ties with the engravers who turned his work into prints, it is at least plausible that there was frequent communication between them.

Haarlem was known for its high-quality printmaking, with such renowned practitioners as Dirck Volckertsz Coornhert and certainly Hendrick Goltzius. Jacob Matham was right at its heart: he was trained at the end of the sixteenth century by his stepfather – none other than Goltzius himself.[45] Publishers and printmakers often collaborated with scholars, who supplied texts for inscriptions, as Schrevelius did in 1598 for a print by Matham.[46] By the time Schrevelius's portrait print was made, engraver and client had thus known each other for about twenty years. Hals and Matham were no strangers to each other either: at the time the painted and printed portraits of Schrevelius were produced, the painter and the engraver were members of the same chamber of rhetoric, De Wijngaertrancken (Vine Tendrils).[47] Moreover, Matham – like Schrevelius, incidentally – had worked with Karel van Mander, Hals's presumed mentor.[48]

We know that Hals was a friend of certain engravers, including Matham's son Adriaen, who learned the craft from his father. Around 1627 Hals painted him as an ensign in his *Banquet of the Officers of the Calivermen Civic Guard* (fig. 65, far left). In addition, Adriaen was a witness at the baptism of Frans Hals's daughter Susanna seven years later.[49] Graphic work after Hals's paintings is also known by Adriaen's brother, Theodoor Matham, as well as by Jan van de Velde the Younger, who was a witness at the birth of Hals's niece Hester (the daughter of his younger brother, Dirck Hals) in 1624 and that of his own son Reynier in 1627.[50] Jonas Suyderhoef also made several portrait prints from small paintings by Hals. Hals and this talented artist, nearly thirty years his junior, certainly knew each other. The archives reveal in particular Hals's connection with Jonas's brother, Adriaen Suyderhoef. In 1641 the latter appeared as a witness in a court case along with Hals's second wife, Lysbeth Reyniers.[51] Ten years later he married the daughter of Dirck Hals, Maria, at whose baptism in 1623 Frans Hals had been a witness.[52]

Hals undoubtedly had an interest in prints made after his own work. Their circulation was good advertising for the artist. The quality of the engravings of Jan van de Velde the Younger, Jonas Suyderhoef and the Matham family would not have let him down: all belonged to the *crème de la crème* of the Haarlem printmaking scene.

Once a portrait was in the hands of the engraver, the image had to be transferred to the copper plate. For this there were tried and tested methods and tools.[53] It was common practice to first make one or more preliminary studies on paper, to which the printmaker would add his own inventions, such as the decorative frame with gods from classical antiquity on the portrait print of Schrevelius (fig. 107). An impression *avant la lettre* of the print of Scriverius has survived, in which the oval frame features two scrolls and a turtle at the top (fig. 109). This invention did not make it to the final print, in which the frame is identical to that painted by Hals (fig. 108).[54]

A painting could be traced with the help of oiled paper (*carta lucida*). In order to transfer the definitive preliminary study to the printing plate, the drawing was laid on the plate and the contour lines would be traced with a metal pen or stylus – a practice known as *doorgriffelen*. Another regularly employed technique was *calqueren*: a thin layer of wax was applied to the copper plate and the back of the design coated with a layer of chalk. The powdery residue would adhere to the places where pressure was applied through *doorgriffelen*, creating a copy in outline.

No preliminary studies for the copper plates made after paintings by Hals have survived. However, drawings made or used by the engravers with whom Hals worked do exist, which show evidence of these methods. Red chalk, for example, has been found on the verso of Adriaen Matham's preliminary study for the portrait print of the clergyman Johannes Polyander van Kerckhoven.[55] Jan van de Velde the Younger traced the drawing made by Pieter Claesz Soutman around 1630 of their old master, Jacob Matham, just before his passing (figs 111, 113).[56] In about 1631 Van de Velde completed the engraving: a posthumous tribute to the man in whose workshop the aforementioned techniques were taught and also likely employed in the production of the portrait prints made after paintings by Hals.

When an ink-covered plate is pressed on to paper, a reverse image is printed. As was common practice in the painting of the time, the light in Hals's paintings always comes from the left. Scriverius apparently wanted this pleasing light orientation in his print as well. Van de Velde the Younger therefore reversed the portrait on the copper plate. He probably traced his preliminary study twice, first on the recto, so that the drawing appeared in reverse on the verso, which was then incised for transfer into the plate.[57]

Who gained ownership of the copper plates varied considerably. Sometimes they were kept by the engraver or publisher. They also occasionally came into the possession of the individual pictured, such as in the case of Rembrandt's etching plates of Jan Six and Pieter Haringh.[58] As far as we know, this happened in two instances with plates made from paintings by Hals. Scriverius gained ownership of the copper plate for his print (fig. 110), which passed through inheritance to the Stichting Fami-

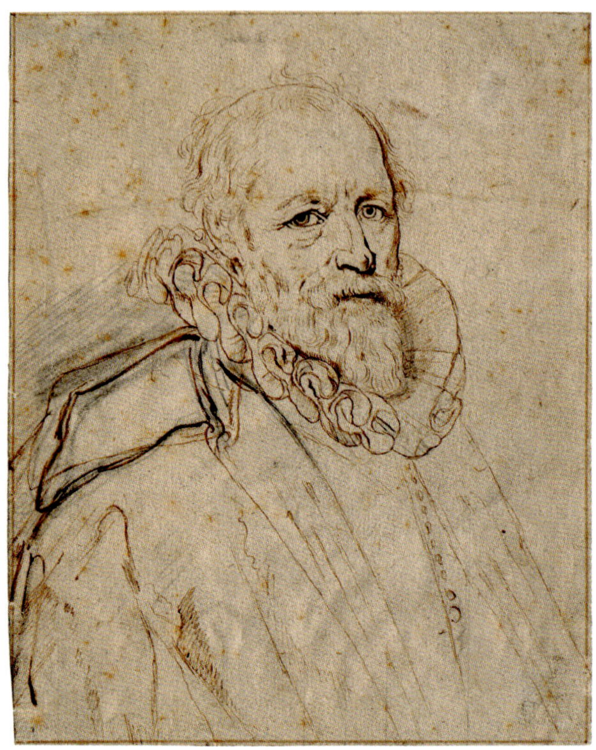

Fig. 111 Pieter Claesz Soutman,
Portrait of Jacob Matham, about 1630
Pen and brown ink, black chalk, 16.9 × 13.8 cm
Print Room, Leiden University

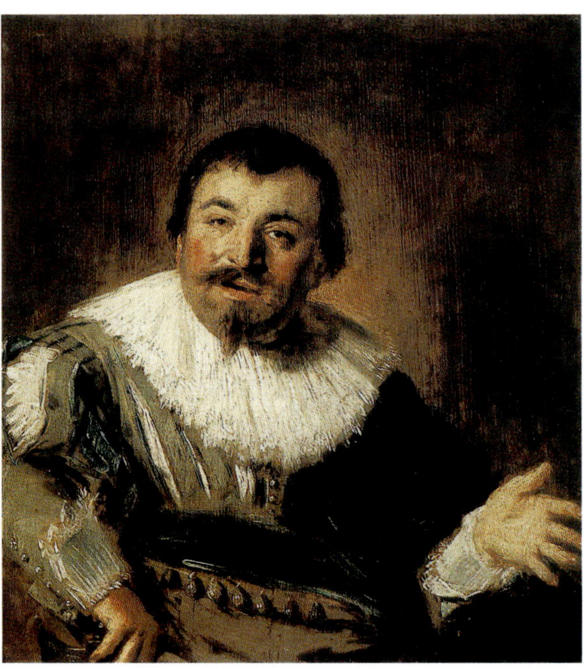

Fig. 112 *Portrait of Isaac
Abrahamsz Massa*, about 1635
Oil on wood, 21.3 × 19.7 cm
The San Diego Museum of Art

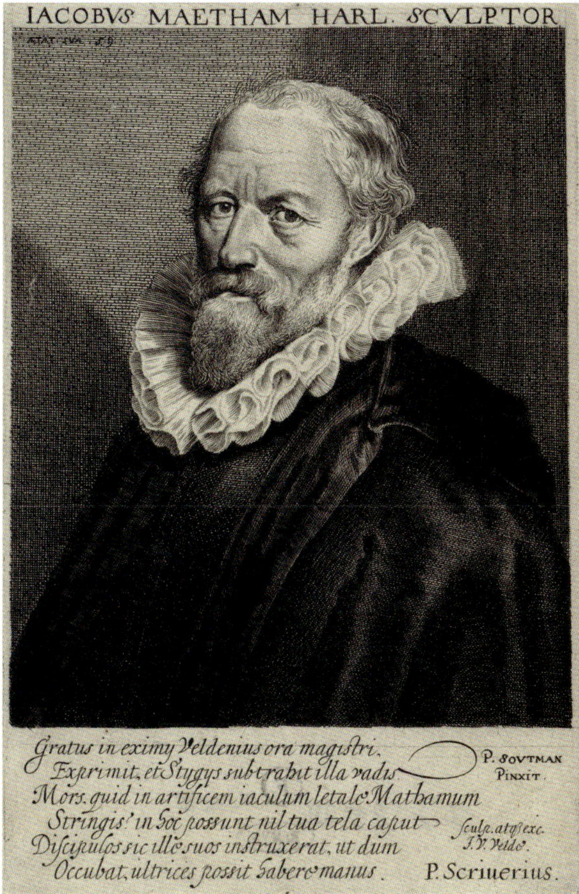

Fig. 113 Jan van de Velde the Younger after Pieter Claesz Soutman,
Portrait of Jacob Matham, 1631. Engraving, 20.4 × 13.5 cm
Rijksmuseum, Amsterdam; D. Franken Bequest, Le Vésinet

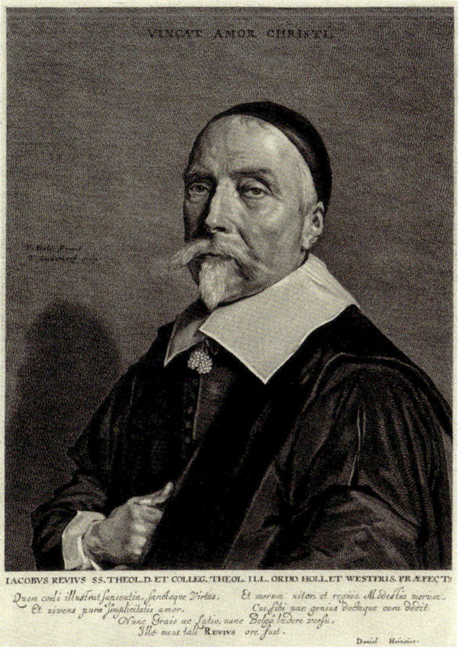

Fig. 114 Jonas Suyderhoef after Frans Hals,
Portrait of Jacobus Revius, about 1642–7
Engraving, 32.8 × 23.8 cm
Rijksmuseum, Amsterdam

lie van Hoogstraten.[59] This is the only copper plate made after a painting by Hals that we know has survived. In addition, a copper plate is mentioned in the 1658 inventory of the clergyman Jacobus Revius, recently discovered by Frans Grijzenhout.[60] The engraving by Jonas Suyderhoef with the inscription by Revius's friend Daniël Heinsius has survived (fig. 114), but neither the location of the original painting by Hals nor that of the copper plate is known. The inventory lists a large portrait without an identified artist; since there is no other known portrait of Revius, it is plausible that this is the portrait by Hals that served as the original for the print. No publisher is indicated on the print, and Revius, as the owner of the plate, may have commissioned the engraving. The fact that a large painting, specifically, was self-published in print form underscores that there are many possible arrangements for the commissioning of portraits and prints. An error at an early stage of the print suggests that an assistant was probably involved in its production process: it reads that not Hals, but 'A. v. Dyck pinxit' – a mistake that Suyderhoef would not have been likely to make himself and that was corrected at a later stage.[61]

DUAL FUNCTION

The painted portraits that were made to scale into prints are small works of art in their own right. Schrevelius's mention in his letter of the 'lively colours' is interesting in this context as well. Prints were almost always printed in black ink; for this reason, painted designs by other artists were often painted in shades of grey or brown.[62] Oil sketches in grisaille and brunaille provide guidance to engravers in the creation of tonal effects. Hals, however, did not adjust his use of colour in any way compared with his larger portraits, providing a visual experience that was independent of the print.

The existence of the portrait of the aforementioned Anna van der Aar is a second persuasive indication that the portrait of Scriverius served not only as a model for a print, but also as a personal keepsake to be shown alongside that of his wife.[63] Based on the inventories and later copies, it is assumed that the portrait of Schrevelius was initially similarly paired with a corresponding image of his wife, Maria van Teylingen.[64] These paintings commissioned by Scriverius and Schrevelius were later included as part of their respective estates.[65] This suggests that the little paintings served as family portraits. This is also true of the small portrait of Isaac Massa (fig. 112), a close acquaintance of Hals, who provided a brief contribution to Scriverius's *album amicorum* and was probably familiar with his portrait print.[66] Massa's little painting served as the model for the print that he self-published, made by Adriaen Matham. Massa had the financial means to have his portrait painted by Hals in a large size several times. As such, the smallest portrait was almost certainly produced as a model for a print and is most probably listed in the recently discovered inventory of his widow, Maria van Wassenbergh, along with the larger portraits.[67]

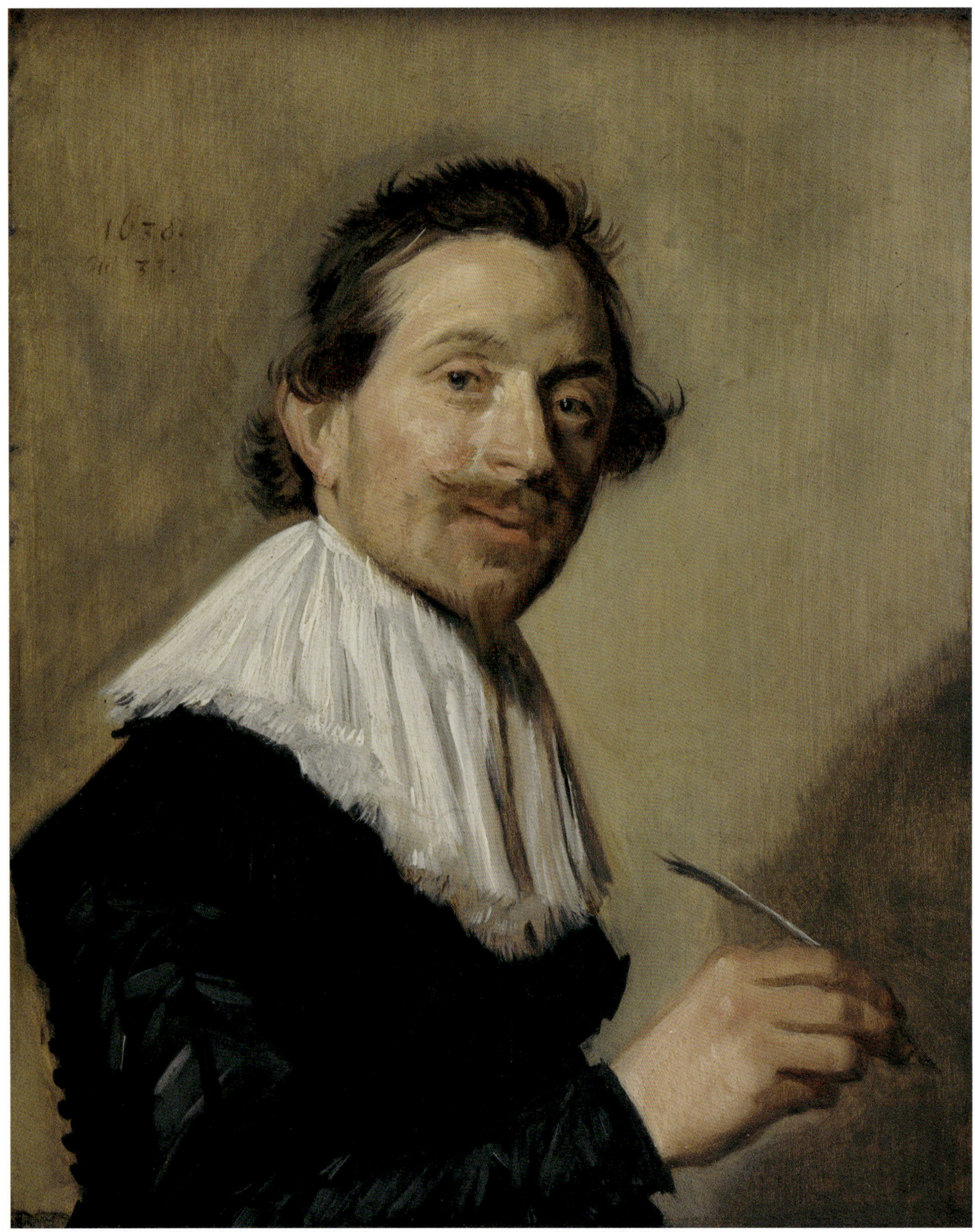

Fig. 115 *Portrait of Jean de la Chambre at the Age of 33*, 1638
Oil on wood, 20.6 × 16.8 cm
The National Gallery, London

Fig. 116 Jonas Suyderhoef after Frans Hals,
Portrait of Jean de la Chambre at the Age of 33, 1638
Engraving, 25.7 × 17.4 cm
Rijksmuseum, Amsterdam

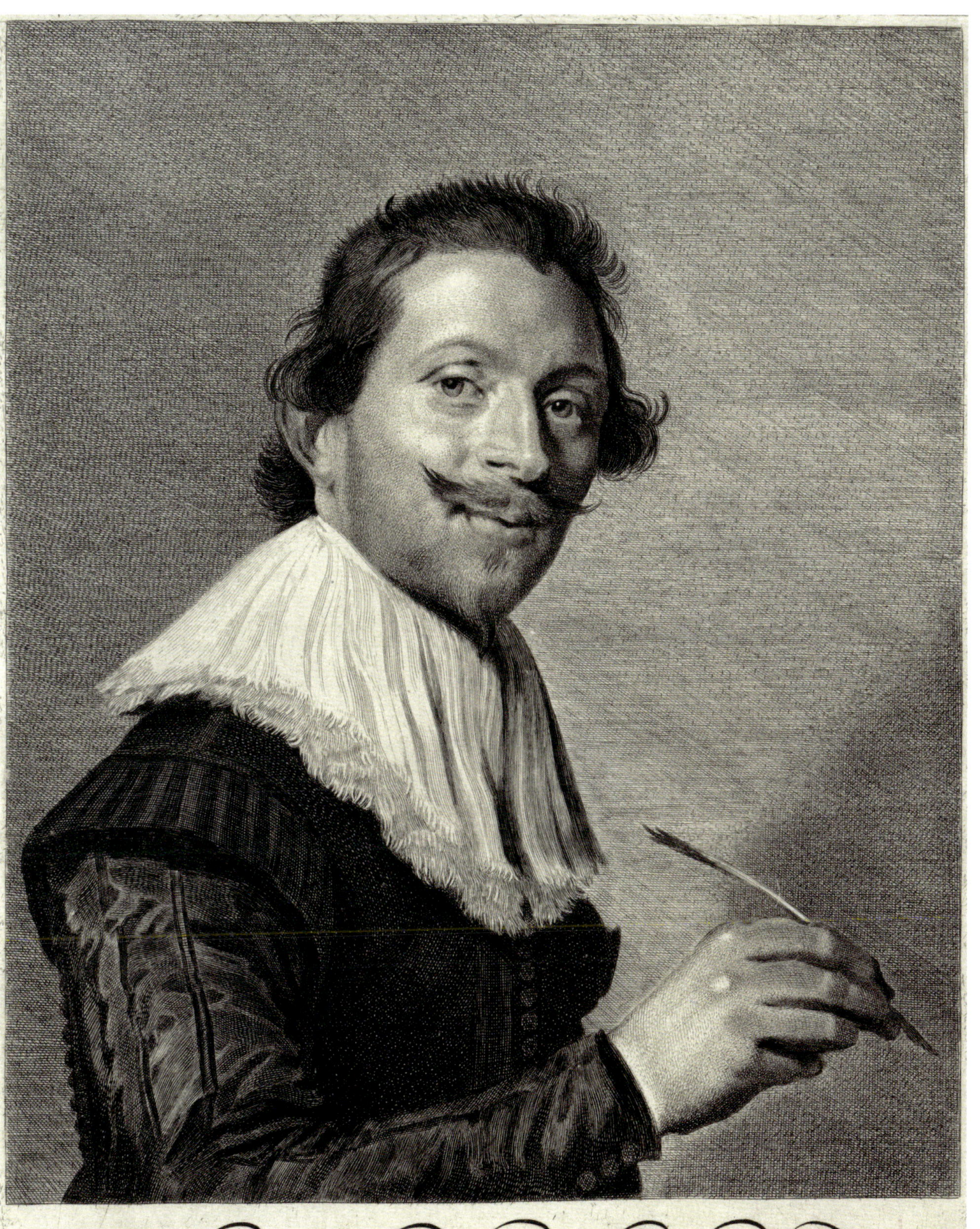

Verscheyden geschriften, geschreven ende int koper gesneden,
door Jean de la Chambre, liefhebber ende beminder der
pennen, tot Haarlem. Anno. 1638.
F. Hals. pinxit.
J. S. Hoef. sculpsit.

That Hals did not take into account the fact that the print would be a reverse image is another indication that his paintings were independent works of art. The extra trouble required to reproduce the engraving in the same orientation as the painting was only taken in a few instances with copper plates made after paintings by Hals, and in each case this was a product of the efforts of the engraver, not of Hals himself (figs 124, 126; 127–8; 134, 136). In the case of the print made after his painted portrait of Jean de la Chambre (figs 115–16, reproduced to scale), this was probably reversed because of the quill in his hand. De la Chambre was a calligrapher and teacher at the French school in Haarlem.[68] Calligraphy was a highly admired skill: the most prominent professional calligraphers were often, like De la Chambre, learned immigrants from the Southern Netherlands, who founded private 'French' schools in Holland, fulfilling a high demand for good education. They generally maintained close ties with scholars and artists.[69] Hals painted De la Chambre's portrait in 1638, after which Jonas Suyderhoef made the print that same year, to serve as the frontispiece of a book on engraved calligraphy by De la Chambre.[70] The 33-year-old looks straight at the viewer, as though he has just been interrupted at his work. The distinguished engraver Hendrick Goltzius took a reverse image into account in his preliminary study drawings for prints. He depicted portrait sitters as left-handed to enable him to represent them as right-handed in the print. The fact that De la Chambre is clearly right-handed in both artworks – undoubtedly an important criterion to the calligrapher for a proper likeness – illustrates the importance of both print and painting. Thanks to contemporary engravings, we know of two other portraits by Hals of calligraphers: Arnold Möller and Theodore Blevet (figs 117–18). The lost originals were probably similarly painted, with the light coming from the left and the quill in the right hand.[71] The same is true, in all probability, of the lost painting of Pieter Christiaansz Bor admired by Théophile Thoré mentioned above (fig. 103).

Nor did Hals modify his brushwork. These paintings may be smaller but they are often proportionally no more finely painted than his larger portraits. His characteristic loose brushstrokes were partly captured in print form by skilled engravers, but this did not make their work any easier. Engraving a copper plate with a burin is a delicate operation using precise lines. In Jean de la Chambre's ruff, Suyderhoef deliberately leaves strips free of line and ink, approximating Hals's white bands of oil paint. Yet even in this high-quality print a great deal of the original is lost in the engraving process. The breezy hairstyle, the almost mobile gaze and the sheen on the black sleeve, which Hals renders with quick streaks of grey – Suyderhoef cannot be blamed for the fact that all of this comes out smoother, more precise and less fluid in print form.

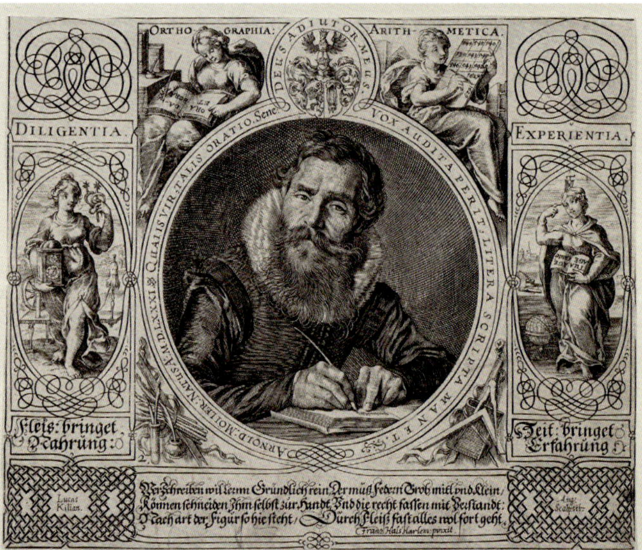

Fig. 117 Lucas Kilian after Frans Hals, *Portrait of Arnold Möller*, 1629
Engraving, 15.3 × 18.6 cm. Herzog Anton Ulrich-Museum, Braunschweig

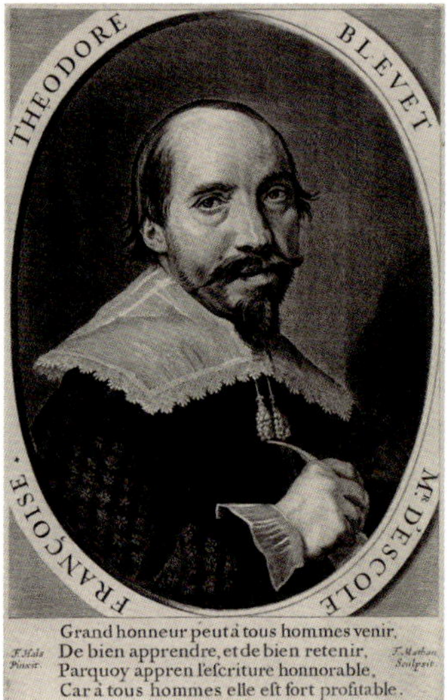

Fig. 118 Theodor Matham after Frans Hals, *Portrait of Theodore Blevet*, 1640
Engraving, 25.8 × 16.4 cm
Rijksmuseum, Amsterdam

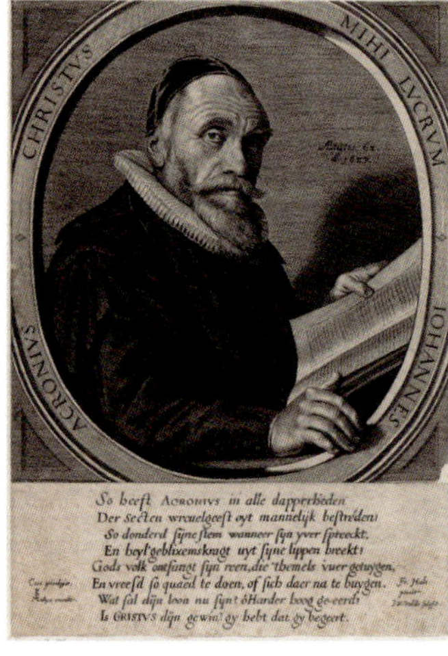

Fig. 119 Jan van de Velde the Younger after Frans Hals, *Portrait of Johannes Acronius*, 1627. Engraving, 23.2 × 16.4 cm
Rijksmuseum, Amsterdam

PORTRAIT PRINTS

The prints made after Hals's small portraits of clergymen in particular raise the question of whether production of a print was intended even as the portrait was painted.[72] In many cases, the interval between the making of the painting and of the print is quite long; sometimes the print was even made posthumously. So these paintings regularly functioned for years as independent portraits, only later serving as designs for prints made to scale. The demand among clergymen for small, independent portraits is illustrated by the existence of a few only slightly larger portraits by Hals of anonymous men with black caps, such as *Portrait of a Man, possibly a Clergyman* (fig. 120). Although it is known that this headgear was not worn exclusively by clergymen, these works are usually identified as portraits of ministers. With heights around 35 cm, these are on the large side to serve as designs for engravings to scale and there are no known prints after them.

The death of a clergyman was frequently the occasion for a portrait print. Those who persuasively preached the Word of God were admired and in some cases adored. Well-attended sermons regularly influenced public debate in this deeply religious society, and in some cases preachers enjoyed local or even national fame. Upon their deaths the grieving community would have had an above average interest in a portrait. In more than one instance, several different stages of these prints are known, for example because a new publisher later released a new print run. The name of the previous publisher (if there was one) would be replaced on the plate by the new name. The recently discovered memory book of Maria van Nesse, a wealthy unmarried, Catholic woman from Alkmaar, reveals that posthumous portrait prints of Catholic priests were distributed as gifts among fellow believers. Van Nesse received several as presents from her brother-in-law.[73] These were made by, among others, Jacob and Adriaen Matham, who were themselves from a Catholic background and engraved numerous portraits of priests with Theodoor Matham.[74] It is feasible that portraits of Protestant clergymen were circulated in similar fashion among followers of their faith.

Portrait prints of Johannes Acronius, who began preaching in Haarlem in 1619, were made from a small painting by Hals from 1627 (figs 119, 127–8). Acronius died on 29 September of that year and it is not known whether Hals made the work before or after his death, perhaps based on a now-lost portrait that was not necessarily painted by him. The engraving, produced by Jan van de Velde the Younger, is most probably posthumous. There are several extant stages of this print. The first bears an inscription in Latin, with no mention of a publisher. The lower part of the plate was then cut off in order to separate the portrait from the caption. A new caption was added using a small, loose plate: the Dutch translation of the original Latin text in verse, praising the thunderous voice and the devotion of Acronius (fig. 119).[75] It also

mentions that the artist Pieter de Molijn has the privilege of publishing this print (*Cum privilegio*). De Molijn would have possibly requested this from the city and, having been granted it, he was the only one authorised to publish this print – copies were forbidden.[76] This indicates that he foresaw a significant demand for it. The translation into Dutch meant that more people could understand the inscription, which no doubt boosted sales.

It was probably appealing to a clergyman to have for his own use a small portrait made by Hals, in order to be able to create a future print for his admirers – on his own or via a publisher, before or after his own death. This may also have been the reason why Suyderhoef's portrait prints of clergymen Hendrick Swalmius and Adrianus Tegularius were commissioned. The portrait of Swalmius was painted by Hals in 1639 and the engraving by Suyderhoef, without an identified publisher, came out about seven years later (figs 139–40).[77] The print made after an undated painting of Tegularius was issued posthumously by publisher and bookseller Robbert Tinneken (figs 145–6).

The painting of Deventer clergyman Caspar Sibelius shows that small portraits of clergymen were sometimes made into prints within a short time-frame and within the lifetime of the portrait sitter. Shortly after it was painted by Hals in 1637, Suyderhoef made an engraving of the portrait to scale (fig. 134–5).[78] Sibelius was in the vicinity that year, since his daughter married a clergyman in Bloemendaal, near Haarlem, on 8 January.[79] He may have been familiar with other work by Hals and Suyderhoef and seized this opportunity. Five years later Suyderhoef produced another, reduced-scale portrait print of Sibelius (fig. 136).[80] This is a reverse image of the original print and of a less refined quality. Perhaps Suyderhoef based this smaller work not on the painting, but on a print from his earlier engraving. The second print was intended as a book illustration, as indicated by the text in letterpress on the verso.

Suyderhoef also made prints of Schrevelius and Ampzing, years after Jacob Matham and Jan van de Velde the Younger, respectively, had produced the same portraits in print (figs 123, 131). The inscription on the undated portrait print of Schrevelius, provided by his good friend Casparus Barlaeus, can be interpreted as a description of an elderly man in retirement, but the comments about 'his silent tongue and his weary old age beseeching heaven for repose' may also suggest that the print was made after the death of Schrevelius in 1649. It would certainly have been made after 1 May 1642, when he was relieved of his headmastership at his own request, with expressions of gratitude for his many services. By this time Schrevelius was, by his own account, old and frail, and no longer derived any pleasure from his work.[81]

Suyderhoef's print of Ampzing, which may have been made around 1640, is an enlarged version of Hals's painting and Van de Velde's print, produced ten and eight years earlier, respectively (figs 129–31).[82] It cannot be determined with certainty with these prints of Schrevelius and Ampzing whether Suyderhoef worked from the

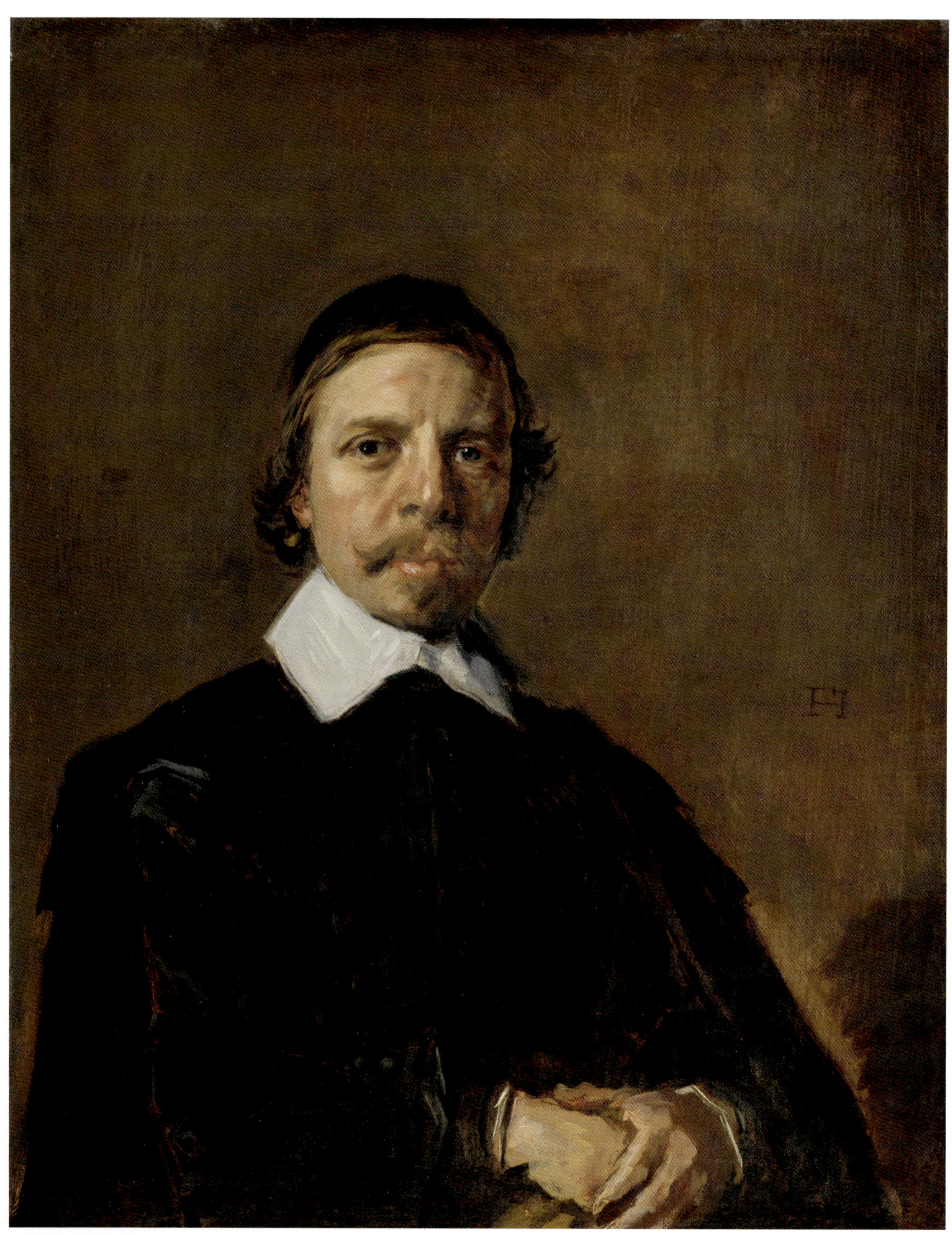

Fig. 120 *Portrait of a Man, possibly a Clergyman*, about 1658
Oil on wood, 37.1 × 29.8 cm
Rijksmuseum, Amsterdam

paintings or the prints, although the fact that his engravings are reverse images of the works by Hals suggests that he may have worked directly from the paintings. There are later known stages of Suyderhoef's prints of Ampzing and Schrevelius that list different publishers.[83] This suggests that demand for them continued for a long time, although nothing is known about the print run totals.

PRINTING FOR POSTERITY

Throughout his entire career Frans Hals produced small portraits on panel and copper, which were made into prints to scale. Around 1655, for example, when already in his seventies, he painted his fellow artist Frans Post, whose portrait was engraved by Suyderhoef (figs 143–4). Hals's models for prints probably began with Schrevelius, who wanted a portrait print of himself for posterity and was no doubt quite pleased to take his place in the appealing tradition of capturing illustrious men on paper.

While this intriguing little group of 11 portraits constitutes only about 5 per cent of Hals's oeuvre, it adds a unique dimension to the artist's work. With Schrevelius, Scriverius, Massa and De la Chambre, it is highly plausible that their portraits were made with the ancillary objective of being turned into prints. Because Hals did not adjust formal aspects like colour, touch and orientation (of light or writing instruments), his clients ended up in possession of a fully fledged and independent little portrait. The surviving pendant portrait of Anna van der Aar and listings in inventories further support the theory that these paintings were used and cherished as independent works of art. With the portraits of clergymen it was sometimes years before the print was produced. Posthumous prints were a frequent phenomenon in this profession and publishers regularly profited from releasing print runs of their portraits on paper.

Scholars, calligraphers, clergymen: the subcategory of portraits that were made into prints illustrates that 'Halsius' – the Latinised name under which Buchelius sang the artist's praises – enjoyed the custom not only of the wealthy bourgeoisie, but also of the intellectual elite. Like Thoré, they had an eye for a jewel, and their portrait prints help ensure that we still know who they were.

THEODORUS SCHREVELIUS

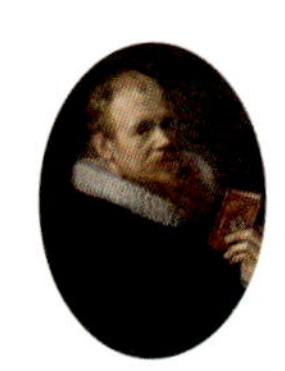

Fig. 121

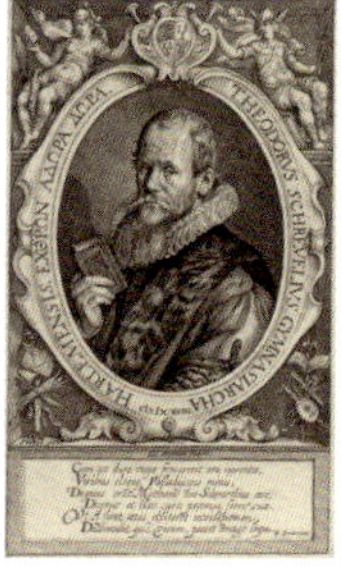

Fig. 122

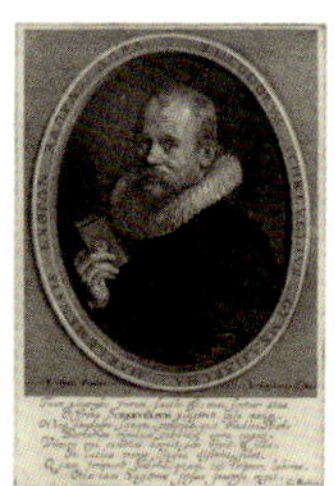

Fig. 123

PETRUS SCRIVERIUS

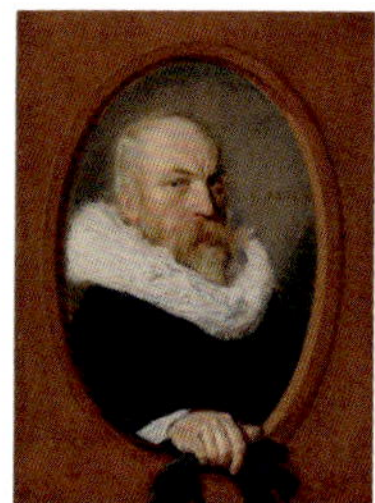

Fig. 124

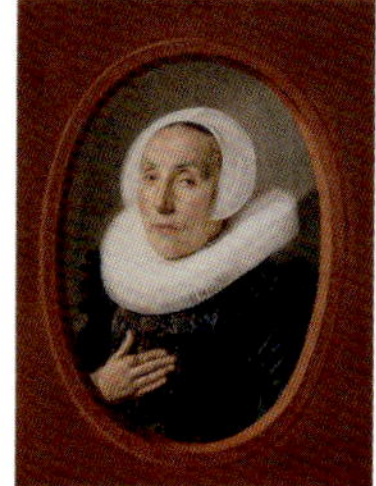

Fig. 125

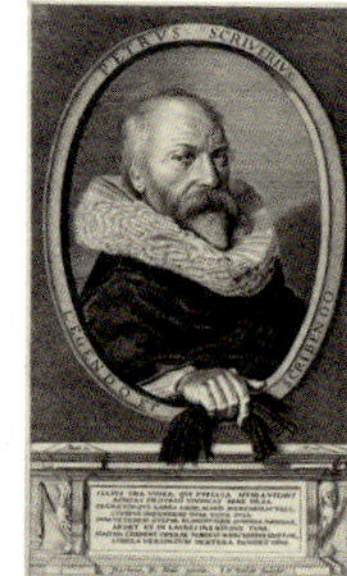

Fig. 126

JOHANNES ACRONIUS

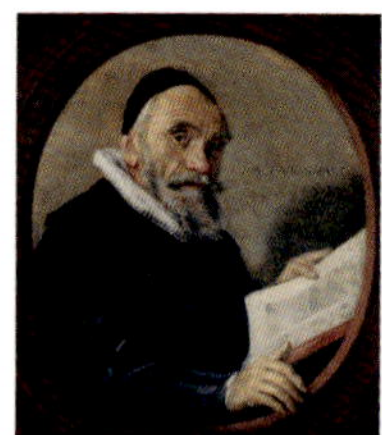

Fig. 127

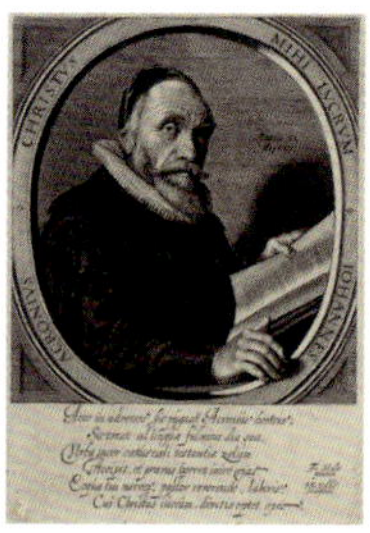

Fig. 128

SAMUEL AMPZING

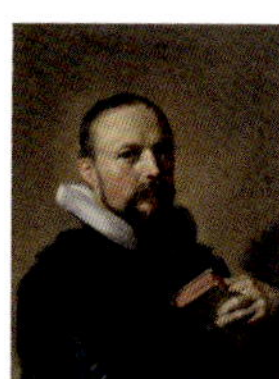

Fig. 129

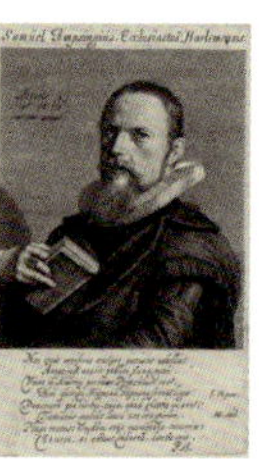

Fig. 130

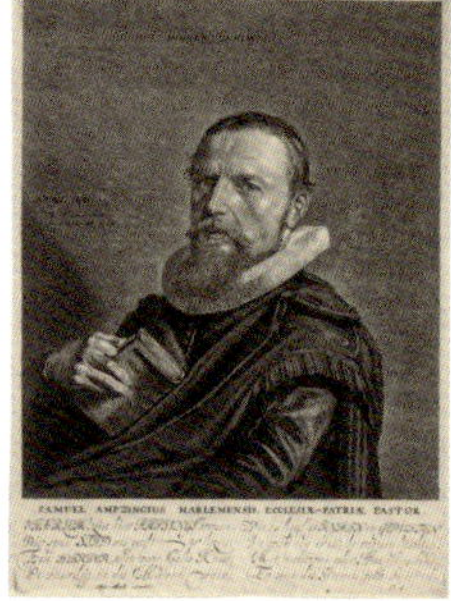

Fig. 131

ISAAC ABRAHAMSZ MASSA

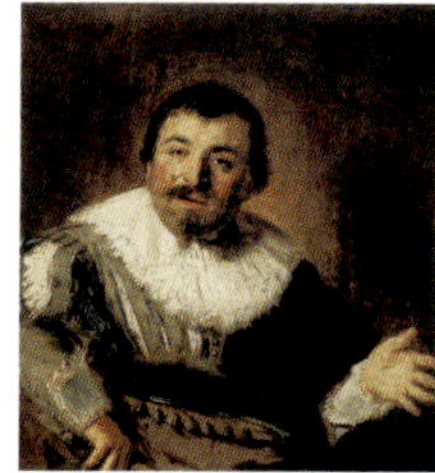

Fig. 132

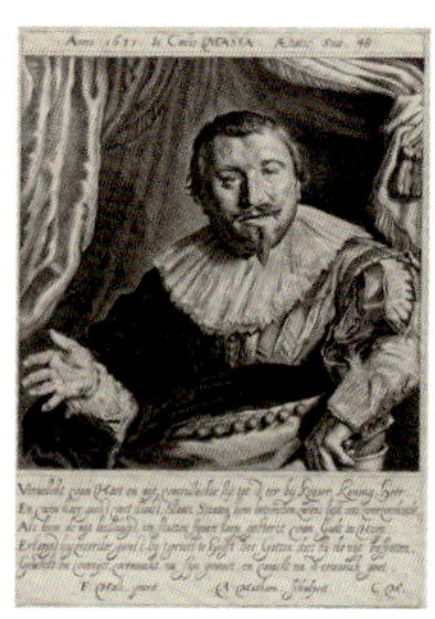

Fig. 133

CASPAR SIBELIUS

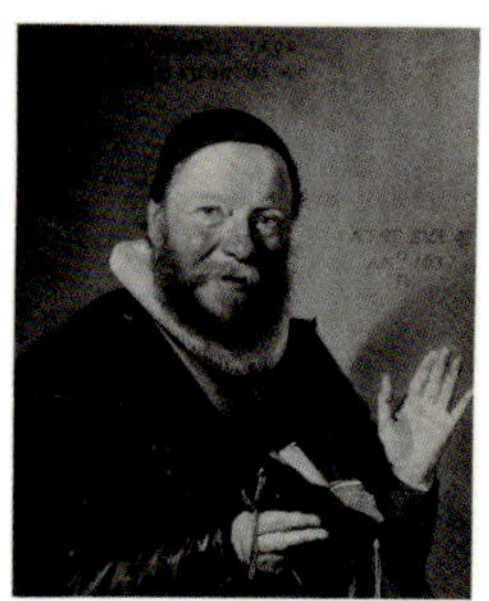

Fig. 134

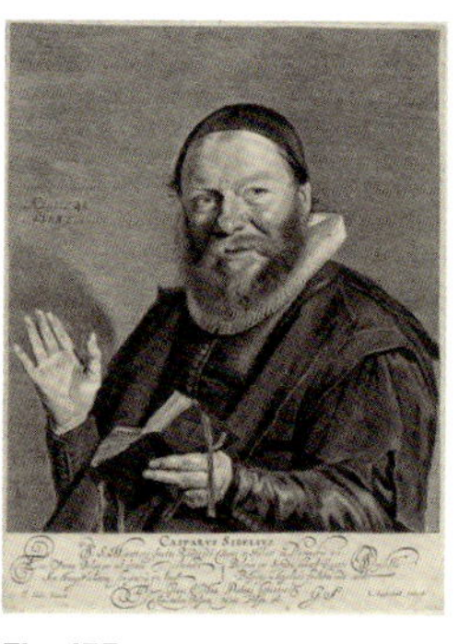

Fig. 135

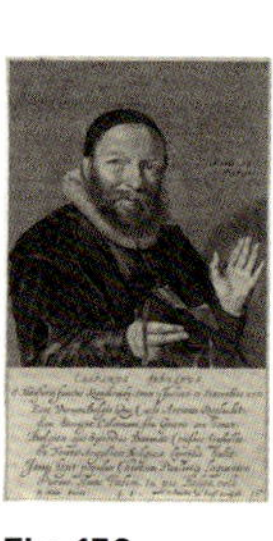

Fig. 136

Fig. 121
Portrait of
Theodorus Schrevelius, 1617
Oil on copper, 14.5 × 12 cm
Frans Hals Museum, Haarlem

Fig. 122
Jacob Matham after
Frans Hals, *Portrait of*
Theodorus Schrevelius, 1618
Engraving, 26.2 × 16 cm
Rijksmuseum, Amsterdam

Fig. 123
Jonas Suyderhoef after
Frans Hals, *Portrait*
of Theodorus Schrevelius,
about 1642–9
Engraving, 21.5 × 14.8 cm
Rijksmuseum, Amsterdam

Figs 124, 125
Portraits of
Petrus Scriverius and
Anna van der Aar, 1626
Oil on wood, 22.2 × 16.5 cm
The Metropolitan Museum
of Art, New York

Fig. 126
Jan van de Velde the Younger
after Frans Hals, *Portrait of*
Petrus Scriverius, 1626
Engraving, 26.9 × 15.6 cm
Rijksmuseum, Amsterdam

Fig. 127
Portrait of
Johannes Acronius, 1627
Oil on wood, 19.4 × 17.2 cm
Staatliche Museen zu Berlin,
Gemäldegalerie

Fig. 128
Jan van de Velde the Younger
after Frans Hals, *Portrait*
of Johannes Acronius, 1627
Engraving, 23.5 × 17 cm
Rijksmuseum, Amsterdam

Fig. 129
Portrait of
Samuel Ampzing, about 1630
Oil on copper, 16.2 × 12.3 cm
Leiden Collection, New York

Fig. 130
Jan van de Velde the Younger
after Frans Hals, *Portrait of*
Samuel Ampzing, 1632
Engraving, 20 × 12.3 cm
Rijksmuseum, Amsterdam;
D. Franken Bequest,
Le Vésinet

Fig. 131
Jonas Suyderhoef
after Frans Hals, *Portrait*
of Samuel Ampzing,
about 1640. Engraving,
16.4 × 12.4 cm. The Leiden
Collection, New York

Fig. 132
Portrait of
Isaac Abrahamsz Massa,
about 1635
Oil on wood, 21.3 × 19.7 cm
The San Diego Museum
of Art; gift of Anne R.
and Amy Putnam

Fig. 133
Adriaen Matham after
Frans Hals, *Portrait of Isaac*
Abrahamsz Massa, 1635
Engraving, 26.3 × 19.2 cm
Rijksmuseum, Amsterdam;
D. Franken Bequest,
Le Vésinet

Fig. 134
Portrait of
Caspar Sibelius, 1637
Oil on wood, 26.5 × 22.5 cm
Lost in a fire in 1956 while in
the private collection of
Billy Rose, New York

Fig. 135
Jonas Suyderhoef after
Frans Hals, *Portrait of*
Caspar Sibelius, 1637
Engraving, 30.1 × 23.2 cm
Rijksmuseum, Amsterdam

Fig. 136
Jonas Suyderhoef
after Frans Hals,
Portrait of Caspar
Sibelius, 1642
Engraving, 20.2 × 12.3 cm
Rijksmuseum, Amsterdam

JEAN DE LA CHAMBRE

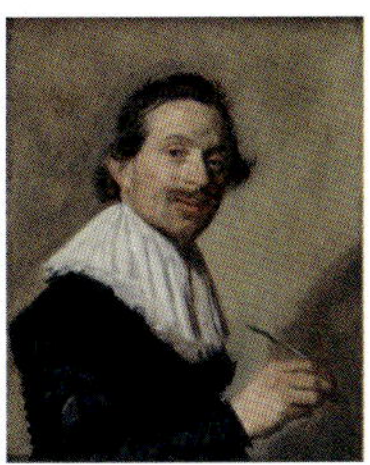

Fig. 137

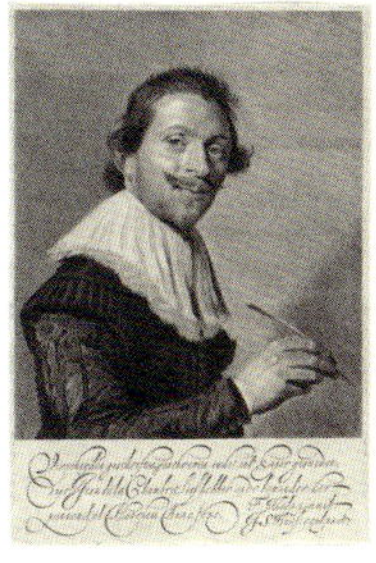

Fig. 138

RENÉ DESCARTES

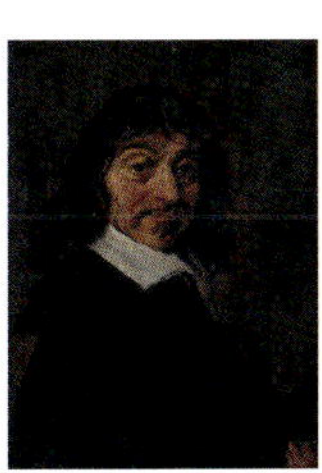

Fig. 141

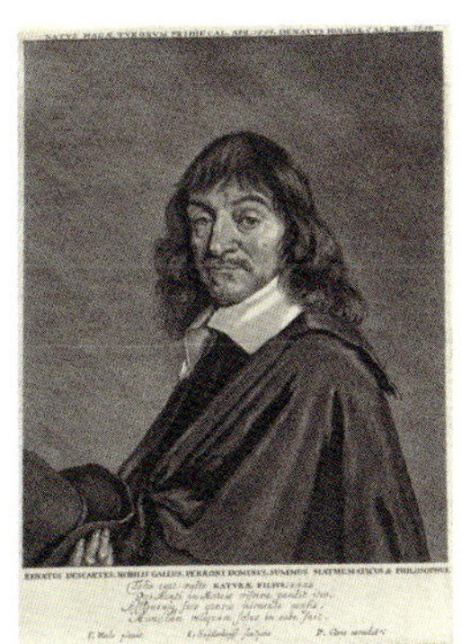

Fig. 142

ADRIANUS TEGULARIUS

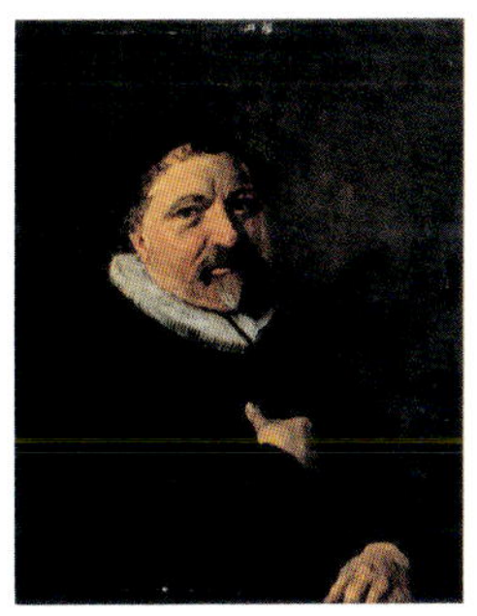

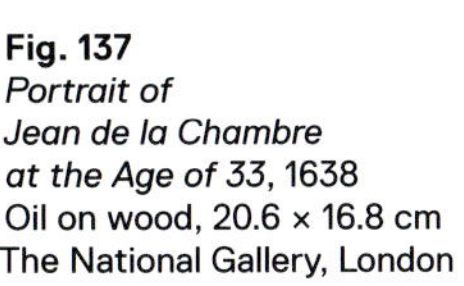

Fig. 145

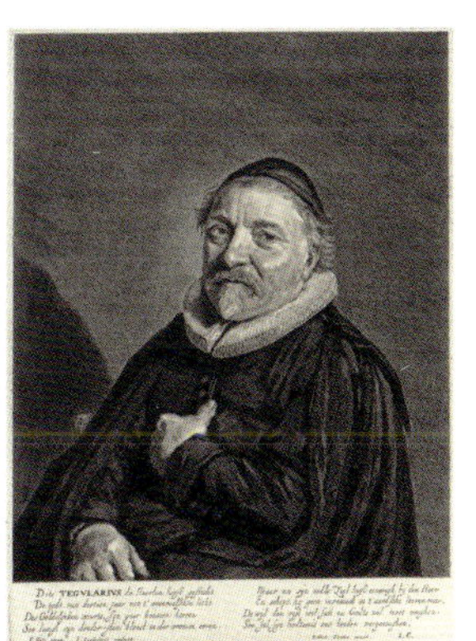

Fig. 146

HENDRICK SWALMIUS

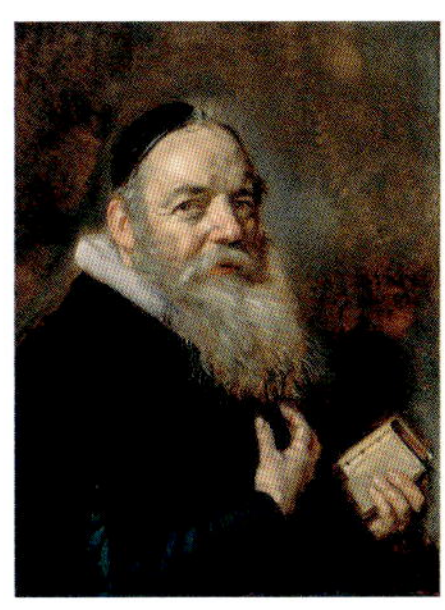

Fig. 139

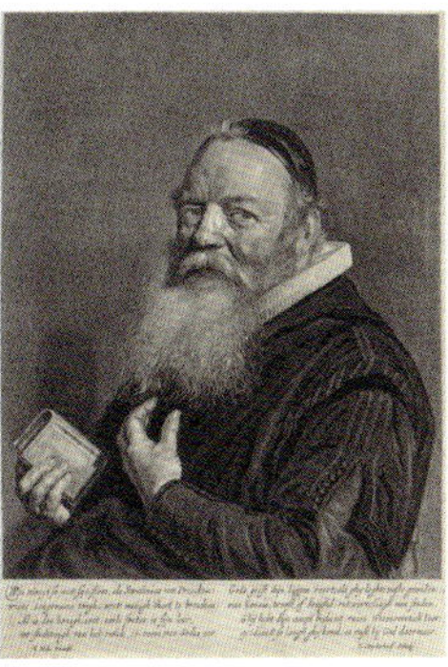

Fig. 140

FRANS POST

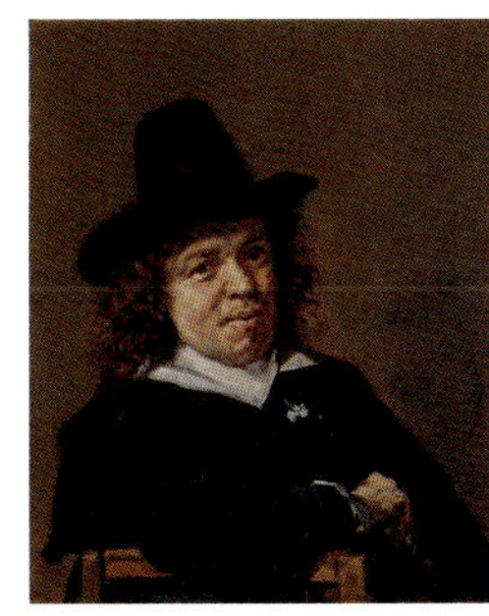

Fig. 143

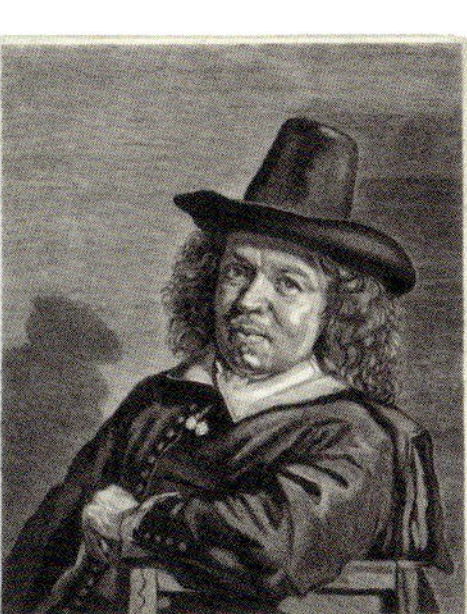

Fig. 144

Fig. 137
*Portrait of
Jean de la Chambre
at the Age of 33*, 1638
Oil on wood, 20.6 × 16.8 cm
The National Gallery, London

Fig. 138
Jonas Suyderhoef after
Frans Hals, *Portrait of
Jean de la Chambre
at the Age of 33*, 1638
Engraving, 25.7 × 17.4 cm
Rijksmuseum, Amsterdam

Fig. 141
*Portrait of
René Descartes*,
about 1649
Oil on wood, 19 × 14 cm
Statens Museum for Kunst,
Copenhagen

Fig. 142
Jonas Suyderhoef after
Frans Hals, *Portrait of
René Descartes*, 1650
Engraving, 31.7 × 22.8 cm
Rijksmuseum, Amsterdam

Fig. 145
*Portrait of
Adrianus Tegularius*,
about 1655–60
Panel, 27.9 × 22.8 cm
Present whereabouts
unknown

Fig. 146
Jonas Suyderhoef after
Frans Hals, *Portrait of
Adrianus Tegularius*, about
1655–60
Engraving, 34.6 × 25.5 cm
Rijksmuseum, Amsterdam

Fig. 139
*Portrait of
Hendrick Swalmius*, 1639
Oil on wood, 27 × 20 cm
Detroit Institute of Art

Fig. 140
Jonas Suyderhoef after Frans
Hals, *Portrait of Hendrick
Swalmius*, about 1646
Engraving, 31.7 × 22.7 cm
Rijksmuseum, Amsterdam

Fig. 143
*Portrait of
Frans Post*, about 1655
Oil on wood, 27.5 × 23 cm
Worcester Art Museum

Fig. 144
Jonas Suyderhoef after
Frans Hals, *Portrait of Frans
Post*, after about 1655
Engraving, 27.8 × 22.9 cm
Rijksmuseum, Amsterdam

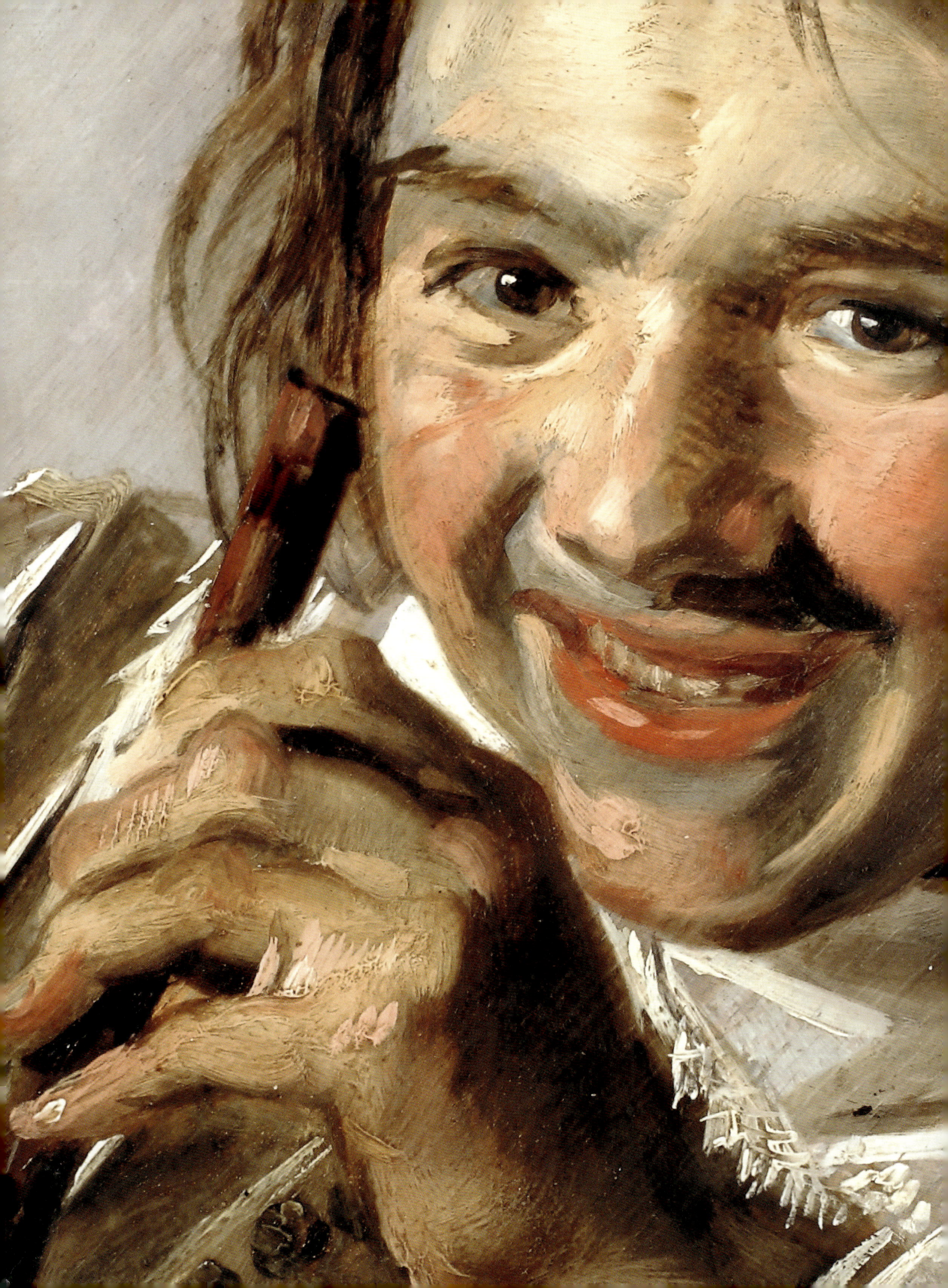

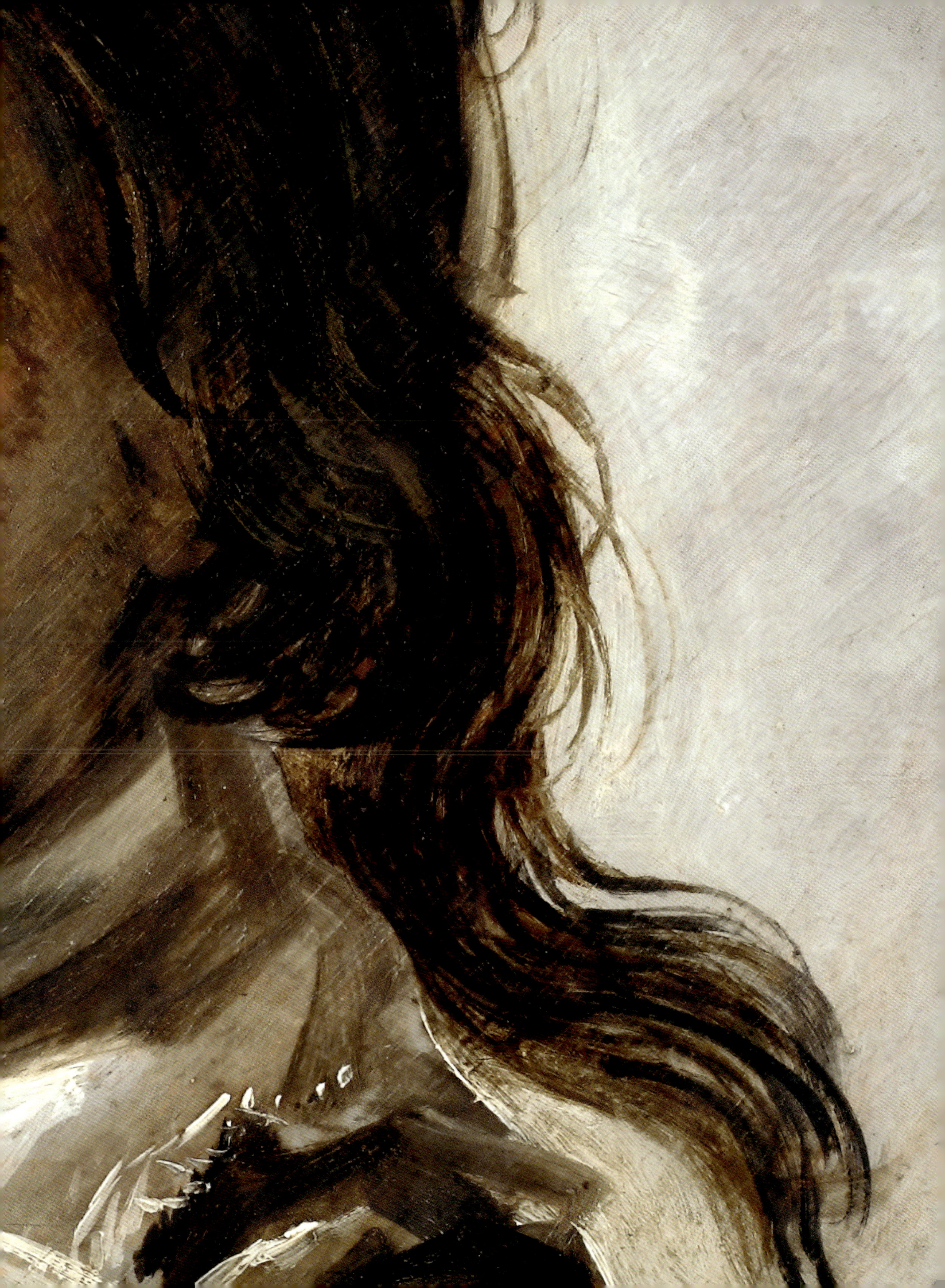

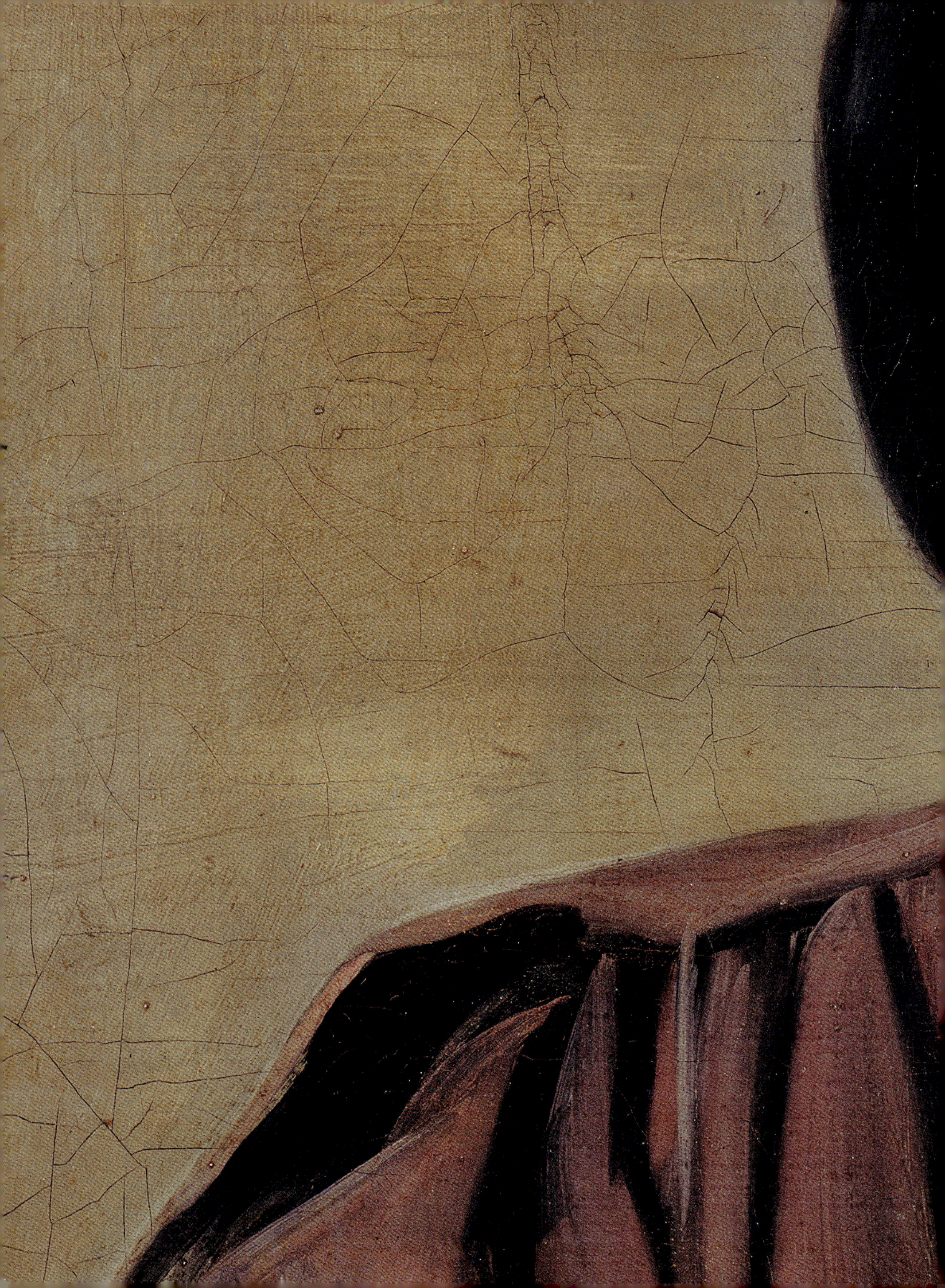

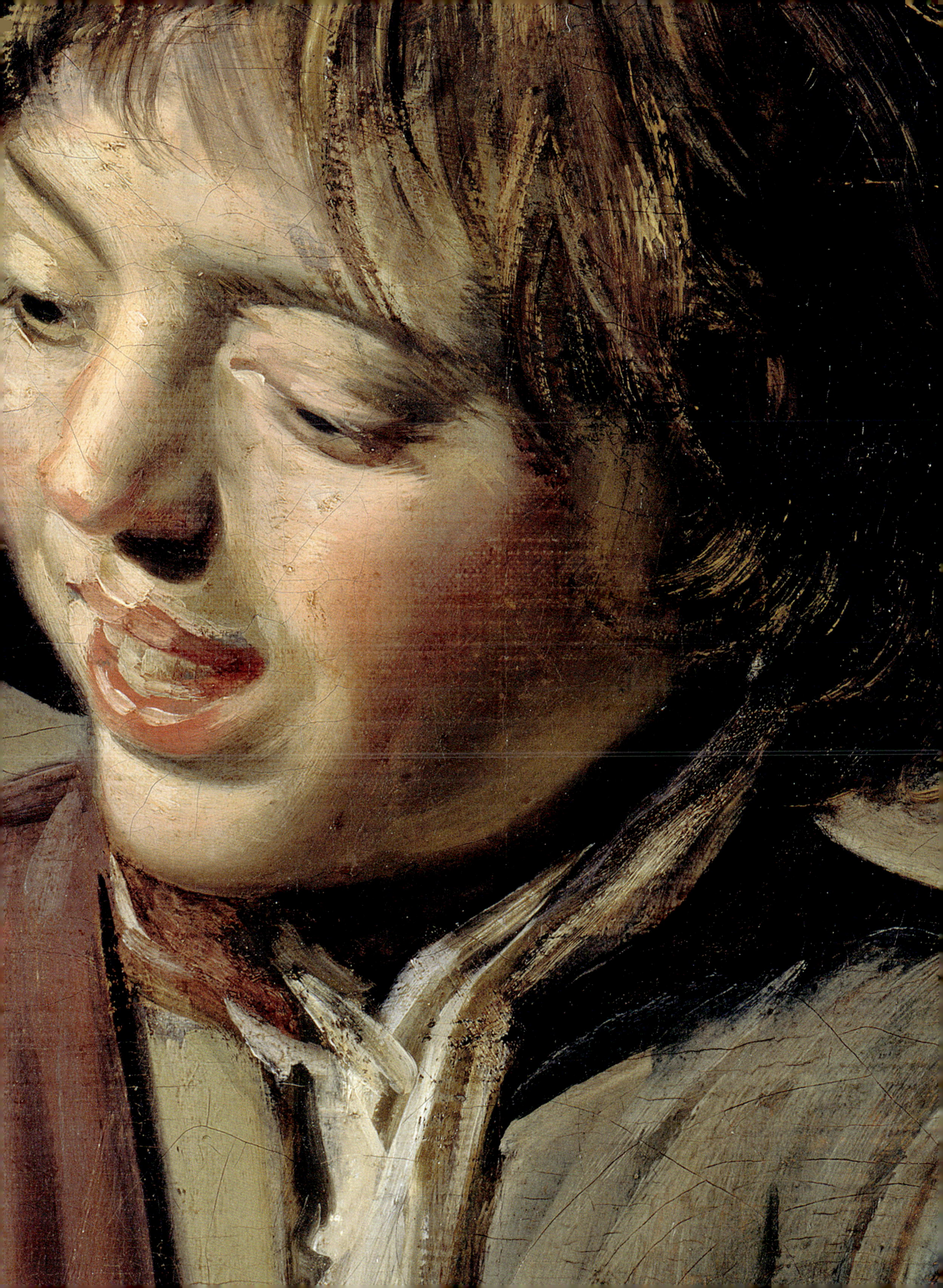

LAUGHTER

FRISO LAMMERTSE

How does one paint a laugh? The mouth and cheeks widen, the eyes are half-closed, creating small wrinkles towards the ears, and the forehead descends. Karel van Mander, Frans Hals's teacher, laid down this rule of thumb in his *Den grondt der edel vry schilder-const* (The Foundation of the Noble, Free Art of Painting), his didactic poem aimed at fledgling painters.[1] He discussed laughter in his chapter on the portrayal of emotions, a crucial aspect of painting if an artist wished to stir the viewer's feelings. If they were depicted convincingly, the observer would be swept up in the emotions of the person portrayed, be they of love, joy, sadness or despair. Depicting a laugh was considered to be particularly difficult, because the associated facial expression was very close to crying.[2] But, according to Van Mander, crying made the cheeks smaller and forced the bottom lip and corners of the mouth down, not up.

We can no longer make out whether Frans Hals knew that passage, but while he was Van Mander's pupil he would undoubtedly have discussed the depiction of emotions with him. He may, even then, have had a particular interest in painting merriment. In any event, as a master painter Hals had a very marked preference for laughter. He was one of the few seventeenth-century artists who regularly gave his portrait sitters a smile, and he very rarely omitted a broad grin in his *tronies* (or study heads) and genre paintings.

TYPES OF LAUGHTER

Laughter, of course, is no respecter of epoch, but in the sixteenth and seventeenth centuries philosophers, medical practitioners and scientists, writers and artists delved increasingly and ever more deeply into its many aspects. They studied how the laugh originated in the human body, who were the most susceptible to it, how melancholic people could be cured by it, and distinguished the varieties of laughter. Books about raising children and etiquette describe when and how laughter was seemly. Apart from a few dogmatic churchmen, who condemned each and every form of laughter with a

reference to the Bible – 'Woe unto you that laugh now' (Luke 6:25) – everyone agreed that it was an emotional response common to all human beings.[3]

That did not mean that one could burst into hysterical laughter at the drop of a hat. It was only fit and proper, according to sixteenth-century humanists such as Desiderius Erasmus, that one should control the body, the emotions and thus laughter. The ideas of this Rotterdam scholar were repeated for centuries afterwards.[4] His 1530 treatise on the rearing of the young (*De civilitate morum puerilium … libellus*) was reprinted and revised until the end of the seventeenth century. According to the title page of a Dutch translation of 1652, *Boecxken, van de borgerlyke beleeftheid der kinderlyke zeden* (A little book of good manners for children), it was also used in schools.[5] Erasmus asserted that:

> It's wrong to smile at obscene words or actions. Raucous laughter and uncontrollable giggles that rock the whole body, and for which reason are known as shaking, are not appropriate. It's improper for anyone when they laugh to make a neighing noise. It's rude when someone opens his mouth in a wide rictus, wrinkling his cheeks and revealing his teeth as if he were a dog.[6]

The face could certainly express merriment as long as it did not dishonour the appearance of the mouth, nor reveal a lack of control. He also disliked 'foolish expressions' such as 'My sides are aching', 'I'm laughing fit to burst' or 'I'm laughing fit to die'. If all else failed, and someone burst out laughing anyway, he recommended covering the face with a cloth or hand.[7]

SWEET LAUGH

Uncontrollable laughter was unbecoming and objectionable but if suppressed it could be the height of attractiveness. The Dutch word for 'smile' (glimlach) was not used in the seventeenth century;[8] if one wanted to stress the charm of a smile, one used words such as 'sweet' and 'gentle', or a diminutive, like 'little laugh'. Daniël Heinsius, a Leiden professor and poet, said of the laugh

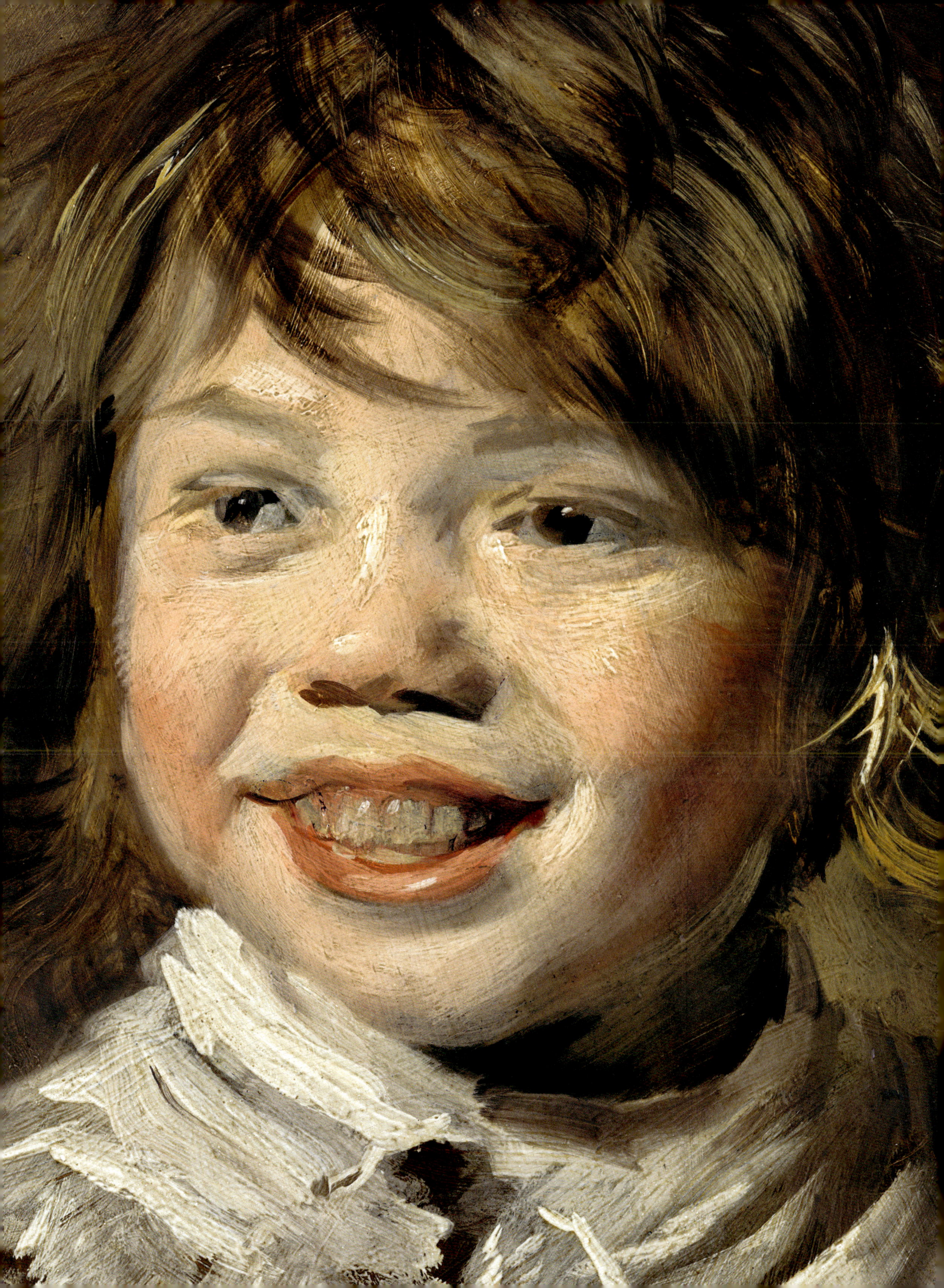

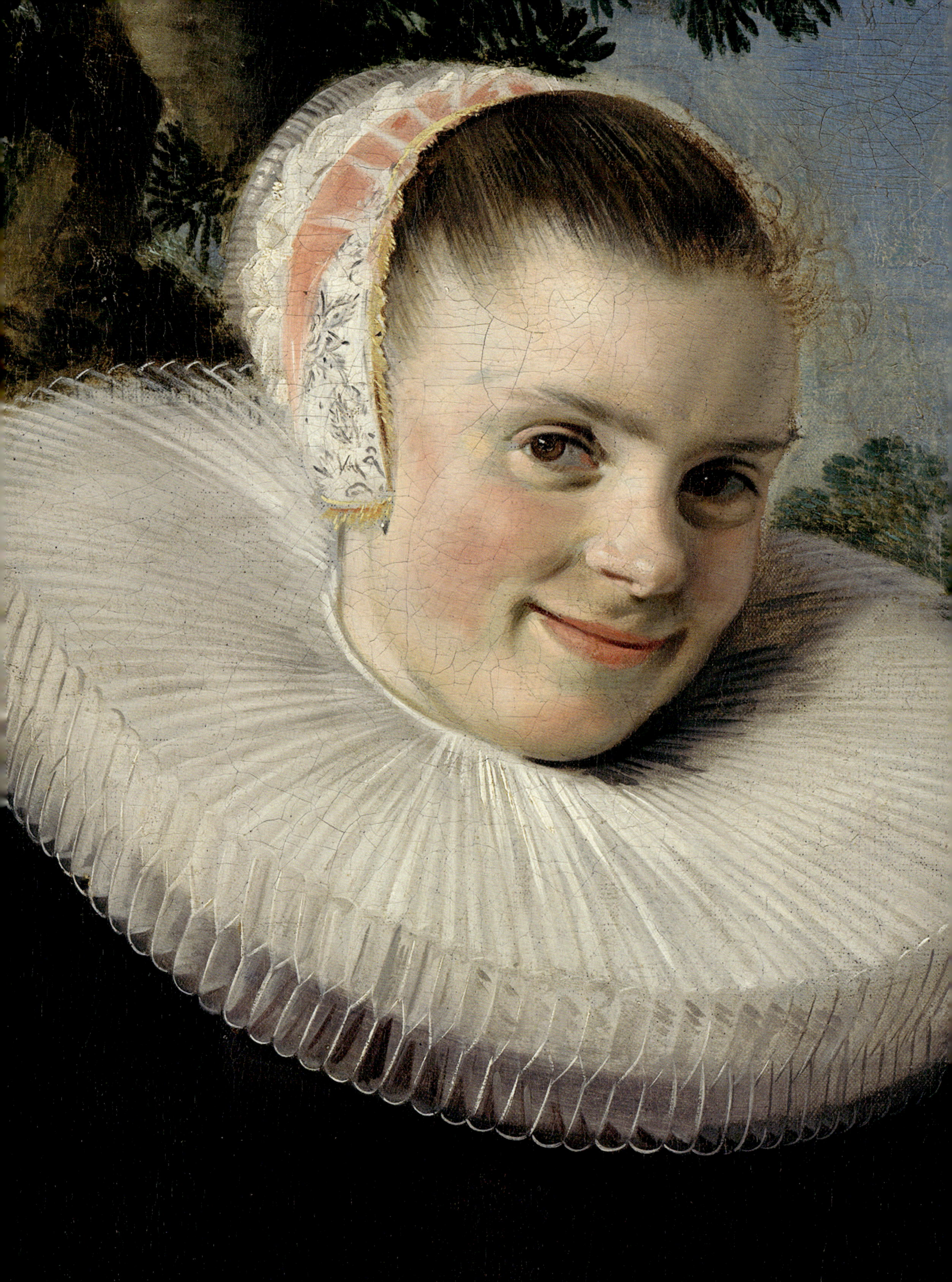

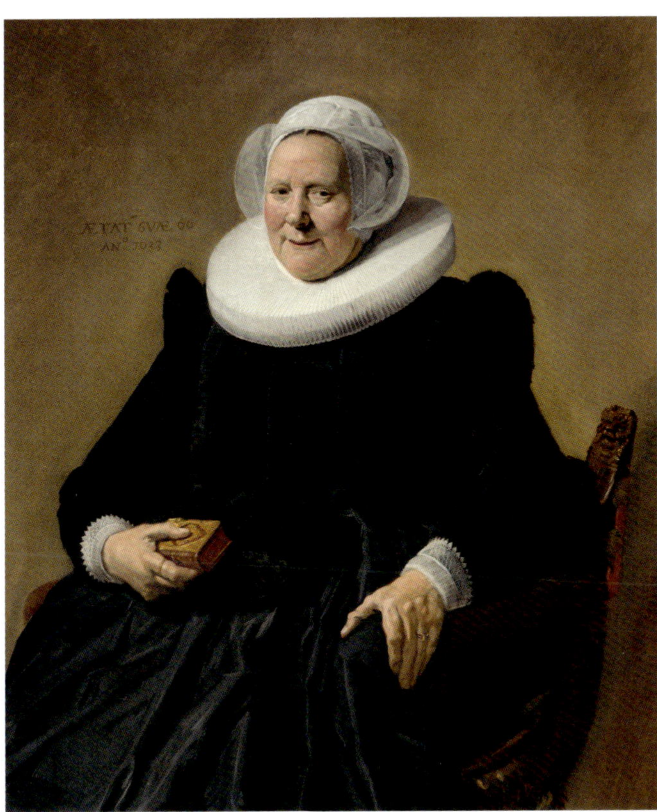

Fig. 147 *Portrait of a Woman Aged Sixty*, 1633
Oil on canvas, 102.5 × 86.9 cm
National Gallery of Art, Washington;
Andrew W. Mellon Collection

of his beloved that 'it could not have been softer'.[9] Jacob Cats had the wife of the biblical commander Potiphar ask 'Whose heart would not be charmed by a sweet laugh?' when she realises with bewilderment that Joseph is rejecting her advances.[10]

Van Mander advises that love between a man and a woman should be depicted 'with a friendly, smiling visage'. Deep affection, he continues, can often reveal itself by a face colouring 'a rosy red'.[11] Frans Hals surpassed everyone in this respect. In a number of his companion pieces of young married couples at least one of the sitters is smiling, the woman more often than the man. In his scene of a garden of love (fig. 61), possibly featuring a double portrait of the newly married Isaac Massa and Beatrix van der Laen, Hals excelled himself.[12] Their laughter, the blush on her cheek and the way she rests her hand on her husband's shoulder convince the beholder that they are indeed 'filled full with love', to quote Van Mander again.[13] The same applies to the equally masterly portraits of Isabella Coymans and her husband, Stephanus Geraerdts, in which she presents him with a rose (figs 82–3).

Of course a smile was suitable for suggesting not only love between a man and woman but also tenderness within a family or between a child and its nurse (fig. 60).[14] Hals almost never showed older people smiling, one of the few exceptions being an unknown 60-year-old woman gazing happily out at us (fig. 147). The general opinion was that laughter was the province of the young. The Italian scholar Cesare Ripa stated in his famous *Iconologia* of 1593 that 'Youth' was to be depicted as a laughing, merry girl, and his personifications of 'Laughter' are invariably young.[15]

The idea that laughter is specifically associated with adolescents and young adults had a 'scientific' foundation in the doctrine of the humours, the idea that the four bodily fluids governed a person's character and states of mind. It was assumed that the young had a great deal of blood, which made them prone to 'laughter and merriment … [being] amusing and witty [and] fond of playing and singing', as Ripa put it.[16] This is why it was appropriate to portray the young with a smile, even when there was no direct connection with love, and why, in Hals's civic guard pieces, in which the figures generally look rather serious, it is above all younger men who cannot suppress a smile. It also accounts for the merry look on the face of Hals's most famous portrait, *The Laughing Cavalier* (fig. 78). That unidentified man, who according to the inscription was 26 at the time, is looking at us with a slightly ironic gaze; his lips are barely parted, but just enough to show that he is in a good mood. Van Mander says that the best way to depict cheerfulness is with 'The mouth somewhat open / sweet / laughing / blithesome', the eyes half-closed, and 'a carefree brow, which is smooth and clear'.[17] The decoration on his luxurious clothing reveals that the man was perhaps thinking of love when he was painted, for the details of the embroidery include a love-knot and Cupid's bow and arrow.[18]

While the sitters in Hals's portraits have lips barely part-ed, their teeth invisible, the figures in his genre scenes roar with laughter, their mouths wide open. These, though, are not the upright citizens who know how to behave but almost invariably characters regarded in the seventeenth century as the embodiment of folly.[19]

The idea that the world was populated with fools was widespread. It was pithily illustrated in prints in which a terrestrial globe is adorned with a fool's cap, like the design by Maarten van Heemskerck for a scene of Heraclitus and Democritus, or the engraving by Jacques de Gheyn II for the fools' festival organised in 1596 by Pieter Cornelisz van der Mersch (see below).[20] Yet fool-ishness was not always in itself foolish: fools could sometimes reveal the truth with their gibbering.

Everyone behaved crazily at times but some were far more inclined to do so than others. In the view of the male urban elite, this was particularly true of people in the lower social classes. They often played the leading roles in farces. An introduction to the work of the famous playwright Gerbrandt Adriaensz Bredero sums them up as 'the dregs of the people, herders, peasants, labourers, innkeepers, women innkeepers, panders, harlots, mid-wives, boatsmen, spendthrifts, female beggars and scroun-gers'.[21] Women and children were also considered to be especially susceptible to foolishness. But even the most serious person could ultimately turn into a fool under the influence of drink and love. As we shall see below, Hals's guffawing figures were of this kind too.

The farces and poems of Bredero and other writers provide good examples of what was considered amusing in the seventeenth century, thus illuminating the comic aspects of genre painting of the period. This is particularly true of the work of Frans Hals, who knew the stage and literature from personal experience.

HALS THE RHETORICIAN

In 1616, when he was in his early 30s, Frans Hals joined one of the three chambers of rhetoric in Haarlem, the Wijngaertrancken (Vine Tendrils).[22] It was flourishing at the time, for in that year it had 14 new members; three years later its membership had grown to 69, a record for the seventeenth century.[23] The members, all men, met on Sunday to drink, discuss the news of the day, declaim poetry they had written and rehearse or perform plays. Occasionally they also held poetry contests. A few times a year, mainly at annual markets, fairs and on other feast days, they put on performances in the streets and squares of the town. The high points were the public theatre and poetry festivals, in which they competed with other rhe-torical societies. The Vine Tendrils had two classes of membership: 'cameristen' (chamberers) and 'beminnaars' (devotees). The former were the central figures within the organisation and provided the chamber's officials. Hals belonged to the second group, which had fewer obligations and rights but far more members.[24]

Hals must have become familiar with the rhetoricians' public performances when he was a child, and he prob-ably began taking an even keener interest in them during his apprenticeship. His teacher, Van Mander, was a pro-lific poet and playwright who played a key role in the Flemish chamber of rhetoric in Haarlem and was also involved with the Vine Tendrils society, although as far as we know he was not a member.[25] When he moved out of Haarlem to a country house in nearby Heemskerk in 1603 or 1604, Van Mander invited enthusiasts and his 'principal friends' for a performance of a play he had written. The actors were his pupils, but it is not known whether Hals was one of them.[26]

No doubt Hals got to know many kindred spirits in the Vine Tendrils, among them the painters Nicolaes de Kemp, Salomon de Bray, Esaias van de Velde and his own brother Dirck, all of whom were members of the chamber during the same period as Hals. In 1626, just after Frans Hals left the chamber, his pupil Adriaen Brouwer joined it.[27] The Vine Tendrils were miscella-neous representatives of a broad, erudite middle class. There were doctors, lawyers, schoolmasters, cloth mer-chants, printers, engravers and gold- and silversmiths, but also wealthy beer brewers such as the alderman and burgomaster Johan Claesz Loo.[28] Hals immortalised Loo in two civic guard portraits, first around 1633 when he was colonel of the Calivermen Civic Guard (fig. 148), and six years later when he had the same function in the St George Civic Guard (fig. 67).[29]

It seems that Hals enjoyed his time with the rhetori-cians, for he remained a member of the Vine Tendrils for ten years,[30] a long time compared with the average of three years.[31] Personifications embodying abstract con-cepts such as love, hate or wisdom, with the aid of identifying attributes, played key roles in their work and were the centrepieces of many of their plays and the parades that marked the openings of their contests. Hals does not seem to have had much interest in such allegorical figures. One of the few paintings in which he depicted them is his portrait of Isaac Massa (fig. 94) – who was, perhaps not coincidentally, a rhetorician him-self – in which Death in the guise of a skeleton and Envy as a woman with snakes in her hair loom up behind the sitter. One of the most important aspects of the rhetori-cians' meetings was the use of discussion to sharpen members' wits. It is possible that Hals debated with his colleagues how certain abstract concepts could be de-picted in such a way as to come closer to everyday life. This applies above all to the five senses, which Hals and his contemporaries no longer portrayed as female alle-gorical figures but as genre scenes.[32]

Above all, Hals was probably interested in the comic side of the rhetoricians: in their poems they loved to scoff and mock, and they regularly staged farces along-side their more serious offerings.[33] Every now and then chambers of rhetoric organised contests together, in which fools battled to determine who was the wittiest and most sophisticated.

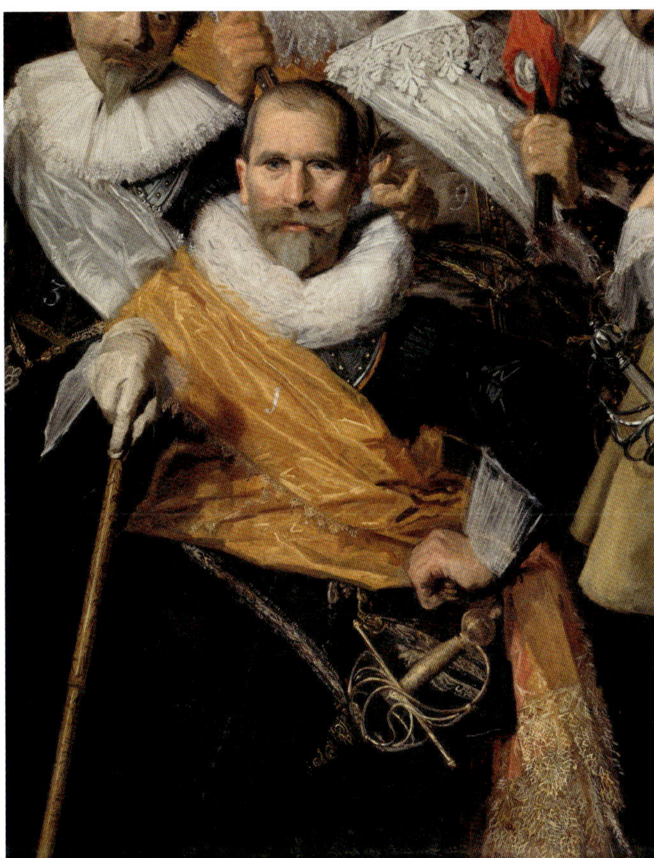

Fig. 148 Detail from *Meeting of the Officers and Sergeants of the Calivermen Civic Guard*, about 1633 (fig. 66), showing Johan Claesz Loo

A PORTRAIT OF A FOOL

Jesters (also known as buffoons) were regarded as supreme fools. They were experts in exaggerating and ridiculing people's everyday behaviour. Laughter was their trademark, not just a seemly chuckle but one that revealed the teeth. They were hired by city authorities, guilds, civic guard companies and city quarters to add merriment to their feasts.[34] Jesters started appearing in prints and paintings in the fifteenth century, and became very popular in the century that followed: by the first half of the sixteenth century, paintings with a jester were by far the commonest of the genre subjects in Antwerp inventories.[35] The jesters from that period are usually immediately recognisable from their colourful costumes and distinctive caps decorated with asses' ears and bells. They were given more varied clothing in the seventeenth century; the typical fool's cap is nowhere to be found in the works of Frans Hals or Judith Leyster.

In the year when Hals joined the Vine Tendrils he painted a portrait of Pieter Cornelisz van der Mersch (fig. 151), probably the most famous Dutch jester of the day.[36] He has a sly, knowing look on his face and is brandishing a kipper in his right hand while clasping a straw-lined basket with several kippers in his left. 'Wie begeert' (Who wants one?) is written in large letters beside him. Typically for rhetoricians, this is an ambiguous question: not whether the viewer wants a fish but a mocking rebuke, known as 'giving someone a kipper' – and Van der Mersch was an expert at that. As the jester in the Leiden Witte Acoleyen (White Columbine) chamber of rhetoric, he was famous for the way he put people in their place. He wrote an elegy for himself that opened with the words 'Hier leyt Piero / Die deelde Bucken' (Here lies Piero. He handed out kippers).[37]

According to the inscription on the portrait, the jester was 73 when it was painted. It is not clear where or how he got to know Hals. Van der Mersch was regularly in Haarlem and is known to have been there in 1606, 1613 and 1615.[38] The two may have met in the latter year, when Van der Mersch entered a poem for the contest organised by the Vine Tendrils chamber.[39] The jester called himself Van der Mersch – nowadays often wrongly called Van der Morsch – the name he assumed for one of his starring roles in the jesters' contest he organised in Leiden in 1596. Clad in a jester's costume in a farce as Joncker Morsch (Squire Bungler), he married Vrou Lors (Dame Cheat).[40] Van der Mersch is presented as a fool in Hals's painting purely because of the kipper, but his clothing proclaims him to be a wealthy citizen, which he was at the time.[41]

SHROVETIDE REVELLERS

Shrove Tuesday, the day before the period of fasting in Lent and given over to feasting and drinking, was one of the most important festivals of the year for rhetoricians.[42] Sometimes masked and costumed, revellers danced and made music as they wended their way through the streets.

Despite its Roman Catholic origins, the festival remained extremely popular, even after the Protestants assumed power in Haarlem in 1581. In order to make the mood even merrier, the rhetoricians organised events of various kinds, both outdoors and in taverns.

In one of his earliest known works Frans Hals painted a group of merrymakers identified in an inscription on the back of a drawn copy of 1660 as 'Vastenavonts-gasten' (Shrovetide revellers; fig. 149).[43] The central figure is a laughing woman being embraced by an older man with a festoon around his shoulder of leaves, sausages, eggs, beans, a pig's foot and a mussel. The woman appears to be more interested in the person on her left, who has tied a sausage to his cap and is making an unmistakable sexual gesture with his hands. Draping an entire meal around yourself in this way appears to have been a common practice. Two beggars in a comedy of 1612 by Samuel Coster describe similar adornments worn by Shrovetide revellers: 'Your hats close-clothed around / with tasty chicken bones / Not forgetting swine buttocks / well-salted / And on your necks make garlands / Of many sausages and bratwurst / tastily peppered. / With which a drink tastes good.'[44]

Some of the details in the painting suggest that Hals set out to accentuate its humorous and erotic elements. For instance, the yolk dripping from the broken egg in the festoon of the man on the left and the flat bagpipes in front of him might be signs that his virility is in question; similar ambiguities are typical of contemporary farces.[45] The contrast between the man's advanced age and the woman's youth suggest the popular theme of the unequal couple.[46] He is emphatically identified as a fool by the fox tail he holds in his right hand.[47] The same figure appears in another composition by Hals that is only known from a copy (fig. 150), again with an arm around a young woman, although this time not draped with food and with the fox tail hanging from his cap.[48] This man, also depicted by Willem Buytewech, was probably a familiar sight in Haarlem and may have been a rhetorician who played a buffoon.[49]

One is left with the question of whether Hals took the subject from a specific stage play, or perhaps it was more a matter of a general image of Shrove Tuesday featuring certain stereotypes.[50] On this day theatrics and festivities regularly merged almost seamlessly. In 1648, for instance, the church council of De Lier, a village near The Hague, scolded several young female members of the congregation for being in a tavern on Shrove Tuesday 'with young men for their play and mealtimes'. Because 'every manner of levity and carnal licentiousness' was committed in such company, they were given a serious warning.[51] A male member of the congregation who had assisted the Shrovetide merrymakers was also reprimanded.

Elsewhere Hals took his inspiration directly from the stage, as is clear from a hitherto unknown mention in an Amsterdam notarised document of 1645. The possessions of Lijsbet Harmens included '1 painting of a farce at/of Santvoort by Frans Hals, with a gilt frame'.[52] It is not clear whether the description was of a comedy of that

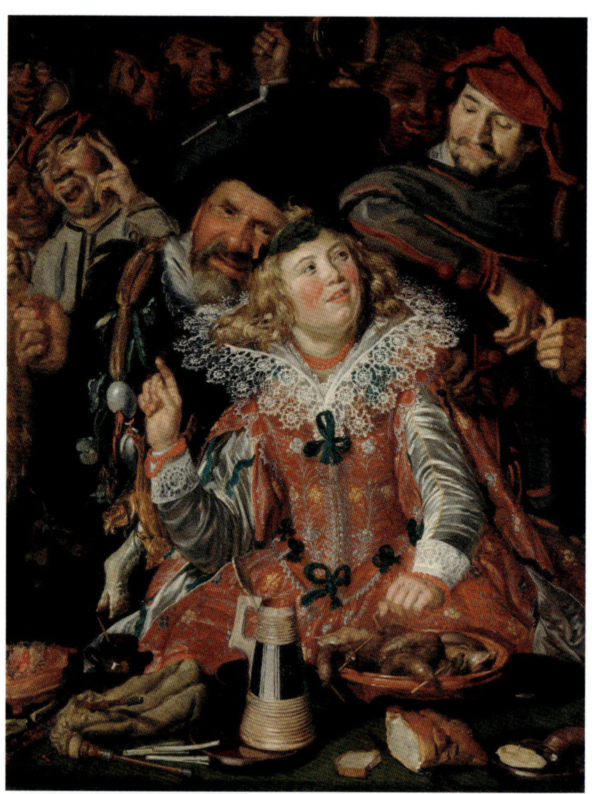

Fig. 149 *Merrymakers at Shrovetide*, about 1616–17. Oil on canvas, 131.4 × 99.7 cm The Metropolitan Museum of Art, New York; Bequest of Benjamin Altman, 1913

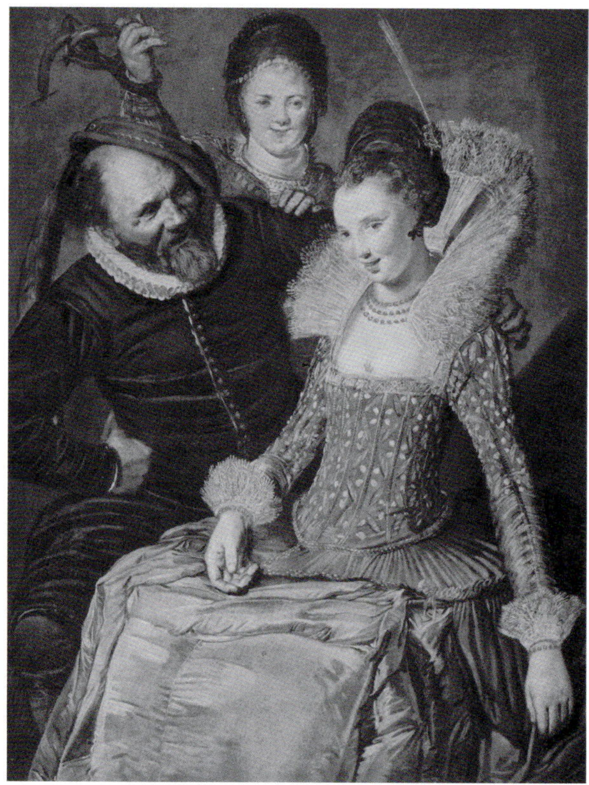

Fig. 150 After Frans Hals, *Merry Trio*, about 1616. Oil on canvas, 81 × 62 cm Previously Kaiser-Friedrich-Museum, Berlin (lost in the Second World War)

LAUGHTER

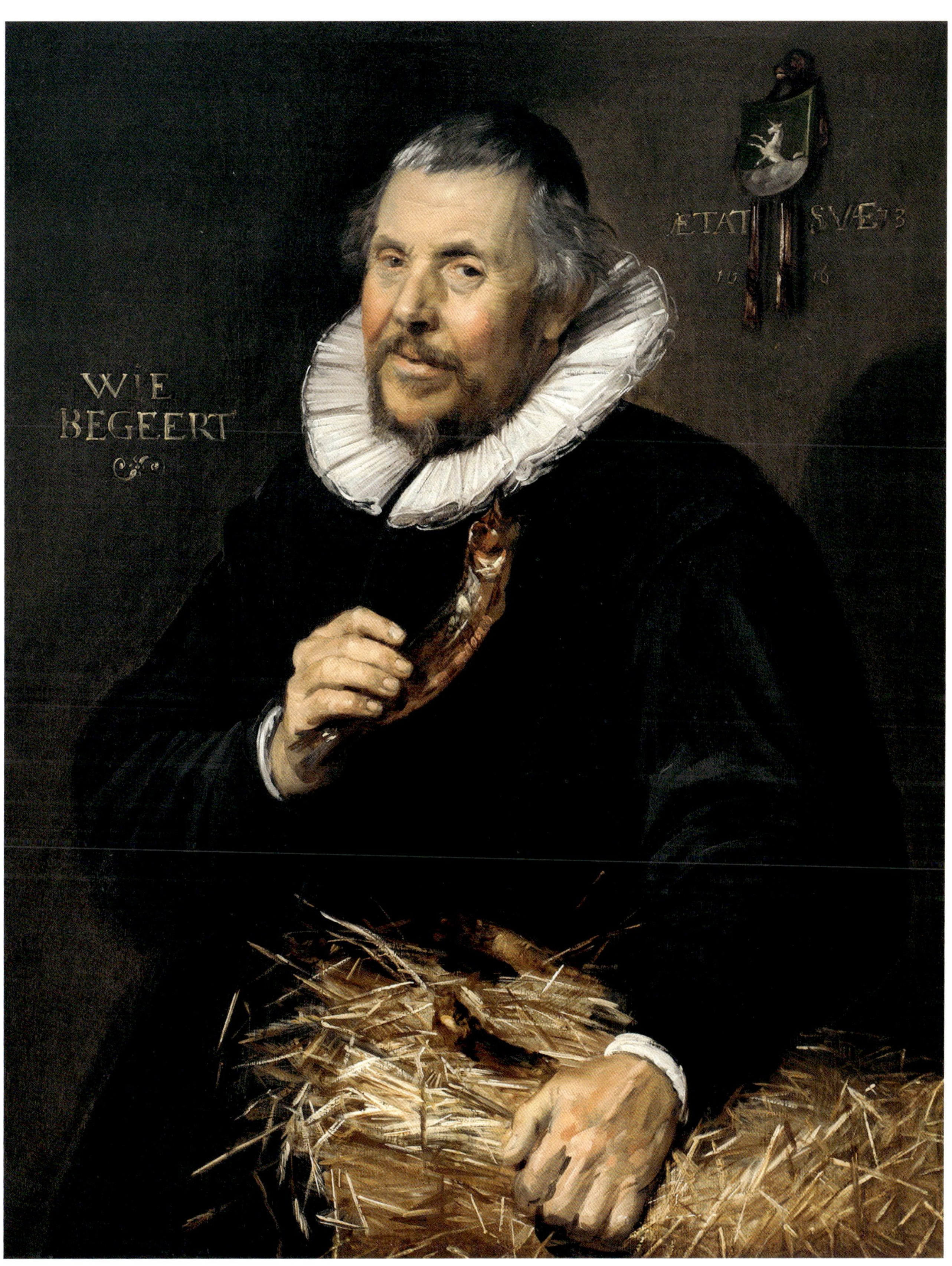

Fig. 151 *Portrait of Pieter Cornelisz van der Mersch*, 1616
Oil on canvas, transferred
from panel, 87.5 × 69.2 cm
Carnegie Museum of Art, Pittsburgh

name, now unknown, or of a performance in Zandvoort, near Haarlem. This village had an active chamber of rhetoric and in August 1616 organised a competition in which all three of the Haarlem chambers took part.[53] Without any further information about the farce it is impossible to say whether this painting can be identified with any of Hals's extant works.

His membership of the Vine Tendrils enabled Hals to take part in the preparation and performance of its stage plays. As well as providing him with subjects for his paintings, it also allowed him to observe the actors and viewers closely, giving him an invaluable opportunity to study their facial reactions and poses during the plays and recitals of humorous poems. While the rhetoricians were amateur actors who organised their performances alongside their daily work, at the end of the sixteenth century and in the early decades of the seventeenth there were also professional English theatre companies touring the Netherlands and German-speaking countries. One of their principal characters, the buffoon Pekelharing (Pickle Herring in English), was the subject of two famous paintings by Hals.

PEKELHARING

'Behold Mr Pickle Herring / He praises a tankard cool and full' are the opening lines of a little poem below an engraving by Jonas Suyderhoef (fig. 152) after a canvas by Frans Hals (fig. 153) now in the Gemäldegalerie alte Meister in Kassel. Because his throat is salty, the four-line poem announces, Pekelharing is in constant need of refreshment.[54] The same guffawing figure, who is immediately recognisable as a fool from his red and yellow costume with large buttons, is also the subject of another painting by Hals (fig. 154). Paintings of the same subject are recorded at early dates. In 1631, for instance, the Haarlem innkeeper Hendrick den Abt owned 'a Pekelharing by Frans Hals', and a few years earlier 'the portrait of Mr Pekelharinck' had been one of the prizes in a dicing lottery held in an Amsterdam tavern.[55]

Every lover of the theatre must have been familiar with Pekelharing, who, despite his Dutch-sounding name, was originally English.[56] As 'Pickle Herring' he was often the star comic turn in the so-called 'jigs', short musicals performed by travelling English theatre companies. His importance can be seen from a collection of English plays published in German in 1620, an anthology of both comedies and tragedies in which he plays the part of a villain and swindler crazy for drink.[57] While improvising, Pekelharing was also expected to react wittily to the proceedings taking place in the play. The stage directions regularly contain prompts for him to react: 'alhier agiret Pickelhering' (action from Pickle Herring here).

The first Dutch play that features Pekelharing only dates from 1637[58] but he must have been a legend long before then. For instance, the poet Jan Jansz Starter wrote in his *Friesche Lust-hof* of 1621 that one of the part-songs had to be sung to the tune of 'Pekelharing', which

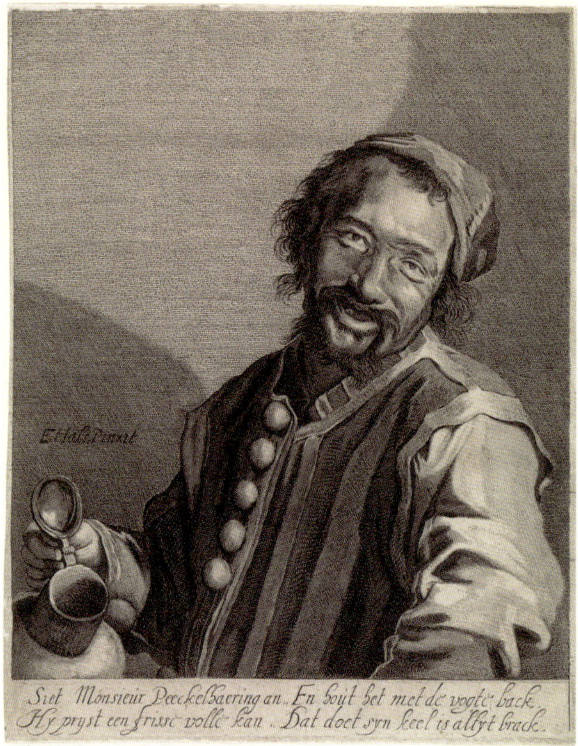

Fig. 152 Jonas Suyderhoef after
Frans Hals, *Pekelharing*, about 1630–40
Engraving, 26.9 × 21.5 cm
Rijksmuseum, Amsterdam

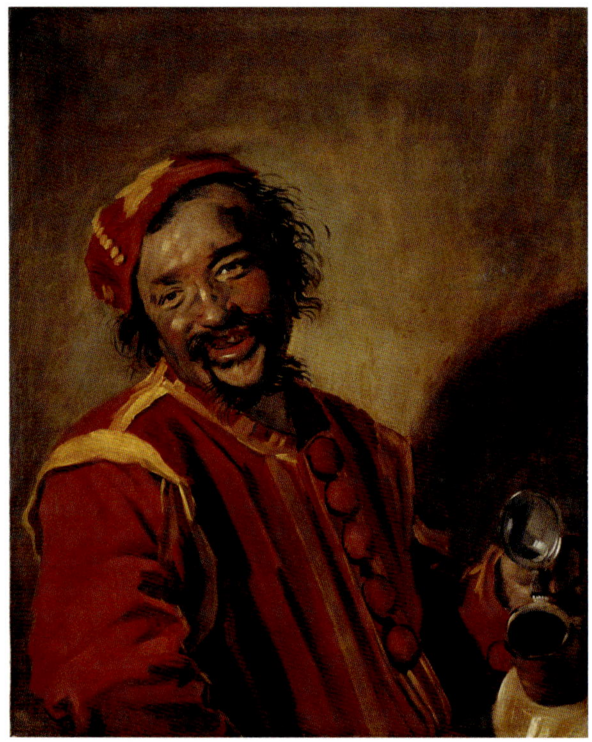

Fig. 153 *Pekelharing*, about 1625
Oil on canvas, 75 × 61.5 cm
Hessen Kassel Heritage

     LAUGHTER

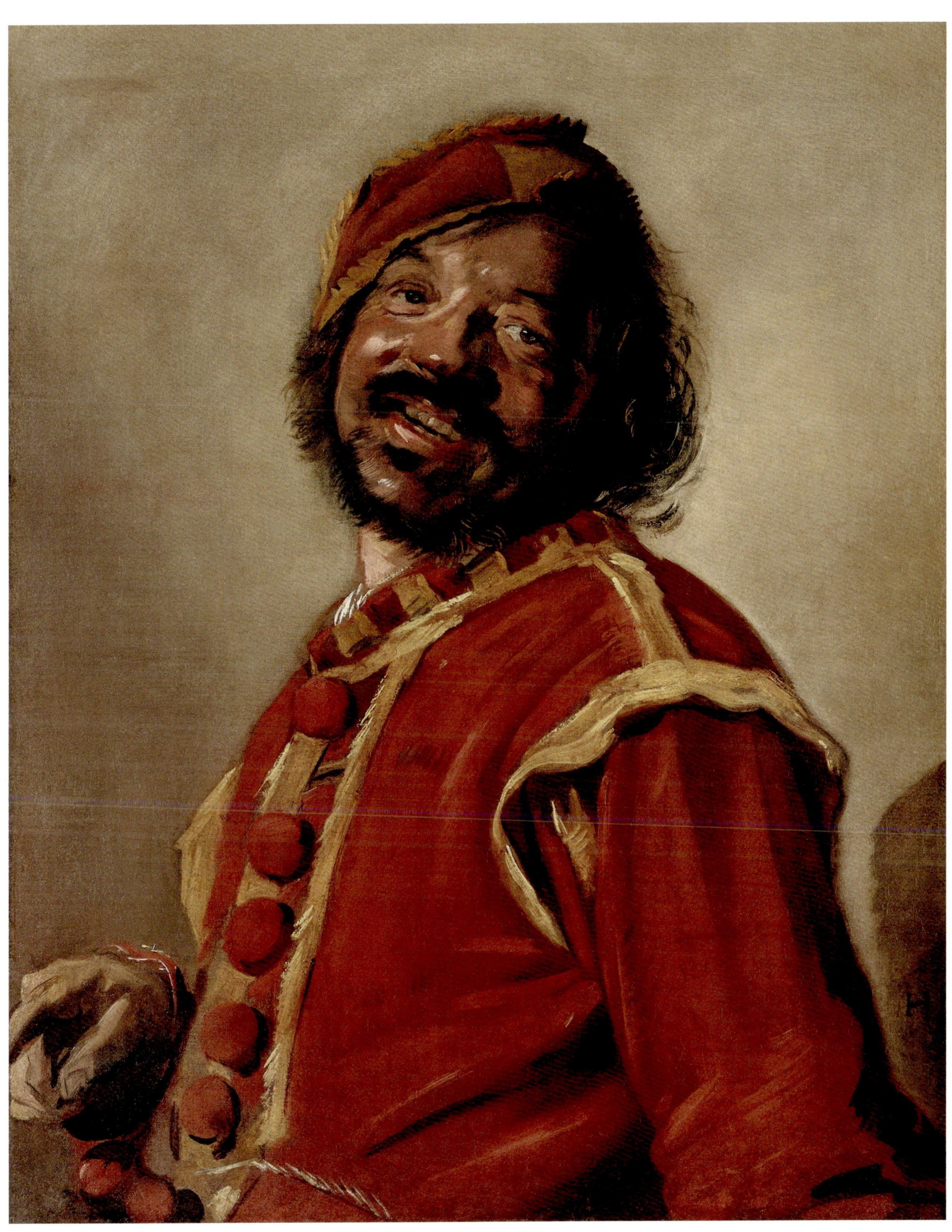

Fig. 154 *Pekelharing (The Merry Drinker)*, about 1625
Oil on canvas, 76.5 × 64 cm
Museum der bildenden Künste Leipzig

was a song in an English jig.[59] The name Pekelharing
also took on a life outside the theatre, with some English
actors adopting it in daily life, as did one or two
Dutchmen.[60]

The question is who Hals was thinking of when he
painted his two surviving Pekelharing pictures. The subject was almost certainly a real person: given the frequent
presence of English touring comedians in the Netherlands, he could be any one of them. One argument is
that the painting in the Museum der bildenden Künste
in Leipzig (fig. 154) or a variant must already have been in
England around 1685, the date of a print made after it,[61]
although it is equally possible that it depicted a Dutch
Pekelharing. The colour of the man's face, as well as that
in the Kassel canvas, is darker than any found in other
portraits and genre figures by Hals.[62] The lighter colour
of the neck, and to a lesser extent of Pekelharing's hand
in Leipzig, suggests that it was theatrical make-up. This
was common in the English theatre of the day, with the
role of the actor often involving foolish behaviour.[63]

Even people who did not know the stage character must
immediately have recognised the figure as a buffoon, so
Pekelharing could have served as a general symbol of
folly. This also seems to be why Hals's painting in the
Gemäldegalerie alte Meister in Kassel (fig. 153) served as
the model for the engraving on the title page of *Nugae
venales*, a collection of comic anecdotes printed in Amsterdam in 1648.[64] It may also be the reason for Jan Steen
depicting it as a painting-in-a-painting in two of his own
works: *The Christening Feast* (fig. 155) and *The Doctor's Visit*.[65]

GUFFAWING 'FOOLS'

Hals's depictions of Pekelharing roaring with laughter
fitted his role as a jester. But he also portrayed many
other people in a similar way. These were specific groups
who, in the eyes of the seventeenth-century elite, showed
a marked tendency to be foolish. Before discussing those
groups I will deal with drink, which taken in excess was
generally regarded as a guarantee of foolish behaviour.

DRINK

Alcohol and idiotic behaviour often go hand in hand. It
was not for nothing that Hals gave Pekelharing a beer
tankard to hold up in the Kassel painting, and the same
goes for the famous *Malle Babbe* (fig. 171). Drink could
turn even the most upright citizen into a fool. In the
words of the Amsterdam printer, publisher and writer
Dirck Pietersz Pers, 'The fool says that if you keep on
drowning yourself in wine then you'll be like me, you'll
be a fool'.[66] This was not a recommendation any more
than the words of the author of a 1623 book of etiquette,
who warned his readers against 'drinking yourself drunk'
because then one would start behaving with 'foolish, silly
and buffoonish stupidity'.[67]

Because fresh water was often too polluted to drink,
everyone, including children, drank light beer. Alcohol
only became a problem if one drank too much. In stage

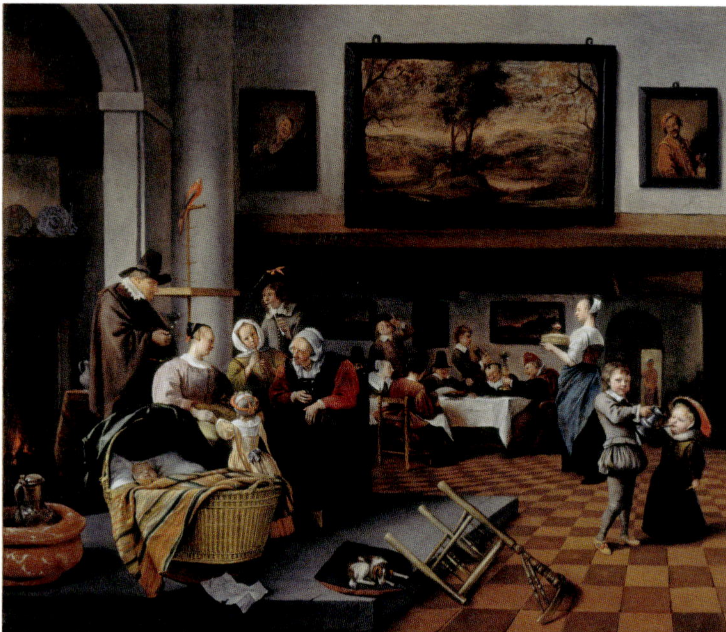

Fig. 155 Jan Steen, *The Christening Feast*,
about 1668. Oil on canvas, 85.1 × 100.5 cm
Staatliche Museen zu Berlin, Gemäldegalerie

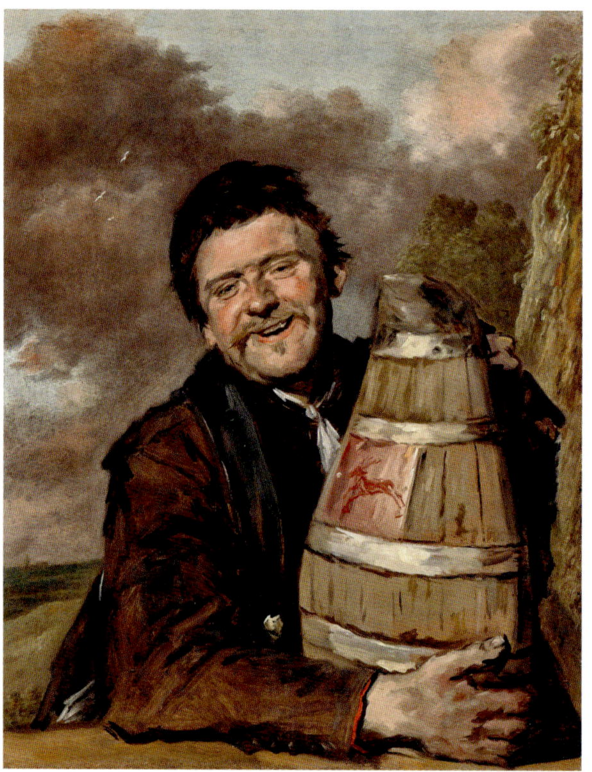

Fig. 156 *Man holding a Beer Jug*,
about 1635. Oil on canvas, 83 × 66 cm
Private collection

LAUGHTER

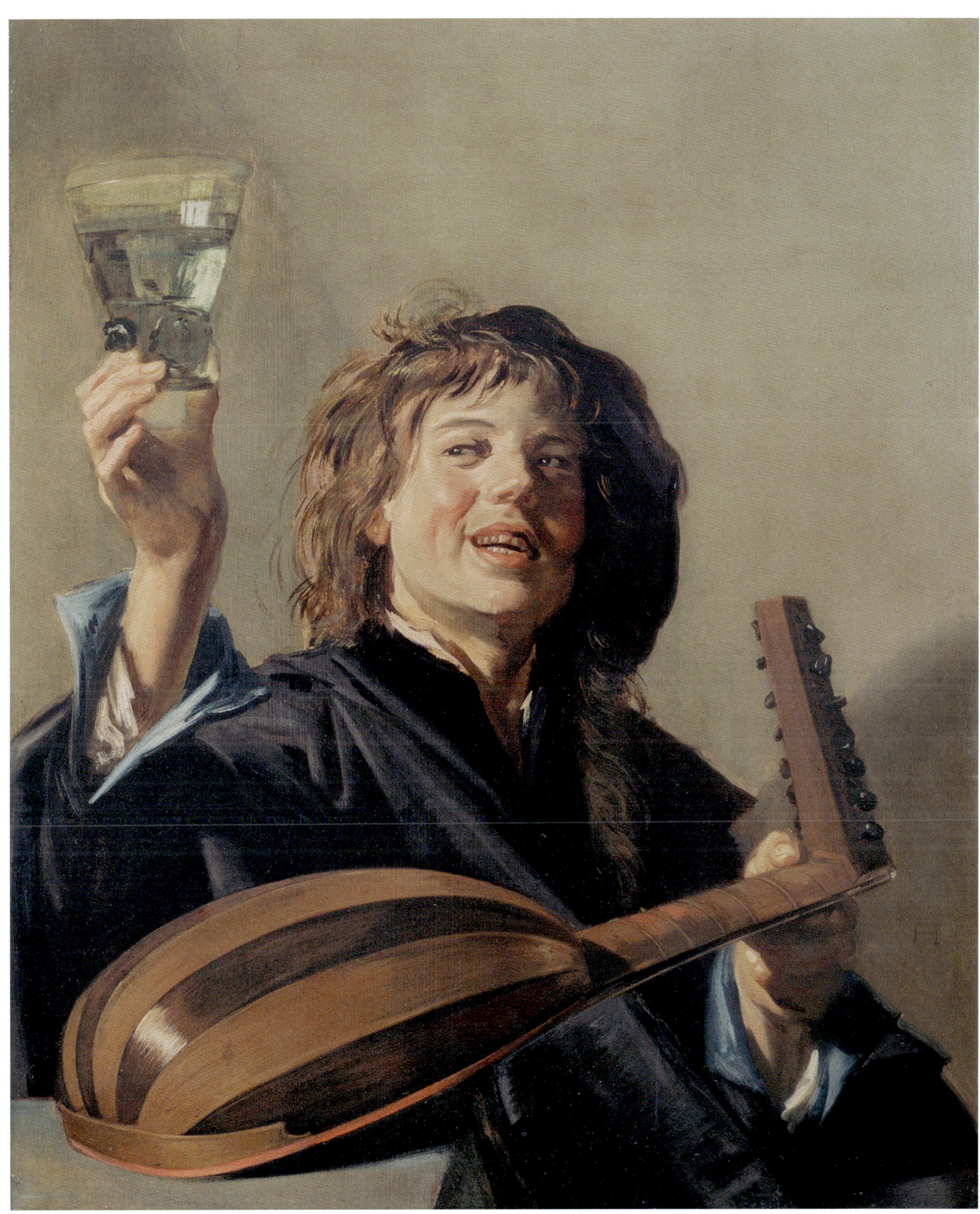

Fig. 157 *The Merry Lute Player*, about 1624–8
Oil on wood, 100 × 90 cm
Guildhall Art Gallery, City of London Corporation

plays it was almost always stereotypes, such as peasants, beggars, innkeepers and young merrymakers, who had a few too many.[68] With the exception of the latter group, about which more below, it was almost always the lower social class who were believed to drink to excess (although to those in the know, the suggestion that their behaviour was so different from that of upright citizens was laughable). We come across those types in Hals's genre painting, showing their teeth when they laugh. In one painting a humbly dressed man (a peasant perhaps, or a fisherman) grasps a gigantic tankard from Haarlem's Het Rode Hert (Red Hart) brewery (fig. 156), while in another the female innkeeper is on the point of refilling the glass (fig. 16).[69]

Excessive drinking was seen as a fairly certain route to stupidity but the effects of alcohol in moderation could be pleasant. It was always served at social gatherings such as christening parties, weddings and funerals, and the same applied to the festivities of civic guards and rhetoricians – and Hals was a member of both.[70] His depictions of laughing drinkers cannot be seen in isolation from the way drink was regarded more widely. Rhetoricians were known as 'tankard gazers' because of their love of a good glass, and painters too were notorious for the quantities that they could consume.[71] If Houbraken is to be believed, Hals was not averse to a dram himself.[72]

The positive view of drink was based on the idea that it brought inspiration as well as merriment. To quote Pers again, 'Wine is the poet's post-horse'.[73] Van Mander wrote that drink awakens the human spirit, which is why Bacchus was often to be found in the company of the Muses.[74] Govert van der Eembd, who was an active member of the Vine Tendrils at the same time as Hals, wondered what the objection was to poets drinking 'quite a lot of' beer and wine, the more so because, according to him, 'water drinkers' could not write decent poetry. He detested writers who claimed at the top of their voices that one had to practise moderation but were as 'drunk as lords' three hours later.[75]

The works of rhetoricians effortlessly combined moralising, satire, humour and self-mockery; the same seems to apply to Hals's genre scenes. It was in the recognition of the behaviour depicted that a great deal of comical element lay. In the *'Merry Drinker'* (fig. 175), by way of an exception, Hals painted a superbly clad gentleman with a glass in his hand who is laughing so uproariously that he is showing his teeth.[76] It is not certain whether this is a portrait or a genre scene, but in either case it would have been intended as a positive, possibly gently mocking image of merriment provoked by drink.[77] The same is possibly true for the *Woman holding a Glass and a Flagon* mentioned above (fig. 16), who may be more than just a stereotypical character, perhaps even an acquaintance of Hals.[78]

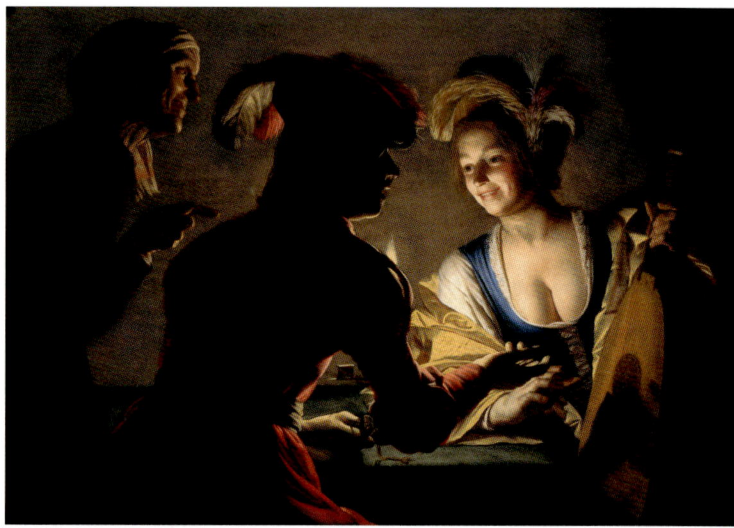

Fig. 158 Gerard van Honthorst, *The Matchmaker*, 1625
Oil on wood, 71 × 104 cm
Centraal Museum, Utrecht

LAUGHTER

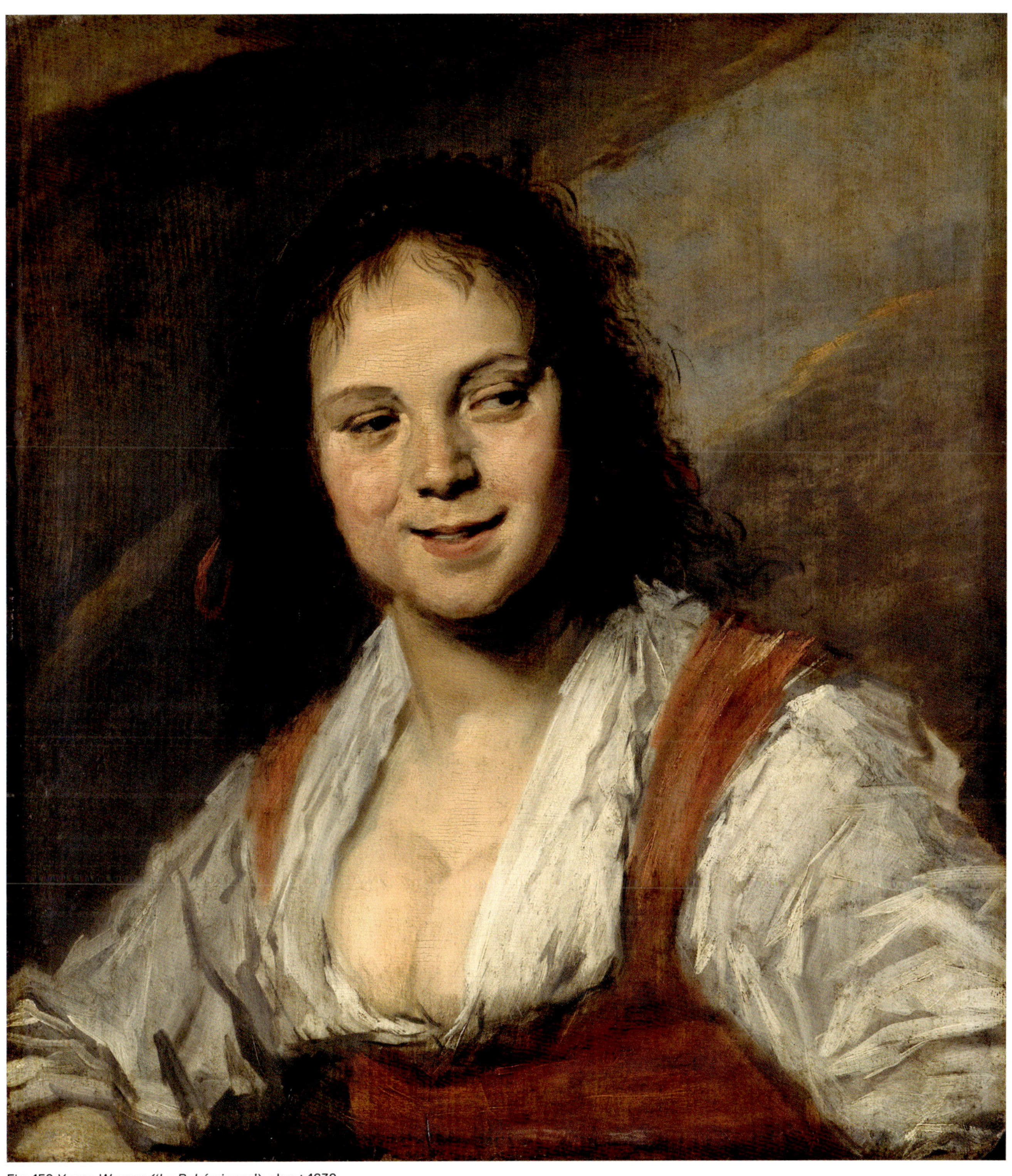

Fig. 159 *Young Woman ('La Bohémienne')*, about 1632
Oil on wood, 58 × 52 cm
Musée du Louvre, Paris, Paintings Department

In the market scene that Frans Hals painted jointly with Claes van Heussen is a young woman with a wide smile (fig. 27). Some contemporaries would undoubtedly have interpreted the fact that she is showing her teeth as a lack of refinement associated with her low social class. It was also believed that women were quicker to laugh because of their 'delicate' constitutions.[79] Furthermore, exuberant laughter was not only improper for women, but could also be seen as a sign of flightiness.[80] Thus sex workers were often depicted laughing immoderately, such as in the paintings of Gerard van Honthorst (fig. 158).[81] Many would no doubt have argued that the young woman laughing merrily in the middle of Hals's *Merrymakers at Shrovetide* (fig. 149) was going far too far.

Women of easy virtue were also depicted with a more restrained laugh. The expression of the woman in another picture by Hals, known by its nineteenth-century title of *La Bohémienne* (fig. 159), may seem at first to resemble the lady in the Rijksmuseum double portrait (fig. 61). But unlike the latter, the former is showing a little more of her teeth and her eyes are slightly narrowed. Some seventeenth-century viewers would undoubtedly have considered her gaze and deep décolleté as sensual, while others would have interpreted it as sly. Writers, in any event, warned against deceitful loose women; to cite Dirck Pers one more time, 'Mirthless laughter, numb caress, / eyeless leer, love loveless'.[82]

La Bohémienne probably hung originally in the house of a wealthy Dutch family but it has been suggested that it might have been intended for a brothel.[83] In certain houses of pleasure the client could make his choice from a painting displaying the charms of the available women. On the title page of the *Spiegel der alderschoonste cortisanen deses tyts* of 1630 by Crispijn van de Passe is a man holding up the portrait of a woman as he contentedly smokes a pipe by a roaring fire.[84] Another visitor in the background points at a series of depictions of women hanging on the wall. Things were taken a step further in the emblem collection *Nebulo Nebulonum* (Rascal of Rascals) by the Lutheran cleric Johannes Flittner, published in 1620 and adapted fourteen years later into Dutch by the Frisian doctor Petrus Baardt. One of the emblems shows a client with his hand in his trousers as he looks at the portraits of two women (fig. 160).[85]

YOUTH

Paintings in which young gentry are seen flirting, dancing and making music were extremely popular in the first half of the seventeenth century.[86] Although there is plenty of drinking going on, the mood is usually civilised. There is barely any sign of excess and there is laughter, but almost never showing the teeth. Frans Hals's brother Dirck specialised almost entirely in this genre, but Frans himself forays into such scenes of gilded youth only occasionally. While Dirck opted for many small figures, Frans almost always painted a few large ones, although he probably did at least once work more in the manner

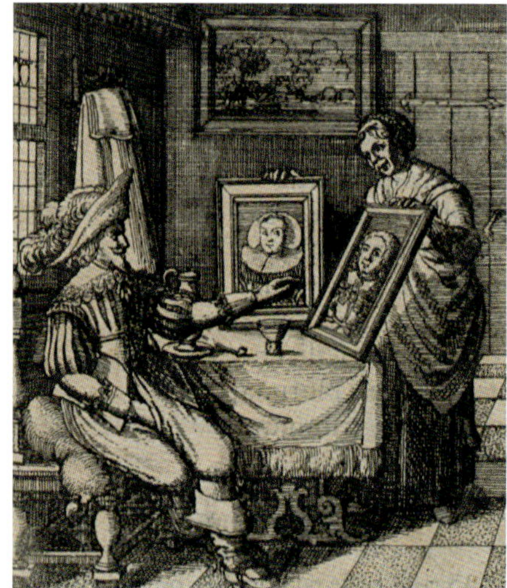

Fig. 160 Anonymous, *Young Man in a Brothel*, in Petrus Baardt, *Nebulo Nebulonum, dat is der vielten affreichten vieltofte boertig ernst*, Leeuwarden 1634, p. 154

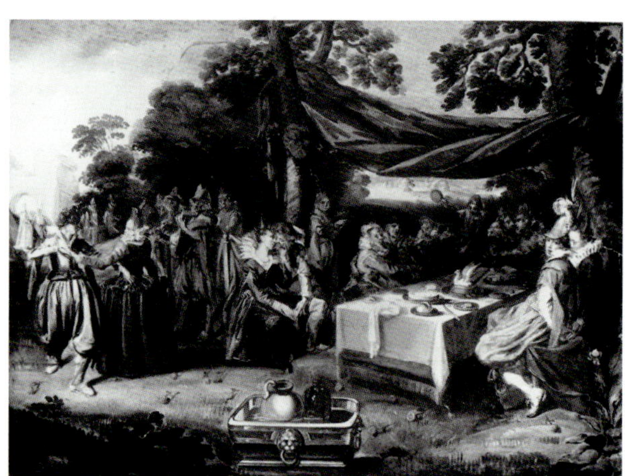

Fig. 161 Frans Hals(?), *Banquet in the Open Air*, about 1610–15. Oil on wood, 65 × 87 cm Previously Kaiser-Friedrich-Museum, Berlin (lost in the Second World War)

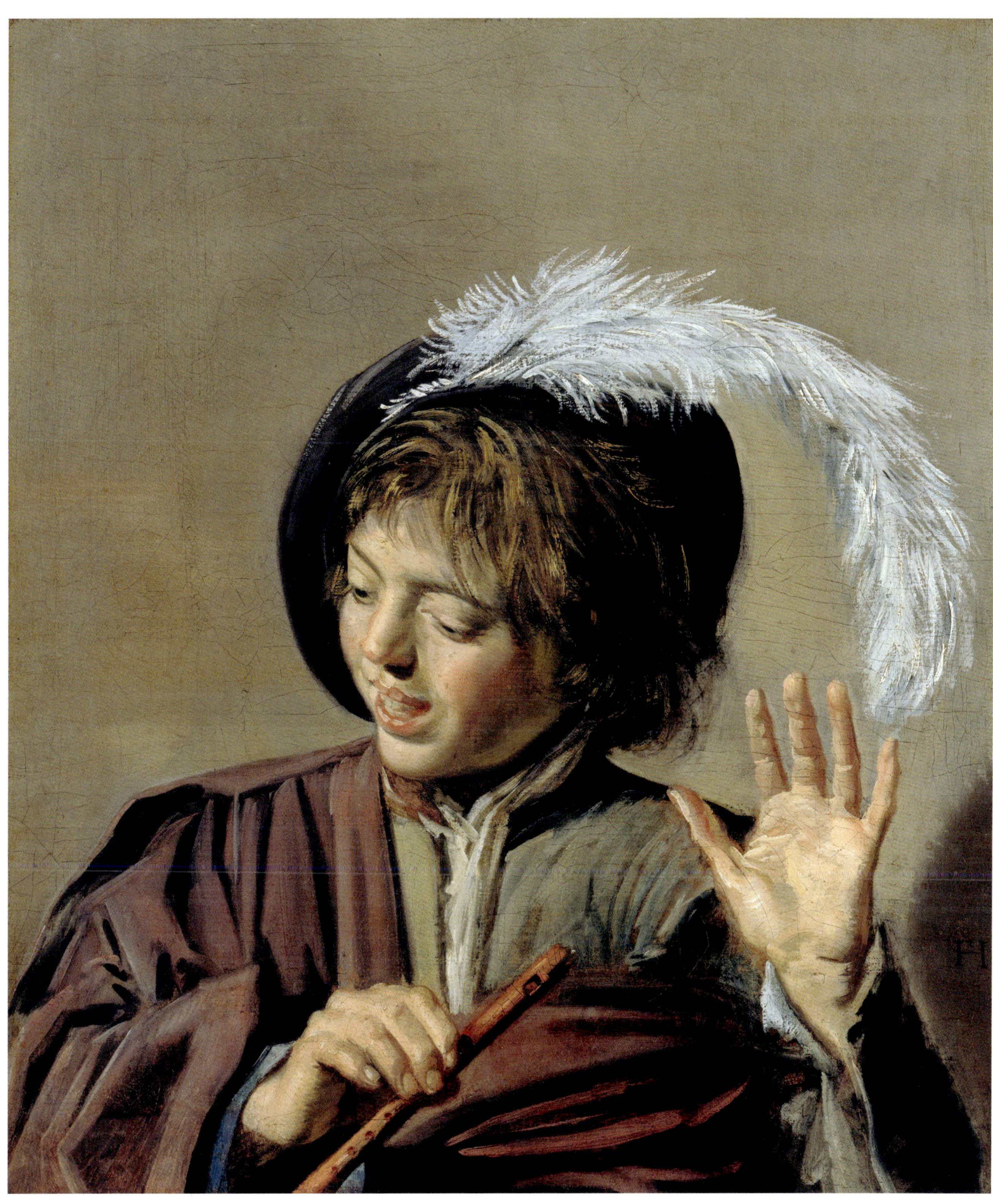

Fig. 162 *Boy with Flute*, about 1627
Oil on canvas, 68.8 × 55.2 cm
Staatliche Museen zu Berlin, Gemäldegalerie

of his younger brother (fig. 161).[87] Another characteristic of Frans's paintings is that most of his figures are so merry that they show their teeth. That is the case, for example, in the dazzling *Boy with Flute* (fig. 162) and two pictures showing a lutenist with a wine glass (fig. 157) and a young man smoking a pipe who is being embraced by an even more exuberant laughing woman.[88]

In one of his most ambitious genre scenes (fig. 163) a richly clad youth holds up a glass of wine with an equally merry woman hanging on his shoulder. This canvas of 1623, one of Frans's rare dated genre paintings, has been associated with two mentions in seventeenth-century inventories of a Prodigal Son by Frans Hals.[89] This biblical parable tells of a rich young man who squanders his inheritance in taverns and brothels. It is clear from certain details that some paintings of festive young people are indeed depictions of the parable.[90] In most cases, though, such references are missing – as they are from Hals's *Young Man and Woman in an Inn* – although this does not mean that some viewers were not immediately reminded of the biblical story. In the eighteenth century, however, the painting had a different name. At an auction in 1786 it was sold as a portrait of 'Squire Ramp and his Mistress',[91] an identification that has been rejected because of its reference to Ensign Pieter Ramp, who was depicted in Hals's 1627 group portrait of the Calivermen Civic Guard (fig. 66). He does not look anything like the young man in this painting; it is also inconceivable that such a wealthy, upright man would ever have allowed himself to be depicted in this way. However, it is possible that the title refers to a now unknown comedy featuring a Squire Ramp, which would translate as 'Squire Disaster'. Such meaningful names were popular in comedies, as can be seen earlier from the Squire Bungler who married Dame Swindler.

CHILDREN

Adolescents and young adults were seen as susceptible to foolishness, and children even more so. The poet Theodoor Rodenburg uses the term 'childish folly' in relation to the ridiculousness of human actions.[92] Children were thus symbols of foolishness, but people were also convinced that they were able to see through the adult world and consequently play a part usually reserved for jesters. On the title page of the comic book *De nieuwe Vaakverdryver* it is children who identify human folly.[93] Stupid behaviour could be excused in children, as distinct from other young people, because they did not yet know better, so they were free to laugh to their hearts's content; in time they would learn how to control their emotions.[94] This explains why children are alone in Hals's portraits (as distinct from his genre paintings and *tronies*) in occasionally revealing their teeth when they laugh (fig. 22). He may have been inspired by the large painting by Maarten van Heemskerck, renowned Haarlem painter of the sixteenth century, in which two children of Pieter Jan Foppesz and his wife, Alijdt Mathijsdr, are laughing fit to burst (fig. 169).

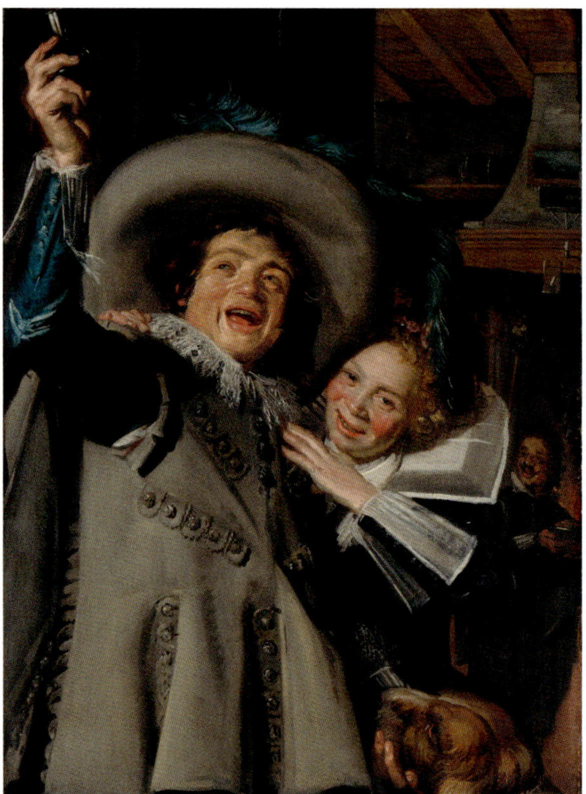

Fig. 163 *Young Man and Woman in an Inn*, 1623
Oil on canvas, 105.4 × 79.4 cm
The Metropolitan Museum of Art, New York;
Bequest of Benjamin Altman, 1913

LAUGHTER

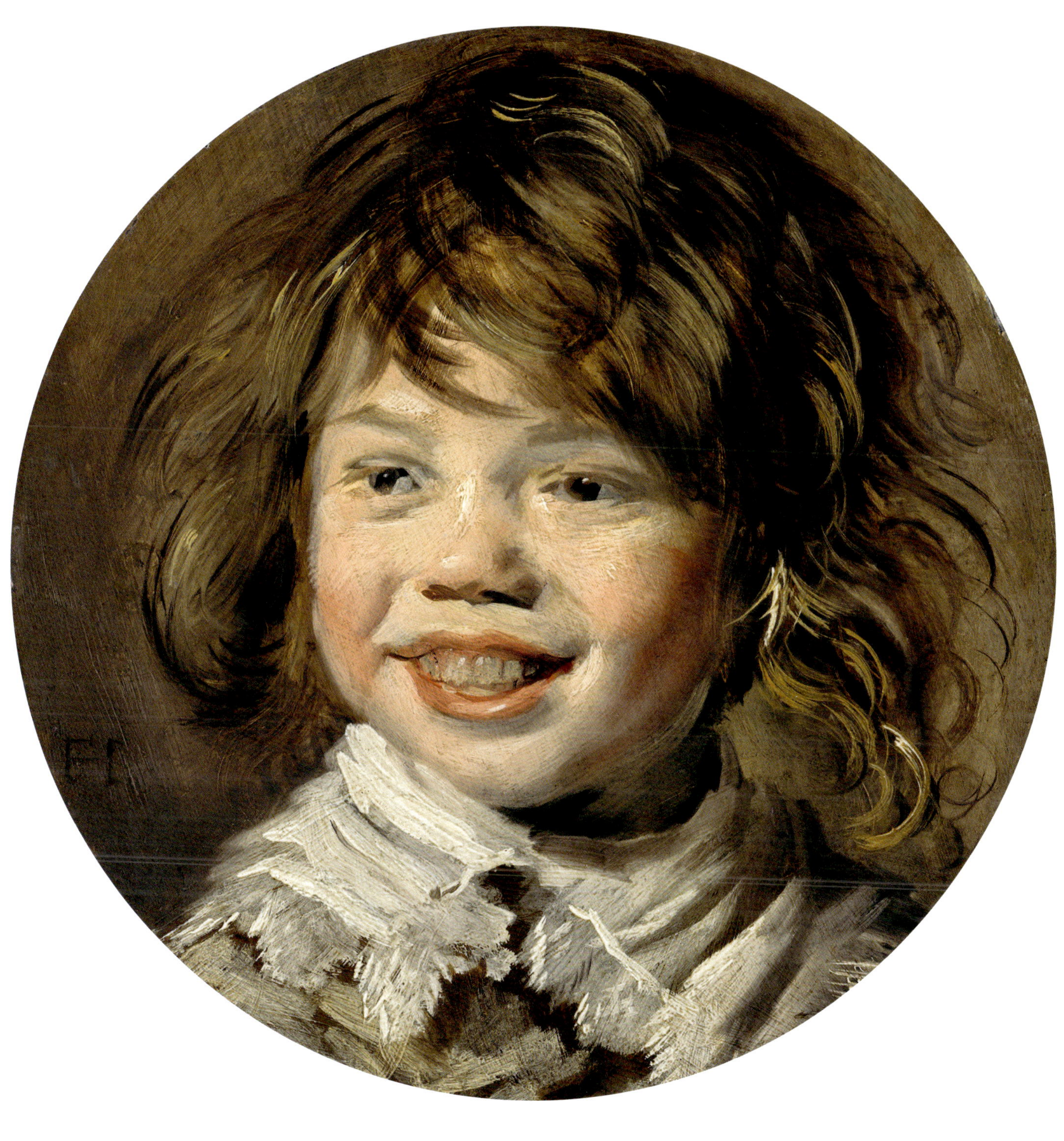

Fig. 164 *Laughing Boy*, about 1630
Oil on wood, 30.4 × 30.4 cm
Royal Picture Gallery Mauritshuis, The Hague

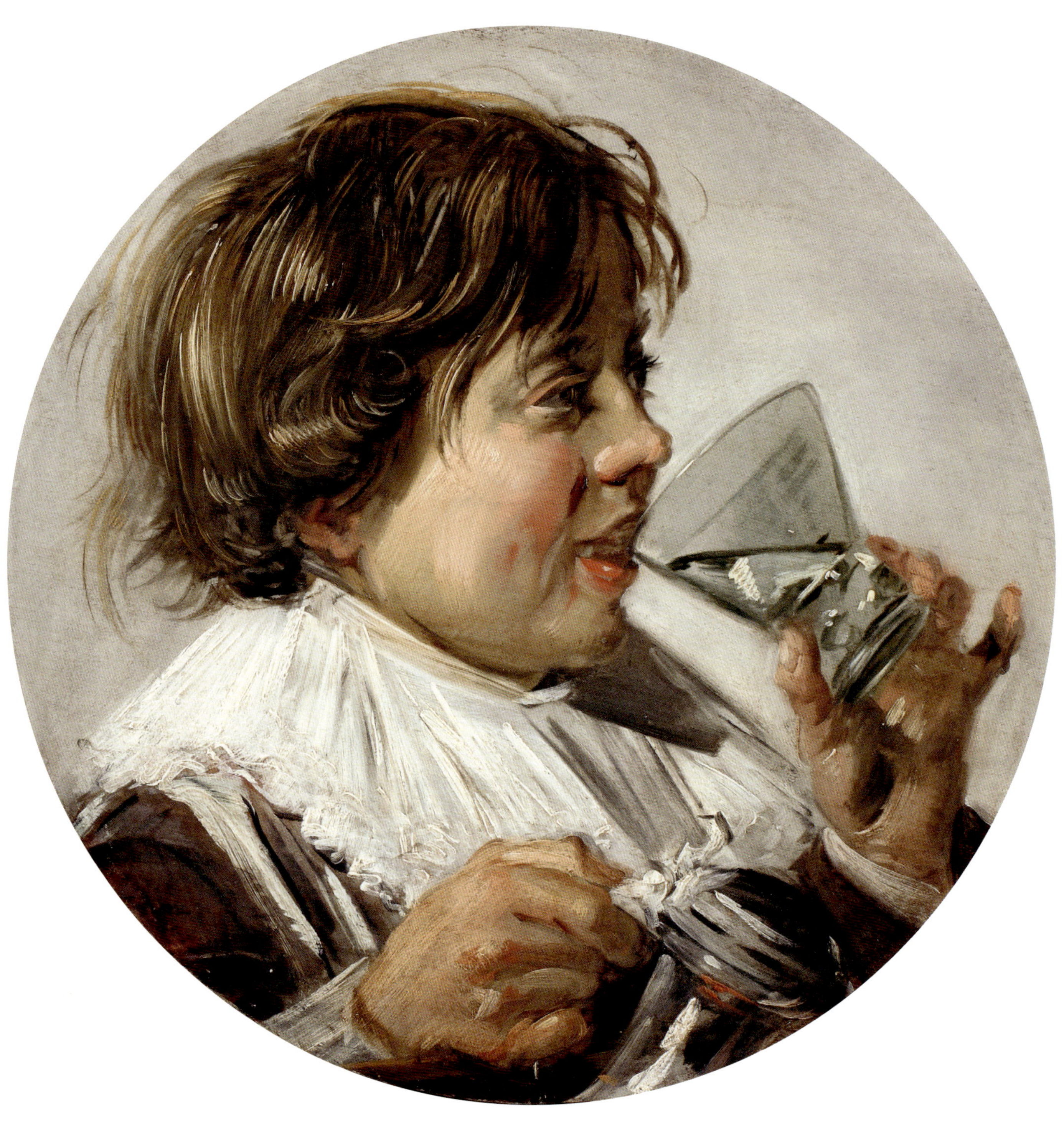

Fig. 165 *Laughing Boy with a Wine Glass*, about 1630
Oil on wood, 38 × 38 cm
Staatliche Schlösser, Gärten und Kunstsammlungen
Mecklenburg-Vorpommern, Schwerin

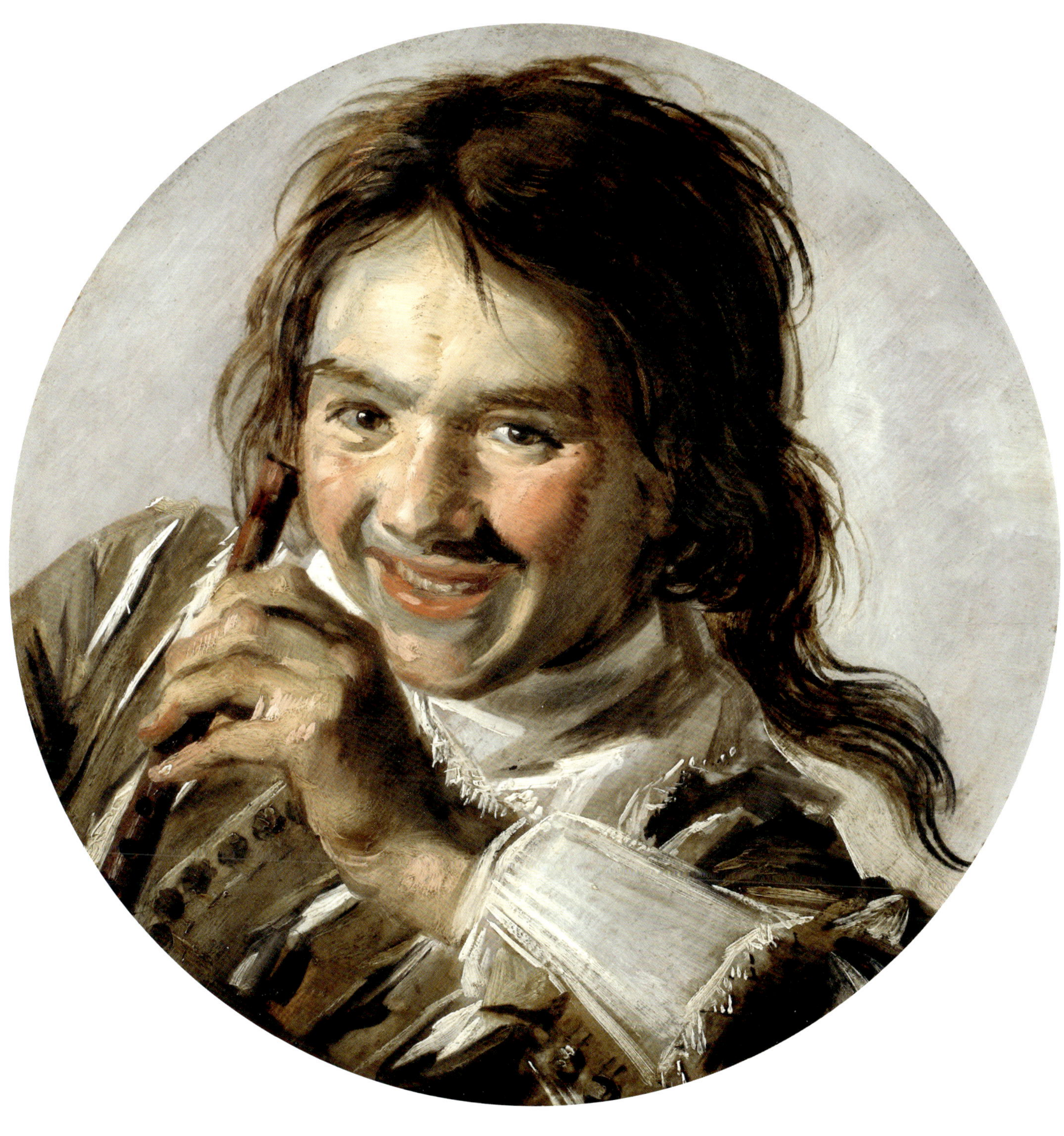

Fig. 166 *Laughing Boy with a Flute*, about 1630
Oil on wood, 37.5 × 37.5 cm
Staatliche Schlösser, Gärten und Kunstsammlungen
Mecklenburg-Vorpommern, Schwerin

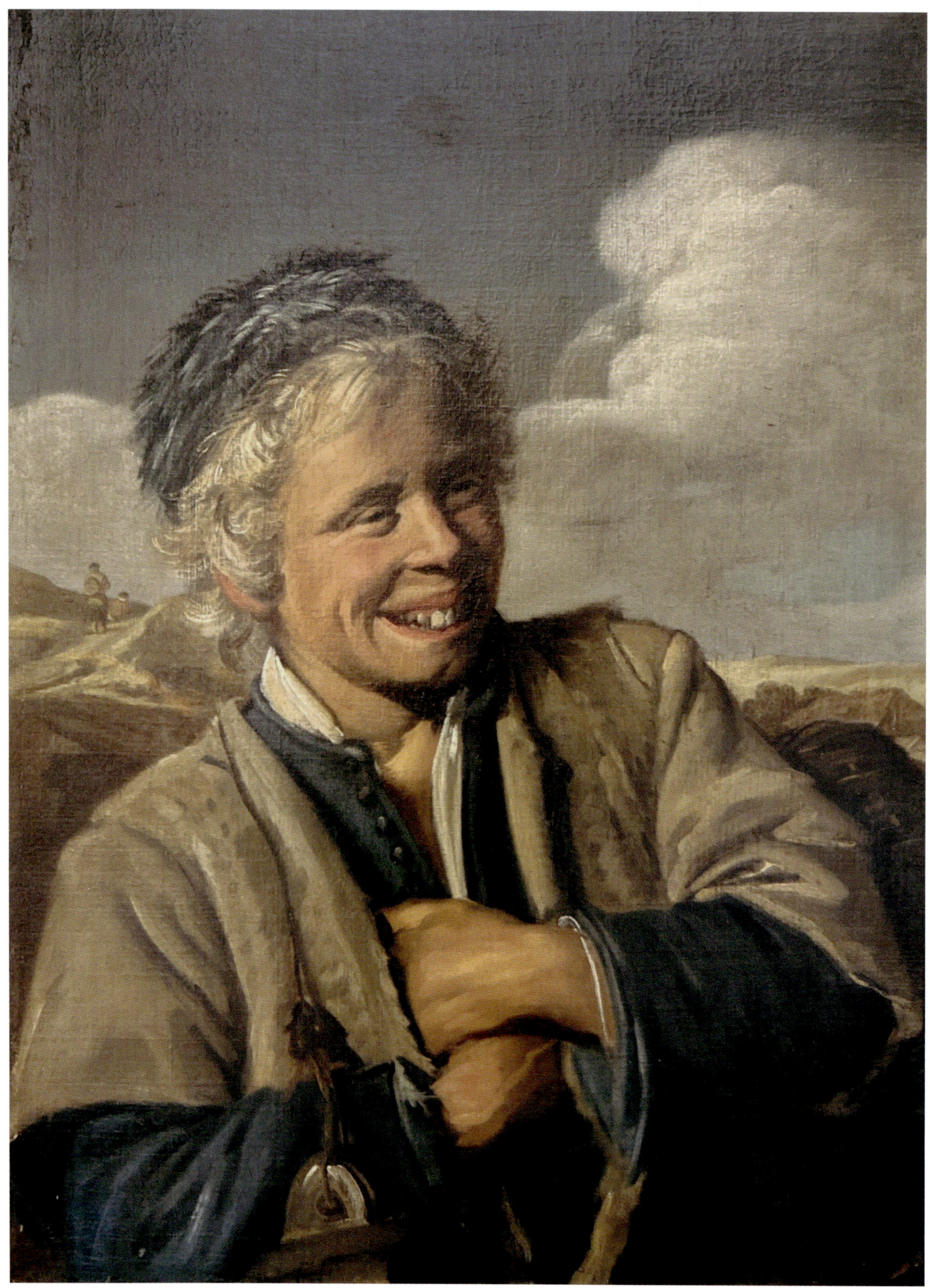

Fig. 167 *Laughing Fisherboy*, about 1630
Oil on canvas, 82 × 60.2 cm
Private collection

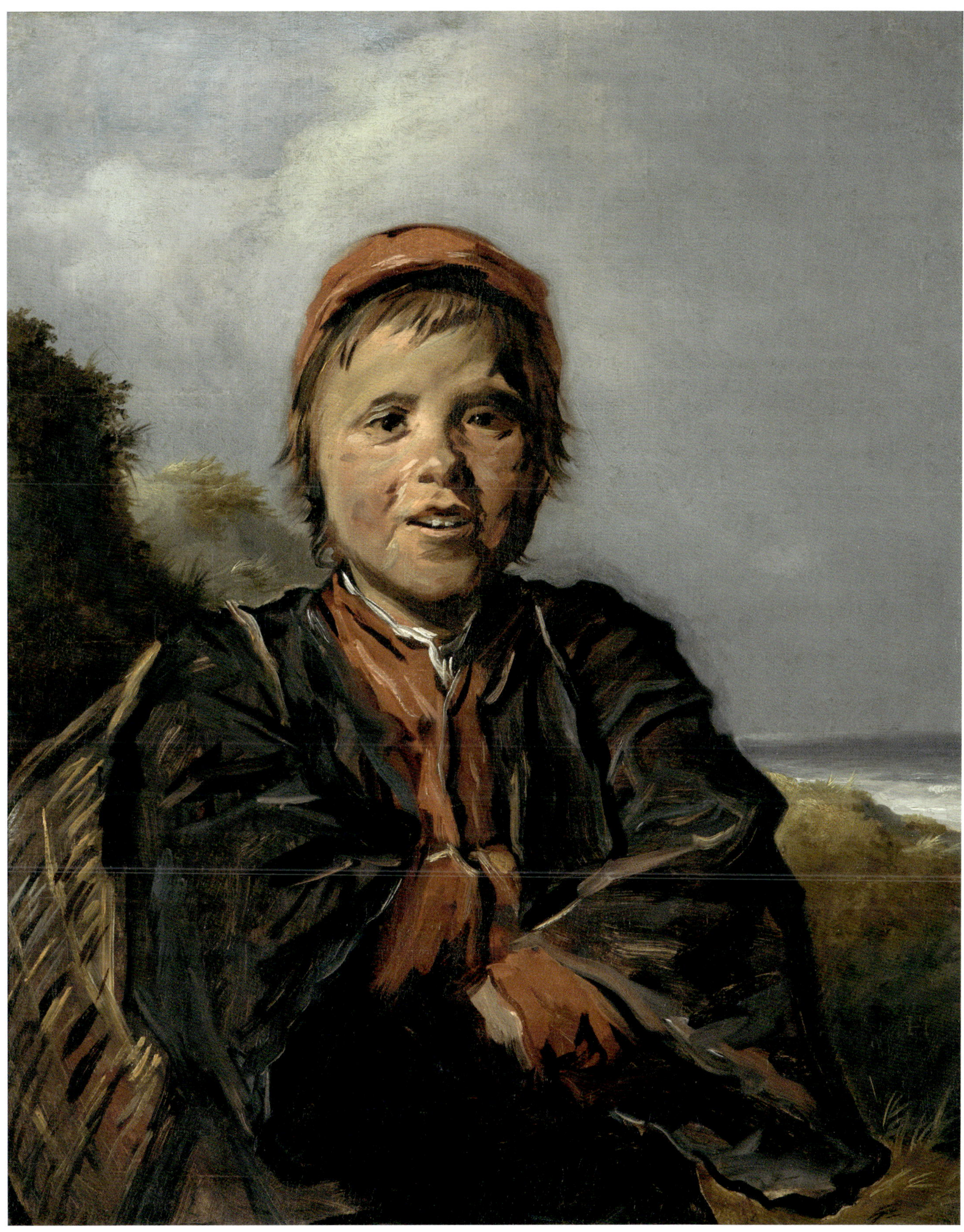

Fig. 168 *Fisherboy*, about 1638
Oil on canvas, 74 × 61 cm
Royal Museum of Fine Arts Antwerp – Flemish Community

The children in Hals's genre scenes and study heads are almost invariably laughing freely. It appears from seventeenth-century inventories that he sometimes used his own children as models.[95] It is not known for certain in which works they appear, but we should probably think of pictures like *Laughing Boy* (fig. 164), *Laughing Boy with a Wine Glass* (fig. 165) and *Laughing Boy with a Flute* (fig. 166), in which the children are well-dressed. The fact that he regarded children, including his own, as symbols of folly is apparent from a lost work by Hals that is known only from an eighteenth-century print (fig. 170), which shows a laughing boy holding an owl, a symbol of madness (see below).

A separate group within Hals's oeuvre consists of paintings of fisher children, whom he would have seen every day at the fish market on Haarlem's Grote Markt (Great Market Square), to which they brought the fish – dab, plaice, herring and cod, as well as shellfish and crustaceans such as shrimps – landed at nearby Zandvoort. The fishing boats were dragged on to the beach and the catch immediately auctioned off and taken to Haarlem in carts and on foot by women and children, who carried them almost 10 km in heavy baskets on their arms, backs or heads. It was these fish porters whom Hals painted (figs 167–8). The fisherboy with a broad grin on his face is probably selling shrimps and shellfish, for at bottom left there is a glimpse of a wooden beaker for measuring out portions.[96] Hals depicted all of them with dunes or a stretch of beach and sea in the background, probably to heighten the sense of a rural idyll.[97]

Similarly, the clergyman and author Samuel Ampzing wrote an ode describing how the Haarlemers treated Zandvoort as a maritime Arcadia.[98] The townsfolk, he said, went there to forget their cares, take their ease and eat fresh fish while their children played and rolled in the dunes until their eyes and necks were full of sand. The local villagers were uncommonly virtuous souls:

> A poor and simple people, not encumbered with splendour, magnificence and pride, / nor with the wickedness and malice of this age, / Simple, innocent and upright, full of fidelity and free of subterfuge, / And where one misses virtue the least and sin the most.[99]

Hals probably regarded the fisherboys and girls as sympathetically as Ampzing, whom he must have known well.[100] As with his paintings of other children, their ever-present grins would have been seen as a sign both of their foolishness and – perhaps even more so – of their undefiled goodness.[101]

MALLE BABBE AND BOONTJE

Terms like 'buffoon', 'fool', 'silly' or 'mad' were used in Hals's day for people 'to whom the path of wisdom was closed'. These are the words of the seventeenth-century physician Johan van Beverwijck who, in his *Schat der ongesontheyt* (Treasure of Disease, 1642), discussed people

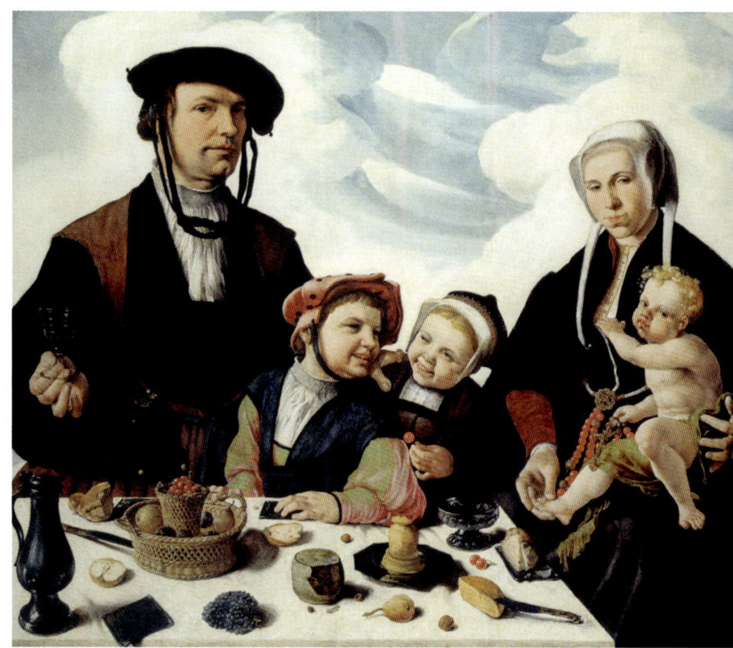

Fig. 169 Maarten van Heemskerck, *Portrait of Pieter Jan Foppesz and his Wife, Alijdt Mathijsdr, called Van Beresteyn, with their Children Jan, Cornelia and Pieter*, about 1530. Oil on wood, 118.7 × 140.2 cm Museumslandschaft Hessen, Gemäldegalerie Alte Meister, Kassel

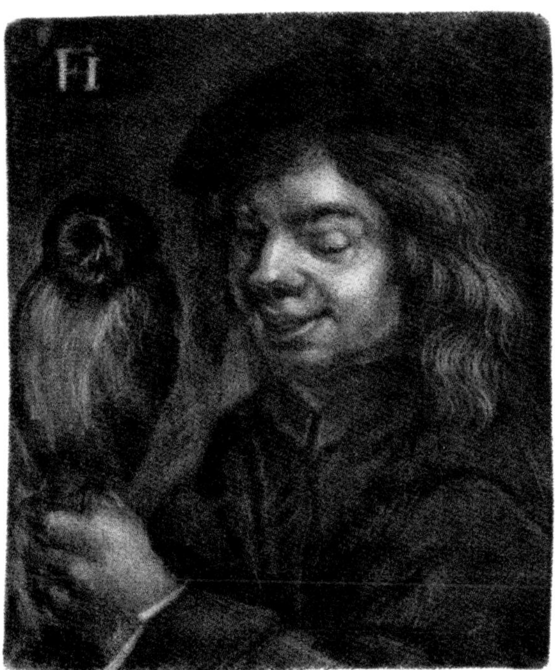

Fig. 170 Johannes de Groot III
after Frans Hals, *Boy with an Owl*,
about 1740. Mezzotint, 10.9 × 9.3 cm
Rijksmuseum, Amsterdam

whose brains lacked 'consultative power'.[102] A broad distinction was made between people with a psychological disorder and those with a mental impairment. The former state, which one could develop at a later age, was typified by an impassioned, often aggressive or even menacing manner, while the second disorder, with which one was born, by calm, unthreatening behaviour. In principle, the family was expected to look after the latter. But if they were a danger to others, or if relatives were unable to care for them, they could be committed to institutions such as hospitals, asylums, workhouses or houses of correction. It was generally considered pointless to try to educate or cure them.[103]

In 1646 'Barbar, also known as Malle Barbar' was committed to the Haarlem workhouse in order to avert any possible further 'dangers of disgrace and dishonour'. She spent the rest of her life there.[104] Hals knew the institution well, because his son Pieter and eldest daughter Sara were taken there four years earlier, the former because he had a mental disability and the latter because of her immoral behaviour, having given birth to her second illegitimate child that year.[105] It is not clear why Malle Barbar or Babbe was committed: people could be confined for very different reasons, as with Hals's two children. The institution was introduced mainly to keep beggars and wastrels off the streets and set them to work, but as time passed the programme was extended to all sorts of other people.[106]

The fact that Hals painted her portrait (fig. 171) suggests that Malle Babbe was a familiar sight around Haarlem before she was rounded up. This is in one of the most loosely brushed works that he ever produced. The sitter is identified by an inscription, probably from the seventeenth century, on the stretcher of the canvas.[107] Furthermore, a hitherto unknown mention of a 'Malle Babbe by Frans Hals' has been discovered in an inventory of 1689, revealing that a painting of the subject was then in Amsterdam, which is evidence that she was also known outside Haarlem.[108]

It has been pointed out that the pewter mug of beer alone might explain Malle Babbe's broad grin, but by adding the owl Hals gave the scene a more general significance. The presence of the bird turned the sitter into a personification of foolishness, fully in the tradition of the rhetoricians. At the fools' festival organised by Van der Mersch, in which the jesters of all three Haarlem chambers participated, three pewter owls were to be awarded for the best aphorisms or mottoes.[109] In order to illustrate the sharp wit and sense of humour of the young Karel van Mander, his biographer relates how the small boy drew portraits on the whitewashed walls of his parents' house of the maids' 'peasant sweethearts or lovers', adding their names below. The portraits tended towards the caricature, one man being given a long, crooked, knobbly nose, and the others club feet, bandy legs, a large hump and an owl on his shoulder.[110]

In view of her nickname and the fact that she had been committed to the Haarlem workhouse, it seems likely

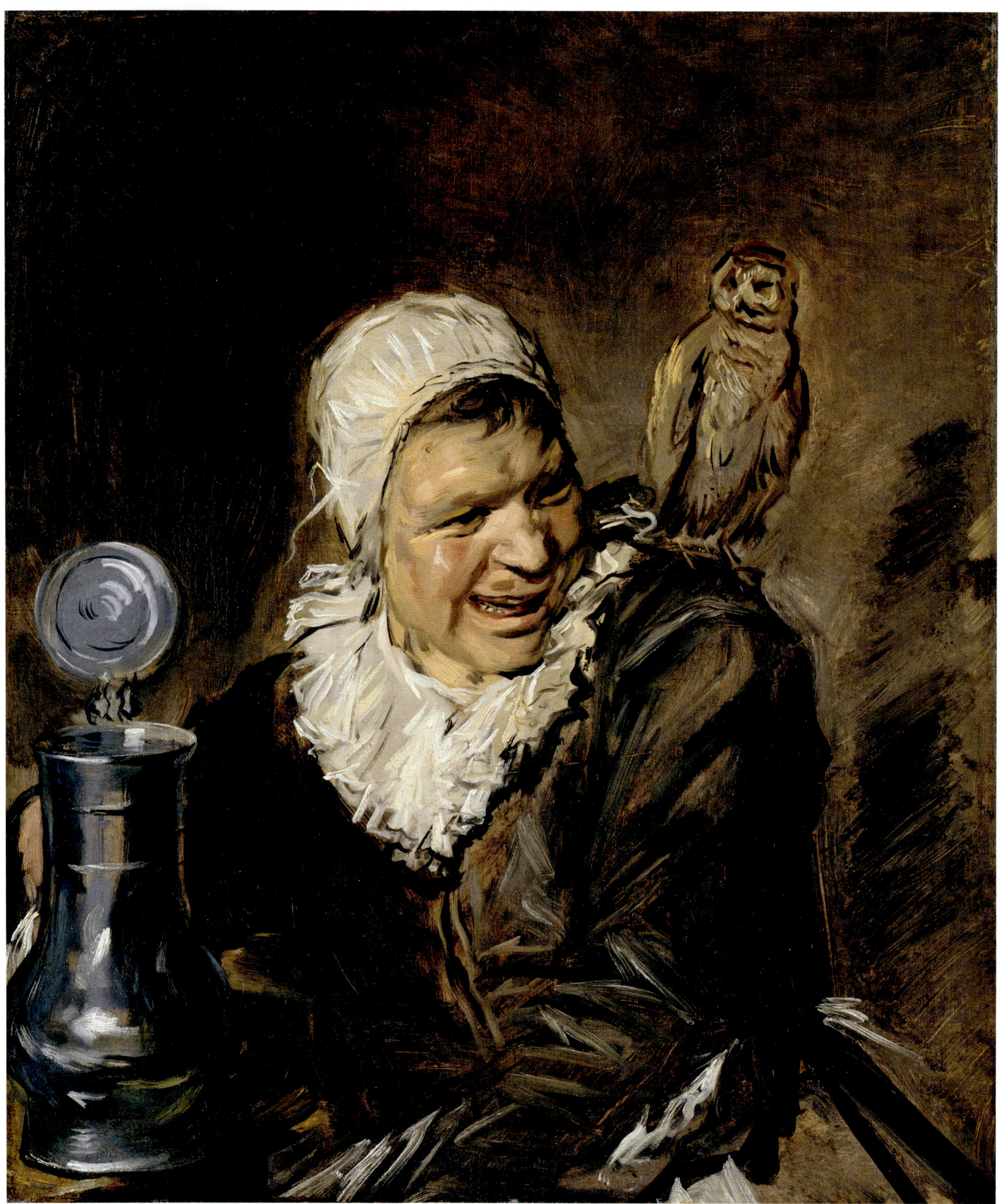

Fig. 171 *Malle Babbe*, about 1640
Oil on canvas, 78.5 × 66.2 cm
Staatliche Museen zu Berlin, Gemäldegalerie

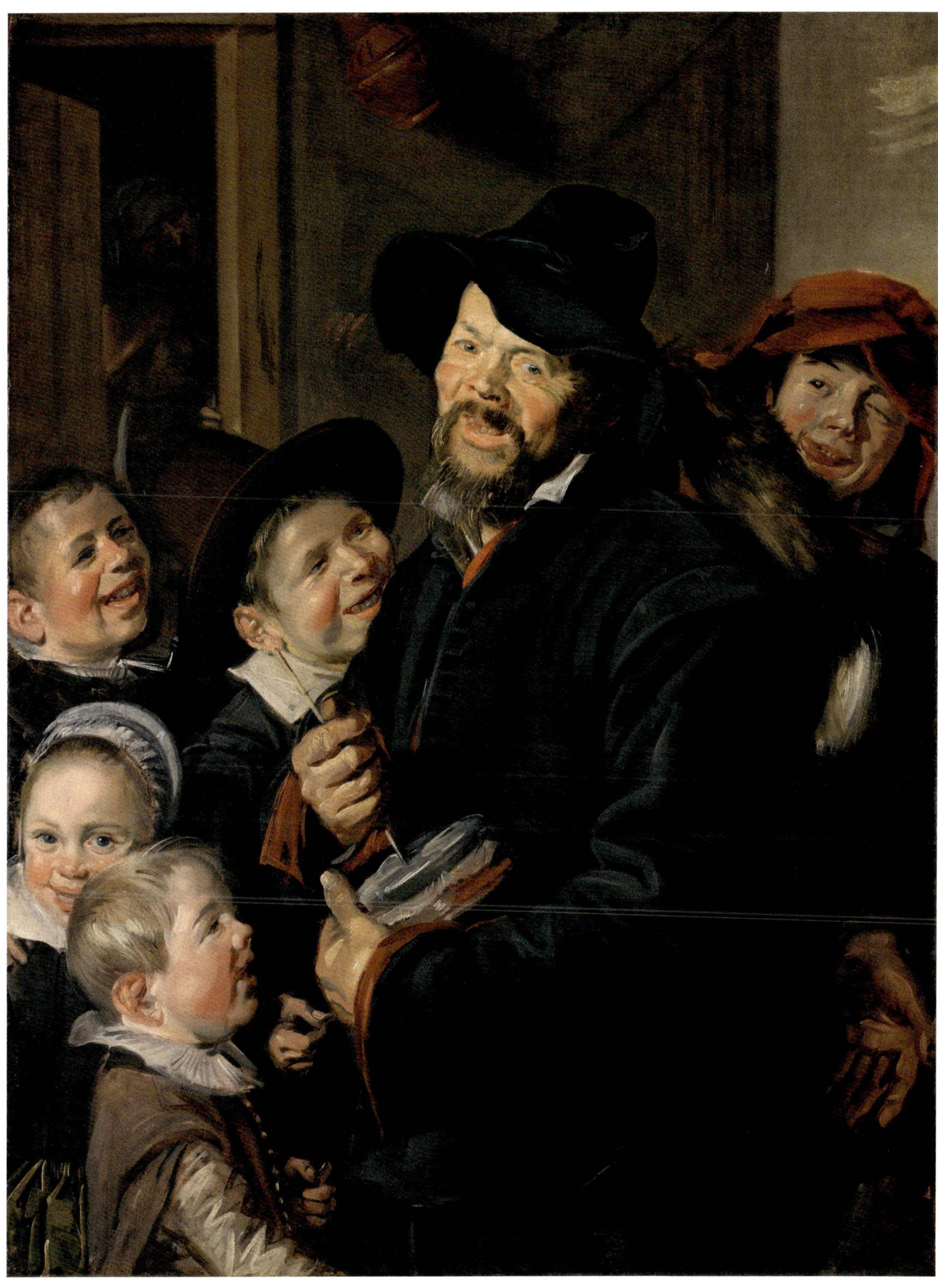

Fig. 172 *The Rommel-Pot Player*, about 1620
Oil on canvas, 106 × 80.3 cm
Kimbell Art Museum, Fort Worth, Texas

that Malle Babbe had a mental disability.[11] The same is probably true of another of Hals's subjects, namely the principal character in *The Rommel-Pot Player* (fig. 172). On the evening of Shrove Tuesday adults, and above all children, went from door to door making music and singing in the hope of being given something tasty to eat or perhaps a little money. They were often accompanied by a *rommelpot*, an earthenware pot with a pig's bladder stretched over the top, pierced by a stick that made a noise like a stuck pig when it was moved up and down.

The inscriptions on prints with a *rommelpot* player almost always refer to the subject as a fool ('zot').[12] In Hals's painting it seems that the man is not behaving foolishly purely for the sake of the festive mood. The catalogue of an eighteenth-century auction states that a drawn copy by the Leiden painter David Bailly depicts someone called Boontje, 'a well-known nutter of Haarlem at the time'.[13] Until now it has not been noticed that this identification is confirmed by the mention of 'a painting of Boontje of Haarlem' that was one of the prizes in the Amsterdam dicing lottery of around 1625 mentioned above. Although the artist is not named, it is very possible that this was Frans Hals as the picture is mentioned together with one of Pekelharing.[14] If this identification is correct, it is very possible that 'Boontje' did indeed go busking in Haarlem surrounded by children on the night before the beginning of Lent. For Hals anyway, the subject gave him the opportunity to combine two kinds of 'fool' – someone with a mental disability and children – in a single painting, and thus display a whole range of different people laughing.

He undoubtedly made other paintings of this kind. In Alkmaar in 1665, for instance, 'the crazies of Haarlem by Frans Hals' was sold for 69 guilders.[15] It is difficult to form a clear idea of what kind of work it was: did it depict mentally unbalanced people or simply more 'fools'?

A SMILE RAISES A SMILE

If you go to the Rijksmuseum's Gallery of Honour and watch the visitors who are looking at Frans Hals's *'Merry Drinker'* (fig. 175), you will often see them start to smile, sometimes without them even being aware of it. A smile raises a smile, as the Latin poet Horace well knew, and later art theorists such as Alberti, Lomazzo and others followed his lead.[16] Hals was undoubtedly aware of the phenomenon and appears to have made every effort to provoke such a reaction through his paintings.

He rarely included groups of figures in his early genre scenes, usually focusing instead on a single person, whom he almost always depicted life-size. This made it easier for the beholder to relate to the sitter, as if they are alone with them. This contact becomes even more direct if the figure is gazing directly at the viewer, as is so often the case with Hals, creating a sense that we are sharing space, time and emotions with the subject.[17] Many of his laughing fools and drinkers were the same types who played leading parts in the farces of his day. However, it appears that

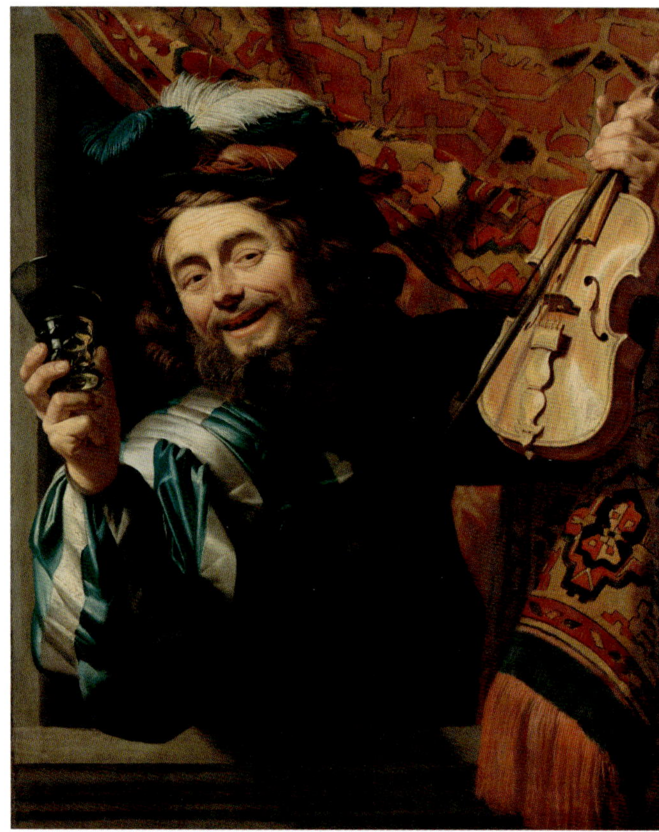

Fig. 173 Gerard van Honthorst, *The Merry Fiddler*, 1623
Oil on canvas, 107.2 × 88.3 cm
Rijksmuseum, Amsterdam

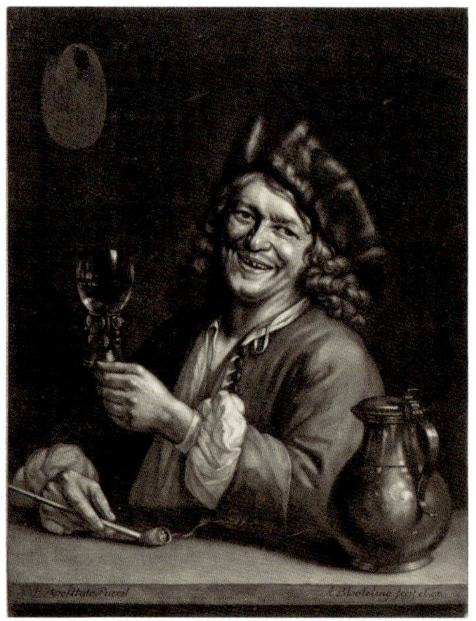

Fig. 174 Abraham Bloteling after Pieter Gerritsz van Roestraten, *Self Portrait*, about 1675
Engraving, 27.5 × 21.1 cm
Rijksmuseum, Amsterdam. On loan from the City of Amsterdam

LAUGHTER

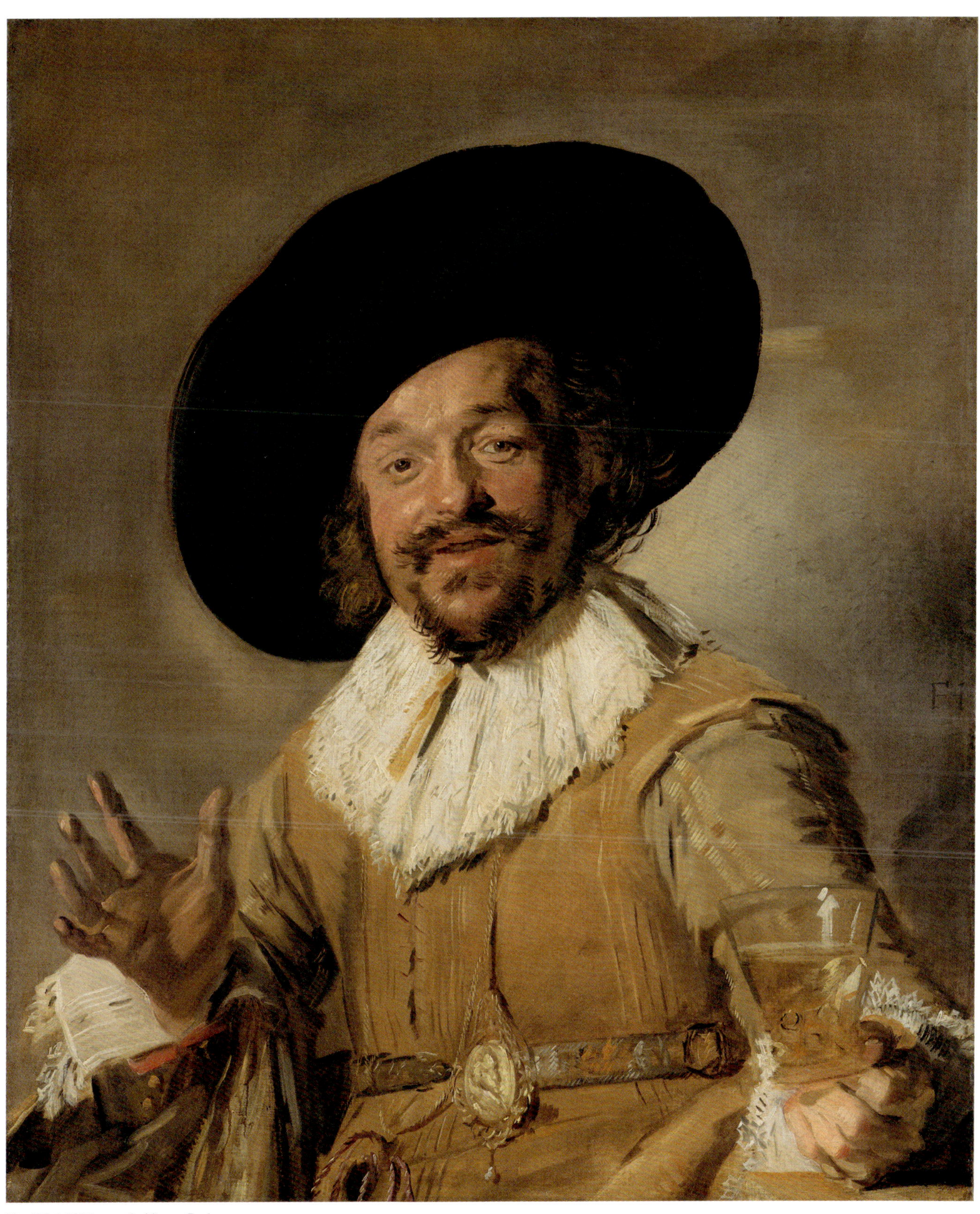

Fig. 175 *A Militiaman holding a Berkemeyer,*
known as the 'Merry Drinker', about 1629
Oil on canvas, 80 × 66.5 cm
Rijksmuseum, Amsterdam

Hals also sought out less obvious individuals to deploy his gift to the best effect. Thus he depicted children, some of them from fishermen's families, and people with a mental disability, who until then had never or rarely been shown in such a way. Some must have been familiar sights in or around Haarlem. These works may be described as portraits, but they were made with very different intentions and purposes than those he made of his affluent clients.[118]

Laughter seems to have been one of Hals's trademarks. His pupils sometimes depicted themselves or each other roaring with laughter (figs 32, 174), not only in self-mockery but also as allusions to their teacher: you learned how to paint a laugh with Frans Hals. His figures appear to be laughing out of merriment and not, for instance, because they were uneasy or malevolent.[119] We cannot be entirely sure about this, because he almost always featured a single figure, seldom adding a narrative element to explain why someone is convulsed with laughter. With Hals, humour and laughter almost invariably coincide. The viewer laughs at paintings in which people are laughing, the contagiousness of a laugh in real life playing a crucial role in his art.

Frans Hals's specialisation in guffawing people was no doubt prompted by his prodigious talent. He was extraordinarily skilful at depicting different expressions and attitudes; he no doubt observed people laughing very closely indeed. Karel van Mander's advice, with which this essay began, might have helped a beginner to paint a laugh, but it would have been of little use to a master painter. Hals's teacher also knew that himself: 'For Nature reveals more about what induces affects / Than one can describe'.[120] What makes it so difficult to paint laughter is that the person's face and pose change fast and continuously, while the essence is to capture a single moment as precisely as possible. The proof that Frans Hals excelled at this is evident in *The Lute Player* (fig. 177), one of his most convincing laughing sitters. The fool's head is turned upwards and at a sharp angle to his torso, his pupils in the extreme corners of his eyes, a position that can only be held very briefly. The fact that it is the details that matter when depicting someone laughing becomes clear from a comparison with Judith Leyster's *The Serenade* (fig. 176), which was heavily influenced by Hals's painting. However beautiful her composition, it does not have the fleeting nature of Hals's, mainly because her musician's body and head are more aligned, thus making him appear more static.

However, Hals's genius for depicting laughter lay above all in his touch. His canvases were described in his own day as being 'farcically painted', which made them ideally suited for merry subjects.[121] He generally worked up a figure's head more than the rest of the body, thereby stressing the facial expression, with the areas of loose brushwork imparting a sense of movement. This is immediately apparent in a comparison of his work with that of another artist who was so fond of laughter, Gerard van Honthorst (fig. 173). His figures have a frozen look, whereas Hals's appear to be bursting with animated life.

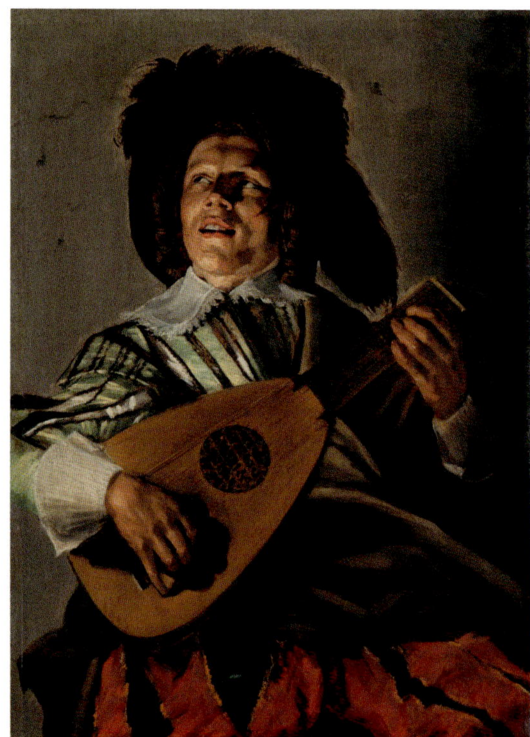

Fig. 176 Judith Leyster, *The Serenade*, 1629
Oil on wood, 47 × 34.5 cm
Rijksmuseum, Amsterdam; purchased with
the support of the Vereniging Rembrandt

Honthorst's detailed and smooth execution, with his meticulous imitation of materials, dispels any illusion of action. It is impossible to observe every detail of someone who is moving around, which is what laughing people do by definition, nor can one see all the decorative details of a glass in their hand or the precise way it catches the light, which naturally changes as the person moves. Hals indicates forms but does not elaborate them. His individual brushstrokes prevent his subjects from looking as if they are standing still, at the same time suggesting that he was working swiftly, as if he recorded his subjects at the very moment when they start laughing. Thus Frans Hals is the undisputed master of the laugh.

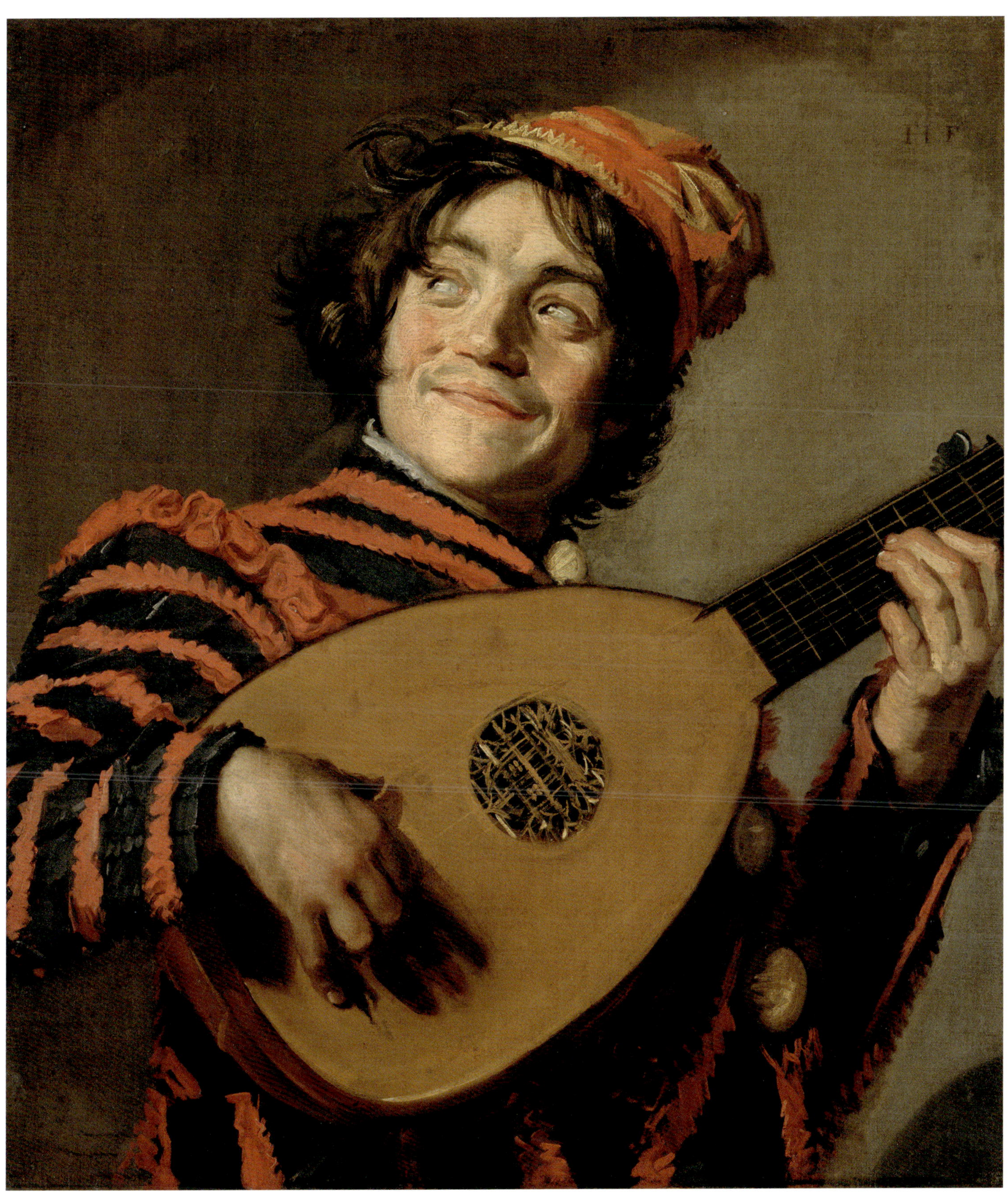

Fig. 177 *The Lute Player*, about 1623
Oil on canvas, 70 × 62 cm
Musée du Louvre, Paris, Paintings Department

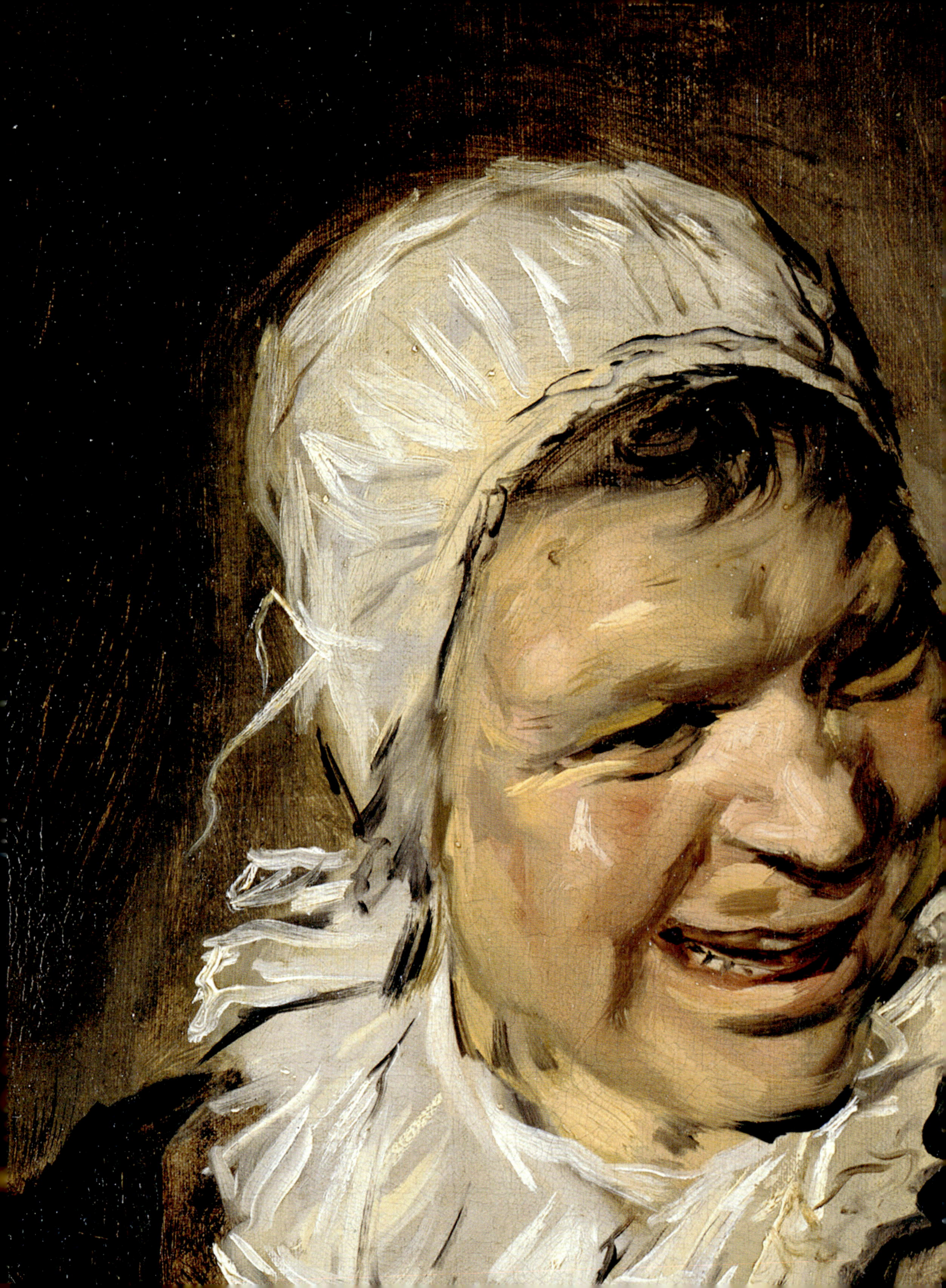

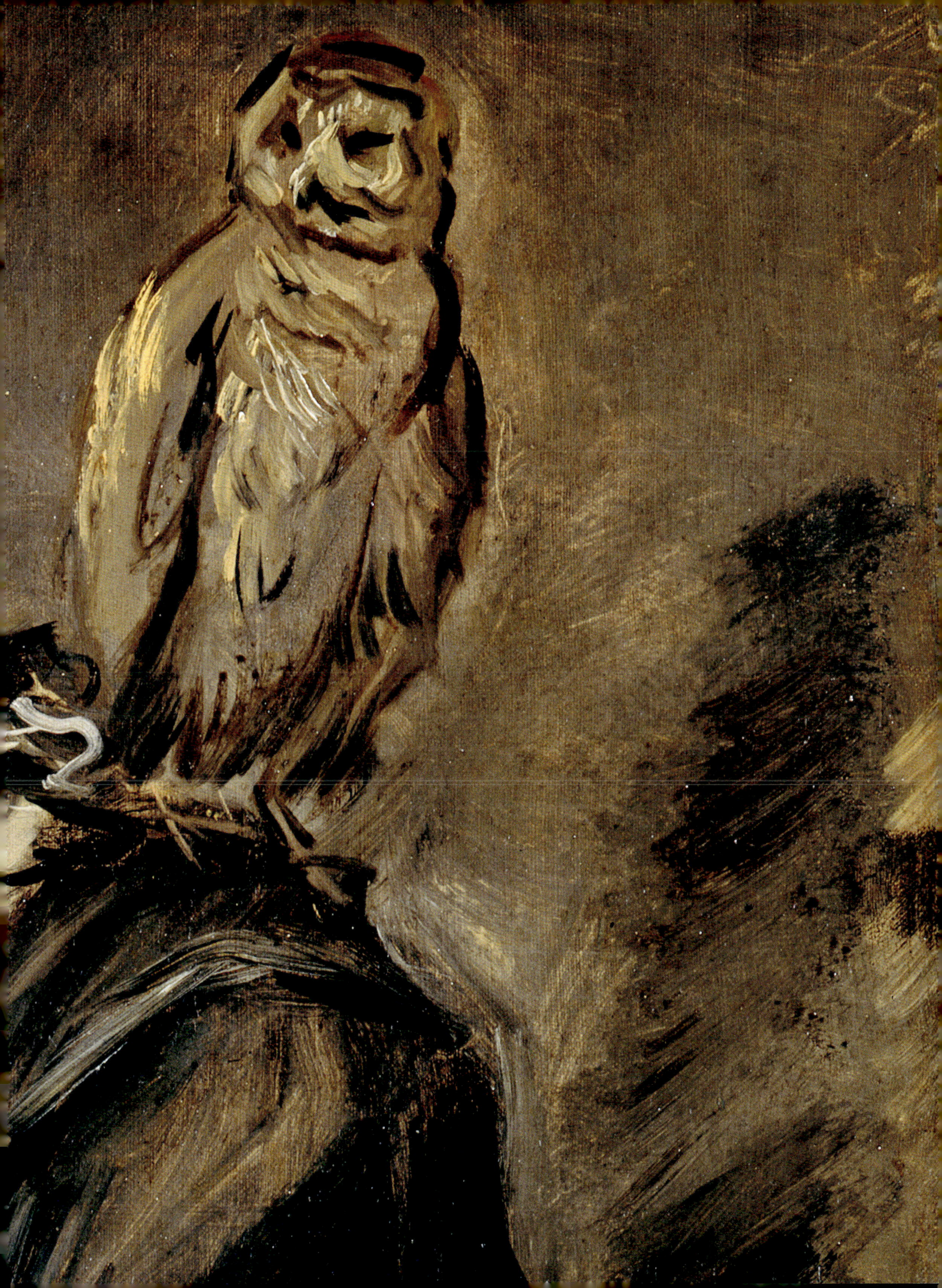

NOTES

HONOURED AND FAMED
FRISO LAMMERTSE AND
BART CORNELIS

1   Robins and Pennell 1908, vol. 2,
pp. 284–6. The authors heard the
account of Whistler's visit to Haarlem from his travelling companion,
the German painter Georg Sauter.
See further F. Jowell in Washington,
London and Haarlem 1989, pp. 61–86,
esp. p. 76.
2   See especially Jowell 1974;
and F. Jowell in Washington,
London and Haarlem 1989, pp. 61–86.
3   Thoré-Bürger 1868, p. 443.
4   In addition to F. Jowell in Washington, London and Haarlem 1989,
pp. 61–86, see Haarlem 2013 and
Haarlem 2018.
5   Thoré-Bürger 1868, p. 443.
6   Demetz 1963; Jowell 1974;
F. Jowell in Washington, London
and Haarlem 1989, pp. 61–86; Ten
Doesschate Chu 1974, pp. 13–15.
7   Vincent van Gogh to Emile
Bernard, 30 July 1888 (letter 651,
see https://vangoghletters.org/vg/
letters/let651/letter.html [accessed
23 March 2023]): 'il s'est peint lui
et sa femme jeunes amoureux dans
un jardin sur un banc de gazon
après la premiere nuit de noce';
and F. Jowell in Washington,
London and Haarlem 1989, p. 78.
8   F. Jowell in Washington,
London and Haarlem 1989, pp. 66–7;
L. Packer in London 2021, pp. 61–8.
9   Thoré-Bürger 1868, p. 222.
10 Ampzing 1621, n.p.; Ampzing 1628,
p. 371; Schrevelius 1647, p. 289;
Schrevelius 1648, p. 383.
11 De Bie 1662, pp. 281–2;
De Monconys 1666, p. 159: 'qui est
avec raison admiré des plus grands
peintres'. De Monconys visited
Haarlem in August 1663.
12 Miedema 1980, vol. 1, p. 309.
13 Houbraken 1718–21, vol. 1,
pp. 90–5.
14 Weyerman 1729, pp. 352–7;
Descamps 1753, pp. 360–2;
Potgieter 1837.
15 Loosjes 1789, p. 12.
16 Thoré-Bürger 1868, p. 424.
17 Robins and Pennell 1908, vol. 2,
p. 285: 'They say he was a drunkard,
a coarse fellow, don't you believe it –
they are the coarse fellows. Just
imagine a drunkard doing these
beautiful things!'
18 See K. Levy-van Halm
in Haarlem 2006, pp. 43–4.
19 See Programma 1900. With
thanks to Tamar van Riessen,
who is preparing an article on
the statue.
20 Haarlem 1937; Haarlem 1962;
Washington, London and Haarlem
1989.
21 See Programma 1900, pp. 29–30.
The words were by Eliza Laurillard
and the music by Willem Robert.
22 Schrevelius 1647, p. 289;
Schrevelius 1648, p. 383; Loosjes 1789,
p. 11; see further pp. 87–90, 139 in the
present volume.
23 Schrevelius 1647, p. 289;
Schrevelius 1648, p. 383; De Bie 1662,
p. 282.

24 See p. 55 in the present volume;
Haarlem 2013.
25 See p. 74 in the present volume.
Recent conservation revealed that
a similar method was employed for
the *Regents of the Old Men's Alms
House*; see L. Abraham in Middelkoop
and Ekkart 2024.
26 Bode 1871a.
27 Schrevelius 1647, p. 289;
Schrevelius 1648, p. 383.
28 Slive 1970–4; Slive 2014; Grimm
1989; Grimm 2023 (in this online
publication, where the attribution of
the paintings is subdivided in a complex way, Grimm is reduced to the
even lower total of about 120 autograph works; our thanks to Ellis
Dullaart for this observation).
29 Episode 8 of the series *Civilisation* (BBC, 1969): 'revoltingly cheerful and odiously skilful'. In his book
Clark's words are 'revoltingly cheerful
and horribly skilful' (see Clark 1969,
p. 195). Clark continued, though, by
saying that he later came to appre-
ciate skill more than he had previously.
30 Robins and Pennell 1908, vol. 2,
p. 285.

THE LIFE OF FRANS HALS
JAAP VAN DER VEEN

1   Bode 1871b, pp. 63–6: 'uytnemende meesters deser konst die ick M.
S. gekent hebbe ende al verby sein'.
2   In 1640 Philips Wouwerman registered as a master with Haarlem's
Guild of St Luke and from that moment was able to take on students;
of Matthias Scheits we know that
he was working as a painter in
Hamburg in 1651 and had therefore
completed his apprenticeship.
3   See p. 68 in the present volume.
4   Among them was Johannes
Voorhout, who worked in Hamburg
between 1672 and 1675 and became
acquainted with Matthias Scheits
there. Voorhout in turn was in close
contact with the art biographer
Arnold Houbraken, who writes that
Scheits had studied painting under
Philips Wouwerman in Haarlem.
Houbraken 1718–21, vol. 3, p. 187
(Scheits) and pp. 224–8 (Voorhout).
5   Bode 1871b, p. 64.
6   Matthias Scheits's copy was
once held in the library of German
art historian Wilhelm Bode, who
published the annotations in 1871
(see note 1): 'Den Treffeliken
Conterfeiter Frans Hals van Harlem
heeft geleert by Carel Vermander
van Molebeke'. The author has been
unable to find the current location
of the book in question, so it is not
yet possible to ascertain whether
Bode, and therefore also Scheits,
owned the first or second edition.
7   The documents were assembled
by Irene van Thiel-Stroman; see
Washington, London and Haarlem
1989, pp. 371–415. Since that publication, virtually no new document
on Frans Hals has been discovered.
8   Under a mezzotint print of a lost
self portrait by Frans Hals, his birth
year is given as 1584: Slive 1970–4,
vol. 3, p. 123 and fig. 93. This source
should not be dismissed out of hand,
for the same caption gives the day
of his death as 24 August 1666. This

date is fairly accurate: Frans Hals was
buried on 1 September of that year.
9   The 'lakenbereider' or 'droog-
scheerder' (cloth-shearer) was
an artisan who shaved the hairs
off woven cloth to give it a smooth
surface.
10 On this see I. van Thiel-Stroman
in Washington, London and Haarlem
1989, pp. 372–3.
11 Haarlem 2006, p. 246.
12 See p. 48 in the present volume.
13 Bode 1871b, p. 64: 'hei is in sein
Jeügt wat lüstich van leven geweest'.
14 J. van B., *Een onderscheyt
Boekje Ofte Tractaetje vande fouten
en dwalingen der Politie in ons
Vaderlant* (A distinguished booklet
or treatise on the errors and aberra-
tions of the police in our fatherland),
Amsterdam 1662: 'dol van geest';
Marieke de Winkel drew attention
to this pamphlet and discussed
'dol van geest': De Winkel 2006,
pp. 145–7, 305 note 59, as well
as Van de Wetering 1995, pp. 221,
237–9.
15 'Den grondt…' is included in Van
Mander 1604, fol. 3r.
16 Neither the application for the
banns nor the date of the wedding
ceremony have been found in
Haarlem.
17 Van Dixhoorn 2009, p. 124. On
Hals as a chamber of rhetoric member, see p. 162 in the present volume.
18 Miedema 1981, pp. 35–6.
19 Schrevelius 1648, p. 383: 'die
hem eygen is', 'ongheloofflijcke veel';
Washington, London and Haarlem
1989, p. 400 doc. 116. The Latin edition of Schrevelius's book, from 1647,
in fact states 'infinita' (infinitely many).
20 In his *Academie der Bau-, Bild-
und Mahlerey-Künste* (Academy of
Architecture, Sculpture and Painting)
published in 1675, Joachim von Sandrart writes about the Delft portrait
painter Michiel van Miereveld: 'Er
hat selbst zum öftern gedacht daß
er wol zehntausend Contrafäte ver-
färtiget' (He himself often thought
that he had made as many as ten
thousand portraits), Peltzer 1925,
p. 171. Houbraken reduced this myth-
ical number by half: see Houbraken
1718–21, vol. 1,
p. 48. What helps achieve a vast
production is reaching a ripe old age,
which is true of both Van Miereveld
and Hals. Van Miereveld confined himself in many cases to painting the face
and hands and left the rest to assistants, an efficient work method that
is not known to this extent for Hals.
21 P. Biesboer in Washington,
London and Haarlem 1989.
22 See also pp. 139, 140
(fig. 106) in the present volume.
23 Haarlem 2006, pp. 215–16;
Washington, London and Haarlem
1989, p. 383 doc. 43, p. 392 doc. 82,
p. 408 doc. 153.
24 For the membership of the
chambers of rhetoric see p. 162
in the present volume.
25 Washington, London and
Haarlem 1989, p. 408 doc. 153.
26 'Schilderyen die ick met my van
Hollandt gebroght hebbe' (Painting
that I have brought with me from
Holland), Kernkamp 1902, pp. 226–37,
esp. pp. 226 (quotation), 217 (De Bray),
229 (Hals).

27 See, for instance, Matham's
signed portrait of Johannes Polyander as a preliminary sketch for his
engraving, in Von Baeyer 2007, no. 6.
28 Washington, London and
Haarlem 1989, pp. 386–7 doc. 62.
29 See pp. 125–7 and fig. 94 in the
present volume.
30 Washington, London and
Haarlem 1989, pp. 379–80 doc. 29.
31 NHA, notary M. de Keijser,
NA 246, 1 March 1652: 'Noch een
conterfeytsel van Ysack Massa met
een swarte vergulde lijst' (Further a
portrait of Ysack Massa with a black
gilded frame), 'noch een cleyn con-
serfeytsel [*sic*] van de voorn. Isack
Massa met een swart ebbenhout
leysie' (further a small portrait of the
aforementioned Isack Massa with a
black ebony frame), 'noch een stuck
schilderij zijnde het conterfeytsel van
de [crossed out: overleden] voorn.
Isack Massa met een swart vergulde
lijst' (further a painting being the portrait of the [crossed out: deceased]
aforementioned Isack Massa with a
black gilded frame), 'noch een conterfeytsel van de [crossed out: overleden, written above:] voorn. Ysack
Massa met een swarte lijst met vergulde letters' (further a portrait of
the [crossed out: deceased, written
above:] aforementioned Ysack Massa
with a black frame with gilt letters)
and 'noch een cleyn conterfeytseltge
met een swart leysie van de voorn.
Ysack Massa' (further a small portrait
with a black frame of the aforementioned Ysack Massa).
32 For the other portraits of Isaac
Massa, a possible painter other than
Hals may be Frans Pietersz de
Grebber. This painter was not only
the next-door neighbour of Isaac's
brother Christiaen Massa for years,
but he had also been one of the two
witnesses who signed the Massa-
Van der Laen will in 1624. In 1655 the
portraits of Christiaen Massa (who
moved from Haarlem to Amsterdam
in 1639) and his wife were on display
in his home, as well as 'een groot
contrefijtsel van Christiaen Massa
op sijn Rus gekleet' (a large portrait
of Christiaen Massa dressed in
Russian clothes), SAA, Archive 5072,
inv. 583, fols 139v–144v, dated
19 December 1655. De Grebber is
the possible maker of this large portrait of the man, presumably attired
in the way Rembrandt had depicted
the Amsterdam merchant Nicolaes
Ruts in 1631 (Frick Collection, New
York, inv. 1943.1.150); De Grebber
painted life-size portraits more
than once; see Van der Veen 2008.
33 See note 31: 'een stuckie schilderij
sijnde een musieckje van meester Hals,
met een swart ebbenhout leysie', 'twee
ronde tronitgens van Frans Hals'.
34 Hessen Kassel Heritage,
inv. GK 215.
35 Slive 1970–4, vol. 3, pp. 35–6
nos 58–9; Washington, London and
Haarlem 1989, pp. 205–7 nos 27, 28.
36 The fact that this happened
is evidenced by early mentions of
paintings in which Hals's children
were identified; see following note.
37 In an inventory of 1644: 'twee
viercante conterfeytsels van de kinderen van Hals tot Haerlem gedaen
door deselve', see p. 72 and note 65

in the present volume; Slive 1970–4, vol. 3, p. 33 nos 53, 54; Washington, London and Haarlem 1989, pp. 202–3 nos 25, 26.

38   NHA, notary F. Swan, NA 226, fol. 319r–v, 21 February 1653: 'groote familiariteyt'.

39   Upon the transfer of the painting it had been agreed that Isaac Massa would have to pay the seller 64 guilders one year and six weeks after the signature of the peace treaty between the Dutch Republic and Spain. Pieter de Molijn requested an acknowledgement of debt, to which Massa replied: 'ick geeff voor soodaenige leurderijen geen schrift, doch ick hebbe de conditie mette requirant [Olivier Jacobsz] aengegaen ende gemaeckt in mijn boeck geschreven' (I will not provide a written bond for such trifles, but I have written the agreement with the petitioner [Olivier Jacobsz] in my books). According to their deal, this sum should have been paid in 1649. The close ties between Massa and De Molijn bring to mind Hals's double portrait in the Rijksmuseum (fig. 61), which is traditionally supposed to depict Massa and his first wife, Beatrix van der Laen, and of which it has been suggested that the landscape was painted by De Molijn; see Bikker et al. 2007, pp. 169–71, esp. p. 171 on its provenance. The 1652 inventory does not list this work, but in theory it could have been displayed elsewhere. The Massa-Van der Laen couple lived in a country house in 1624.

40   Olivier Jacobsz is listed in the membership list of the Guild of St Luke as an art seller in 1634: Miedema 1980, vol. 2, p. 422. He is presumably the father of the painters Jacob Oliviers, who was a member of the guild in 1632 and 1634, and François Oliviers, who cleaned and varnished paintings for the city of Haarlem and was also commissioned to prepare canvases.

41   Washington, London and Haarlem 1989, pp. 376–7 doc. 15.

42   On this issue see pp. 62, 71 in the present volume.

43   In their notification to Hals of 19 March 1636, his clients refer to 'de penningen die op 't voors. stuck alreede betaelt sijn' (the money already paid for the piece in question); Washington, London and Haarlem 1989, p. 389.

44   In 1617 Hals lived in the Peuzelaarsteeg, in 1636 in a house on the Groot Heiligland, in later years in a house by a city gate looking out on the Lange Begijnestraat, then in the Kleine Houtstraat and on the Oude Gracht – on the corner with the Jacobijnestraat – and at his last known address around 1660 in a house in the Ridderstraat. I. van Thiel-Stroman in Washington, London and Haarlem 1989, pp. 378–9, 390, 393, 395, 396, 397, 399, 401, 402, 403, 405–6, 407 and 409 and ibid., p. 24, and Haarlem 2006, pp. 179–80.

45   Washington, London and Haarlem 1989, p. 390: 'binnenshuys'.

46   Van Deursen 1994, pp. 111–12, 126–7, 146–7.

47   Washington, London and Haarlem 1989, p. 406 doc. 147.

48   Ibid., pp. 407–8 doc. 152: 'gene ofte seer weynige goederen tot sijnen huwelycke aengebracht te hebben' (having brought no or very few assets into his marriage).

49   Bode 1871b, p. 64: 'ende mit sein Schildern (het welck nu nit meer wass als weleer) nit meer de Kost verdienen kon', 'om de deugt seinder Konst'. 'Deugd' should be interpreted as quality. It means that the city of Haarlem had profited from the high-quality art that Hals had produced in the preceding years. This must in particular refer to the civic guard group portraits that could be admired in the Doelen, the civic guard's target hall.

50   Washington, London and Haarlem 1989, pp. 411–13 docs 170, 171, 174, 175, 176, 177, 178, 181: '… in zijn hoochdringende noot'.

51   Bode 1871b, p. 64: 'Na myn gissen … wel 90 Jaren off niet veel minder out geworden'.

52   Houbraken 1718–21, vol. 1, pp. 90–5: 'in den ouderdom van 5 of 86 jaren'.

53   Hofstede de Groot 1893; Emmens 1979, pp. 101–11; Carasso 1998; Cornelis 1995; Cornelis 1998; Horn 2000; Bikker 2009.

54   Houbraken 1718–21, vol. 1, pp. 89–90: 'Gy zyt van Dyk, want geen mensch anders kan zulks doen', 'een fynen trek', 'want niemant anders kan zulks doen', 'trek', 'minnelyk bejegende', 'Men zegt', 'slegte wyze van leven'.

55   Ibid., vol. 1, p. 93: 'Lieve Heer, haal my vroeg in uwen hoogen Hemel'.

56   Ibid.: 'Zoo haastig niet, lieve Heer, zoo haastig niet', 'dikwils stof tot lachen'.

57   Ibid., vol. 1, pp. 93–4. In vol. 3, p. 309, Houbraken names Dirck van Delen as a student of Frans Hals, according to Hofstede de Groot 1893 and others based on an erroneous reading of De Bie.

58   Houbraken 1718–21, vol. 2, p. 191: 'dikwijls om de klugt'. A similar incident is described later by Houbraken, in which engraver Joseph Mulder claimed to have played a prank on a baby he was watching over. Houbraken judged that this was not particularly original, but 'merely copied. Adriaan Brouwer played this prank first'. This suggests that Brouwer's prank was known among his contemporaries: such stories, sometimes exaggerated, appear to have been circulating in artists' studios. Houbraken 1718–21, vol. 3, pp. 247–8: 'dit was maar nageaapt. Adriaan Brouwer heeft dergelyke vieze Pots 't eerst gespeelt'.

59   Ibid., vol. 2, pp. 75, 263; vol. 3, pp. 76–7.

60   Besides on Adriaen Brouwer, Karel de Moor also provided information on Jan Porcellis, Nicolaes Berchem and Jan Steen; see Houbraken 1718–21, vol. 1, respectively pp. 318, 213; vol. 2, p. 110; vol. 3, p. 25. Houbraken met De Moor in his early years in Dordrecht; ibid., vol. 3, p. 343.

61   Houbraken 1718–21, vol. 1, p. 322: 'eene van Zomeren toen waard in 't schilt van Vrankryk', 'nam hem in, en zette hem te schilderen'.

62   Bredius 1915–22, vol. 3, pp. 804–5; Oudenaarde 2018, p. 43.

63   Bredius found both the 1626 document and the 1635 auction record and made the connection with Houbraken's text: Bredius 1915–22, vol. 3, pp. 795–805.

64   Washington, London and Haarlem 1989, p. 385 doc. 57; the other witness, Judith Jans, is probably Judith Leyster.

65   Houbraken 1718–21, vol. 1, pp. 95, 325. In his biography of Philips Wouwerman, Houbraken says that he obtained Wouwerman's funeral notice on which 'de oude Vincent vander Vinne in dien tyd, op geschreven had, dat hy was gestorven in zyn 48 jaar' (old Vincent vander Vinne at the time had written that Wouwerman had died at 48 years of age): ibid., vol. 2, p. 70. On the funeral notice that has survived of Laurens van der Vinne, the year of his birth and the full name of his father have been added; NHA, Beeldcollectie (access no. 1100), inv. 49957. A copy of the printed funeral notice of Claes Hals is included in the auction catalogue Oud-Amsterdam, [uit de] verzamelingen Wurfbain, Slagregen, Kroese e.a., Amsterdam (Frederik Muller & Co), 6–11 May 1912, p. 137, no. 1292.

66   Houbraken 1718–21, vol. 1, p. 95: 'een Mestys, of halve Zwartinne', 'op de Hollandse wyze'.

67   The Orphan Chamber was responsible for overseeing the administration of the estates of children when one of their parents had died.

68   SAA, Orphan Chamber Archives (access no. 5073), inv. 808 (Input register 37), 1725, dated 20 April 1689, with later registrations of 14 December 1694 and 26 November 1699: 'den zoldaet Jacob Hals, zoon van Reynier Hals en Elisabet Groen', 'sig in dese landen ter neer te setten', 'vrijburger'.

69   SAA, Orphan Chamber Archives (access no. 5073), inv. 184, letter dated 31 January 1699 in Colombo and documents of 22 January and 13 November 1699; ibid., inv. 187, with a last mention of Jacob Hals as Orphan Chamber Commissioner in 1731; he is no longer listed as such in 1733.

70   No further information could be found on Jan Hals. The name appears more than once in documents drawn up in Amsterdam in the first decades of the eighteenth century. In 1725 a Johannes Hals, 'master painter', is listed, a year before a son of Martinus Hals (a grandson of Dirck Hals) married under this name, and a person of the same name died in March 1725.

71   Slive 1970–4, vol. 3, pp. 123–5, no. L15 and figs 93–6.

72   Houbraken 1718–21, vol. 1, p. 95: 'J. Wieland, een oud Liefhebber, en die de meeste der zelve gekent heeft, getuigt: dat al de kinderen van F. Hals luchtig van geest, en beminnaars van Zang- en Speelkonst geweest hebben.'

73   Miedema 1980, vol. 2, p. 948, and Van der Willigen 1870, pp. 329–30, who owned a portrait of Joan Wielant dated 1690, with an inscription indicating that he was born in Haarlem and died there in 1717.

74   SAA, Baptismal, Marriage and Burial Registers (access no. 5001), inv. 495, p. 356, dated 10 October 1670; his bride, Geesje Jans, had previously been married to Olivier Stevens, also a schoolmaster. The schoolmaster–painter combination was common at this time: De Beer 2019, vol. 3, pp. 1051–2 and note 9.

75   Houbraken 1718–21, vol. 1, p. 93: 'gemeenlyk allen avond tot de keel toe vol met drank'.

76   Rembrandt, for example, was not someone, according to Houbraken, 'who spent a lot of time in the pub or with cronies', while Nicolaes Maes even had 'an extraordinary aversion to pubs' and to 'those who loitered there'; Houbraken 1718–21, vol. 1, p. 272, vol. 3, p. 275.

77   Ibid., vol. 3, p. 248: 'het plegen van onvoeglyke bedryven, en inzonderheid 't overdadig wynzwelgen, onder de Konstschilders byster in zwang ging, en gelyk als een mode ingekropen was', 'dat het zedert allengs heeft afgenoomen'.

78   NHA, notary W. Crousen de Jonge, NA 159, fol. 1r–v, 11 January 1637: 'van moderne beelden'; Bredius 1923–4, p. 60.

79   In 1631 Den Abt claimed money from the painter Frans Pietersz de Grebber for costs incurred: NHA, Oud-Rechterlijk Archief (access no. 3111), inv. 978, fols. 122v, dated 11 March 1631, and 141, dated 28 March 1631.

80   See p. 67 in the present volume.

81   The Hals brothers did not sign any other documents for the notary who drew up the statement in question and were undoubtedly asked to do so by Den Abt, presumably because they were present in his inn anyway (compare Brouwer's role as a witness; see note 62); NHA, notary W. Crousen de Jonge, NA 155, fol. 208, 29 March 1630; Bredius 1923–4, p. 22; Washington, London and Haarlem 1989, p. 384 doc. 52.

82   Washington, London and Haarlem 1989, p. 403 docs 135, 136: 'van verteert gelach'.

83   Slive 1970–4, vol. 3, p. 15 no. 22. In Haarlem 2017, p. 73 no. 4, Jasper Hillegers considers it conceivable that Hals's innkeeper represents Den Abt's wife, without referring to the 1662 inventory (cited in the next note).

84   First 'twee contrefeytsels met ebbenhoute lijsten van Pot sijnde Hendrick Willemsz den Abt ende Josina van Nesten selff' (two portraits with ebony frames by Pot being Hendrick Willemsz den Abt and Josina van Nesten themselves) and then 'twee conterfeytsels van Josina van Nesten ende haer man sa: met vergulde lijsten' (two portraits of Josina van Nesten and her late husband: with gilded frames), NHA, notary H. van Gellinckhuijsen, NA 341, 4 September 1662; Biesboer 2001, pp. 162–3 (with the erroneous reading 'en haer moer sa' [and her deceased mother]). The second pair of portraits is listed without the maker's name, probably because the first pair was already provided with an artist's name.

ANTWERP AND HAARLEM
FRISO LAMMERTSE AND
JAAP VAN DER VEEN

1 Washington, London and Haarlem 1989, p. 377 doc. 17.
2 Ibid., p. 378 docs 19–22.
3 It emerges from a document of 15 November 1616 that Hals was back in Haarlem by then; see ibid., p. 378 doc. 22.
4 Lee 1972, p. 218.
5 Groenveld 2009.
6 SAA, notary P. Mathijsz, NA 456, fols 515–16, 20 November 1614; De Beer 2019, vol. 1, pp. 183–4.
7 For this inundation of Southern Netherlandish paintings see, for example, Sluijter 1999, pp. 118–21.
8 Ampzing 1628, p. 372; Miedema 1980, vol. 2, pp. 420 (the guild list of 1634), 423 (an update to the membership roll from 1637 on, with the annotation 'wt' [dead] after Andries Snellingh's name, due to his death in 1638).
9 'van Antwerpen geboortich'; 'tegenwoordich'; as recorded in the will that Andries Snellingh drew up with his first wife, Paulina Wolphaerts, in Haarlem: NHA, notary A. Willemsz, NA 49, fols 236–7v, 27 March 1613.
10 De Grebber was also active as an art dealer outside Haarlem, in Amsterdam and elsewhere, where he was referred to as Frans Pietersz van Haarlem; at the auction of Gillis van Conincxloo on 1 March 1607 as 'Frans Pietersz. van Haerlem'; after that simply as 'Frans Pietersz.'; at the auction of Claes Rauwaert on 28 August 1612 as 'Frans Pietersz. de Grebber van Haerlem'; and thereafter always without his place of origin and surname.
11 Washington, London and Haarlem 1989, p. 384 doc. 47.
12 Andries Snellingh was related to the De Robiano family of Antwerp, through his first marriage (see note 9), members of which were art and tapestry dealers.
13 NHA, Oud-Rechterlijk Archief (access no. 3111), inv. 986, 16 March 1640: 'oock 17 jaere niet en is aengesproocken oft gemaent' (and also has not been exhorted nor pressed [for payment] in 17 years).
14 Rooses and Ruelens 1898, pp. 130, 136.
15 Ibid., pp. 130–94.
16 Peter Paul Rubens, *Achilles and the Daughters of Lycomedes*, about 1617, Museo Nacional del Prado, Madrid, inv. 1661; Peter Paul Rubens, *Daniel in the Lions' Den*, about 1614–16, National Gallery of Art, Washington, inv. 1965.13.1.
17 Rooses and Ruelens 1898, pp. 130, 161: 'galantuomo'.
18 Van der Veen 2002, p. 73 (for Delft); Gruber and Tomášek 2018 (for Rubens's *Head of Medusa*).
19 Grijzenhout 2021, pp. 183–4.
20 For Buytewech see Haverkamp Begemann 1959, pp. 7, 165–7, nos vG 2, 6 and 7, which indicates that the attribution to Buytewech should be treated with caution. For De Bray and De Grebber see above all Rotterdam and Frankfurt 1999, pp. 84–111, 116–43; for De Grebber see also Hemmer 2015; for Soutman see Barrett 2012; for Rubens and Goltzius see Vermeylen and De Clippel 2012.

21 Davies et al. 2018.
22 Quoted in Denucé 1949, p. 28: 'Het konterfyt van Van Dyck na my wort soo hooch gheestimeert, als imant ietz van Van Dyck gesien heeft, 't welck oock wt myn handen niet sal gaen ofte moet 300 guld. gelden' (My portrait by Van Dyck is regarded as highly as anyone who has seen anything by Van Dyck, and it will not leave my hands for anything less than 300 guilders).
23 For this topic the following were consulted: Briels 1976; Briels 1985; De Schepper 1987; Biesboer 1996a; Briels 1997.
24 Quoted in Briels 1976, p. 124: 'eenijghe goede luijden van buijten heure residentie binnen Haerlem'.
25 Van Mander 1604, fols 229r, 251v; De Bie 1662, p. 282: 'Const-baerende Stadt Haerlem'.
26 Lee 1972, p. 218.
27 Miedema 1980, vol. 2, pp. 1035, 1036, 1040.
28 For Esaias van de Velde's loose touch in the same period see Sluijter 1999, pp. 130–3.
29 For the apprenticeship of these painters see De Beer 2019, vol. 2, p. 363 (Van Goyen); The Hague and Münster 1974, p. 222 (Ter Borch); Bredius 1919, p. 216 (Potter).
30 De Beer 2019, vol. 1, pp. 219–21.
31 The year 1612 is based on the report by Roger de Piles in his life of Rubens (published in 1677), in which he states that the artist went to the Dutch Republic four years after his marriage. Rubens married Isabella Brant in 1609. In a letter of 20 June 1612 her father, Johannes Brant, wrote that his son-in-law had returned to Antwerp from 'Batavia' a few days before, and had spoken there to the Leiden professors Grotius, Baudius and Heinsius; see De Smet 1977.
32 Rutgers 2019.
33 A possible reason for the journey is that the artists wanted to go to Amsterdam to look at a famous painting by Caravaggio and were possibly prepared to make an offer for it. His so-called 'Madonna of the Rosary' had been bought around 1607 in Naples jointly by the painter Louis Finson (about 1575–1617) and the Antwerp-born artist Abraham Vinck (about 1575–1619), both of whom worked there. It is not clear when the painting came to Amsterdam. Vinck stayed there from 1610, Finson from 1615. In 1617 Finson left two paintings by 'Michiel Angel Crawats' (Caravaggio) to Vinck in his will: a Judith and Holofernes and a Madonna of the Rosary, 'waervan de wederhelft den voorn. mr. Abraham Vinck is toecomende' (of which the other half belongs to the aforenamed Master Abraham Vinck): Briels 1976, p. 256 note 7, p. 258 doc. c. After Vinck's death in 1619 the latter work was bought by Rubens, Brueghel, Van Balen, Jan Baptist Coymans and others, and transferred to Antwerp. On Vinck and Finson see especially Osnabrugge 2019, pp. 63–122; and for the sale to Antwerp see Sammut 2020.
34 Belkin 2009, vol. 1, pp. 217–20 nos 107–10; Logan 2021, pp. 50–3 nos 15–18.

35 Rubens is described as the god of painters ('de god van de schilders') in a letter of 1611 from the Antwerp merchant Jan Le Grand; see Monballieu 1965, p. 195.
36 Gerbier 1620, p. 44: 'Rubens, Breughel, Van Baelen ende sommige meer in Hollant zijnde, werden rijsende van Haerlem van Goltzius en andere gheesten derselver Stadt in een Dorp (hun boertighs onbekent toeghemaeckt hebbende), gearesteert om de Eedele Gheesten Eer aen te doen, ende om voor het letste uyt eenen onbeweynsden boertighen Roomer malcanderen de Vrientschap ende de foy [afscheidsmaal] toe drincken' (Rubens, Brueghel, Van Balen and various others, being in Holland, journeyed from Haarlem and were arrested in a village by Goltzius and other minds of the same city [who had made themselves unrecognisable as a manner of joke] in order to pay these Noble Minds respects and drink to each other, in friendship and a last farewell banquet from an unfeigned peasant glass). The poem, which appeared in print in 1620, was already complete in 1618.
37 Slive 1970–4, vol. 1, p. 68.
38 In addition to individual portraits, one can think of Van Dyck's double portraits and the portraits that Jordaens made of his family. For Van Dyck see Barnes et al. 2004, nos I.108, I.113, I.114, I.115; Madrid 2012; Alsteens 2014. For Jordaens see Antwerp 1993, vol. 1, nos A5, A6, A30.
39 Liedtke 2011, p. 17.
40 Van Mander 1604 (1973), fol. 48r–v.
41 The following has been said about this: 'Rubens's touch is smooth and flowing, while in Van Dyck the brush strokes are clearly visible, a technique which is distinctly reminiscent of Frans Hals – who is known to have been in Antwerp in 1616'; Vlieghe 1998, p. 124. See also Liedtke 2011.
42 Houbraken 1718–21, vol. 1, pp. 90–2; see also p. 42 in the present volume.
43 For Van Dyck's visit to The Hague see Van Gelder 1959, and especially Baudouin 2001.
44 See p. 42 in the present volume.

THE STUDIO
FRISO LAMMERTSE AND
JAAP VAN DER VEEN

1 NHA, notary E. van Bosvelt, NA 63, fol. 80, 20 March 1636: 'ende dat het met meerder lust tot Haerlem als tot Amsterdam sal gedaen worden, overmits hij dan binnenshuys ende bij zijn volck zijnde 't oge oock daerop mach hebben'. This is one of the four documents dealing with the genesis of the painting. It was first published in Bredius 1917, and a transcription later appeared in Haarlem 1988, pp. 383–4 and cat. 194, and in Washington, London and Haarlem 1989, pp. 389–90 doc. 74.
2 Van Mander 1604, fol. 239v: 'wat hij daer voor volck had op zijn winckel?' Van Mander also uses the term 'volck' in this sense in his biographies of Italian painters. He re-

lates that 'Pierijn', the painter Perino del Vaga, an industrious draughtsman, left the practical work to his assistants, thus 'keeping many people in work' ('veel volck in't werck houdende'), gaining financial profit rather than honour. See Van Mander 1604, fol. 142r.
3 On the training of artists see Miedema 1986–7 and other articles in Boschloo 1986–7; De Jager 1990; Van de Wetering 1995, pp. 223–9; Franken 1997.
4 Louis de Pret, 'resident assistant' ('knecht in huys') of Cornelis van der Voort of Amsterdam, was around 35 years old when his master died; see SAA, Archief 5073, inv. 952, 30 August 1625, and Bredius 1915–22, vol. 4, p. 1180. In 1609 Van der Voort's wife drew up a codicil that was jointly signed by the journeyman ('schildersgesel') Hendrick van Mer; SAA, notary J. Gijsbertsz, NA 27, p. 31, 14 March 1609. Van der Voort testified a few months later that he had known Van Mer for a long time, and that he was 'learning the practice of painting from and in the house of the aforesaid Cornelis van der Voort, his master' ('die practycque van 't schilderen is lerende bij ende ten huyse van den voorsz. Cornelis van de Voorde, sijn meester'); see SAA, notary J. Franssen Bruijningh, NA 196, cover 16, fol. 1gr–v, 23 July 1609, and Bredius 1915–22, vol. 4, p. 1183. The latter document states that Van Mer was between 23 and 24 years old. A document drawn up in Haarlem in 1634 in the house of Frans Pietersz de Grebber was signed by 'his assistant' ('sijnen knecht') Vincent Casteleijn, who was around 25 years old.
5 The new statutes of 1590, which were first printed in Briels 1976, pp. 159–62, and then in Miedema 1980, vol. 1, pp. 57–61, were made necessary by the Alteration (the replacement of the Catholic city government with a Protestant one), which abolished the guild's religious functions, such as the upkeep of the altar or chapel in the church and holding processions.
6 This is demonstrated in Miedema 1980, vol. 1, pp. 1, 8, 9, 93 and note 49; for the integral text of the draft see ibid., vol. 1, pp. 91–135. Goosens 2001 regards the draft statutes of 1631 as an indication of a tendency circulating among some circles within the guild. For the guild system in Haarlem see also Van der Ree-Scholtens 1995, pp. 59–60, 127–30, 284–6.
7 See p. 53 in the present volume.
8 Miedema 1980, vol. 2, pp. 497, 505, 514: 'onaengegeeven discipulen', 'sijn gasten', 'hoeveel knechts dat hij hadde die niet betaelt en hebben'. In the case of Frans Pietersz de Grebber, this does not seem to have been due to forgetfulness or nonchalance but rather a question of sheer obstinacy. His administration of his pupils was perfectly adequate. In 1620 he claimed 22 guilders from a woman who owed him 'tuition fees' for teaching her son. She replied that she had already paid, whereupon he was ordered 'to bring his book', which he did; see NHA, Oud-Rechterlijk Archief (access no. 3111), inv. 970,

NOTES

fol. 117v, 5 May 1620, and fol. 124v, 8 May 1620. A document of 1642 states that De Grebber was still owed 64 guilders and 7 stuivers by 'Van Rasenburgh', as recorded in an 'oblong book' of his; NHA, notary E. van Bosvelt, NA 64, 3 February 1642. The credit was made up of two sums: 56 guilders for (one year's) tuition fees, and 8 guilders and 7 stuivers (extra tuition time). The debtor was Reynier van Rasenbergh, who was apprenticed to De Grebber around 1640–2, at the same time as Peter Lely (on whom see p. 53 in the present volume).

9 For the documentation on this incident see Bredius 1917; Miedema 1980, vol. 2, pp. 430–4.

10 The formulation 'in accordance with the contract signed between the two of them, namely to be allowed to part from the other' ('volgens de besteedingh tusschen haer beyden gedaen te weeten dan van den andere te moghen scheyden') seems to indicate a written agreement.

11 Bredius 1919.

12 For Frans Pietersz de Grebber see notes 4, 8 and 21.

13 De Jager 1990 provides an initial inventory of contracts between masters and pupils but does not cover Haarlem.

14 Chris Atkins in Oudenaarde 2018, p. 208, note 11.

15 Schatborn 1973; Amsterdam and Washington 1981, pp. 74–5; Nehlsen-Marten 2003, pp. 223–7.

16 Nehlsen-Marten 2003.

17 Oudenaarde 2018.

18 Houbraken 1718–21, vol. 1, pp. 319, 347, and vol. 2, p. 191: 'die toen nog jong was, en by F. Hals de Konst leerde', 'wanneer zy nog jong was, bescheet, en die van Brouwer weer bescheten werd'. See also p. 42 in the present volume.

19 Ibid., vol. 1, p. 320: 'afgescheiden van zyn andere leerlingen'.

20 See p. 42 in the present volume.

21 Von Schneider 1922 was the first to draw attention to the Caravaggist lighting in Judith Leyster's early work. Wijnman 1932 discovered the year of her birth and details about her parents moving to Vreeland. In Ampzing 1628, in a description of Haarlem, the name Judith Leyster is written in the margin of a remark about Frans Pietersz de Grebber and his daughter Maria. Wijnman stresses that this was merely in passing, but Ellen Broersen, in Worcester and Haarlem 1993, pp. 19–20, attaches greater weight to it. She suggests that Leyster could have received some training from De Grebber, and that in those days an artist in Haarlem could also be exposed to a Caravaggesque or 'Utrecht' influence. See also Pieter Biesboer in Worcester and Haarlem 1993, p. 77. However, no such markedly 'Utrecht' influence as detected in Leyster's work can be observed in that of any other Haarlem painter. All the same, it is possible that Leyster had had drawing lessons in Haarlem before receiving any training in painting, from De Grebber, for example. Haarlem and Washington 2009 supports this De Grebber hypothesis. Geurts 2020 stresses the Caravaggist elements in Leyster's work.

22 Judith Leyster, *A Fool holding a Jug, known as 'The Jolly Drinker'*, 1629, oil on canvas, 88.2 × 87.9 cm, Rijksmuseum, Amsterdam, inv. SK-A-1685.

23 See note 30 for the lost portrait of Leyster. It is not certain that the Judith Jans who witnessed the baptism of Hals's daughter Maria on 11 November 1631 was Judith Leyster or a namesake, but the first is the most likely.

24 Haarlem and Washington 2009, p. 22, suggests the possibility that the portrait of a woman in the Frans Hals Museum (Haarlem 2006, no. 284, pp. 536–7) dated 1635 depicts a sister of Judith Leyster, possibly Catharina Jansdr Leyster. She married an Amsterdam real estate agent in 1639 and had a list of possessions that she transferred from Haarlem to Amsterdam in connection with her forthcoming marriage. These included 'twee conterfeytsels van haer eygen persoon' 'two portraits of her own person', SAA, notary G. Vliet, NA 1624, fols 10–11v, 6 July 1639. It can be assumed that one (or both) were by her sister Judith Leyster.

25 Weller 1992, pp. 11–12; D.P. Weller in Raleigh, Indianapolis and Manchester 2002, pp. 4, 10–11. The author is a little more cautious in a later publication: Molenaer 'trained in the circle of Frans Hals' and calls Dirck Hals 'one of Molenaer's probable teachers in the mid-1620s'; Weller 2007, p. 147.

26 Weller 2007, pp. 147–9.

27 The work is comparable or perhaps even identical to a 'student van Jan Meynssen' ('student by Jan Meynssen'), meaning an artist's pupil, described in an Amsterdam inventory; SAA, notary W. Hasen, NA 1598, fols 31–69v, 21 December 1639, closed 17 January 1640.

28 Miedema 1980, pp. 136–7. See also p. 70 in the present volume.

29 Among the entries in the Amsterdam inventory of 1639 mentioned in note 27 are a study head by Frans Hals, a large work with 'modern' figures by Dirck Hals – meaning that they wore contemporary dress – two paintings by Adriaen Brouwer and four copies after him, including a 'tobacco drinker' ('tobackdrincker'), immediately followed by 'a tobacco drinker by the young [Harmen] Hals' ('een tobacqdrincker van de jongen Hals'), by whom there was also a small work with 'some peasants' ('met eenige boertjens') and a barber's shop. In addition to the 'student' by Jan Miense Molenaer mentioned above, the estate also contained a 'cat scratcher' ('kattekrabber') by him, two works by Pieter Codde and one by Dirck van Delen. See also note 57.

30 They are described in the probate inventory as '2 portraits of Jan Molenaer and his wife by Frans Hals, without frames' ('2 conterfeytsels van Jan Molenaer ende sijn huysvrou van Frans Hals, sonder lijst'), NHA, notary W. van Kittensteyn, NA 313, 10 October 1668 (our reading of this item differs from that in Washington, London and Haarlem 1989, p. 389, where Bredius is corrected,

in our opinion wrongly). For this inventory see Bredius 1915–22, vol. 1, pp. 2–9; Hofrichter 1989, pp. 85–103; Raleigh, Indianapolis and Manchester 2002, pp. 181–7; GPI N-5314.

31 In the same room as this 'piece dead-coloured by Brouwer and completed by Molenaer, trictrac players' ('stuckje van Brouwer gedootverruwt en van Molenaer opgemaeckt, verkeerdertjes') there was also 'an old piece by Molenaer with cards [card players]', ('een out stuckje van Molenaer met de kaert') and 'an old piece with tric-trac players' ('een out stuck met verkeerderen').

32 Houbraken 1718–21, vol. 1, p. 347: 'Adriaen [van Ostade] was born in the year 1610 and died in 1685. Adr. Brouwer and he were pupils of Frans Hals at the same time' ('Adriaan … is geboren in 't jaar 1610, en gestorven 1685. Adr. Brouwer en hy waren op een tyd Leerlingen van Frans Hals'). He adds that Isaac van Ostade was Adriaen's younger brother and pupil. Houbraken was undoubtedly basing his account on information from the collector Constantijn Sennepart, in whose Amsterdam house Adriaen van Ostade lived for a while. Sennepart owned many works of art by Adriaen, which according to his own account, Houbraken was allowed to view on several occasions.

33 NHA, notary J. Steyn, NA 162, fol. 2v, 8 June 1632. In this deed he is referred to as 'mr. schilder' (master painter), so he must already have become a member of the guild, but the year of his admission is not known.

34 Robinson 2015, pp. 15–16, fol. 10, and pp. 40–1, fol. 38.

35 Van de Wetering pointed out that in those days artists used tablets or *tafeletten*, small prepared sheets of wood or parchment that could be drawn on with a stylus. They could be reused after the application of a new prepared layer. This might explain why not a single drawing by artists like Johannes Vermeer and Frans Hals has come down to us. See Van de Wetering 1991, p. 214 and *passim*; Van de Wetering 1995, pp. 227–8.

36 De Bie 1662, pp. 281–2.

37 Bredius 1890–5, vol. 1, p. 8; Philips Wouwerman is mentioned a second time in this notebook, with the statement that he painted landscapes and animals (ibid., vol. 6, p. 115).

38 Houbraken 1718–21, vol. 2, p. 75.

39 SAA, notary P. van Velsen, NA 1788, pp. 554–5, 6 October 1651: 'vijff jaren bij de requirante ende haren man gewerct heeft'. Washington, London and Haarlem 1989, p. 404 doc. 138, with earlier literature.

40 Miedema 1980, p. 1038; this membership roll states that he was born in 1627 and died in 1698, the very years given by Houbraken, which he must have copied from that list.

41 Houbraken 1718–21, vol. 2, pp. 191–2.

42 Pieter van Roestraten, *Head of an Old Fisherman of Haarlem (Kopf eines alten Fischers aus Haarlem)*, oil on wood, 32 × 25 cm, sale Berlin (Mandelbaum und Kronthal), 18 March 1936, no. 131. Its present whereabouts are unknown.

43 Houbraken 1718–21, vol. 2, pp. 210–11.

44 I. van Thiel-Stroman in Haarlem 2006, pp. 325–8; Biesboer 2017 discusses a self portrait of 1649.

45 The data accompanying the lot numbers in the auction catalogue of the Jacob van der Marck collection were supplied on the basis of notes that the collector kept through the years. Among other pieces of information, the notes state that Vincent van der Vinne was a 'disciple of the famous Frans Hals' ('Discipel van den Beroemden Frans Hals'), see Amsterdam 1773, p. 164, and that there was a painted portrait of him holding a drawing that was 'forceful, in the manner of F. Hals' ('Kragtig in de manier van F. Hals', no. 472).

46 The painted model for this drawing is in Museum Boijmans Van Beuningen, where it is attributed to Pieter Codde; see Rosen 2020, pp. 225–7.

47 NHA, notary L. Baert, NA 372, doc. 373, 9 December 1668; Bredius 1923–4, pp. 30–1; Washington, London and Haarlem 1989, p. 401, note 123, and p. 187, note 12.

48 Reynier Hals married in Amsterdam in 1653. At the bottom of the marriage licence is his signature, with that of Pieter Gerritsz van Roestraten crossed out. Because the groom declared that he was 22 years old, his father had to consent to the marriage, even though Reynier Hals had been born in 1627 and, strictly speaking, was no longer a minor. Due to this – alleged – minority, he had to be accompanied by someone, and we suspect that Van Roestraten signed in error, since witnesses to a notice of an intended marriage did not sign the document; see SAA, DTB 472, p. 260, 27 December 1653. Six months later, Van Roestraten, assisted by Claes Hals, married Ariaentje Hals. In that same year he and the painter Daniel Boone signed an affidavit that was also signed by Reynier Hals, 'schilder', as the witness; SAA, notary Joh. Hellerus, NA 2053, fol. 125, 21 September 1654.

49 SAA, notary G. van Schoonderwoert, NA 6864, fol. 376, 24–25 November 1700: 'tabacqsrookertje'.

50 NHA, notary L. Baert, NA 387, doc. 68, 19 December 1669; Biesboer 2001, pp. 218–19 doc. 64.

51 Rudi Ekkart identified a third candidate: Johannes Verspronck, who was born in Haarlem. Ekkart detected the influence of Frans Hals in Verspronck's earliest work, leading him to suspect that he was in Hals's studio before joining the guild; see Haarlem 1979, p. 15. In another publication he observes that Verspronck borrowed poses from works by Hals in his own portraits, and postulates an apprenticeship around 1630; see Ekkart 1979, p. 109. For Verspronck's technique see also Hendriks 1998; Krekeler et al. 2014.

52 Van Eeghen 1974.

53 SAA, notary J. Bruijningh, NA 836, pp. 1360–76, 5 February 1636; Bredius 1888, pp. 188–90.

54 This was previously pointed out by Bredius in his article cited in note 53. Bredius also saw elements in paintings by Pieter Codde that

reminded him of works by Hals. There is no available information on Codde's training, and Houbraken does not mention him.

55 Biesboer 2001, p. 235, respectively Stadsarchief Delft, ONA (access no. 161), notary W. van Assendelft, NA 1867, doc. 3107, pp. 564–6, d.d. 29 April 1659, esp. p. 564.

56 Houbraken 1718–21, vol. 3, p. 309, plainly states that Dirck van Delen 'was a pupil of Frans Hals' ('was een Leerling van Frans Hals'). This assertion is supposedly based on an incorrect reading of a passage in De Bie 1662, pp. 281–2. See Schmidt 1874, who also denied that Brouwer was trained by Hals.

57 They are *Elegant Company in a Dutch Renaissance Room*, Frans Hals Museum, Haarlem (signed by Dirck van Delen), *Elegant Company in a Palatial Loggia*, Gemäldegalerie der Akademie der bildenden Künste, Vienna (signed by Dirck Hals), and *Elegant Company in a Palatial Room*, private collection (signed by Dirck Hals). All three are reproduced in Rikken 2021. According to her, all these works are collaborations between Dirck Hals and Dirck van Delen. According to Vermet (see note 58), the first work is entirely by Dirck van Delen (that is, both architecture and figures) and in the other two the figures are by Dirck Hals and the architecture by Bartholomeus van Bassen. It is noteworthy that the above-mentioned Amsterdam inventory of 1639/40 (see notes 27, 29) lists not only paintings by Frans, Dirck and Harmen Hals, Adriaen Brouwer and Jan Miense Molenaer, but also 'a perspective, palace by Van Belen [i.e. Delen]' ('een perspectyff, palys van Van Beelen [= Delen]') and 'a small temple by Van Bassen' ('een tempeltje van Van Bassen'). Almost no works by Van Delen are recorded in inventories prior to 1650. Could the palace interior have been acquired from the Hals studio?

58 With thanks to the art historian Bernard Vermet, who gave us access to an as yet unpublished manuscript in which he discusses the three paintings of 1628.

59 See also p. 42 in the present volume.

60 For examples by Hals see p. 68 in the present volume and notes 27, 29 and 57.

61 See also p. 38 in the present volume.

62 NHA, Van Sypesteyn family archive, 1437–1937 (no. 1614), inv. 923 (2); first published in Dudok van Heel and Bok 2013, pp. 14–15, then later by Pieter Biesboer, GPI N-6696. In addition to Frans Hals's portraits of Olycan and Hanemans, this inventory lists portraits of Aletta Hanemans and her second husband, Nicolaes Loo, by Johannes Verspronck.

63 See p. 39 in the present volume.

64 Houbraken 1718–21, vol. 2, p. 165: 'I was then the oldest pupil among his disciples, placed above his painting room, the others in a room below, over the central courtyard, where we, I above and they below, often spoke together when he went out' ('Ik was toenmaals onder zyne Discipelen de oudste Leerling, geplaatst boven zyn Schilderkamer, d'andere [leerlingen] in een vertrek beneden over de middelplaats, daar wy, ik van boven, en zy van beneden, elkander dikwijls toespraken, wanneer hy was uitgegaan').

65 Similar numbers are mentioned in documents about other studios. In 1657 Pieter Verelst in The Hague had at least four pupils, and in 1641 Joachim Sandrart in Amsterdam had at least three pupils between 16 and 18 years old, as well as an assistant some ten years older.

66 Erfgoed Leiden, notary W. van Leeuwen, NA 785, doc. 13, 10–23 February 1644 (not mentioned in Washington, London and Haarlem 1989). In the same estate there was 'the painting of Peeckelhaering' ('het conterfeytsel van Pekelharing'); see note 102, without the name of the maker but undoubtedly from Hals's studio.

67 See p. 38 in the present volume.

68 Houbraken 1718–21, vol. 2, p. 211 (biography of Vincent van der Vinne): 'Gy moet maar stout toesmeeren: als gy vast in de Konst word zal de netheid van zelf wel komen'.

69 Van Mander 1604 (1973), vol. 1, fol. 48v, chap. 12, no. 26.

70 Ibid., vol. 1, fol. 5r–v, and vol. 2, p. 391: 'helpen onderhouden [van] Winckels gherechten'.

71 Activities of this kind are often mentioned in pupils' contracts; see De Jager 1990.

72 About 70 per cent of Hals's known oeuvre is painted on canvas. Although the sizes of his paintings differ considerably (the smallest and the largest measuring 58.4 by 47 cm and 218 by 421 cm, respectively; see Slive 1970–4, vol. 3, nos 178, 124), a preference can be detected for canvases with a height between about 68 and 83 cm, and a width between about 73 and 88 cm. Approximately one third of Hals's works on canvas fall within these dimensions.

73 Copying works by other masters was highly recommended by Van Mander; see Miedema 1981, pp. 18–20. Orlers 1641, p. 371, writing for instance about David Bailly's apprenticeship, says that Cornelis van der Voort, his Amsterdam teacher, owned many good paintings by other masters, and that Bailly spent most of his time in his studio copying them. He remained with Van der Voort for six years. In 1625 the latter's art collection was auctioned, and included 'a laugher, original' ('een lachertgen, principael') with no fewer than six copies after it, and 11 works by and above all after Cornelis Cornelisz van Haarlem.

74 In 1654 Frans Hals owned a *Gathering of Manna* by Maarten van Heemskerck and a *John the Baptist preaching* by Karel van Mander, and in 1634 he bought a painting by Hendrick Goltzius; see I. van Thiel-Stroman in Washington, London and Haarlem 1989, nos 147, 66, pp. 387–8, 406 respectively. See also p. 39 in the present volume.

75 Delft 2011, p. 51, mention no fewer than 42 versions of Maurits and 36 of Frederik Hendrik.

76 Slive 1970–4, vol. 3, no. 175, pp. 89–91, mentions eight copies.

77 Ibid., nos 128–9, pp. 68–70; Dudok van Heel and Bok 2013, pp. 5–7, 22–4. The copies are on panel (both 66.2 × 56.2 cm) and show the sitters as half-lengths with their arms in different positions from the originals, which are on canvas and depict the sitters as three-quarter-lengths. Another example is the so-called *Portrait of Theodorus Schrevelius*; see Slive 1970–4, vol. 3, nos 49, 50, 51, pp. 31–3.

78 Speet 1995, p. 30; Biesboer 1996b; Martin Bijl and Pieter Biesboer in London and The Hague 2007, no. 20, pp. 118–19.

79 Slive 1970–4.

80 Miedema 1980, vol. 1, p. 137; Erfgoed Leiden, notary A. Joachimsz Raven, NA 755, doc. 50, 15 March 1649; Biesboer 2001, pp. 109–11 respectively.

81 Such works are occasionally called 'satellites', a term coined by Ernst van de Wetering; see Van de Wetering 2011.

82 For *The Rommel-Pot Player* in the Art Institute of Chicago, which has been attributed to Judith Leyster, see in particular Worcester and Haarlem 1993, no. 40, pp. 356–61.

83 Erfgoed Leiden, Archief van de Weeskamer (acc. no. 0518), inv. 13479, 1640, fol. 7: 'een bordeeltgen bij Hals overschildert'.

84 Houbraken 1718–21, vol. 1, p. 92: 'vet en zachtsmeltende aan te leggen', 'Nu moet 'er het kennelyke van den meester noch in'.

85 Martin Bijl and Pieter Biesboer in London and The Hague 2007, no. 20 pp. 118–19. Even the first version of Willem van Heythuysen's portrait is not an entirely secure work. Some people believe that the curtain in the top right corner and the background are not good enough to have been painted by the master himself.

86 For David Bailly's drawing in the Clement Moore collection, with the artist's signature on the back, see New York 2012, no. 15 pp. 40–1. A second drawn copy, but now signed and dated 'D. baillij. delin. Ao. 1626' on the front, is in the Rijksmuseum, while a third drawn version from 1628 is listed in the Simon Fokke auction of 1782. For the painting in the Rijksmuseum see especially J. Bikker in Bikker et al. 2007, no. 113 pp. 183–4, and the literature cited there. In the past the copy has been rather unconvincingly attributed by turn to Dirck Hals, one of Frans Hals's sons and Judith Leyster.

87 The tiny differences are in the locks of hair near the left eye and to the left of the musician's cap, and the position of his left little finger (which initially was the same as in the Louvre picture but was reworked to the present position).

88 Liedtke 2007, vol. 1, no. 69 pp. 299–302.

89 Slive and Grimm regard both as original; see Slive 1970–4, vol. 3, nos 64, 65, pp. 39–41; Grimm 1989, pp. 21, 223, 275.

90 For these paintings see Slive 1970–4, vol. 3, no. D-32 p. 140, and Stukenbrock 1993, pp. 110–16. Martin Bijl and Pieter Biesboer make a very far-fetched attribution to Frans Hals the Younger, with a few dabs by his father, of the small panel in a private

collection (fig. 48) in the catalogue of sale Vienna (Dorotheum), 10 November 2020, no. 72. Dendrochronology shows that the panel could have been used at the earliest from 1629 onwards.

91 SAA, notary P. de Bary, NA 1681 (B), pp. 1431–49, 15 September 1642.

92 Van der Veen 2011, pp. 105–6.

93 Slive 1970–4, vol. 1, pp. 168–74; Slive 2014, pp. 259–61.

94 Slive 1970–4, vol. 1, p. 183, vol. 3, no. 179 p. 94; Slive 2014, pp. 303–4.

95 According to Slive 1970–4, vol. 3, p. 69, neither the copy of Olycan's portrait nor that of Vooght is by Frans Hals, but Biesboer and Bijl say that the former is; see Biesboer and Bijl 2006.

96 The second version of *The Laughing Cavalier* was auctioned at Bonhams in London on 7 July 2010, lot no. 34, as 'School of Haarlem, c. 1630' and then in Sydney (Leonard Joel), 25 August 2020, lot no. 420, as 'after Frans Hals'.

97 Van Mander 1618, fol. S3r: 'rijckdom van vindingen en stoutheyt van Schilderen en tekenen'. In his biographies of artists Van Mander is at pains to stress how important it is for a master to stimulate the inventiveness of his pupils and ensure that he teaches them 'courage and boldness of execution' ('stoutheyt en handelinghe'), as did the Antwerp painter Frans Floris; see Van Mander 1604, fol. 242r–v. See also Miedema 1981, pp. 16–18.

98 Houbraken 1718–21, vol. 1, pp. 319–21.

99 Subjects of this kind are no longer known in Hals's oeuvre, but an inventory of 4 December 1662 of the belongings of Gerrit Willemsz Verstraeten and Anna Schuts lists a 'peasant wedding by Frans Hals' ('boere bruijloft van Frans Hals') that was appraised at 20 guilders; see Biesboer 2001, p. 168. See Oudenaarde 2018 for Brouwer's early work.

100 Slive 1970–4, vol. 1, pp. 141–4; Stukenbrock 1993, pp. 106–9; Slive 2014, p. 186.

101 It is clear from an early record that Jan Miense Molenaer did indeed paint this subject. In 1653 the stock of an Amsterdam art dealer who had quite a few paintings by artists active in Haarlem included a beach scene 'by Jan Miense Molenaer in Haarlem' ('gedaen bij Jan Miensz. Molenaer tot Haerlem'). The final clause means that it must have been painted before 1636/7, the period in which Molenaer moved from Haarlem to Amsterdam.

102 A Leiden probate inventory of 1666/7 lists 'a company in which there is Torrentius with his hand on his hip by Dirck Hals' and 'a head of Peeckelhaering by F. Hals' ('een geseltschap waerin Torentsius met de hant in sijn sij van Dirc Hals' and 'een trony van Pekelharing van F Hals'); see Erfgoed Leiden, notary L. van Swieten, NA 1005, doc. 10, 30 March 1667.

103 The most important example of a genre scene with small figures, thus more in the style of Dirck Hals, was a *fête champêtre* in the Kaiser-Friedrich-Museum in Berlin that was destroyed in the Second World War (fig. 161); see Slive 1970–4, vol. 3, no. L1 pp. 114–15.

NOTES

104 A reduced copy by Dirck Hals of Frans Hals's *Merrymakers at Shrovetide* that is signed and dated 1639 is in the Fondation Custodia (Frits Lugt Collection) in Paris. Figures from that painting are found in pictures in the Louvre and in the Städel Museum in Frankfurt, both from the early 1620s and signed by Dirck Hals; see Nehlsen-Marten 2003, nos 19, 37, pp. 265, 268, and above all, Frankfurt 2005, pp. 135–43. The Leipzig *Pekelharing* can be seen in a painting by Dirck Hals, signed and dated 1639, in the Nationalmuseum in Stockholm; see Stockholm 2005, no. 217 pp. 218–19.
105 Lunsingh Scheurleer et al. 1986–92, vol. 5A, p. 225: 'als was [het] van Brouwer geschildert'.
106 SAA, notary P. Carelsz, NA 732 (B), pp. 583–4, 2 December 1642: 'ick salder u twaalf stucx leveren, ider so goet als die voor twaalf pont', 'ja ende nogh beter'.
107 See especially Honig 1998; Newman and Nijkamp 2021. See also p. 55 in the present volume.
108 In 1656 Nicolaes de Kemp received from his brother Jan de Kemp and nieces Magdaleentje and Antoinette de Croon the two portraits of his grandparents painted by Frans Hals, 'and the compartment by Buytewech, otherwise called Ingenious Willem' ('ende het comparcquement bij Buytewegh ofte anders genaemt Geestige Willem'); see NHA, notary Z. van der Pullen, NA 240, fol. 65v, 6 November 1656; Van Hees 1959; I. van Thiel-Stroman in Washington, London and Haarlem 1989, no. 153 p. 408.
109 Houbraken 1718–21, vol. 1, p. 93: 'groote agtinge'.

PORTRAITURE INTO ART
BART CORNELIS

1 Van Mander 1604, fol. 281r: 'desen sijd-wegh der Consten (te weten, het conterfeyten nae t'leven)' (this side-road of art [that is: portrait painting after life]). The English translation is based on Miedema 1994–9, p. 382.
2 'Hy verdient in onse Const loflijck gherucht, en afghescheyden te wesen van alle verachtinghe, die ten minsten in eenigh deel daer in uytnemende, en anderen overtreffende is' and 'Daerom segh ick, datmen van een Conterfeytsel ooc wel wat goets can maken, dat een tronie, als t'heerlijckste deel des Menschen lichaems, vry wat in heeft, om daer mede te openbaren, en toonen de deughden en crachten der Consten', Van Mander 1604, fols 280v and 281r. For the English translation, see Miedema 1994–9, pp. 381–2.
3 Delft 2011. For the two portraits illustrated here, see ibid., nos 11a and 11b.
4 Both were treated in preparation for the exhibition in the National Gallery's Conservation Department by Larry Keith. Dendrochronological examination by Ian Tyers carried out at the same time (report at the National Gallery, London) has confirmed that the panels are from the same tree and that they are bookmatched,

as was long suspected from the visible grain in both panels. The latest surviving tree-ring is from 1590 and the panels would have been ready for use by about 1600.
5 See Leesberg 1993–4.
6 Among the forebears of the early twentieth-century owner of the male portrait we find Jan Anthonisse de Jonge (1546–1617), who in January 1606 married his third wife, Elisabeth van Hertsbeeck (1573–1653). In 1606 they were exactly the ages inscribed on the pendants. However, Jan Anthonisse de Jonge's coat of arms (see Wijnaendts van Resandt 1924, pp. 16–17) looks nothing like the one seen in the male portrait. It must therefore be a bizarre coincidence. For the provenance, see Sewter 1952; Washington, London and Haarlem 1989, p. 136; and Van Thiel 1993, pp. 86–8. It has not been noted before that on the back of the panel of the female portrait the year 1617 is inscribed in what appears to be seventeenth-century handwriting. It is unlikely to refer to the year Hals painted the portraits, which most scholars put earlier than that. In what must be a further coincidence, this is also the year in which De Jonge died.
7 See p. 163 in the present volume.
8 'maer soude doch raden u eerst te quellen, En u te wennen, met vlijtighe sinnen, Een suyver manier, end' een net beginnen', Van Mander 1604, fol. 48v.
9 'het welck verscheyden Meesters willende volghen in't arbeyden, En hebbender niet van ghemaeckt te deghe, Dan een deel leelijck goets ghebracht te weghe', ibid., fol. 48r–v.
10 'Hoe wacker schilderd Frans de luyden naer het leven!', Ampzing 1628, p. 371.
11 '... deur een onghemeyne manier van schilderen, die hem eyghen is, by nae alle overtreft, want daer is in sijn schildery sulcke forse ende leven, dat hy te met de natuyr selfs schijnt te braveren met sijn Penceel, dat spreecken alle sijne Conterfeytsels, die hy ghemaeckt heeft, ongheloofelijcke veel, die soo ghecolereert zijn, dat se schijnen asem van haer te gheven, ende te leven', Schrevelius 1648, p. 383. The English translation is taken from Washington, London and Haarlem 1989, p. 400.
12 As has been pointed out on numerous occasions; see De Jongh and Vinken 1961, p. 145, and De Jongh in Haarlem 1986, p. 124.
13 A rare contemporary account of what such sessions could be like can be found in Samuel Pepys's diary entry for 17 March 1666, in which he describes how he was sitting for his portrait by John Hayls (now in the National Portrait Gallery, London): 'I do almost break my neck looking over my shoulders to make the posture for him'; cited by Slive in Washington, London and Haarlem 1989, pp. 215 and 358–60.
14 See pp. 181, 184 in the present volume.
15 E.H. Gombrich's 1970 lecture 'The Mask and the Face: The Perception of Physiognomic Likeness in Life and Art', published in Gombrich 1982, pp. 105–36, remains by far the

best analysis of the complex phenomena related to this question.
16 As Gombrich put it (ibid., p. 114), 'We shall never know whether we would recognize Mona Lisa or the Laughing Cavalier if we met them in the flesh'.
17 In this context it is worth mentioning a contemporary description of such a moment of recognition in the diary of the English tourist Robert Bargrave (1628–1661), who on 23 and 24 February 1653 visited the Doelen in Amsterdam, where Rembrandt's *Night Watch* and other group portraits could be seen: 'The Principle Roome, adorned with Hangings, with Pictures of Burghomasters, Burghers, and chief Officers, in theyr severall postures, drawen to the life in full proportion: and so like persons, that I knew divers of them, as I met them in the Streets', cited in Van de Wetering 2017, p. 579.
18 See pp. 36–8 in the present volume.
19 See Slive 1970–4, vol. 1, pp. 110–11; Washington, London and Haarlem 1989, p. 215; Bikker et al. 2007, pp. 171–3 no. 105.
20 For an overview of the various backgrounds of Hals's sitters see Pieter Biesboer's essay 'The Burghers of Haarlem and their Portrait Painters', in Washington, London and Haarlem 1989, pp. 23–44.
21 J. Paul Getty Museum, Los Angeles.
22 See Spicer 1992. See also London 2021.
23 In bronze and in marble, both in the Museo Nazionale del Bargello, Florence.
24 First identified as Willem Jansz Cock by E. Domela Nieuwenhuis, see ibid. in Buijsen, Dumas and Manuth 2012, pp. 99–108, esp. p. 102.
25 Duparc 2022.
26 See also p. 194, note 102 in the present volume.
27 For an in-depth exploration of the painting, see London 2021.
28 Waagen 1854, vol. 3, p. 36.
29 Ibid., vol. 2, p. 4.
30 See Biesboer 2001, p. 118. It is interesting, however, that in 1653 Hals was asked to paint a replica of this informal portrait to represent Willem van Heythuysen in the regents' room of the Van Heythuysen hofje, an alms house that was built after Van Heythuysen's death on the land where his manor, Middenhout, had stood, as he had stipulated in his will. This later version is now in the Royal Museum of Fine Arts, Brussels, inv. 2247; see also fig. 49.
31 Dirck Hals, *Seated Man with Sword*, about 1630, oil on paper, 27 × 16.8 cm, Rijksmuseum, Amsterdam, inv. RP-T-1989-99. Schatborn 1973.
32 M. de Winkel in Buijsen, Dumas and Manuth 2012, pp. 141–50.
33 Women depicted in similarly assertive poses often lead to refreshingly original pictures; see, for example, Thomas de Keyser's portrait of a seated lady sold at Christie's, London, 6 December 2007, lot 4.
34 Although Van Mander's remarks are made in the context of history

painting, the sentiment will no doubt have extended to portraiture; see Van Mander 1604, fol. 14v: 'Oock Vrouwen, als onghewoone t'arbeyden, Haer postueren en zijn niet seer te prijsen, Als sy een Mannelijck ghewelt bewijsen' (And so it is with women, who are not accustomed to work, Their postures are not very praiseworthy, If they testify to a manly strength).
35 See p. 62 in the present volume.
36 See F.S. Jowell, 'The Rediscovery of Frans Hals', in Washington, London and Haarlem 1989, p. 76; Jansen, Luijten and Bakker 2009, letter 534.
37 See p. 128 in the present volume.
38 See Slive 1970–4, vol. 3, no. 168; Washington, London and Haarlem 1989, p. 306.
39 De Jongh and Vinken 1961; Haarlem 1986, no. 20.
40 See p. 38 in the present volume.
41 As pointed out in Slive 1970–4, vol. 1, pp. 54–5, vol. 3, p. 26; and Washington, London and Haarlem 1989, p. 190.
42 See De Jongh and Vinken 1961, p. 150; Washington, London and Haarlem 1989, p. 192.
43 We can be sure that the two paintings belong together, which has occasionally been doubted: both pictures have similar inscriptions attached to their backs identifying the sitters as Pieter Tjarck and Marie Larp, while we know that the works remained together with the sitters' descendants until they were sold at auction in 1889 (for full details of the provenance see Marandel and Walsh 2019, p. 106). Such incontrovertible evidence puts paid to the doubts raised in Slive 1970–4, vol. 3, no. 108, and MacLaren and Brown 1991, vol. 1, pp. 159–60.
44 See p. 163 in the present volume.
45 Van Thiel 1980.
46 See Washington, London and Haarlem 1989, p. 192; Boston and Kansas City 2015, p. 149.
47 The literature on Isaac Massa is extensive; the salient details of his biography are summarised in De Jongh and Vinken 1961; Haarlem 1986, no. 20; and Washington, London and Haarlem 1989. See also p. 38 in the present volume.
48 For a very full account of how soon after Massa's appointment in 1614 fellow merchants turned to the States General with their complaints about Massa, see Raptschinsky 1937, pp. 75–80.
49 'Vervolcht van Haet en nijt, voorvluchte hij tot d'eer bij keijser, koning, heer / En won haer gonst met dienst, Slants Staaten hem betrouden, wiens liefd' eens weer verkoude / Als hem de nijt belaagd, om stutten sijnen loop gesterct van Godt in Hoop / Erlangd hij meerder gonst, bij 't grootste hooft der Gotten, dies hij de nijt bespotten / Geadelt on verrijct, vernoucht nu sijn gemoet en wacht na d'eeuwich goet'. The English translation is largely based on Washington, London and Haarlem 1989, p. 268.
50 Slive remained sceptical of the identification; see ibid., no. 13.
51 Ibid., p. 166.
52 The conservation treatment was carried out by Paul Ackroyd. The technical examination was carried

out by Marika Spring, Joanna Russell, Catherine Higgitt and Rachel Billinge, the last carrying out infrared reflectography using the Apollo digital infrared scanning camera.
53   Macro XRF scanning of the picture more clearly shows that the coat of arms has ribbons on top and tassels hanging down below, and that the shield is divided horizontally into two colour fields, with some sort of motif – perhaps a lion or a dragon – crossing both fields. A combination of stereomicroscopy, paint cross-sections and macro XRF scanning established that the coat of arms is red in the upper field and that the lower field probably contains a blue or green copper-containing pigment. We have no other record of Massa's coat of arms to check it against. It is also clearer from macro XRF scanning that the scroll underneath may have had some lettering on it, but it cannot be deciphered.
54   Since age cracks run through the brown overpaint that covers the attributes it seems to have been applied at an early stage. The canvas has been mounted on to an oak panel. Dendrochronological examination has determined that the latest surviving tree ring is from 1638, so accounting for the sapwood that has been removed, the panel must date from the 1650s or a little later (report by Ian Tyers at the National Gallery, London). This significant intervention may have been the moment when the overpaint was applied in the background, but the pigments identified in the overpaint are not especially helpful for dating this layer as they would have been available to Hals, as well as to anyone working at a later date. There were further layers of a slightly darker brown colour on top of the first brown overpaint layer, although again the analysis could not categorically prove that these were applied much later.
55   See Jowell in Washington, London and Haarlem 1989, pp. 76–7; Jansen, Luijten and Bakker 2009, letters 535–6 and 651.

PORTRAIT PRINTS
JUSTINE RINNOOY KAN

1   Thoré-Bürger 1860, pp. 198–9.
2   Turner 2014, vol. 1, no. 47.
3   For the unconvincing theory that these portraits are copies of lost originals, or made by Hals's sons Frans or Jan, see Grimm 1971, 1972 and 1989 (*passim*). For the attribution to Frans Hals followed in this essay and for criticism and rebuttals of Grimm's view, see, among others, Slive 1970–4 (*passim*); Washington, London and Haarlem 1989, no. 5, note 1; Bijl 2005, pp. 47–52; Liedtke 2007, vol. 1, p. 283 note 1.
4   For the works on copper, see Slive 1970–4, vol. 3, nos 8, 48, 76.
5   Although a few large panels form an exception to this general rule, there are no known smaller paintings on canvas. The larger panels, ranked from small to large, are: Slive 1970–4, vol. 3, nos 98 and 99 (pendants), 100 and 101 (pendants), 159, 6, 27, 2 and 3 (pendants), 115 and 116

(pendants), 77 and 79 (pendants). Only 13 of Hals's paintings are in a horizontal format. These are all among his larger work on canvas; the smallest is 140 × 166.5 cm. See, from small to large: Slive 1970–4, vol. 3, nos 17, 176, 140, 70, 222, 7, 221, 46, 45, 177, 79, 80, 124.
6   Paintings with a height of less than 27 cm that were not produced in print are Slive 1970–4, vol. 3, nos 35, 37 (portrait of Anna van der Aar), 48, 49, 50 and 51 (pendants), 91 and 92 (often discussed as a group), and D37.
7   Ibid., no. 48.
8   For the earliest mention of the dimensions of this painting, see Rotterdam 1849, p. 17 no. 93.
9   The publisher of this print was David van Hoorenbeeck, a writing master at the Latin school in Haarlem. For his professional title, see Ampzing 1628, p. 133, and again on an unnumbered page.
10   Slive 1970–4, vol. 3, no. L8.
11   *Courante uyt Italien ende Duytslandt, &c.*, 11 June 1650: 't' Amsterdam by Pieter Goos op 't Water op de nieuwe Brugh in de vergulde Zee-Spiegel wort uytghegheven het Effigies van den alderhooghsten Wiskonstenaer en Wijsgierighen Edelman Renatus Descartes na 't leven geschildert door F. Hals en ghesneden door J. Suyderhoef.' With thanks to Jaco Rutgers and Jaap van der Veen for sharing this information.
12   Slive 1970–4, vol. 3, no. 175.
13   See, among others, ibid., nos 38 (portrait of Michiel Jansz van Middelhoven, engraving by Jan van de Velde the Younger) and 165 (portrait of Johannes Hoornbeek, engraving by Jonas Suyderhoef). The size ratio between, for example, the painted portrait of Verdonck (his first name is unknown) (fig. 90) and the corresponding print by Jan van de Velde the Younger (see for example Rijksmuseum, Amsterdam, inv. RP-P-OB-15.290) is about 1:3. For the argument that, because of the differences in size between print and painting, the portrait was not made as an original for prints, see Van Thiel 1980, pp. 117–18.
14   Utrecht 1991, pp. 11–12; Berkvens-Stevelinck 2001, p. 55.
15   One catalyst for this was Petrarch's *De viris illustribus*, the book of collected biographies of historical figures in prose from 1337; see Joost-Gaugier 1982, pp. 97–100.
16   An early and renowned example of a physical collection that was later published in print form is the collection of Paolo Giovio, bishop of Nocera dei Pagani. Starting in 1521, he assembled 350 painted portraits, divided into categories: statesmen and military men, artists, deceased poets and scholars, and living poets and scholars. His collection was partially published in print during the last quarter of the sixteenth century. For Paolo Giovio and his portrait collection, see Hagedorn 2020.
17   Berkvens-Stevelinck 2001, p. 55.
18   Waquet 1991, pp. 22–8; Van Deinsen 2022, p. 85.

19   For a large selection of portrait prints, see Muller 1853, Van Someren 1888–91.
20   For the classification of portrait prints according to function, see Ekkart 1987, pp. 12–13.
21   For an early history of collected prints in book form during the Renaissance, see Pelc 2002. Many prints were also published in series, as loose sheets as well as in book form. For the distinction between uniformly arranged portrait series of holders of the same office (for example popes, monarchs, noblemen or scholars) on the one hand and more heterogeneous series of all kinds of celebrities, see Utrecht 1991, pp. 11–12.
22   The majority of the portrait etchings for which Rembrandt was commissioned, for instance, were intended for private distribution. Ekkart 1987, p. 19.
23   Van de Venne 2009, p. 343.
24   Widerkehr 2007, vol. 2, no. 255. For the margin inscription in the oval around the print, see Van de Venne 2009, p. 246 note 47.
25   For an annotated chronicle of the life of Schrevelius, see Van de Venne 2009, pp. 241–92.
26   Having been appointed deputy headmaster, Schrevelius lightened the duties of Cornelius Schonaeus, under whose inspired direction he had once been a pupil himself. Schonaeus enjoyed international renown as the author of Latin school dramas that were performed by pupils on the Grote Markt as an aid to their mastering the language. Langereis 2001, p. 110.
27   University of Amsterdam, Special Collections, MS H 103: 'D. Scriveri praefata salutisdictione / Sculptor Maethamius operi inchoato iampridem, / summam tandem manum imposuit Minerva et Mercurio / faventibus: quippe effigiem meam vivis coloribus expressam / aeri insculpsit, et simul Memoriae consecravit: Huius / πρωτότυπον author mittere me tibi voluit, ut memorem monerem, / Huic si accesserit epigrammatis honos, lucem sperabimus / et vitam, aspirante videlicet genij tui amica aura. / Cui rei ut vigilem praestes operam rogare multis / verbis non debeo; ne extorquere videatur id importunitas / mea, quod sponte obtulit benignitas tua. Vale / 17 Jun. An. 1618. / Tuus, ut uno verbo, / T. Schrevelius'; 'Dear Scriverius, first a greeting. The engraver Matham has at long last put the final touches to a work that he began long ago [and placed] under the protection of Minerva and Mercury, for he has engraved my portrait, painted in lively colours, in copper and so preserved it for posterity. The maker of this prototype wished me to send it to you in order to remind you [of something] that you [without that certainly] remember. If this portrait is to be honoured with an epigram, light and life, we expect, will come into it, blown into it in friendship by the breath of your mind. It is not necessary for me to clothe my question of whether you are willing to supply "night work" towards this with many words, in order to avoid it seeming that my immodesty extorts

from you what your generosity has offered of its own volition. Greetings. 17 June 1618. As one word, your T. Schrevelius.' The English translation is based on that of P. Tuynman in Roscam Abbing 2014, pp. 65–9 (including complete transcript and translation). I would like to thank Machteld de Kok and Siward Tacoma for their help with the interpretation of the Latin for this essay. See Langereis 2001, p. 328; Van de Venne 2009, p. 266 note 194; M. Roscam Abbing in Haarlem 2013, p. 137 no. 42.
28   M. Roscam Abbing in Haarlem 2013, no. 42; Roscam Abbing 2014, pp. 65–9.
29   Buchelius c.1588–1631.
30   Tuynman 2006, p. 217; Van de Venne 2009, pp. 266–71.
31   Erfgoed Leiden, SA II, inv. 3338, fols 103v–106v. For a transcript of the contract of the appointment, see Van de Venne 2009, pp. 373–5.
32   Buchelius c.1588–1631, fol. 1ov: 'een tronie van Screvelio, cleyn, seer wel gewerckt tot Haarlem'. See Tuynman 2006, p. 222 note 23.
33   Buchelius c.1588–1631, fol. 17r. See Tuynman 2006, p. 221. Buchelius writes that the portrait was painted on panel rather than on copper, but this is probably based on an error.
34   For Ampzing as a pupil of Schrevelius, see Van de Venne 2009, p. 259 note 143.
35   Ampzing 1621, n.p.; I. van Thiel-Stroman in Washington, London and Haarlem 1989, p. 379 doc. 28.
36   Ampzing 1628, p. 371: 'Hoe wacker schilderd Frans de luyden naar het leven!'; I. van Thiel-Stroman in Washington, London and Haarlem 1989, p. 382 doc. 41.
37   Schrevelius 1648, p. 383: 'soo ghecolereert zijn, dat se schijnen asem [adem] van haer te geven, ende te leven'. The Latin version of the book came out a year earlier (Schrevelius 1647). See I. van Thiel-Stroman in Washington, London and Haarlem 1989, p. 400 doc. 116.
38   'Because he bridled so many hard mouths of wayward youths, With the force of his eloquence and his Palladian discipline, Schrevelius was worthy, Mathamius, of your copper, Worthy too to win this reward for his conscientious care, So that if perchance envious time should blot out his name and hide the man, his likeness may speak for him.' Washington, London and Haarlem 1989, no. 5 p. 141.
39   Portraits of more famous women, such as queens, but also the humanist Anna Maria van Schurman, for example, were produced. See, among others, Van Deinsen 2022.
40   See Roscam Abbing and Tuynman 2018. Scriverius received several poems about his portrait written by acquaintances, no doubt in response to received copies of the print; see Roscam Abbing 2014, p. 76.
41   Buchelius c.1588–1631, fol. 17r. The translation of the word *geminam* has been reason for debate in recent literature, because it had prompted the problematic hypothesis that Buchelius had received one portrait print of Scriverius, as well as one (highly unlikely and unknown) portrait print of Anna van der Aar (see

Tuynman 2006, pp. 223–4; Liedtke 2007, pp. 275–8; Roscam Abbing 2014, p. 75). Historian Peter van der Eerden poses that the word *geminam* in this case means that Buchelius received two prints of Scriverius's portrait print. With thanks to Michiel Roscam Abbing for sharing this new interpretation.
42   The dating on the painting is not quite legible; it either says 1630 or 1631 and that Ampzing's age is 40. The etching gives his age as 41 and is dated 1632, but he was then 42. For Van Thiel this is reason enough to assume that the print was made prior to his death; Liedtke keeps open the possibility that it was posthumous, which is conceivable based on the inscription. Van Thiel 1996, pp. 198–9; Liedtke 2017.
43   Ampzing 1628, pp. 108 (Scriverius), 125 (Schrevelius), 137 (Bogaert), 140 (Acronius).
44   For the theory that Ampzing's congregation may have been the commissioner for this edition, see Van Thiel 1996, pp. 198–9; Liedtke 2017. This theory is not backed by archival evidence.
45   Widerkehr 2007, vol. 1, pp. xxv–xxvii. For portrait engravings and drawings by Goltzius, see M. Schapelhouman in Amsterdam, New York and Toledo 2003–4, pp. 33–56.
46   On an engraving made from Goltzius's drawing of a beached sperm whale at Berkhey (see, for example, Rijksmuseum, Amsterdam, inv. RP-P-1885-A-9446). See Amsterdam, New York and Toledo 2003, pp. 183–4; Liedtke 2007, p. 278.
47   For Hals and Jacob Matham, see Widerkehr 2007, vol. 1, under 'Frans Hals', pp. lvi–lvii. For Hals as a member of a chamber of rhetoric, see also p. 162 in the present volume.
48   Matham made, among other things, engravings for Karel van Mander's *Schilder-Boeck* of 1604. See Widerkehr 2007, vol. 1, under 'Jacob Matham and Haarlem', pp. xlvii–liii. Schrevelius played an organisational role for the liminary verses in Van Mander's book, which also contains his own poetry. See Roscam Abbing 2014, pp. 63–5.
49   I. van Thiel-Stroman in Washington, London and Haarlem 1989, doc. 62. The name given is Adriaen Jacobs. Despite the absence of the family name, this is almost certainly Adriaen Matham. Pieter van den Broecke was also a witness. A year before this baptism, Adriaen made an engraving from Hals's life-size painting of Van den Broecke (fig. 11) to serve as the frontispiece of the book in which he recorded his travel adventures (Rijksmuseum, Amsterdam, inv. RP-P-OB-23.167X).
50   I. van Thiel-Stroman in Washington, London and Haarlem 1989, p. 373, under doc. 4, p. 382 doc. 38.
51   Ibid., p. 380, under doc. 30.
52   Ibid., p. 399 doc. 114.
53   For an overview, see Leeflang 2003, pp. 4–6.
54   There is an even earlier known stage in which only the oval is visible and the turtle has not yet been added. The ornament on the

frame was removed from the third stage. See Luijten and Schuckman 1989, vol. 1, p. 129 no. 407.
55   *Old Master Drawings*, sale London (Bonhams), 7 July 2004, lot 44: 'Adriaen Matham, Bust-length portrait of Poliander … black chalk and leadpoint, the verso reddened in chalk for transfer'.
56   The print inscription 'P. Soutman *pinxit*' (painted) shows that Soutman's preliminary study drawing was probably made from a painting. Leeflang 2003, p. 79 nos 30A, B.
57   For this technique, see ibid., pp. 4, 36–7.
58   Ekkart 1987, p. 13.
59   Tuynman 2006, p. 224 note 29; Roscam Abbing 2014, pp. 72–88.
60   With thanks to Frans Grijzenhout, who shared this information and the substantive discussion of this inventory before the publication of F. Grijzenhout in Middelkoop and Ekkart 2024, note 30: Erfgoed Leiden, ONA Leiden, inv. 898, notary Pieter Gerardsz van Tielt, act nr. 160, 19 December 1658; see also ibid., inv. 899, act nos 149–153, 14 January–11 December 1659.
61   Slive 1970–4, vol. 1, pp. 197–8. See the impression of the print kept at the Graphische Sammlung Albertina in Vienna, inv. H/I/61/26.
62   For examples of painted print designs in grisaille see Van Thiel 1980, p. 117 note 16 (including engraving originals painted in oil grisaille on paper by Maarten van Heemskerck and Goltzius, and originals on panel by Cornelis Cornelisz van Haarlem and Rubens, who also frequently added some colour). See also Leeflang 2003, pp. 14, 25 note 49, who also mentions Anthony van Dyck, Rembrandt, Dirck Barendsz and Anthonie Blocklandt.
63   Liedtke 2007, p. 278.
64   For the later copies and the inventories, see Washington, London and Haarlem 1989, p. 143; Roscam Abbing 2014, pp. 69–71. The great similarity between the small portraits of Maria van Teylingen, about which it is speculated that they are lost copies made from paintings by Hals, and her portrait that is part of the family portrait by Pieter de Grebber is remarkable (compare with De Grebber's *Theodorus Schrevelius and His Family Having a Meal*, Stedelijk Museum, Alkmaar, inv. 20982). The small portraits of Van Teylingen may have been based on the painting by De Grebber. The resulting pendant portraits (probably made for their descendants) would then consist of a copy of Schrevelius from a painting by Hals and a copy of Van Teylingen from a painting by De Grebber.
65   Roscam Abbing 2014, pp. 69–88. For a transcript of the estate inventory of Schrevelius, drawn up by Bregitta Schrevelius on 2 October 1652, see Van de Venne 2009, pp. 376–8 (including 'Vader en moeders conterfeytsels' [Father and mother's portraits]). NHA, notary Jacob Steyn, ONAH 163, fols 68r–69r. See also Van de Venne 2009, p. 344 note 2.
66   *Album amicorum* of P. Scriverius, The Hague, National Library of the Netherlands (KB), 133 M 5, fol. 152r.

For Isaac Massa's biography and portrait print, see p. 38 in the present volume.
67   With thanks to Jaap van der Veen. NHA, notary M. de Keijser, NA 246 [no folios], 1 March 1652: 'Inventaris van de naergelaten goederen van wijlen joffr. Maria van Wassenbergh, in haer leven wede. van de E. Isack Massa, die sij beseten ende op den 26e february 1652 metter doot ontruymt ende ter werelt naergelaten heeft, als volcht … Noch een cleyn conterfeytseltge met een swart leysie van de voorn. Ysack Massa' (Inventory of the goods left by the late Miss Maria van Wassenbergh, in her life widow of E. Isack Massa, which she possessed and on the 26th February 1652 left behind in the world through death, as followed … And a small portrait with a black frame seen frontally. Ysack Massa) or 'Noch een cleyn conterfeytseltge met een swart leysie van de voorn. Ysack Massa' (And a small portrait with a black frame seen frontally). Although it is not specified that these works were painted by Hals, it is plausible that one of these two small paintings is fig. 112.
68   Washington, London and Haarlem 1989, no. 50; MacLaren and Brown 1991, pp. 158–9.
69   For information on calligraphy in Holland and the developments described see Broos 1971, p. 151.
70   See De la Chambre 1638. In 1873 an edition was sold containing the frontispiece followed by 19 sheets of calligraphy by Jean de la Chambre, see *Catalogue d'une Collection Précieuse de Calligraphie*, sale Amsterdam (Frederik Muller), 1 September 1873, lot 39. At the National Art Library in London a volume is kept containing calligraphy by Jean de la Chambre as well as Jan van de Velde the Elder (father of Jan van de Velde the Younger). Possibly originally bound in the seventeenth century, it consists of the 1638 frontispiece by Suyderhoef followed by 26 sheets of calligraphy by Jean de la Chambre, then followed by a frontispiece for Van de Velde's work and 26 sheets by him (see Van de Velde 1607). Buyers could most likely pick and choose loose quires at publishers and dealers and bind their own selections in volumes, resulting in volumes of different lengths. Convolutes were also put together, and bound copies could probably be bought at bookstores.
71   Washington, London and Haarlem 1989, p. 273. The portrait of Acronius is also displayed in reverse on the plate (fig. 128).
72   See F. Grijzenhout in Middelkoop and Ekkart 2024 for an extensive discussion of the portraits of clergymen by Hals.
73   Noorman and Van der Maal 2022, pp. 90–3, 170–1. For Maria van Nesse's memory book, see www.regionaalarchiefalkmaar.nl/mariavannesse and www.regionaalarchiefalkmaar.nl/images/Documenten/Transcriptie_memorieboek_Maria_van_Nesse.pdf, fols 21r, 50v (accessed 23 March 2023).
74   Turner 2014, pp. xxiv–xxx.
75   Luijten and Schuckman 1989, vol. 1, p. 120 no. 384.

76   For privileges, see Orenstein 1996, pp. 90–4.
77   Swalmius became a clergyman in 1600. The inscription says that he had already held this office for more than 46 years, which is why it is presumed that the print dates from 1646 or later. Slive 1970–4, vol. 3, no. 126. In 1646, Swalmius legitimised the marriage of Hals's daughter Sara, who had previously borne two children out of wedlock. I. van Thiel-Stroman in Washington, London and Haarlem 1989, docs 91–3, 110. For the print see De Hoop Scheffer and Keyes 1984, p. 253 no. 121.
78   De Hoop Scheffer and Keyes 1984, p. 251 nos 116 and 117. The painting bears a legend stating that it was painted in 1637 and that he was 47 years old. The print gives his age as 48; the year 1637 is unchanged.
79   See Slive 1970–4, vol. 3, no. L12. Slive bases this on Moes 1909, p. 52.
80   The second small print states 1642 and an age of 53.
81   See Van de Venne 2009, pp. 284–6. For the full inscription, see Washington, London and Haarlem 1989, p. 141.
82   Liedtke 2017.
83   See Bijl 2005, pp. 53–4, for the same conclusion on the print of Schrevelius being based on the painting, following on a theory about paint loss on the original. For the different stages of the two prints, see De Hoop Scheffer and Keyes 1984, p. 227 no. 59, Ampzing: second stage 'C. Banheynigh excudit', third stage 'Hugo Allerdt excudit', fourth stage 'Carolus Allard excudit'; p. 250 no. 114, Schrevelius: third stage 'Cornelius Banheinningh excudit', fourth stage 'H. Focken exc'. It is noteworthy that both prints were published by Cornelis Banheyning.

LAUGHTER
FRISO LAMMERTSE

I would like to thank Arjan van Dixhoorn and Lotte Kokkedee for their helpful comments.

1   Van Mander 1604 (1973), vol. 1, fol. 25v, pp. 168–9. For Frans Hals as a pupil of Van Mander see pp. 28, 30 in the present volume, and for his partiality for laughter, Schiller 2010.
2   This peculiarity was remarked upon quite often, by Leon Battista Alberti, Leonardo da Vinci and Gualtherus Rivius among others. See Van Mander 1604 (1973), vol. 2, p. 501; Schiller 2006, pp. 64–8.
3   See Dekker 1997, and especially Verberckmoes 1998.
4   In addition to Erasmus, it was above all the Spanish humanist Juan Luis Vives who carried out important research into laughter with his *De anima et vita* published in Bruges in 1538; see Verberckmoes 1998, pp. 53–7.
5   Erasmus 1652: 'In eenige plaetzen bequamelijck gevoeght tot het gebruyk der Schoolen van Hollandt en West-Vrieslandt, ende door openbare last in druk uytgegeven' (Fittingly added for the use of schools in various places in Holland and West

Friesland, and issued in print by public order).

6 Ibid., pp. 11–12: 'Het misstaet ook dat zommige / als zy lacchen een gebries maken. Oock onbetaamlijk is die lach / welke de opsperring van de mond / met gerimpelde wangen en naakte tanden wydt van een strekt / welke hondelijck is'.

7 Ibid.: 'de gestaltenisse der mondt niet onteere / noch een ongebonden gemoedt te kennen geeve', and 'zotte praatjes' like 'Ik lach my slap / ik lach my te barsten / ik lach my doodt'.

8 However, the word 'grim-lachje', which could mean bitter laugh or smile, was used by Ritsart in *Moortje*; see Bredero 1620, n.p., 'Vierde uytkomen, Het darde bedrijf' (act 3, scene 4).

9 Heinsius 1616, p. 16, in the poem 'Dominae servitium libertatis summa est': 'die niet sachter wesen mach'.

10 Cats 1620, p. 90: 'Wien soud' een soeten lach niet innerlijk becooren?'.

11 Van Mander 1604 (1973), vol. 1, fol. 23r, pp. 158–9 nos 7–8: 'Met een vriendelijck toelachend aenschouwen', 'een Roose rootheyt'; Melion 2023, p. 261.

12 For this portrait see also p. 90 and note 39 on p. 191 in the present volume.

13 See note 11, 'vol Liefden doorgoten'.

14 For the family portraits see Toledo, Brussels and Paris 2018. See Grijzenhout 2021 for the identification of the *Portrait of Nicolaes van den Heuvel, his Wife Susanna van Halmael, their Daughter Maria and an Unknown Daughter*, painted around 1635 (Cincinnati Art Museum, inv. 1927.399). See fig. 22 in the present volume.

15 Ripa (1593) 1644, pp. 222: 'Ionckheyd' (Youth), 278: 'De Lach wort longh geschildert, om dat de teere en jonge leughd, meest tot lacchen is genegen' (Laughter is painted young, because tender and young youth is the most inclined to laugh). Ripa's book was translated into Dutch in 1644 by the writer and publisher Dirck Pers.

16 Ibid., p. 76 (under 'Sanguigno of Blygeestige'): 'lach en vrolijckheyt … vermaecklijck en boertig [zijn, en], beminnende het speelen en singen'.

17 Van Mander 1604 (1973), vol. 1, fol. 25r, pp. 166–7 no. 28: 'Den mondt wat open / soet / lachende / vrolijck'; Melion 2023, p. 266.

18 See especially L. Packer in London 2021, pp. 42–8.

19 The fact that the adults in portraits do not show their teeth could also be due to widespread poor dental hygiene in the seventeenth century. Against that, painters often flattered their sitters and were certainly not content to be slaves to reality. So the demands of etiquette that it was uncivilised to show one's teeth must still have been a weighty consideration in portraiture. Painters, after all, were perfectly capable of giving their sitters a gleaming set of teeth.

20 Koppenol 2001, p. 236; Schiller 2006, pp. 78–89; for the payment to De Gheyn see Van Boheemen and Van der Heijden 1999, p. 541. See engraving and etching by Dirck Volckertsz Coornhert after a design by

Maarten van Heemskerck, *Heraclitus and Democritus*, 1557 (Veldman 1994, vol. 2, no. 475 p. 160; one impression of this print is in the Noord-Hollands Archief, Haarlem, inv. 143); Jacques de Gheyn II, *The World in a Fool's Cap*, engraving, 1596 (Filedt Kok and Leesberg 2000, vol. 2, no. 257 p. 117; the engraving was also included in publications in 1613 and 1614: an edition of *Const-riick beroep ofte antwoort…*, Leiden 1614, with the print, is in the Rijksmuseum Research Library, 332 D 13).

21 According to Cornelis Luidewijck van den Plasse in his dedication to Albrecht Koenraed; see Bredero 1638, fol. A3v: 'het schuim des volckx, harders, boeren, werckluiden, waerden, waerdinnen, koppelaersters, snollen, vroedwyven, bootgezellen, opsnappers, schoisters en panlickers'. See further Westermann 1997, p. 99.

22 NHA, 3162 Aloude Rhetorijkamer De Wijngaardranken onder de zinspreuk Liefde Boven Al te Haarlem, inv. 597, n.p., under the year 1616. See especially Van Dixhoorn 2009; Van Boheemen and Van der Heijden 1999, pp. 341–456.

23 Van Dixhoorn 2009, pp. 75–7.

24 Ibid., p. 73.

25 Vermeer 1993; Miedema 1994–9, vol. 2, pp. 10–168. Van Mander made the designs for an engraving of their device for the Vine Tendrils and for a New Year's print; see Leesberg 1999, nos 161, 162 pp. 184–5.

26 Van Mander 1618, fol. S3r.

27 See note 22.

28 See Van Dixhoorn 2009 for the members of the chambers of rhetoric. Loo and Hals must have known each other well, since they were members of the Vine Tendrils at roughly the same period. They joined in 1616 and Loo remained until 1626, one year longer than Hals. A painting of 1653 recently sold at auction has been identified as a portrait of Loo (Sotheby's, London, 9 December 2021, lot 136; Biesboer 2023).

29 Köhler and Levy-van Halm 1990, pp. 32–45.

30 Hals is last recorded as a member of the Vine Tendrils in 1625; see note 22.

31 Van Dixhoorn 2009, p. 85.

32 It has been assumed that some of Hals's paintings of children belonged to a series of the Five Senses (see Slive 1970–4, vol. 1, pp. 79–80). No complete series by him has survived, but it is clear from seventeenth- and eighteenth-century records that he did make them. It is sometimes not clear whether Frans or his brother Dirck was the artist, as in the case of 'Vijff cleyne vijff sinnen bortjes van Hals' (Five small five Sense panels by Hals, SAA, notary F. Uijttenbogaert, NA 1915, pp. 1–23, 13 January 1654'; ibid., pp. 24, 25–33; see I. van Thiel-Stroman in Washington, London and Haarlem 1989, doc. 146 p. 406, as not seen); 'Drie schilderijtjes van de vijff sinnen door Hals gedaen' (Three small paintings of the Five Senses done by Hals, inventory of Wilhelmus Scriverius, son of Petrus, SAA, notary H. Westfrisius, NA 2804 [B], pp. 971–84, 26 October 1661; see Bredius 1915–22, pp. 216, 369–73, 1301); 'Vijff sinnebeeltjes van Hals'

(Five allegories by Hals, inventory of Maria van Strijp, widow of Eduard Wallis, 1707; see Biesboer 2001, pp. 323–6); '37 Vyf Stuks, zynde de Vyf Zinnen van F. Hals.' (37. Five pieces, being the Five Senses by F. Hals, see Amsterdam 1734). Dirck Hals was identified in 'De vijff sinnen van D. Hals, met ebbe binnenlijsten' (The Five Senses by D. Hals, with ebony frames) in 1634 in a list of paintings for a lottery organised by Cornelis Kittensteijn (about 1600–after 1638) and Dirck Hals (see Miedema 1980, pp. 157–9); and 'Noch vijff stucken schilderije met ebbenhoute lijsten, de vijff sinnen van Dirck Hals' (A further five paintings with ebony frames, the Five Senses by Dirck Hals, inventory of Josina van Neste, the widow of Hendrick Willemsz den Abt, 1662; see Biesboer 2001, pp. 162–3).

33 For the comical elements in the rhetoricians' work see especially Pleij 2007; Van Dixhoorn 2009; Kramer 2009.

34 See especially Verberckmoes 1998 and Dorren 2001, p. 79.

35 Martens and Peeters 2006, pp. 49–50.

36 The classic article on this painting is Van Thiel 1961; see also various articles in Koppenol 2001, 2003 and 2004.

37 Van Thiel 1961. Piero was Van der Mersch's nickname.

38 The *Portrait of a Fool with a Yellow Fool's Cap* painted by Cornelis van Haarlem around 1596 (Theater Instituut Nederland, Amsterdam) has been regarded since at least the eighteenth century as a portrait of Van der Mersch. However, the resemblance to the subject of Hals's portrait is slight, so at most it seems to have been inspired by the famous Leiden fool and not a true portrait. For Cornelis van Haarlem's painting see Van Thiel 1999, no. 221 pp. 378–9, and the literature listed there under note 14; J. Hillegers in Haarlem 2017, no. 2 pp. 68–9.

39 Koppenol 2004, p. 8.

40 For the name see ibid., p. 2. For the marriage see especially Koppenol 2001, p. 236. The costume, like all the expenses for the feast, was paid for by the City of Leiden; for the invoice see Van Boheemen and Van der Heijden 1999, pp. 535–7.

41 Van Thiel 1961, p. 167, suggested that the coat of arms, like the monkey holding it, was intended to be humorous. However, the present author believes it more likely that it was Van der Mersch's official coat of arms.

42 On the Shrovetide festivities see Mezger 1991; Den Bosch 1992; Kruijswijk and Nesse 2004, and the Shrovetide songs in the Dutch song database (www.liederenbank.nl, accessed 27 February 2023).

43 For the painting, which is undated, see Slive 1970–4, vol. 3, no. 5 pp. 3–4; Liedtke 2007, no. 58 pp. 251–9. The drawing of 1660 is signed by Matthijs van den Bergh (Fondation Custodia, Paris, inv. 6310A).

44 Coster 1633, n.p., 'tweede uytcomst, van 't vierde deel' (act 4, scene 2): 'U hoeden rondom dight bekleedt / met lecker hoender

bouten / De varckens billen niet vergeet / al zijnse wat ghesouten / En an u halsen kransen maeckt / Van worsten en sausysen veel / ghepepert eel. / Daer wel een dronck op smaeckt'. The play was first performed in 1612. In the engraving made by Cornelis Bloemaert around 1625 after a painting by his father Abraham, a boy has a sausage around his shoulder. The inscription states that he is a 'Vastel-avonts Sot' (Shrovetide Fool). See Hollstein 1949, no. 287 p. 79; Rijksmuseum, Amsterdam, inv. RP-P-BI-1444. For the painting see Haarlem 2017, no. 6 pp. 75–7.

45 For the use of eggs in an ambiguous, often risqué sense, see Bostoen in Haarlem and Hamburg 2003, pp. 43–9. For the ambiguity of bagpipes, see for example a painting by Pieter Huys (Gemäldegalerie, Berlin, inv. 693) in which the bagpiper says to a woman in the inscription that his 'pijp [is] al uyt ghepepe[n]' (pipe has stopped piping); see M. Ubl in Rotterdam 2015, pp. 157–75, esp. p. 165.

46 Stewart 1978. A painting that is very similar but lacks the Shrovetide elements is *Merry Company* of about 1633, attributed to Hendrick Pot (Museum Boijmans Van Beuningen, Rotterdam, inv. 1678); see Lammertse 1998, no. 48, pp. 140–2.

47 See especially Mezger 1991, pp. 258–68, for the fox tail as an attribute of fools and a symbol of flattery, gossip and dishonesty.

48 The original was dated 1616, according to Bode 1883, p. 46, who stated that it was in a Belgian collection and later sold to America. Its present whereabouts are unknown. Bode attributed the copy formerly in the Kaiser-Friedrich-Museum, Berlin (but lost in the Second World War), to Willem Buytewech. See also Slive 1970–4, vol. 3, no. L.2, pp. 115–16.

49 Haverkamp Begemann 1959; Rotterdam and Paris 1974, nos 2, 26, 27 pp. 5–7, 25–7. The figure is also found in Dirck Hals's work (see p. 195, note 104 in the present volume). For the painting by Willem Buytewech (*Merry Company*, about 1620, Museum Boijmans Van Beuningen, Rotterdam, inv. 1103), see Lammertse 1998, no. 9, pp. 33–5.

50 The two men flanking the central figure of *Merrymakers at Shrovetide* are often identified as Pekelharing (left) and Hans Worst (right), among others; see Slive 1970–4, vol. 1, pp. 33–6, vol. 3, no. 5, pp. 3–4; Liedtke 2007, no. 58, pp. 251–9; and Liedtke 2011, pp. 17–18. However, this identification is unconvincing, based only on the food that they are carrying: the man on the left could equally be Hans Worst because of the sausages round his neck. In addition, his herrings are not pickled but smoked, so they are kippers. Sausages were a popular food at Shrovetide; see Mezger 1991.

51 Van Boheemen and Van der Heijden 1999, p. 642: 'de jonghluydens op deselver spel ende maeltijden', 'allerley lichtveerdigheyt ende vleeschelijcke ongebondenheden'.

52 SAA, notary G. Coren, NA 1004 (B), pp. 753–67 (undated); ibid.,

NOTES

pp. 768–9, 30 October 1645, inventory of Elisabeth Hermans (Lijsbet Harmens), widow of Coenraet Willemsz van Ceulen, who then married Jan Dorhout. The painting is listed on p. 762: '1 schilderij sijnde een cluch van Santvoort van Frans Hals met een vergulde lijst'.

53   Van Boheemen and Van der Heijden 1999, pp. 408–9. It is not known which plays were performed at the competition. The event was in August 1616, so it is unlikely that Hals was present because he was already in Antwerp on 6 August of that year and did not return until between 11 and 15 November, see I. van Thiel-Stroman in Washington, London and Haarlem 1989, pp. 377–8. See also p. 48 in the present volume.

54   The full rhyme is: 'Siet Monsieur Peeckelhaering an, / Hy pryst een frisse volle kan, / En hout het met de vogte back, / Dat doet syn keel is altyt brack' (Behold Monsieur Pickled Herring, / He praises a tankard cool and full, / And goes on and on about the wet jar, / For his throat is always dry).

55   For the list of Hendrick den Abt's paintings see Miedema 1980, vol. 1, pp. 136–7 no. A45; and I. van Thiel-Stroman in Washington, London and Haarlem 1989, doc. 58 p. 386. For the dicing lottery of around 1625 organised by the Amsterdam painter Laurens Mauritsz Hellewech see De Roever 1886, p. 196; Bok 2008, pp. 16–18. The booklets for the dicing lottery are in the library of the Amsterdam City Archives, inv. U00.3101. The full entry reads: 'No. 14 Eene schilderije van Boentijen t'Haerlem met noch het conterfeijtsen van mr Pekelharinck kluchtich geschildert is geestimeert op 5 ponden Vlaems' (No. 14. A painting by Boontje of Haarlem, together with the likeness of Mr Pickle Herring, farcically painted, is appraised at 5 pounds Flemish). Later in the seventeenth century, too, there are mentions of paintings of Pekelharing. The probate inventory of the great Leiden collector Hendrick Bugge van Ring (died 1667) listed 'Een trony van Pekelharing van F. Hals' (A head of Pekelharing by F. Hals, Erfgoed Leiden, notary L. van Swieten, NA 1005, akte 10, 30 March 1667). In 1680, the probate inventory of Joris van Hasselt, widower of Trijntje Arents, lists 'Een kontrefeytsel van monsieur Peeckelharingh' (A portrait of Monsieur Peeckelharingh, SAA, notaris J. de Winter, NA 2411 [B], pp. 1–19, d.d. 4 November 1680, especially p. 9), and in 1684–5 the probate inventory of Cornelis van Lodensteyn and Maria van der Haer mentions '[no.] 95 Joncheer Peeckelhaeringh f 2:-:-' ([No.] 95, Squire Peeckelhaeringh, 2 guilders, The Hague City Archives, notary M. Beeckman, NA 290, pp. 121–268, 20 April 1685, especially p. 252). See also notes 66 and 102 on p. 194 in the present volume.

56   Pekelharing's English nationality is expressly spelled out in a German treatise of 1631; see Alexander 2007, p. 470. There is very extensive literature on Pekelharing, for example Worp 1886; Weber 1987; Schrickx 1983; Albach 1990; Alexander 2003,

2007 and 2015; Katritzky 2007, 2013 and 2018; Buijsen 2016.

57   The probable author of this anthology of translated English plays was Friedrich Menius; see Alexander 2007, p. 463; Brauneck 1970.

58   Jan Zoet, *Jochem-Jool ofte Jalourschen-Pekelharing*, Amsterdam 1637. It is not known whether the play was ever performed. See Cordes 2008, pp. 62–9.

59   Starter 1621, n.p., 'kluchtigh t'samen-gesang van dry personagien' (Comical part-song for three characters). The full reference to the melody is 'Pekelharings. Ofte, Pots hondert tausent Slapferment' (Pekelharing, or Pot's hundred thousand weak fermentation), which was a bastardisation of 'Gods allerheiligst sacrament' (God's most holy sacrament). This melody reference occurs, with or without the mention of Pekelharing, no fewer than 25 times in Dutch songs before 1645; see www.liederenbank.nl (accessed 27 February 2023). The earliest reference dates from 1615 but does not mention Pekelharing. See further Grijp 1991, pp. 135–9.

60   In 1615 the English comedian 'Georg Vincint alias pickelhering' is mentioned in Braunschweig; see Alexander 2007, pp. 468–9. The records of paintings of 'mr.' or 'Monsieur' Pekelharing (see note 55) make it clear that they were portraits and not pictures of an imaginary person.

61   The engraving *The Mountebank Doctor and his Merry Andrew* was made by Edward (Le) Davis (active 1671–98); see S. Slive in Washington, London and Haarlem 1989, pp. 220–3, and British Museum, London, inv. 1945,0512.56.

62   The Leipzig painting has been referred to as 'the mulatto' since the late nineteenth century, but there is no source for that. S. Slive in Washington, London and Haarlem 1989, p. 220.

63   For the 'Moor' as a symbol of folly, see Hornback 2001 and 2007.

64   *Nugae venales, sive thesaurus ridendi & jocandi…*, Amsterdam 1648, of which a copy is in the Koninklijke Bibliotheek, The Hague (KW 224 G 16 [1]). As can be seen from its Latin title, this book was for a learned readership. Starting in 1632, it was published in various countries and compilations; see Tomarken 2015.

65   For an overview of images with Pekelharing see Haarlem 2017, p. 15. Jan Steen, *The Doctor's Visit*, about 1660 (Apsley House, Wellington Museum, London, inv. WM.1525-1948); Jan Steen, *The Christening Feast*, about 1668 (Staatliche Museen zu Berlin, Gemäldegalerie, inv. 795D). The latter painting contains not only a picture of Pekelharing but also of a pipe-smoking Malle Babbe. Steen was undoubtedly working after a model by Frans Hals, which now seems to be lost.

66   Pers 1628a, p. 35: 'De Sot seght, als ghy blijft bedoven in den wijn, / Dan suldy zijn als ick, een Narre suldy zijn'.

67   Boot 1623, p. 467: 'droncken te drincken' and 'sotte, malle ende narrachtighe geckernien'.

68   Schiller 2006, pp. 15–16; Van Bruaene and Van Bouchaute 2017, p. 13. See also note 21.

69   Slive 1970–4, vols 2, 3, nos 22, 74, figs 63, 118.

70   For civic guardsmen and alcohol see Knevel 1994, pp. 295–304.

71   Adam van der Hagen, member of the Vine Tendrils, lamented in 1613 that 'Retorijckers / Wijvensmijters / Kannen-kijckers' (Rhetoricians / Wife Beaters / Tankard Gazers) had become a general term for many rhetoricians; see Van Dixhoorn 2009, p. 186; Van Bruaene and Van Bouchaute 2017. For painters' love of drink see Miedema 1981 and p. 44 in the present volume.

72   Houbraken 1718–21, vol. 1, pp. 90–5.

73   Pers 1628a, p. 8: 'De Wijn is der Poëten post-paerd'.

74   Van Mander 1604, fol. 24r.

75   Van der Eembd 1621, fol. 2v: 'vrij wat', 'water-drinkers' and 'vol ende beschoncken'; Van Dixhoorn 2009, p. 187.

76   J. Bikker in Bikker et al. 2007, no. 105, pp. 171–3.

77   There is a drawing in the Rijksmuseum of a man laughing with his teeth exposed, with a (later) inscription identifying the sitter as Frans Hals. If this is a copy after a (lost) self portrait it could be an example of his self-mockery. For the drawing see Middelkoop and Van Grevenstein 1988, p. 93, and Rijksmuseum, Amsterdam, inv. RP-T-1961-51.

78   See p. 45 in the present volume.

79   Verberckmoes 1998, p. 86, with references to the books of Juan Luis Vives and the French physician Laurent Joubert, who wrote a long treatise on laughter, *Traité du ris*, in 1579.

80   Ibid. It was also said that exuberant laughter made women look older and uglier before their time.

81   See Schiller 2010 for laughing prostitutes.

82   Pers 1628b, p. 113: 'lacchen sonder lach, met streelen sonder sin, / Met loncken sonder oogh, met lieven sonder min'. See also Verlaan and Grootes 1978.

83   Slive 1970–4, vol. 1, pp. 91–4; Slive 2014, pp. 119–20.

84   Crispijn van de Passe, *Les miroir des plus Belles courtisannes de ce temps / Spiegel der alderschoonste cortisanen deses tyts*, Utrecht 1630; a copy of the 1631 edition is housed at the Koninklijke Bibliotheek, The Hague, inv. KW 343 J 8.

85   For other examples see Van de Pol 1996, p. 318. A farce of 1650 mentions a woman with 'bortjes' (panels) of prostitutes who were summoned when a client had made his choice. A notarised document of 1697 speaks of a woman who had her portrait hanging in an Amsterdam gaming house for seven years so that those who 'wanted to have' her could 'get' her there. See further Kolfin 2001.

86   Kolfin 2005; Roberts 2012.

87   There are doubts as to whether this work was by Hals: it has also been attributed to Willem Buytewech in the past. It was destroyed in the Second World War. See Slive 1970–4, vol. 3, no. L1, pp. 114–15.

88   *Boy with a Lute* and *The Smoker*, both Metropolitan Museum of Art, New York (Slive 1970–4, vol. 3,

nos 21, 24 pp. 14–15, 16–17; Liedtke 2007, nos 60, 61 pp. 266–8, 269–72), and *The Merry Lute Player*, Guildhall Art Gallery, London (Slive 1970–4, vol. 3, no. 26 p. 17).

89   SAA, notary S. van der Piet, NA 1027 (A), pp. 253–4, 24 March 1646: Cornelia van Lemens, wife of Abraham Macaree, is in arrears with her rent owed to Nicolaes Duysentdaelders and transfers household goods to him, including 'Een groot stuck schilderij affbeeldende de verlooren soon, gedaen bij Frans Hals, bij provisie geëstimeert f 48:-:-' (A large painting of the Prodigal Son by Frans Hals, appraised on commission at 48 guilders), SAA, notary J. van de Ven, NA 1081, fol. 66r–v, 28 March 1647: agreement between Andries Aeckersloot and Marten van den Broeck, whereby the first-named delivers goods to Van den Broeck, who in return provides him with paintings, including 'Een verloren soon van Frans Hals' (A Prodigal Son by Frans Hals). See I. van Thiel-Stroman in Washington, London and Haarlem 1989, docs 115 (as unverified), 119, pp. 399–400, 400–1. For the painting see especially Liedtke 2007, no. 59, pp. 263–5. The mentions have also been associated with the lost *Banquet in the Open Air* (fig. 161).

90   Kolfin 2005.

91   Sale Johannes Enschede collection, Haarlem (Taco Jelgersma and Vincent van der Vinne), 30 May 1786, no. 87, 'Jonker Ramp en zyn Matres'.

92   Rodenburg 1619, p. 377 (poem titled 'Humana fumus'): 'kindse zotterny'.

93   Dekker 1997, pp. 49–50; *De nieuwe Vaakverdryver, of Neederlandze verteller*: samengesteld door K.A.P.S.M., Amsterdam 1651.

94   Verberckmoes 1998, p. 49.

95   See pp. 38, 72 in the present volume.

96   Compare the engraving of the Hague kermis (or local fair) in Adriaen van de Venne's *Tafereel van de belacchende werelt* (The Hague 1635), in which the boy is very similar to the one in Hals's painting. He is identified in the text as 'Fopje', a 'Garnaerts-Jongen' (shrimp boy), selling hot shrimps, crabs and winkles from his basket (pp. 49, 50). In Gerrit Dou's famous *Quacksalver* of 1652 (Museum Boijmans Van Beuningen, Rotterdam, inv. St 4) there is a fisherwoman carrying a basket with a similar wooden beaker; see Lammertse 1998, no. 19 pp. 63–8, with more examples. See also Royalton-Kisch 1988, pp. 324–5.

97   For other depictions of fish porters see above all the series by Gillis van Scheyndel after Jan Porcellis, *Miscellaneous Beach and Water Views*, 1645 (Keyes 1980, nos 144–60, 163, 164, pp. 247, 249, and Rijksmuseum, Amsterdam). See also the prints by Claes Jansz Visscher (*View of Zandvoort*, 1612; see Schuckman 1991, vol. 1, no. 151, p. 85, vol. 2, p. 88, Rijksmuseum, Amsterdam, inv. RP-P-1879-A-3464); Jan van de Velde the Younger after Willem Buytewech, *Aqua* (two versions, one of them dated 1622; see Luijten and Schuckman 1989, vol. 1, nos 21, 24 pp. 16, 17, vol. 2, pp. 17, 19,

and Rijksmuseum, Amsterdam, invs RP-P-OB-15.324, 15.320); Jan van de Velde the Younger, *View of Zandvoort*, 1627 (see ibid., vol. 1, no. 451 p. 144, vol. 2, p. 114, and Rijksmuseum, Amsterdam, inv. RP-P-1898-A-20532; the print was an illustration in I. Robbertsen, *Herders-Zanghen*, Amsterdam 1627). In Hendrick Sorgh's *Fish Market* of 1650–70 (Rijksmuseum, Amsterdam, inv. SK-C-227) there are two young children with large baskets.

98 Ampzing 1621; Ampzing 1628. See also, for example, Van Wesbusch 1636, for a delightful poem about a trip to Zandvoort. The prints that Jan van de Velde the Younger (?), Willem Buytewech and Claes Jansz Visscher made of and around Zandvoort evoke an image similar to Ampzing's; see previous note and especially Amsterdam 1993, pp. 54–5, 76–7; Leeflang 1997.

99 Ampzing 1621, fol. B4v, almost identical to Ampzing 1628, pp. 71, 76: 'Een arm, en simpel volck, met prael, en pracht, en prangen, / En slimheydt deser eeuw' en boosheydt niet behangen, / Eenvoudich, slecht, en recht, vol trouw', en sonder list, / En daermen minst de deugd, en meest de sonde mist'.

100 Hals painted Samuel Ampzing's portrait around 1630 (Leiden Collection, New York, inv. FH-100; see Liedtke 2017). Ampzing, in his turn, mentioned Hals in his books about Haarlem (Ampzing 1621; Ampzing 1628). See also p. 139 in the present volume.

101 Jacob Cats had a similarly affirmative view, this time of the fishermen of Scheveningen, on which see S. Slive 1970–4, vol. 1, p. 144; Slive in Washington, London and Haarlem 1989, p. 232; Slive 2014, p. 186.

102 Van Beverwijck 1642, p. 328: 'de wegh tot de Wijsheyt gesloten', 'over-leggende kracht'.

103 See Mans 1998 and Aan de Kerk 2019 for people with mental disabilities and psychological disorders in the seventeenth century and later.

104 NHA, 3993, no. 498, Resoluties van de burgemeesters, 17 February 1646, fol. 61r–v: 'Barbar, alias Malle Barbar', 'swarichheden van schande en oneere'. The burgomasters present were Pieter Olycan and Floris van der Hoeff, the first of whom had his portrait painted by Hals (see p. 72 in the present volume). Barbar, also called Malle Barber, Barbar or Babbe, lived in the workhouse until her death in December 1663, and was supported financially by the governors of St Elizabeth's Hospital in Haarlem until she died; see NHA, 3305 Sint Elisabeths Gasthuis of Groote Gasthuis te Haarlem, inv. 37, alimentatieregister, fol. 27r–v. With thanks to Floris Mulder, who is preparing an article on Malle Babbe and kindly shared his findings with me. In 1653 the Leper House also paid to support 'Malle Babbe int Tuchthuijs' (Malle Babbe in the workhouse), 65 guilders; see I. van Thiel-Stroman in Washington, London and Haarlem 1989, doc. 94 p. 395.

105 In 1637 Frans Hals received financial support for his 'innocente soone' (son with a mental disability),

Pieter, enabling him to be housed outside the city. In 1642 Pieter was moved to the workhouse on the orders of the burgomasters, where he was allocated quarters 'buyten de gemeenschap' (separate from the community). He was only required to work if he was 'fit' ('bequaem') to do so. See I. van Thiel-Stroman in Washington, London and Haarlem 1989, docs 80, 81, 94, pp. 392, 395. It appears that Pieter Hals was only briefly in the workhouse and then went to live with a private individual. From 1643 until his death in 1667 the financial support he received from St Elizabeth's Hospital was paid to Aert Boom(en), who also received money for other people supported by the hospital (see NHA, 3305 Sint Elisabeths Gasthuis of Groote Gasthuis te Haarlem invs 35, 36, 37, alimentatieregister). Sara Hals was placed in the workhouse at her mother's request; see I. van Thiel-Stroman in Washington, London and Haarlem 1989, docs 91, 92, 93, p. 394.

106 See Hallema 1928, pp. 76–80, for the 1613 workhouse regulations.

107 Slive 1970–4, vol. 3, no. 75, pp. 45–6.

108 SAA, notary L. Fruijt, NA 3909, pp. 165–7, 13 June 1689, Cornelis van den Driessche(n) transfers goods to Leendert van Dulcken, among them a 'Malle Babbe van Frans Hals', '1 trony van Frans Hals' and '1 copy na Frans Hals' (Malle Babbe by Frans Hals; 1 head by Frans Hals and 1 copy after Frans Hals).

109 Koppenol 2001, p. 237; Van Boheemen and Van der Heijden 1999, p. 539.

110 Van Mander 1618, fol. R2v: 'boere-vryers oft minnaers'. For other examples of the owl as a symbol of folly see S. Slive in Washington, London and Haarlem 1989, no. 37 pp. 236–41.

111 The fact that people with a mental disability were often called 'malle' (foolish) emerges from the burgomasters' resolutions, which in 1646, the year when Malle Babbe was taken to the workhouse, also refer to Pieter and Cornelis Aerentsse, 'beijde malle soonen' (both foolish sons, 22 February 1646) and the 'malle kint' (foolish child) of Hendrick Willemse (5 March 1646); see NHA, 3993, no. 498, Resoluties van de burgemeesters, fols 62r–v, 65r.

112 See, for example, the engraving by Cornelis Bloemaert mentioned in note 44, with the inscription: 'Siet de Vastel-avonts Sot / Comt hier met de Rommelpot, / Hoort hem singen, lieve man / Geeft een Koeckjen wt de pan' (Behold the Shrovetide fool / Coming here with his rommelpot / Hear him sing, the dear man / Give him a biscuit from the pan); an engraving by Jan van de Velde, inscribed: 'Op vasten-avont loopt menich Sotje / Om duytjes gnorren op 't Rommelpotje' (Many fools walk around at Shrovetide / Grunting for farthings on the rommel pot', Luijten and Schuckman 1989, vol. 1, no. 132, p. 47, vol. 2, p. 70; Rijksmuseum, Amsterdam, inv. RP-P-OB-15.301); an engraving by J. Dubois after J. Matham, inscribed: 'k'speel voor Sot om 't genot van dees Pot'

(I play the fool for the profit from this pot), Hollstein 1952, no. 2, p. 6; Rijksmuseum, Amsterdam, inv. RP-P-BI-1959). It is also clear that *rommelpot*, fool and Shrovetide were mentioned in the same breath from Reynier's monologue in Bredero's *Moortje*: 'Ja wel het is te mal / de geck is seecker sot / Hier schort niet dan een blaas / of soo een romel-pot / Om voor de luyer duer te rasen en te singhen / De neske-deuntjes met de kinderlijcke dingen: / Als; gheeft my een Panck-koeck uyt de pan / ho man / ho: / De Vastelavondt die komt an: so, mijn Heer, also:' (Aye it really is too foolish / The fool is clearly mad / All that's missing is a bladder / Or a rommelpot / With which to make a racket outside people's doors / The foolish ditties with the childish things: / Such as: give me a pancake from the pan / Ho man / Ho / Shrovetide is coming / so, my lord, just so), Bredero 1620, n.p., 'Vierde uytkomen, Het darde bedrijf' (act 4, scene 3). The play was first performed in 1615.

113 'Het afbeeldzel van *Boontje* enz, in dien tijd een bekend gekje te Haarlem, speelende op de rommelpot … door W. [sic] Bailli, 1624' (The likeness of *Boontje* etc, at the time a well-known nutter of Haarlem, playing on a rommelpot … by W. [sic] Bailli, 1624); see Utrecht 1792, no. 19 p. 83; Bruyn 1951, p. 223. Hals may have portrayed this Boontje eating gruel. In any event, there is mention of a drawing, once again by Bailly, from which this could be concluded, namely Amsterdam 1754, no. 51 p. 70, 'The Gruel Eater, a nutter of Haarlem, drawn with the pen and washed, by Bailly'; and Amsterdam 1767, no. 22 pp. 8–9, 'Boontje or Gruel Eater, A nutter of Haarlem, very detailed and finely drawn'. See Bruyn 1951.

114 See note 55.

115 Memorandum book of the patrician Alkmaar Van Egmond van de Nyenburg family. The painting was bought with others, which included three 'little pieces' by Jan Miense Molenaer (costing a total of 28 guilders) and 'a night piece' by Claes Hals (11 guilders) from the 'house of the deceased Beekom', probably a reference to Pieter van Beeckum, who was buried in Alkmaar on 21 April 1665. See Van Gelder 1906, p. 63. It seems possible that instead of 'de gecken van Haerlem' (the crazies of Haarlem), the document in fact read 'de geckin van Haerlem' (the crazy woman from Haarlem), in which case it presumably referred to a version of *Malle Babbe*. However, as long as the original document has not been found, this cannot be ascertained.

116 De Hemelaer 1612, n.p.: 'Zulx ist / dat als een lacht / hem werd ook toegelacht' (It is thus that those who laugh invite laughter). In 1612 J. De Hemelaer was the first person to translate Horace's *Ars poetica* into Dutch. It was published in Haarlem and was dedicated to Karel van Mander. For Alberti see Sinisgalli 2011, p. 61, and for Lomazzo and other examples see Ciardi 1973–4, vol. 2, p. 95; Schiller 2006, pp. 63, 64, 68, 69.

117 On this phenomenon see Shearman 1992; Schiller 2006, p. 39.

118 Westermann 1997, pp. 267–71.

119 Research into the reasons why people laugh has been vastly expanded since the seventeenth century: it would be going too far to explore this in the current essay on Frans Hals. For a recent general introduction on the subject see Trumble 2004.

120 Van Mander 1604 (1973), vol. 1, fol. 23r, pp. 158–9, no. 5: 'Want al wat d'affecten moghen bedrijven / Wijst Natuer al meer / dan men can beschrijven'; Melion 2023, p. 261.

121 See note 55: 'kluchtich geschildert'. No artist's name is mentioned but the paintings must almost certainly have been made by Frans Hals.

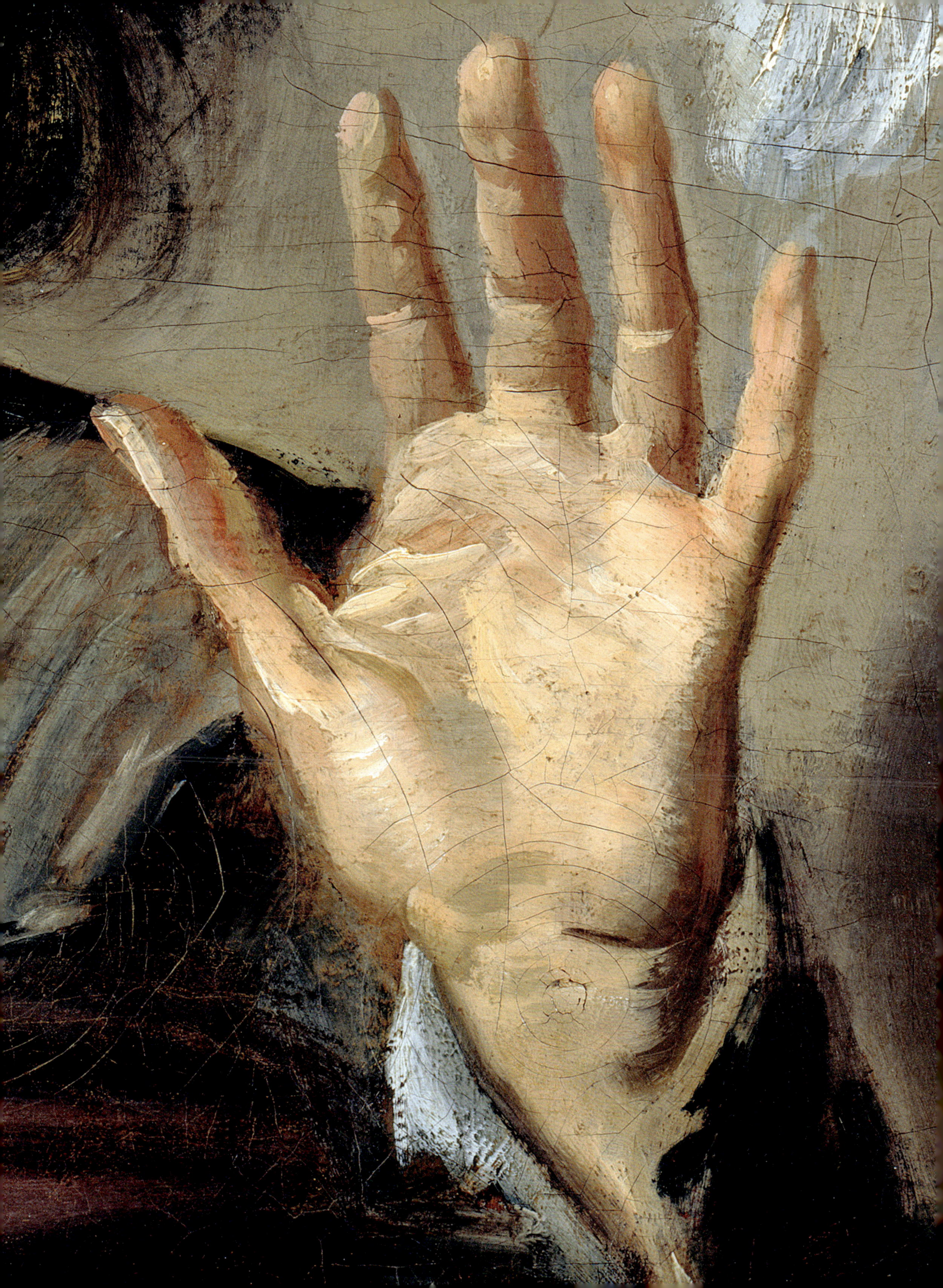

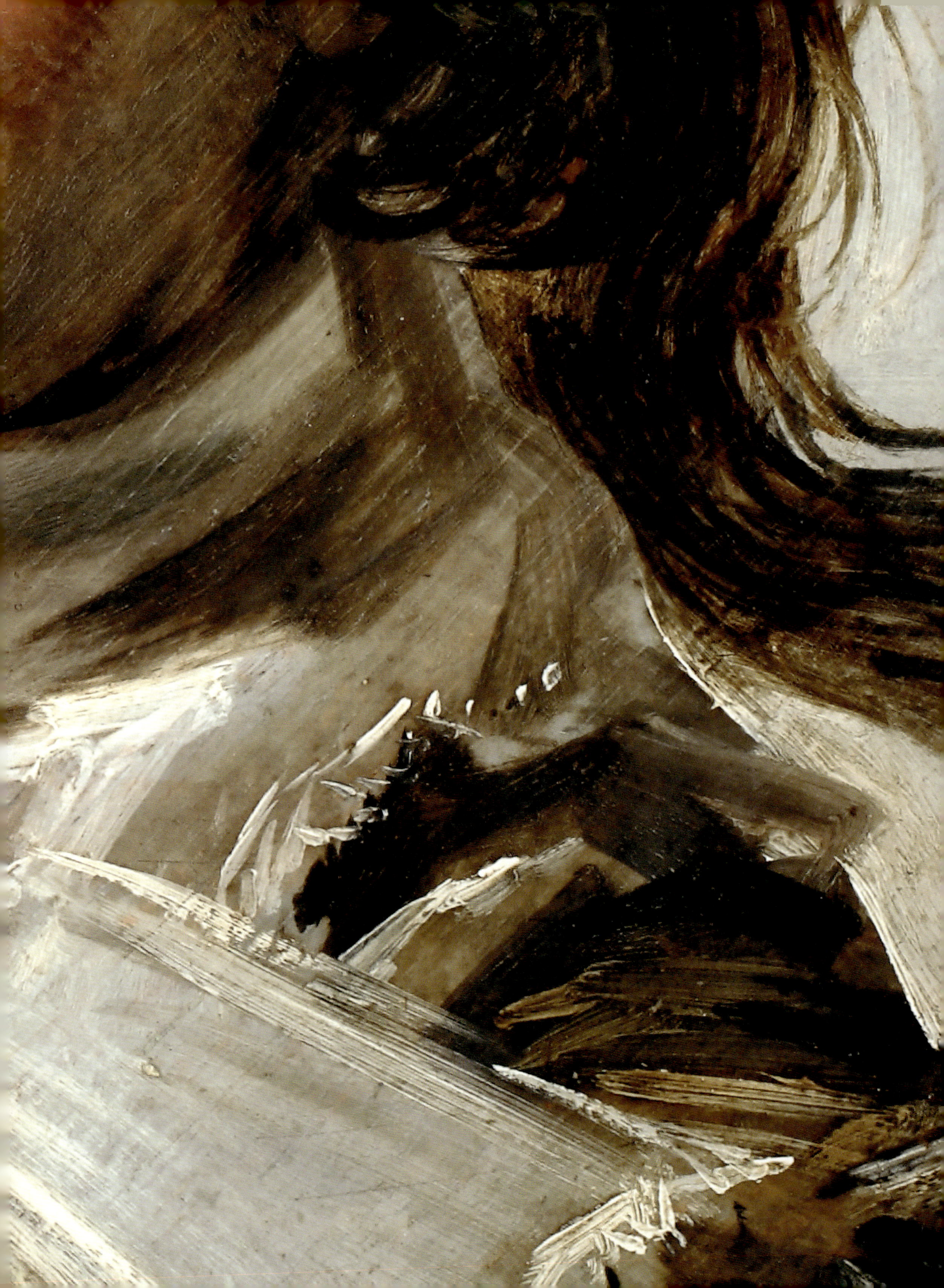

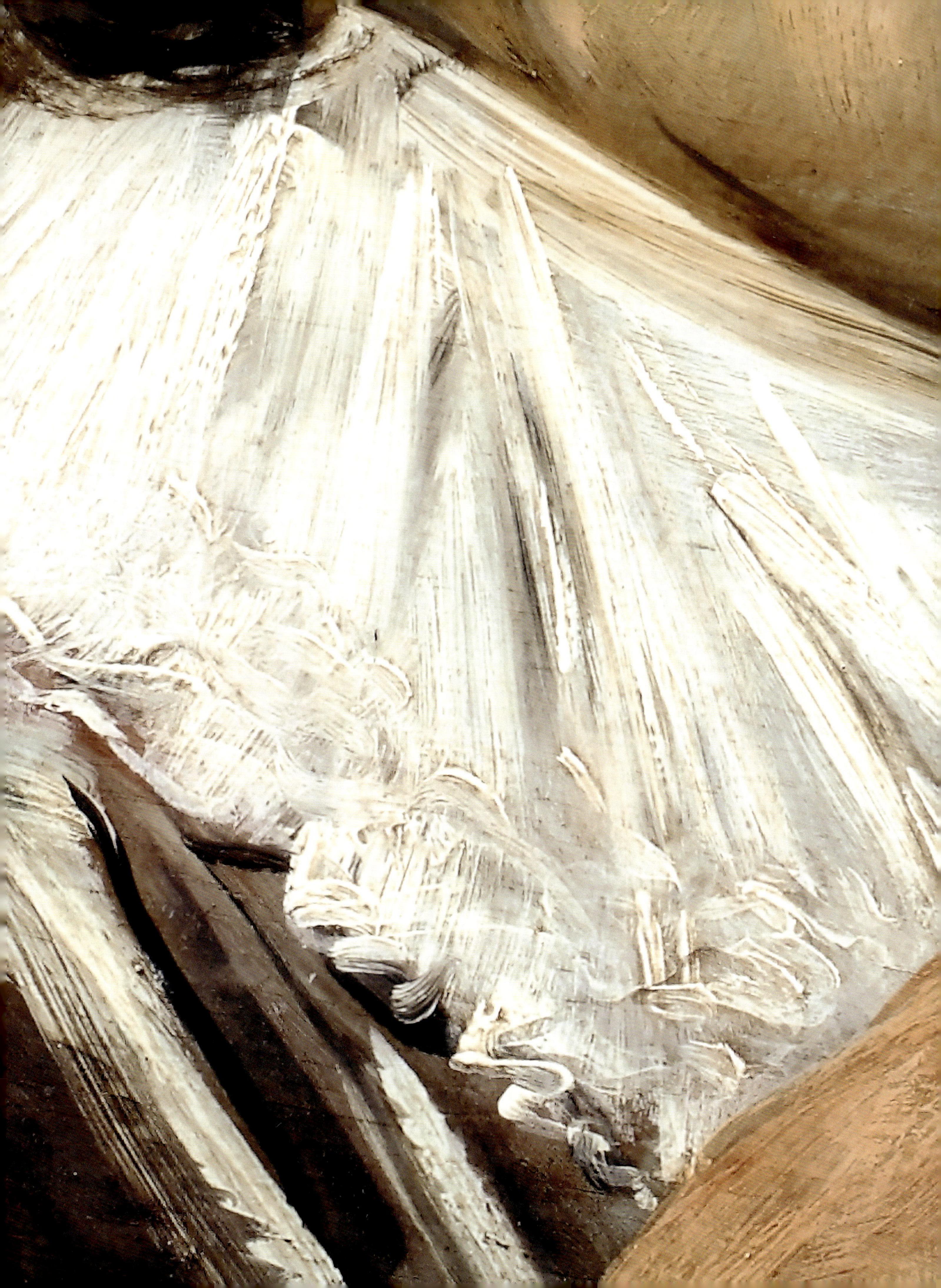

BIBLIOGRAPHY

ABBREVIATIONS

GPI Getty Provenance Index (www.getty.edu/research/tools/provenance/search.html)
NA Notarieel Archief (Notarial Archive)
NHA Noord-Hollands Archief Haarlem
ONA Oud Notarieel Archief (Old Notarial Archive)
ONAH Oud Notarieel Archief Haarlem (Old Notarial Archive, Haarlem)
SAA Stadsarchief Amsterdam (Amsterdam City Archive)
SAR Stadsarchief Rotterdam (Rotterdam City Archive)

A

Albach 1990
B. Albach, 'Pekelharing: personage en potsenmaker', *Literatuur*, 7 (1990), pp. 74–80

Alexander 2003
J. Alexander, 'The Dutch Connection: On the Social Origins of the Pickelhering', *Neophilologus*, 87 (2003), pp. 597–604

Alexander 2007
J. Alexander, 'Will Kemp, Thomas Sacheville and Pickelhering: A Consanguinity and Confluence of Three Modern Clown Personas', *Daphnis*, 36 (2007), pp. 463–86

Alexander 2015
J. Alexander, 'Peter van Durant (ca. 1514–1584) alias Pickle Herring: A Contribution to the Possible Genesis of an Early Modern Clown Persona', *Philologica Jassyensia*, 11 (2015), no. 2, pp. 111–23

Alsteens 2014
S. Alsteens, 'A note on the young Van Dyck', *The Burlington Magazine*, 156 (2014), pp. 85–90

Ampzing 1621
S. Ampzing, *Het Lof der stadt Haerlem in Hollandt*, Haarlem 1621

Ampzing 1628
S. Ampzing, *Beschryvinge ende lof der stad Haerlem in Holland...*, Haarlem 1628

Amsterdam 1734
Catalogus van een konstig kabinet schilderyen, dewelke verkogt zullen werden ... den 10. Augustus 1734..., Amsterdam 1734

Amsterdam 1754
Catalogus van 't uitmuntend kabinet schilderijen, craionnen, tekeningen, miniaturen, en printen, van de beste Italiaansche, Nederlandsche, Fransche, Engelsche en andere meesters ... Alles met veel kennis en groote naaukeurigheid, in veele jaren byeen vergaderd, en nagelaten door den heere Jeronimus Tonneman, auction cat., Amsterdam (Oude Zyds Heeren Logement, Huibert de Wit and Hendrik de Leth), 21 October 1754 and following days

Amsterdam 1767
Catalogus van een fraaije verzaameling schilderyen, teekeningen, en prenten ... in veele jaaren by een ver-zaameld en nagelaten door Jeronimo de Bosch, auction cat., Amsterdam (Jan and Bernardus de Bosch), 5 October 1767 and following days

Amsterdam 1773
Catalogus van een uitmuntend en overheerlyk kabinet konstige schilderyen ... in veele w byeen verzamelt en nagelaaten door ... mr. Johan van der Marck Ægidz...., auction cat. Amsterdam (Hendrik de Winter and Jan Yver), 25 August 1773 and following days

Amsterdam 1993
B. Bakker and H. Leeflang, *Nederland naar 't leven. Landschapsprenten uit de Gouden Eeuw*, exh. cat., Museum Het Rembrandthuis, Amsterdam 1993

Amsterdam and Washington 1981
P. Schatborn, *Dutch Figure Drawings from the Seventeenth Century*, exh. cat., Rijksmuseum, Amsterdam, and National Gallery of Art, Washington, The Hague 1981

Amsterdam, New York and Toledo 2003
H. Leeflang and G. Luijten (eds), *Hendrick Goltzius (1558–1617): Drawings, Prints and Paintings*, exh. cat., Rijksmuseum, Amsterdam, Metropolitan Museum of Art, New York, and Toledo Museum of Art, Toledo, Amsterdam 2003

Antwerp 1993
R.-A. d'Hulst, N. De Poorter and M. Vandeneven, *Jacob Jordaens (1593–1678)*, 2 vols, exh. cat., Royal Museum of Fine Arts, Antwerp, Brussels 1993

Atkins 2012
C.D.M. Atkins, *The Signature Style of Frans Hals: Painting, Subjectivity, and the Market in Early Modernity*, Amsterdam 2012

B

Von Baeyer 2007
E. von Baeyer, *Drawings, Watercolours, Bozzetti, Paintings, 1530–1880*, London 2007

Barnes et al. 2004
S.J. Barnes, N. De Poorter, O. Millar and H. Vey, *Van Dyck: A Complete Catalogue of the Paintings*, New Haven and London 2004

Barrett 2012
K. Barrett, *Pieter Soutman: Life and Oeuvre*, Amsterdam and Philadelphia 2012

Baudouin 2001
F. Baudouin, 'Van Dyck in The Hague', in *Van Dyck 1599–1999: Conjectures and Refutations*, ed. H. Vlieghe, Turnhout 2001, pp. 53–64

De Beer 2019
G. de Beer, *The Golden Age of Dutch Marine Painting: The Inder Rieden Collection*, 4 vols, Leiden 2019

Belkin 2009
K.L. Belkin, *Copies and Adaptations from Renaissance and Later Artists: German and Netherlandish Artists (Corpus Rubenianum Ludwig Burchard*, 26), London 2009

Berkvens-Stevelinck 2001
C. Berkvens-Stevelinck, *Magna Commoditas: Geschiedenis van de Leidse Universiteitsbibliotheek 1575–2000*, Leiden 2001

Van Beverwijck 1642
J. van Beverwijck, *Schat der ongesontheyt ofte genees-konste van de sieckten*, Dordrecht 1642

De Bie 1662
C. de Bie, *Het gulden cabinet vande edele vry schilder-const...*, Antwerp 1662

Biesboer 1996a
P. Biesboer, 'De Vlaamse immigranten in Haarlem 1578–1630 en hun nakomelingen', in *Vlamingen in Haarlem*, eds P. Biesboer, G. Kolthof and H. Rau, Haarlem 1996, pp. 35–60

Biesboer 1996b
P. Biesboer, 'Willem van Heythuysen en zijn twee portretten', in *Hart voor Haarlem: Liber Amicorum voor Jaap Temminck*, eds H. Brokken et al., Haarlem 1996, pp. 113–26

Biesboer 2001
P. Biesboer, *Collections of Paintings in Haarlem 1572–1745*, ed. C. Togneri, Los Angeles 2001

Biesboer 2012
P. Biesboer, 'De identificatie van een familiegroep door Frans Hals', *Haerlem Jaarboek 2012* (2013), pp. 63–83

Biesboer 2017
P. Biesboer, 'Een zelfportret door Vincent Laurensz. van der Vinne (Haarlem 1628–1702 Haarlem)', *Haerlem Jaarboek 2016* (2017), pp. 95–105

Biesboer 2023
P. Biesboer, 'The Loo family of Haarlem in portraits by Hals and Verspronck', *The Burlington Magazine*, 165 (2023), pp. 109–19

Biesboer and Bijl 2006
P. Biesboer and M. Bijl, *A Portrait of Pieter Jacobsz. Olycan: Frans Hals Re-discovered*, Zurich 2006

Bijl 2005
M. Bijl, 'The Portrait of Theodorus Schrevelius', in *The Learned Eye: Regarding Art, Theory, and the Artist's Reputation. Essays for Ernst van de Wetering*, eds M. van den Doel et al., Amsterdam 2005, pp. 47–55

Bikker 2009
J. Bikker, 'Sir Joan Reynst, his good acquaintance, neighbour, and landlord: truth and fantasy in Houbraken's life of Karel du Jardin', *The Burlington Magazine*, 151 (2009), pp. 92–7

Bikker et al. 2007
J. Bikker, Y. Bruijnen, G. Wuestman, E. Korthals Altes, J.P. Filedt Kok and T. Dibbits, *Dutch Paintings of the Seventeenth Century in the Rijksmuseum Amsterdam*, vol. 1: *Artists Born Between 1570 and 1600*, Amsterdam and New Haven 2007

Bode 1871a
W. Bode, *Frans Hals und seine Schule. Ein Beitrag zu einer kritischen Behandlung der holländischen Malerei*, Leipzig 1871

Bode 1871b
W. Bode, 'Frans Hals und seine Schule', *Jahrbücher für Kunstwissenschaft*, 4 (1871), pp. 1–66

Bode 1883
W. Bode, *Studien zur Geschichte der holländischen Malerei*, Brunswick 1883

Bode and Binder 1914
W. Bode and M.J. Binder, *Frans Hals: Sein Leben und seine Werke*, Berlin 1914

Van Boheemen and Van der Heijden 1999
F.C. van Boheemen and T.C.J. van der Heijden, *Retoricaal Memoriaal. Bronnen voor de geschiedenis van de Hollandse rederijkerskamers van de middeleeuwen tot het begin van de achttiende eeuw*, Delft 1999

Boot 1623
G. Boot, *Eene bvrgherlycke onderrechtinge. Ofte anders ghenaemt: Eene beleefde Raedtghevinghe*, Amsterdam 1623

Boschloo 1986–7
A.W.A. Boschloo (ed.), *Academies of Art between Renaissance and Romanticism*, The Hague 1986–7 (*Leids Kunsthistorisch Jaarboek*, 5–6)

Boston and Kansas City 2015
R. Baer et al., *Class Distinctions: Dutch Painting in the Age of Rembrandt and Vermeer*, exh. cat., Museum of Fine Arts, Boston, and Nelson-Atkins Museum of Art, Kansas City, Boston 2015

Brauneck 1970
M. Brauneck (ed.), *Spieltexte der Wanderbühne*, vol. 1: *Engelische Comedien und Tragedien*, Berlin and Boston 1970

Bredero 1620
G.A. Bredero, *G.A. Brederoos Moortje, waar in hy Terentii Eunuchum heeft nae-ghevolght*, Amsterdam 1620 (1st impression 1617)

Bredero 1638
G.A. Bredero, *Alle de spelen, werken en brieven van Gerbrand Adriaensz Bredero, Amsterdammer*, Amsterdam 1638

Bredius 1888
A. Bredius, 'Iets over Pieter Codde en Willem Duyster', *Oud Holland*, 6 (1888), pp. 187–94

Bredius 1890–5
A. Bredius, 'Het schildersregister van Jan Sysmus, Stads Doctor van Amsterdam', I, II, III: *Oud Holland*, 8 (1890), pp. 1–17, 217–34, 297–313; IV: *Oud Holland*, 9 (1891), pp. 137–49; V: *Oud Holland*, 12 (1894), pp. 160–71; VI: *Oud Holland*, 13 (1895), pp. 112–20

Bredius 1914
A. Bredius, 'De ouders van Frans Hals', *Oud Holland*, 32 (1914), p. 216

Bredius 1915–22
A. Bredius, *Künstler-Inventare: Urkunden zur Geschichte der holländischen Kunst des XVIten, XVIIten und XVIIIten Jahrhunderts*, 7 vols, The Hague 1915–22

Bredius 1917
A. Bredius, 'Een conflict tusschen Frans Hals en Judith Leyster', *Oud Holland*, 35 (1917), pp. 71–3

Bredius 1919
A. Bredius, 'Het schetsboek van Jacob de Wet', *Oud Holland*, 37 (1919), pp. 215–22

Bredius 1923–4
A. Bredius, 'Archiefsprokkels betreffende Frans Hals', 'Archiefsprokkels betreffende Dirck Hals', 'Archiefsprokkels betreffende Herman Hals', 'Eenige gegevens over Frans Hals den Jonge', 'Oorkonden over Reynier Hals', 'Oorkonden over Jan Hals', *Oud Holland*, 41 (1923–4), pp. 19–31, 60–2, 215, 258–62, 263–4

Briels 1976
J. Briels, *De Zuidnederlandse immigratie in Amsterdam en Haarlem omstreeks 1572–1630*, dissertation, University of Utrecht, 1976

Briels 1985
J. Briels, *Zuid-Nederlanders in de Republiek 1572–1630. Een demografische en cultuurhistorische studie*, Sint-Niklaas 1985

Briels 1997
J. Briels, *Vlaamse schilders en de dageraad van Hollands Gouden Eeuw, 1585–1630*, Antwerp 1997

Broos 1971
B.P.J. Broos, 'The "O" of Rembrandt', *Simiolus*, 4 (1971), no. 3, pp. 150–84

Van Bruaene and Van Bouchaute 2017
A.-L. Van Bruaene and S. Van Bouchaute, 'Rederijkers, Kannenkijkers: Drinking and Drunkenness in the Sixteenth and Seventeenth-Century Low Countries', *Early Modern Low Countries*, 1 (2017), pp. 1–29

Bruyn 1951
J. Bruyn, 'David Bailly', *Oud Holland*, 66 (1951), pp. 212–27

Buchelius c.1588–1631
A. Buchelius, Aantekeningen betreffende meest Nederlandse schilders en kunstwerken, c. 1588–1631, manuscript, Universiteit Utrecht UBU Hs. 1781 (Hs 5 J 21)

Buijsen 2016
E. Buijsen, '"Foolish Wisdom": Adriaen van de Venne and Frans Hals's "Pekelharing"', *The Burlington Magazine*, 158 (2016), pp. 94–100

Buijsen, Dumas and Manuth 2012
E. Buijsen, C. Dumas and V. Manuth (eds), *Face Book: Studies on Dutch and Flemish Portraiture of the 16th–18th Centuries. Liber Amicorum presented to Rudolf E.O. Ekkart on the occasion of his 65th Birthday*, Leiden 2012

C

Carasso 1998
D. Carasso, 'Houbrakens "Groote schouburgh". Enkele beschouwingen over de invloed van de *Groote schouburgh* op ons beeld van de Noord-Nederlandse schilderkunst in de Gouden Eeuw', in *In de ban van het beeld. Opstellen over geschiedenis en kunst*, Hilversum 1998 (*Amsterdamse Historische Reeks. Grote serie*, 24), pp. 111–23

Cats 1620
J. Cats, *Self-stryt, dat is crachtighe bewheginghe van Vlees en Gheest…*, Middelburg 1620

De la Chambre 1638
J. de la Chambre, *Verscheyden geschriften, geschreven ende int Koper gesneden, door Jean de la Chambre, liefhebber ende beminder der pennen, tot Haarlem anno 1638*, Haarlem 1638

Ciardi 1973–4
R.B. Ciardi (ed.), *Gian Paolo Lomazzo, Scritti sulle arti*, 2 vols, Florence 1973–4

Clark 1969
K.M. Clark, *Civilisation: A Personal View*, London 1969

Cordes 2008
R. Cordes, *Jan Zoet, Amsterdammer 1609–1674. Leven en werk van een kleurrijk schrijver*, Hilversum 2008

Cornelis 1995
B. Cornelis, 'A reassessment of Arnold Houbraken's *Groote schouburgh*', *Simiolus*, 23 (1995), pp. 163–80

Cornelis 1998
B. Cornelis, 'Arnold Houbraken's *Groote schouburgh* and the canon of seventeenth-century Dutch painting', *Simiolus*, 26 (1998), pp. 144–61

Coster 1633
S. Coster, *Boere-Klucht van Teeuwis de Boer, en men Juffer van Grevelinckhuysen*, Amsterdam 1633 (1st impression 1612)

D

Davies et al. 2018
J. Davies, G. Gruber, I. Slama and E. Goetz, *Ein Maler als Modell: Van Dycks Porträt von Pieter Soutman*, Vienna 2018 (*Ansichtssache Kunsthistorisches Museum Wien*, 21)

Van Deinsen 2022
L. van Deinsen, 'Female Faces and Learned Likenesses: Author Portraits and the Construction of Female Authorship and Intellectual Authority', in *Memory and Identity in the Learned World Community Formation in the Early Modern World of Learning and Science*, eds K. Scholten, D. van Miert and K.A.E. Enenkel, Leiden and Boston 2022, pp. 81–116 (*Intersections: Interdisciplinary Studies in Early Modern Culture*, 81)

Dekker 1997
R. Dekker, *Lachen in de Gouden Eeuw. Een geschiedenis van de Nederlandse humor*, Amsterdam 1997

Delft 2011
A. Jansen et al., *De portretfabriek van Michiel van Mierevelt (1566–1641)*, exh. cat., Museum Het Prinsenhof, Delft, Zwolle 2011

Demetz 1963
P. Demetz, 'Defenses of Dutch Painting and the Theory of Realism', *Comparative Literature*, 15 (1963), pp. 97–115

Denucé 1949
J. Denucé, *Na Peter Pauwel Rubens. Documenten uit den kunsthandel te Antwerpen in de XVII eeuw van Matthijs Musson*, Antwerp and The Hague 1949

Descamps 1753
J.B. Descamps, *La vie des peintres Flamands, Allemands et Hollandois…*, vol. 1, Paris 1753

Van Deursen 1994
A.T. van Deursen, *Een dorp in de polder. Graft in de zeventiende eeuw*, Amsterdam 1994

Van Dixhoorn 2009
A. van Dixhoorn, *Lustige geesten. Rederijkers in de Noordelijke Nederlanden (1480–1650)*, Amsterdam 2009

Ten Doesschate Chu 1974
P. ten Doesschate Chu, *French Realism and the Dutch Masters: The Influence of Dutch Seventeenth-Century Painting on the Development of French Painting between 1830 and 1870*, Utrecht 1974

Dorren 2001
G.M.E. Dorren, *Eenheid en verscheidenheid. De burgers van Haarlem in de Gouden Eeuw*, Amsterdam 2001

Dudok van Heel 1975
S.A.C. Dudok van Heel, 'Een minne met een kindje door Frans Hals', *Jaarboek van het Centraal Bureau voor Genealogie*, 29 (1975), pp. 146–59

Dudok van Heel and Bok 2013
S.A.C. Dudok van Heel and M.J. Bok, 'Frans Halsen' aan de muur: omgang met familieportretten in Haarlem: Voocht-Olycan-Van der Meer, The Hague 2013

Duparc 2022
F.J. Duparc, 'Frans Hals's "Portrait of a young man holding a pair of gloves"', *The Burlington Magazine*, 164 (2022), pp. 578–80

E

Van Eeghen 1974
I.H. van Eeghen, 'Pieter Codde en Frans Hals', *Maandblad Amstelodamum*, 61 (1974), pp. 137–40

Van der Eembd 1621
G. van der Eembd, *Treur-spel Sophonisba*, The Hague 1621

Ekkart 1979
R.E.O. Ekkart, 'Johannes Verspronck, een Haarlemse portretschilder uit de zeventiende eeuw', *Antiek*, 14 (1979), no. 2, pp. 105–16

Ekkart 1987
R.E.O. Ekkart, 'Inleiding / Introduction', in R.E.O. Ekkart and E. Ornstein-van Slooten, *Oog in oog met de modellen van Rembrandts portret-etsen / Face to Face with the Sitters for Rembrandt's Etched Portraits*, exh. cat., Museum het Rembrandthuis, Amsterdam 1987, pp. 4–19

Emmens 1979
J.A. Emmens, *Rembrandt en de regels van de kunst*, Amsterdam 1979

Erasmus 1652
D. Erasmus, *Boecxken van de borgerlyke beleeftheid der kinderlyke zeden*, Amsterdam 1652 (translation of *De civilitate morum puerilium … libellus*, 1530)

F

Filedt Kok and Leesberg 2000
J.P. Filedt Kok and M. Leesberg, *The New Hollstein Dutch and Flemish Etchings, Engravings and Woodcuts ca. 1450–1700*, vol. 9: *The De Gheyn Family*, 2 vols, Rotterdam and Amsterdam 2000

Franken 1997
M. Franken, '"Aen stoelen en bancken leren gaen". Leerzame vormen van navolging in Rembrandts werkplaats', in *Album Discipulorum J.R.J. van Asperen de Boer*, eds P. van den Brink and L.M. Helmus, Zwolle 1997, pp. 66–73

Frankfurt 2005
M. Neumeister, *Holländische Gemälde im Städel 1550–1800*, vol. 1: *Künstler geboren bis 1615*, collection cat., Städelsches Kunstinstitut, Frankfurt 2005

G

Van Gelder 1906
H.E. van Gelder, 'Schilderijen te Alkmaar en Hoorn', *Oud Holland*, 24 (1906), pp. 63–4

Van Gelder 1959
J.G. van Gelder, 'Anthonie van Dyck in Holland in de zeventiende eeuw', *Bulletin Koninklijke Musea voor Schone Kunsten*, 8 (1959), pp. 43–86

Gerbier 1620
B. Gerbier, *Eer ende claght-dicht: ter eeren van den lofweerdighen constrijcken ende gheleerden Henricus Goltius, constrijcken schilder, plaetsnijder, ende meester van de penne, overleden tot Haerlem, den 29. december anno 1617*, The Hague 1620

Geurts 2020
L. Geurts, 'Enkele Caravaggeske elementen in het oeuvre van de Hollandse meester-schilderes Judith Leyster', *Desipientia*, 27 (2020), no. 1, pp. 10–16

Gombrich 1982
E.H. Gombrich, *The Image and the Eye: Further Studies in the Psychology of Pictorial Representation*, Oxford 1982

Van Gool 1750–1
J. van Gool, *De Nieuwe Schouburg der Nederlantsche kunstschilders en schilderessen…*, 2 vols, The Hague 1750–1

Goosens 2001
M.E.W. Goosens, *Schilders en de markt, Haarlem 1605–1635*, Leiden 2001, dissertation, University of Leiden, 2001

Gosselink and De Goede 2008
M. Gosselink and J. de Goede (eds), *At Home in the Golden Age: Masterpieces from the SØR Rusche Collection*, exh. cat., Kunsthal, Rotterdam, Zwolle 2008

Van Greevenbroek 1981
J.T.R. van Greevenbroek, *De Bank van Lening te Haarlem. Een instelling van weldadigheid*, Haarlem 1981

Grijp 1991
L.P. Grijp, *Het Nederlandse lied in de Gouden Eeuw*, Amsterdam 1991

Grijzenhout 2021
F. Grijzenhout, 'Adriaen van Ostade, Frans Hals, and the Art-Loving Van den Heuvel Family', *Simiolus*, 43 (2021), no. 3, pp. 170–89

Grimm 1970
C. Grimm, 'Ein Meisterliches Künstlerporträt: Frans Hals' Ostade-Bildnis', *Oud Holland*, 85 (1970), pp. 170–6

Grimm 1971
C. Grimm, 'Frans Hals und seine "Schule"', *Münchner Jahrbuch der bildenden Kunst*, 22 (1971), pp. 146–78

Grimm 1972
C. Grimm, *Frans Hals: Entwicklung, Werkanalyse, Gesamtkatalog*, Berlin 1972

Grimm 1989
C. Grimm, *Frans Hals: Das Gesamtwerk*, Stuttgart and Zurich 1989

Grimm 2023
C. Grimm, *RKD Study: Frans Hals and his Workshop*, The Hague 2023 (www.rkdstudies.nl)

Groenveld 2009
S. Groenveld, *Het Twaalfjarig Bestand, 1609–1621. De jongelingsjaren van de Republiek der Verenigde Nederlanden*, The Hague 2009

Gruber and Tomášek 2018
G. Gruber and P. Tomášek, *Albtraumhaft Schön: Rubens' Wiener Medusenhaupt trifft auf die Brünner Fassung*, Vienna 2018 (*Ansichtssache Kunsthistorisches Museum Wien*, 23)

H

Haarlem 1937
Frans Hals Tentoonstelling, exh. cat., Frans Halsmuseum, Haarlem 1937

Haarlem 1962
Frans Hals, exh. cat., Frans Halsmuseum, Haarlem 1962

Haarlem 1979
R.E.O. Ekkart, *Johannes Cornelisz. Verspronck. Leven en werken van een Haarlems portretschilder uit de 17-de eeuw*, collection cat. Frans Halsmuseum, Haarlem 1979

Haarlem 1986
E. de Jongh, *Portretten van echt en trouw. Huwelijk en gezin in de Nederlandse kunst van de zeventiende eeuw*, exh. cat., Frans Halsmuseum, Haarlem 1986

Haarlem 1988
M. Carasso-Kok and J. Levy-van Halm (eds), *Schutters in Holland. Kracht en zenuwen van de stad*, exh. cat., Frans Halsmuseum, Haarlem 1988

Haarlem 2006
P. Biesboer and N. Köhler (eds), *Painting in Haarlem 1500–1800: The Collection of the Frans Halsmuseum*, collection cat., Frans Halsmuseum, Haarlem 2006

Haarlem 2013
A. Tummers (ed.), *Frans Hals: Eye to Eye with Rembrandt, Rubens and Titian*, exh. cat., Frans Halsmuseum, Haarlem 2013

Haarlem 2017
A. Tummers, E. Kolfin and J. Hillegers (eds), *The Art of Laughter: Humour in Dutch Paintings of the Golden Age*, exh. cat. Frans Halsmuseum, Haarlem 2017

Haarlem 2018
M. Rikken and J. Rozenbroek (eds), *Frans Hals en de modernen*, exh. cat., Frans Halsmuseum, Haarlem 2018

Haarlem and Hamburg 2003
P. Biesboer and M. Sitt (eds), *Satire and Jest: Dutch Genre Painting in the Age of Frans Hals*, exh. cat., Frans Halsmuseum, Haarlem, and Hamburger Kunsthalle, Hamburg, Haarlem 2003

Haarlem and Washington 2009
A. Tummers, *Judith Leyster (1609–1660): The First Woman to Become a Master Painter*, exh. cat., Frans Halsmuseum, Haarlem, and National Gallery of Art, Washington 2009

Hagedorn 2020
L. Hagedorn, *Das Museum im Buch: Paolo Giovios Elogia und die Porträtsammelwerke des 16. Jahrhunderts*, Berlin 2020

The Hague and Münster 1974
G. Langemeijer and P. Pieper, *Gerard ter Borch, Zwolle 1617–Deventer 1681*, exh. cat., Mauritshuis, The Hague, and Landesmuseum für Kunst unde Kultureschichte, Münster, Münster 1974

Hallema 1928
A. Hallema, *Haarlemsche gevangenissen. Een bijdrage tot de geschiedenis der detentie- en strafgestichten in de grafelijke stad Haarlem*, Haarlem 1928

Haverkamp Begemann 1959
E. Haverkamp Begemann, *Willem Buytewech*, Amsterdam 1959

Van Hees 1959
C.A. van Hees, 'Archivalia betreffende Frans Hals en de zijnen', *Oud Holland*, 74 (1959), pp. 36–42

Heinsius 1616
D. Heinsius, *Dan. Heinsii Nederduytsche Poemata*, Amsterdam 1616

De Hemelaer 1612
J. de Hemelaer, *Q. Horatii Flacci Latijnschen poeets boexken / De Arte Poetica, dat is: vande weldichtens kunst…*, Haarlem 1612

Hemmer 2015
M.W. Hemmer, 'Artistic transmission in the Low Countries: De Grebber's creative imitation of Rubens', *De Zeventiende Eeuw*, 31 (2015), pp. 191–210

Hendriks 1998
E. Hendriks, 'Johannes Verspronck: The Technique of a Seventeenth Century Haarlem Portraitist', *Looking Through Paintings*, Baarn 1998 (*Leids Kunsthistorisch Jaarboek*, 11), pp. 227–68

's-Hertogenbosch 1992
C. de Mooij (ed.), *Vastenavond–Carnaval. Feesten van de omgekeerde wereld*, exh. cat., Noordbrabants Museum, 's-Hertogenbosch, Zwolle 1992

Hofrichter 1989
F.F. Hofrichter, *Judith Leyster: A Woman Painter in Holland's Golden Age*, Doornspijk 1989

Hofstede de Groot 1893
C. Hofstede de Groot, *Arnold Houbraken und seine 'Groote Schouburgh' kritisch beleuchtet*, The Hague 1893

Hofstede de Groot 1910
C. Hofstede de Groot, *Beschreibendes und kritisches Verzeichnis der Werke der hervorragendsten Holländischen Maler des XVII. Jahrhunderts, nach dem Muster von John Smith's catalogue raisonné*, vol. 3: *Frans Hals, Adriaen van Ostade, Isack van Ostade, Adriaen Brouwer*, Esslingen 1910

Hollstein 1949
F.W.H. Hollstein, *Dutch and Flemish Etchings, Engravings and Woodcuts*, vol. 2: *Berckheyde–Bodding*, Amsterdam 1949

Hollstein 1952
F.W.H. Hollstein, *Dutch and Flemish Etchings, Engravings and Woodcuts*, vol. 6: *Douffet–Floris*, Amsterdam 1952

Honig 1998
E.A. Honig, *Painting and the Market in Early Modern Antwerp*, New Haven and London 1998

De Hoop Scheffer and Keyes 1984
D. de Hoop Scheffer and G.S. Keyes, *Hollstein's Dutch and Flemish Etchings, Engravings and Woodcuts ca. 1450–1700*, vol. 28: *Louis Spirinx to M. Suys*, Blaricum 1984

Horn 2000
H.J. Horn, *The Golden Age Revisited: Arnold Houbraken's Great Theatre of Netherlandish Painters and Paintresses*, 2 vols, Doornspijk 2000

Hornback 2001
R. Hornback, 'Emblems of Folly in the First "Othello": Renaissance Blackface, Moor's Coat and "Muckender"', *Comparative Drama*, 35 (2001), no. 1 pp. 69–99

Hornback 2007
R. Hornback, 'The Folly of Racism: Enslaving Blackface and the "Natural" Fool Tradition', *Medieval and Renaissance Drama in England*, 20 (2007), pp. 46–84

Houbraken 1718–21
A. Houbraken, *De groote schouburgh der Nederlantsche konstschilders en schilderessen: waar van 'er vele met hunne beeltenissen ten tooneel verschynen, en hun levensgedrag en konstwerken beschreven worden: zynde een vervolg op het Schilderboek van K. v. Mander*, 3 vols, Amsterdam 1718–21

J

De Jager 1990
R. de Jager, 'Meester, leerjongen, leertijd. Een analyse van zeventiende-eeuwse Noord-Nederlandse leerlingcontracten van kunstschilders, goud- en zilversmeden', *Oud Holland*, 104 (1990), pp. 69–111

Jansen, Luijten and Bakker 2009
L. Jansen, H. Luijten and N. Bakker (eds), *Vincent van Gogh: The Letters. The Complete, Illustrated and Annotated Edition*, 6 vols, Amsterdam 2009

BIBLIOGRAPHY

De Jongh and Vinken 1961
E. de Jongh and P.J. Vinken, 'Frans Hals als voortzetter van een emblematische traditie: Bij het Huwelijksportret van Isaac Massa en Beatrix van der Laen', *Oud Holland*, 76 (1961), pp. 117–52

Joost-Gaugier 1982
C.L. Joost-Gaugier, 'The Early Beginnings of the Notion of "Uomini Famosi" and the "De Viris Illustribus" in Greco-Roman Literary Tradition', *Artibus et Historiae*, 3 (1982), no. 6, pp. 97–115

Jowell 1974
F.S. Jowell, 'Thoré-Bürger and the Revival of Frans Hals', *The Art Bulletin*, 56 (1974), pp. 101–17

K

Katritzky 2007
M.A. Katritzky, '"Some tymes J have a shillinge aday, and some tymes nothinge, so that J leve in great poverty": British Actors in the Paintings of Frans Hals', in *Others and Outcasts in Early Modern Europe: Picturing the Social Margins*, ed. T. Nichols, London 2007, pp. 197–214

Katritzky 2013
M.A. Katritzky, '"A Plague o' these Pickle Herring": From London Drinkers to European Stage Clown', in *Renaissance Shakespeare/ Shakespeare Renaissances: Proceedings of the Ninth World Shakespeare Congress*, eds M. Procházka, A. Hoefele, H. Scolnicov and M. Dobson, Newark 2013, pp. 116–22

Katritzky 2018
M.A. Katritzky, 'Stefanelo Botarga and Pickelhering: Fishy Italian and English Stage Clowns in Spain and Germany', in *Theatre Cultures within Globalising Empires: Looking at Early Modern England and Spain*, eds J. Kuepper and L. Pawlita, Berlin and Boston 2018, pp. 15–39

Aan de Kerk 2019
M. aan de Kerk, *Madness and the City: Interaction between the Mad, Their Families and Urban Society in Amsterdam, Rotterdam and Utrecht, 1600–1795*, dissertation, University of Amsterdam, 2019

Kernkamp 1902
G.W. Kernkamp, 'Memoriën van ridder Theodorus Rodenburg betreffende het verplaatsen van verschillende industrieën uit Nederland naar Denemarken, met daarop genomen resolutiën van koning Christiaan IV (1621)', *Bijdragen en Mededeelingen van het Historisch Genootschap*, 23 (1902), pp. 189–257

Keyes 1980
G.S. Keyes, *Hollstein's Dutch and Flemish Etchings, Engravings and Woodcuts ca. 1450–1700*, vol. 24: *Salomon Savery to Gillis van Scheyndel*, Amsterdam 1980

Knevel 1990
P. Knevel, 'De vele gezichten van Frans Hals. Een eeuw Frans Hals-onderzoek doorgelicht', *Holland*, 22 (1990), pp. 73–82

Knevel 1994
P. Knevel, *Burgers in het geweer. De schutterijen in Holland, 1550–1700*, Hilversum 1994 (*Hollandse studiën*, 32)

Köhler and Levy-van Halm 1990
N. Köhler and K. Levy-van Halm, *Frans Hals. Schuttersstukken*, The Hague 1990

Kolfin 2001
E. Kolfin, 'Portretten van liefde en lust. Portretten en portretteren in illustraties uit Noord- en Zuidneder-landse boekjes over liefde, c.1600–1635', *De Zeventiende Eeuw*, 17 (2001), pp. 121–37

Kolfin 2002
E.E.P. Kolfin, *Een geselschap jonge luyden. Productie, functie en betekenis van Noord-Nederlandse voorstellingen van vrolijke gezel-schappen 1610–1645*, dissertation, University of Leiden, 2002

Kolfin 2005
E. Kolfin, *The Young Gentry at Play: Northern Netherlandish Scenes of Merry Companies 1610–1645*, Leiden 2005

Koppenol 2001
J. Koppenol, 'Piero, de zot van Leiden', *Literatuur*, 18 (2001), pp. 234–43

Koppenol 2003
J. Koppenol, 'Pieter Cornelisz van der Mersch en de ingekeerde Leidse rederijkerij', in *Conformisten en rebellen. Rederijkerscultuur in de Nederlanden (1400–1650)*, ed. B. Ramakers, Amsterdam 2003, pp. 228–39

Koppenol 2004
J. Koppenol, 'Het zakboekje van Piero: profiel van een rederijker', *Neerlandistiek.nl*, 3 (2004), pp. 1–20

Kramer 2009
F. Kramer, *Mooi vies, knap lelijk. Grotesk realisme in rederijkers-kluchten*, Hilversum 2009

Krekeler et al. 2014
A. Krekeler, E. Smeenk-Metz, Z. Benders and M. van de Laar, 'A Technical Study of Johannes Cornelisz Verspronck's Portraits in the Rijksmuseum', *The Rijksmuseum Bulletin*, 62 (2014), pp. 2–23

Kruijswijk and Nesse 2004
M. Kruijswijk and M. Nesse, *Nederlandse jaarfeesten en hun liederen door de eeuwen heen*, Hilversum 2004

L

Lammertse 1998
F. Lammertse, with contributions from J. Giltaij and A. Janssen, *Nederlandse genreschilderijen uit de zeventiende eeuw. Eigen collectie Museum Boijmans Van Beuningen*, Rotterdam 1998

Lange, Gerkens and Lukatis 2023
J. Lange, D. Gerkens and C. Lukatis, *Frans Hals inspiriert. Der Mann mit dem Schlapphut*, Berlin and Munich 2023 (*Hessen Kassel Heritage, Wissenschaftliche Reihe*, 5)

Langereis 2001
S. Langereis, *Geschiedenis als am-bacht. Oudheidkunde in de Gouden Eeuw: Arnoldus Buchelius en Petrus Scriverius*, Hilversum 2001

Lee 1972
M. Lee Jr, *Dudley Carleton to John Chamberlain 1603–1624: Jacobean Letters*, New Brunswick, NJ, 1972

Leeflang 1997
H. Leeflang, 'Dutch Landscape: the urban view: Haarlem and its environs in literature and art, 15th–17th century', in *Natuur in landschap in de Nederlandse kunst 1500–1850/ Nature and Landscape in Nether-landish Art 1500–1850*, eds R. Falkenburg et al., Zwolle 1997 (*Nederlands Kunsthistorisch Jaarboek/Netherlands Yearbook for History of Art*, 48), pp. 53–115

Leeflang 2003
H. Leeflang, 'Van ontwerp naar prent. Tekeningen voor prenten van Nederlandse meesters (1550–1700) uit de collectie van het Prenten-kabinet van de Universiteit Leiden', special issue, *Delineavit et Sculpsit* 27 (2003), pp. 1–108

Leesberg 1993–4
M. Leesberg, 'Karel van Mander as a painter', *Simiolus*, 22 (1993–4), pp. 5–57

Leesberg 1999
M. Leesberg, *The New Hollstein Dutch and Flemish Etchings, Engravings and Woodcuts 1450–1700*, vol. 6: *Karel van Mander*, Rotterdam and Amsterdam 1999

Liedtke 2007
W. Liedtke, *Dutch Paintings in The Metropolitan Museum of Art*, 2 vols, collection cat., Metropolitan Museum of Art, New York 2007

Liedtke 2011
W. Liedtke, 'Frans Hals: Style and Substance', *The Metropolitan Museum of Art Bulletin*, 69 (2011), pp. 1, 4–48

Liedtke 2017
W. Liedtke, 'Portrait of Samuel Ampzing' (2017), in *The Leiden Collection Catalogue*, eds A.K. Wheelock Jr. and L. Yeager-Crasselt (3rd edn New York 2020–) (https://theleidencollection.com/ artwork/portrait-of-samuel-ampzing/)

Logan 2021
A.M. Logan with the cooperation of K.L. Belkin, *The Drawings of Peter Paul Rubens: A Critical Catalogue*, Turnhout 2021

London 2021
L. Packer and A. Roy, *Frans Hals: The Male Portrait*, exh. cat., Wallace Collection, London 2021

London and The Hague 2007
R. Ekkart and Q. Buvelot (eds), *Dutch Portraits: The Age of Rembrandt and Frans Hals*, exh. cat., National Gallery, London, and Koninklijk Kabinet voor Schilderijen Mauritshuis, The Hague, London 2007

Loosjes 1789
A. Loosjes Pz., *Frans Hals. Lierzang*, Haarlem 1789

Luijten and Schuckman 1989
G. Luijten and C. Schuckman, *Hollstein's Dutch and Flemish Etchings, Engravings and Woodcuts ca. 1450–1700*, vol. 33: *Jan van de Velde I to Dirk Vellert*, 2 vols, Roosendaal 1989

Lunsingh Scheurleer et al. 1986–92
T.H. Lunsingh Scheurleer, C.W. Fock and A.J. van Dissel, *Het Rapenburgh. Geschiedenis van een Leidse gracht*, 6 vols with separate index, Leiden 1986–92

M

MacLaren and Brown 1991
N. MacLaren and C. Brown, *The Dutch School 1600–1900*, 2 vols, National Gallery Catalogues, London 1991

Madrid 2012
A. Vergara and F. Lammertse, *The Young Van Dyck*, exh. cat., Museo Nacional del Prado, Madrid 2012

Van Mander 1604
K. van Mander, *Het Schilder-Boeck…*, Haarlem 1604

Van Mander 1604 (1973)
K. van Mander, *Den grondt der edel vry schilder-const*, ed. H. Miedema, 2 vols, Utrecht 1973

Van Mander 1618
K. van Mander, *Het Schilder Boeck…*, Amsterdam 1618 (2nd impression)

Mans 1998
I. Mans, *Zin der Zotheid. Vijf eeuwen cultuurgeschiedenis van zotten, onnozelen en zwakzinnigen*, Amsterdam 1998

Marandel and Walsh 2019
J.P. Marandel and A. Walsh et al., *Gifts of European Art from The Ahmanson Foundation*, vol. 3: *Dutch Painting, Flemish Painting, Spanish Painting and Sculpture*, Los Angeles 2019

Martens and Peeters 2006
M.P.J. Martens and N. Peeters, 'Paintings in Antwerp Houses (1532–1567)', in *Mapping Markets for Paintings in Europe 1450–1750*, eds N. De Marchi and H.J. van Miegroet, Turnhout 2006 (*Studies in European Urban History [1100–1800]*, 6), pp. 35–51

Mechelen 1621
De Schadt-Kiste Der Philosophen Ende Poeten…, Mechelen 1621

Melion 2023
Walter S. Melion, *Karel van Mander and his Foundation of the Noble, Free Art of Painting*, first English translation, with introduction and commentary, Leiden and Boston 2023 (*Brill's Studies on Art, Art History, and Intellectual History*, 62)

Mezger 1991
W. Mezger, *Narrenidee und Fastnachtsbrauch. Studien zur Fortlebben des Mittelalters in der europäischen Festkultur*, Constance 1991

Middelkoop and Ekkart 2024
N.E. Middelkoop and R.E.O. Ekkart (eds), *Frans Hals: A Survey of Current Research*, to be published in 2024

Middelkoop and Van Grevenstein 1988
N. Middelkoop and A. van Grevenstein, *Frans Hals. Leven, werk, restauratie*, Amsterdam 1988

Miedema 1980
H. Miedema, *De archiefbescheiden van het St. Lukasgilde te Haarlem, 1497–1798*, 2 vols, Alphen aan den Rijn 1980

Miedema 1981
H. Miedema, *Kunst, kunstenaar en kunstwerk bij Karel van Mander. Een analyse van zijn levensbeschrijvingen*, Alphen aan den Rijn 1981

Miedema 1986–7
H. Miedema, 'Over vakonderwijs aan kunstschilders in de Nederlanden tot de 17de eeuw', *Academies of Art Between Renaissance and Romanticism*, The Hague 1986–7 (*Leids Kunsthistorisch Jaarboek*, 5–6), pp. 268–82

Miedema 1994–9
H. Miedema (ed.), *Karel van Mander: The Lives of the Illustrious Netherlandish and German Painters from the First Edition of the Schilder-boeck (1603–1604)*, 6 vols, Doornspijk 1994–9

Moes 1909
E.W. Moes, *Frans Hals: sa vie et son œuvre*, Brussels 1909

Monballieu 1965
A. Monballieu, 'P.P. Rubens en het "Nachtmael" voor St. Winoksbergen (1611), een niet uitgevoerd schilderij van de meester', *Jaarboek Koninklijk Museum voor Schone Kunsten Antwerpen*, 5 (1965), pp. 183–205

De Monconys 1666
B. de Monconys, *Journal des voyages de Monsieur de Monconys…*, vol. 2, Lyons 1666

Muller 1853
F. Muller, *Beschrijvende catalogus van 7000 portretten van Nederlanders…*, Amsterdam 1853

N

Nehlsen-Marten 2003
B. Nehlsen-Marten, *Dirck Hals 1591–1656: Oeuvre und Entwicklung eines Haarlemer Genremalers*, Weimar 2003

New York 2012
J.S. Turner (ed.), *Rembrandt's World: Dutch Drawings from the Clement C. Moore Collection*, exh. cat., The Morgan Library and Museum, New York 2012

Newman and Nijkamp 2021
A.D. Newman and L. Nijkamp (eds), *Many Antwerp Hands: Collaborations in Netherlandish Art*, Turnhout 2021

Noorman and Van der Maal 2022
J. Noorman and R.J. van der Maal, *Het unieke memorieboek van Maria van Nesse (1588–1650). Nieuwe perspectieven op huishoudelijke consumptie*, Amsterdam 2022

O

Offenberg 2005
G.A.M. Offenberg, 'Boudewijn van Offenberg, de vaandrig van Frans Hals', *Haerlem Jaarboek 2004* (2005), pp. 83–106

Orenstein 1996
N.M. Orenstein, *Hendrick Hondius and the Business of Prints in Seventeenth-Century Holland*, Rotterdam 1996

Orlers 1641
J.J. Orlers, *Beschrijvinge der stadt Leyden…*, Leiden 1641

Osnabrugge 2019
M. Osnabrugge, *The Neapolitan Lives and Careers of Netherlandish Immigrant Painters (1575–1655)*, Amsterdam 2019

Oudenaarde 2018
K. Lichtert (ed.), *Adriaen Brouwer: Master of Emotions: Between Rubens and Rembrandt*, exh. cat., Stedelijk Museum Oudenaarde, 2018

P

Pelc 2002
M. Pelc, *Illustrium Imagines: das Porträtbuch der Renaissance*, Leiden, Boston and Keulen 2002 (*Studies in Medieval and Reformation Traditions*, 88)

Peltzer 1925
A.R. Peltzer, *Joachim von Sandrarts Academie der Bau-, Bild- und Mahlerey-Künste von 1675*, Munich 1925

Pers 1628a
D.P. Pers, *Bacchus Wonder-wercken: waer in het recht gebruyck en misbruyck des wijns…*, Amsterdam 1628

Pers 1628b
D.P. Pers, *Suyp-Stad of Dronckaerts Leven…*, Amsterdam 1628

Pleij 2007
H. Pleij, *Het gevleugelde woord. Geschiedenis van de Nederlandse literatuur 1400–1560*, Amsterdam 2007

Van de Pol 1996
L.C. van de Pol, *Het Amsterdamse hoerdom. Prostitutie in de zeventiende en achttiende eeuw*, Amsterdam 1996

Potgieter 1837
E.J. Potgieter, 'Frans Hals en zijne dochter', *De Gids*, 1 (1837), pp. 423–44

Programma 1900
Anoniem, *Officieel programma der feestelijkheden bij gelegenheid der onthulling van het standbeeld van Frans Hals op 14 juni 1900*, Haarlem 1900

R

Raleigh, Indianapolis and Manchester 2002
D.P. Weller (ed.), *Jan Miense Molenaer: Painter of the Dutch Golden Age*, exh. cat., North Carolina Museum of Art, Raleigh, Columbus Gallery of the Indianapolis Museum of Art, Indianapolis, and The Currier Museum of Art, Manchester, NH, Raleigh 2002

Raptschinsky 1937
B. Raptschinsky, 'Uit de geschiedenis van den Amsterdamschen handel op Rusland in de XVIIe eeuw. Georg Everhard Klenck', *Jaarboek Amstelodamum*, 34 (1937), pp. 57–83

Van der Ree-Scholtens 1995
G.F. van der Ree-Scholtens (ed.), *Deugd boven geweld. Een geschiedenis van Haarlem, 1245–1995*, Hilversum 1995

Rikken 2021
M. Rikken, 'Feest in Haarlem', *Bulletin van de Vereniging Rembrandt*, 31 (2021), pp. 14–17

Ripa (1593) 1644
C. Ripa, *Iconologia of uytbeeldingen des Verstands: van Cesare Ripa van Perugien… uyt het Italiaens vertaelt door D.P. Pers*, Amsterdam 1644 (1st Italian edn 1593)

Roberts 2012
B.B. Roberts, *Sex and Drugs before Rock 'n' Roll: Youth Culture and Masculinity during Holland's Golden Age*, Amsterdam 2012

Robins and Pennell 1908
E. Robins and J. Pennell, *The Life of James McNeill Whistler*, 2 vols, London and Philadelphia 1908

Robinson 2015
W.W. Robinson, 'The Abrams Album: An Album Amicorum of Dutch Drawings from the Seventeenth Century', *Master Drawings*, 53 (2015), no. 1, pp. 1–58

Rodenburg 1619
T. Rodenburg, *Eglentiers poëtens borst-weringh*, Amsterdam 1619

De Roever 1886
N. de Roever, 'Rijfelarijen', *Oud Holland*, 4 (1886), pp. 190–7

Van Roey 1957
J. van Roey, '"Frans Hals van Antwerpen". Nieuwe gegevens over de ouders van Frans Hals', *Antwerpen: Tijdschrift der Stad Antwerpen*, 3 (1957), pp. 117–20

Van Roey 1972
J. van Roey, 'De familie van Frans Hals. Nieuwe gegevens uit Antwerpen', *Jaarboek Koninklijk Museum voor Schone Kunsten Antwerpen*, 12 (1972), pp. 145–70

Rooses and Ruelens 1898
M. Rooses and Ch. Ruelens, *Correspondance de Rubens et documents épistolaires concernant sa vie et ses oeuvres*, vol. 2, Antwerp 1898

Roscam Abbing 2014
M. Roscam Abbing, 'Theodorus Schrevelius, Petrus Scriverius en Frans Hals. Opmerkingen bij enkele nieuwe Hals-documenten', *Haerlem Jaarboek 2013* (2014), pp. 63–98

Roscam Abbing and Tuynman 2018
M. Roscam Abbing and P. Tuynman, *Petrus Scriverius Harlemensis (1567–1660): A Key to the Correspondence, Contacts and Works of an Independent Humanist*, Leiden 2018

Rosen 2020
J. Rosen, *Pieter Codde (1599–1678): Catalogue Raisonné*, Newcastle-upon-Tyne 2020

Rotterdam 1849
A. Lamme and A.J. Lamme, *Catalogus van schilderijen enz. in het museum te Rotterdam, gesticht door Mr. F.J.O. Boymans*, collection cat., Museum Boymans, Rotterdam 1849

Rotterdam 2015
P. van der Coelen and F. Lammertse (eds), *De ontdekking van het dagelijks leven. Van Bosch tot Bruegel*, exh. cat., Museum Boijmans Van Beuningen, Rotterdam 2015

Rotterdam and Frankfurt 1999
A. Blankert et al., *Dutch Classicism in Seventeenth-Century Painting*, exh. cat., Museum Boijmans Van Beuningen, Rotterdam, and Städelsches Kunstinstitut, Frankfurt, Rotterdam 1999

BIBLIOGRAPHY

Rotterdam and Paris 1974
M. van Berge, J. Giltay, C. van
Hasselt and A.W.F.M. Meij (eds),
Willem Buytewech 1591–1624,
exh. cat., Museum Boymans-van
Beuningen, Rotterdam, and Institut
Néerlandais, Paris, Rotterdam
and Paris 1974

Royalton-Kisch 1988
M. Royalton-Kisch, *Adriaen van de
Vennes' Album in the Department of
Prints and Drawings in the British
Museum*, London and Amsterdam
1988

Rutgers 2019
J. Rutgers, 'Rubens's early
involvement in printmaking', in *Early
Rubens*, exh. cat., Art Gallery of
Ontario, Toronto, and Legion of
Honour, San Francisco, Ontario
2019, pp. 103–14

S

Sammut 2020
A. Sammut, 'With a little help
from his friends. Rubens and the
acquisition of Caravaggio's *Rosary
Madonna* for the Dominican church
in Antwerp', in *Ars Amicitiae: The
Art of Friendship in the Early
Modern Netherlands / Ars
amicitiae: de kunst van de
vriendschap in de vroegmoderne
Nederlanden*, eds H. Perry
Chapman et al., Leiden 2020
(*Netherlands Yearbook for History
of Art / Nederlands Kunsthistorisch
Jaarboek*, 70), pp. 119–58

Schatborn 1973
P. Schatborn, 'Olieverfschetsen van
Dirck Hals', *Bulletin van het Rijks-
museum*, 21 (1973), pp. 107–16

De Schepper 1987
H. de Schepper, *'Belgium Nostrum'
1500–1650. Over integratie en
desintegratie van het Nederland*,
Antwerp 1987

Schiller 2006
N.G. Schiller, *The Art of Laughter:
Society, Civility and Viewing
Practices in the Netherlands,
1600–1640*, dissertation, University
of Michigan, Ann Arbor 2006

Schiller 2010
N.G. Schiller, 'Desire and dis-
simulation: laughter as an expressive
behavior in Karel van Mander's *Den
grondt der edel vry schilder-const*
(1604)', in *De hartstochten in de
kunst in de vroegmoderne Nederlanden / The Passions in the Arts of
the Early Modern Netherlands*, eds
S.S. Dickey and H. Roodenburg,
Zwolle 2010 (*Nederlands Kunsthistorisch Jaarboek / Netherlands
Yearbook for History of Art*, 60),
pp. 82–107

Schmidt 1874
W. Schmidt, 'Dirk van Deelen und
Adriaen Brouwer', *Zeitschrift für
bildende Kunst*, 9 (1874), pp. 95–6

Von Schneider 1922
A. von Schneider, 'Gerard Honthorst
und Judith Leyster', *Oud Holland*, 40
(1922), pp. 169–73

Schrevelius 1647
T. Schrevelius, *Harlemum, sive urbis
Harlemensis incunabula, incrementa,
fortuna varia, in pace, in bello…*,
Leiden 1647

Schrevelius 1648
T. Schrevelius, *Harlemias, ofte,
om beter te seggen, de eerste
stichtinghe der stadt Haerlem…*,
Haarlem 1648

Schrickx 1983
W. Schrickx, '"Pickleherring"
and English Actors in Germany',
Shakespeare Survey Online, 36
(1983), pp. 135–47

Schuckman 1991
C. Schuckman, *Hollstein's Dutch
and Flemish Etchings, Engravings
and Woodcuts ca. 1450–1700*,
vol. 39: *Claes Jansz Visscher to
Claes Jansz Visscher II (Nicolaes
Visscher II)*, 2 vols, Roosendaal 1991

Seifert 2020
C. Seifert, 'A "Burgomaster and his
wife" indeed: Two portraits by Frans
Hals identified', in *Connoisseurship:
Essays in Honour of Fred G. Meijer*,
eds C. Dumas, R. Ekkart and
C. van de Puttelaar, Leiden 2020,
pp. 275–80

Sewter 1952
A.C. Sewter et al., *Catalogue of the
Paintings, Drawings and Miniatures
in the Barber Institute of Fine Arts,
University of Birmingham*,
Cambridge 1952

Shearman 1992
J. Shearman, *Only Connect: Art
and the Spectator in the Italian
Renaissance*, Washington and
Princeton 1992

Sinisgalli 2011
R. Sinisgalli, *Leon Battista Alberti:
On Painting. A New Translation and
Critical Edition*, Cambridge 2011

Slive 1970–4
S. Slive, *Frans Hals*, 3 vols, London
1970–1974 (*Kress Foundation
Studies in the History of Art*, 4),
London 1970–4

Slive 2014
S. Slive, *Frans Hals*, 2nd edn,
London 2014

Sluijter 1999
E.J. Sluijter, 'Over Brabantse
vodden, economische concurrentie,
artistieke wedijver en de groei van
de markt voor schilderijen in de
eerste decennia van de zeventiende
eeuw', in *Kunst voor de Markt / Art
for the Market, 1500–1700*, eds
R. Falkenburg et al., Zwolle 1999
(*Nederlands Kunsthistorisch
Jaarboek / Netherlands Yearbook
for History of Art*, 50), pp. 113–43

De Smet 1977
R. De Smet, 'Een nauwkeuriger
datering van Rubens' eerste reis
naar Holland in 1612', *Jaarboek
Koninklijk Museum voor Schone
Kunsten Antwerpen*, 17 (1977),
pp. 199–220

Van Someren 1888–91
J.F. van Someren, *Beschrijvende
catalogus van gegraveerde
portretten van Nederlanders:
vervolg op Frederik Mullers catalogus van 7000 portretten van
Nederlanders*, 3 vols, Amsterdam
1888–91

Speet 1995
B.J.M. Speet, *Het hofje van Willem
van Heijthuijsen*, Haarlem 1995

Spicer 1992
J. Spicer, 'The Renaissance elbow',
in *A Cultural History of Gesture:
From Antiquity to the Present Day*,
eds J. Bremmer and H. Roodenburg,
Ithaca 1992, pp. 84–128

Starter 1621
J.J. Starter, *Friesche Lust-hof*,
Amsterdam 1621

Stewart 1978
A.G. Stewart, *Unequal Lovers:
A Study of Unequal Couples in
Northern Art*, New York 1978

Stockholm 2005
G. Cavalli-Björkman, *Dutch and
Flemish Paintings*, vol. 2: *Dutch
Paintings, c.1600–1800*, collection
cat., Nationalmuseum, Stockholm
2005

Stukenbrock 1993
C. Stukenbrock, *Frans Hals:
Fröhliche Kinder, Musikanten und
Zecher: Eine Studie zu ausgewählten
Motivgruppen und deren Rezeptions-
geschichte*, Frankfurt am Main 1993

T

Van Thiel 1961
P.J.J. van Thiel, 'Frans Hals' portret
van de Leidse rederijkersnar Pieter
Cornelisz. van der Morsch, alias
Piero (1543–1628)', *Oud Holland*, 76
(1961), pp. 153–72

Van Thiel 1980
P.J.J. van Thiel, 'De betekenis van
het portret van Verdonck door Frans
Hals', *Oud Holland*, 94 (1980),
no. 2/3, pp. 112–40

Van Thiel 1993
P.J.J. van Thiel, 'Het portret van
Jacobus Hendricksz. Zaffius door
Frans Hals', *Oud Holland*, 107 (1993),
pp. 84–96

Van Thiel 1996
P.J.J. van Thiel, 'For Instruction
and Betterment: Samuel Ampzing's
"Mirror of the Vanity and Unrestrained-
ness of Our Age"', *Simiolus*, 24,
no. 2/3, pp. 182–200

Van Thiel 1999
P.J.J. van Thiel, *Cornelis Cornelisz
van Haarlem 1562–1638: A Monograph and Catalogue Raisonné*,
Doornspijk 1999

Thierry de Bye Dólleman 1974a
M. Thierry de Bye Dólleman,
'Nieuwe gegevens betreffende
Anneke Harmansdr., de eerste
echtgenote van Frans Hals',
Haerlem Jaarboek 1973 (1974),
pp. 249–57

Thierry de Bye Dólleman 1974b
M. Thierry de Bye Dólleman,
'Vier verschillende families "Hals"
te Haarlem', *Jaarboek van het
Centraal Bureau voor Genealogie*,
28 (1974), pp. 182–211

Thoré-Bürger 1860
E.J.T. Thoré-Bürger, *Musées de
la Hollande*, vol. 2: *Musée van
der Hoop, à Amsterdam et musée
de Rotterdam*, Paris 1860

Thoré-Bürger 1868
W. Bürger, 'Frans Hals', *Gazette des
Beaux-Arts*, 24 (1868), pp. 219–32,
431–48

Toledo, Brussels and Paris 2018
L.W. Nichols, L. De Belie and
P. Biesboer, *Frans Hals Portraits:
A Family Reunion*, exh. cat., Toledo
Museum of Art, Toledo, Royal
Museums of Fine Arts of Belgium,
Brussels, and Fondation Custodia,
Paris, Brussels 2018

Tomarken 2015
A. Tomarken, 'Borrowed Nonsense:
The *Nugae Venales* and the
Prologues of Bruscambille',
Humanistica Lovaniensia,
64 (2015), pp. 321–37

Trivas 1941
N.S. Trivas, *The Paintings
of Frans Hals*, New York 1941

Trumble 2004
A. Trumble, *A Brief History
of the Smile*, New York 2004

Turner 2014
S. Turner, *The New Hollstein Dutch
and Flemish Etchings, Engravings
and Woodcuts 1450–1700*, vol. 29:
Adriaen, Jan and Theodoor Matham,
2 vols, Ouderkerk aan den IJssel and
Amsterdam 2014

Tuynman 2006
P. Tuynman, 'The earliest extant
judgement on Rembrandt. Schrevelius and Buchelius, with an aside
on Scriverius', in *Rembrandt 2006:
Essays and New Rembrandt Documents*, ed. M. Roscam Abbing,
Leiden 2006, pp. 217–27

U

Utrecht 1792
*Catalogus van eene uitmuntende
Verzameling kostbare schilderyen …
Zijnde dit kostbaar kabinet nagelaten door den Hoog Welgeb. Heere
J.W. Barchman Wuytiers*, auction
cat., Utrecht (at the home of the
deceased), 7 September 1792 and
following days

Utrecht 1991
R.E.O. Ekkart et al., *Knappe koppen.
Vier eeuwen professorenportret*,
exh. cat., Centraal Museum and
Universiteitsmuseum, Utrecht 1991

V

Van Vaeck 1992
M. van Vaeck, 'De Schadt-Kiste
Der Philosophen Ende Poeten
(Mechelen 1621): een blazoenfeest
aan de vooravond van het einde van
het Bestand', De Zeventiende Eeuw,
8 (1992), pp. 75–80

Valentiner 1923
W.R. Valentiner, Frans Hals:
Des Meisters Gemälde in 322
Abbildungen, 2nd edn, Stuttgart,
Berlin and Leipzig 1923

Van der Veen 2002
J. van der Veen, 'Delftse
verzamelingen in de zeventiende
en eerste helft van de achttiende
eeuw', in Schatten in Delft.
Burgers verzamelen 1600–1750,
eds E. Bergvelt, M. Jonker and
A. Wiechmann, exh. cat., Stedelijk
Museum Het Prinsenhof, Museum
Lambert van Meerten and Museum
Nusantara, Delft, Zwolle 2002,
pp. 47–89

Van der Veen 2008
J. van der Veen, 'Bij het bereiken
van het zeventigste levensjaar.
Een opdracht aan Frans Pietersz
de Grebber voor de levering van
een portret in 1622', in De verbeelde
wereld. Liber amicorum voor Boudewijn Bakker, eds J.E. Abrahamse,
M. Carasso-Kok and E. Schmitz,
Bussum 2008, pp. 123–6

Van der Veen 2011
J. van der Veen, 'Danckerts en
Zonen. Prentuitgevers, plaatsnijders
en kunstverkopers te Amsterdam,
ca. 1625–1700', in Gedrukt tot
Amsterdam. Amsterdamse prent-
makers en -uitgevers in de Gouden
Eeuw, eds E. Kolfin and J. van
der Veen, exh. cat., Museum het
Rembrandthuis, Amsterdam 2011,
pp. 58–119

Van de Velde 1607
J. van de Velde, Exemplaer-boec,
inhoudende alderhande gheschrif-
ten zeer bequaem ende dienstelyck
voor de joncheydt ende allen lief-
hebbers der pennen, Amsterdam
1607

Veldman 1994
I.M. Veldman, The New Hollstein
Dutch and Flemish Etchings,
Engravings and Woodcuts
1450–1700, vol. 1: Maarten van
Heemskerck, 2 vols, Roosendaal
and Amsterdam 1994

Van de Venne 2009
H. van de Venne, Sol et sal vitae
amicitia. Het album amicorum van
Theodorus Schrevelius 1597–1602.
Met een overzicht van zijn leven
en werken, Amersfoort 2009

Verberckmoes 1998
J. Verberckmoes, Schertsen,
schimpen en schateren.
Geschiedenis van het lachen in de
Zuidelijke Nederlanden, zestiende
en zeventiende eeuw, Nijmegen
1998

Verlaan and Grootes 1978
J.E. Verlaan and E.K. Grootes (eds),
Dirck Pietersz. Pers: Suyp-stad of
dronckaerts leven. Tekstuitgave
met inleiding en aantekeningen,
Culemborg 1978

Vermeer 1993
W. Vermeer, '"Den Nederduytschen
Helicon"', in Haarlems Helicon.
Literatuur en toneel te Haarlem vóór
1800, ed. E.K. Grootes, Hilversum
1993, pp. 77–92

Vermeylen and De Clippel 2012
F. Vermeylen and K. De Clippel,
'Rubens and Goltzius in Dialogue:
Artistic Exchanges between
Haarlem and Antwerp during the
Revolt', De Zeventiende Eeuw, 28
(2012), pp. 138–60

Vlieghe 1998
H. Vlieghe, Flemish Art and
Architecture 1585–1700, New Haven
and London 1998

W

Waagen 1854
G. Waagen, Treasures of Art in
Great Britain being an Account of
the Chief Collections of Paintings,
Drawings, Sculptures, Illuminated
Mss., &c. &c., 3 vols, London 1854

Washington, London
and Haarlem 1989
S. Slive (ed.), Frans Hals, exh. cat.,
National Gallery of Art, Washington,
DC, Royal Academy of Arts, London,
and Frans Halsmuseum, Haarlem,
London 1989

Waquet 1991
F. Waquet, 'Les savants face à leurs
portraits', Nouvelles de l'estampe,
117 (1991), pp. 22–8

Weber 1987
G. Weber, '"'t Lof van den
Pekelharingh". Von alltäglichen und
absonderlichen Heringsstilleben',
Oud Holland, 101 (1987), pp. 126–40

Weller 1992
D.P. Weller, Jan Miense Molenaer
(ca. 1609/10–1668): The Life and
Art of a Seventeenth-Century
Dutch Painter, dissertation,
University of Maryland, College
Park 1992

Weller 2007
D.P. Weller, 'The Drawings of Jan
Miense Molenaer', Master Drawings,
45 (2007), no. 2, pp. 147–66

Van Wesbusch 1636
C.P. van Wesbusch, Haerlemsche
Duyn-Vreucht…, Haarlem 1636

Westermann 1997
M. Westermann, The Amusements
of Jan Steen, Zwolle 1997

Van de Wetering 1991
E. van de Wetering, 'Verdwenen
tekeningen en het gebruik van
afwisbare tekenplankjes en
"tafeletten"', Oud Holland, 105
(1991), pp. 210–27

Van de Wetering 1995
E. van de Wetering, 'De schilder',
in Gestalten van de Gouden Eeuw.
Een Hollands groepsportret, eds
H.M. Beliën et al., Amsterdam 1995,
pp. 219–39

Van de Wetering 2011
E. van de Wetering, A Corpus
of Rembrandt Paintings, vol. 5,
Dordrecht 2011

Van de Wetering 2017
E. van de Wetering, Rembrandt's
Paintings Revisited: A Complete
Survey, Heidelberg 2017

Weyerman 1729
J.C. Weyerman, De levens-
beschryvingen der Nederlandsche
konst-schilders en konst-schilde-
ressen…, vol. 1, The Hague 1729

Widerkehr 2007
L. Widerkehr, The New Hollstein
Dutch and Flemish Etchings,
Engravings and Woodcuts
1450–1700, vol. 16: Jacob Matham,
3 vols, Ouderkerk aan den IJssel
and Amsterdam 2007

Wijnaendts van Resandt 1924
W. Wijnaendts van Resandt,
Geschiedenis en genealogie van
het geslacht De Jonge uit Zierikzee
van pl.m. 1420 tot heden, n.p. 1924

Wijnman 1932
H.F. Wijnman, 'Het geboortejaar van
Judith Leyster', Oud Holland, 49 (1932),
pp. 62–5

Van der Willigen 1870
A. van der Willigen Pzn., Les artistes
de Harlem. Notices historiques avec
un précis sur la Gilde de St Luc,
Haarlem and The Hague 1870

De Winkel 2006
M. de Winkel, Fashion and Fancy:
Dress and Meaning in Rembrandt's
Paintings, Amsterdam 2006

Worcester and Haarlem 1993
J.A. Welu and P. Biesboer (eds),
Judith Leyster: A Dutch Master and
Her World, exh. cat., Worcester Art
Museum, Worcester, MA, and Frans
Halsmuseum, Haarlem, London and
New Haven 1993

Worp 1886
J.A. Worp, 'Engelsche toneelspelers
op het vasteland in de zestiende en
zeventiende eeuw', Nederlandsch
Museum, 13 (1886), pp. 65–113

     BIBLIOGRAPHY

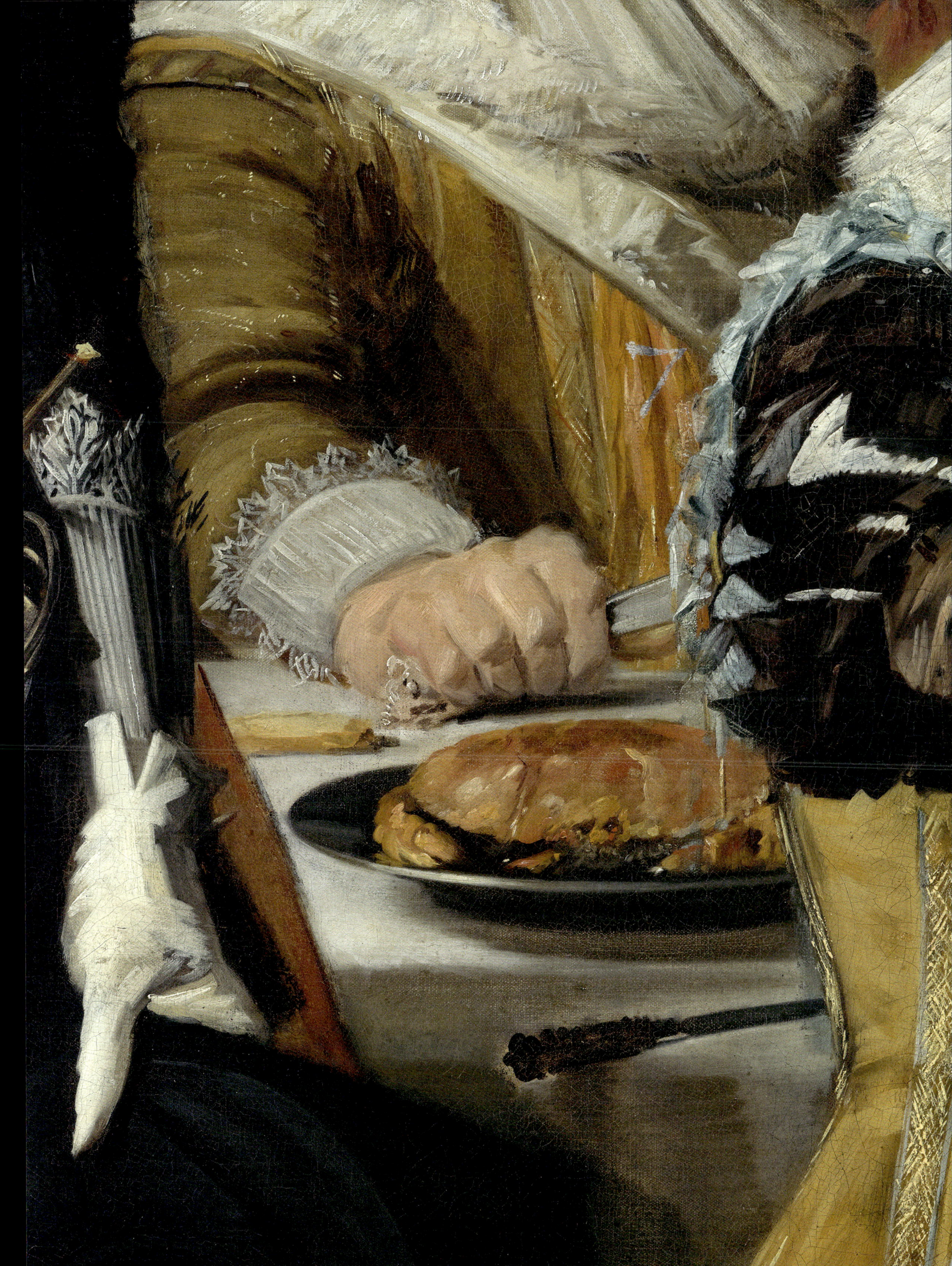

LIST OF EXHIBITED WORKS

Compiled by Tamar van Riessen
with the contribution of Justine
Rinnooy Kan.

Works are in chronological order
and then listed alphabetically by title,
apart from pendant portraits, which
are listed together.

Portrait of a Man holding a Skull,
about 1612
Oil on wood, 92.8 × 71.2 cm
The Henry Barber Trust, the Barber
Institute of Fine Arts, University of
Birmingham
Selected literature
Bode and Binder 1914, no. 88;
Valentiner 1923, p. 4; Trivas 1941,
no. 2; Slive 1970–4, no. 2; Grimm
1989, no. 6; Washington, London
and Haarlem 1989, no. 2.
[fig. 58]

Portrait of a Woman standing,
about 1612
Oil on wood, 94.2 × 71.1 cm
The Devonshire Collections,
Chatsworth
Selected literature
Bode 1883, no. 145; Moes 1909,
no. 197; Hofstede de Groot 1910,
no. 382; Bode and Binder 1914,
no. 91; Valentiner 1923, p. 48; Trivas
1941, no. 3; Slive 1970–4, no. 3;
Grimm 1989, no. 7; Washington,
London and Haarlem 1989, no. 3.
[fig. 59]

**Banquet of the Officers of the
St George Civic Guard,** 1616
Oil on canvas, 175 × 324 cm
Frans Hals Museum, Haarlem
Selected literature
Bode 1883, no. 1; Moes 1909, no. 1;
Hofstede de Groot 1910, no. 431;
Bode and Binder 1914, no. 92;
Valentiner 1923, no. p. 8; Trivas 1941,
no. 4; Slive 1970–4, no. 7; Grimm
1989, no. 4; Köhler and Levy-van
Halm 1990, no. 1.
[Amsterdam only, fig. 68]

**Portrait of Pieter Cornelisz van
der Mersch,** 1616
Oil on canvas, transferred from panel,
87.5 × 69.2 cm
Carnegie Museum of Art, Pittsburgh.
Acquired through the generosity
of Mrs Alan M. Scaife (61.42.2)
Selected literature
Bode 1883, no. 143; Moes 1909,
no. 259; Hofstede de Groot 1910,
no. 205; Bode and Binder 1914, no. 89;
Valentiner 1923, p. 11; Van Thiel 1961;
Slive 1970–4, no. 6; Grimm 1989,
no. 3; Washington, London and
Haarlem 1989, no. 4.
[fig. 151]

**Portrait of a Young Man holding
a Pair of Gloves,** about 1619
Oil on wood, 24.5 × 19 cm
Rose-Marie and Eijk de Mol
van Otterloo Collection
Selected literature
Moes 1909, no. 167; Hofstede de
Groot 1910, no. 260; Bode and Binder
1914, no. 87; Valentiner 1923, p. 7;
Slive 1970–4, no. D 37 (as attributed
to Willem Buytewech); Duparc 2022.
[fig. 73]

**Portrait of Catharina Hooft
with her Nurse,** 1619–20
Oil on canvas, 91.8 × 68.3 cm
Staatliche Museen zu Berlin,
Gemäldegalerie
Selected literature
Bode 1883, no. 87; Moes 1909,
no. 92; Hofstede de Groot 1910,
no. 429; Bode and Binder 1914,
no. 131; Valentiner 1923, p. 15; Trivas
1941, no. 1; Slive 1970–4, no. 14;
Grimm 1989, no. 5; Washington,
London and Haarlem 1989, no. 9.
[fig. 60]

The Rommel-Pot Player,
about 1620
Oil on canvas, 106 × 80.3 cm
Kimbell Art Museum, Fort Worth,
Texas
Selected literature
Hofstede de Groot 1910, no. 137, 5;
Bode and Binder 1914, no. 10;
Valentiner 1923, p. 24; Trivas 1941,
no. 3; Slive 1970–4, no. L3-1 (as a
copy); Washington, London and
Haarlem 1989, no. 8 (as by Hals).
[fig. 172]

**Portrait of Isaac Abrahamsz
Massa,** 1622
Oil on canvas mounted on wood,
107 × 85 cm
The Devonshire Collections,
Chatsworth
Selected literature
Bode 1883, no. 137; Moes 1909,
no. 156; Hofstede de Groot 1910,
no. 287; Bode and Binder 1914,
no. 152; Valentiner 1923, p. 41; Trivas
1941, no. 9; Slive 1970–4, no. 18;
Grimm 1989, no. 16; Washington,
London and Haarlem 1989, no. 13.
[fig. 94]

**Portrait of a Couple, probably
Isaac Abrahamsz Massa and
Beatrix van der Laen,** about 1622
Oil on canvas, 140 × 166.5 cm
Rijksmuseum, Amsterdam
(SK-A-133)
Selected literature
Bode 1883, no. 15; Moes 1909,
no. 90; Hofstede de Groot 1910,
no. 427; Bode and Binder 1914,
no. 96; Valentiner 1923, p. 20; Trivas
1941, no. 13; Slive 1970–4, no. 17;
Grimm 1989, no. 26; Washington,
London and Haarlem 1989, no. 12;
Bikker et al. 2007, no. 104.
[fig. 61]

The Lute Player, about 1623
Oil on canvas, 70 × 62 cm
Musée du Louvre, Paris, Paintings
Department (RF 1984 32)
Selected literature
Bode 1883, no. 45; Moes 1909,
no. 216; Hofstede de Groot 1910,
no. 98; Bode and Binder 1914, no. 71;
Valentiner 1923, p. 29; Trivas 1941,
no. 4; Slive 1970–4, no. 19; Grimm
1989, no. 24; Washington, London
and Haarlem 1989, no. 14.
[fig. 177]

The Laughing Cavalier, 1624
Oil on canvas, 83 × 67.3 cm
The Wallace Collection, London
Selected literature
Bode 1883, no. 141; Moes 1909,
no. 120; Hofstede de Groot 1910,
no. 291; Bode and Binder 1914, no. 100;
Valentiner 1923, p. 38; Trivas 1941,
no. 12; Slive 1970–4, no. 30; Grimm
1989, no. 18; London 2021.
[fig. 78]

The Merry Lute Player, about 1624–8
Oil on wood, 100 × 90 cm
Guildhall Art Gallery, City of London
Corporation
Selected literature
Moes 1909, no. 241; Hofstede de
Groot 1910, no. 82; Bode and Binder
1914, no. 58; Valentiner 1923, p. 58;
Trivas 1941, no. 27; Slive 1970–4,
no. 26; Grimm 1989, no. 33.
[fig. 157]

Pekelharing (The Merry Drinker),
about 1625
Oil on canvas, 76.5 × 64 cm
Museum der bildenden Künste Leipzig
(Museum of Fine Arts Leipzig)
Selected literature
Moes 1909, no. 268; Hofstede de
Groot 1910, no. 96; Bode and Binder
1914, no. 65; Valentiner 1923, p. 143;
Trivas 1941, no. 34; Slive 1970–4,
no. 65; Grimm 1989, no. 58;
Washington, London and Haarlem
1989, no. 32.
[fig. 154]

Portrait of Michiel de Wael,
about 1625
Oil on canvas, 118.8 × 95.3 cm
Taft Museum of Art, Cincinnati, Ohio.
Bequest of Charles Phelps and Anna
Sinton Taft (1931.450)
Selected literature
Bode 1883, no. 73; Moes 1909, no. 83;
Hofstede de Groot 1910, no. 242;
Bode and Binder 1914, no. 168; Valen-
tiner 1923, p. 120; Slive 1970–4, no. 85;
Grimm 1989, no. 29; M. de Winkel
in Buijsen, Dumas and Manuth 2012.
[fig. 84]

Portrait of Cunera van Baersdorp,
about 1625
Oil on canvas, 123.8 × 95.3 cm
Susan and Matthew Weatherbie
Collection
Selected literature
Moes 1909, no. 195; Hofstede de
Groot 1910, no. 391; Bode and Binder
1914, no. 101; Valentiner 1923, p. 183;
Slive 1970–4, no. 120; Grimm 1989,
no. 50; M. de Winkel in Buijsen,
Dumas and Manuth 2012.
[fig. 85]

**Portrait of Willem van
Heythuysen,** about 1625
Oil on canvas, 204.5 × 134.5 cm
Bayerische Staatsgemäldesamm-
lungen München – Alte Pinakothek
Selected literature
Bode 1883, no. 123; Moes 1909, no. 44;
Hofstede de Groot 1910, no. 191;
Bode and Binder 1914, no. 220;
Valentiner 1923, p. 153; Trivas 1941,
no. 64; Slive 1970–4, no. 31; Grimm
1989, no. 23; Washington, London
and Haarlem 1989, no. 17.
[fig. 81]

**Portrait of Isaac Abrahamsz
Massa,** 1626
Oil on canvas, 79.7 × 65.1 cm
Collection Art Gallery of Ontario,
Toronto. Bequest of Frank P. Wood,
1955 (54/31)
Selected literature
Moes 1909, no. 122; Hofstede de
Groot 1910, no. 246; Bode and Binder
1914, no. 108; Valentiner 1923, p. 45;
Trivas 1941, no. 20; Slive 1970–4, no.
42; Grimm 1989, no. 30; Washington,
London and Haarlem 1989, no. 21.
[fig. 93]

**Banquet of the Officers of the
St George Civic Guard,** about 1627
Oil on canvas, 179 × 257.5 cm
Frans Hals Museum, Haarlem
Selected literature
Bode 1883, no. 2; Moes 1909, no. 2;
Hofstede de Groot 1910, no. 432;
Bode and Binder 1914, no. 113; Valen-
tiner 1923, p. 63; Trivas 1941, no. 31;
Slive 1970–4, no. 46; Grimm 1989,
no. 36; Köhler and Levy-van Halm
1990, no. 3.
[fig. 69]

Boy with Flute, about 1627
Oil on canvas, 68.8 × 55.2 cm
Staatliche Museen zu Berlin,
Gemäldegalerie
Selected literature
Bode 1883, no. 90; Moes 1909,
no. 218; Hofstede de Groot 1910,
no. 81; Bode and Binder 1914, no. 56;
Valentiner 1923, p. 55; Trivas 1941,
no. 25; Slive 1970–4, no. 25; Grimm
1989, no. 37; Washington, London
and Haarlem 1989, no. 15.
[fig. 162]

Portrait of Pieter(?) Verdonck,
about 1627
Oil on wood, 46.7 × 35.5 cm
National Galleries of Scotland.
Presented by John J. Moubray
of Naemoor, 1916
Selected literature
Moes 1909, no. 80; Hofstede de
Groot 1910, no. 235; Bode and
Binder 1914, no. 297; Trivas 1941,
no. 10; Slive 1970–4, no. 57; Van
Thiel 1980; Grimm 1989, no. 39;
Washington, London and Haarlem
1989, no. 24.
[fig. 90]

**Young Man holding a Skull
(Vanitas),** about 1627
Oil on canvas, 92.2 × 80.8 cm
The National Gallery, London.
Bought 1980 (NG6458)
Selected literature
Hofstede de Groot 1910, no. 102;
Bode and Binder 1914, no. 64;
Valentiner 1923, p. 227; Trivas 1941,
no. 26; Slive 1970–4, no. 61; Grimm
1989, no. 34; Washington, London
and Haarlem 1989, no. 29.
[fig. 64]

Boy playing the Violin, about 1628
Oil on wood, 20.3 × 20.3 cm
The Jordan and Thomas A. Saunders
III Collection, on loan to the Virginia
Museum of Fine Arts (L2020.6.15)
Selected literature
Moes 1909, no. 237; Hofstede de
Groot 1910, no. 87; Bode and Binder
1914, no. 45; Valentiner 1923, p. 68;
Slive 1970–4, no. 53; Washington,
London and Haarlem 1989, no. 26.
[fig. 13]

Girl singing, about 1628
Oil on wood, 20.3 × 20.3 cm
The Jordan and Thomas
A. Saunders III Collection, on loan
to the Virginia Museum of Fine Arts
(L2020.6.14)
Selected literature
Moes 1909, no. 238; Hofstede de
Groot 1910, no. 118; Bode and Binder
1914, no. 46; Valentiner 1923, p. 68;
Slive 1970–4, no. 54; Grimm 1989,
no. 52; Washington, London and
Haarlem 1989, no. 25.
[fig. 12]

A Militiaman holding a Berkemeyer, known as the 'Merry Drinker',
about 1629
Oil on canvas, 80 × 66.5 cm
Rijksmuseum, Amsterdam (SK-A-135)
Selected literature
Bode 1883, no. 17; Moes 1909, no. 264;
Hofstede de Groot 1910, no. 63; Bode
and Binder 1914, no. 53; Valentiner
1923, p. 61; Trivas 1941, no. 32; Slive
1970–4, no. 63; Grimm 1989, no. 51;
Washington, London and Haarlem
1989, no. 30; Bikker et al. 2007,
no. 105.
[fig. 175]

Portrait of a Man, 1630
Oil on canvas, 116.7 × 90.2 cm
The Royal Collection / HM King
Charles III
Selected literature
Bode 1883, no. 134; Moes 1909,
no. 125; Hofstede de Groot 1910,
no. 286; Bode and Binder 1914,
no. 126; Valentiner 1923, p. 84;
Trivas 1941, no. 37; Slive 1970–4,
no. 68; Grimm 1989, no. 53;
Washington, London and Haarlem
1989, no. 38.
[London only, fig. 80]

Frans Hals and Claes van Heussen
**Young Woman with a Display
of Fruit and Vegetables**, 1630
Oil on canvas, 157 × 200 cm
Private collection
Selected literature
Hofstede de Groot 1910, no. 121c;
Slive 1970–4, no. 70; Grimm 1989,
no. 54; Washington, London and
Haarlem 1989, no. 33.
[fig. 27]

Laughing Boy, about 1630
Oil on wood, 30.4 × 30.4 cm
Royal Picture Gallery Mauritshuis,
The Hague. Purchased with the sup-
port of the Rembrandt Association,
the Prince Bernhard Culture Fund
and the Friends of the Mauritshuis
Foundation, 1968 (1032)
Selected literature
Bode 1883, no. 113; Moes 1909,
no. 235; Hofstede de Groot 1910,
no. 28; Bode and Binder 1914, no. 29;
Valentiner 1923, p. 31; Slive 1970–4,
no. 29; Grimm 1989, no. 19; Washing-
ton, London and Haarlem 1989, no. 16.
[Amsterdam only, fig. 164]

**Laughing Boy with
a Wine Glass**, about 1630
Oil on wood, 38 × 38 cm
Staatliche Schlösser, Gärten und
Kunstsammlungen Mecklenburg-
Vorpommern, Schwerin
Selected literature
Bode 1883, no. 117; Moes 1909,
no. 229; Hofstede de Groot 1910,
no. 11; Bode and Binder 1914, no. 8;
Valentiner 1923, p. 52; Trivas 1941,
no. 29; Slive 1970–4, no. 58; Grimm
1989, no. 46; Washington, London
and Haarlem 1989, no. 27.
[fig. 165]

**Laughing Boy with
a Flute**, about 1630
Oil on wood, 37.5 × 37.5 cm
Staatliche Schlösser, Gärten und
Kunstsammlungen Mecklenburg-
Vorpommern, Schwerin

Selected literature
Bode 1883, no. 118; Moes 1909,
no. 230; Hofstede de Groot 1910,
no. 32; Bode and Binder 1914, no. 9;
Valentiner 1923, p. 53; Trivas 1941,
no. 30; Slive 1970–4, no. 59; Grimm
1989, no. 47; Washington, London
and Haarlem 1989, no. 28.
[fig. 166]

Laughing Fisherboy,
about 1630
Oil on canvas, 82 × 60.2 cm
Private collection
Selected literature
Moes 1909, no. 253; Hofstede de
Groot 1910, no. 50; Bode and Binder
1914, no. 74; Valentiner 1923, p. 114;
Slive 1970–4, no. 55.
[Amsterdam only, fig. 167]

Young Woman ('La Bohémienne'),
about 1632
Oil on wood, 58 × 52 cm
Musée du Louvre, Paris, Paintings
Department (MI 926)
Selected literature
Bode 1883, no. 41; Moes 1909,
no. 263; Hofstede de Groot 1910,
no. 119; Bode and Binder 1914,
no. 73; Valentiner 1923, p. 130;
Trivas 1941, no. 36; Slive 1970–4,
no. 62; Grimm 1989, no. 28.
[fig. 159]

**Militia Company of District XI
under the Command of Captain
Reynier Reael, known as
'The Meagre Company'**, 1633
(completed by Pieter Codde, 1637)
Oil on canvas, 209 × 429 cm
Rijksmuseum, Amsterdam. On
loan from the City of Amsterdam
(SK-C-374)
Selected literature
Bode 1883, no, 19; Moes 1909, no. 5;
Hofstede de Groot 1910, no. 428;
Bode and Binder 1914, no. 159;
Valentiner 1923, p. 119; Slive 1970–4,
no. 80; Grimm 1989, no. 70;
Washington, London and Haarlem
1989, no. 43; Bikker et al. 2007,
no. 112.
[fig. 70]

Portrait of Pieter van den Broecke,
1633
Oil on canvas, 68.3 × 54.9 cm
English Heritage, The Iveagh
Bequest (Kenwood, London)
Selected literature
Bode 1883, no. 67; Moes 1909,
no. 21; Bode and Binder 1914,
no. 181; Valentiner 1923, p. 163;
Trivas 1941, no. 42; Slive 1970–4,
no. 84; Grimm 1989, no. 61;
Washington, London and Haarlem
1989, no. 44.
[fig. 11]

Portrait of Tieleman Roosterman,
1634
Oil on canvas, 117 × 87 cm
The Cleveland Museum of Art,
Leonard C. Hanna Jr. Fund
(1999.173)
Selected literature
Bode 1883, no. 126; Moes 1909,
no. 131; Hofstede de Groot 1910,
no. 354; Slive 1970–4, no. 93;
Grimm 1989, no. 76.
[fig. 9]

Portrait of Catharina Brugman,
1634
Oil on canvas, 115 × 85 cm
Private collection
Selected literature
Bode 1883, no. 59; Moes 1909,
no. 66; Hofstede de Groot 1910,
no. 218; Bode and Binder 1914,
no. 143; Valentiner 1923, p. 122;
Slive 1970–4, no. 94; Grimm 1989,
no. 77.
[fig. 10]

Portrait of Lucas de Clercq,
about 1635
Oil on canvas, 121.6 × 91.5 cm
Rijksmuseum, Amsterdam. On loan
from the City of Amsterdam, 1891
(SK-C-556)
Selected literature
Moes 1909, no. 24; Hofstede de
Groot 1910, no. 165; Bode and Binder
1914, no. 160; Valentiner 1923, p. 138;
Trivas 1941, no. 22; Slive 1970–4,
no. 104; Grimm 1989, no. 45;
Washington, London and Haarlem
1989, no. 46; Bikker et al. 2007,
no. 108.
[Amsterdam only, fig. 7]

**Portrait of Feyntje van
Steenkiste**, 1635
Oil on canvas, 121.9 × 91.5 cm
Rijksmuseum, Amsterdam. On loan
from the City of Amsterdam, 1891
(SK-C-557)
Selected literature
Moes 1909, no. 25; Hofstede de
Groot 1910, no. 166; Bode and Binder
1914, no. 161; Valentiner 1923, p. 139;
Trivas 1941, no. 58; Slive 1970–4,
no. 105; Washington, London and
Haarlem 1989, no. 47; Bikker et al.
2007, no. 109.
[Amsterdam only, fig. 8]

Portrait of a Man, about 1635
Oil on canvas, 79.5 × 66.5 cm
Rijksmuseum, Amsterdam. Gift
of Jonkheer J.S.R. van de Poll,
Arnhem, 1885 (SK-A-1246)
Selected literature
Moes 1909, no. 42; Hofstede de
Groot 1910, no. 186; Bode and Binder
1914, no. 115; Valentiner 1923, p. 102;
Trivas 1941, no. 60; Slive 1970–4,
no. 86; Grimm 1989, no. 73; Bikker
et al. 2007, no. 106.
[Amsterdam only]

Portrait of a Woman, about 1635
Oil on canvas, 81.5 × 68 cm
Rijksmuseum, Amsterdam. Gift of
Jonkheer J.S.R. van de Poll,
Arnhem, 1885 (SK-A-1247)
Selected literature
Moes 1909, no. 43; Hofstede de
Groot 1910, no. 187; Bode and Binder
1914, no. 116; Valentiner 1923, p. 103;
Trivas 1941, no. 61; Slive 1970–4,
no. 87; Grimm 1989, no. 74; Bikker
et al. 2007, no. 107.
[Amsterdam only]

Portrait of Pieter Dircksz Tjarck,
about 1635
Oil on canvas, 85.3 × 69.9 cm
Los Angeles County Museum of Art.
Gift of The Ahmanson Foundation
Selected literature
Moes 1909, no. 77; Hofstede de
Groot 1910, no. 231; Bode and Binder
1914, no. 178; Valentiner 1923, p. 172;
Trivas 1941, no. 65; Slive 1970–4,
no. 108; Grimm 1989, no. 92.
[London only, fig. 91]

Portrait of Marie Larp,
about 1635
Oil on canvas, 83.4 × 68.1 cm
The National Gallery, London.
Presented by the Misses Rachel
F. and Jean I. Alexander; entered
the collection 1972 (NG6413)
Selected literature
Moes 1909, no. 78; Hofstede de
Groot 1910, no. 232; Bode and
Binder 1914, no. 179; Valentiner 1923,
p. 173; Trivas 1941, no. 66; Slive
1970–4, no. 112; Grimm 1989, no. 82.
[London only, fig. 92]

**Portrait of a Man, possibly
Nicolaes Pietersz Duyst
van Voorhout**, about 1637
Oil on canvas, 80.6 × 66 cm
The Metropolitan Museum of Art,
The Jules Bache Collection, 1949
(49.7.33)
Selected literature
Bode 1883, no. 153; Moes 1909,
no. 33; Hofstede de Groot 1910,
no. 176; Bode and Binder 1914,
no. 114; Valentiner 1923, p. 154;
Trivas 1941, no. 62; Slive 1970–4,
no. 119; Grimm 1989, no. 81;
Washington, London and Haarlem
1989, no. 52.
[fig. 79]

**Portrait of Jean de la Chambre
at the Age of 33**, 1638
Oil on wood, 20.6 × 16.8 cm
The National Gallery, London.
Presented by the Misses Rachel
F. and Jean I. Alexander; entered
the collection 1972 (NG6411)
Selected literature
Moes 1909, no. 50; Hofstede de
Groot 1910, no. 164; Bode and Binder
1914, no. 166; Valentiner 1923, p. 169;
Slive 1970–4, no. 122; Grimm 1989,
no. 89; Washington, London and
Haarlem 1989, no. 50.
[fig. 115]

Jonas Suyderhoef after Frans Hals
**Portrait of Jean de la Chambre
at the Age of 33**, 1638
Engraving, 25.7 × 17.4 cm
Rijksmuseum, Amsterdam.
Transfer of the Royal Library, 1816
(RP-P-OB-60.744)
Selected literature
De Hoop Scheffer and Keyes 1984,
no. 96-2.
[London only, fig. 116]

Fisherboy, about 1638
Oil on canvas, 74 × 61 cm
Royal Museum of Fine Arts
Antwerp – Flemish Community
Selected literature
Bode 1883, no. 37; Moes 1909,
no. 254; Bode and Binder 1914,
no. 76; Valentiner 1923, p. 117; Slive
1970–4, no. 71; Washington, London
and Haarlem 1989, no. 34.
[fig. 168]

**Portrait of Willem van
Heythuysen seated in a Chair**,
about 1638
Oil on wood, 47 × 36.7 cm
Private collection, Courtesy
Richard Nagy Ltd., London
Selected literature
Bode 1883, no. 44; Moes 1909,
no. 45; Hofstede de Groot 1910,
no. 190; Bode and Binder 1914,
no. 221; Trivas 1941, no. 5; London
and The Hague 2007, no. 20.
[fig. 50]

Malle Babbe, about 1640
Oil on canvas, 78.5 × 66.2 cm
Staatliche Museen zu Berlin,
Gemäldegalerie
Selected literature
Bode 1883, no. 92; Moes 1909,
no. 260; Hofstede de Groot 1910,
no. 108; Bode and Binder 1914,
no. 68; Valentiner 1923, p. 142;
Trivas 1941, no. 33; Slive 1970–4,
no. 75; Grimm 1989, no. 111;
Washington, London and Haarlem
1989, no. 37.
[fig. 171]

Portrait of Jasper Schade, 1645
Oil on canvas, 80 × 67.5 cm
National Gallery Prague
Selected literature
Bode 1883, no. 124; Moes 1909, no.
68; Hofstede de Groot 1910, no. 221;
Bode and Binder 1914, no. 244;
Valentiner 1923, p. 226; Slive 1970–4,
no. 168; Grimm 1989, no. 126;
Washington, London and Haarlem
1989, no. 62.
[fig. 88]

Portrait of François Wouters,
about 1645
Oil on canvas, 115 × 86.1 cm
National Galleries of Scotland.
Presented by William McEwan, 1885
Selected literature
Moes 1909, no. 109; Hofstede de
Groot 1910, no. 274; Bode and Binder
1914, no. 169; Valentiner 1923,
p. 206; Slive 1970–4, no. 156;
Washington, London and Haarlem
1989, no. 57; Seifert 2020.
[London only, fig. 86]

Portrait of Susanna Baillij,
about 1645
Oil on canvas, 115 × 85.8 cm
National Galleries of Scotland.
Presented by William McEwan, 1885
Selected literature
Moes 1909, no. 110; Hofstede de
Groot 1910, no. 377; Bode and Binder
1914, no. 170; Valentiner 1923,
p. 207; Slive 1970–4, no. 157;
Washington, London and Haarlem
1989, no. 58; Seifert 2020.
[London only, fig. 87]

Family Group in a Landscape,
about 1646
Oil on canvas, 202 × 285 cm
Museo Nacional Thyssen-
Bornemisza, Madrid
Selected literature
Moes 1909, no. 89; Hofstede de
Groot 1910, no. 441; Bode and
Binder 1914, no. 272; Valentiner
1923, p. 229; Slive 1970–4, no. 177;
Washington, London and Haarlem
1989, no. 67; Toledo, Brussels and
Paris 2018.
[fig. 62]

A Family Group in a Landscape,
about 1648
Oil on canvas, 148.5 × 251 cm
The National Gallery, London.
Bought from Lord Talbot of
Malahide, Malahide Castle,
near Dublin, 1908 (NG2285)
Selected literature
Moes 1909, no. 88; Hofstede
de Groot 1910, no. 439; Bode and
Binder 1914, no. 271; Valentiner 1923,
p. 248; Slive 1970–4, no. 176; Toledo,
Brussels and Paris 2018.
[London only]

Portrait of a Man, about 1650
Oil on canvas, 110.5 × 86.4 cm
The Metropolitan Museum of Art,
Marquand Collection, Gift of Henry
G. Marquand, 1890 (91.26.9)
Selected literature
Moes 1909, no. 184; Hofstede de
Groot 1910, no. 297; Bode and
Binder 1914, no. 260; Valentiner
1923, p. 266; Slive 1970–4, no. 190;
Grimm 1989, no. 136; Washington,
London and Haarlem 1989, no. 70.
[London only, fig. 89]

**Portrait of a Man, possibly
a Clergyman**, about 1658
Oil on wood, 37.1 × 29.8 cm
Rijksmuseum, Amsterdam.
Purchased with the support of the
Vereniging Rembrandt (SK-A-2859)
Selected literature
Valentiner 1923, p. 269; Trivas 1941,
no. 88; Slive 1970–4, no. 208;
Grimm 1989, no. 138; Bikker et al.
2007, no. 111.
[fig. 120]

Portrait of a Young Woman,
about 1658
Oil on canvas, 60 × 55.5 cm
Ferens Art Gallery: Hull Museums
Selected literature
Slive 1970–4, no. 196; Washington,
London and Haarlem 1989, no. 74.
[London only, fig. 63]

Portrait of a Man in a Slouch Hat,
about 1660
Oil on canvas, 79.5 × 66.5 cm
Hessen Kassel Heritage
Selected literature
Bode 1883, no. 101; Moes 1909,
no. 174; Hofstede de Groot 1910,
no. 268; Bode and Binder 1914,
no. 280; Valentiner 1923, p. 289;
Trivas 1941, no. 107; Slive 1970–4,
no. 217; Grimm 1989, no. 145;
Washington, London and Haarlem
1989, no. 83; Lange, Gerkens and
Lukatis 2023.
[fig. 101]

Portrait of an Unknown Man,
about 1660
Oil on canvas, 80 × 67 cm
The Syndics of the Fitzwilliam
Museum, University of Cambridge
Selected literature
Moes 1909, no. 152; Hofstede de
Groot 1910, no. 264; Bode and
Binder 1914, no. 240; Valentiner
1923, p. 287; Slive 1970–4, no. 218.
[London only, fig. 102]

**Regents of the Old Men's Alms
House**, about 1664
Oil on canvas, 172.3 × 256 cm
Frans Hals Museum, Haarlem
Selected literature
Bode 1883, no. 7; Moes 1909, no. 8;
Hofstede de Groot 1910, no. 437;
Bode and Binder 1914, no. 287;
Valentiner 1923, p. 290; Trivas 1941,
no. 108; Slive 1970–4, no. 221;
Grimm 1989, no. 143; Washington,
London and Haarlem 1989, no. 85.
[fig. 3]

**Regentesses of the Old Men's
Alms House**, about 1664
Oil on canvas, 170.5 × 249.5 cm
Frans Hals Museum, Haarlem
Selected literature
Bode 1883, no. 8; Moes 1909, no. 9;
Hofstede de Groot 1910, no. 438;
Bode and Binder 1914, no. 286;
Valentiner 1923, p. 291; Trivas 1941,
no. 109; Slive 1970–4, no. 222;
Washington, London and Haarlem
1989, no. 86.
[Amsterdam only, fig. 4]

PHOTOGRAPHIC CREDITS

LIST OF LENDERS

Amsterdam
Rijksmuseum

Antwerp
Royal Museum of Fine Arts Antwerp

Bakewell
The Devonshire Collections,
Chatsworth

Berlin
Staatliche Museen zu Berlin,
Gemäldegalerie

Birmingham
The Henry Barber Trust,
the Barber Institute of Fine Arts,
University of Birmingham

Cambridge
The Fitzwilliam Museum

Cincinnati
Taft Museum of Art

Cleveland
The Cleveland Museum of Art

Edinburgh
National Galleries of Scotland

Fort Worth
Kimbell Art Museum

Haarlem
Frans Hals Museum

Hull
Ferens Art Gallery

Kassel
Museumslandschaft Hessen Kassel,
Gemäldegalerie Alte Meister

Leipzig
Museum of Fine Arts Leipzig

London
Guildhall Art Gallery, City of London
Corporation
His Majesty The King
Kenwood House
The National Gallery
The Wallace Collection

Los Angeles
Los Angeles County Museum of Art

Madrid
Museo Nacional Thyssen-
Bornemisza

Munich
Bayerische Staatsgemälde-
sammlungen München –
Alte Pinakothek

New York
The Metropolitan Museum of Art

Paris
Musée du Louvre,
Paintings Department

Pittsburgh
Carnegie Museum of Art

Prague
National Gallery Prague

Richmond
The Jordan and Thomas A. Saunders
III Collection, on loan to the Virginia
Museum of Fine Arts

Schwerin
Staatliche Schlösser, Gärten und
Kunstsammlungen Mecklenburg-
Vorpommern, Schwerin

The Hague
Royal Picture Gallery Mauritshuis

Toronto
Art Gallery of Ontario

Rose-Marie and Eijk de Mol van
Otterloo Collection
Susan and Matthew Weatherbie
Collection
Private collection, Courtesy Richard
Nagy Ltd

And all those private collectors who
wish to remain anonymous

ACKNOWLEDGEMENTS

Liesbeth Abraham
Paul Ackroyd
Janneke van Asperen
Christopher Atkins
Piet Bakker
Maria del Mar Borobia
Xavier Bray
Alexander de Bruin
Quentin Buvelot
Sabine Craft-Giepmans
Sara van Dijk
Arjan van Dixhoorn
Blaise Ducos
Ellis Dullaart
Frits Duparc
Adam Eaker
Bernd Ebert
Frans Grijzenhout
Gerlinde Gruber
Dagmar Hirschfelder
Willem Jan Hoogsteder
Nico van Hout
Jacobine Huisken
Larry Keith
Katja Kleinert
Lidewij de Koekkoek
Lotte Kokkedee
Justus Lange
Leah Lehmbeck
Fred Meijer
Norbert Middelkoop
Floris Mulder
Otto Naumann
Jan Nicolaisen
Charles Noble
Carlo van Oosterhout
Rose-Marie and Eijk van Otterloo
Lelia Packer
Marrigje Rikken
Pieter Roelofs
Michiel Roscam Abbing
Jaco Rutgers
Alysia Sawicka
Eddy Schavemaker
Elizabeth Scott
Gero Seelig
Tico Seifert
Marika Spring
Cécile Tainturier
Emilie den Tonkelaar
Anna Tummers
Bernard Vermet
Henrietta Ward
Susan and Matthew Weatherbie
Dennis Weller
Robert Wenley
Arthur K. Wheelock Jr.
Charlotte Wytema

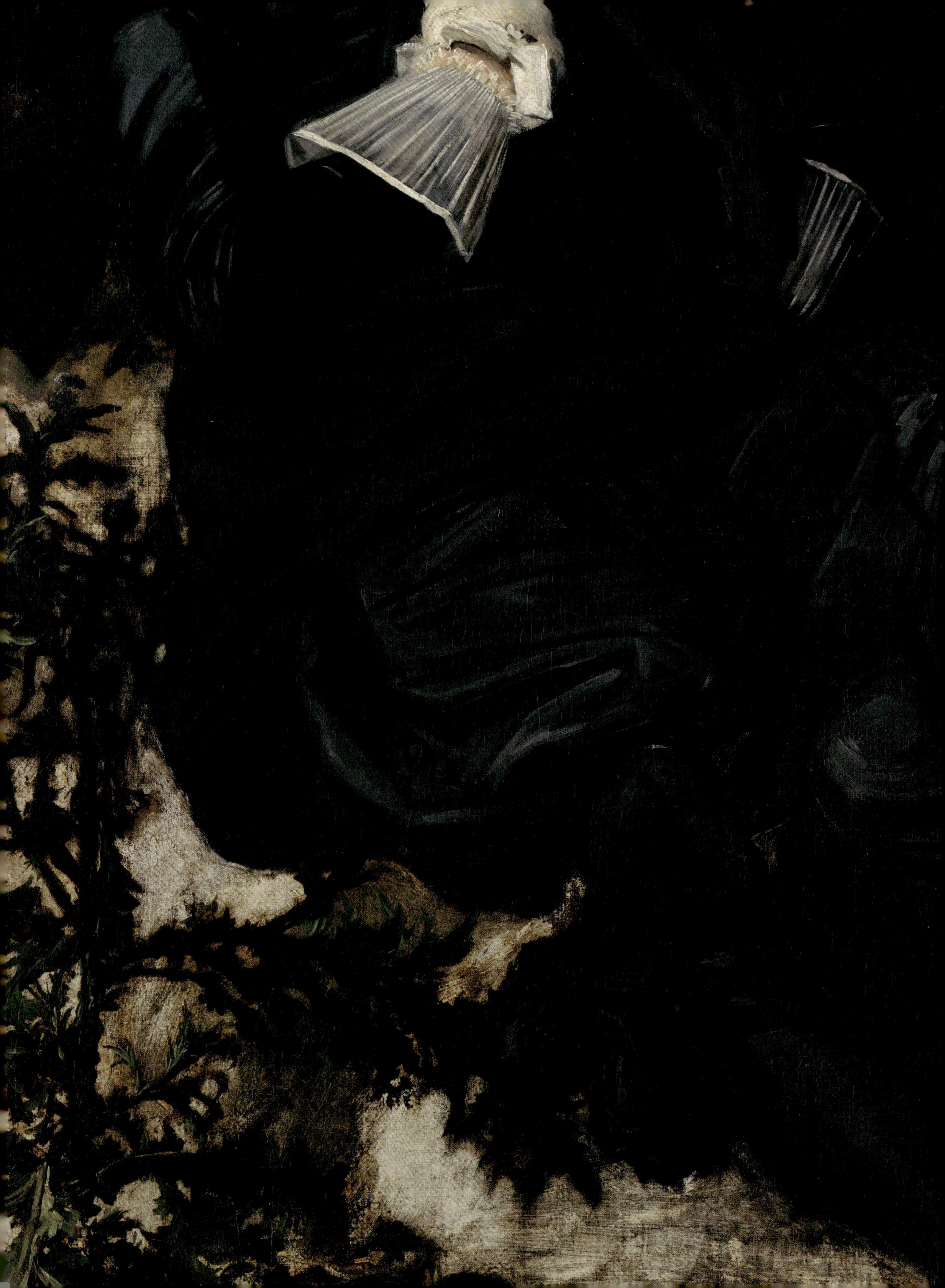

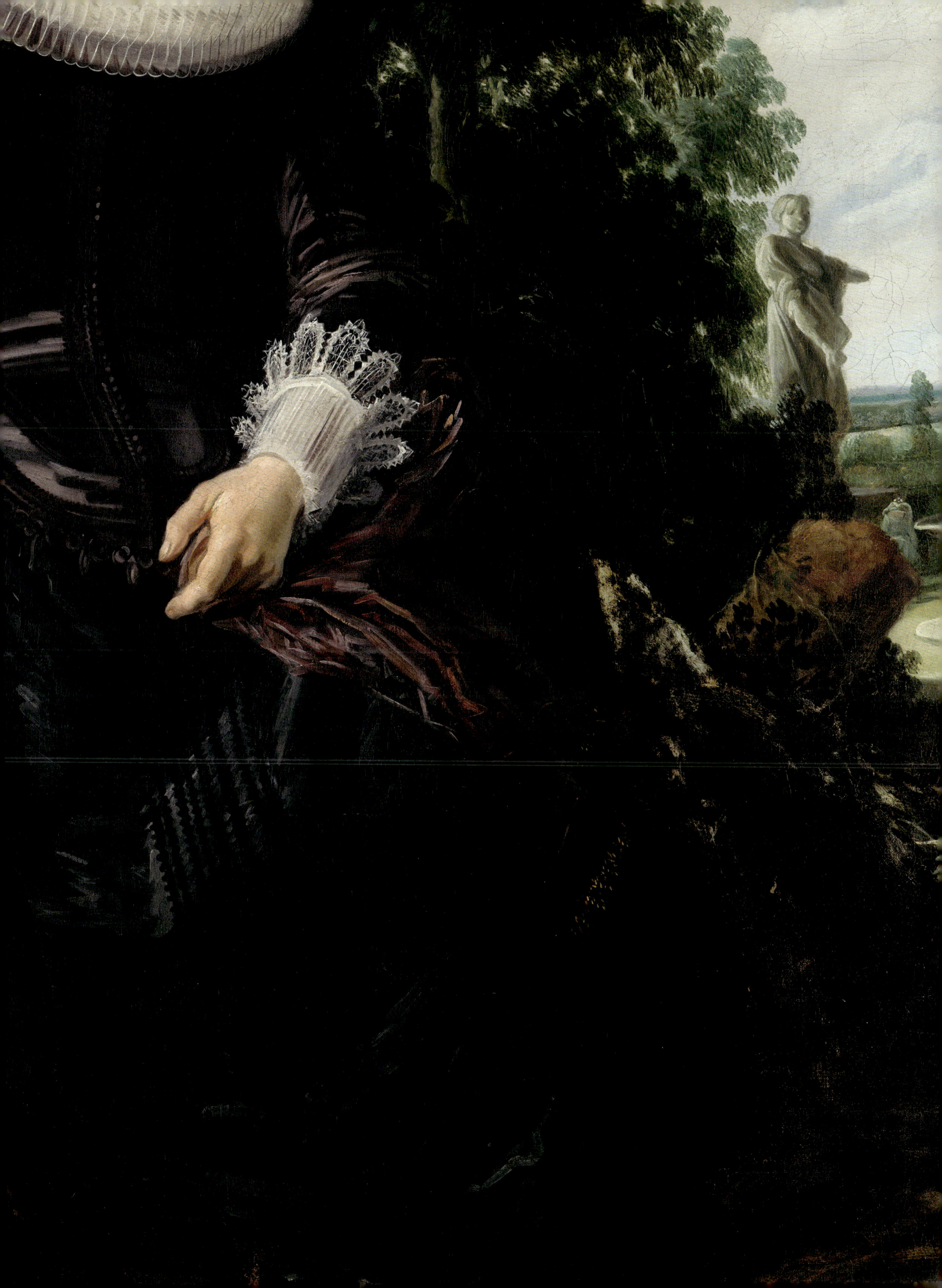

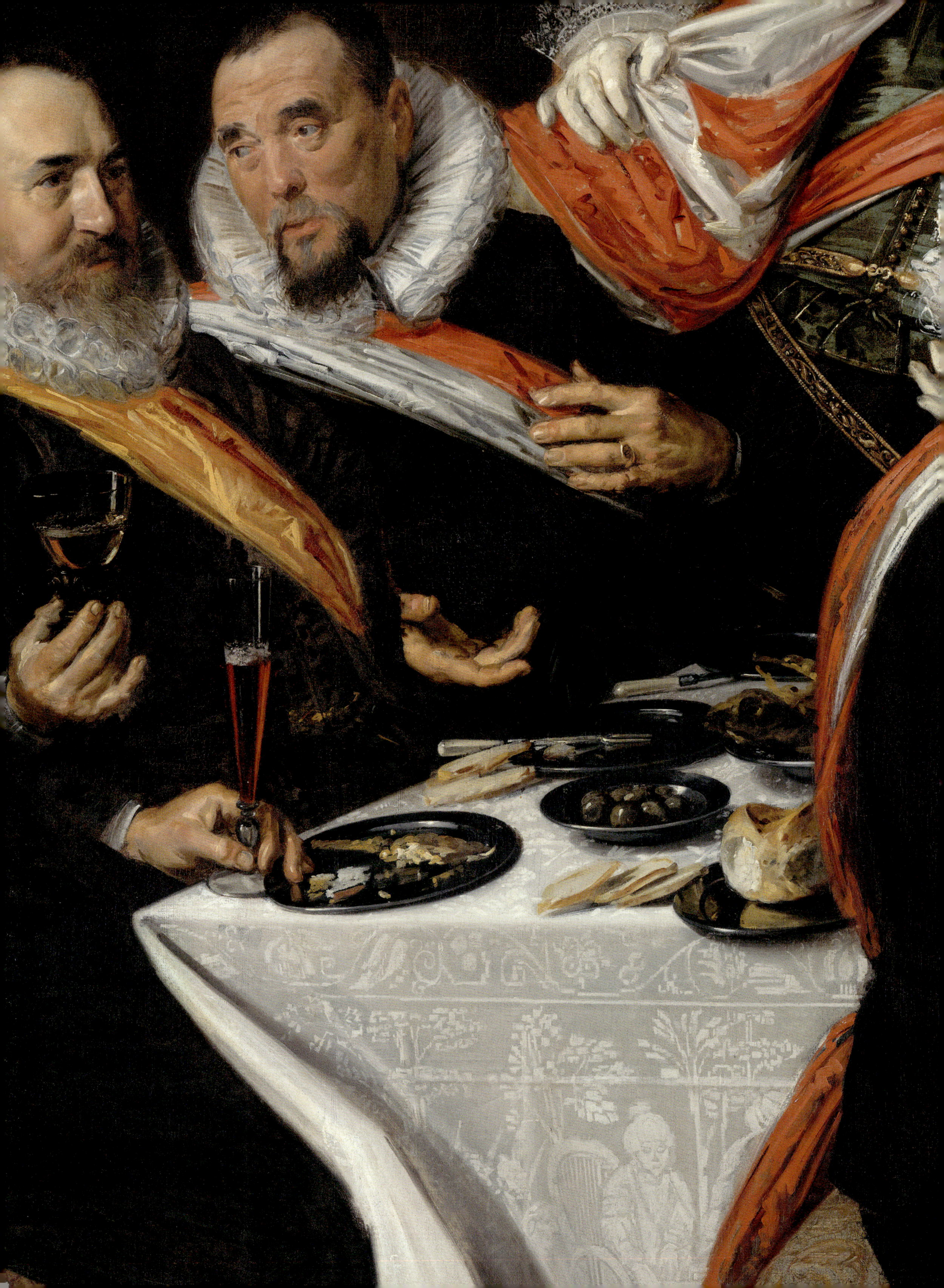

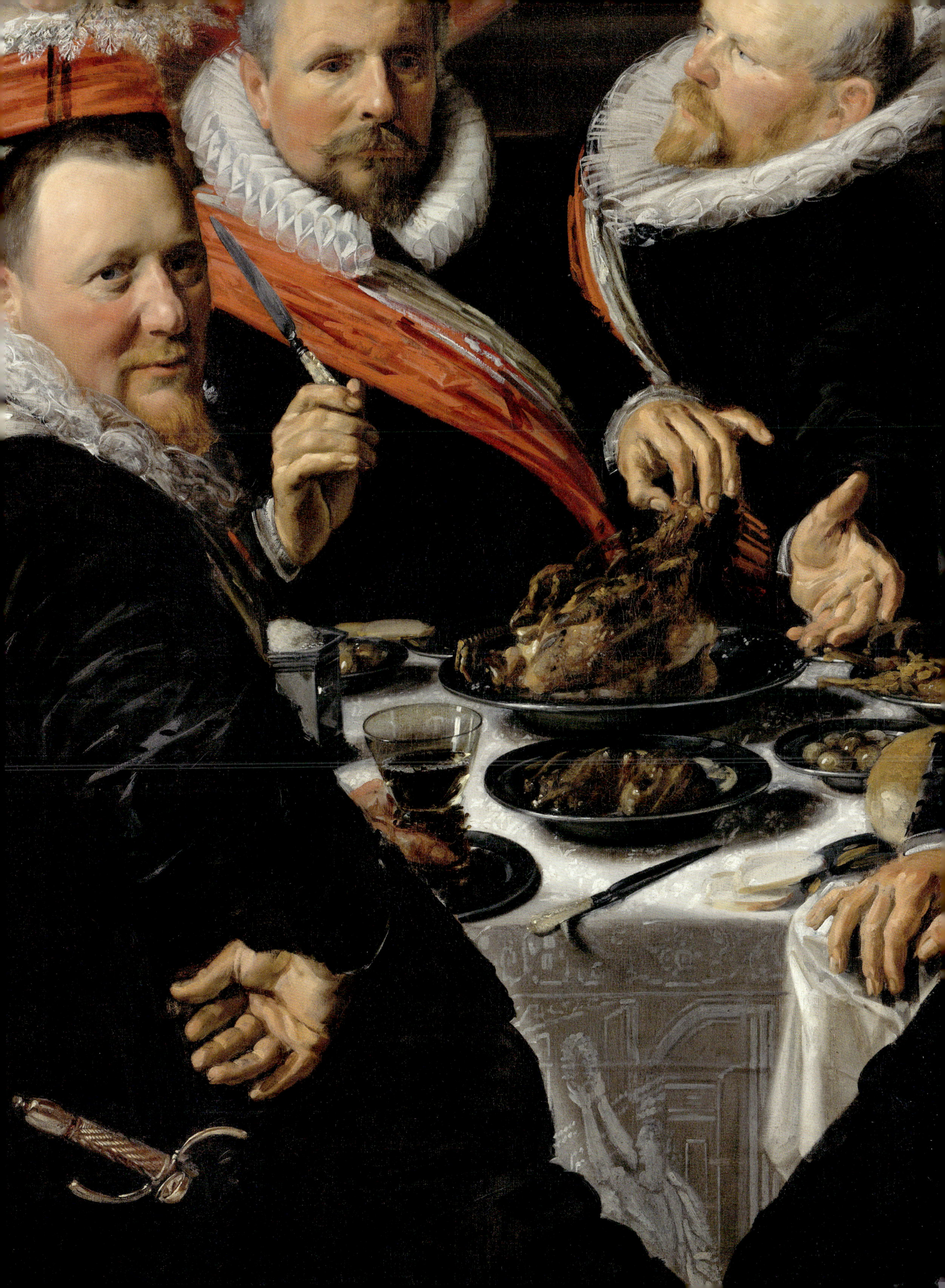

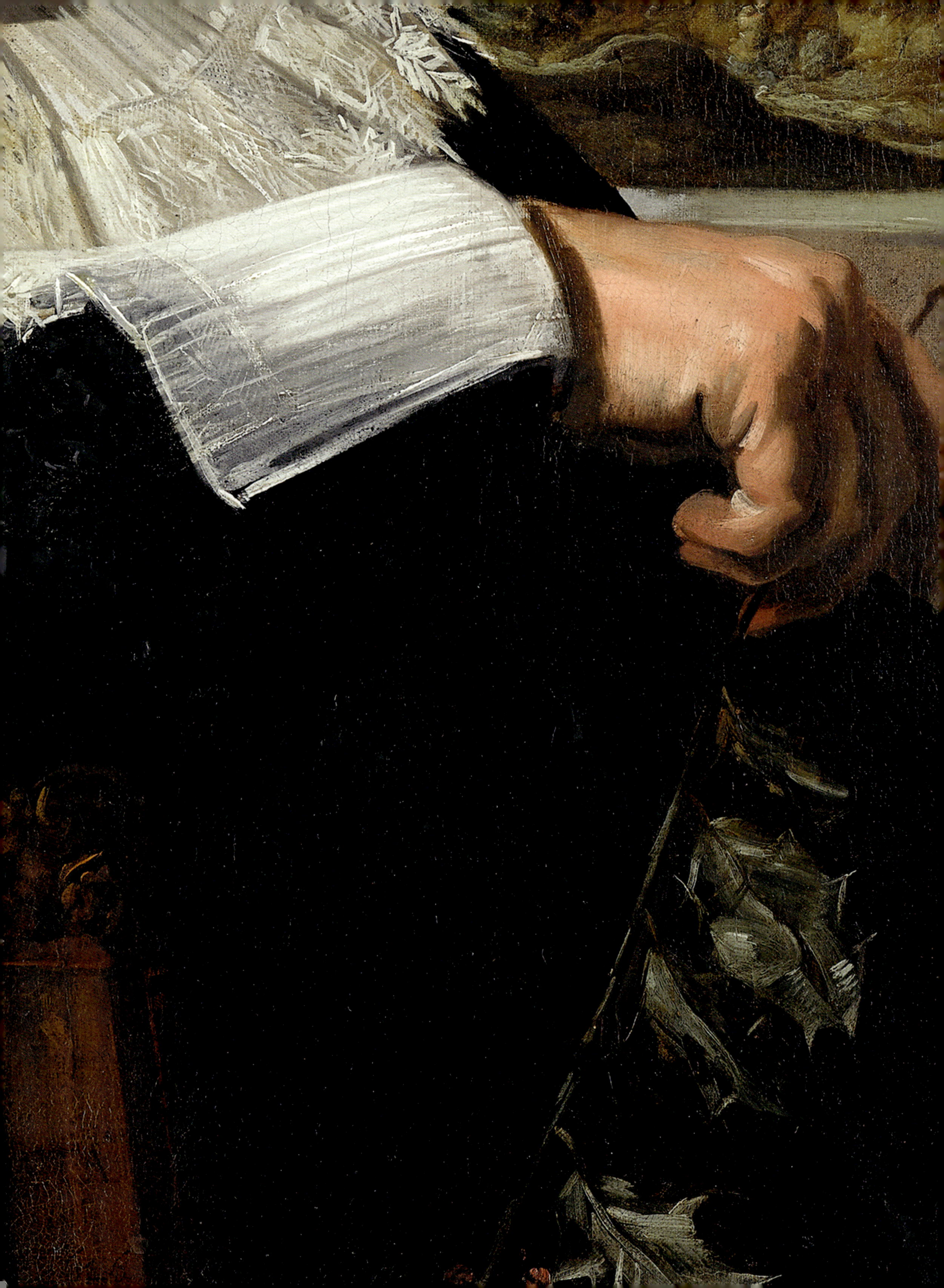